SOCIAL PSYCHOLOGY
OF DRESS

SOCIAL PSYCHOLOGY OF DRESS

SHARRON J. LENNON

Indiana University

KIM K.P. JOHNSON

University of Minnesota

NANCY A. RUDD

The Ohio State University

FAIRCHILD BOOKS

NEW YORK · LONDON · OXFORD · NEW DELHI · SYDNEY

FAIRCHILD BOOKS
Bloomsbury Publishing Inc
1385 Broadway, New York, NY 10018, USA
50 Bedford Square, London, WC1B 3DP, UK
29 Earlsfort Terrace, Dublin 2, Ireland

BLOOMSBURY, FAIRCHILD BOOKS and the Fairchild Books logo are trademarks
of Bloomsbury Publishing Plc

First published in the United States of America 2017
Reprinted 2018
Reprinted 2019
Reprinted 2021
Reprinted 2022

Cover design: Alice Marwick
Cover image © Alice Marwick

Library of Congress Cataloging-in-Publication Data
Names: Lennon, Sharron J., author. | Johnson, Kim K. P., author. | Rudd, Nancy A. (Nancy Ann), author.
Title: Social psychology of dress / Sharron J. Lennon, Kim K.P. Johnson, Nancy A. Rudd.
Description: New York : Fairchild Books, 2017.
Identifiers: LCCN 2016039919 | ISBN 9781501313561 (paperback)
Subjects: LCSH: Clothing and dress—Social aspects. | Clothing and dress—Psychological aspects. |
Social psychology. | BISAC: DESIGN / Fashion. | DESIGN / Textile & Costume. | SOCIAL SCIENCE /
Anthropology / Cultural.
Classification: LCC GT525 .L46 2017 | DDC 391—dc23 LC record available at
https://lccn.loc.gov/2016039919

ISBN: PB: 978-1-5013-1356-1
ePDF: 978-1-5013-1357-8

Typeset by Lachina
Printed and bound in the United States of America

To find out more about our authors and books visit www.fairchildbooks.com
and sign up for our newsletter.

CONTENTS

EXTENDED CONTENTS

**PART THREE
SOCIOLOGICAL PERSPECTIVES
ON DRESS** 235

PREFACE

Throughout human history, research has been conducted on WHY people dress the way they do and HOW people put together their personal appearance, including factors that impact decision making about hairstyle, makeup, clothing, and accessories. Further, many have often wondered WHAT people want to communicate through their appearances, and WHO is willing to take a risk via their appearance, as well as who is comfortable blending in with the crowd. Over the course of this research, plenty of light has been shed on WHEN and WHERE humans first began wearing clothing and WHAT human interaction would be like if people dressed differently than they do. *The Social Psychology of Dress* explores these and many other questions related to the phenomenon of dress, provides examples from multiple cultures and subcultures, and discusses how multiple facets of our identities are expressed and influenced through our dress. In this book we summarize and synthesize the findings of the aforementioned research, we present major theories and concepts that are important to understanding relationships between dress and human behavior, and we make application of this information to the fashion and related industries. We supplement our research-based presentation with contemporary examples of why people do what they do by way of constructing their appearances and how dress influences everyday behaviors.

We propose this book for a survey class in dress and human behavior that addresses dress primarily from the perspectives of three areas of the social sciences (e.g., anthropological, psychological, sociological). This approach situates decision making about dress as a complex process wherein the individual, the social groups that individual participates in, and the culture wherein one resides all must be considered to understand why people dress their bodies the way that they do. Other textbooks may be focused on one of these perspectives (e.g., psychological, anthropological) or may include two, but few textbooks include discussion of all three of the major influences on decision making concerning dress.

The content presented in this textbook is frequently required for undergraduate majors in retail merchandising, apparel design, or textiles and clothing. It is intended for use by students in an introductory level course with no prerequisite courses and, depending on how the course is structured and supplemented, can be offered to students during the second, third, or fourth year of an undergraduate degree. It can be used in a traditional lecture course, hybrid course, or as an online course. It can also be used for a first year graduate level course if supplemented with readings from the research literature.

COVERAGE AND ORGANIZATION

The book features three perspectives: anthropological, psychological (and social psychological), and sociological. We begin our introductory chapters with the connection between culture and dress, since culture is perhaps the biggest single influence on our behavior. In Chapter 1 we define dress as the total arrangement of all outwardly detectable modifications of the body and all material objects added to it. Broad topics covered in Chapters 1 and 2 include definitions and classifications of dress, culture, origins and functions of dress, and sources of information about dress. Chapter 3 introduces research processes as another way to learn about dress.

The psychological (and social psychological) unit includes Chapters 4 through 9. Chapter 4 focuses on social perception and social cognition, Chapter 5 examines the way we form impressions and formulate meaning about others based on dress. Chapter 6 examines physical appearance and concentrates on body modifications as dress, while Chapter 7 explores body image perceptions, attitudes, and appearance management behaviors. Chapter 8 focuses on dress and personality and Chapter 9 distinguishes among aspects of the self and connections to dress.

A sociological view of dress is presented in Chapters 10 through 12. Chapter 10 concerns relationships between dress and identity, Chapter 11 focuses on the role of dress in our socialization, and Chapter 12 focuses on how dress helps us to function in social groups. Chapters 13 and 14 bring the discussion back to dress and culture. Chapter 13 addresses cultural aesthetics of dress and how those are influenced by norms of behavior and technology. Chapter 14 focuses on cultural rituals involving dress including those related to religion, health, and hygiene.

Although the chapters have been ordered in a way that moves discussion of dress from introductory material to individual influences on dress, group influences, and cultural influences, instructors may find that this organization is not one that works for their students. If this is the case, chapters can be assigned in any order that enables flow for students or better matches with existing approaches course instructors have to the study of dress. Some chapters may not be assigned at all to students or offered as supplementary reading. For example, in some undergraduate programs a separate course in research methods is required; therefore instructors may not assign Chapter 3 to students in these circumstances. Instructors may wish to spend more or less time on a specific approach so that only sections of chapters might be assigned as required reading with other parts assigned as optional. A review of the chapter objectives at the beginning of each chapter will facilitate instructor's customized use of the textbook.

FEATURES

Even though emphasis has been placed on three major perspectives, the textbook content provides opportunities to examine dress from other perspectives (e.g., communication, clothing, and textiles). Along with the summaries of empirical research provided, content is derived from the popular press, the news, and/or popular culture. We do this by integrating our discussion of content with the theories that support them and by providing in-class activities, discussion questions, photographs, illustrations where relevant (e.g., tables, figures), and a list of related readings that supplement textbook content. Our goal is to make this book relevant to your student's experience, reading level, and intellectual inquiry. We intersperse conceptual and theoretical content with examples from daily life and with applications to the fashion and beauty industry. Notable features include:

- *Learning Objectives* at the beginning of each chapter that outline student outcomes for the chapter, providing a roadmap for study.
- *Dress in the News* feature boxes highlight events from daily life related to each chapter's topic. For example, in Chapter 10, "Dress and Identity," we discuss a J. Crew ad controversy in which J. Crew's president and creative director is shown in an ad applying pink nail polish to her son's toenails. The controversy generated by this ad included speculation about whether or not a mother painting her son's toenails is an influence on his gender identity. In other words, could he grow up to be gay or transgendered as a result of this experience?
- *Industry Application* feature boxes connect a chapter's topic to real world industry scenarios. For example, in Chapter 6, "Dress and Physical Appearance" we discuss how hiring workers who convey the image of the company has proven problematic for Abercrombie and Fitch. In 2008, they chose not to hire a woman as a sales associate because her hijab did not conform to their looks policy. However, the woman was not told about the policy, and in June 2015 the Supreme Court ruled that the company's failure to accommodate her violated her civil rights concerning religious accommodation.
- *In-Class Activities* give students the opportunity to examine their own dress habits either individually or in small groups, to uncover the mysteries behind why they dress the way they do, and what it says about themselves and others.

- *Discussion Questions* at the end of each chapter allow students to assess their mastery of the chapter's main concepts.
- *Suggested Readings* enable instructors and students to study further chapter concepts and theories and develop course projects.

INSTRUCTOR AND STUDENT RESOURCES

Social Psychology of Dress STUDiO

We are pleased to offer an online multimedia resource to support this text—*Social Psychology of Dress STUDIO*. The online *STUDIO* is specially developed to complement this book with rich media ancillaries that students can adapt to their visual learning styles to better master concepts and improve grades. Within the *STUDIO*, students will be able to:

- Study smarter with self-quizzes featuring scored results and personalized study tips

- Review concepts with flashcards of essential vocabulary
- Download worksheets to complete chapter activities

STUDIO access cards are offered free with new book purchases and also sold separately through Bloomsbury Fashion Central (www.BloomsburyFashionCentral.com).

Instructor Resources

- Instructor's Guide provides suggestions for planning the course and using the text in the classroom, supplemental assignments, and lecture notes
- Test Bank includes sample test questions for each chapter
- PowerPoint® presentations include images from the book and provide a framework for lecture and discussion

Instructor's Resources may be accessed through Bloomsbury Fashion Central (www.BloomsburyFashionCentral.com).

ACKNOWLEDGMENTS

The work contained herein is the result of many years of studying, teaching graduate and undergraduate courses focusing on the social psychology of dress, conducting research on dress, and discussing dress research with colleagues. In writing this textbook, our ideas have been influenced and shaped by the ideas of a generation of scholars that came before us, our immediate colleagues, and our students. The list is too long to include all of them, but we recognize the many ways they contributed to our thinking and thus, this textbook.

A group of colleagues directly impacted the content and format of this textbook. We thank Jennifer Ogle and Kathryn Reilly who utilized early versions of the book in their courses and provided their direct feedback about the book contents; we also thank them for the feedback they collected from their students. Their suggestions were helpful in revising early versions of the text. In addition, we thank our many colleagues who have shared ideas and references to research as well as offered words of wisdom and encouragement during the writing and revision process, including Joanne B. Eicher, Jennifer Ogle, Andrew Reilly, LuAnn Lafrenz, Jennifer Harmon, Wendy Goldstein, Hyunjoo Im, Becky Yust, Elizabeth Bye, and Carl Maresh. We also thank our research partners and colleagues whose work has shaped our thinking about the social psychology of dress, including Leslie Davis Burns, Margaret Rucker, Joanne B. Eicher, Mary-Ellen Roach-Higgins, and each other.

The authors are especially grateful to their spouses Larry Lennon, Mark Johnson, and Tom Rudd for their continuous support and understanding during the writing of this book. Special thanks to Tom for time spent taking many photographs used in the book.

The Publisher wishes to gratefully acknowledge and thank the editorial team involved in the publication of this book:

Acquisitions Editor: Amanda Breccia
Development Editor: Corey Kahn
Assistant Editor: Kiley Kudrna
Art Development Editor: Edie Weinberg
In-House Designer: Eleanor Rose
Production Manager: Claire Cooper
Project Manager: Morgan McClelland

Fairchild Books wishes to gratefully acknowledge and thank the reviewers who contributed their ideas to this textbook: Carrie Brezine, University of Michigan, US; Willie Tolliver, Agnes Scott College, US; Charlette T. Padilla, University of Arizona, US; Amy Meadows, Columbia College Chicago, US; Jessica Strubel, University of North Texas, US; Joanne B. Eicher, University of Minnesota, US; Jaehee Jung, University of Delaware, US; Jose Blanco, Dominican University, US; Jay Yoo, Baylor University, US; Janna Eggebeen, Ryerson University, CAN; Jade R. Bettin, University of North Carolina, US; Jennifer Ogle, Colorado State University, US; Evonne Bowling, Mesa Community College, US; Katalin Medvedev, University of Georgia, US; Dr. Lalon Alexander, University of the Incarnate Word, US; Caroline Alexander, London College of Fashion, UK; and Karen Cross, Robert Gordon University, UK.

PART 1

INTRODUCTION TO THE STUDY OF DRESS

CHAPTER

1

WHY STUDY DRESS?

After reading and reflecting on the content of this chapter students should be able to:

- Provide an overview of the concept of dress.
- Define terms commonly used in the study of dress.
- Use a schema for analyzing dress cross-culturally.
- Distinguish among artifacts, mentifacts, and sociofacts of culture.
- Employ a contextual perspective in the study of dress.

INTRODUCTION

Dress is one of the most interesting aspects of human behavior we can study. Everyone in the world "dresses" their body. Dress has long been a means to communicate information about the self to others, to express the self creatively, and to protect the self from physical and psychological harm.

WHY STUDY DRESS?

Dress is one of many **artifacts** of culture, or those material items that are produced by a culture. Like other artifacts of culture that we use to learn about the practices of cultures, dress represents human workmanship, cultural beliefs, aesthetic sensibilities, and lifestyle practices. Dress can situate a culture in terms of time, geography, technical skill, and level of cultural complexity. Dress is also a reflection of our **mentifacts**, or our guiding beliefs, mores, and values that shape culture; and our **sociofacts**, or social institutions and **norms** that direct human behavior. Thus, dress is worthy of our attention in explaining and understanding cultural identities, differences, and similarities.

Dress is also important to our understanding of self and others, to our daily behavior and decisions. At first, this may not occur to us. Yet, on a subconscious level, we evaluate what we should wear, we assign meanings to people and situations by their dress, and we come to know what things in our own culture are expressed through appearance. For example, how would we act and how would others respond to us if we were dressed in an entirely different manner than we typically dress? What if we wore a nun's habit or the clothing of a cloistered religious sect? Or a graphic T-shirt with an inflammatory message? What about a restrictive corset or another form of restrictive dress such as five-inch high heels?

Do you think we have a preconceived notion of what certain people should look like based on their position or social role within a community? Consider, for example, a doctor, a corporate executive, a toddler, a sorority member, a college professor in fine arts versus a professor in chemistry, or a fashion designer. Do we have preconceived ideas about the type of person who might wear false eyelashes, or padded rear-end extenders, or a bustier? Do we consider certain types of dress appropriate for some occasions or people, yet not for others?

The answers that we give to any of these questions underscore that we do pay a considerable degree of attention to the appearance and dress of ourselves and others. The **social psychology of dress** is the study of dress and adornment in the larger context of appearance in human behavior in general. Why is it important to study dress? Dressing the body is a behavior that we learn, and we evaluate the end result (i.e., the dressed body) in our personal and social interactions. Dressing the body is similar to other behaviors that we learn and evaluate in our personal and social interactions, including language (verbal and body), physical skills, and social skills of others. Dressing the body influences the interactions we have because dress is used as a symbol. People attach meanings to dress and those meanings influence the nature and scope of our interactions. Dress carries meaning which we respond to, form opinions about, and that influences our behavior toward self and towards others.

There are many approaches to studying variations in behavior concerning dress from one culture or subculture to another. The disciplines of **cultural anthropology**, sociology, and psychology are devoted to the examination of these factors. For example, cultural anthropology focuses on the variations in human cultures as they are impacted by economics, politics, trade, and belief systems. **Sociology** is the study of humans in groups that are smaller than entire cultures, focusing on social structures, organization, interaction, and deviance. **Psychology** is the study of individuals who live in social groups within a larger culture and focuses on the perceptions, motivations, and understandings of individuals that contribute to behavior. While these definitions may be rather simplistic distinctions of these broad and widely respected social science disciplines, they help to explain the breadth and depth of the study of human behavior. Many other disciplines add their own unique focus to the understanding of factors explaining cultural variation: women's studies and gender studies that focus on the social constructions of gender and sexuality; critical race and ethnic studies that focus on the social constructions of race and ethnicity, and social justice movements that transform the negative impacts of discrimination; philosophy that deals with issues of human existence such as knowledge, values, reason and language; linguistics that deals with the study of human language; communication that concerns patterns of sharing information among individuals and groups. We will draw from these varied disciplines to examine cultural complexity and patterns of culture that impact dress.

WHAT IS DRESS?

Dress is the total arrangement of all outwardly detectable modifications of the body and all material objects added to it. *Dress* used as a noun is defined as the assemblage of body modifications and body supplements worn by an individual at a specific moment in time (Roach & Eicher, 1973; Roach-Higgins & Eicher, 1992; Roach-Higgins, Eicher, & Johnson, 1995). This definition is described by Roach-Higgins and Eicher as "culturally neutral," so that the term *dress* can be used to describe body modifications and body supplements of any group of people in any location and at any point in time. The term *dress* does not carry surplus meaning (additional meaning) or judgment. **Body modifications** are changes made directly to the body itself, such as changes in shape (teased hair), color (paint or cosmetics), texture (making the skin smooth or rough), surface embellishment (piercing, tattooing), etc. (Figure 1.1, Figure 1.2). These modifications can be permanent or temporary. They affect one or all of the five human senses of sight, sound, smell, taste, or touch. **Body**

Figure 1.1
Body modifications include tattoos; pierced holes in lip, septum, eyebrow, and ears; styled head and facial hair. Body supplements include handwoven bracelet, shirt, jacket, and jewelry inserted through pierced holes.

Figure 1.2

Body modifications of this Suri woman include pierced holes in lip and ear, scarification on arm, cut of hair, and removal of lower teeth to accommodate plug. Body supplements include lip plug made of wood or clay, bead necklaces, bracelets, body covering tied on shoulder. Suri culture, Oma Valley, Ethiopia.

Figure 1.3

Scottish men in traditional tartan dress at a bagpipe and dance festival, Stirling, Scotland. Dress items include kilts, trousers, jackets, vests, ties, socks, garters, shoes, shirts, tams (hats), sporrans (hanging pouches), and clan pins.

supplements are additions of items to the body such as jewelry, clothing, and accessories. They relate to the body form in any of several different ways, including being wrapped around the body (e.g., a head wrap), being suspended from the body (e.g., a necklace), being shaped to the body (e.g., a pair of jeans), being attached to the body (e.g., earrings), being attached to garments (e.g., buttons), or being held by the body (e.g., a purse).

Equally important to the descriptive terms that we use to discuss dress is the evaluative language that we use in discussing or perceiving dress. It is this evaluation that helps us to derive meaning from what we see—terms such as *pretty, fashionable, cool, tight, droopy, inappropriate,* and *sexy* reflect judgments that we make. These judgments are made in relation to cultural and social norms or general guidelines for behavior that are time-specific, place-specific, and related to particular reference groups. For example, we can describe a garment as a body supplement in neutral, descriptive terms (e.g., a white tank top worn with black, fitted pants and heels); but when it is worn by someone to a job interview, we can evaluate its fit on the body, its appropriateness to the situation, how fashionable are the accessories worn with it, and how trendy or expensive it is (e.g., "That top is too tight and too revealing," "No one should wear yoga pants to a job interview," and

"Those stiletto Jimmy Choo shoes are hot, but definitely not good in a Disney store."). Beyond this, and perhaps most importantly or with the greatest ramifications, is that visual evaluation may be used by the interviewer to establish how well-qualified the person so appearing is to hold the job. (e.g., "As a recruiter, I see some strange people coming in to interview, but this person clearly isn't interested in our company because she doesn't understand our audience at all.") Even though people can be counseled not to use appearances in interview settings as a barometer of ability, or in a dating setting as a barometer of lifelong compatibility, they often do.

Dress used as a verb refers to all the behaviors undertaken to create an appearance or to modify the body in some way. These behaviors include bathing or cleansing,

Figure 1.4
Pakistani Muslim women get henna painting in preparation of the upcoming religious celebration of Ramadan; Lahore, Pakistan.

perfuming or altering the natural scent of the body (e.g., use of deodorant, cologne or perfume, mouthwash), changing the color of the body (e.g., use of hair dye, cosmetics or other colorants, tattoos), changing the texture of the body (e.g., use of lotions, hair products, dermabrasion, shaving, scarring), changing the size and shape of the body (e.g., dieting, exercising, weight-training, cosmetic surgery), and adding items of dress to the body. All of these behaviors stem from choices that people make to change their appearances.

What, when, and how often we engage in behaviors all vary on the basis of culture. For example, daily behaviors and materials associated with dressing the body for people living in an industrialized society may include bathing, applying deodorant and body moisturizers, brushing teeth, applying cosmetics (many females), styling hair, applying fragrance, and adding body supplements including garments and accessories. Members of another cultural group, one that relies on hunting and is fairly isolated from other communities, are likely to engage in different behaviors and use different materials to modify their appearance. They might bathe infrequently, chew on a fragrant piece of wood to clean teeth, use animal fat to style hair, apply paint to change body color, and wear the same body supplement daily. The point is that all people make choices to modify their appearances, and they each engage in specific behaviors to do so. Thus, *dress* is both noun and verb, or both product and process (Eicher & Evenson, 2015.) *Dress* as a noun is *what* is done to the body, and *dress* as a verb is *how* it is done.

CROSS-CULTURAL CLASSIFICATIONS OF DRESS

In order to neutrally describe all types of human dress worldwide, without making any judgments about meaning, appropriateness, or types of interaction among individuals, a classification system of dress was developed in the 1970s and refined by other scholars of dress over the next thirty years (Roach & Eicher, 1973; Roach & Musa, 1980; Roach-Higgins & Eicher, 1992; Eicher & Evenson, 2015). As you can see, opposite, body modifications and body supplements form the two categories of dress. This classification system allows us to simply describe elements of dress, regardless of their contextual meaning.

The vertical axis (left hand column) of Figure 1.5 designates the categories of body modifications or body supplements, with sub-categories under each, such as hair, skin, and nails under body modifications, and wrapped, suspended, or fitted under body supplements that enclose the body. The horizontal axis describes the properties of the body modification or body supplement. Let us consider the category of body modifications. For example, hair can be transformed via hair dye or bleach or other coloring such as mud or ochre. Its texture, as well as volume and proportion, can be transformed through chemical means such as a permanent wave or straightening, a particular style of haircut would transform its shape, and scented shampoo or other products would transform its odor. The body could be transformed in shape and volume with long-term weight training, with a weight-loss or weight-gain program, by binding a body part while it is still growing, or through cosmetic surgery. Body color could be altered via tattooing, tanning, painting,

Figure 1.5 Forms of dress

A model for classifying body modifications and supplements and their properties. (Copyright permission granted from International Textiles and Apparel Association, Nancy J. Rutherford, Executive Director.)

Properties: Body Modifications	Color	Shape & Volume	Structural Design	Surface Design	Texture	Odor	Sound	Taste
Hair								
Skin								
Nails								
Head								
Trunk								
Limbs								
Teeth								
Breath								

Properties	Color	Shape & Volume	Structural Design	Surface Design	Texture	Odor	Sound	Taste
Body Supplements								
Enclosures								
a. Wrapped								
b. Suspended								
c. Pre-shaped								
d. ab, ac, bc								

Properties	Color	Shape & Volume	Structural Design	Surface Design	Texture	Odor	Sound	Taste
Attachments to Body								
a. Inserted								
b. Clipped								
c. Adhered								

Properties	Color	Shape & Volume	Structural Design	Surface Design	Texture	Odor	Sound	Taste
Attachments to Body Enclosures								
a. Inserted								
b. Clipped								
c. Adhered								
Hand-held								
a. By self								
b. By other								

and application of cosmetics. Scarification changes the texture of the body, as does shaving, and application of lotions. Body odor can be changed through fragrances of many types.

Under the category of body supplements, there are three distinct ways that a supplement can enclose the body: suspended from it, wrapped around it, or fitted to its contours. Examples of **suspended dress** items include a necklace that hangs from the neck, a loin cloth that hangs loosely from the hips, or an apron that hangs from the waist. **Wrapped dress** items are often long pieces of fabric that are wrapped around the body or head and pleated or knotted to hold them in place (e.g., an Indian sari, an Indonesian sarong) or ribbons and ties that go around the body or hair. **Fitted dress** items are pre-shaped to the contours of the body through seams, darts, and other means; examples include much of the clothing in Europe and North America and perhaps your own wardrobe (e.g., pants, jeans, coats, shirts, hats, and shoes). Finally, some items of dress use a combination of methods to enclose the body. For example, a bathrobe may have a few seams on the side (fitted), have a sash at the waist (wrapped), but may hang loosely from the shoulders and waist (suspended).

Regardless of the item of dress and how it encloses the body, it can be described in terms of color, volume, proportion, shape and structure, surface design, texture, odor or scent, sound, and taste. For example, a pair of fitted German leather shorts (lederhosen) (Figure 1.6) could be described as grey-green in color, proportioned to fit to mid-thigh, with a buttoned drop-front panel, with leather piping, made of suede (slightly soft, bumpy

Figure 1.6

German lederhosen.

List the body modifications and supplements you show today in your dress.

Body part	Modification	Details
Ex., Hair	Washed, Conditioned	Styled, Sprayed
Ex., Limbs (legs)	Shaved	Moisturized
Ex., _____		
Ex., _____		
Ex., _____		

Supplement	Type	Details
Ex., V Neck Top	Fitted (knitted)	Fits Bust & Waist
Ex., Jeans	Fitted (stretch, woven)	5-Pocket, Cropped
Ex., Necklace	Suspended	Chain with Pendant
Ex., Belt	Wrapped	Leather with Buckle
Ex., _____		
Ex., _____		
Ex., _____		
Ex., _____		
Ex., _____		
Ex., _____		

texture), with a slight animal odor, and perhaps creating a "brush, brush" sound when walking in them. A shoe could be described by its characteristics as well.

Items of dress may be **attached to the body** via insertion into a body part (such as an earring that is inserted into a pierced ear), via clipping (hair barrettes and other hair ornaments), or adhering to the body (false eyelashes adhered with glue). Items of dress may also be **attached to a garment** (or body enclosure) via these same techniques: insertion (as in fringe on a vest), clipping (suspenders), or adhering (glued-on patches on a jacket).

Finally, there are items of dress that are **handheld** or held by the hand, such as purses or briefcases, umbrellas, and canes. Sometimes these items are held for the individual by others, as in the case of a mother carrying an umbrella over her child's head, or carrying a child's backpack on the way to the school bus.

WHAT IS CULTURE?

The widely accepted definition of **culture** is a complex whole that includes knowledge, beliefs, art, morals, laws, customs, and other capabilities and habits, which is acquired by humans as members of society (Tylor, 1974). It is the fundamental determinant of how we live as we do and how that life is shaped. When we contemplate how our lives are shaped and how they are different from the lives of others, we see that they are shaped by our values and view of the world, language, lifestyle, traditions, products of human workmanship that we use and that surround us (e.g., tools, transportation, housing, works of art, utilitarian items, and dress). Our lives are also shaped by our creative endeavors (e.g., music, dance, theater), food habits, and social institutions (e.g., family, education, government, religion).

These material and nonmaterial aspects of culture are learned from and reinforced by individuals around us, beginning from our earliest years of life. These individuals include nuclear and extended family members, neighbors, caregivers, teachers, religious leaders and congregations, peer groups, and the media. Our accumulation of knowledge is dynamic and cumulative over our lifespan. As a result, certain aspects of culture may become more firmly entrenched in our psyche (e.g., our religious beliefs) than others. Not only is what we know open to change, but culture itself is dynamic. The "American" culture, or the Hmong culture in Southeast Asia (Figure 1.7), or Yanomami culture of the Amazon in South America (Figure 1.8), or any culture for that matter, will continue to change and evolve. What a culture is at one point in time is never what it is at another point in time. Some cultures change more slowly than others, while some cultures change more rapidly.

An experience you may have had that reflects the dynamic nature of culture occurs when you experience differences in beliefs from your parents or your grandparents. The term **generation gap** is used to refer to a difference in opinions and understandings between children and their parents or their grandparents or between large groups of people whose formative years were influenced by different events and beliefs in different time periods. Take, for instance, the following groups of individuals. There is the baby boomer generation in America that consists of individuals who were born between 1946 and 1964 (approximately 81 million). Many of their children were born between 1965–1976 (approximately 46 million) who are referred to as generation X, or who were born between 1977–1994 (~75 million) and referred to as generation Y or millennials, or those born after millennials known as generation Z. What will we call those born after generation Z? The term *generation Alpha* has been proposed. An examination of the cultural influences on these broad groups of individuals during their formative years can explain some of their differences in beliefs. (Bump, 2014; Fry, 2016).

Baby boomers were influenced by the Cold War with Russia in the 1950s and by political and racial unrest in the 1960s–1970s. They are, therefore, a typically politically activist generation; their mores, music, clothes, and politics were much different in the 1960s and 1970s from their parents' generation. In the 1980s and 1990s, many assumed corporate positions and redefined corporate directions (i.e., social responsibility, materialism, credit

Figure 1.7

H'mong girl in traditional dress at New Year's celebration in a Northeastern province of Vietnam.

Figure 1.8

Yanomami of the Amazon rainforest, a hunter-agriculturalist culture of some 23,000 in Brazil and Venezuela, South America.

cards). In the twenty-first century, they are redefining retirement and living choices, health care, and consumer behavior (Fry, 2016).

Generation Xers were raised when divorce, smaller-size families, AIDS, recreational drug use, and daycare were common. Therefore, they are characterized as independent, pragmatic, and take-control individuals who often want to work for themselves. They tend to be conservative financially, highly educated and media savvy, and are practical and economical in their consumption habits (Stein, 2013).

Generation Yers are sometimes referred to as the "warp speed generation" because they are doing more and moving faster than any previous generation. They were raised in an environment of group sports participation, extensive homework, "play dates," and high technology use (computers, MP3 players, video game systems, cellular phones). They have had fairly structured time schedules all their lives, are very socially engaged (even using the Internet as a social space, as in Facebook) and hold a strong sense of social responsibility and sensitivity to war, the environment, race, and gender (Fry, 2016; Stein, 2013).

Generation Zers are still relatively too young (children, tweens, teens) to know much about their consumption habits, but we do know that they are considered to be digital natives raised with cell phones and constant access to social media, taking in information instantaneously and losing interest in it just as fast. Regarding attitudes, they are thought to embrace multicultural and gender equality, personal safety, pragmatism, and individuality (including "creating" their own brands as unique individuals on social media) (Bump, 2014; Williams, 2015).

Given the cultural parameters in which each generation was raised, we can see how attitudes would vary dramatically between the generations on such topics as military service, advertising, use of free time, education, humanitarian service, corporate greed, and healthy living. Yet each of these generations as well as others existing during the same time period contribute to the diversity of beliefs, attitudes, and behaviors that cause the continual evolution of culture.

When we think of culture, we may assume that the same culture exists across an entire nation or state. Indeed, there are some cultural beliefs that are shared across all or most members of a nation or country. However, in reality, the United States and other countries encompass a series of small cultures, each reflecting similarities yet distinctive differences. For example, traveling across the United States, you experience components of the national culture because the nation shares rules concerning traffic and where and how to drive a car. But you also experience regional differences in language, food, dress, and housing that reflect both material and non-material aspects of culture as well as the physical environment.

Subculture or society refers to smaller groups of individuals who interact with each other and share commonalities such as a similar geographic area, language, lifestyle, interests, beliefs, social structure, and language. Any group of people held together by commonalities can comprise a subculture. So the basis for a subculture could reflect a variety of factors including ethnicity, hobbies, religion, neighborhood, athletics, education, or occupation, among others.

These groups are smaller than the dominant culture in which they exist and may vary in size from many individuals to few. Depending on the size of the subculture, individuals may all know each other in a small subculture, or they may rarely if ever know all of the other members in a larger subculture. Consider the Amish, for example. The Amish are a religious subculture that originally existed in Europe in Switzerland in the 1600s, and to escape religious persecution, migrated to North America. They are one of several Anabaptist religious sects. Many of the Amish live in the states of Ohio, Pennsylvania, and Indiana (Powell, 2010). There are, however, Amish communities in many other states of the United States, as well as in various Canadian provinces.

Likewise, there are many distinct groups of Amish (such as Old Order Amish and Beachy Amish), and there are also many other Anabaptist religious sects who have similar but not identical characteristics, including Mennonites and Hutterites. Some of the distinguishing characteristics include dress that is simple in design and not fashionable by current standards, often plain in color, and modest. Other commonalities include living a lifestyle that is functional and not materialistic. They live a lifestyle that revolves around farming in many communities, that focuses on spiritual beliefs and religious observance, and that is basically separated from the larger, mainstream culture which is driven by change, technology, and consumption. These communities recognize one another often by their dress, and they recognize that they are different from other Anabaptist groups and from mainstream US culture. However, they all live within that larger culture and take great pride in being "in the world, but not of the world" (Ruth, 2000).

We learn our subcultural or societal behaviors and belief system through **socialization**. Socialization occurs as a result of observing, listening to, and engaging in conversations and other interactions with other members of the group. We learn from **role models** first, typically in the nuclear or extended family. Role models are individuals that we aspire to be like and we may often imitate their behaviors. Some of our first role models might be our parents, grandparents, caregivers, or teachers. Then as our interaction broadens to include other groups of people, we learn from leaders in those groups as well. We learn and repeat the same behaviors, or "model" the behaviors of these groups, including language, actions, dress, and rituals. Gradually, we continue to engage in these behaviors because we believe they are right to do and because we are praised and rewarded for doing so. We are encouraged to engage in some behaviors and discouraged from engaging in others depending on the beliefs of the groups to which we want to belong. In other words, we are socialized into different groups and accept the commonalities that bind us together with other members of the group and separate us from non-members of the group. For example, on the first day we began school, we probably learned how to address the teacher, how to say the Pledge of Allegiance, how to get into a line to go to the lunchroom or outside to recess, and so on.

We often belong to several different groups or subcultures concurrently (Figure 1.9). Each of these groups has its own beliefs, customs, "language" (e.g., verbal expressions), social structure, and expectations for appearance. We learn how to function successfully in each of these groups. For example, your nuclear family exists as a unit within other family units in an extended family, and your extended family exists within the context of all families within a culture. Within your nuclear family, there are behaviors you engage in that are somewhat unique.

Consider birthday celebrations as one example of a family's behavior. In one family, they might be celebrated with great pomp and circumstance, with each person in that family recognized with special cards, food, and gifts. In another family, it is only the individual with the birthday who receives attention. That person alone receives

Figure 1.9
Your nuclear family in relation to other families.

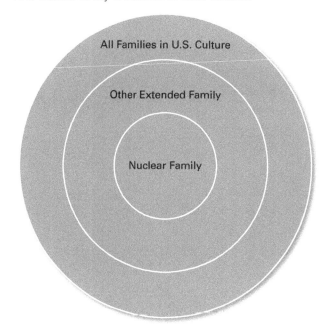

special treatment, gifts, special foods, and may be excused from daily tasks. Within another family, birthdays may not be celebrated at all. Each of these forms of celebrating birthdays is learned from the nuclear family itself, and each family knows that their way of celebrating may be different from other families, even those families that exist within their extended circle of family members (e.g., cousins, grandparents). They also understand that their views may vary from or align with those of the dominant culture. Continuing with our example, evidence that other members of the dominant culture value birthday celebrations may exist in the forms of birthday cards made available in the marketplace or the predominance of others' birthday celebrations.

Figure 1.10 represents the different interests, beliefs, social structure, language, and customs for each of the family subcultures individuals belong to.

Figure 1.11 represents an example of several subcultures to which an individual may belong simultaneously, including social groups, educational groups, occupational groups, and others. Consider how many groups of subcultures you belong to and how the commonalities and people may differ or overlap for each.

Figure 1.10
Overlap of nuclear, extended, and procreational family units.

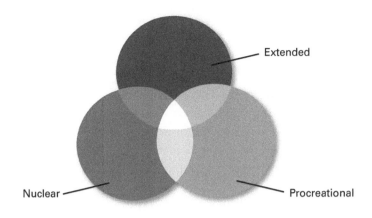

Extended

Nuclear

Procreational

Figure 1.11
Subcultures you may belong to.

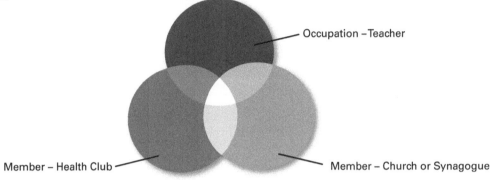

Occupation – Teacher

Member – Health Club

Member – Church or Synagogue

The relationships depicted in Figures 1.9, 1.10, and 1.11 reflect simple membership structures; in reality, if you were to construct a diagram of the groups you participate in, it would be more complex than these. Particularly, if you live in large societies, you are likely to be a member of a large array of groups. For example, in Figure 1.11, the teacher might also be a member of the university graduate faculty, a member of an academy of teaching fellows, a member of a university wellness collaborative, the chair of a university task force, a church, a health club, a parents' group, and a musical group.

IN-CLASS ACTIVITY
Construct a Diagram That Reflects the Various Groups to Which You Belong

Using Figures 1.9, 1.10, and 1.11 as a model, construct a diagram that reflects the various groups to which you belong, including family, peer, social, occupational, and religious organizations.

We must also consider cultural diasporas as part of our discussion of subcultures (Eicher & Evenson, 2015), A **diaspora** represents a group of people who have moved to new or different locations from their original geographic location but continue to show strong cultural connection to their heritage. The cause of the move may be due to opportunity or force, but the result is often the same, which is a strong identity with the original subculture. Many major metropolitan areas have large enclaves of diasporas. These groups speak their indigenous language, socialize primarily within their groups, follow long-established food habits, and send their children to cultural immersion classes so they will learn the group's traditions and continue to practice and appreciate those traditions. At the same time, individuals in this enclave are members of and function in a larger culture. They attend school, work and buy products within the dominant culture, and subsequently their lives are shaped by both groups.

Living within two cultures simultaneously can obviously create conflict personally and culturally. Let us consider two real-life examples:

(1) A young woman of Ukrainian descent grew up in a family who lived in Chicago. While she was born in the

US, her parents emigrated from the Ukraine. As she grew up, she attended Ukrainian language classes each Saturday, vacationed with other Ukrainian families in Florida, and spent a year of education and preparation for her public presentation as a Ukrainian debutante, thus making her eligible to date other (preferably) Ukrainian men.

She went away to college, dating men of many cultural backgrounds, and eventually met a Polish man and fell in love. She agreed to marry him only if he consented to raise any children they might have as Ukrainian, which caused him great distress as he weighed his decision. They did marry and their wedding was very lavish, combining elements of both a traditional American wedding (bridal gown, decorations, flowers, banquet, and honeymoon) and a Ukrainian wedding (special bridal cap, Ukrainian vows, songs, and dances). Actually, the dress traditions were merged more easily than other rituals and practices of daily life. It has been a cultural struggle for them in their early years of marriage to merge traditions and decide which traditions and practices trump others in the name of matrimonial harmony.

(2) A young woman grew up in an Italian-American family in Cleveland, where she was raised as devoutly Roman Catholic, attended private girls-only schools even through college, ate and learned to cook Italian food, and developed a strong sense of her Italian lineage. She dated very few men because her parents and older sisters insisted the men had to be Italian. Eventually, she married an Italian man and had three children, all of whom were given Italian names. However, as the children have grown up and gone away to college, they are attending public schools and are dating non-Italian people, to the dismay of their mother. She is fearful that her Italian culture is being lost among her children, particularly because the children do not devoutly practice their religion, nor are likely to marry fellow Italians. In each case, we can see how conflict arises and behaviors are undertaken to minimize that conflict.

ARTIFACTS, MENTIFACTS, AND SOCIOFACTS

Cultures and subcultures are made up of both material and nonmaterial components. Material components include things like articles of dress, tools, housing, home furnishings, pottery, equipment, and vehicles. These are products of human workmanship and are called artifacts or "facts of art." These products are tangible and can be studied in terms of their material properties, method of construction, and use (refer to figures 1.3, 1.6, and 1.7 earlier in chapter).

Whereas the commonly understood term *artifact* refers to material aspects of culture, Sir Julian Sorell Huxley, an English evolutionary biologist living from 1880–1975, is generally credited with coining the terms *mentifact* and *sociofact* to explain the non-material aspects of culture ("Julian Huxley," n.d.). Spradley (1972) corroborated these terms in describing non-material aspects of culture.

Mentifacts are "facts" of the mind, such as beliefs, values, attitudes, goals, and world view. They are the guiding principles of groups of people and of individuals. For example, two major world views are *independence* and *interdependence*, originally identified in the 1990s (Markus and Kitayama, 1991). *Independence* refers to believing that one's worth comes from being self-sufficient and

DRESS IN THE NEWS
Sarkozy Bans Burqas

On April 11, 2011, French President Nicholas Sarkozy and his government, banned the public wearing of the burqa (and a similar garment, the niqab) in his country. The burqa is an outer garment that hides the female wearer from view, and typically covers the entire body and the face except for the eyes. The motivation was stated as the need to see the face of all people, for security reasons; further, Sarkozy is reported to have said it "is a sign of enslavement and debasement" (Price, 2011).

Since then, Barcelona, Spain has banned the wearing of burqa in government buildings, and Belgium has enacted a similar ban. Muslims, who typically wear this item, as well as many others, believe this action violates religious expression. Blogs and newscast reporters have wondered why this particular garment, worn by Muslim women, is any more a security issue than apparel such as baseball caps, sunglasses, or other items such as scarves that may be wrapped around the neck and face in cold weather. Why would a secular government want to become involved in religious sociofacts or the mentifacts influencing these symbols of expression?

DUBAI

We have discussed acculturation, assimilation, and ways culture is transformed. Dubai, United Arab Emirates, has recently undergone a huge transformation in commercial building, including high-rise office buildings (with the tallest building in the world, Burj Khalifa, 2,723 feet tall), retail stores, and entertainment venues. International companies are anxious to establish a presence in this emerging market and send employees overseas.

However, UAE mentifacts of modesty suggest that a very modest form of dress should be worn in the workplace and often in public generally, so international employees who have moved to Dubai are advised to be sensitive to cultural norms, to be conservative in their workplace dress by not wearing figure-hugging styles or revealing much skin. The long flowing, black gown ("abaya") that female citizens often wear need not necessarily be worn by internationals. Yet, sociofacts in Dubai would suggest that modest workplace dress codes may be loosened in clubs and other social venues, where jeans or more skin could be shown. UAE female citizens also wear Western dress under their abayas.

How do international employees relocated to Dubai know what can and cannot be worn in the workplace or in social venues? How do apparel companies wanting to locate here understand what product assortment can reasonably be marketed to both citizens and internationals? If you were a buyer planning to move into this international market for Abercrombie, the Gap, or Levi's, what would you include in your product assortments and promotional campaigns? American stores that already have a presence in Dubai include Adidas, Bennetton, Burberry, Armani jeans, Banana Republic, Calvin Klein, and Cartier, among others.

being in control of one's own choices and life. Individuals who believe in being independent value their autonomy. In contrast, *interdependence* refers to believing that one's success is based on how well one contributes to the group effort. It is collaboration rather than autonomy that is valued. Many Western cultures, including US culture, hold a world view of independence. However, many Asian and African cultures hold a world view of interdependence.

One universal of culture, or something that is held by each culture, is ideology. **Ideology** refers to the principle beliefs and values of a culture, a group, or a social movement. For example, Taoism is a Chinese philosophy based on simplicity and balance; the universe is balanced among five life forces (fire, water, wood, metal, rock). Environmentalism is a social movement that supports the protection and preservation of the environment for future generations and supports an arena in which industries can thrive in a sustainable manner without depleting the world's natural resources. Social justice is a social and political ideology that supports the equal distribution of goods and opportunities to all members of a social system regardless of any arbitrary factors such as race, ethnicity, or gender.

Understanding a group's ideology is important because the ideology of a group directs much of the decision-making of group members. For example, an environmentalist might purchase apparel made from natural or recycled fibers because she believes this practice will be better for the environment as a whole.

Sociofacts are the facts of social organization, including religion, education, government, family, economy, crime and punishment, and social status. For example, in the US, children are expected to begin formal education in public or private schools by age five. The first year of education is called kindergarten, followed by elementary school (generally grades 1 through 5 or 6), middle school (generally grades 6 or 7 through 8), and high school (grades 9 through 12). Post-secondary education is optional, but is pursued by the majority of students in the US, who attend a four-year college or university, or a community college or trade school for one to two years. These social organizations provide a means of organizing people's interactions so that the culture runs more smoothly. These facts of beliefs shape individuals' behaviors including their behavior concerning dress.

CONTEXT FOR THE STUDY OF DRESS

Whenever we study human behavior, including the behavior of dress, we do so in a context. That context will help us understand the rich nature of the behavior. Context can consist of:

- A physical setting
- A relationship with two or more people
- Social circumstances
- Historical time period

To understand why a specific item of dress is worn, we need to consider the context within which it is worn, along with the sociofacts and ideology of a group of people. Take, for example, a gut-skin parka or kamlaykas (or kamleika) worn by Inuit groups of the North (and other groups, including those in Labrador, Siberia, and the Aleutian Islands). The harsh and frozen conditions of most circumpolar regions of the world would necessitate wearing protective clothing that can withstand extremely cold temperatures and still keep the wearer warm, dry, and able to carry out his/her activities. In that harsh and frozen environment, there are many large sea and land mammals that provide materials for clothing; their large intestines can be cleaned and stitched together with a unique waterproof stitch using animal tendon or grass (Hickman, 2015) to create a lightweight, waterproof garment to be worn over a heavier fur parka in a kayak in wet, frigid water while fishing or on land in a wet snowstorm while hunting or traveling (Figure 1.12).

The context can be further explained through understanding the sociofacts of the group. In this example, it is important to know that the kamlaykas is typically made by a woman from the intestines of a sea animal that men have killed. Social circumstances of the context might include group hunting or fishing expeditions or the fact that there are many versions of the gut skin garment found among different cultures in the Arctic. Gut skin garments also have a spiritually protective function, worn by shamans during ceremonies (Hickman, 2015). The sound that dry gutskin makes is considered symbolic of contact with the spirit world and is worn to keep away evil spirits. Gut skin garments have also been part of Arctic dress across many time periods, perhaps as long as 4,000 years (Fitzhugh & Crowell, 1988).

If we were to compare another artifact, the beautiful tiny shoes for bound feet that existed for a period of about 1,000 years, from the tenth century to the early twentieth century (Jackson, 1997), we would have an entirely different context. The physical setting would be China, which encompasses a diverse geographic terrain. Girls whose feet were bound during this time period were usually members of the landowning class of more elite people, as opposed to farmers whose ability to walk the field would be impeded by bound feet. There were several interactions among individuals surrounding the phenomenon of binding the feet: among the female relatives in the young girl's family who carried out the binding, among female relatives and peers who taught the girl how to embroider and make beautiful slippers to occupy her time, and the interaction

Figure 1.12

Waterproof parkas (likely of seal or walrus intestine), worn over other layers of warm clothing, circa 1929.

between husband and wife who would use the bound foot in lovemaking (Jackson, 1997). Social circumstances dictated that middle and upper class girls were expected to bind their feet, although there were instances where farmers wanted their daughters' feet bound to attract suitors of higher socio-economic classes. Foot binding was outlawed in 1911 (Jackson, 1997), but it was still practiced into the early years of the twentieth century among Chinese living in Singapore and other areas (Figure 1.13).

Before we begin our study of dress, it is important to share our approach or perspective. Every situation is viewed through a particular point of view or perspective. Say, for example, you are watching a game at a football stadium. Your seat in the upper deck of the stadium causes you to see some of the events happening in the stadium with complete clarity (e.g., the actions of the people seated immediately in front of you), but your view of other events (e.g.,

Figure 1.13
Eighty-six-year-old Chinese woman whose feet were bound as a child shows how the bones of her four small toes were broken and re-shaped under her big toe, China's southern Yunnan province.

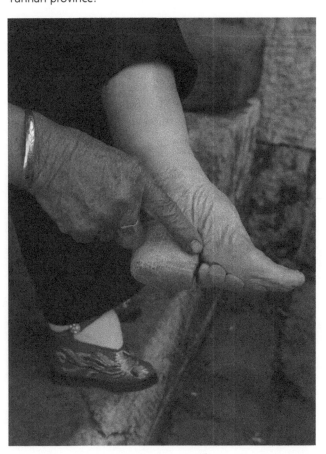

the coaching staff) is limited due to the location of your seat. This example illustrates how your physical location can influence your view of a football game. Individuals' observations of others' behavior are also impacted by their point of view. Your point of view causes you to see some aspects of an event and limits your ability to see others.

It is not possible for an individual to see all aspects of a situation simultaneously. Having a perspective is basic to our everyday existence because it is needed to make sense out of what is seen and experienced.

A good definition of perspective is **conceptual framework**. A framework provides us with a set of words to use to make sense out of our experiences. The words we use "cause us to make assumptions and value judgments about what we are seeing and not seeing" (Charon, 1992, p. 3). Because our perspective narrows what we see, whatever we know "must be seen as a truth gained from a certain perspective" (p. 4). The perspective we take guides our perceptions. Reality is interpreted by people in many different ways based on their perspective.

To complicate the matter, perspectives change throughout our lives. They also vary from situation to situation. Each situation we find ourselves in places us in a different role and causes us to change our perspective. As a student, you may have experienced a change in perspective as you moved from one role (e.g., student) to another (e.g., employee) throughout the day. The process of your college education has undoubtedly exposed you to a variety of perspectives. One such perspective that can be used to study and interpret behaviors is that of **social science**. Social scientists make certain assumptions about what to study and how to study it. Our approach in this textbook is a social science approach. The social sciences include many different disciplines (e.g., sociology, psychology, social psychology, anthropology, women's studies, cultural studies), each providing a perspective with which to view and interpret human behavior. Researchers interested in understanding dress have drawn from these various disciplines as well as others. In this book, we attempt to share a sampling of the variety of perspectives used to understand dress.

CONTEXTUAL PERSPECTIVE

A **contextual perspective of dress** (Kaiser, 1997) is well known among scholars as one method to study the social meanings of dress. There are three components that, together, create this approach: (1) a cognitive perspective, (2) a symbolic-interaction perspective, and (3) a cultural/historical perspective. These perspectives fit together to explain how people think about dress, how they negotiate meaning from dress in encounters with others, and how they use dress to shape their behaviors and others' behaviors. Following is a brief overview of each perspective.

Cognitive Perspective

A cognitive perspective is derived from psychology and focuses on what we know about appearance. We gather information about someone by looking at the forms of dress being worn and their specific configuration in color, style, or embellishment. The term used for this process is **appearance perception**. Appearance perception refers to the process of observing and interpreting the appearance of others (as well as interpreting one's own appearance). We use the information we gain from interpreting another's appearance to assign the individual appearing before us an **identity** (e.g., a definition of who they are). Assigning them an identity allows us to place them as a member of society and to shape our behavior toward them based on the assigned identity. We make inferences on the basis of numerous aspects of their appearance, including various aspects of their clothing such as its fashionability or whether it presents a pleasing sense of design. The inferences we draw can be related to numerous traits, including intelligence, friendliness, desirability, responsibility, whether they represent a threat, and so forth. Identities are further discussed in this book in Chapter 10.

As we interpret dress, we access the mental categories we have developed over the years representing stored information regarding appearance traits and their meanings; when we perceive someone, we quickly compare the characteristics they demonstrate to the mental categories we have developed, to see if there is a match. If so, then we have some idea how to "interpret" this appearance. Some key assumptions in the cognitive perspective are:

- We use numerous aspects of appearance to categorize individuals.
- We strive to be consistent in our appearance perceptions.
- We acknowledge that people use creativity and novelty in their appearances.
- We try to explain why people behave as they do in part on the basis of appearance cues.

Symbolic Interaction

This perspective is derived from sociology and focuses on how people construct their appearance as well as how others perceive an appearance. Key to this perspective is the idea that what dress means is negotiated between individuals. We interact with others in a setting, and we use symbols presented through appearance to fit our actions together. We use symbols because symbols convey meaning. In numerous first encounter situations, people come to conclusions about others on the basis of the symbols they present and decide whether or not to pursue any interaction. The decision on whether or not to interact could be based on the level of appearance similarity between the two people or whether the symbols worn by one person meet the expectations of the other, or a variety of other criteria.

For example, two of the authors of this book had their initial encounter during a break at a professional conference where they were each presenting research on the social psychology of appearance; both people were dressed similarly in professional, conservative suits that were navy blue, yet they wore different accessories. In an instant interaction, each person knew her own appearance management somewhat "matched" that of the other person, and each perceived the other's appearance as similar, yet distinctive. This similarity reduced any perceived threat and allowed them to engage in a conversation that became the start of a long friendship. Many other interactions are similarly carried forward or halted in such a short period of time based upon the way two people present themselves and perceive the presentation of others. Basic assumptions of this perspective are:

- We present information about ourselves to others via our appearance.

- We use symbols in our appearance to fit our communication together with others.
- We respond to others in part on the basis of appearance.
- We learn meanings of symbols through social interactions.
- Meanings of symbols are constantly modified.

Cultural/Historical Perspective

Derived from a number of disciplines, including anthropology, consumer behavior, gender studies, ethnic studies, and communications, this perspective focuses on culture and history as determinants of human behavior. A basic tenet of this perspective is that our cultural frame of reference gives us an understanding of our actions, since culture is shared with others. History also gives us a certain frame of reference; our cultural frame of reference is not the same today as it was five years ago, or ten, or one hundred.

Culture constantly evolves. Thus, our cultural/historical perspective acts as a screen or filter in understanding meaning and in interacting with others based on appearance. Our codes of communication stem from our shared beliefs, feelings, and values at a given point in time. Take, for example, our constantly changing standards of male and female beauty, which are heavily influenced by media and cultural icons. Appearances that were considered beautiful twenty years ago are not the same as what is considered beautiful today. What we consider to be ideal body shapes, body embellishments (e.g., cosmetics, tattoos, piercing, hairstyles), and body care (e.g., hair removal, tanning, scenting, exercise) change continually.

Specific assumptions of this perspective, as discussed by Kaiser (1997), are:

- Cultural forms (i.e., bodies, appearances, artifacts) represent shared cultural values.
- Cultural values are either perpetuated or questioned via dress and appearance.
- We can create our own realities by manipulating our dress.
- Culture uses abstract or fantasy representations of social life (media).
- We use culturally-constructed codes to send and receive messages about appearance.

By combining these three different perspectives, we have a comprehensive contextual framework for examining appearance and interpretations of appearance. This contribution to the field provides us with a useful means to dissect the myriad ways in which humans negotiate interactions on the basis of appearance.

CULTURAL VIEWPOINTS

As we noted earlier, our cultural frame of reference gives us a certain slant or understanding of our actions because we share culture with others. Thus, we come to understand our own behaviors concerning dress in light of our belief system and cultural practices. These behaviors seem "right" or "normal" to us, and we feel comfortable with them. However, their familiarity can also breed a feeling that a certain lifestyle, behaviors, or belief system is the only standard by which people should conduct their lives. Practicing **ethnocentrism**, or judging another culture by one's own standards, may lead to drawing incorrect conclusions about people or cultural groups who are different from us, and we may be prone to interpreting any differences as negative. Also, if a culture is relatively isolated from other cultures, either geographically or technologically, there is little contact with people whose beliefs, behaviors, or social institutions are different from their own, and this can lead to little understanding of practices different from their own when there is contact.

In contrast to ethnocentrism is the position of cultural relativity. **Cultural relativity** refers to finding worth in all cultural practices, since these practices arise from the universals of culture. Cultural relativity is a viewpoint that is objective and allows us to observe the behaviors of groups of people who are different from us and conclude that they have reasons for their behaviors, just as we have reasons for ours, that are grounded in their unique belief system and cultural practices. Taking the view of cultural relativity, along with greater contact with a variety of cultural groups (via travel, reading, global communications), we are able to draw better conclusions about others and use a less biased lens through which to view other people and their behavior.

For example, cultural relativity can be demonstrated in the following case. There is wide variety in human body modifications around the world—piercings, tattoos, scarification, shaping of body parts, cosmetics or body paint, hair coloring and shaping, and use of scented products. If it is not common practice in one's culture to pierce the lip and insert a large wooden plug, or to add many neck rings to elongate the neck (Figure 1.14), we may look at these modifications and have a strong negative response (an ethnocentric response). Yet, we might look at these same examples and marvel at the nature of the modifications and how they resemble the Western types of body piercing or how the neck rings resemble multiple layers of jewelry around the neck worn by many people of the world (a culturally relative response).

The more contact a culture has with another culture, the greater its familiarity with the beliefs and cultural practices of that culture. When two cultures have extensive contact and interaction with each other, they each learn to some extent the traditions, practices, and belief systems of the other. They may even share some cultural artifacts, such as clothing. This process is referred to as **acculturation**—cultural contact that may affect either or both cultures (Teske & Nelson, 1974). In Western cultures, we have many apparel artifacts that we adopted that originated in other cultures—the pajama (India), kimono style robe (Japan), and the kilt (Scotland) are all examples.

The level of sharing is not always equal when cultures interact, but there is typically some degree of sharing. For example, when one group is captured and transported to another culture, the captured individuals have no say in how they will be treated or what behaviors they will be forced to practice. Often, as a matter of survival, they must learn some of the captors' language and behaviors; their original cultural dress may be removed and they may be given dress from the culture that captured them. This was often the practice with the capture of individuals to serve as slaves within the US culture. However, US slave records have suggested that, even with the provision of elements of dress from the enslaving culture, the enslaved found ways to modify dress to present and preserve their own cultural aesthetics, as in tying a headscarf to approximate a "wrapper" from their West African roots (Hunt and Sibley, 1994). What was a symbol of oppression from plantation owners' perspectives may have actually been a symbol of identity among female slaves, carrying forward into modern culture as various ornate wrapped headdresses.

Some of the time, contact between cultures can result in **assimilation**. Assimilation occurs when a subculture

Figure 1.14
Neck rings on woman of Padaung tribe, north Thailand.

is gradually accepted into larger culture (Teske & Nelson, 1974). An example of assimilation is the migration of various cultural groups into the United States. As many people immigrated to the United States from European and Asian countries in the nineteenth and twentieth centuries, they often relinquished their indigenous dress in favor of US dress at the time of their immigration. This act, seemingly a small thing, served for some as a major step in blending in with other citizens—becoming less distinguishable as "other" and more distinguishable as part of the US melting pot of cultures. As immigrants became fluent in English, acquired jobs and housing, attended public schools and community events, they gradually became part of the social fabric of American culture.

CHARACTERISTICS OF CULTURE THAT AFFECT DRESS

Dress is only one behavior, but it is valuable in studying and learning about different cultures because, first, it is a visible manifestation of a culture. In addition, all cultures engage in dressing the body; it is possible to make comparisons between cultures on the basis of dress. Dress provides information about the social and cultural development of a group of people. Dress is a complex communication system that is influential in determining behaviors and their meanings. As we begin to dissect human behavior concerning dress, it is helpful to remember the following points.

First, culture is transmitted from one generation to another generation and from long-term members of the culture to newcomers. Culture may be transmitted via dress, values, ideologies related to appearance and group interaction, and many other means such as media, social institutions (religion, education, the family), and interpersonal communications.

Second, culture is learned. It is taught by some members and absorbed by others. All members of a culture or subculture are active players in the transmission and learning of culture. We learn many beliefs and behaviors from our families when we are young; we continue to learn from our peers and other influential members of culture as we develop into adulthood. We pass our cultural beliefs and behaviors on to others as we become models for younger or newer members of the culture.

Third, culture is shared via dress and other behaviors with all those we come into contact with and through mass media with those we may never have contact with.

Fourth, culture is transformed via dress and other behaviors since culture is always dynamic. Standards of beauty continually change, as do standards of modesty, norms of adornment, and displays of social status. Consider what a transformation may occur when a non-Western culture adopts Western practices of dress or Western standards of beauty. For example, double eyelid surgery in South Korea is the single most popular form of surgery, undertaken to create an eyelid shape that many Americans have, yet few Koreans have (Lee & Rudd, 1999). This practice has altered what is considered an attractive face.

The adoption and eventual rejection of apparel styles and ways of behaving transform culture. We have seen many changes in the speed of fashion movement and the variety of products available and consumed. Inventions may include (1) a whole new category of appearance such as street fashion like grunge clothing, or hip-hop clothing that corresponds to a music genre; (2) a new way of wearing something, such as jeans worn at hip level or below, intentionally exposing underwear; (3) new meanings attached to old items or practices, such as the co-opting of a classic style element such as a work shoe by a subculture who imbues it with new meaning.

The introduction and adoption of new technology also transforms a culture. Consider what the introductions of electricity and water power meant to communities and the production of goods in the eighteenth and nineteenth centuries. The introduction of home computers, the internet, micro-technology, and data mining of consumer habits represent an equivalent leap in technology for the late twentieth and early twenty-first centuries.

Chapter Summary

As seen in this chapter, one way to learn about dress is to study individuals from various cultures. Several questions might be asked, including what materials are used for dress, how dress is made, and how it is used. You may even explore further the material of dress by asking whether the dress adopted by members of the culture is simply a function of the environment in which the people live. (e.g., Fiji islanders are unlikely to wear sealskin garments (a) because seals are not available from which to make the garments, and (b) Fiji Islanders do not need fur garments to keep warm.)

It might also be useful to learn about the social norms concerning dress held by the cultural group. Clearly, what is considered appropriate or inappropriate to wear will impact several aspects of dressing the body, including what material is appropriate to use for dress. In the US, it is considered appropriate to use cow hide for shoes and belts, but this is not the case in India. Finally, the social institutions of a culture are also sometimes associated with the dress of that culture (e.g., the military and the judiciary often wear distinctive dress).

We have examined what we know about the origins of dress, as well as common functions that dress serves. A cross-cultural classification schema was provided to allow the reader to describe the body modifications and supplements of any person in any culture in any time period. Finally, we have discussed where we gather our information about dress and human behavior, noting advantages and biases with each source.

Key Terms

acculturation
appearance perception
artifacts
assimilation
attached to a garment
attached to the body
body modifications
body supplements
conceptual framework

contextual perspective of
    dress
cultural relativity
culture
diaspora
dress
ethnocentrism
fitted dress
generation gap

handheld dress
identity
ideology
mentifacts
norms
psychology
role models
socialization
social psychology of dress

social science
sociofacts
sociology
subculture or society
suspended dress
wrapped dress

Discussion Questions

1. What examples can you give of appearance making a difference to high school or college students on spring break?

2. What examples can you give of appearance and meaning during the Academy Awards, MTV Awards, or numerous other award shows?

3. What appearance issues are you most interested in— for example, school violence over clothing items, uniforms, body sculpting procedures and processes? Why?

4. How useful is the classification system in Figure 1.5 to analyze current body modifications and supplements seen in popular culture? Are there any examples you have difficulty classifying?

5. What aspects of your own identity are critical to the way you construct your appearance?

6. How are artifacts, mentifacts, and sociofacts important in your own culture? How are these reflected in your own dress or the dress of other members of your culture?

STUDiO™

Visit your book's STUDIO for additional quiz questions, vocabulary flashcards, and chapter worksheets!

Suggested Readings

Eicher, J., & Evenson, S. (2015). *The visible self: Global perspectives on dress, culture, and society* (4th ed.). New York, NY: Fairchild Books.

Fry, R. (2016, April 25). Millennials overtake Baby Boomers as America's largest generation. Pew Research Center. Retrieved from http://www.pewresearch.org /fact-tank/2016/04/25/millennials-overtake-baby -boomers

References

Bump, P. (2014, March 25). Here is when each generation begins and ends, according to facts. *The Atlantic*. Retrieved from http://www.theatlantic.com/national /archive/2014/03/here-is-when-each-generation- begins-and-ends-according-to-facts/359589

Charon, J. (1992). *The meaning of sociology*. New York, NY: Prentice Hall.

Eicher, J., & Evenson, S. (Eds.). (2015). *The visible self: Global perspectives on dress, culture, and society* (4th ed.). New York, NY: Fairchild Books.

Fitzhugh, W. & Crowell, A. (1988). *Crossroads of continents: Cultures of Siberia and Alaska*. Washington, DC: Smithsonian Institution.

Fry, R. (2016, April 25). Millennials overtake Baby Boomers as America's largest generation. Pew Research Center. Retrieved from http://www.pewresearch.org /fact-tank/2016/04/25/millennials-overtake-baby -boomers

Hickman, P. (2015). Innerskins/outerskins: Gut and fishskin. In Eicher, J., & S. Evensen (Eds.) *The visible self: Global perspectives on dress, culture, and society* (4th ed.) (pp. 171–176). New York, NY: Fairchild Books.

Hunt, P. & Sibley, L. (1994). African American Women's Dress in Georgia, 1890–1914: A Photographic Examination, *Clothing and Textiles Research Journal, 12*(2), 20–26.

Huxley, J. (n.d.). In *Wikipedia*. Retrieved January 5, 2010 from http://en.wikipedia.org/wiki/ Julian _Huxley

Jackson, B. (1997). *Splendid Slippers: A thousand years of an erotic tradition*. Berkeley, CA: 10 Speed Press, Inc.

Kaiser, S. (1997). *The social psychology of clothing: Symbolic appearances in context* (Rev. 2nd ed.).New York, NY: Fairchild Books.

Lee, S. H. & Rudd, N. A. (1999). Beneath the skin: Body image and cosmetic surgery among Korean and American females. *International Journal of Costume Culture, 2*(1), 21–30.

Markus, H. R. & Kitayama, S. (1991). Culture and the self: Implications for cognition, emotion, and motivation. *Psychological Review, 98*, 224–53.

Powell, A. (2010). Amish 101: Amish culture, beliefs, and lifestyle: History of the Amish. About Travel: Pittsburgh. Retrieved from http://pittsburgh.about.com/cs /pennsylvania/a/amish_2.htm

Price, R. C. (2011). Banning the burqa: Behind the veil of France's new law. *The Huffington Post*. Retrieved from http://www.huffingtonpost. com/robyn-carolyn-price /banning-the-burqa-behind-_b_849937.html

Roach, M. E. & Eicher, J. (1973). *The visible self: Perspectives on dress*. Englewood Cliffs, NJ: Prentice Hall.

Roach, M. E. & Musa, K. (1980). *New perspectives on the history of western dress*. New York, NY: Nutriguides.

Roach-Higgins, M. E. & Eicher, J. (1992). Dress and identity. *Clothing and Textiles Research Journal, 10*(4), 1–8.

Roach-Higgins, M. E., Eicher, J. & Johnson, K. (1995). *Dress and identity*. New York, NY: Fairchild.

Ruth, J. L. (Writer). (2000). *The Amish: A people of preservation* [Motion picture]. (Available from Heritage Productions, US).

Spradley, J. (1972). *Culture and cognition: Rules, maps, and plans*. San Francisco, CA: Chandler Publishing.

Stein, J. (2013, May 20). Millennials, the me-me-me generation. *Time*. Retrieved from http://time.com/247 /millennials-the-me-me-me-generation

Teske, Jr., R. & Nelson, B. (1974). Acculturation and assimilation: A clarification. *American Ethnologist, 1*(2), 351–367.

Tylor, E. B. 1974. *Primitive culture: researches into the development of mythology, philosophy, religion, art, and custom*. New York: Gordon Press. (Original work published 1871)

Williams, A. (2015, September 18). Move over millennials, here comes generation Z. *The New York Times*. Retrieved from http://www.nytimes.com/2015/09/20/fashion /move-over-millennials-here-comes-generation -z.html?_r=0

ORIGINS AND FUNCTIONS OF DRESS

After reading and reflecting on the content of this chapter, students should be able to:

- Distinguish between origins and functions of dress.
- Consider evidence of origins of dress.
- Consider cross-cultural modifications of dress.
- Explore where and how we gather information about dress.

INTRODUCTION

Using our working definition of dress to include all body modifications and body supplements, people have dressed for hundreds of thousands of years (Anawalt, 2007). While early records are not as accurate or as complete as records since the invention of the written word, and early evidence of dress has often been partially destroyed by the passage of time, we still have very strong evidence of the beginnings of dress and the role it has played in human behavior. This is a rich area of study that has been informed by anthropology, archaeology, ethno-history, history of art, linguistics, textiles, and clothing, among others. In this chapter we will examine how people began to dress, the purposes that dress serves, and how we know what we know about dress. We rely on major findings that occurred in the last part of the twentieth century as well as early pioneering findings that changed our knowledge about the origins of dress.

ORIGINS OF DRESS

We rely on both visual and written records to document dress. Visual records consist of actual artifacts or remnants of artifacts, and visual representations of dress

such ancient cave drawings, illustrations, paintings, photographs, and sculpture, among others. Written records include historians' accounts, records of anthropologists and explorers, diaries from travelers and private individuals, and published research. Of course, before written language, which is thought to have originated in Mesopotamia around 3200 BCE (Collins, 2003), we have only visual records to guide our understanding. When it comes to actual artifacts of dress made of animal skins, plant and animal fibers, many of those have not lasted because they are made of organic materials that decompose over time.

We established in Chapter 1 that dressing the body includes any modifications made to the body or supplements added to the body. Thus, a basic question that is easy to ask and difficult to answer concerns the **origins of dress**, or when and where humans began dressing the body.

We first turn to **archaeology**, the study of past civilizations and ancient people for evidence concerning early forms of dress. There is ample evidence that ancient cultures dressed the body using a variety of techniques and materials. For example, a grave in Lake Mungo, New South Wales, Australia dated to about 40,000–60,000 years ago, was found with ochre next to human bones, suggesting that the powdery mineral substance may have been used on the body as a means of body decoration (Gilligan, 2011). A similar grave with ochre exists in France (Figure 2.1). Beads were used as decoration on fitted garments and on necklaces from Sungir burials (present-day Russia) dating to the Upper Paleolithic period, about 35,000 BCE–8000 BCE (Anawalt, 2007, p. 81). A beaded necklace probably made of kangaroo bones around 12,000–19,000 years ago was also found in Australia (Collins, 2003). Other evidence of early body coverings includes stone scrapers dating back 60,000–100,000 years ago, found in many parts of the world, including Africa, Europe, and Asia (Collins, 2003). One probable use was to scrape tissue and muscle away from animal hides to prepare them

Figure 2.1

Paleolithic burial of young adult woman, St. Germain-le-Ridiere, France, showing red ochre around body.

for body coverings. Eyed needles carved of bone, dating to the Upper Paleolithic period (35,000–8000 years BCE), have been found in southern France (Collins, 2003) and in what is now the state of Washington (Lyman, 2015). These early needles were likely used to sew animal skins together using pieces of animal intestines or tendons, thus creating a more fitted garment than wrapping flat skins around the body. Such garments were warmer and accommodated body movement because they were shaped to the body's configuration.

We also have archaeological evidence of textiles that were created in early cultures. For instance, people located in Scandinavia and eastern southern Europe used heavy stones to weight the ends of yarn in upright vertical looms about 18,000 BCE; these stones have indentations on both sides to suggest that warp yarns were wrapped around them tightly in an effort to keep them taut as the fabric was woven (Barber, 1994). Remains of linen fibers were found in Anatolia (modern day Turkey) dating to about 6500 BCE; woven silk in China dating to about 2700 BCE; and twined and knotted textiles in Peru before 1100 BCE (Collins, 2003). Other finds from archaeological digs have found carved figurines some 22,000 years old that depict **string skirts** or aprons worn by women in Lespugue, France (Collins, 2003), in Austria (Barber, 1994), and even older finds in Moravia (modern Czech Republic) dating from about 24,000–29,000 years ago (Park, 2000.)

In North America, archeological sites in New York have produced small samples of diagonally twined fabric dating to about 10,000 years ago and a woven sandal in Missouri dating to about 8,000 years ago (Adovasio & Hyland, 2000).

Evidence of other potential body coverings comes from mummies found around the world. For instance, in northern Chile, burial sites of the Chinchorro people dating to 8000 BCE indicated evidence of string or grass skirts worn by women (Oakland, 2008). These Chinchorro people practiced mummification until about 1700 BCE. By contrast, the Egyptian culture did not begin the practice of mummification until about 2500 BCE (Wilcox, 1998), even though the mummies from the Nile Valley are perhaps the best known in the world. **Mummies** are preserved human remains that are intentionally preserved by other humans; human remains may also be unintentionally preserved by the environment. Mummies preserved by humans have revealed many different styles of mummification, including removing organs, drying the body with different salts (Wilcox, 1998), sometimes stuffing the body with materials such as grass or dirt and reinforcing the body structure with sticks (Arriaza, 1995), and sealing the skin with tree sap, or a paste of ashes, or paint (Arriaza, 1995). Mummies have been found covered in linen wrappings, wrapped in "bundles" made of leather or twined reeds, and often have elements of dress included. The

Chinchorro mummies included wrapped cords around the waist and reed shrouds that covered the shoulders; cactus needles with cord attached were also found, perhaps used for fishing or making nets or twined fabrics (Arriaza, 1995). Textile scholars believe that the shrouds were probably made using a warp-weighted loom and a twining technique; they may have been painted in earlier times, but by 6000 BCE they were probably embroidered with geometric designs using dyed hair of animals in the llama, alpaca, and vicuñ a family (Cassman, Odegaard, & Arriaza, 2008).

Other mummies dating some 3,200–4,000 years old were found around Ürümqi, in the vast desert in China (Barber, 1999). They contained dyed woolen garments, felt hats and boots, twined belts, and carved bone pins that may have been used to hold garments closed on men, women, and children (Barber, 1999; Hadingham, 1994). An interesting side note is that these carefully preserved mummies were Caucasian (probably of Celtic origin from northwest Europe), not Asian, causing speculation that they were travelling an ancient trade route between China and Europe.

The tomb of the Egyptian pharaoh, Tutankhamun, was discovered in the early twentieth century, and revealed a massive collection of shrines, funerary objects, and the pharoah's three coffins dating to 1325 BCE (Gilbert, Holt, & Hudson, 1976). In the innermost coffin was the mummy of the boy-king, thought to have died around age twenty, covered by a solid gold mask (Figure 2.2) showing his eyes lined with a black substance, pierced ears, an elaborate headdress with a cobra above the forehead, and a gold necklace with inlaid glass. Many other personal objects were found, including both items he had used in his lifetime and items thought to be needed in his next life. Ornate daggers, protective necklaces, bracelets, and other amulets were rich with symbols signifying life, infinity, devotion to parents, the sun god, and safe passage through the underworld. Sadly, the mummy was very badly decomposed.

Fur and skin garments have been found from the Late Stone Age, some 2500–5000 years BCE, and the Bronze Age, about 2000–2500 years BCE, in burial sites in Russia. Ornaments composed of animal teeth and beads of ivory were also found in these sites. Another rare find was the Iceman, "Ötzi," so named because he was found in the Ötztal region in the Italian Alps of Italy in 1991 and dated to about 3300 years BCE (Ryder, 1996). He was

Figure 2.2
Solid gold mask found in tomb of King Tuthankhamen, Egyptian pharaoh, dating to about 1300 years BCE.

found partially clothed, wearing a bearskin cap, a tunic or vest made of strips of deerskin and goatskin, a cloak woven with grass and bast fibers from the bark of a linden tree, leggings and moccasins of both bear skin and deer hide (Dickson, Oeggl, & Handley, 2005; Jaroff, 1992; Ryder, 1996). See Figure 2.3 for an artist's rendering of these items. His shoes were stuffed with grass for insulation from cold. The body was also tattooed; tattooing was speculated to be a mark of puberty (Jaroff, 1992).

Another discovery, that of the Siberian Ice Maiden of the Pazyryk horse-riding culture of the Eurasian steppes, dates to about 2,400 years ago. She had an ornate headdress made of hair and felt, a silk blouse, a woolen skirt, and blue tattoos of horned animals (Polosmak, 1994).

Figure 2.3

Artist's rendering of Iceman mummy remnants found in Italian Alps, dating to about 3000 years BCE.

In North America, remains from the Spirit Man Cave in Nevada revealed a Paleo-Indian human of about 9,400 years ago who wore a constructed blanket woven of twisted strips of rabbit fur and cords of hemp (Wright, 1999).

Aside from a few remaining actual remnants of prehistoric dress, we also have depictions of early dress from carbonized textiles in Çatal Hüyük, Anatolia (modern Turkey) dating to about 6000 BCE. Other finds were fossilized clay textile impressions found in the Czech Republic that dated to about 27,000 years ago (Soffer, 2004).

Artwork has also recorded the dress of ancient peoples. A 20,000 year-old sculpture (female figure) of carved bone found in France depicts a skirt made of fibers twisted into string (Barber, 1994,). Many figurines elsewhere have also shown elaborate braided hairstyles or beard shapes. Petroglyph carvings in stone found among many indigenous peoples around the world (North and South America, South Pacific, Scandinavia, Australia) have often depicted the clothing and bodily adornment of men and women and are considered to be a form of expression predating writing, often between 3,000–12,000 years old.

What does all this evidence tell us? It confirms that we know with some degree of certainty that people have been wearing clothing and decorating the body as early as the Paleolithic Period. Archaeologists have uncovered some tremendous finds related to the early existence of forms of dress and the technology to produce those early forms. The few examples mentioned above provide evidence of body supplements that were suspended (string skirts), wrapped (hides wrapped around the shoulders or torso), fitted (animal skins sewn together in shaped garments), and attached (feathers attached to the body or to garments). Evidence of ochre in burial sites, clay figurines depicting coiled hairstyles, cave paintings showing feathered headdresses, and mummies with tattoos are evidence of early body modification.

While these archeological finds are very exciting, and slowly put together a picture of the origins of human dress much as one finds all the pieces to a jigsaw puzzle, these finds also raise considerable discussion concerning the reasons behind the phenomenon of dress. We turn next to a discussion of functions of dress.

FUNCTIONS OF DRESS

Scientists have considered the wide variety of **functions** or purposes that dress serves. Scholars began studying functions of dress in the early twentieth century, and identified distinct functions of dress as physical protection, psychological protection, modesty, attraction, status or display of success, and adornment or aesthetics (Hiler, 1929; Hirn, 1900). These same functions of dress were confirmed by scholars writing in the latter part of the century, although with slightly different names. These were ornamentation, concealment, protection, social identification, and adornment (Horn & Gurel, 1981; Schwartz, 1979; Taylor, 1973). While we cannot truly know why humans began to dress their bodies, it is interesting to speculate on functions of dress as possible explanations. Here we present various ideas about origins of dress stemming from two broad functions: dress as a form of protection and as a form of communication.

Protection

Protection refers to dress that maintains physical comfort in hostile environments (e.g., extreme cold, heat) and dress that provides psychological comfort to ward off harm or bring good luck. Given that humans have limited capacity to adapt to their surrounding physical environments in terms of temperature, geographical landscape, and harm caused by insects or animals, dress that helps to mediate these environments and serves as a form of physical protection (Figure 2.4) has been developed by nearly all cultures that have been discovered. Examples include warm clothing that allows humans to maintain their

body temperature while exposed to cold temperatures, or shoes that protect the feet from the impact of walking and allow us to walk over rocky, prickly, or other inhospitable terrain. Of course, those dress adaptations vary widely according to perceived need, available resources, and skill in using the resources. Dress enables humans to expand their capabilities, to move and be active in circumstances otherwise not possible (e.g., space suits that allow movement in deep space or sunscreen lotions that allow prolonged exposure to the sun). By protecting the body, dress extends the body's capabilities in these instances, allowing humans to do things that otherwise would not be possible.

Protection from supernatural forces or evil spirits is also a motivation for dress. These forces are believed to cause illness, death, or bad luck, among other misfortunes. Thus, items of dress may ward off evil spirits or negative

Figure 2.4
Mexican highlands poncho for physical protection.

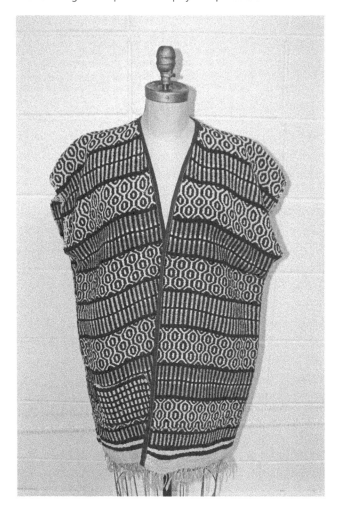

Figure 2.5
Blue-eyed bracelet provides psychological protection.

Figure 2.6
Modesty in celebrity fashion, Gwen Stefani.

forces, help to ensure positive forces, and may seem "magical." A blue-eyed bracelet (Figure 2.5) worn by a small baby or attached to a crib may ensure protection in Turkey and Egypt; a mustard seed pendant worn by an American girl may bring good luck before an exam; a sheer veil worn during a Western wedding ceremony may protect a new bride from the evil eye or any evil spirits that might torment her during the ceremony.

Communication

Many things can be communicated through dress, including modesty, immodesty, adornment, and status. **Communication** is the exchange of information.

Modesty and immodesty. Modesty refers to covering certain body parts out of a sense of shame or embarrassment. It is a cultural and social construct that is learned from one's peers. Different cultures believe that different parts of the body should be covered. To leave these body parts uncovered could result in experiencing shame or embarrassment. Areas of the body that are covered are often linked with reproduction, or sexual attraction, but not always. Thus, in some cultures, body parts that should be concealed are centered on primary and secondary sexual characteristics such as the breasts and genitalia. For other cultures, what is concealed are the feet or the face. Covering these body parts for these cultures may be an attempt to control sexual activity between humans. The body parts to be concealed may be based not only on ideas concerning what comprises sexual attraction or seduction, but may also be related to religious beliefs stated in widely-accepted

texts, or may be related to common cultural practices. Beliefs about what comprises a modest appearance change over time, as illustrated by the amount of skin covered or revealed in Western women's dress over the last two centuries, and even in the last two decades (Figure 2.6).

Rather than concealing the body, individuals can also use dress to call attention to specific body parts that are associated with sexual characteristics and behaviors. **Immodesty** refers to dressing the body to draw attention to these parts of the body by uncovering them or

Figure 2.7
Sumo wrestlers, Japan.

exaggerating them. It is the opposite of modesty and is also a cultural and social construct. An early writing on the codpiece, an article of male dress worn in Europe about 1450, states that the most obvious function of this genital covering was to attract attention to the male genitals (Benedict, 1931). Concealment may increase interest, while full exposure may result in indifference.

Which aspect of the body is revealed or concealed varies by culture and time period. Women's cleavage has been the focus of attention in some cultures and times, while the back of the neck has been the focal point in others, and also feet or other body parts. Calling attention to the body may be for non-sexual reasons as well. The bulk of a Sumo wrestler (Figure 2.7) or the shape of a competitive body builder is the focus of attention when appearing in a relative state of undress. While we might consider modesty as we dress ourselves, it is unlikely that modesty was why dress originated. Since many humans appeared nude in tropical regions of the world, it was unlikely that dress was first used for purposes of appearing either modest or immodest. Modesty and immodesty are learned behaviors that have their roots in whatever is the accepted fashion of the times.

Adornment/Ornamentation. Many writers believe that adornment is the one universal communicative function of dress, given that we have more evidence of this practice than the other functions of dress. **Adornment** refers to dressing the body in order to make it aesthetically pleasing, communicating knowledge of the aesthetic ideals of the culture. Adorning the body may be rooted in our primate heritage,

since other species embellish themselves with beads, berries, rags, and other available resources. Adornment also allows us to express our creativity by decorating, shaping, altering, or covering the body. Adorning the body can take many forms, including painting, tattooing, scarring, reshaping, piercing, scenting, retexturing, and adding to or subtracting from body size. Adornment is often culturally determined, in that the practice of a behavior such as piercing will vary from culture to culture in what is considered beautiful, who may be adorned in this manner, and how it is carried out. Consider these variations in piercing in Figure 2.8, for example.

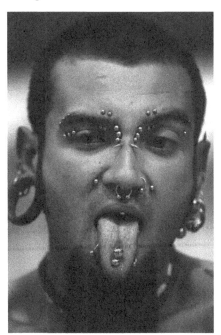

Figure 2.8
Adornment seen in piercings of Bulgarian man.

Status. Human beings place different value on various human attributes and various social positions, such that rulers are often differentiated from those they rule. In one culture, it might be more valuable to be old than to be young. In another culture, it might be the reverse. Dress can be used to communicate one's **status** (rank, importance, achievement) within a culture, because we assign meanings to dress and use dress to communicate both human and cultural attributes including age, sex, class, caste, or accomplishments. For example, only the Tuareg men of the Sahara desert of Africa (nomads who rely on camels for transport across dry and sandy terrain) wear dark blue veils dyed with indigo. Certainly physical

protection is offered by the veil, which shields wearers from the intense sun glare of the desert sand, yet women do not veil themselves (Beckwith & Fisher, 2002). Therefore, the veil distinguishes men from women.

Another example of status can be seen in crowns, usually decorated with valuable jewels, which have historically been used to indicate a person with a royal title (Figure 2.9). The use of fur has also indicated status in many cultures. Although the use of fur has received much public outcry as a fashion item since the late twentieth century, a fur coat in Western cultures is frequently interpreted as a symbol of wealth. Yet another example of status can be seen in military uniforms. Various embellishments on a military uniform indicate the wearer's position within the military. Human attributes that increase or decrease the status of an individual vary from culture to culture, but dress is often used as a means of communicating status.

Figure 2.9
Queen Elizabeth II of England wears her Imperial State Crown and the crown jewels for the opening of Parliament, London, England.

WHERE DOES INFORMATION ABOUT DRESS COME FROM?

Information about dress comes from a variety of sources. As we noted earlier, artifacts of dress provide certain types of information. There are also written and visual sources of information, as well as our own "lived experience" of constructing our appearance and making observations about the appearance of others. Each of these sources of information is described briefly.

Artifacts of Dress

Whole garments or accessories, or surviving fragments of dress located in archaeological sites, can provide us with a wealth of information about the dress of a group of people. Artifacts can provide information about the materials used, the type of construction or processing of materials, the forms of dress, their embellishment, and other information about the cultural context. For example, the bark vest in Figure 2.10 is worn by a tribe in the Borneo rain forest. It was acquired by one of the book authors. By examining the artifact closely, we can see that it is made of the bark fiber of a tree; chances are good that it came from the inner side of the bark on a tree, since the fibers were soft and more easily processed than the outer rough bark. While the people in the market where it was sold did not know what tree bark was used, we could surely discover

Figure 2.10
Bark vest from Borneo.

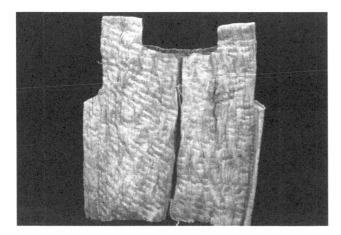

this information with additional analysis conducted by botanists. We do know that the process used to produce the garment was to soak the bark fiber until it was soft, pound it with a rock or hard object to flatten it, and repeat this process until the bark was soft and flexible enough to form around the body.

Simple hand stitching was used to attach the two front pieces and the back pieces together; an overcast stitch was used and the material appears to be very narrow strips of bark fiber twisted into a cord. There were no dyes used, and the only embellishment on the garment is two tiny strings that are used to tie the garment closed at the front. The form of dress, using the classification scheme in Figure 1.5 in Chapter 1, is a combination of suspended and fitted forms of dress, and the strings on the front are attachments. Because we purchased this artifact in the environment where it is worn, we know that it is worn by men, women, and children. We also know it serves a function of physical protection in the tropical rain forest, where it is both hot and humid.

It is fortunate when we have whole garments or other artifacts of dress, such as accessories, available to analyze, because the information they provide is often more complete than that provided by only a few surviving fragments of dress. However, information has also been gleaned from small fragments that have survived. Dress of the past is limited in availability, because it was made from perishable organic materials such as plant and animal fibers (cotton, linen, silk, wool), leather, and fur.

Textile scientists, who specialize in archaeological textiles, study remaining fragments of dress and are often able to put together small pieces of information into a fairly comprehensive analysis of the products and the people who wore them. Textiles survive in archaeological contexts for many reasons:

- They may be desiccated or preserved through drying, as in the case of Egyptian tomb artifacts, clothing artifacts found in the Chinese desert, and textile artifacts found in the Paracas Peninsula of Peru (Paul, 1991). The human remains in Ürümqi China, discussed in this chapter, were dug up from burial sites between the arid foothills and the desert. Naturally dry conditions of the desert sand, with daytime temperatures over 100 degrees, dried out the bodies and clothes, thus leaving their skin, hair, and artifacts fairly intact. In Peru, some 420 mummy bundles from the Paracas culture (about 750 BCE to 100 CE) were discovered in the mid-twentieth century in subterranean burial chambers, well preserved by dry, sandy conditions. These human remains had many layers of cloaks wrapped around them. Fragments of these textiles indicate that the cloaks are made of cotton, are woven in a tapestry technique with additional wool fibers, and feature many small human and animal figures in brightly colored yarns (Paul, 1991).

- They may be frozen, as in the Iceman mummy of the Italian Alps discussed in this chapter. Scholars believe that this man was wounded by an arrow, fell into a trench, and died during a snowstorm. The trench became filled with water and was frozen for thousands of years during the Ice Age, thus protecting him. He is estimated to be about 5,000 years old and was found partially sticking out of the ice by mountain climbers in 1991. Officials damaged the body and some of the clothes in their attempt to free it from the ice. Tourists quickly visited the site before the body was freed and took fragments of garments and tools as souvenirs. However, enough fragments remained to determine a likely scenario of his dress as discussed in this chapter (Jaroff, 1992).

- They may be immersed in fluid with certain chemical characteristics. Human remains between 1,500 and 2,000 years old have been found in bogs in Denmark and Germany. They have been preserved due to the acidic, wet, swampy conditions that exist in bogs (Wilcox, 1998).

ARCHAEOLOGY, CONSERVATION, AND FORENSICS

by Dr. Kathryn Jakes, Textile Scientist Emeritus, The Ohio State University

Through multiple analytical methods, archaeological scientists learn the composition of the objects that have been recovered from sites. The results of these analyzes help them to identify such information as the types of fibers and dyes used or whether the items were worn and used prior to their burial. The same analyzes are necessary for a conservator to understand the object and determine the best way to preserve it for the future. Cellulosic fibers (plant fibers), for example, require different treatment than proteinaceous fibers (protein materials like silk or wool).

The same analyzes are also used by forensic scientists to identify and understand materials recovered from criminal cases. Not only can the fibers and dyes be identified, but the results derived from the analysis of the fiber will provide evidence for stains, such as blood. They can also provide evidence for mechanical activity, such as cutting with a knife versus cutting with scissors versus tearing.

Bogs form in low-lying land where water collects and cannot drain off. Plants grow in these fertile swamps, and when they die they decompose, forming acids. These acids preserve protenaceous objects (things with protein) in the bogs. Thus, skin and leather objects are preserved, but plant materials such as sewing thread on boots, are destroyed (Sibley & Jakes, 1984).

- They may have been charred or carbonized by fire in burning ceremonies long before being found by archeologists. This charring destroys the organic components of the textiles, yielding carbon products that are not subject to microbial degradation. Charred textile fragments recovered from Seip Mound in Ohio were likely formed through burning ceremonies practiced by the people of the Hopewell Culture. The charred remains, though blackened and fragile, display the features of the twined textiles; gradations of black are indicative of a former pattern of coloration on the fabric surfaces (Thompson & Jakes, 2005).
- They may become mineralized through association with metals. For example, a prehistoric bronze spear point corroded and created mineral decomposition products that fused into the silk wrapping around the spear point (Jakes & Sibley, 1984). The organic composition of the silk was replaced with copper products to form a "**pseudomorph**" (false form) (Figure 2.11). Over time, the bronze caused the silk fabric

Figure 2.11
Magnified pseudomorph of woven fabric with silk fibers, 3500 BCE, mineralized by a Chinese bronze spearpoint. Individual silk filaments are about 28–37 microns in diameter.

to mineralize, leaving fragments that could be examined. Fragments from the Etowah mounds in Georgia revealed twined textiles with feathers included in them (Sibley & Jakes, 1989; Sibley, Jakes, & Swinker, 1992).

Written Sources

Written sources include all written historical records, diaries and personal accounts; travelers' ethnographic accounts; novels, catalogs, songs, poetry, and scholarly journal articles. These sources may be purely descriptive, such as diaries that may record the items, colors, and embellishments of dress that have been observed, and they may contain a narrow point of view that describes artifacts as different, strange, or offensive. Ethnographic accounts (**ethnographies**) may be more objective in their descriptions, although they too run the risk of bearing the biases and values of the authors. They may be interpretive of behavior as well, and they may be accompanied by hand-drawn illustrations or photographs. A well-known early ethnographic account was produced by Edward S. Curtis (n.d.), the first person who photographed numerous North American Indian tribes in the early 1900s, and wrote about them in his journals. These twenty volumes depicting American and Canadian tribes in the American Southwest, California, Northwest, Western Canada, and Alaska were produced between 1907 and 1930. Long before the advent of digital photography and computers, Curtis went through a painstaking process of taking still photographs of his subjects on a large camera, etching the images onto metal plates for printing books, and developing the prints himself. He also took notes about the subjects he photographed to compile one of the first complete ethnographies of North American tribes.

Another early pioneering study was done by Captain James Cook, an explorer who made copious notes and drawings during his three voyages in the Pacific in the late 1700s and early 1800s (Aughton, 2002; Collingridge, 2003). The intent of this British explorer was to navigate and map the islands and continents in the Pacific Ocean, which he did, including Australia and New Zealand, Antarctica, Tahiti, the Hawaiian archipelago, and also the coastline of North America from Oregon to the Bering Strait in the mid-1700s. Yet he also kept journals with extensive notes about the indigenous people he met in these locations. His crew included botanists, artists, and other scientists who identified thousands of plant species, illustrated the terrain, and gathered a wealth of other scientific information.

Such written records, observations, images, and commentaries are secondary sources, subject to interpretation by the author. They report things as they see them, but are influenced by their own experiences. Thus, the drawings of Native Americans by early travelers to the North American continent appear more European than Indian. For example, images of Pocahontas changed over time. The American Indian princess, Pocahontas, lived in the early 1600s along the James River in what is now Virginia

(Ross, 1999). She was born with the name Matoaka, and was the daughter of Powhatan, a powerful chief of the Tidewater Algonquin tribes. It is thought that Pocahontas was a pet name, meaning frolicsome. The first known depiction of her is a 1616 engraved portrait in the National Portrait Gallery of the Smithsonian Institute in Washington, DC, in which she was depicted with high cheekbones and intense eyes but dressed in an English stovepipe hat and lacy ruff collar. Over a century later, an oil painting was done by an unknown artist who saw the first engraving. In this color painting, Pocahontas is shown with more Anglicized facial features and brown hair. The point made by the author is that depictions of Pocahontas probably imbued her with more European virtues and characteristics over the years because it is believed that she assisted the English who settled in the area, eventually married a tobacco grower there, and moved to England (Ross, 1999).

One of your book authors kept a personal diary in seventh grade, in which she recorded who she talked with each day, ate with in the school lunchroom, how her classes went, what assignments she had, what boy she silently admired, and, most importantly, how she dressed each day. She recorded her efforts to walk in her first pair of high heels, her new haircut, wearing nylon stockings, and details about her clothing such as the color, style, fit, and accessories.

Costume historians provide an interpretive analysis of dress as part of the overall social, political, or economic context of the time period in which it was worn. Analytical examinations of dress utilize historical methodology in connecting dress to the broader behavior of the time. For example, a very complete history of world dress was undertaken by Anawalt (2007), and covers what is known about dress in various regions of the world, including the Middle East, Europe, Central Asia, East Asia, South Asia, Southeast Asia, Oceania, North America, South America, and Africa. It includes over 1,000 illustrations and photographs and draws from a rich bibliography of scholars who have studied the history of dress in each of these regions.

Textile historians, by contrast, focus primarily on the textiles used in dress, examining the materials from which textiles were made, their properties (such as weaving, knitting, knotting, crochet, lace-making, plaiting, etc.), their dyeing materials (natural or synthetic dyes), dyeing techniques (such as tie-dye, ikat, batik), and embellishments (such as embroidery, needlepoint, mirror-work, printing, pleating, tufting, etc.). For example, Ginsburg

(1991) edited a complete volume on historic textiles from early times through the current world textile industry. Her contributors are all textile scholars who specialize in specific time periods and the influence of these time periods on the textile industry (such as the Industrial Revolution) or they specialize in specific textile manufacturing techniques (i.e., embroidery, tapestry, lace-making). Other historians focus on a specific type of textile. For example, a volume on the Scottish tartan (Zaczek & Phillips, 2004) examines the origins of the tartan, suppression by the British during the 1700s, and the specific designs and colors of tartans indicating the different highland family clans.

Literature (novels, poems, short stories) often use verbal images of dress of the characters in an attempt to "paint" their true nature. Dress may also be used as a metaphor for something else. For example, this quote from the epic book, *Gone with the Wind*, describes how Scarlett realizes that she was never in love with Ashley, a former boyfriend who married her friend Melanie, but only with the thought of loving him.

> "He never really existed at all, except in my imagination," she thought wearily. "I loved something I made up, something that's just as dead as Melly is. I made a pretty suit of clothes and fell in love with it. And when Ashley came riding along, so handsome, so different, I put that suit on him and made him wear it whether it fitted him or not. And I wouldn't see what he really was. I kept on loving the pretty clothes—and not him at all." (Mitchell, 1936, p. 1016)

Also, we could read the following passage from *Memoirs of a Geisha* to get a strong impression of how a young geisha, who had been in training for two years, grew into a young woman and what this meant to her as she was fitted in her first kimono:

> Finally Mameha [geisha house mother] asked Tatsumi [assistant] to take me into the back room and put me into a proper kimono. I'd arrived in the blue and white cotton robe I'd worn that morning to my lessons at the school, but Tatsumi changed me into a dark blue silk covered with a design of tiny carriage wheels in shades of brilliant yellow and red. It wasn't the most beautiful kimono you would ever see, but when I looked at myself in the full-length mirror as Tatsumi was tying a bright green obi into place around my waist, I found that except for my

plain hairstyle, I might have been taken for a young apprentice geisha on her way to a party. I felt quite proud when I walked out of the room, and thought Mameha would gasp again, or something of the sort. But she only rose to her feet, tucked a handkerchief into her sleeve, and went directly to the door, where she slipped her feet into a green pair of lacquered zori [clogs] and looked back over her shoulder at me.

> "Well?", she said. "Aren't you coming?" (Golden, 1997, p. 156)

Words to songs may create similar images and evoke strong feelings, as word choice gives us a quick clue to the characters or to the setting. It is true that these words are not read by the reader to him or herself, but are sung by the artist with the accompaniment of music. However, the written words, as sung, still convey meaning about dress or appearance. Consider the first two verses of the song, "Blue Velvet," by Bobby Vinton (Wayne & Morris, 1963). We can easily picture a woman wearing an elegant gown of blue velvet, who has blue eyes, in a romantic setting. Maybe we picture ourselves.

> She wore blue velvet.
> Bluer than velvet was the night.
> Softer than satin was the light
> From the stars.

> She wore blue velvet.
> Bluer than velvet were her eyes.
> Warmer than May her tender sighs.
> Love was ours.

Written descriptions in merchandise catalogs use descriptive terms for their products, together with visual representations such as photographs or line drawings, to convey meaning to customers. If a garment from Land's End is described as a no-iron, 100 percent combed cotton long sleeve shirt, we know that it is a fine grade cotton shirt fabric. If the description says naturally soft cotton with added ease, 96 percent cotton, 4 percent spandex, we know that the shirt has a little bit of stretch built in and may better fit female curves. Or when we read these words in a Chico's catalog, "This is my absolute favorite jean ever. I love it even more paired with our ikat blazer" by Cher Canada, Chico's "style expert" (Chico's, January 2012, p. 6), we may pay attention to that particular featured jean and also check out the ikat blazer she is talking about. Whether or not Cher Canada actually exists, or is simply a fictional character created as a marketing ploy to convince readers that Chico's knows what they are talking about, the written description and purported credentials of its author give weight to the claim.

Visual Representations

Visual representations of dress, as opposed to the artifacts themselves, include hand-drawn illustrations, photographs, tapestries, sculpture, pottery, carvings, films, movies, television shows, catalogs (print and online), websites, magazines, and advertisements. For example, tomb paintings, pottery painting, jade and pottery figurines, and even animal bone hairpins have provided us with information about early Chinese dress (Shang Dynasty in the Bronze Age, 1500–1000 BCE, and Zhou Dynasty, 1000 BCE–200 BCE), indicating robes with ornate patterns and narrow sleeves, caps, and hairstyles (Zhou & Gao, 1984). An incredible find occurred in the late twentieth century when an entire army of warriors, horses, and chariots sculpted of terracotta was found in China, dating to about 200 BCE, during the time of the first Chinese emperor (Figure 2.12). It is thought they were sculpted to guard him in the afterlife.

The Bayeux Tapestry, so named because it was first mentioned in an inventory in 1476 in the Bayeux Cathedral in France and rediscovered in the early eighteenth century, from the early Norman era, reflects details of both the Norman and English men of this time, including trouser style, tunics, hair style, and battle costume. The Normans were people from the "North" of Europe, probably Vikings from Scandinavia, who settled in the northern part of France in the 800s CE and then moved into England (1066 AD) and other parts of Europe. The Bayeux Tapestry consists of seventy-nine embroidered scenes with some 600 figures and 700 animals depicting not only the infamous Battle of Hastings, resulting in a Norman duke (known as William, the Conqueror) becoming the king of England, but also everyday activities of farming, hunting, sailing, feasting, and building (Ginsburg, 1991). This artwork provides a wealth of information about dress of the time.

Statues can also depict the dress of a particular person or time period. A statue from the Old Kingdom in Egypt (2700–2200 BCE) indicates that one king wore a cloak, a wig, and a striped head cloth. Other Old Kingdom statues dated about 2600 BCE show men in pleated skirts, and those of 1,000 years later show a similar pleated skirt for men, but longer in length (Anawalt, 2007). Statues from ancient Sumeria (present-day Syria), dating to 3000 BCE, depict men in calf-length skirts of a fleecy material, decorated with a tassel on the back; about 500 years later, statues from the same area depict men wearing a cloak wrapped around the body, a beard, and a fitted skull cap (Anawalt, 2007). Most cultures, past and present, use

Figure 2.12
The terracotta soldiers dating to about 200 BCE discovered in 1974 in Shaanxi Province, China—some 8,000 soldiers, 100 chariots, and more than 600 horses.

statues as a means of artistic expression to represent themselves, which include the details of dress.

Fashion illustrations over time have depicted current fashions of the time period, as well as fantasy design ideas. *Godey's Lady's Book* was published from 1830–1878, as a lifestyle magazine for women (Blum, 1985). It carried poetry, stories, and artwork of the time, as well as an illustration of a popular dress each month and often a pattern so that readers could sew the dress at home. Piano sheet music was also included for home entertainment. It served primarily as an arbiter of taste, rather than to delve into controversial issues such as the Civil War (Douglas, 1998). However, there were stories about women in the workforce, wearing white for weddings, and other social issues.

In contrast to the fashion illustrations depicted in this monthly magazine, Erté (a French pseudonym he derived from his initials, R.T., for Romain de Tirtoff) is known for his ornate and often fantastical fashion designs in the 1920s and 1930s. He moved from Russia to Paris, to pursue design, and became the cover illustrator for the well-known fashion magazine, *Harper's Bazaar* (Riding, 1990). He also designed costumes and stage sets for the *Ziegfield Follies*, the ornate music and dance stage productions of the time, and for Hollywood movies. His designs were influenced by the Art Deco movement and its controlled lavishness; he published many of his designs in the 1970s and 1980s when the Art Deco influence was seen again in fashion. Some of his illustrations were considered to be so complicated that they couldn't be produced.

Films, videos, and television shows all utilize representations of dress, although these representations are typically as accurate as the actual medium (film, digital, or still photography) will allow. Consider the importance of costumes in conveying a character in a movie. If we have seen *The Wizard of Oz*, originally made in 1939 and still shown annually on television, we can easily recall Dorothy's blue-checkered pinafore, her reddish-brown hair in high pigtails, and her ruby slippers. In contrast, we recall the costumes of the Scarecrow, the Tin Man, the Cowardly Lion, Glinda (the good witch), the Munchkins, and many others (Figure 2.13). Each of these costumes conveys a wide range of personal characteristics and qualities about the individual characters. Or think about a popular contestant show, such as *Dancing with the Stars*. The costumes are designed for each contestant according to the type of dance (waltz, fox trot, jive, etc.) and the particular persona of the dancer. This phenomenon is why films

Figure 2.13

The Wizard of Oz movie shown at the Sydney Opera House, Australia, with live accompaniment from the Sydney orchestra.

and television shows all have costume designers to create, for the viewing audience, the "image" of each character through dress.

However, other artwork that does not depend on photography (i.e., illustrations, carvings, sculpture, digital artwork, etc.) may take liberties with the accuracy of representation if the artist so chooses. In fact, even photography, especially digital photography, can be greatly altered. Images and advertisements in magazines and online may also be quite distorted through digital manipulation such as airbrushing to alter size, color, texture, or detail. Thus, artistic style, technique, and choice of art medium may affect the accuracy of the visual representation of items or people.

Lived Experiences

While not technically a "record" of dress, our personal **lived experiences** (living in our bodies and our dress) can provide useful insights into dress and human behavior. We draw upon these collective experiences to interpret our own behavior and the behavior of others. How we perceive our bodies, and the choices we make to construct our appearances as we present them publicly, can allow us to draw conclusions about the use of dress in establishing and maintaining identity. For example, one of the authors loves the color purple in almost any variation. Probably half or more of her current wardrobe is clothing and accessories that are purple, lavender, mauve, burgundy, violet, heather, plum, orchid, wine, or some other variant of the color. She has often wondered why purple is such a personal favorite and why it is so much a part of her identity. Upon reflection, she remembers a time when she was three years old, and her family received a box of "hand-me-down" clothes from her cousins who were just two years older. The box arrived just before Easter, and in it was a beautiful lavender dress made out of a crispy, crunchy fabric that had soft little flowers all over it (probably flocked organdy), and a beautiful ribbon around the waist. There was also a hat and socks. Well, this little three year old girl fell in love with that dress, and thought she was a little princess (a fleeting dream for many girls at some point in early childhood) as she got dressed for church that Easter. As she grew up, her mother made her other clothes out of purple or lavender fabric, including a special dress for her choir performance when she was ten years old and in fifth grade. She also remembers her grandmother making her a school dress of purple plaid fabric with a white collar in third grade, and a skirt to go with a pale lavender angora sweater in seventh grade. Somewhere along the way, she became so fond of purple that she saw it as one characteristic of herself that was unique. Other people acknowledged that uniqueness when they made or gave her purple gift items. When she began to design and sew her own clothing in high school, she frequently made garments in one purple fabric or another, and acquired many purple accessories as well. This young girl grew up to be a college professor, and her identity grew to encompass many more unique characteristics, yet her aesthetic sense still focuses on the color purple. From this lived experience, she believes that her self-identity does indeed match some of the characteristics that are typically described in the literature about the color purple (bold, outspoken, mysterious, both reserved and dynamic in interactions). This self-observation has contributed to her understanding and appreciation of worldwide dress as expressions of personal and social identity.

Another way we come to view our lived experiences about dress may include our bodies and how we "inhabit" them, or experience living in them. Body image, discussed in Chapter 7, is a very personal experience comprised of our perceptions of our bodies, our attitudes or feelings about them, and our behaviors related to those perceptions and feelings. As these personal experiences are shared with others (for example, through conversations with friends and family, or through personal interviews with scholars studying body image), we have learned that most people in Western culture and perhaps the world, feel some degree of anxiety about their physical bodies and how they are evaluated by other people.

As we think back over our own experiences of living within our bodies, we realize that we think of them as having certain characteristics related to attractiveness, height, weight, muscularity, sexual appeal, coloring, texture, and features. Thus, our lived experiences in our bodies may shape what we "know" about others and their appearance. We may believe that hair should be dyed blond because it is a valued appearance characteristic in our culture, or that we should constantly strive to be thin, or that we should have large breasts or well-defined abdominal muscles. To the extent that we document feelings in personal diaries, letters, or digital messages to others, notes by physicians or mental health professionals, or research articles in professional journals, these lived experiences become sources of information about dress as human behavior.

IN-CLASS ACTIVITY
With a Partner, Discuss Your Favorite Color

What is the color, and why is it your favorite?

1. Can you remember a specific occasion when your feelings began?
2. How do you create your appearance using this favorite color?
3. How is this preference symbolic of your identity or personality?

Chapter Summary

In compiling what we know about dress, it is useful to consider where the information comes from. One way to learn about a culture's dress is to study existing groups and their practices regarding dress. To do this, we could study actual items of dress (i.e., artifacts) or other materials that provide information about dress. For example, movies, television shows, letters, catalogs, magazines, artwork, poetry, songs, and novels all provide information about how people dress.

A second way to gather information about dress is to study the dress of past cultures. Because the dress of past cultures was typically made from natural fibers, it was often biodegradable. As a result, dress artifacts were often obliterated from the archeological record. Yet, some actual artifacts as well as indirect artifacts of dress have survived through a variety of natural processes, including drying, freezing, immersion in liquid, mineralization, charring, and impressions formed by contact with other materials such as clay. For example, Ötzi (the Iceman) was preserved in ice. Research determined that he was well outfitted, both with equipment and dress.

By studying fragmentary textile products, researchers are able to make inferences about the people who created those products and their culture (i.e., Sibley & Jakes, 1994; Sibley, Jakes & Swinker, 1992). In addition to these natural processes that have allowed fragments of textiles and dress to survive, we can also learn about the dress of past cultures by studying other artifacts from the culture that provide information about dress such as written or pictorial records.

In this chapter, we have differentiated between the origins or "beginnings" of dress and functions or "purposes" served by dress. While there is limited physical evidence of early dress prior to the written word, there are many archaeological examples of prehistoric dress, and we have been able to draw limited conclusions about its origins in various parts of the world. As we continue to find much more physical evidence, as well as written records, we can continue to draw more complex conclusions about the origins of dress as well as the functions served by dress. These functions can basically be grouped into two main categories: protection and communication. Protection may be from physical elements in the environment or psychological elements such as spirits. Communication includes shared meaning regarding modesty, immodesty, adornment, and status. With continued research by archaeologists, costume historians, and textile historians, and other social scientists, we will likely draw even richer conclusions about the myriad functions served by dress of past peoples of the world.

Key Terms

adornment	functions	origins of dress	textile historians
archaeology	immodesty	protection	Venus figurines
communication	lived experiences	pseudomorph	visual representations
costume historians	modesty	status	written sources
ethnographies	mummies	string skirts	

Discussion Questions

1. When you select a representative artifact of dress from any culture, how can you determine the
   - materials used?
   - processes used?
   - forms of dress?
   - probable function of dress?

2. What archaeological evidence exists regarding the earliest dress?

3. Can you identify an example from your current dress that exemplifies the functions of
   - protection (physical, psychological)?
   - communication (modesty, immodesty, adornment, status)?

STUDIO

Visit your book's STUDIO for additional quiz questions and vocabulary flashcards!

Suggested Readings

Anawalt, P.R. (2007). *The worldwide history of dress*. New York, NY: Thames and Hudson, Inc.

Dickson, J.H., Oeggl K., & Handley L.L. (2005) The iceman reconsidered. *Scientific American, Special Archaeology Volume, 15*, 4–13.

References

Adovasio, J. M. & Hyland, D. C. (2000, January/February). The need to weave. *Scientific American: Discovering Archaeology, 2*(1), 36–37.

Anawalt, P. R. (2007). *The worldwide history of dress*. New York, NY: Thames and Hudson, Inc.

Arriaza, B. (1995, March). Chile's Chinchorro mummies. *National Geographic, 187*(3), 68–89.

Aughton, P. (2002). *Endeavour: The story of Captain Cook's first great epic voyage*. London: Cassell & Co.

Barber, E. (1994). *Women's work: The first 20,000 years*. New York, NY: W.W. Norton & Co.

Barber, E. (1999). *The mummies of Ürümchi*. New York, NY: W.W. Norton & Co.

Beckwith, C. & Fisher, A. (2002). *African ceremonies*. New York, NY: Harry N. Abrams, Inc.

Benedict, R. (1931). Dress. In *Encyclopedia of the Social Sciences* (Vol 5, pp. 235–237). New York, NY: Macmillan.

Blum, S. (1985). *Fashions and costumes from Godey's Lady's Book*. New York, NY: Dover Publications.

Cassman, V., Odegaard, N., & Arriaza, B. (2008). *Chinchorro twined shrouds* [PDF document.]. Textile Society of America Symposium Proceedings, 11th Biennial symposium: Textiles as Cultural Expressions, September 4–7, 2008, Honolulu, Hawai'i. Retrieved from Digital Commons @ University of Nebraska Web site: http://digitalcommons.unl.edu/tsaconf/226/

Chico's (January 2012.) *Closet confidential*. Fort Myers, FL: Chico's.

Collins, H., (Ed.) (2003). *Past worlds: Atlas of archeology*. Ann Arbor, MI: Borders Press.

Collingridge, V. (2003). *Captain Cook: The life, death and legacy of history's greatest explorer*. London: Ebury Press.

Curtis, E. S. (n.d.). *The North American Indian*. Reproduced by BiblioBazaar, 2008. (Sold by subscription only from 1907–1930; then acquired by Charles Lauriat Co., Boston, in 1935.) Now held by Northwestern University and made available as a digital edition through *Northwestern University* libraries, nai@northwestern.edu.) Retrieved from http://curtis.library.northwestern.edu/index.html

Dickson, J.H., Oeggl K, & Handley L.L. (2005) The iceman reconsidered. *Scientific American Special Archaeology Volume, 15*, 4–13.

Douglas, A. (1998). *The feminization of American culture*. New York, NY: Farrer, Strauss & Giroux.

Gilbert, K., Holt, J. & Hudson, S. (1976). *Treasures of Tutankhamun*. New York, NY: Metropolitan Museum of Art.

Gilligan, I. (2011). Clothing and modern human behaviour in Australia. *Bulletin of the Indo-Pacific Prehistory Association, 30*. Retrieved from https://journals.lib.washington.edu/index.php/BIPPA/article/view/10916

Ginsburg, M. (Ed.) (1991). *The illustrated history of textiles*. New York, NY: Portland House.

Golden, A. (1997). *Memoirs of a geisha*. New York, NY: Alfred P. Knopf, Inc.

Hadingham, E. (1994, April). The mummies of Xinjiang. *Discover, 15*(4), 68–77.

Hiler, H. (1929). *From nudity to raiment*. New York, NY: E. Weyhe Publishers.

Hirn, Y. J. (1900). *Origins of art: A psychological and sociological inquiry*. New York, NY: Macmillan and Co. Limited.

Horn, M. & Gurel, L. (1981). *The second skin: An inter-disciplinary study of clothing* (2nd ed.). Boston, MA: Houghton Mifflin.

Jakes, K. A., and Sibley, L. R., (1984). An examination of the phenomenon of textile fabric pseudomorphism, In, J.B. Lambert (Ed.), *Archaeological Chemistry III, Advances in Chemistry, No. 205*, American Chemical Society, Washington, D.C., 403–424.

Jaroff, L. (1992, October 26). Iceman. *Time, 140*(17), 62–66.

Lichfield, J. (December 10, 2011). The earth mother of all Neolithic discoveries. *The Independent.* Retrieved from http://www.independent.co.uk/news/world/europe /the-earth-mother-of-all-neolithic-discoveries -6275062.html

Lyman, R. (2015). North American paleoindian eyed bone needles: Morphometrics, sewing, and site structure. *American Antiquity, 80*(1), 146–160.

Mitchell, M. (1936). *Gone with the wind.* New York, NY: Macmillan.

Oakland, A. (2008). *The string or grass skirt: An ancient garment in the southern Andes* [PDF document.]. Retrieved from Digital Commons @ University of Nebraska Web site: Textile Society of America Symposium Proceedings, 11th Biennial symposium: Textiles as Cultural Expressions, September 4-7, 2008, Honolulu, Hawai'i. Retrieved from http://digitalcommons .unl.edu/tsaconf/index.html

Park, L. (2000, January/February). The eclectic: A former fashion maven digs into Russian mammoth fields and ancient textiles. *Scientific American: Discovering Archeology, 2*(1), 26–28.

Paul, A. (1991). Paracas: An ancient cultural tradition on the south coast of Peru In A. Paul (Ed.), *Paracas art and architecture: Object and context in south coastal Peru* (pp. 1–34). Iowa City, IA: University of Iowa Press.

Polosmak, N. (1994, Ocotober). A mummy unearthed from the pastures of heaven. *National Geographic, 186*(4), 80–103.

Riding, A. (1990, 22 April). Erté, a master of fashion, stage and art deco design is dead at 97. *New York Times.* Retrieved from http://www.nytimes.com/1990/04/22/ obituaries/erte-a-master-of-fashion-stage-and-art -deco-design-is-dead-at-97.html

Ross, J. (1999 January). Picturing Pocahontas. *Smithsonian, 29*(10), 34–36.

Ryder, M. (1996). Fibres and fashions of a Stone Age man. *Textiles Magazine, 2,* 12–14.

Schwarz, R. A. (1979). Uncovering the secret vice: Toward an anthropology of clothing and adornment. In Cordwell, J. & Schwarz, J. (Eds.). *Fabrics of culture.* (pp. 23–47.) The Hague: Mouton Press.

Sibley, L. R., and Jakes, K. A. (1984). Survival of protein fibers in archaeological contexts. *Science and Archaeology, 26,* 17–27.

Sibley, L. & Jakes, K. (1989). Etowah textile remains and cultural context: A model for inference. *Clothing and Textiles Research Journal, 7*(2), 37–45.

Sibley, L. & Jakes, K. (1994). Coloration in Etowah textiles from Burial No. 57. In D. Scott and P. Meyers (Eds.), *Archaeometry of Pre-Columbian sites and artifacts: Proceedings of a symposium organized by the UCLA Institute of Archaeology and the Getty Conservation Institute, March 23–27, 1992.* (pp. 395-418.) Los Angeles, California: The Getty Institute.

Sibley, L., Jakes, K., & Swinker, M. (1992). Etowah feather remains from Burial 57: Identification and Context. *Clothing and Textiles Research Journal, 10*(3), 21–28.

Soffer, O. (2004). Recovering perishable technologies through use wear on tools: Preliminary evidence for Upper Paleolithic weaving and net making. *Current Anthropology, 45*(3), 407–413.

Taylor, R. (1973). *Introduction to cultural anthropology.* Boston, MA: Allyn & Bacon, Inc.

Thompson, A. & Jakes. K. A. (2005 Winter). Textile evidence for Ohio Hopewell burial practices. *Southeastern Archaeology, 24*(2), 137–141.

Wayne, B. & Morris, L. (1963). Blue velvet [Recorded by Bobby Vinton]. On *Blue on blue.* New York, NY: Epic Records.

Wilcox, C. (1998). *Mummies and their mysteries.* New York, NY: Barnes & Noble Books, Inc.

Wright, K. (1999, February). The first Americans. *Discover, 20*(2), 52–62.

Zaczek, I. & Phillips, C. (2004). *The complete book of tartan.* London: Hermes House, Anness Publishing, Ltd.

Zhou, X. & Gao, C. (1984). *5000 years of Chinese costume.* Hong Kong: China Books and Periodicals, Inc.

CONDUCTING RESEARCH ON DRESS

After reading and reflecting on the content of this chapter students should be able to:

- **Explain the research process used to study dress related behaviors.**
- **Compare and contrast different research strategies.**
- **Use appropriate research terminology.**
- **Conduct original research on dress.**

INTRODUCTION

Dressing the body is an important phenomenon to study. So how do we learn about this behavior? We all dress our bodies, so we all know something about the process from our first-hand experiences. However, when approaching any topic in a scholarly manner, it is important to gather facts, determine relationships, and offer explanations via an active, thorough, and systematic process. The name of such a process is called **research**. Conducting research involves the formulation of questions, the gathering of data, the analysis and interpretation of that data, and the formulation of conclusions. Research is concerned with gathering reliable information that can be used to make **generalizations** or general statements which are obtained by inferring from specific research results. Research is a process that results in (a) discovery; (b) an interpretation of facts, events, behaviors, or theories; and sometimes in (c) practical applications.

There are several ways in which research and knowing how to conduct research is potentially useful to students. First of all, a typical student assignment might be to develop a product line, create a brand, construct a position map, and develop a marketing strategy. Although many steps are required to complete such a project, one of the first steps is to assess the target market for preferences and

product acceptance. This step requires market research, research that assesses, for example, the target market's preferences, perceptions of the product line, perceived risk, and purchase intent. To get this kind of information, one might use a survey research strategy and develop a questionnaire.

In addition, students are often required to complete a research project involving collection of original data for class projects. This type of project is called **empirical research**, which is distinct from doing library research. When assigned to complete empirical research projects related to dress, students can use any of the four strategies: fieldwork, non-reactive research, experimentation, or survey methodology. In addition, undergraduates in some programs have theses to complete and these often require empirical research.

Finally, knowing how to conduct research makes it much easier to understand research articles, which are often required reading for undergraduate course assignments. The principles of how to do anything are always understood better after a "hands-on" activity. Conducting research is a "hands-on" activity that is best learned through participation, trial, and error.

To conduct research, a researcher often needs ideas or directions before beginning the research process. Ideas and directions often come from **theory**, a "set of ideas that describe, explain, and predict outcomes and relationships;" such theories then "guide(s) the development of research hypotheses" (Kaiser, 1997, p. 33) (Figure 3.1). Some researchers actually develop theory or modify existing theory through their research. As you read this book, you will be introduced to many theories that have been used by researchers to provide guidance in what they attempt to research. Other times, theory is used to explain research results. For example, in Chapter 7, "Dress and Body Image" you will learn about cultivation theory (Gerbner, Gross, Morgan, Signorielli, & Shanahan, 2002). Also in Chapter 6, "Dress and Physical Appearance," you will discuss social

Look for the following characteristics, many of which can usually be found in the abstract at the beginning of the article.

Characteristics of an empirical research article:

1. Statement about the methodology being used
2. Research questions or hypotheses to be addressed
3. Definition of the group or phenomena being studied
4. Process used to study the group or phenomena, including controls or instruments such as tests or surveys

Use the following article and fill in the chart below to decide if it represents empirical research.

Howlett, N., Pine, K., Orakcioglu, I., & Fletcher, B. (2013). The influence of clothing on first impressions: Rapid and positive responses to minor changes in male attire. *Journal of Fashion Marketing and Management: An International Journal, 17*(1), 38-48.

	In Abstract?	In Text?	Page #	What Was Found?
Statement about the methodology being used				
Research questions or hypotheses to be addressed				
Definition of the group or phenomena being studied				
Process used to study the group or phenomena				

Figure 3.1

The Trickle Down Theory of Fashion (Simmel, 1904) explains that fashions move down the socioeconomic scale from the elite class to the adjacent class below.

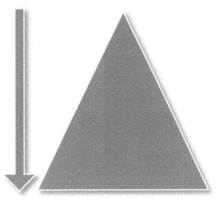

Trickle Down Theory

comparison theory (Festinger, 1954). In each case, the theory is used to explain body image issues and sometimes to predict research outcomes. As you conduct your own research, you will find that theory is not only useful to help guide your research but also to explain your results.

Paradigms

In social science research, there are two main research **paradigms** or world views about what research is and how it should be conducted (Willis, Jost, & Nilakanta, 2007). Paradigms help us to understand the world and have their roots in different philosophies of knowledge. As such, the two paradigms make different assumptions about what are legitimate topics of study and what criteria constitute proof or evidence of a phenomenon (Creswell,

1994). In Chapter 1, "Why Study Dress" we defined *perspective* and noted that your perspective allows you to see some aspects of a situation, while limiting your ability to see other aspects. In a similar way, the research paradigm you use allows you to focus on some aspects of research but limits your ability to focus on others. Without going into the philosophical nature of the paradigms, suffice it to say that the terms *qualitative* and *quantitative* are widely used today to describe two different paradigms, models, or world views for research (Willis et al., 2007).

Researchers who study the social psychology of dress gather data from participants, textiles, artifacts, documents, or media in the course of their research. That data collected can be qualitative or quantitative, as a function of whether or not the data are numerical or non-numerical. "Using those terms implies that the big difference between the two paradigms is in the type of data collected: Quantitative researchers use numbers as data, whereas qualitative researchers do not. In fact, that is not true. Number-based research methods often are used by qualitative researchers, and a growing number of quantitative researchers use qualitative data" (Willis et al., 2007, p. 7).

A **qualitative study** is an inquiry into a social problem that is "based on building a complex, holistic picture, formed with words, reporting detailed views of informants, and conducted in a natural setting" (Creswell, 1994, p. 2). So in a qualitative study, the data collected are typically qualitative and are treated qualitatively. So for example, suppose we are interested in why people dress the way they do. We ask people to tell us in their own words why they dress as they do, record their answers, and transcribe the responses. Here we are collecting qualitative data. Then we read through all of the data, find themes in the data, and organize the data into those themes. When reporting the data, we list the themes that we have identified and within each theme we present some examples of what was said. If we do that, we have treated the qualitative data qualitatively. However, we might instead decide to count how frequently each of our themes is mentioned by participants. Then when reporting the data, we may not only list the themes and examples of the themes (what participants actually said), we can also report the frequencies with which each of our themes was mentioned by participants. In this case, we still have collected qualitative data, but now we are also treating it quantitatively since we are reporting numbers.

A **quantitative study** is an inquiry into a social problem, which is based on testing a theory of variables and their relationships (Creswell, 1994). In quantitative studies, variables are measured with numbers (called quantitative treatment of data) and analyzed with statistics to determine if predictions of the theory can be verified. Thus, in quantitative studies the data collected are typically quantitative in nature but do not have to be (Willis et al., 2007). Returning to the previous example, we could ask the same question, "Why do you dress the way you do?" However, suppose that you are given a list of ten responses to select from and I ask you to rank those responses (see Table 3.1 for response choices). So you would give a 1 to the most likely reason for why you are dressed as you are, give a 2 to the second most likely reason, and so forth. In this case, we have collected quantitative data. In a research

| TABLE 3.1 | STUDIO |

SAMPLE CHOICES FOR "WHY DO YOU DRESS THE WAY YOU DO?"

In the table below please indicate why you dress the way you do by ranking each item from 1 to 10. So you would give a 1 to the most likely reason for why you are dressed as you are, give a 2 to the second most likely reason, and so forth.

	To be attractive
	To be fashionable
	To attract the opposite sex
	To increase my confidence
	To look professional
	To look competent
	To look honest
	To be modest
	To look clean
	To be comfortable

report from this data, we might then report how many respondents selected each of the ten possible choices. In this instance we have treated the data quantitatively. To treat these data qualitatively, we might categorize the ten response choices into themes. The choices to be attractive, fashionable, and attract the opposite sex, could be grouped into a social reasons theme. The choices to increase confidence, to look professional, to look competent, and to look honest could be grouped into a task-related theme. The choices to be modest, look clean, and be comfortable could be grouped into a general appearance theme. Suppose that the first seven items in Table 3.1 receive the most low numbers and that the last three items receive the most high numbers. In our research report we might say that people dress the way they do for social reasons and task-related reasons, rather than for general appearance reasons. So here we have collected quantitative data and treated it qualitatively.

Institutional Review Boards

In the US, research is monitored at the college and university levels. An **institutional review board (IRB)** of a university is a group of people or committee that has been formed to approve, monitor, and review medical and behavioral research involving people. The purpose of the IRB is to oversee that the rights and welfare are protected of the people who are studied. In the US, regulations give IRBs the power to approve, disapprove, or require modifications in planned research. Therefore, any research with human participants conducted by faculty or students of US universities that studies human behavior, including behavior toward dress, must first receive IRB approval. This involves an extra step in the research procedure not required by research that does not rely on human participants. Because research on dress related behaviors (e.g., buying, wearing, altering, embellishing) often involves human participants, it must receive IRB approval.

RESEARCH STRATEGIES

Lennon and Burns (2000) suggested that the type of **strategy** utilized in research is an effective way to organize studies focusing on human behavior as it is related to dress. Major strategies that we present to you in this chapter include fieldwork, survey research, experimentation,

and non-reactive research. Fieldwork, survey research, and experimentation all differ from non-reactive research in that they all "involve some level of intrusion by the researcher into the lives of those being studied" (Lennon & Burns, 2000, p. 214). Although these strategies have been separated for our discussion, research strategies are sometimes combined by researchers to meet their research objectives. For example, researchers investigating Black Friday shopping conducted a content analysis of news articles about Black Friday, conducted fieldwork at retail stores on Black Friday, and surveyed Black Friday shoppers (Lennon, Johnson, & Lee, 2011).

Fieldwork

Fieldwork is also referred to as field studies or field research. When using this strategy, researchers study actions, behaviors, relationships, and situations of people in their everyday lives. The goal of the researcher is to understand phenomena that you cannot directly ask people about. For example, if you ask salespeople directly if they are willing to help any customer regardless of appearance, they will most likely respond that they are willing to help anyone. However, you can find out for sure if salespeople actually do help all customers regardless of their appearance if you design a field study. As will be illustrated in the following examples, salespeople do treat customers differently as a function of their appearance.

In research using the strategy of fieldwork, researchers found that sales clerks engage in interpersonal discrimination against large-size male shoppers. The discrimination included less smiling, less eye contact, less friendliness, less nodding, and more rudeness (Ruggs, Hebl, & Williams, 2015). In other fieldwork well-dressed and well-groomed plus-size women were found to receive friendlier and, in some cases, faster service from salesclerks, as compared to plus-size women who were not so well-dressed or well-groomed (Kim & Lennon, 2005). The researchers discreetly observed interactions between customers and salesclerks at three large-sized women's clothing stores, timing how long clerks took to greet customers and rating the clerks' friendliness. As customers entered the stores, the researchers rated them on characteristics of dress including attractiveness of clothing, fashionability, formality, femininity, overall grooming, hair grooming, make-up, clothing fabric quality, accessory quality, and purse quality. To rate friendliness, the researchers

IN-CLASS ACTIVITY
Are Salespeople Affected
by Customer Dress?

Have you ever been ignored or served slowly by a salesperson? Could that treatment have been related to your dress? Explain your answer.

determined whether and how much the salespeople smiled at the shoppers, how closely they approached the shoppers, and whether they continued to do other work (e.g., fold clothes) or gave full attention to customers. The researchers also used a stopwatch to determine how long it took clerks to greet customers. Nearly all characteristics of customer dress affected clerk's friendliness, but only subtle cues (e.g., hair grooming, fabric quality, accessory quality, and purse quality) influenced how quickly the customers were approached. Thus, dress may not be as important in affecting speed of service as it is in influencing friendliness

of service. This difference may be due to training. At specialty clothing stores employees are trained to greet customers quickly. However, friendliness may not be an integral part of training.

Field studies are conducted in a variety of settings such as schools, shopping malls, athletic events, or other situations of daily life (i.e., the field). Fieldwork is the best strategy when a behavior cannot be studied outside of its natural context. Some research questions that can be addressed using fieldwork are presented in Table 3.2.

Fieldwork allows researchers to study the meanings associated with dress and dress practices in situations of daily life. For example, in field research a researcher from the UK studied the meanings girls attribute to their own clothing consumption (Pilcher, 2010). Fieldwork has also been used in studies of the meanings attributed to tattoos (Mun, Janigo, & Johnson, 2012). Meanings were also studied in fieldwork that focused on masquerade dress (Copeland & Hodges, 2014).

Sometimes fieldwork is short-term involving little contact with those being studied, and in these instances the data are usually treated quantitatively; for example the

TABLE 3.2

SAMPLE RESEARCH QUESTIONS THAT COULD BE ADDRESSED IN FIELDWORK

Research Question	People Observed	Behaviors Observed
Do men receive faster (or better) service in retail stores than women?	Sex of shopper (male, female)	Observe customer–salesperson interactions; using an unobtrusive stop watch, time how long it takes a shopper to be approached by a salesperson.
Do people from one ethnic group receive faster restaurant service than people from a different ethnic group?	Ethnicity of restaurant patron	Observe waitperson–patron interactions; using an unobtrusive stop watch, time how long it takes people to be served (from when they sit down until the meal arrives).
Do men leave dressing rooms messier than women?	Sex of shopper (male, female)	Observe condition of dressing rooms; enter and rate messiness of dressing room after shopper exits.
Do preschool teachers comment more on preschool girls' appearances than preschool boys' appearances?	Sex of preschooler (male, female)	Observe preschooler–teacher interactions and code any comment about appearance of the preschoolers.
Do well-dressed people get friendlier service than poorly-dressed people?	Dress of shopper (well-dressed, poorly-dressed)	Observe customer–salesperson interactions and rate the friendliness of the salesperson on a rating scale.

research conducted by Kim and Lennon (2005). In that study, the only contact between the researchers and the salespeople was a brief interview of the salespeople by the researchers to ascertain that the salespeople were unaware that they had been observed. This study also illustrates two ways in which data are collected in fieldwork: **structured observations** and **interviews**. The observations in this instance were structured because the researchers determined what specifically they were watching for before they began to observe at the shopping malls. When interviews are conducted in field research, the people being interviewed are often referred to as **informants** because they supply information to the researcher.

On the other hand, sometimes data are collected and there is no direct contact between researchers and those being studied; this process of data collection is called **unobtrusive observation**. With this type of data collection, the people being studied are unaware that they are part of a research project. A researcher uses this process because he or she is interested in understanding a behavior as it occurs. Observations may be made at one point in time or multiple observations might be made over time. Returning to the Black Friday shopping example, Pilot Study 2 in that research consisted of fieldwork in the form of unobtrusive observation at retail stores on Black Friday (Lennon, Johnson, & Lee, 2011). The researchers observed shoppers inside and outside a store. The observation was unobtrusive because the shoppers did not know they were being observed and there was no contact between the researchers and the shoppers being observed.

Finally, fieldwork can last for extended periods of time. For example, one researcher spent eight months of field research studying how former prisoners change their dress style to avoid negative stereotypes (Halushka, 2016). Similarly another research team engaged in two years of fieldwork to learn how clothing is used for impression management by former prisoners (Smiley & Middlemass, 2016). Fieldwork has also been used to study textile, apparel, and fashion businesses. For example, South African home textile designers were studied by a South African scholar using fieldwork (Bonnin, 2013). A UK researcher conducted fieldwork to study the ethicality of the second-hand clothing market in India (Norris, 2015). In other field research focusing on the nonprofit organization *Dress for Success*, eight months of observations were made of personal shopping experiences (Cummins & Blum, 2015). To study fashion models, two and one-half years were spent conducting fieldwork as a fashion model (Mears, 2011).

Researchers can vary in the amount of involvement they have with the individuals that they are studying. Being separated from or not being a member of the group of people you are studying reflects the least amount of involvement. In this instance, the researcher approaches the group to be studied and indicates that she/he is conducting research. For example, the organizational culture of small Guatemalan textile and apparel businesses that produce products for export to the US were investigated by Dickson and Littrell (1998). These researchers spent three weeks in the field conducting interviews and making observations. They had an **outsider's perspective** or view of the phenomenon they were studying. When researchers conduct fieldwork in other cultures, they are typically recognized as outsiders and because of that must gain rapport with those being studied for their cooperation and assistance.

In contrast to this approach to doing research, **participant observers** are researchers who participate in the activities of the group being observed. In fieldwork, researchers' involvement in the activities of the group being studied varies greatly. Researchers can observe the phenomenon under investigation from the perspective of a group member or an insider's perspective. When the researcher is a member of the group studied, this is called being a **true insider**. An example of an individual who was a true insider when conducting her research is Liza Dalby. Dalby is an anthropologist specializing in Japanese culture. She decided to investigate the place of the geisha in modern Japan for her dissertation research. She spent six months gathering data concerning geisha. Her informants thought Dalby could present their perspective to a Western audience and suggested that she become a geisha. She accepted their offer and became in effect, a member of the group that she was studying. She shared her research findings through two books: *Geisha* (1983) and *Kimono, Fashioning Culture* (1993). A more recent example of participant observation is related in *Pricing Beauty: The Making of a Fashion Model* written by Ashley Mears (2011). Mears is a sociologist who became a model and used her 2.5-year experience modeling as the basis of her dissertation. Like Liza Dalby, Ashley Mears was a true insider.

Sometimes researchers simply *"act as if"* they belong to the group that they are studying. An example of this approach is research conducted by Runying Chen. Chen was a Chinese graduate student at a US university when she was hired by a Chinese-owned garment factory in New York City as a garment worker (Chen & Behling, 1994). She was working on a research project that focused on labor conditions in the US apparel industry. In this instance, Chen acted as if she was a member of the group of garment workers at that particular factory, and no one suspected that she was actually also studying conditions at the factory.

Sometimes a researcher might not know what to expect when studying something for the first time. The term **exploratory research** is used to describe research in which the researcher is just beginning to examine a phenomenon. In this situation, researchers might make **unstructured observations** to gather their data. They would record everything they observed using descriptive words and avoiding evaluative ones. For example, a clothing ensemble might be described as bright and colorful or, alternatively, as gaudy. The "bright and colorful" phrase is descriptive. The "gaudy" term is evaluative because it has negative connotations so it is not appropriate. On the other hand, to make structured observations, coding sheets might be developed. For example, in the study of plus-size shoppers by Kim and Lennon (2005) mentioned previously, the researchers might have developed a coding sheet (see Table 3.3 for a coding sheet) and recorded

information about speed of service and ratings of dress features in each column: attractiveness of clothing, fashionability, formality, femininity, overall grooming, hair grooming, make-up, clothing fabric quality, accessory quality and purse quality.

As we noted previously, field researchers can also collect their data by interviews or one-on-one questioning. Their goal is to gather data that reflects people's experience and is expressed in their own words. By using interviews, researchers are able to ask about things that cannot be directly observed, such as the meaning of an article of dress. For example, researchers use the strategy of fieldwork and interview World Cup soccer fans about their dress (see Figure 3.2).

Interviews also allow researchers to compile a large amount of focused information. Interviews are called **structured** or semi-structured if the interviewer conducts the interview using a list of **a priori questions**, that is, questions developed before the interview.

Alternatively, **unstructured interviews** are flexible. The researchers may have only an outline of suggested topics that they are interested in discussing. These topics are introduced to participants in any order appropriate for the situation (Touliatos & Compton, 1988). Interviewees are typically encouraged to respond freely and express their feelings. Using this approach, a researcher

TABLE 3.3

SAMPLE OF CODING SHEET

Shopper	#1	#2	#3	#4 . . .
Attractiveness of Clothing				
Fashionable				
Formal				
Feminine				
Hair Grooming				
Make-Up				
Fabric Quality				
Accessory Quality				
Purse Quality				
Time to Approach				

Figure 3.2
Researchers could conduct fieldwork and interview World Cup soccer fans about their dress.

is looking for depth of response, not just yes/no responses or simple answers. Conducting unstructured interviews requires greater skill than conducting structured interviews (Selltiz, Wrightsman, & Cook, 1976). For example, the researcher does not use a predefined list of questions but explores topics (or poses questions) based on detailed knowledge and preparation and instead generates questions in response to interviewee comments. Thus, for the unstructured interviews, researchers are required to "think on their feet," in ways unnecessary for structured interviews. Regardless of the type of interview, the researcher should listen, establish a connection with the interviewee, and be non-judgmental.

Non-Reactive Research

Dress can also be studied using a **non-reactive research** strategy. This strategy is reflected in many types of historic research, content analyzes, and secondary analyzes of survey or other data. *Non-reactive research* is an umbrella term for research that does not intrude on the people being studied. Because non-reactive research does not typically require the participation of humans, it typically does not require IRB approval. What is used for the data of non-reactive research varies. For example, if you were a dress historian, you might use pictures or paintings of dress. In this instance, this form of data would allow you to study an inaccessible object if the dress depicted existed only in the pictures or paintings. A picture or a painting could also allow researchers to study some past behaviors related to dress. Thus, non-reactive research has some distinct advantages.

In non-reactive research, the data collection technique does not affect the behavior being studied. Researchers conducting non-reactive research may study material artifacts produced by cultural groups including textiles and other aspects of dress. Examples include the study of fragmentary remains like those found in 1991 with Ötzi (the Iceman). See Chapter 2, "Origins and Functions of Dress" for more information about Ötzi (the Iceman). These remains were located in the Ötztal Alps of Northern Italy and reflect individuals who lived about 5,300 years ago (Dickson, Oeggl, & Handley, 2005).

Another example is a bra that was discovered in 2008 during a reconstruction of an Austrian castle. Apparently, the castle had added a second floor in the Fifteenth Century. A space below the floor of a second floor room was found to contain wood, leather shoes, and textiles. Because the conditions were dry, the items were preserved and contained fragments that resembled modern bras. This find was unexpected because bras were not thought to have been worn so long ago (Nutz, 2012). Also as Figure 3.3 shows, dress researchers could study garments depicted in art as a type of non-reactive research.

A non-reactive strategy includes examining information about the dress of a culture found in other material artifacts such as fashion magazines, diaries, archives, and official statistics (e.g., court documents; records of items on ships, planes, or trucks). In addition, studying the physical effects of a behavior might offer information regarding that behavior. For example, if you were interested in finding out which museum exhibit was the most popular with patrons, you could study the wear patterns on the carpeting of the museum. This study would be considered non-reactive research.

A non-reactive strategy used routinely in dress research is **content analysis**. Content analysis is defined as "the

Figure 3.3

Content analyzing art such as this mosaic of a woman practicing at a gym is a type of non-reactive research that can give researchers information about dress in the fourth century. (Detail from the mosaic of the *Ten Maidens,* fourth century).

objective, systematic, and quantitative description of the manifest content of communication" (Berelson, 1952, p. 18). Content analysis is a research technique that focuses on the content of media (either verbal or nonverbal). Media to be analyzed includes books, stories, magazines, films, television shows, diaries, clothing, furniture, advertisements, letters, newspapers, music lyrics, and catalogs. Researchers use content analysis of various types of media as a means of making inferences about the culture that produced the items (e.g., Jung & Lee, 2009; Kim & Lennon, 2006). In content analysis the researcher codes what is seen, read about, or heard into numbers.

Whatever is being counted is the **unit of analysis or recording unit**. It can be a word, fiber content information, a theme, a color, a hairstyle, or a particular garment feature. Easily observable content that resides on the surface of communication is called **manifest content** (Lynch & Peer, 2002). Specific words, garment features, colors, or the revealing nature of clothing are examples of manifest content. Coding of manifest content is highly **reliable** (i.e., two people coding the same content are very likely to get the same results) because counting the number of times something occurs or whether or not it occurs is objective. For example, the number of products an online retailer displays within a given merchandise category is an example of manifest content. It is easily observable and countable

so coding this content is generally reliable. The number of times a character wears a skirt or dress in a television episode would also be manifest content (Figure 3.4).

Coding words such as *organic cotton* is also highly reliable because words are easily observable. Thus, when two people code the same manifest content (i.e., *organic cotton*) they are very likely to arrive at the same outcomes because the number of occurrences of the phrase *organic cotton* is objective. Consider another example. Suppose you are interested in whether or not the host of a television shopping show segment discusses a product's fiber content. This can be easily determined by recording and then transcribing the segment. Two different coders can easily record the same segment and arrive at the same conclusions regarding whether or not fiber content was mentioned. Thus, this type of coding is highly reliable.

Content that is not manifest is called **latent content**. Some authors believe that the use of content analysis should be restricted to manifest content because coding is reliable (Berelson, 1952; Holsti, 1969; Riffe, Lacy, & Fico, 1998). However, many consumer behavior researchers have coded latent content. Coding of latent content

Figure 3.4

Women's appearances in TV sitcoms such as *Leave it to Beaver* were analyzed by Lennon (1990) and found to contain more masculine aspects in the 1980s than in the 1950s.

requires some knowledge of the subject and is less reliable and more subjective than coding manifest content. In coding latent content, the researcher must judge **implicit content** or the indirect content. In comparing both types of content, manifest content refers to concrete things, whereas latent content is subtle, not concrete. Manifest content is easy to measure; latent content requires extensive training and reliability testing (Lynch & Peer, 2002). A simple example of assessing latent content is coding dress as feminine. Suppose a researcher is interested in determining whether or not women's dress in television situation comedies has changed over time from very feminine to less feminine. Some definition of what aspects of dress are feminine must be determined before coding can occur. For example, we may decide that ruffles, floral prints, lace, and bows are feminine aspects of dress. For guidelines on aspects of appearance considered masculine and feminine see Table 10.6 in Chapter 10, "Dress and Identity" or Workman and Johnson (1993). It should be noted that all aforementioned aspects of dress have at one time or another been considered appropriate for men, so what constitutes aspects of a feminine appearance change over time.

We could also code clothing ads in terms of the sexiness of the women in the ads. This project would require coding latent content. The women in such ads might be coded as sexy due to the sexiness of their dress, their poses, and their facial expressions. This kind of coding might be difficult for coders to agree on (Figure 3.5).

Content analysis has advantages and disadvantages. Its advantages include providing a way to unobtrusively assess communications and serving as a starting point for developing new research ideas regarding the nature of specific media (Kolbe & Burnett, 1991). However, content

Figure 3.5
This Calvin Klein ad featuring Kate Moss might be part of a content analysis in which researchers coded the sexiness of women in clothing in ads.

TABLE 3.4

SAMPLE RESEARCH QUESTIONS THAT COULD BE ADDRESSED IN CONTENT ANALYSIS

Research Question	Media to Analyze	Method of Enumeration
Do women's magazines have more ads for diet preparation than men's magazines?	Select all issues of two men's and two women's magazines from the past one year	Count # of ads and # of ads for diet preparations
Are women more likely to be shown in sexy clothing in ads than men?	Videotape all television ads during primetime on one channel for two weeks	Count women and men in ads who are wearing sexy clothing
How is merchandise presented on retail apparel websites?	Choose ten retail apparel websites targeting young women	Check all clothing categories to determine if clothing is displayed flat, on a mannequin, or on a model
Do women's magazines contain more fitness articles than men's magazines?	Select all issues of two men's and two women's magazines from the past one year	Count the # of fitness articles in each type of magazine
Do television shopping hosts provide more intrinsic apparel attributes (e.g., color, fiber content, fabric structure) than extrinsic attributes (e.g., price, country of origin, brand name)?	Videotape all QVC segments selling apparel in a one week period	Watch the tapes and count how many times the hosts mention intrinsic attributes and how many times they mention extrinsic attributes

analyzes, especially as applied to manifest content, are restricted to reporting specific elements of communications. While such data are useful for classification and description, the type of exploratory approach this necessitates is essentially **atheoretical** or not based on theory (Kolbe & Burnett, 1991).

To conduct a content analysis, the researcher must first formulate research questions or hypotheses. See Table 3.4 for a sample of possible research questions to investigate using content analysis. Continuing with our feminine appearance example, the research question might be "Did women's dress become less feminine over the years from 1950 to 1990?" The second step is to select the content to be analyzed and define the unit of analysis. The researcher might decide to code women's dress from television situation comedies from the forty-year time period. Specific programs would need to be identified that represent the time period and that feature female lead characters whose dress can be coded. For example, *Leave It to Beaver* (representing the 1950s), *Dick Van Dyke Show* (representing the 1960s), *The Brady Bunch* (representing the 1970s),

and *Family Ties* (representing the 1980s) could be used as sources of data, assuming that the programs are available to the researcher. Then the unit of analysis would need to be defined. If the unit(s) of analysis were defined as feminine aspects of women's dress, it might include the presence of floral prints, ruffles, bows, and lace.

The third step is to read, watch, or listen to, and then code the content according to the unit(s) of analysis. Applying this step to our example, the researcher would watch the television programs and count how many times the lead female character's (or perhaps all female characters') dress contained floral prints, ruffles, bows, and lace (i.e., defined feminine elements). To make this step manageable, one could develop coding sheets consisting of a matrix (see Table 3.5 for sample matrix). Step four consists of quantifying or assigning numbers to the coded data. One approach is simply to add up the frequencies of the feminine elements of dress for the lead female character for each episode (if there is more than one female character, separate matrices could be developed for each). However, this approach does not take into account that some

TABLE 3.5

SAMPLE MATRIX

	Floral Prints	Ruffles	Bows	Lace
Leave It to Beaver, episode 1				
Leave It to Beaver, episode 2				
Leave It to Beaver, episode 3				
Leave It to Beaver, episode 4				
Leave It to Beaver, episode 5				
Leave It to Beaver, episode 6				
Leave It to Beaver, episode 7				
Leave It to Beaver, episode 8				
Leave It to Beaver, episode 9				
Leave It to Beaver, episode 10				
Leave It to Beaver, episode 11				
Leave It to Beaver, episode 12				
Totals				

characters might have more costume changes than others, which would likely inflate their numbers relative to other characters. In this example, the researcher would need to consider how many changes of dress occurred and perhaps take this into consideration by averaging the number of feminine elements of dress by the number of costume changes per female character per program. The last step is to analyze and interpret the findings.

Before beginning to count, the researcher needs to decide on the **method of enumeration**, that is, how the counting is done. One strategy is simply to code whether or not something appears. We could watch one episode and if the lead female character wore a dress with a lace collar and a bow, we would count that lace was present and a bow was present, for a total of two feminine elements of appearance. If the same character later in the program wore a different dress with lace and a bow, we would not change our count (e.g., lace was present, bow was present). However, in the previous example using the matrix, the researcher was counting the frequency of specific elements of women's dress. Using this second method

of enumeration, we could watch one episode and if the lead female character wore a dress with a lace collar and a bow, we would count that lace was present once and a bow was present once. If the same character later in the program wore a different dress with lace and a bow, we would change our count (e.g., lace was present twice, bow was present twice).

Continuing with our example of using content analysis to answer our research question, "Did women's dress become less feminine over the years from 1950 to 1990?" we need to consider another question. What exactly can a researcher glean from coding women's dress in television situation comedies? Do ordinary people dress like the women seen on television? These questions are important because most of us would agree that what we see on television is not a perfect reflection of reality. In fact, in using content analysis to answer this research question the researcher is making two assumptions. The first assumption is that media content reflects the society that produced it. For example, if television programs present appearance stereotypes, it is reasonable to assume that many people in the culture hold those stereotypes. The second assumption is that the more space or time devoted to a topic, the more important the topic. This is why we do the counting of the unit of analysis. In other words, we assume that as compared to unimportant topics, important topics in a culture will be written about more and take up more space in the media.

When content analyzing text that might appear in a book or magazine, researchers have the option of measuring the amount of space taken up by a topic to indicate how important that topic is. For example, suppose you are interested in the changing popularity of dress codes in the US workplace. You could start your research by identifying several publications to analyze that appeal to working professionals (e.g., *Working Woman, BusinessWeek*) and acquire copies of all issues for the last thirty years. Your next step could be to select specific issues to analyze. You might select February, May, August, and November issues because they represent all four seasons of a year. Then you could decide to measure the square inches of text devoted to articles about dress codes in each issue. You could average this number over the four issues per year. By looking at the yearly averages you could get a sense of whether or not the popularity of dress codes has increased, decreased, or remained steady over the thirty years. By measuring the amount of space taken up by a topic, the researchers get a better sense of the importance of a topic than by simply counting articles devoted to the topic.

A variant of these methods of enumeration relies on using multiple raters. Instead of counting some aspect of the content to be analyzed, multiple raters can code that same content using rating scales. For example, let's re-examine the research on whether or not women's dress in television situation comedies has changed from very feminine to less feminine. Instead of defining what aspects of dress are feminine (e.g., floral prints, ruffles, bows, lace) and then counting them, the researcher could train a group of raters regarding feminine elements of appearance so that each rater or coder had the same understanding of what constitutes a feminine appearance. The raters would then view the situation comedies and rate the femininity of each female character's appearance; these raters could view a series of episodes and rate the female character's appearance for each episode (Figure 3.6). Then these scores could be averaged for the character in question. See Table 3.6 for a sample coding sheet that consists of a series of **rating scales** that could be used in this type of content analysis. A rating scale is a method of assigning a value to a stimulus along a dimension. For example, in Table 3.6 we can assign a value (in this case a number) to a stimulus (Mrs. Cleaver's appearance) along the dimension of femininity.

Figure 3.6
In 1950s television, mothers were depicted in light colored shirtwaist dresses with tight fitting bodice, often wearing aprons, and never wearing pants.

TABLE 3.6

SAMPLE CODING SHEET

	Mrs. Cleaver's Appearance							
Leave It to Beaver, episode 1	feminine	6	5	4	3	2	1	Not feminine
Leave It to Beaver, episode 2	feminine	6	5	4	3	2	1	Not feminine
Leave It to Beaver, episode 3	feminine	6	5	4	3	2	1	Not feminine
Leave It to Beaver, episode 4	feminine	6	5	4	3	2	1	Not feminine
Leave It to Beaver, episode 5	feminine	6	5	4	3	2	1	Not feminine
Leave It to Beaver, episode 6	feminine	6	5	4	3	2	1	Not feminine
Leave It to Beaver, episode 7	feminine	6	5	4	3	2	1	Not feminine
Leave It to Beaver, episode 8	feminine	6	5	4	3	2	1	Not feminine
Leave It to Beaver, episode 9	feminine	6	5	4	3	2	1	Not feminine
Leave It to Beaver, episode 10	feminine	6	5	4	3	2	1	Not feminine
Leave It to Beaver, episode 11	feminine	6	5	4	3	2	1	Not feminine
Leave It to Beaver, episode 12	feminine	6	5	4	3	2	1	Not feminine
Average	feminine	6	5	4	3	2	1	Not feminine

Suppose a researcher rates Mrs. Cleaver's appearance on the twelve episodes and the ratings are 5, 6, 5, 4, 6, 5, 5, 5, 6, 4, 6, and 5. Then we would average those twelve scores for a mean of 5.17. If a second researcher rates Mrs. Cleaver's appearance on the twelve episodes and the ratings are 6, 6, 5, 5, 6, 6, 5, 4, 6, 4, 6, and 5, we could average those twelve scores for a mean of 5.33. Both raters are evaluating her appearance as strongly feminine.

Experimentation

A third research strategy is **experimentation**. In experimental research, the researchers produce a **manipulation** of one variable (the **independent variable**) and observe its effect on some outcome (the **dependent variable**). Typically the independent variable is under the control of the researcher and the dependent variable is what is measured as a result of the manipulation. Experimentation is very different from fieldwork, where there is no manipulation and the researchers attempt to understand the situations of people in their everyday lives. It is only in experiments that the researcher can create a controlled situation and deliberately impose conditions in order to examine cause and effect relationships between variables.

There are two types of experiments: **laboratory experiments** and **field experiments**. In laboratory experiments, research participants engage in tasks in a neutral environment such as a laboratory; hence the name. In laboratory experiments, participants know they are participating in research in contrast to field experiments where participants typically do not know they are participating in research. Generally, in both types of experiments there is some type of manipulation (treatment, intervention) and the researcher wants to find out if that manipulation (treatment, intervention) affected the dependent variable. The researcher controls the manipulation or independent variable. In a popular experimental design, called the **post-test only control group design**, one group of individuals is exposed to a manipulation (i.e., the **treatment group**) and measured (or observed). A second group of individuals, the **control group**, is simply measured (or observed) without exposure to the manipulation. Then the

1. Go to www.firstview.com. Click on fashion shows; then click on "Browse men's collections by date."
2. Search through men's collections.
3. Find ten examples of men's jackets, each from a different year going back in time from the current year.
4. Make sure all your examples are from the same designer.
5. Compare the lengths, widths, garment fit (loose, snug), and details (lapels, pockets) during the ten-year period.
6. Use the content analysis chart below to record your findings.
7. Identify patterns of change and make a prediction for the following year.
8. Save each picture you content analyze and paste them into a PowerPoint. Include the year on each slide.
9. Submit your PowerPoints on our course site.

	Year 1	Year 2	Year 3	Year 4	Year 5	Year 6	Year 7	Year 8	Year 9	Year 10
Jacket Length										
Lapel Width										
Pocket Width										
Fit of Jacket										
Single/Double Breasted										
Type of Lapel										

two groups' responses are compared for differences. Differences between the groups are attributed to the manipulation or treatment. The term *post-test only control group design* is used to distinguish this design of an experiment from other designs in which both groups of individuals are given pretests, then exposed to the manipulation, and then given a post-test.

Experimental studies can vary in their complexity. An experimental study that is more complex than the post-test only control group could employ three conditions: two treatment conditions and one control condition. Researchers conducted an impression formation laboratory experiment that used three conditions (Johnson, Crutsinger, & Workman, 1994). People were asked to view stimuli and make judgments of the person depicted in the stimuli (or **stimulus person**). In their study, the appearance of a female stimulus person was changed to create three conditions reflecting two treatments and one control condition. The stimulus person was described to research

participants as a middle manager of a retail firm. In all conditions the stimulus person wore a white button-down collar shirt with a navy blue jacket. The independent variable was the neck treatment worn by the stimulus person. In the control condition, the female stimulus person simply had the neck of the shirt unbuttoned, in the second condition a scarf was worn around the neck, and in the third condition a necktie[1] was worn. Each research participant was shown a photograph depicting the stimulus person in one of the three neckwear conditions. The participants rated the stimulus person on a series of traits that previous researchers had found to be important to promotability and success in the workplace. In summary, in this study the independent variable was neck treatment and the dependent variables were traits related to

[1] At the time the study was conducted, it was fashionable for professional women to wear neckties styled similarly to men's, but often in floral prints or using more feminine colors than men wore.

TABLE 3.7

DETAILS ON THE JOHNSON ET AL. (1994) RESEARCH

Procedure. In Johnson et al. (1994), research participants saw one of three photos of a female stimulus person and read the following description: "The woman pictured works for a large retail firm in a middle management position. Her job responsibilities include writing reports, supervision and training of salespeople, research/market analysis, conducting meetings with top management, seminar presentations, developing budgets, developing long range strategies and plans, meeting with manufacturers' reps, and public relations" (p. 28).

Dependent Variables. Participants also rated the female stimulus person on a series of sixty-eight traits, some of which follow below. They were given the following written instructions: "indicate the likelihood that the manager pictured possesses each trait" (p. 28). By selecting the numbers below, participants could indicate their ratings of each trait.

		Speaks and Writes Effectively							
	Likely	7	6	5	4	3	2	1	Not Likely
		Stays Well Informed							
	Likely	7	6	5	4	3	2	1	Not Likely
		Gets Things Done							
	Likely	7	6	5	4	3	2	1	Not Likely
		Is a Leader							
	Likely	7	6	5	4	3	2	1	Not Likely
		Intelligent							
	Likely	7	6	5	4	3	2	1	Not Likely
		Likelihood of Being Promoted							
	Likely	7	6	5	4	3	2	1	Not Likely

promotability and success in the workplace. See Table 3.7 for examples of the dependent variables used in that study together with instructions to the participants as they completed their experimental task.

It may be evident that to conduct a laboratory experiment the researcher must carefully structure the study in advance. In the previous study about neckwear, the researchers reviewed the literature on traits related to executive success and promotability to develop the list of dependent variables to present to the research participants (Johnson et al., 1994). The researchers also had to give considerable thought to the development of the treatment conditions (white shirt with open-collar, white shirt with scarf, and white shirt with necktie). The authors noted that professional women were being advised to adopt the man's business suit but that there was reason to believe that such

a look might be "too masculine." The two experimental neck treatments were selected because neckties are traditional male symbols, while scarves are more "soft." The open neck shirt was the control condition. As of 2016, it is no longer fashionable for professional women to wear neckties.

To verify that the neckwear treatment conditions were perceived as the researchers intended, the researchers might have pretested their stimuli (treatment levels) (Johnson et al., 1994). A **pretest** can mean an evaluation of procedures, learning if people understand the questions in a questionnaire, or a trial run of the experiment administered to identify or verify the identification of different treatments (Dillman, 2000). As applied to the Johnson et al. study, the researchers might have conducted a pretest to verify that respondents rated the model (1) as more masculine when wearing the necktie than in the other two conditions and (2) as more feminine when wearing the scarf than in the other two conditions. The term **pilot test** or **pilot study** can be used to mean a pretest used by experimental researchers for stimulus development (e.g., Johnson, Ju, & Wu, 2016; Kim & Lennon, 2012).

Another way the researchers had to structure the study was to carefully manipulate the photos. First of all, they employed a professional photographer to guarantee high-quality photos. They took pictures of the same model in all three conditions to be sure that the only thing that varied between the photographs was the neck treatment in question. Then they carefully held all other appearance variables constant across the pictures (i.e., hairstyle, cosmetics, facial expression). It should be obvious that in studies with multiple independent variables there are even more aspects that the researcher must structure in advance.

In all experimental research it is important to randomly assign research participants to treatments; this is called **random assignment or randomization**. Continuing with the previous example of the neckwear study, participants were randomly assigned to treatment conditions (Johnson et al., 1994). This was possible because all participants were given packets of information including a photo, a description of job responsibilities, and lists of traits on which to rate the person depicted in the photo. However, for practical reasons, instead of using photos a researcher might want to use slides of the stimulus person and to show the same slide to a group of people at one time. This arrangement might reduce costs of developing the stimulus materials because, for one thing, the researcher would not have to pay for printing multiple photos. In this case, everyone in the same room would be exposed to the same treatment condition so that random assignment to treatment conditions at the participant level would not be possible. When random assignment at the individual participant level is not possible, the researcher should randomly assign groups of participants to treatments. See Table 3.8 for some sample research questions that could be investigated using laboratory experiments.

A special type of experimental research is called a field experiment because it is an experiment conducted in the field or in a real-life setting. In field experiments, participants cannot be randomly assigned to treatment

---

TABLE 3.8

SAMPLE RESEARCH QUESTIONS THAT COULD BE ADDRESSED VIA LABORATORY EXPERIMENTS

Sample Research question	Independent Variable	Dependent Variable
Are people wearing glasses perceived to be more intelligent than people not wearing glasses?	Glasses (presence or absence)	Ratings of Intelligence
Are women wearing short skirts perceived to be sexier than women wearing longer skirts?	Skirt Length (mini skirt, moderate length skirt, long skirt)	Ratings of Sexiness
Are fashionably dressed women thought to be friendlier than less fashionably dressed women?	Fashionability of Dress (fashionable, less fashionable)	Ratings of Friendliness
Are women wearing clothing with sorority insignia perceived to be snobbier than women wearing clothing without the insignia?	Sorority Insignia (T-shirt with sorority insignia, T-shirt without sorority insignia)	Ratings of Snobbishness
When men have tattoos, do we attribute more negative traits to them than to men without tattoos?	Tattoos (man with visible tattoos, man without visible tattoos)	Ratings of Negative Traits (e.g., likelihood of being a troublemaker, likelihood of getting in fights, likelihood of juvenile delinquency)

conditions, but the researcher still has some degree of control over the independent variable. Field experiments use groupings of people in their natural environments (e.g., schools, hospitals, retail stores, malls, or on the street). The lifelike nature of the field experiment is considered to be an advantage because it allows the researcher to study naturally occurring behaviors. As is the case with laboratory experiments, in field experiments the researcher manipulates an independent variable and studies its effects on one or more dependent variables. In field experiments, the dependent variable is often an observable behavior and the researcher is interested in determining whether the independent variable can cause a change in that observable behavior.

Just as in laboratory experiments, in field experiments the researcher carefully structures the study in advance. However, field experiments involve intruding into the natural environment where the effects of the independent variable are studied to determine its effect. A popular field experiment design occurs when one group of individuals is exposed to a treatment and measured (usually observed) and another group of individuals is simply measured (observed) without exposure to the treatment. Then the two groups' responses can be compared and any differences are attributed to the independent (treatment) variable.

A field experiment was conducted in two department stores in the Pacific Northwest (Lennon & Davis, 1989). There were two independent variables: age and dress. Two women (aged twenty-four and thirty-two) posed as shoppers at the stores. The first independent variable was age of the women posing as shoppers (e.g., the stimulus persons). One appeared older than the other. The other independent variable, dress, had two levels: the dress of the women either conveyed high status or it conveyed low status. The dependent variable was the length of time before the shoppers were acknowledged by a salesperson in the department store. Time was measured by hidden stopwatches. High- and low-status clothing items worn by the stimulus persons were selected based on a pilot study in which participants were asked to list high- and low-status clothing items. For the low-status condition both models wore poorly-fitted polyester pants, worn out shoes, unfashionable inexpensive sweaters, and carried inexpensive purses. In the high-status condition both models wore expensive pants and jackets/sweaters, with new leather shoes, gold accessories, and expensive purses.

More recently researchers investigated discrimination against obese shoppers in a Houston mall. In that field experiment ten average-sized female women posed as shoppers (King, Shapiro, Hebl, Singletary, & Turner, 2006). There were two independent variables: clothing (casual or professional) and size of shoppers (average or obese). Each of the ten women wore a "fat suit" in the obese condition, so that they appeared to be a size 22. The four experimental conditions were: average-weight shoppers wearing casual clothing, average-weight shoppers wearing professional clothing, shoppers wearing fat suit (i.e., obesity prosthesis) under casual clothing, and shoppers wearing fat suit under professional clothing. Each of the ten women visited stores in each condition. When dressed in the fat suit shoppers were subject to more interpersonal discrimination, which was subtle (rudeness, lack of friendliness), especially when wearing casual clothing.

More recently, the research on interpersonal discrimination has been extended to obese male shoppers (Ruggs, Hebl, & Williams, 2015). As in the previous study, the men wore fat suits in one condition and did not wear fat suits in the control condition. When dressed in the fat suit, the men experienced more interpersonal discrimination (less friendliness, less eye contact, less smiling, less nodding, and more rudeness) than when not wearing the fat suit.

Other researchers have conducted field experiments in contexts other than retail stores, such as in health care facilities. For example, researchers from Iran have studied how wearing a nurse's uniform affects anxiety in hospitalized children (Roohafza et al., 2009). In that study, children whose nurses wore white uniforms had higher anxiety than children whose nurses wore colored uniforms. Other researchers studied the effects of uniform color and style on preferences for nurses' uniforms at a Midwestern health care center (Wocial et al., 2010). Child hospital patients preferred uniforms that were brightly colored. In both of these field experiments the hospitalized children reacted more positively to colored nurses uniforms. See Table 3.9 for sample research questions that could be addressed via field experiments.

The people acting as stimulus persons in a field experiment (i.e., those whose appearances are altered) must be careful to behave the same way in all conditions, regardless of how they are dressed. The researcher wants to be able to ensure that any differences that occur are a result of the treatment and not a result of changes in the behavior of the stimulus persons.

TABLE 3.9

SAMPLE RESEARCH QUESTIONS THAT COULD
BE ADDRESSED VIA FIELD EXPERIMENTS

Sample Research Question	Independent Variable	Dependent Variable
Do men receive faster service in retail stores than women?	Sex of customer (men vs. women)	Speed of service
Do well-dressed women receive better restaurant service than poorly-dressed women?	Dress of customer (well-dressed vs. poorly dressed)	Friendlier service, quicker service
Do attractive servers get better tips than less attractive servers?	Attractiveness of server (attractive vs. less attractive)	Bigger tips
Are attractively dressed people approached more than unattractively dressed people?	Dress of customer (attractively dressed vs. unattractively dressed)	Number of times people approach
Are similar people (similarity could be based on ethnicity, or clothing, or sex) approached more than dissimilar people?	Clothing similarity (similar vs. dissimilar)	Number of times people approach
Is compliance to a request (answering questions, filling out a form, taking a tourist's picture) related to the appearance of the requester?	Appearance of requester (attractive vs. unattractive)	Complying with a request (e.g., filling out a questionnaire, answering questions, loaning a dime)
Do older people get better service in retail stores?	Age of customer (old vs. young)	Friendlier service, quicker service

Experimental research always involves the manipulation of at least one variable of interest. This is very different from other types of research (e.g., fieldwork or content analysis) that may involve no type of researcher intervention or manipulation. The lifelike nature of the field experiment is considered an advantage because the researcher is studying naturally occurring behaviors.

The primary advantage of experimental research is that if properly executed, experimentation allows the researcher to make inferences about cause and effect relationships (i.e., that the independent variable "causes" the dependent variable). Other advantages include the researcher has control over which variables are to be studied. Disadvantages include that the findings may not apply to other situations and may be difficult to replicate. Pretesting can sensitize participants to the research being conducted and they may respond to stimuli in a socially desirable way rather than how they might normally respond.

Survey Research

In **survey research** a group of people is asked to respond to questions or statements (also called items). See Table 3.10 for sample questions and sample items that might be included in a survey about shopping. Survey research assesses existing phenomena; true survey research does not involve the manipulation of variables like experimental research does. In survey research, the variables of interest are measured via questions or items. The questions and items can be compiled into a **questionnaire** which is a written set of self-administered questions or items. (See Figure 3.7 for an example of questionnaire items from a study that investigated rural consumers' use of the Internet to purchase food and fiber products (Johnson, Lennon, Jasper, Damhorst, & Lakner, 2003). Responses to questionnaire items from consumers who purchased online were compared to those of consumers who had not

TABLE 3.10

SAMPLE QUESTIONS AND SAMPLE ITEMS FROM A STUDY USING THE STRATEGY OF SURVEY METHODOLOGY

Suppose you visited an online store, found a pair of jeans that you liked, at a price that was great, and then found that the garment was out of stock in your size. Indicate your immediate reaction using the scales below.

Items (Statements)

Statement									
I would feel angry.	Agree	7	6	5	4	3	2	1	Disagree
I would feel upset.	Agree	7	6	5	4	3	2	1	Disagree
I would feel sad.	Agree	7	6	5	4	3	2	1	Disagree

Questions

How likely is that you will shop via this online store?	Very likely	7	6	5	4	3	2	1	Not Likely
How likely is that you will purchase apparel via this online store?	Very likely	7	6	5	4	3	2	1	Not Likely
How likely is that you will recommend this store to your friends?	Very likely	7	6	5	4	3	2	1	Not Likely

purchased online. Survey research is the most common research strategy used by researchers studying dress and human behavior (Lennon, Burns, & Rowold, 1995).

Surveys can be administered by mail or email, by handing them out in person, by phone, or by posting them online (Figure 3.8). In some cases, the questions can be read to participants (i.e., a one-to-one interview). The surveys were mailed in the research by Johnson et al. (2003). In other research, women were recruited to study reactions to body scanning (Loker, Cowie, Ashdown, & Lewis, 2004). The participants came to either a university campus or a retail store in New York City to be scanned and after the scanning procedure were handed a questionnaire to complete.

Advantages to the use of survey research include: Data are usually easy to summarize and analyze, it is fairly easy to sample a large number of people, it is fairly low in cost, it is convenient, and it allows the respondents to remain anonymous. Disadvantages include that there are often low response rates (i.e., ratio of number of respondents to the number who could have responded); respondents may misinterpret items/questions; respondents often must rely on memory, which can be faulty; and the researcher may not know who actually completed the survey. For example, in the previously discussed study of online shoppers, the cover letter requested that the person responsible for apparel shopping complete the questionnaire, however, it is possible that a child could have completed the questionnaire (Johnson et al., 2003).

When surveys are handed out to consumers at a mall, we call the technique a **mall intercept**. This technique was used to collect data from a large number of teen consumers in shopping malls in New York, Houston, and Los Angeles (Kim, Kang, & Kim, 2005). Another popular method of collecting survey data is by posting questionnaires online. For example, researchers obtained a random sample of female students' emails from a university registrar (Chattaraman & Rudd, 2006). Potential participants were sent an invitation to participate, which included a URL. By clicking on the URL, participants could access the posted questionnaire. As participants completed the questionnaires, the data were saved electronically and stored for the researchers, which is a major advantage of online surveys.

Figure 3.7
Sample questionnaire items.

Sample questionnaire items from Johnson et al. (2003)

19. How often do you use the following sources **TO PURCHASE**?
    [circle number]

B. Clothing Purchases (clothes and accessories):

	Never	Once or Twice a Year	Every Few Months	Every Month	At Least Once a Week
a. Internet	1	2	3	4	5
b. Television shopping channels	1	2	3	4	5
c. Mail-order catalogs	1	2	3	4	5
d. Local retail stores	1	2	3	4	5
e. Non-local retail stores	1	2	3	4	5

20. Think about the purchases you have made in the last month in the categories listed in question 19. ESTIMATE how much you spent on products from the following sources. *[place response in open corresponding line]*

A. TV shopping channels $ _____

B. Mail-order catalogs $ _____

C. Internet $ _____

D. Local retail stores and restaurants $ _____

E. Non-local retail stores and restaurants $ _____

Figure 3.8
An online survey.

Tell us about tanning using the following system:
1 = very infrequently, 2 = infrequently, 3 = somewhat infrequently, 4 = neither infrequent or frequently, 5 = somewhat frequently, 6 = frequently, 7 = very frequently

	1	2	3	4	5	6	7
How often do you tan?	●	●	●	●	●	●	●
How often have you burned while tanning?	●	●	●	●	●	●	●
How often do you wear sunscreen when you tan?	●	●	●	●	●	●	●
How often have you tanned in the last month?	●	●	●	●	●	●	●

Do you tan?

On occasions when you tan, how long are your tanning sessions in minutes?

> >

Survey research is designed to provide accurate information as it exists in a population. **Descriptive surveys** are used to describe a population. Descriptive surveys are used as a source of information regarding incidence of unemployment, disease, crime, and so forth, according to Touliatos and Compton (1988). Thus, when researchers investigated the incidence of dermatological health problems attributed to contact with textiles, they conducted descriptive survey research (Davis, Markee, Dallas, Harger, & Miller, 1990). These researchers mailed questionnaires to a sample of 750 households in each of five western states. The purpose of their research was to provide baseline data regarding the percentage of respondents who perceived skin irritation problems from fabrics. Often descriptive survey research examines associations between demographic variables (e.g., income, sex, age) and the variables of interest (Touliatos & Compton, 1988). Continuing with the example of the Davis et al. study, the researchers determined that differences existed between men and women in terms of perceived incidence of dermatological health problems associated with fabrics. Women perceived more problems than did men.

DRESS IN THE NEWS
Survey Research about Steroids

Jay Hoffman, chair of health and exercise science at the College of New Jersey, conducted confidential survey research with students in grades 8 to 12. He was interested in the extent to which the students would risk drug and supplement use to change their bodies and enhance their success in sports. He collected responses from over 3,200 students in twelve states. Of those who admitted to using steroids, 57 percent reported being influenced by professional athletes and 63 percent had friends who were influenced by professional athletes to use the drugs. Most of the steroid users (80 percent) said that they thought the steroids would help their athletic performance. In addition, 65 percent of the users (versus 6 percent of non-users) were willing to take extreme risks to achieve athletic success. This descriptive survey research was published in *Medicine & Science in Sports & Exercise* in 2008 and the news story about it appeared on MSNBC (Stenson, 2008).

Analytic surveys or explanatory surveys are used when the researcher intends to explain relationships among variables within a population (Touliatos & Compton, 1988). The primary goal of analytic or explanatory surveys is to explain relationships between variables, whereas the primary goal of descriptive surveys is to describe phenomena and to assess their incidence. The online shopping survey research previously reviewed is an example of an analytic survey (Johnson et al., 2003). The researchers were interested in whether or not online purchasers of apparel, home furnishings products, and food differed from non-purchasers with respect to their perceptions of characteristics of online shopping.

Thus, researchers studying dress and human behavior have used four research strategies: fieldwork, experimentation, non-reactive research such as content analysis, and survey methodology. Each strategy has its advantages and disadvantages, so the researcher must take these into account when selecting a strategy. See Table 3.11 for advantages and disadvantages of each of the four strategies.

SAMPLING

For any research strategy, the researcher must determine or define the groups to be studied. For example, researchers interested in retail customer service might unobtrusively observe customer-salesperson interactions in retail stores. In this case, the group being studied might be defined as salespeople at retail stores selling apparel. In any study, the group of "things" being studied is the **population** of interest. The things being studied are called **elements** and could consist of people, artifacts, or businesses. In survey research, the population is made up of people. In conducting a content analysis, the population might be fashion magazines.

It is usually not possible for the researcher to assess every element of a population, thus, the researcher selects a subset of the population to study, called a **sample**. This procedure of selecting the subset of the population to study is called **sampling**. Thus, through sampling a researcher chooses a portion of a population to participate in the research.

The type of research strategy employed along with the goal of the research are used to determine the type of sample that is drawn. For example, to elicit information from a sample that accurately represents a population,

TABLE 3.11

ADVANTAGES AND DISADVANTAGES OF RESEARCH STRATEGIES

Research Strategy	Advantages	Disadvantages
Fieldwork	Can study meanings of dress in daily life (i.e., in their contexts of daily use)	Extended time often needed to gather data Intrudes on the behavior being studied Can only study existing relationships
Content analysis (as a type of non-reactive research)	Does not affect the behavior being studied May allow the researcher to study inaccessible objects Does not require IRB approval	Is atheoretical Is descriptive (the researcher can say what was found, but can only speculate on why)
Experimentation: laboratory	Allows the researcher to determine cause and effect relationships Allows the researcher to maintain control over variables	Intrudes on the behavior being studied Variables and stimuli may be unrealistic or artificial in nature Results may not apply to other situations (i.e., may be difficult to replicate)
Experimentation: field	Allows the researcher to determine cause and effect relationships More realistic than laboratory experiments	Intrudes on the behavior being studied Not as much control over variables as lab experiment
Survey methodology	Data may be easy to summarize and analyze Fairly easy to obtain a large sample Fairly low in cost Allows respondents to remain anonymous If respondents are randomly selected, results are generalizable	Intrudes on the behavior being studied Possibility of low response rate Respondents may misinterpret items May not know who actual respondents are May rely on memory

participants in the sample should be randomly selected from that population. **Random selection** occurs when every element of the population has an equal chance of being selected for the research. When survey respondents are randomly selected, the research may be **generalizable** or representative of the entire population from which the data came. Random selection is a type of probability sample. A **probability sample** is characterized by the ability to specify the probability at which each individual within a population will be included in a sample. In the simplest case, all members of a population have an equal probability of being included in a sample. For example, suppose you are interested in drawing conclusions about the 1,500 students that are enrolled full-time in your college. You do not have enough money to gather data from

all members of your college. If you have a list of the names of all the students and you draw a sample of names from this list, you can determine the probability of any one student being included in your sample. The probability is 1/1,500 or .0006. Since descriptive surveys in general are used to provide accurate information about a population, it is especially important to gather data from a random selection of respondents.

However, random selection is not important or even possible for all types of research investigating dress and human behavior. For example, in field experiments or in research studying past peoples and their dress, true random selection is simply not possible. For example, suppose you are studying helping behavior and you are interested in determining whether women who are wearing school

MYSTERY SHOPPING

Mystery shopping has become very popular. For example, if you search Google for "mystery shopping" you will get around 24,300,000 hits. Mystery shoppers can even belong to a professional organization. Typically, mystery shoppers are customers or people who act like customers and visit businesses to conduct research for a company. Businesses use mystery shoppers to determine the level of customer service delivered to customers. In effect, the mystery shoppers are conducting *fieldwork* in the business, such as a restaurant or a retail store. In addition, by requiring the mystery shoppers to complete a questionnaire about the perceived level of service, the business gets a sense of how customers (i.e., the mystery shoppers) perceive the business. In this instance, the business is using the research strategy of *survey methodology*.

Mystery shoppers can call the business before visiting and ask a series of questions (or *interview* the employees), to evaluate employee telephone skills. In addition, such calls can be recorded so that the business team can listen to and evaluate them. Other services, such as how fast customers are waited on, how clean the establishment is, and how friendly the employees are, can also be provided by mystery shoppers. The results of mystery shopping can be used to recognize the need for training in a certain area; for example, do all employees follow the employee handbook? If not, then some type of intervention training program could be designed and executed.

logo sweatshirts will get more help when they have a flat tire than women who are not wearing school logo clothing. You set up your field experiment in a parking lot on your campus. Your participants are people walking by the woman who needs help. In this type of research, you have no idea exactly who will participate in your research because you do not know in advance who is going to walk by on the days you conduct your research and gather your data. Similarly, if you are studying historical dress artifacts, you do not know what artifacts will be available to you. For example, suppose you were interested in investigating gender differences in children's dress during the 1970s. In the population of all possible items of children's dress that were worn, some items might simply not be available because they were not considered worth saving, such as pacifiers, socks, hairbows, or sandals. This type of sample is referred to as a **non-probability sample** because the researcher does not know the likelihood that any one person (in the first example) or artifact (in the second example) could be included in the sample. In addition, in these instances a researcher would not typically try to generalize his/her findings, based on the sample data, to a population. Thus, the type of sampling for research depends on the research strategy employed and the goals of the research.

INFORMATION LITERACY

Definition

As a student in this class, you will be reading about research in this textbook. This task will require you to be able to evaluate the information you read. You may also be asked to read and report on empirical research articles. This task may require you to locate the appropriate research articles, possibly access them via an online source, and evaluate the article. You may be required to develop a research topic, collect data, and write a research paper. This task requires not only finding, accessing, and evaluating information but also using that information. We use the term **information literacy** to describe the set of abilities that includes finding, accessing, evaluating, and using information (American Library Association, 2000). Information literacy is especially important in the contemporary world due to the exponential growth of information sources and availability of new technology to use in finding information. With many sources available to students, and many of them unfiltered (e.g., blogs), it is important to be able to evaluate the authenticity, validity, and reliability of the information. For example, with so much digital information today, it is easy to do a database search to locate information. A **database search** uses a search engine and operates on material stored in a digital **database**, a collection of information stored in a computer system that is organized for easy access ("What is a database?," n.d.).

A few examples should shed light on what is meant by information literacy. Suppose you need a new pair of running shoes and you want some information to use to evaluate them. You could Google "running shoes." In so doing, you find that the first sixteen hits are ads for brands of running shoes or for stores that sell running shoes. Since you know that ads and stores are motivated to sell products, you might decide not to rely on that information. Finding information that you might use in a research paper also requires that you evaluate that information before you use it. For example, suppose that you need to cite a source that reports that make-up affects judgments of competence for a research paper. Further, suppose that you find an article in the *New York Times* that reports on research about make-up and judgments of competence, but by doing a database search you find the original research on which the *New York Times* piece was based. In a research paper you will need to cite the original study, not the *New York Times* piece which is one step removed from the research and could be inaccurate, biased, or misrepresented. Also, if you find that the research in question was funded by Cover Girl cosmetics, that information should make you question the results of the study. This is what is meant by evaluating the reliability of the information.

Evaluation of Source Material

When writing a research paper, it is important to use scholarly sources. **Scholarly sources** are intended to disseminate research and academic discussion within a discipline. There are some easy ways to determine if a source is scholarly. Scholarly sources tend to be written and read by scholars and experts in the field and authors' credentials are provided. These types of articles should be peer-reviewed or refereed, which means that they have been evaluated by other experts in the field. This you can determine by visiting the website of the publication. Not all scholarly articles are empirical, but empirical articles are published in scholarly journals. In scholarly journals you will find copious references, but you are unlikely to find advertisements. Scholarly sources may use **jargon**, or special words used in a discipline that may be difficult to understand and may not be commonly used outside research publications in one's field.

Articles from the **popular press** are written for the general public as opposed to being written for a scholarly audience. Examples of the popular press include online and offline newspapers, magazines, and blogs. Popular press sources are not to be used as evidence in a research paper and also have some easily recognized characteristics. They can be written or read by anyone and tend to use less technical language and jargon. These sources are often accompanied by much commercial advertising and many glossy photos. Popular press sources are published more often—sometimes once a week or every day and rarely include references. They can serve as a good source for a broad perspective on a topic or a popular slant and may be used in the introduction of a research paper if used for that purpose.

Another source of information important to dress scholars is trade publications. **Trade publications** can be considered somewhere between scholarly and popular sources. Trade publications cover apparel and textile industry news, provide product information, and report trends in the field. Authors tend to be authorities in the industry. The audience for trade publications consists of professionals in the industry, researchers, and the general public. The language used in trade publications may be technical and uses the jargon of the industry. These publications do include advertising, as well as a combination of text, graphs, charts, and photos. Trade publications may be cited in empirical research to establish the importance of the fashion industry (for example, number of workers involved in or value in dollars of the industry).

Chapter Summary

In this chapter you have learned that dress is studied through the research process. To conduct research we formulate research questions, gather data, analyze data, interpret results, and reach conclusions. To study dress and human behavior from a social science perspective, researchers have relied on four main strategies: fieldwork, non-reactive research, experimentation (subcategories: laboratory and field), and survey methodology. In all these types of research the researcher selects a sample to be studied. In random selection, every element of the population has an equally likely chance of being selected for study.

Information literacy is a set of abilities that includes finding, accessing, evaluating, and using information. Information literacy is an important concept that must be applied when conducting research and writing about research. Sources used in empirical research must be evaluated for their authenticity, validity, and reliability. Sources can be located using database searches.

Key Terms

a priori questions
analytic or explanatory surveys
atheoretical
content analysis
control group
database
database search
dependent variable
descriptive surveys
elements
empirical research
experimentation
exploratory research
field experiments
fieldwork
generalizable
generalizations

implicit content
independent variable
informants
information literacy
institutional review board (IRB)
interviews
jargon
laboratory experiments
latent content
mall intercept
manifest content
manipulation
method of enumeration
non-probability sample
non-reactive research
outsider perspective
paradigms

participant observers
peer-reviewed or refereed
pilot test or study
popular press
population
post-test only control group design
pretest
probability sample
qualitative study
quantitative study
questionnaire
random assignment or randomization
random selection
rating scale
reliable
research

sample
sampling
scholarly sources
stimulus person
strategy
structured interview
structured observation
survey research
theory
trade publications
treatment group
true insider
unit of analysis or recording unit
unobtrusive observation
unstructured interview
unstructured observation

Discussion Questions

1. What does "participant observers" mean? Give an example.

2. A sociologist plans to conduct a study to analyze the status of the kimono (a traditional Japanese garment) in Japan's modern society. Which strategy would you choose if you are assigned to design this study? Explain your choice.

3. What is content analysis? What is unit of analysis? Design your own content analysis study by describing a research purpose, coding objects, and unit of analysis.

4. A researcher designs an experiment to examine whether fashion therapy (a program developed to help people improve their appearance) would affect

people's self-esteem and social interaction. Identify the independent variables and dependent variables. Identify the population from which to draw a sample. Develop a specific experimental design to test the relationship between the independent and dependent variable.

5. A research survey found that college women's self-esteem is negatively correlated with their exposure to fashion magazines. Suppose you were interested in conducting a similar study with adolescents. What kind of survey would you use for this study: descriptive survey or explanatory survey? Explain your choice.

6. What does "random sampling" mean? A researcher wants to analyze the relationship between college women's favorite dress color and their self-perceptions. She may select a group of female students from a class as the research subjects. Could you identify the "population" and the "elements"? Did the researcher use a random sampling method? Why, or why not?

STUDiO™

Visit your book's STUDIO for additional quiz questions, vocabulary flashcards, and chapter worksheets!

Suggested Readings

Johnson, K. K. P., Crutsinger, C., & J. E. Workman (1994). Can professional women appear too masculine? The case of the necktie. *Clothing and Textiles Research Journal, 12*(2), 27–31.

Johnson, K. K., Ju, H. W., & Wu, J. (2016). Young adults' inferences surrounding an alleged sexual assault alcohol consumption: Gender, dress, and appearance schematicity. *Clothing and Textiles Research Journal, 34*(2), 127–142.

Johnson, K. K. P., Lennon, S. J., Jasper, C., Damhorst, M. L., Lakner, H. (2003). An application of Rogers's Innovation Model: Use of the internet to purchase apparel, food, and home furnishing products by small community consumers. *Clothing and Textiles Research Journal, 21*, 185–196.

Kim, M., & Lennon, S. J. (2005). The effects of customers' dress on salesperson's service in large-sized clothing specialty stores. *Clothing and Textiles Research Journal, 23*(2), 78–87.

King, E. B., Shapiro, J. R., Hebl, M. R., Singletary, S. L., & Turner, S. (2006). The stigma of obesity in customer service: A mechanism for remediation and bottom-line consequences of interpersonal discrimination. *Journal of Applied Psychology, 91*(3), 579–593.

References

American Library Association. (2000). *Information literacy competency standards for higher education.* Retrieved from: http://www.ala.org/acrl/sites/ala.org.acrl/files/content/standards/standards.pdf

Berelson, B. (1952). *Content analysis in communication research.* New York, NY: Free Press.

Bonnin, D. (2013). Global integration, new technologies and the work of South African textile designers, *South African Review of Sociology, 44*(2), 112–130.

Chattaraman, V., & Rudd, N. A. (2006). Preferences for aesthetic attributes in clothing as a function of body image, body cathexis, and body size. *Clothing and Textiles Research Journal, 24*(1), 46–61.

Chen, R., & Behling, D. (1994, October). Paper presented at the International Textiles and Apparel Association meeting: *Chinese immigrant garment workers in New York City: A field study.* Minneapolis, MN.

Copeland, R., & Hodges, N. (2014). Exploring masquerade dress at Trinidad Carnival: Bikinis, beads, and feathers and the emergence of the popular *pretty mas*. *Clothing and Textiles Research Journal, 32*(3), 186–201. DOI: 10.1177/0887302X14531452.

Creswell, J. (1994). *Research design: Qualitative, quantitative, and mixed methods approaches.* Thousand Oaks, CA: Sage Publications.

Cummins, E. R., & Blum, L. M. (2015). "Suits to self-sufficiency": Dress for success and neoliberal maternalism. *Gender & Society, 29*(5), 623–646.

Dalby, L. (1983). *Geisha.* Berkeley, CA: University of California Press.

Dalby, L. (1993). *Kimono, fashioning culture.* New Haven, CT: Yale University Press.

Davis, L. L., Markee, N., Dallas, M.J., Harger, B., & Miller, J. (1990). Dermatological health problems attributed by consumers to contact with textiles. *Home Economics Research Journal, 18*, 311–322.

Dickson, J. H., Oeggl, K., & Handley, L. L. (2005). The Iceman reconsidered. *Scientific American Special Edition, 15*(1), 4–10.

Dickson, M. A., & Littrell, M. A. (1998). Organizational culture for small textile and apparel businesses in Guatemala. *Clothing and Textiles Research Journal, 16*(2), 68–78.

Dillman, D. A. (2000). *Mail and internet surveys: The tailored design method* (Vol. 2). New York, NY: Wiley.

Festinger, L. (1954). A theory of social comparison processes. *Human Relations, 7*(2), 117–140.

Gerbner, G., Gross, L., Morgan, M., Signorielli, N., & Shanahan, J. (2002). Growing up with television: Cultivation processes. *Media Effects: Advances in Theory and Research, 2*, 43–67.

Halushka, J. (2015). Work wisdom: Teaching former prisoners how to negotiate workplace interactions and perform a rehabilitated self. *Ethnography, 17*(1), 72–91. DOI: 10.1177/1466138115609625.

Holsti, O. (1969). *Content analysis for the social sciences and humanities.* Reading, MA: Addison-Wesley Publishing Company.

Howlett, N., Pine, K., Orakcioglu, I., & Fletcher, B. (2013). The influence of clothing on first impressions: Rapid and positive responses to minor changes in male attire. *Journal of Fashion Marketing and Management: An International Journal, 17*(1), 38–48.

Johnson, K. K. P., Crutsinger, C., & J. E. Workman (1994). Can professional women appear too masculine? The case of the necktie. *Clothing and Textiles Research Journal, 12*(2), 27–31.

Johnson, K. K. P., Lennon, S. J., Jasper, C., Damhorst, M. L., Lakner, H. (2003). An application of Rogers's Innovation Model: Use of the internet to purchase apparel, food, and home furnishing products by small community consumers. *Clothing and Textiles Research Journal, 21*, 185–196.

Jung, J., & Lee, Y-J. (2009). Cross-cultural examination of women's fashion and beauty magazine advertisements in the United States and South Korea. *Clothing and Textiles Research Journal, 27*(4), 274–286.

Kaiser, S. B. (1997). *The social psychology of clothing: Symbolic appearances in context* (Rev. 2nd ed.). New York, NY: Fairchild Publications.

Kim, Y. K., Kang, J., & Kim, M. (2005). The relationships among family and social interaction, loneliness, mall shopping motivation, and mall spending of older consumers. *Psychology & Marketing, 22*(12), 995–1015.

Kim, J. H., & Lennon, S. (2012). Music and amount of information: Do they matter in an online apparel setting?. *The International Review of Retail, Distribution and Consumer Research, 22*(1), 55–82.

Kim, M., & Lennon, S. J. (2005). The effects of customers' dress on salesperson's service in large-sized clothing specialty stores. *Clothing and Textiles Research Journal, 23*(2), 78–87.

Kim, M., & Lennon, S. J. (2006). Content analysis of diet advertisements: A cross-national comparison of Korean and U.S. women's magazines. *Clothing and Textiles Research Journal, 24*, 345–362.

King, E. B., Shapiro, J. R., Hebl, M. R., Singletary, S. L., & Turner, S. (2006). The stigma of obesity in customer service: A mechanism for remediation and bottom-line consequences of interpersonal discrimination. *Journal of Applied Psychology, 91*(3), 579–593.

Kolbe, R. H., & Burnett, M. S. (1991). Content-analysis research: An examination of applications with directives for improving research reliability and objectivity. *Journal of Consumer Research, 18*, 243–250.

Lennon, S. J. (1990). Clothing and changing sex roles: Comparison of qualitative and quantitative analyzes. *Home Economics Research Journal, 18*, 245–254.

Lennon, S. J., & Burns, L. D. (2000). Diversity of research in textiles, clothing, and human behavior: The relationship between what we know and how we know. *Clothing and Textiles Research Journal, 18*, 213–226.

Lennon, S. J., Burns, L. D., & Rowold, K. L. (1995). Dress and human behavior research: Sampling, subjects, and consequences for statistics. *Clothing and Textiles Research Journal, 13*, 262–272.

Lennon, S. J., & Davis, L. L. (1989). Customer service as a function of customer appearance and salesperson goals. *Home Economics Forum, 9*, 9–11, 18.

Lennon, S. J., Johnson, K. K. P., & Lee, J. (2011). A perfect storm for consumer misbehavior: Shopping on Black Friday. *Clothing and Textiles Research Journal, 29*, 119–134.

Loker, S., Cowie, L., Ashdown, S., & Lewis, V. D. (2004). Female consumers' reactions to body scanning. *Clothing and Textiles Research Journal, 22*(4), 151–160.

Lynch, S., & Peer, L. (2002). Analyzing newspaper content: A how-to guide, including national comparison data for US daily newspapers. *Readership Institute Media Management Center at Northwestern University, Chicago.*

Mears, A. (2011). *Pricing beauty: The making of a fashion model.* Berkeley, CA: University of California Press.

Mun, J. M., Janigo, K. A., & Johnson, K. K. P. (2012). Tattoo and the self. *Clothing and Textiles Research Journal, 30*(2), 134–148. DOI: 10.1177/0887302X12449200.

Norris, L. (2015). The limits of ethicality in international markets: Imported second-hand clothing in India. *Geoforum, 67*, 183–193.

Nutz, B. (2012). Medieval lingerie. *History Extra.* Retrieved from: http://www.historyextra.com/lingerie

Pilcher, J. (2010). What not to wear? Girls, clothing, and 'showing' the body. *Children and Society, 24*, 461–470.

Riffe, D., Lacy, S., & Fico, F. (1998). *Analyzing media messages: Quantitative content analysis.* New Jersey: Lawrence Erlbaum Associates, Inc.

Roohafza, H., Pirnia, A., Sadeghi, M., Toghianifar, N., Talaei, M., & Ashrafi, M. (2009). Impact of nurses' clothing on anxiety of hospitalised children. *Journal of Clinical Nursing, 18*(13), 1953–1959.

Ruggs, E. N., Hebl, M. R., & Williams, A. (2015). Weight isn't selling: The insidious effects of weight stigmatization in retail settings. *Journal of Applied Psychology, 100*(5), 1483–1496.

Selltiz, C., Wrightsman, L. S., & Cook, S W. (1976). *Research methods in social relations.* New York, NY: Holt, Rinehart, and Winston.

Smiley, C. J., & Middlemass, K. M. (2016). Clothing makes the man: Impression management and prisoner reentry. *Punishment & Society, 18*(2), 220–243.

Stenson, J. (2008, March 3). Kids on steroids willing to risk it all for success. NBC News.com. Retrieved from: http://www.msnbc.msn.com/id/22984780/

Touliatos, J., & Compton, N. H. (1988). *Research methods in human ecology/home economics.* Ames, IA: Iowa State University Press.

What is a database? (n.d.). In *Access 2010: Introduction to Databases.* Retrieved from: http://www.gcflearnfree.org/access2010/1.2

Willis, J. W., Jost, M., & Nilakanta, R. (2007). *Foundations of qualitative research: Interpretive and critical approaches.* Thousand Oaks, CA: Sage Publications.

Wocial, L., Albert, N. M., Fettes, S., Birch, S., Howey, K., Na, J., & Trochelman, K. (2010). Impact of pediatric nurses' uniforms on perceptions of nurse professionalism. *Pediatric Nursing, 36*(6), 320–326.

Workman, J. E., & Johnson, K. K. P. (1993). Cultural aesthetics and the social construction of gender. In S. J. Lennon & L. D. Burns (Eds.), *Social science aspects of dress: New directions* (pp. 93–109). Monument, CO: ITAA.

PART 2

PSYCHOLOGICAL/SOCIAL PSYCHOLOGICAL PERSPECTIVES ON DRESS

CHAPTER

4 DRESS AND SOCIAL COGNITION

After reading and reflecting on the content of this chapter students should be able to:

- **Explain how dress is used as a cue in social perception processes.**

- **Analyze how dress is used in forming stereotypes.**

- **Use the Livesley and Bromley model to explain social perception as a function of dress.**

INTRODUCTION

In our daily lives, we often find ourselves in situations in which we have to assess others or make judgments about them, sometimes based on very little information. Those judgments have very powerful consequences. For example, jurors may make judgments concerning guilt or innocence based not only on defendant testimony but also on defendant demeanor and appearance. Recruiters may use physical appearance cues as they make their hiring decisions because new college graduates often have very similar resumes and experiences. In both of these instances, the people making the judgments are engaging in **social cognition**, the use of mental or cognitive processes to think, perceive, judge, and make inferences about people. The social part of social cognition refers to a focus on people in interpersonal situations. The cognitive part of

social cognition means that the process is mental. Thus, social cognition consists of mental processes that focus on how people make sense of themselves and others. Another way to think about these mental processes is that social cognition focuses on the influence of social and cognitive variables on each other (Higgins, 2000). The part of social cognition that is concerned with perceptual processing of information including dress and appearance cues is called **social perception**.

Social perception is a general term and includes several specific processes: categorization, impression formation, impression management, stereotyping, and prejudice. In this chapter we discuss social perception generally. We review the way that dress variables have been used in studying social perception processes including categorization, schema, stereotyping, and prejudice.

SOCIAL PERCEPTION

The study of how and what we perceive about people has been referred to with several terms including social perception, **person perception**, or **impression formation**. The terms social perception and person perception are synonymous, since social refers to people. Impression formation subsumes them because we form impressions of both people and other entities including stores and brands. For example, the impression or perception of a store is

Figure 4.1

A Steampunk enthusiast attends a Steampunk picnic during the annual Wave-Gotik-Treffen (WGT) music festival on June 7, 2014 in Leipzig, Germany.

called **store image** (Jacoby & Mazursky, 1984; Zimmer & Golden, 1988). The impression of a brand is called **brand image** (Aaker, 1997; Dobni & Zinkhan, 1990).

Since our sense of sight is our most developed sense, we often rely on visual information in forming social perceptions. When using visual information (e.g., aspects of appearance) to form a social perception, there is a significant amount of information available on which to base perceptions. As a result of the amount of information available, individuals selectively attend to some information and ignore others. Therefore, some pieces of information about a person you may not even notice (e.g., hair color, eye color), while other pieces of information you may attend to closely (e.g., cleanliness, neatness, appropriateness). For example, **steampunk** fashion is likely to attract attention in most contexts. Steampunk fashion is deconstructed (the *punk* part) neo-Victorian looks that incorporate technological aspects from the nineteenth century (the *steam* part) (Higham, 2011; "Steampunk picnic at park," 2015). Figure 4.1 illustrates an example of steampunk fashion.

What Makes Us Pay Attention to Some Cues and Ignore Others?

There are a number of factors that cause people to pay more attention to some aspects of appearance when forming perceptions and to ignore others. Berlyne (1960) noted that people tend to pay attention to novel cues or stimuli.

A dress cue, like any other type of cue, can be novel and attract attention. Dress and appearance cues are novel and attract attention when they are innovative, unusual, unexpected, or unfamiliar (Kaiser, 1990). Outside a college or high school campus, cues that might be identified as unusual include deviations from an expected appearance such as purple hair, ear gauges, or facial tattoos.

Novel Cues

Innovativeness has been studied in research investigating fashionability (Clayton, Lennon, & Larkin, 1987; Lennon & Clayton, 1992; Thurston, Lennon, & Clayton, 1990). In this series of related studies, the researchers defined style features of women's professional dress as innovative if they were newly introduced (within the last year or less). In those studies, innovative cues were attended to but were not always perceived as fashionable. Unexpectedness as a cue is represented in research that addresses unfashionable, startling, and inappropriate dress. When faced with unexpected stimuli our attention is drawn to those stimuli (McGuire, 1976). Inappropriate, unexpected, and unfashionable forms of dress have all been found to affect perceptions (Cooper, Darley, & Henderson, 1974; Johnson, Nagasawa, & Peters, 1977; McPeek & Edwards, 1975; Workman, 1984–85). Thus, dress cues that are unusual, innovative, unexpected, or inappropriate are likely to capture the attention of perceivers and to be used in subsequent social cognitive processing. Clearly, what is considered unusual, innovative, unexpected, or inappropriate is a function of the cultural context and changing social mores. An example of dress that might currently be considered unusual and unexpected is the fashion for skirts for men (Figure 4.2) seen in some designers' 2016 collections ("Man skirts," 2015).

Salience

The **salience** or relevance of a dress cue also affects perception because when stimuli are salient we pay attention to them and are likely to use them in our cognitive processing (Lennon & Miller, 1984; Wingate, Kaiser, & Freeman, 1985–86). People with physical difficulties or who are just learning to dress themselves may need clothing with **self-help features**. Self-help features are aspects of clothing that make the clothing easy to put on and take off. For example, toddlers and senior citizens with arthritis can easily put on

Figure 4.2
Gucci—Men's Spring 2016 Runway—Milan Menswear Fashion Week.

their own shoes if the shoes have Velcro closures instead of shoelaces. Dress stimuli in the form of self-help features are salient if they are unexpected or if they draw attention to a person's physical abilities (Wingate et al., 1985–86). Other characteristics of dress cues that draw attention to a wearer and affect perception include coloration (bright colors) and pattern (Miller, 1982).

Do We Have To Be Aware Of Cues That Affect Us?

While salient, innovative, and unusual cues attract our attention and so are used in social perception, other cues affect social perception without our being aware of them. When this occurs we say that some cues affect us below our conscious level of awareness. For example, fragrance has been found to affect consumers' perceptions even when the consumers are unaware of the presence of a fragrance (Laird, 1932; Miller, 1991). More recently, UK researchers conducted a field experiment and studied ambient scents in the retail environment (Ward, Davies, & Kooijman, 2007). In that study, when the store was scented it was perceived to be darker, busier, more inviting, more formal, and more stimulating that when the store was not scented. Thus, we do not have to be consciously aware of cues for them to affect us. Because cues can affect us below our conscious level of awareness, we may not be able to accurately report on which cues actually affect our perceptions.

In a typical social perception situation, there is a person (i.e., an observer or perceiver) who perceives a second person (i.e., the **target**) within some kind of context or physical setting, a relationship, or a historical time period. Consider the first day of class in a typical university classroom. The classroom is the context and the historical time period is the first day of class. A student enrolled in the class arrives a few minutes early and sees the professor standing at the front of the room. In this case, we can consider the student as the perceiver or observer, the university professor as the stimulus person or target (of the perception). Recall from Chapter 3, "Conducting Research on Dress," that a stimulus person is a person depicted in stimuli about whom judgments are made in experimental research. Researchers have documented that social perception is affected by stimulus variables (Johnson & Roach-Higgins, 1987a; 1987b). **Stimulus variables** are aspects of the stimulus person that affect social perception. Social perception is also affected by **perceiver variables** (Rowold, 1984). Perceiver variables are aspects of the perceiver that affect what he/she perceives. Finally, **context variables** also influence social perception (Damhorst, 1984–85). Context variables in social perception are variables contained in the setting within which the stimulus person is perceived. Thus social perception depends upon characteristics of the individual being perceived (stimulus or target person), characteristics of the perceiver (observer), and characteristics of the setting or context in which the perception occurs. In the next sections we outline a process of person perception that highlights how individuals are able to use aspects of dress and appearance as a basis for their assessments and perceptions of others.

PERSON PERCEPTION

Livesley and Bromley (1973) proposed a four-stage process of person perception. They discuss the process as if one stage followed the next. There is no evidence that each stage follows the next in a sequential manner. It is very possible that stage four follows immediately after stage one. However, we present the stages as originally discussed by Livesley and Bromley because this presentation facilitates understanding of the process.

The first stage was labeled **cue selection**. During this stage, a perceiver selects, from information available about another person (i.e., stimulus), the particular information (i.e., cues) that will be used as a basis for forming perceptions of the stimulus person. The perceiver may not be consciously aware of the cues that he or she selectively perceived or aware of the reasons for selection of those particular cues. If the perceiver is aware of the cues selected, it is assumed that the cues selected have personal relevance or significance to the perceiver. A variety of cues could be selected. For example, in one study, researchers asked women what dress cues they routinely used when forming perceptions of others (Johnson, Schofield, & Yurchisin, 2002). Cues identified were classified as clothing, suits, shoes, jewelry, glasses, appropriateness of dress, body form, body surfaces, body motions, make-up, and piercings among others (Figure 4.3).

Although actual cue selection (i.e., specific cues people select) has not been measured, we do know that judgments of others are affected by dress cues (Glick, Larsen, Johnson, & Branstiter, 2005; Grabe & Samson, 2010; Lennon & Miller, 1984–85). As previously demonstrated, judgments are also influenced by the context within which the cue is presented and by perceiver characteristics. Thus, the reason a specific dress cue is selected can be something about the cue itself (e.g., it might be a novel cue), something about the setting in which the cue is selected (e.g., the setting might be formal and the dress cue might be informal such as jeans), or something about the perceiver (e.g., the perceiver might be a fashion leader who notices dress cues that are unfashionable). All of these variables may affect what cue individuals select to form the basis of their perceptions. So even though we do not know how people select cues, we know that cue selection occurs because in these studies judgments were shown to be a function of manipulated dress cues. This assumption is consistent with perceivers' reports of how they form perceptions of others (Johnson et al., 2002).

Figure 4.3
During the cue selection stage of Livesley and Bromley's model of person perception, perceivers select cues such as hair style or clothing style for further processing.

The second stage of person perception is **interpretative inference**. During this stage, a perceiver infers traits of the stimulus person presumably on the basis of the selectively perceived dress cue(s) and on what meaning(s) the individual has linked to the selected cue(s). In a classic person perception study people viewed and then rated a stimulus person on a variety of traits. The stimulus person either wore or did not wear glasses (Thornton, 1944). When the stimulus person wore glasses, people rated the stimulus person as more intelligent than when not wearing glasses. In a more recent similar study, children aged six to ten judged other children from photos (Walline, Sinnott, Johnson, Ticak, Jones, & Jones, 2008). The children were judged smarter and more honest when wearing

Figure 4.4

Possible link between the dress cue (eye glasses) and the inferred trait of intelligence.

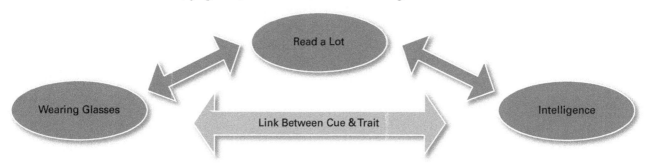

glasses. The ratings in these two studies may be a result of inferences linked to wearing glasses, namely that (a) people who need glasses have poor vision because they read a lot and (b) people who read a lot are intelligent. Thus, a cognitive link was formed between the dress cue (i.e., glasses) and the trait (i.e., intelligence) such that one of the meanings signaled by wearing glasses was that the person wearing them was intelligent (Figure 4.4).

Inferences may be inaccurate (Bruner, 1957). This happens because, as we have seen, the association of specific personal characteristics with dress cues is a function of perceiver characteristics as well as stimulus characteristics (Burns & Lennon, 1993). In our eye glass example people may wear glasses not because they read a lot but simply because they need to see! So the linking of glasses with the trait of intelligence may be wrong. In fact, we know that inferences about people are sometimes accurate and sometimes inaccurate (Neuberg, 1989; Schneider, Hastorf, & Ellsworth, 1979). Regardless, individuals often assume that the inferences they form about others are accurate (Johnson et al., 2002) and this assumption shapes their perceptions accordingly.

The third stage involved in person perception is called **extended inference**. During this stage, characteristics are thought to be assigned to people not on the basis of selected cues and immediate links to associated meanings but on the basis of interpretative inferences. An example of an extended inference would be to assume that a fifteen-year-old girl holding a Gucci handbag has wealthy parents. Such an inference is an extended inference because instead of making an inference about the stimulus person (the girl), you have made an inference about someone associated with the stimulus person (her parents).

Employers may attempt to strategically manipulate extended inferences through dress codes and other rules. For example, at Walt Disney World costumed workers

must proceed to their place of work underground so as not to appear out of context to guests (e.g., wearing a French costume walking through the "China" region of the EPCOT complex) and thus possibly reflect poorly on the facility. Workman (1991) noted that consideration of company image is one of the criteria to be considered when designing uniforms for foodservice workers. Uniforms represent a substantial investment by a company and if well designed can enhance the company's image. Inconsistencies between employee dress and desired image may result in extended inferences about a company that a company may find unacceptable. Thus, in order to control extended inferences about a business made on the basis of an employee's clothing, many companies may require uniforms or enforce a dress code.

Research demonstrates that people do make extended inferences on the basis of at least two aspects of dress: physical attractiveness and clothing. For example, in one study teachers inferred that attractive children had parents who were more interested in their education than unattractive children (Clifford & Walster, 1973). In other research, adults made inferences about the childrearing practices of a child's parents, on the basis of information about the child's conduct and physical attractiveness (Adams & LaVoie, 1975). Researchers found that voters were willing to ascribe more radical opinions to an unseen candidate who was represented by a campaign worker with a deviant appearance (e.g., long hair, beard, jeans, and old army jacket) as compared to an unseen candidate represented by a campaign worker with a conventional appearance (e.g., short hair, coat, and tie) (Darley & Cooper, 1972). In qualitative research mothers were interviewed about the appearances of their young children (Collett, 2005). These women believed that the way their children looked and dressed did reflect on them. In other words, the mothers believed that others formed extended inferences concerning them based on their children's appearance. Many of the mothers explained this belief by saying that they themselves made these (extended) inferences about other moms based on their children's appearance.

Researchers have documented that people are willing to make extended inferences about things that are simply associated with other people. For example, people make extended inferences about a city based on the clothing of their taxi drivers (Workman & Johnson, 1989a). These researchers found that appropriately dressed taxi drivers were attributed more favorable traits than inappropriately dressed drivers; in addition, people did make extended inferences about the city for whom the driver worked on the basis of the driver's clothing. The inferences about the city were more favorable when the driver wore appropriate as compared to inappropriate clothing. Many cities regulate taxi driver appearance. For example, New York City requires taxi drivers to maintain an appearance that is neat and professional or face a $25 fine ("NYC votes to change," 2011) and Montreal, Canada requires cabbies to wear dark pants or shorts and white shirts ("Dress code," 2015).

Others have conducted qualitative research and reported findings that do not support the idea that people make extended inferences. Johnson and her colleagues (2002) interviewed women about the perceptions they formed of others based on dress and what specific dress cues they used in forming those perceptions. None of the participants reported forming perceptions that extended beyond the initial perceived person. Perhaps the explanation for these discrepant results is simply that we are not always aware of making extended inferences.

The final stage in person perception is **anticipatory set** (expected behaviors) or **verbal report**. Based on inferences about a person and things associated with the person, expectations may be formed regarding how that person will behave. These expectations may be made explicit through the perceiver's behavior toward that individual. Behaviors could include the verbal expression of an opinion about another or a physical act such as the amount of physical distance maintained from another. Anticipatory set is important because it presumably affects actual behavior towards people and, more than that, it affects the interpretation of others' behavior. Several researchers have demonstrated that if people expect others to possess certain characteristics and to act in a certain way, then they are likely to find those characteristics and interpret those behaviors in that way (Snyder, Campbell, & Preston, 1982; Snyder & Swann, 1978). This process is due to the way in which these individuals go about gathering information (Snyder & Gangestad, 1981) and is called **expectancy confirmation**.

In other words, the kind of information we pay attention to (i.e., that we gather) about another *affects how we interpret* that person's behavior and can ultimately affect that person's behavior (Snyder, Tanke, & Berscheid, 1977). For example, suppose a young woman is wearing fashionable clothing and the fashion is for bare midriffs and low-waisted pants. One could interpret this behavior as sexy or as fashionable. A male observer might initiate different responses to the young woman as a function of whether her behavior (i.e., dress) is interpreted as sexy or fashionable. Slutwalk (Figure 4.5), described in more

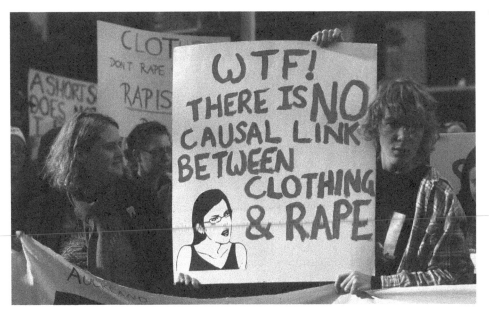

Figure 4.5
Protesters during a Slutwalk march in 2011 for the right of women to wear what they want without sexual assault in New Zealand.

detail in Chapter 5, "Dress and Impression Formation," is a movement that advocates an end to rape culture and victim blaming (Rizzo, 2015), such as blaming a survivor of sexual assault for how she was dressed.

Researchers have found that our expectations for others' behavior can influence our judgments of them even in the face of clear contrary evidence (Traut-Mattausch, Schulz-Hardt, Greitemeyer, & Frey, 2004). For example, the term *teflon* was used to describe President Reagan (Schroeder, 2004), to mean that he was not blamed for various short-comings or scandals in his administration. In the 2016 US presidential campaign that term has been applied to Donald Trump to mean that his supporters do not hold him accountable for his many egregious and sometimes false statements and flip-flops on issues (Haq, 2015). According to Haq, his staff call him bulletproof. In other words, Trump's supporters ignore information that suggests he is untruthful or blameworthy. In each of these examples, followers have actively ignored data that disconfirmed people's expectations for a president or presidential candidate.

Anticipatory set and expectancy confirmation are potentially important during perception when interpreting the dress of another person. For example, Abbey, Cozzarelli, McLaughlin, and Harnish (1987) found that when wearing body-revealing clothing, female models were judged to be more sexy, seductive, and promiscuous than when wearing non-revealing clothing. Returning to the notion of anticipatory set, suppose that you are a jury member hearing a case concerning an alleged rape. If the victim was said to have been wearing body-revealing clothing at the time of the alleged rape, you might infer that at the time of the rape she appeared "sexy," behaved "seductively," and acted "promiscuously" (Figure 4.6). This collection of inferred traits concerning the victim might influence your anticipatory set (i.e., how you expect that she behaved) and those expectations are likely to be confirmed by your interpretation of her behavior (Snyder et al., 1982; Snyder & Swann, 1978). You might assume that she was at least somewhat responsible for the alleged rape because she choose to dress in body-revealing clothing.[1]

Figure 4.6

If a survivor of sexual assault was dressed like Maria Menounos at the time of the assault, jurors might infer that she had appeared "sexy," behaved "seductively," and acted "promiscuously."

Social perception is a complex process that involves a perceiver, a stimulus person, and that takes place in a specific context. In the next sections we review dress variables (i.e., purposeful manipulations of body supplements) that affect social perception as they relate to each of these three broad categories of variables. Although body type and overall attractiveness of a stimulus person are also stimulus variables and do affect social perception, they are discussed in Chapter 6, "Dress and Physical Appearance."

SOCIAL PERCEPTION AND STIMULUS VARIABLES

Stimulus variables are aspects of the stimulus person that affect social perception. Continuing with our first day of class example, the professor in that class may have gray

[1] The consequences of focusing on how dress cues are used within the legal system are non-trivial. In most states, the clothing of sexual assault victims is admissible in court as evidence of "consent," that is, as evidence that the victim agreed to have sexual relations with the offender. Certain dress cues, including "immodest" dress and heavy makeup that have been historically associated with women in the sex business (i.e., prostitutes) (Banner, 1983) may be highlighted by the defense attorney in an attempt to redefine a rape as consensual sex.

hair and wrinkles. A student may associate gray hair with advanced age, and advanced age could be associated by the student with traits such as wisdom and experience. In this case, gray hair and wrinkles are the stimulus variables that influence the student's perception of the professor. Other stimulus variables that might also affect social perceptions of the professor include clothing, odor, hair, height, and ethnicity. Of these stimulus variables, the clothing worn by the professor is generally viewed as being under the control of the professor. In order to make a good first impression, the professor may elect to wear a suit in a subdued color on the first day of class. The professor decides to wear a suit, believing that students will associate wearing a suit within the context of a university classroom with traits such as professionalism and competence. Since researchers investigating relationships between dress and social perception are interested in clothing as a stimulus variable, clothing has been the focus of a great deal of research. Several aspects of clothing have been investigated for their influence on social perception. These aspects include clothing style, the fashionability of clothing, and the attractiveness of clothing. In addition, researchers have examined general appearance variables including how well-groomed individuals appeared overall or how clean they appeared for their influence on social perceptions.

Clothing Style

As noted in Chapter 1, "Why Study Dress?" clothing style refers to apparel items that represent different shapes or types of clothing. A researcher interested in studying the effects of clothing style on social perception might investigate the influence of wearing feminine designs (e.g., skirted suit, blouses with a scarf) as compared to the influence of masculine designs (e.g., skirted suit, a blouse with a necktie). These kinds of studies were of applied interest when women returned to the workplace in the 1970s and 1980s and were interested in what styles might be perceived as more professional. Much of the early research on social perception and dress was of this type. When researchers have studied the influence of clothing style as well as other aspects of the stimulus person that could influence perceptions formed, they have often used experimental research methods.

Researchers have studied competency-related perceptions of women as a function of clothing style. In these studies, clothing style has been manipulated using line drawings, photos, and videos (Damhorst, 1984–85;

Forsythe, 1987; Forsythe, Drake, & Cox, 1984; Johnson & Roach-Higgins, 1987b). Overall, clothing style influences perceptions of women's competencies. As compared to stimulus persons wearing dresses or casual clothing, stimulus persons wearing suits were perceived to have more occupational success, to have a more professional image, to be more competent, and to be more independent (Davis, 1987; Johnson & Roach-Higgins, 1987a; 1987b; Scherbaum & Shepherd, 1987; Thurston et al., 1990). Stimulus persons wearing masculine clothing, formal clothing, or clothing appropriate for an interview were perceived to be more likely to possess managerial traits than stimulus persons wearing dresses or casual clothing (Bardack & McAndrew, 1985; Damhorst, 1984–85; Forsythe, 1987; Forsythe, Drake, & Cox, 1984; Johnson & Roach-Higgins, 1987a; 1987b).

Fashionability

Researchers have studied the effects of apparel fashionability (Clayton et al., 1987; Davis, 1984; Johnson et al., 1977; Thurston et al., 1990; Workman, 1987). Fashionability answers the question: To what extent would the majority of individuals in a given time and place find a specific clothing style to be acceptable or unacceptable for wear? Fashionable styles consist of clothing that is up to date and currently acceptable for wear. Clothing considered unfashionable includes clothing that is not up-to-date and is not worn by most people at a given point in time and place.

Generally when studying apparel fashionability, garment details are varied either using drawings or photos (Clayton et al., 1987; Davis, 1984; Johnson et al., 1977; Thurston et al., 1990; Workman, 1987). Overall, fashionably dressed stimulus persons have tended to be judged more favorably than unfashionably dressed persons. For example, fashionably dressed stimulus persons were rated as more sociable than unfashionably dressed persons by college students (Johnson et al., 1977). In research featuring three levels of garment fashionability, models wearing moderately fashionable clothing were judged to be more professional by businessmen than models wearing either the most fashionable or least fashionable clothing (Thurston et al., 1990), Thus, researchers have consistently found that the fashionability of clothing influences social perceptions but the influence of fashionability varies depending on who is forming the perceptions. For example, these studies and others suggest that, in general, when being judged by professionals, wearing highly fashionable clothing may be inadvisable for the workplace (Kimle & Damhorst, 1997).

Clothing Color

A theory of color psychology called **color-in-context theory** has recently been developed (Elliot & Maier, 2007). The theory proposes that like other variables that influence social perception, color conveys meaning and its meaning varies based on its context (i.e., the context in which it is perceived). For example, researchers proposed that in US culture we associate red with female sexuality (e.g., red light district, sexy red lingerie) (Pazda, Elliot, & Greitemeyer, 2014).

Dress that is red has been found to affect perceptions. Guéguen (2012) investigated the extent to which shirt color affected men's perceptions of women's sexual intent and attractiveness. The men saw a picture of a woman who wore a colored T-shirt. When the woman wore the red T-shirt, she was perceived to have greater sexual intent and was judged as more attractive than when wearing any of the other colors. In other research, men rated women as more attractive when wearing red as compared to other colors (Pazda, Elliot, & Greitemeyer, 2014). Thus, the color red, at least, affects social perception. Other researchers wondered if clothing color might also affect the wearer (e.g., do women act in a more sexy way when wearing red?) (Roberts, Owen, & Havlicek, 2010). Their results showed that clothing color affects both the perceiver and the wearer.

Attractive Dress

Attractive dress refers to judgments concerning the beauty or aesthetic appeal of the dress of the stimulus person. Researchers have developed attractive and unattractive stimulus persons by manipulating the clothing of the stimulus person (Buckley, 1983; Buckley & Haefner, 1984; Lapitsky & Smith, 1981; Lennon, 1990) or by varying clothing and makeup usage (Dabbs & Stokes, 1975; Hartnett, Gottlieb, & Hayes, 1976). With these types of manipulations, researchers have found that perceptions of attractively dressed individuals are more positive than perceptions of unattractively dressed individuals. For example, college students perceive attractively dressed stimulus persons to be more intelligent, higher in morality, better

adjusted, more competent, and more sociable than less attractively dressed stimulus persons (Buckley & Haefner, 1984; Lennon, 1990). Applied research in the content area of clothing attractiveness is potentially useful, since research shows that by simply wearing attractive clothing an individual can elicit positive responses (Buckley & Haefner, 1984; Lapitsky & Smith, 1981; Lennon, 1990). Disadvantaged groups could benefit by intervention programs aimed at increasing self-confidence and self-esteem through lessons in wardrobe selection and coordination. An example of such a program is Dress for Success ("Dress for success," n.d.).

General Appearance Variables: Grooming, Cleanliness, Shabbiness

In the US, there is a general belief that people should keep their clothing and their bodies free from dirt and tidy. It is not too surprising to learn that researchers have repeatedly found that less desirable social perceptions are linked to a poor general appearance (e.g., dirty, untidy) (Figure 4.7). For example, early researchers surveyed Midwestern US adults and found that people dressed in shabby clothing were thought to be members of low-income families (Form & Stone, 1957). Others studied law enforcement officers and school counselors; in that study people who were poorly groomed were also perceived as low in socio-economic

Figure 4.7
People tend to form negative impressions of others who are stained or dirty.

status (Littrell & Berger, 1985–86). Senior citizens wearing stained clothing have been perceived by college students to have poorer memory skills than senior citizens wearing unstained clothing (Workman & Johnson, 1989b). Furthermore, individuals with a poor general physical appearance, aspects of which include grooming and clothing, are more likely to be perceived as delinquent than individuals with a more pleasing appearance (Agnew, 1984).

SOCIAL PERCEPTION AND PERCEIVER VARIABLES

Perceiver variables are aspects of the perceiver that affect what is perceived. For example, a fashion innovator is likely to notice the extent to which others are fashionably dressed, while someone who has no interest in fashion would not necessarily use that particular cue as the basis of their perceptions. Examples of perceiver variables that have been shown to affect social perception include self-monitoring, self-consciousness, lifestyle, and visual acuity. Perceiver variables are sometimes called **individual difference variables** because individuals differ in the extent to which they exhibit these variables.

Self-monitoring reflects the extent to which a person pays attention to interpersonal cues in social environments. Self-monitoring as a perceiver variable has not been studied in the context of social perception, although there are reasons to believe that self-monitoring is likely to affect social perception. However, level of self-monitoring has been shown to affect consumer behavior and hiring decisions. For example, individuals who are high self-monitors are influenced by dress cues that reflect style, beauty, and image in advertisements, whereas people who are low self-monitors are not so affected (Lennon, Davis, & Fairhurst, 1988; Snyder, Berscheid, & Matwychuk, 1988). Researchers studied the effects of decision makers' self-monitoring and applicant attractiveness on hiring decisions (Jawahar & Mattsson, 2005). They found that high self-monitors were more influenced than low self-monitors by applicant attractiveness in their hiring decisions. More recently, in a study conducted in Italy, researchers investigated the relationship between self-monitoring and interest in breast cosmetic surgery (Matera, Nerini, Giorgi, Baroni, & Stefanile, 2015). Data analysis showed that people who scored higher in self-monitoring also had more interest in breast cosmetic surgery. Although the influence of self-monitoring on social perception has not been studied, it is reasonable to assume that dress cues that reflect style, beauty, and image are more likely to affect the social perceptions of high rather than low self-monitors. Future researchers might study to what extent self-monitoring influences the social perception process to determine if this assumption is true and extend the literature on social perception and perceiver variables.

Self-consciousness refers to the degree to which a person's attention is focused on one's self (Fenigstein, Scheier, & Buss, 1975). Self-consciousness is related to stereotyping (Ryckman et al., 1991). In that study as compared to people who were not self-conscious of their own appearance, people who were self-conscious of their appearance were more apt to classify others as a function of their physiques. Thus, evidence exists that self-consciousness may affect what particular appearance cues might be selected as a basis for social perceptions. Studying self-consciousness as a perceiver variable in social perception would require that research participants be divided according to their level of self-consciousness. Then researchers could determine if people high and low in self-consciousness differed in their social perceptions.

Certain perceiver characteristics, which are often categorized as **demographic characteristics**, can also affect social perceptions. Age, sex, and body type have all been shown to affect social perceptions (Kamtsios & Digelidis, 2008; Macapagal, Rupp, & Heiman, 2011; Posthuma & Campion, 2009; Shah & Ogden, 2006). For example, in a study conducted in the U.K., age and gender affected impressions of a doctor much more strongly than ethnicity (Shah & Ogden, 2006). In other research, Greek scholars recently studied children's self-impressions and found that obese and overweight children rated themselves lower on body attractiveness than normal weight children (Kamtsios & Digelidis, 2008).

SOCIAL PERCEPTION AND CONTEXT VARIABLES

Context variables are variables contained in the setting within which the stimulus is perceived. In other words, context variables are those that are present in the environment at the time social perception occurs. For example, whether a stimulus person is perceived on a street corner, in a classroom, or at a wedding can affect other's perceptions of her. Dress that is appropriate when worn in a classroom (e.g., jeans) might be viewed as inappropriate when worn at a formal occasion, such as a wedding. In fact, by wearing jeans to attend a wedding, a person might be perceived as thoughtless, inconsiderate, or even disrespectful. See Figure 4.8 for an example of appropriate dress.

The idea that dress cues can be interpreted to indicate respect has been supported. In qualitative research, the tendency of African Americans to dress up has been found to indicate respect (O'Neal, 1998). The author explained that dressing up "refers to the tradition found in the African-American community to make distinction between categories of apparel and to give special consideration to dress. Dress is used to signify that which is set apart, reverenced, or respected, and that which is not to be made common" (p. 171). Dressing up could be done for oneself or others and for secular or sacred occasions.

In a series of experiments, Hebl and Mannix (2003) found that context variables affected judgments related to hiring (i.e., perceptions of professional and interpersonal skills). In particular, when a male job applicant was seated next to an obese woman as compared to a normal weight woman in a waiting room, research participants were less willing to hire him. They also rated him lower on professional and interpersonal skills. In this study, the proximity of an obese woman was the context that affected perceivers' judgments of the male job applicant. Other research has also found effects for context on social perception (e.g., Damhorst, 1984–85; Lennon & Miller, 1984–85). Damhorst studied the effects of context on social perception by focusing on an interaction context. Male and female white-collar employees viewed pictures of men and women who were interacting in office settings and who were either professionally (formally) or casually dressed. Participants were asked to describe what was happening in the pictures. The interaction context did affect social perceptions.

Thus far we have presented social perception as a process that occurs when a perceiver makes inferences about a target person in a particular environment. We have acknowledged that all three aspects (perceiver, stimulus person, context) contribute to the process. In the next section we present an interactional view of the person perception process. In this view, both the perceiver and the target person play active roles in the process.

Figure 4.8
This type of dress (i.e., body paint) is *not* inappropriate in the context of sporting events such as World Cup soccer.

PERSON PERCEPTION PROCESS: AN INTERACTIONAL VIEW

At the beginning of this chapter we noted some everyday examples of instances when we engage in social perception: jurors making judgments of defendants and recruiters making judgments concerning future employees. Although these are two very important real-life situations, when researchers have studied them, they have not reproduced the situations as they would have occurred in real life. In the courtroom context, researchers often presented participants with a scenario that described a

Figure 4.9
Diagram of the one-way view of the person perception process.

crime, showed a picture of the alleged perpetrator, and asked participants to infer guilt or innocence. In the hiring situation, researchers often provided participants with a resume, presented a picture of the interviewee, and asked participants to make judgments about managerial traits and share their hiring intent. What is missing in these approaches is the interaction of the target with the perceiver (Figure 4.9). In real life, a juror would see and hear the perpetrator. A juror would also hear testimony. In a real hiring situation, a recruiter would interview people, read their resumes, and check their references.

Research that is conducted in this way removes the perceiver from the person perception process (Swann, 1984; 1987). In this approach there is the assumption that perceivers' actions have little or no effect on the characteristics and behaviors of the target (the perceived person). This seems like a reasonable assumption, since we do not expect to affect inherent characteristics in others, rather we simply expect to be able to assess them. Swann, however, takes an interactional view of person perception and argues that, "the activities of perceivers exert a powerful channeling influence on the identities that targets assume" (1984, p. 460) (Figure 4.10). Swann explains that the behaviors perceivers and targets engage in to negotiate the target's identity are very important aspects of person perception.

People expect their world and the people in it to be predictable. We observe our own behaviors, how others react to us, and over time develop self-concepts as well as identities. See Chapter 10, "Dress and Identity" for more specific information about identities. Used here, the term *identity* includes various aspects that make us who we are: personality characteristics, group memberships, and roles we engage in. In this process of developing self-concepts

and more broadly in the process of person perception, we attempt to verify or confirm our views of ourselves. Because we expect the world to be predictable, we want to know that others see us as we see ourselves so we engage in a process called self-verification. **Self-verification** is an interactive process in which we (as targets) attempt to confirm who we are with other people (i.e., perceivers) through negotiation.

There are two sets of ways that we can verify aspects of our self. The first way is that we (as targets of other's perceptions) can create an environment that confirms our self-views. To create a confirming environment, we typically decide where and with whom to interact. To take an extreme example, assuming we are not part of a street gang we are probably not going to interact with street gang members: We have decided not to interact with them. Instead in many situations both targets and perceivers seek out interaction partners who are similar, familiar, and predictable to them (Swann, 1984; 1987). Targets may display **identity cues** to suggest to the perceivers the identity they wish to acknowledge and increase the likelihood that perceivers will form impressions of them that accurately predict their behavior. Examples of identity cues are clothing, makeup, and possessions.

Not all aspects of the self can be displayed through identity cues. For example, it is hard to think of a cue to friendliness or honesty. If identity cues presented do not lead to acknowledgment of the desired identity, then targets can provide feedback to perceivers to shape their impressions. For example, suppose you are interviewing for a position that requires friendliness. In the interview to try to establish that you are a friendly person, you might make certain you have good eye contact, smile, adopt a positive tone of voice, and respond to questions in an

Figure 4.10
The interactional view of the person perception process.

engaging way. Should the interviewer indicate to you that this position requires someone who is quite friendly, that is a clue that your desired identity is not accepted. In that case you might mention that even though you are somewhat quiet, you are the chair of the social committee for your sorority.

During the social perception process, perceivers have expectations of targets (the perceived) and respond to them according to those expectations. In a seminal study, teachers were told that some of their students were "late bloomers," that is they were provided with expectations for certain students (Rosenthal & Jacobson, 1968). In fact, the "late bloomers" were no more gifted than any other students but by the end of the school term the "late bloomers" were performing better than the other students. This finding demonstrates that a perceiver's expectations can actually affect how a target behaves.

Targets want to know if perceivers' expectations are compatible with an identity the target actually wants to acknowledge. In the friendliness example, the interviewer did not acknowledge that the interviewee was friendly. After perceivers have made the first move in this process of negotiation of identity, targets can acknowledge or reject the identity offered by the perceiver. In our example, the interviewee (target) rejected the "not-friendly" identity by providing further evidence that she is indeed friendly (chair of social committee). Targets typically accept identities that confirm their views of themselves. If the identity offered does not confirm a self-view, then negotiation occurs. Perceivers try to evoke behaviors that confirm expectations, while targets continue to try to verify their self-views.

The second method to self-verify is to distort our perceptions (Swann, 1984; 1987). This is a mental way to make ourselves think that our views of self are verified, when in fact they are not. In these instances targets interpret feedback from perceivers to be consistent with their views of themselves. Referring to our previous interview example, the interviewee could have interpreted the feedback from the interviewer that the position required someone who was friendly as acknowledgment that the interviewee was indeed friendly. Another way that targets can make inconsistent feedback harmonious with self-views is to simply ignore information that is discrepant from their self-views. Supporting this idea is a study in which people were provided with both discrepant and consistent information about themselves (Swann, 1987).

In that study, people were likely to recall the information that was consistent with their self-views.

A final way that we self-verify is through selective interpretation of the feedback we receive. Researchers have found that when people receive disconfirming feedback they often discount the source of the information rather than change their self-views (Swann, Griffin, Predmore, & Gaines, 1987). So returning to the interview example, if you do not get the job after providing so much information about your high level of friendliness, you might discount the interviewer ("What does he know anyway?") or the company. It is unlikely that you would change your self-view and decide that you are unfriendly. For example, suppose you graduated with a degree in apparel design and were excited to be interviewed with American Apparel. If you are not hired, you may decide that you really do not want to work for a company whose CEO (now fired) has figured in multiple sexual harassment suits and other misconduct, such as choking an employee (Bruni, 2014; Ferro, 2015).

We stated earlier that social or person perceptions (i.e., inferences about people) may be accurate or inaccurate (Neuberg, 1989; Schneider, Hastorf, & Ellsworth, 1979). It is likely that much of the inaccuracy is a function of how we study person perceptions (Swann, 1984; 1987). When we only consider the target and do not acknowledge the effects of the perceiver on the target's behavior, inaccurate person perceptions may be common.

The previous discussion outlined the kinds of variables that have been shown to influence social perceptions and different models of the social perception or person perception process. In the next sections we highlight several perceptual processes and their relationships to dress.

CATEGORIZATION

Categorization of Objects

Categorization, a part of the perception process, is the process we use to mentally classify things into groups so that non-identical things are treated as equivalent (Medin, Wattenmaker, & Hampson, 1987). The grouping of objects into categories is one way to reduce and organize all the stimuli we are bombarded with every day (Hamilton, 1979). Most of the research on categorization occurred in the 1970s and 1980s, but the process has implications for retailers today. Retailers use categorization to organize merchandise into departments in stores, sometimes with more success than others. For example, backpacks are often found in the same departments as purses, occasionally are found with luggage, and are sometimes found with "Back to school" merchandise. If the categorization helps shoppers find desired merchandise, it has reduced and organized stimuli in the form of merchandise.

In general, a category is conceptualized as two or more distinguishable "things" (e.g., cars, animals, clothing items, people) which are treated equivalently and which are similar perceptually or functionally (Mervis & Rosch, 1981). For example, boots, sandals, athletic sneakers, and pumps are non-identical objects, but are all types of footwear. They can all be placed within the one category of footwear. By placing all of these types of footwear into one category we have simplified our perceptions of (thought processes concerning) the four different items by recognizing a **within group similarity** (i.e., all items are footwear). Just as in this example, in the process of categorizing the numerous items we encounter daily, we organize our perceptions by identifying how items are similar (i.e., within group similarities) (Rosch, 1973). In forming these mental categories we may rely on visual similarities as well as past experience with the items to provide useful information helpful to us in the categorization process. For example, in the previous example our past experience may have shown that all of these items can protect the feet.

We also organize our perceptions by recognizing how items are different (i.e., **between group differences**). For example, consider how you might organize your laundry after taking it out of the dryer. When you organize the clean laundry by sorting it you are perceiving between group differences. So you do not pair up a white crew sock and red mitten because they are dissimilar—one protects

your hands, the other protects your feet. Categorization allows you to both organize and simplify stimuli. Continuing with the laundry example, you may store all the towels together in the bathroom but store the sheets in a linen closet in the hall. You store them in different locations as a way to organize them and simplify your job of finding these items when you want them. Because we cannot perceive a thing without categorizing it as a "something," categorization is an inescapable process (Lennon & Davis, 1989). It is a basic function of all living things (Rosch, Mervis, Gray, Johnson, & Boyes-Braem, 1976).

In addition to recognizing within group similarities and between group differences as part of the categorization process, researchers have documented that our cultural context affects categorization. For example, color categorization differs across cultures. English has a basic color word for each focal color (e.g., black, white, red, green, yellow, blue, brown, purple, pink, orange, and gray) (Anderson, 1990). However, the Dani, a Stone Age people of New Guinea, have only two basic color words in their language: **mili** for dark or cold colors and **mola** for bright or warm colors (Heider, 1970). How we and the Dani actually physically perceive color is the same but we categorize those colors quite differently.

Categorization of Dress

How then do we categorize items of dress? Since categorization is part of perception, it is reasonable to expect that variables which affect perception (e.g., stimulus variables, perceiver variables, and context variables) will also affect categorization. In fact, researchers have documented that visual characteristics of garments (i.e., what they look like) affect how they are categorized (Buckley, 1984–85; Damhorst, Ekman, & Stout, 1986; Lennon & Clayton, 1992). This is not surprising given how much people rely on their sense of vision. In her research, Buckley identified three basic categories of dress. She gave people black and white sketches of outfits and asked them to "put similar sketches together in piles" (p. 4). Each sketch illustrated a female model wearing an outfit typically worn on a college campus. One of the three categories was named "special occasion dress" suggesting that people may have categorized based on the assumed context for which the particular outfit might be worn. Another category consisted entirely of pants suggesting people were also using structural aspects of the garments to categorize as well.

IN-CLASS ACTIVITY
Sportswear Categorization

Some objects are more representative of a category than others. For example, robins are considered more representative of the category *birds* than chickens. Which of the following brands is more representative of the category of *sportswear*? MUDD, Croft & Barrows, Levi, Wrangler, or Charter Club?

Using a similar procedure, the way people categorize women's skirted suits was studied by Damhorst et al. (1986). Research participants were told to sort women's suits according to how appropriate they were to be worn as business dress for retail managers; thus, they were provided a context for their categorization. People tended to sort the suits based partly on structural aspects of the suits (e.g., how symmetric the garment was or whether or not it had an emphasis on the neck). Other researchers have also found that context variables affect how forms of dress are categorized and that people will also infer or assume a context to guide their categorization when it is not explicitly provided (Buckley, 1984–85; DeLong, Minshall, & Larntz, 1986; Lennon & Clayton, 1992) (Figure 4.11). Summarizing this research on how forms of dress are categorized, it appears that both stimulus characteristics (i.e.,

structural features) and context characteristics are important to the process.

Another study highlighting the importance of context in the categorization process was conducted by Lennon and Clayton (1992). They designed a series of laboratory experiments to assess the degree of fashionability conveyed by women's professional style clothing. Participants were a large number of businessmen, businesswomen, homemakers, college women, high school women, and junior high women who judged the fashionability of professional clothing ensembles. Models who systematically varied in age and body type were photographed wearing professional clothing and served as stimulus persons. In addition, the garments were systematically varied in terms of their style features to represent three different levels of fashionability. Judgments of clothing fashionability were based on the age and body type of the model wearing the clothing, as well as on actual garment features. In fact, age and body type conveyed fashionability of clothing to a greater extent than garment features! The authors concluded that age and body type of the person wearing the clothes may be considered as markers (i.e., features) of the category "fashionable garment."

Categorization of Textiles

The previously reviewed studies focused on visual categorization of forms or items of dress. However, another equally important means of categorizing forms or items of dress is by the way they feel (e.g., tactile sensations). From an applied perspective, human perceptual response to the textile component of dress is an important factor guiding judgments of comfort, warmth, and skin wetness. Information regarding factors that affect such judgments has important practical implications for manufacturers of exercise wear, incontinence products, feminine hygiene products, underwear, and medical garments. To understand how people categorize garments, we first begin by considering how people categorize fabrics.

To investigate how people categorize fabrics, researchers asked volunteers to sort fabric samples into groups based on how the fabric samples felt (Brandt et al., 1998). Some of the volunteers sorted the fabrics but were not allowed to see the fabrics (non-viewers). A screen was placed between them and the fabrics so that their view of the fabrics was blocked. The rest of the volunteers (viewers) did not have their view blocked by the screen. Viewers seemed to sort the fabrics by their probable end use (a

Figure 4.11
What stimulus characteristics of these shoes suggest that they are for casual wear?

context) while non-viewers seemed to sort by fiber content and fabric structure. The authors also asked participants to describe the fabrics in each sorted group. Viewers were likely to use terms reflecting end use and appearance while non-viewers were likely to use terms reflecting fiber content and texture. To summarize, viewers seemed to rely on inferred properties such as end use and non-viewers relied on physical properties. These results seem to suggest that vision overrides touch and that in a consumption situation, such as buying a new clothing item, people may be more influenced by the appearance of the item than by how it feels.

Businesses are also interested in how the categorization process influences our ideas about product categories. A significant amount of money is spent to position products to appeal to particular market segments. At the consumer level, product positioning translates to a judgment of a product's (or brand's) category membership. The outcome of product positioning is not only a particular identification of a product but increased salience of information relevant to that category and the category-based inferences that result. For example, men might resist or ignore items if they are categorized as "purses," yet might consider buying them if categorized as "portfolios." Therefore, factors that affect how consumers decide what an object is (i.e., what category it belongs to) is of concern to consumer researchers (Loken, 2006). How store personnel decide category membership for products has implications for consumers. Sales may be lost if consumers' categorizations do not match with the store personnel's categorizations.

Social Categorization

Just as we categorize objects we also categorize people. When we categorize people, the process is called **social categorization** or categorization of social objects (i.e., people). When categorizing people we often use immutable physical characteristics (e.g., age, sex, race, body type). When sorting people into categories, children first sort by sex and by race (Davey, 1983; Katz, 1982; Ramsey, 1987). Using a variety of strategies to assess categorization, many researchers have found that adults also categorize others on the basis of sex and race (e.g., Stangor, Lynch, Duan, & Glass, 1992; Taylor, Fiske, Etcoff, & Ruderman, 1978). In fact, categorizing people along the dimensions of race, sex, and age is thought to be automatic (Nelson, 2005). People have also been found to use body size to categorize others (Lennon, 1992).

DRESS IN THE NEWS
Categorization by Dress and Ethnicity

A Bangladeshi Muslim wearing traditional shalwar kameez was beaten in the Bronx in New York. He had been walking with his niece when he was attacked by teenagers who were apparently reacting to his ethnicity and clothing, because they were shouting "ISIS, ISIS." The man suffered bruises on his face and neck. The teens were charged with assault and hate crimes (Cavallier, 2016; "Muslim man who was 'pummeled' by," 2016).

Because visual characteristics can be manipulated through the use of clothing, the part clothing plays in the categorization process is useful to understand. If we use physical characteristics such as age, race, sex, and body type to categorize others, people might also use clothing as a basis for categorization. The rationale is that clothing, like immutable physical features, is also visible and may be relevant to category judgments. Researchers interested in studying the role of clothing in categorizing people have not clearly demonstrated that people use clothing to categorize others. In one study, a researcher attempted to measure categorization as a function of clothing attractiveness but found that participants did not categorize people on the basis of how attractive their clothing was (Lennon, 1990). However, when given a goal to identify a person from a group "who would make a good media representative" (p. 214) participants formed categories based on whether the person was formally or informally dressed (i.e., style of dress) (Stangor et al., 1992). Participants did not categorize based on clothing color. The authors suggested that clothing style provided information about the underlying personality traits of the wearer that were useful in identifying "good media representatives" but clothing color did not.

SCHEMA

A concept similar to a category is **schema**. A schema is a mental knowledge structure containing information about a concept or stimulus, including its attributes and how they are related to each other (Wyer, 1980). See

Figure 4.12

Example of a wedding schema, its attributes, and their relationships.

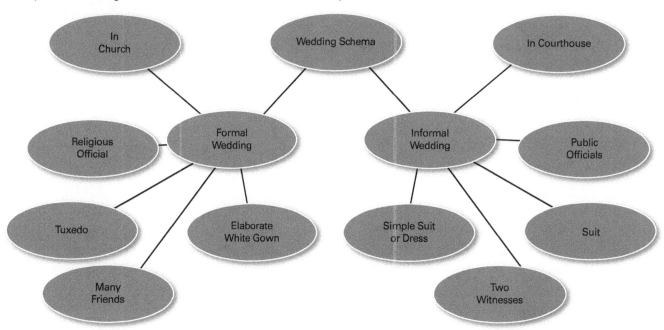

Figure 4.12 for an example of wedding schemas. Categories and schemas are ways to explain expectations and their effects (Fiske & Taylor, 1991). For example, we have schemas about shopping. Our shopping schema tells us that when we want to purchase something, we enter a store, find a desirable product, and exchange money for the product based on an amount indicated on the product. Expectations such as this can be beneficial and help us to organize our world; they are functional and we would be unable to operate without them. Such expectations, assumptions, and prior knowledge allow us some sense of prediction and control, which is essential to well-being.

Expectations evoked by categories and schemas can also be costly by misleading us (Higgins, 2000). For example, suppose you are recruiting new college graduates and you judge the attractive candidates as more capable than those who are less attractive. Here you have associated being attractive with being capable. If the attractiveness of the candidate is the only basis for your decision to hire, then you are being misled by your schema that attractive people are also capable.

To demonstrate how a schema works, imagine being in situations with people about whom you have no information or prior knowledge. Consider arriving in a foreign country. You want to go shopping, but there are no prices on things and you cannot determine who exactly the seller

is. The entire process could seem mysterious. With a guide to explain that you are expected to bargain for what you want, you might form some idea about how to shop and buy. Before you can apply your schematic prior knowledge about shopping to this situation, you have to identify the seller. This is difficult. How can we visually classify salespersons in a retail store? There may not be any appearance characteristics for classifying. Salespeople do not all necessarily wear the same clothing or share any other appearance characteristic. You may not have a schema for salesperson that includes appearance cues. However, you might have a salesperson schema that contains information about behavior. So while you cannot identify who the seller is by appearance, you can determine by behaviors. Who is helping other people make selections? Who is taking money in exchange for products? Not being able to determine who people are and what they do can have practical implications. For example, if a shopper is unable to identify a salesperson to ask for help or to pay for a purchase, she may give up, and leave the store without purchasing.

Consumers' knowledge about products and brands forms a partially integrated structure in memory that could arguably be called a product or **brand schema**. Such structures are composed of similarly perceived objects and both object-based (i.e., knowledge about the object) and category-based (i.e., what you know about the brand) knowledge. Through branding businesses try to shape our schemas about their products. A **consideration set** is a set of products or brands that an individual consumer considers interchangeable (Mehta, Rajiv, & Srinivasan, 2003). Consider your schema for what is appropriate to wear to work. You are shopping and are wondering whether or not to purchase a pair of black denim jeans because you want to be able to wear them to work. Generally, you have not worn blue jeans to work. The style you are considering is not the typical five-pocket jean style and is made of black denim fabric. If you accept this black pair of jeans as appropriate for work, then you have extended your expectations for appropriate work clothing—your consideration set—to include black jeans. This updating or revision of your schema for what is appropriate for workplace dress has implications for the kinds of clothes you buy to wear to work.

There are four basic types of schema: person schema, self-schema, role schema, and event schema (Fiske & Taylor, 1991). **Person schemas** contain information on what traits seem to go together in people. This concept is discussed in Chapter 5, "Dress and Impression Formation" as implicit personality theory. We may think that honesty and dependability co-occur in people. We think this because it has been our experience that these traits occur together in people. People that we know are honest are also dependable. **Self schemas** are trait dimensions along which we have clear self-conceptions (i.e., we are **self-schematic**), while dimensions along which we are less clear are termed *aschematic*. People tend to be self-schematic along dimensions they consider important. For example, anorexics are self-schematic on topics related to food (Johansson, Ghaderi, & Andersson, 2005). Individuals with eating disorders develop schema containing maladaptive and dysfunctional attitudes and beliefs about eating, food, and appearance. An example of a dysfunctional belief is that individuals with eating disorders (particularly anorexics) may often think they are fat, even if they are emaciated. When we say anorexics are self-schematic on topics related to food, we mean that they consider food, weight, and shape to be important to their daily lives. In laboratory experiments, anorexic individuals are more likely than non-anorexic individuals to pay attention to and express concern about food-related topics, body and weight-related topics, and shape-related topics. Women who are self-schematic on appearance are likely to pay too much attention to appearance information (Jung

& Lennon, 2003). This kind of attention to appearance may make them more vulnerable to the effects of ideal images in the media.

Role schemas are the sets of behaviors expected of a person in a particular social position. A role schema is the cognitive structure that organizes knowledge about those behaviors. When you see a young child, you may expect certain behaviors from that individual simply because of your schema for "young child." For example, you may not become disturbed if the child has food stains on her clothing in the same way that it might disturb you to see an adult wearing clothing with food stains. In the case of the young child, you might assume the child does not yet know how to feed herself without spilling. On the other hand, you might expect adults to eat without staining their clothing. Role schemas have associated with them role-based expectations for social positions based on gender, age, and ethnicity. For example, some items or colors of garments have not been considered appropriate for all ages (age role). A girl had to be considered fairly "grown up" to wear high heels. At one time the color black was not considered appropriate for all ages. Since black is considered a somber color, young people seldom wore it. However, today it is not uncommon to see black velvet used in children's clothing, even in very small sizes.

Event schemas or scripts describe sequences of events for well-known situations. People in the same culture share expectations for what should happen at a restaurant, a concert, or when shopping at a retail store. Schemas are often cued or brought to mind by visual triggers such as dress or aspects of visual merchandising (Fiske & Taylor, 1991; Stanforth & Lennon, 1997; Ward, Bitner, & Barnes, 1992).

IN-CLASS ACTIVITY
Consideration Set

Make a list of the brands of makeup or clothing you buy. List the attributes of those brands. Are there other brands you would buy and use, but have not? List those and their attributes. Are there brands you will not consider buying? List those brands and the attributes you associate with those brands. Compare your list to a classmate's list. The items in your list form your consideration set.

STEREOTYPING

The existence of schemas can contribute to stereotypes and stereotyping. **Stereotypes** are mental images that arise from past experience and which are used to place people into social categories. Stereotypes can be thought of as mental representations of a group and its members; stereotypes derive from the cultural construction of social groups, are molded by and reflect the actual social position of groups, and operate in basic psychological ways.

Stereotyping is thought to be related to categorization. In stereotyping, individuals are often grouped or categorized according to similar visual characteristics. Accordingly, it is supposed that categorization will facilitate one's ability to know the personality and behavioral characteristics of the individuals associated with the stereotype. Stereotyping has been found to be based upon such visual characteristics as perceived age, body type, hair color, ethnicity, and sex (Brochu & Morrison, 2007; Kiefer & Sekaquaptewa, 2007; Rupp, Vodanovich, & Crede, 2006; Takeda, Helms, & Romanova, 2006; Yu & Bairner, 2012). Since the aforementioned research was conducted in Canada, Taiwan, the UK, and the US, it is clear that stereotyping occurs in many parts of the world.

Scholars from Australia maintain that stereotypes are both a cause and an effect of **prejudice**, "an evaluation of an out-group and its members" (Augoustinos & Walker, 1995, p. 208). For example, based on past experiences with a few sorority members, we might associate the trait "ditzy" with sorority members. If so, then we have formed a stereotype of those specific individuals. As a result of that association we might form an evaluation of all sorority members (i.e., prejudge them, hence prejudice is formed). That prejudice might then be used as a basis for judging other people we meet in the future who are sorority members (i.e., she must be ditzy since she is a sorority member).

Stereotypes are different from other schemas due to their social consequences. There are two major types of stereotypes: Individual stereotypes and social stereotypes (Augoustinos & Walker, 1995). **Individual stereotypes** are stereotypes an individual has of a social group. An individual stereotype is an exaggerated belief associated with a social group; it justifies our conduct in relation to that social group (Allport, 1954). Individual stereotypes are cognitive concepts; they serve a purpose in helping us reduce the complexity of the stimulus world and are thought to be objective. These stereotypes are based on our knowledge and experience with others.

Individual stereotypes can be useful. For example, as you were growing up and attending school, you learned about a category of people called teachers. You might have learned that teachers have certain traits (e.g., helpful, welcoming). The next time you are introduced to a stranger and in the introduction that person is referred to as a "teacher" this information triggered your individual stereotype "teacher" and you immediately assumed this individual will be helpful and outgoing. To the extent this individual actually is helpful, your individual stereotype is confirmed.

Much like the situation outlined, the assignment of traits based on information contained in stereotypes is frequently done in first impression situations when people are unknown to each other. We often assume that the information contained in our individual stereotypes is accurate and applies to everyone who is a member of the category. So in a first contact situation when meeting someone for the first time, we try to use what we know (our individual stereotypes) and assume as much information as possible to be able to communicate effectively with the new person we are meeting. We have pre-judged the individual. In other words, based on certain visual characteristics we have linked that individual with a schema and applied information contained in that schema to the individual.

Sometimes the information applied is accurate. We think the person will be helpful and the person is helpful. Sometimes the information we apply is not accurate. While the process of treating all objects that look alike in a similar manner works fairly well with objects, people are more complex and vary to a much greater extent than do objects. So treating people that share some visual characteristics as "all the same" can be very ineffective.

Stereotypes can contain positive traits and they can contain negative or less desirable traits. Undesirable traits (e.g., lazy, unintelligent) are often linked with large-sized people. These are examples of negative stereotypes. While no one generally minds being assigned positive traits, when you assign negative traits based on your individual stereotype people generally think of that process as reflecting prejudice. In other words, just like assuming people have positive traits, when we assume people have less desirable traits without interacting with them or getting to know them we have pre-judged them.

Prejudice occurs when we pre-judge others without learning about them through interpersonal contact. Prejudice can also be thought of as an attitude (Augoustinos & Walker, 1995). Prejudice does not have to be negative, as can be seen in our example, but that is what most people mean by it and what many people study. Prejudice may occur when stereotypes are rigid and information inconsistent with or contrary to the stereotype is ignored. In such a case, the contrary information is not allowed to alter the stereotypes. Racism and sexism are two types of prejudice associated with social groups. Both prejudice and stereotyping can result in discrimination.

Discrimination is a behavior and therefore is not a social perceptual process, although it may be a consequence of stereotyping and prejudice. Discrimination occurs when negative actions are taken with respect to a social group. In the US, some discrimination is banned by law. For example, there are **statutes** (i.e., laws passed by governing bodies) that outlaw discrimination in hiring based on race, religion, sex, color, or national origin (Title VII of the Civil Rights Act of 1964). Michigan bans discrimination in hiring on the basis of appearance. Title III of the Americans with Disabilities Act (ADA) outlaws discrimination in hiring on the basis of disability. Title 29 of the Age Discrimination in Employment Act (ADEA) bans employment discrimination as a function of age and protects people aged 40 and over.

However, even with these protections, discrimination still occurs in the US *Price Waterhouse v. Hopkins* (1989) is a famous discrimination case in the US that was heard by the Supreme Court and in which dress played a role. Ann Hopkins was denied partnership in the accounting firm Price Waterhouse even though she had the second highest number of billable hours in the firm (the gold standard in accounting firms). One of the partners took her aside and explained that her chances of partnership the following year would improve if she would walk, talk, and dress more femininely. Hopkins resigned and since walking, talking, and dressing more femininely were unrelated to her ability to do her job, she sued the firm for discrimination on the basis of sex (violation of Title VII of the Civil Rights Act of 1964). Eventually, the Supreme Court decided the case in Hopkins's favor and she was offered re-instatement in the firm. Subsequently she wrote a book called *Making Partner the Hard Way*. A more recent example of an appearance discrimination suit that also went all the way to the Supreme Court (*EEOC v. Abercrombie & Fitch*, 2015) is the case of Samantha Elauf. Elauf won that case based on a violation of her civil rights. For more information including pictures and a video, search online for *A Muslim Woman Beat Abercrombie*.

As noted, in addition to individual stereotypes there are social stereotypes. **Social stereotypes** are

---

DRESS IN THE NEWS
Sex Discrimination Continues

Joanna Grossman, an attorney with expertise in sex discrimination and workplace equality, has written about sex-stereotyping and dress (Grossman, 2009). In the 1989 *Price Waterhouse v. Hopkins* decision, employers were barred from disciplining their employees for nonconformity to gender stereotypes associated with their biological sex. Yet according to Grossman, courts still uphold employers' dress and grooming guidelines that differentiate by sex and, in so doing, mandate that their employees conform to stereotypical appearance standards assigned to their sex. An example of this is the case of *Jespersen v. Harrah's* (2006).

At Harrah's Casino all employees had to wear the same uniform, and all were required to be "well groomed, appealing to the eye, be firm and body toned, and be comfortable with maintaining this look while wearing the specified uniform" (Grossman, 2009). Also, men and women had different grooming requirements. Men had to have short hair, their nails trimmed, and could not wear makeup or nail polish. Women were required to have hair that was styled, curled, or teased. They also had to wear stockings, colored nail polish, and facial makeup. An image consultant made up each female employee, photographed them, and then the female employees were compared to that standard each day at work.

Darlene Jespersen was a longtime, well-liked bartender at Harrah's, who challenged the appearance requirements for women. Jespersen did not tease her hair or wear makeup and held that being forced to do so constituted sex discrimination. In this case, the court ruled against Jespersen. According to Grossman (2009) this decision did a great disservice to sex equality. Dress and grooming codes may not seem important, but they mirror social stereotypes and prejudice about how men and women should look. Hence they punish people who do not fit traditional appearance expectations associated with their sex.

constructive and subjective and consist of social or cultural representations of a social group (Augoustinos & Walker, 1995). Consider the caste system in India; in that system the lowest of the castes, the untouchables, was considered to be ritually unclean. This stereotype was shared within that culture or social group. Social stereotypes serve to justify the social position of the stereotyped group and of the system that produces that position. To continue with the same example, because untouchables were considered ritually unclean, they were considered only fit for certain types of employment such as street sweepers, latrine cleaners, or tanners of leather. Social stereotypes are also affective and there is an evaluation associated with the cognitive representation of the associated social group (i.e., one group believes it is better/smarter/more pure than another). Within a culture, the stratification associated with social stereotypes produces cultural categories. Cultural categories are categories of people based on differences that are culturally relevant (Kaiser, 1997).

Chapter Summary

Social cognition is the study of how we process information about people. We have focused on information conveyed by dress. Social perception is concerned with perceptual processing of information about people including dress. In this chapter, we have concentrated on the social perception processes of person perception, categorization, stereotyping, and prejudice as a function of dress. We reviewed literature showing that dress variables in the forms of stimulus, context, and perceiver variables all affect social perception. We have considered the interactional view of person perception to explain how dress influences perception as well as a model of social perception (Livesley & Bromley, 1973). Finally, we have discussed individual and social stereotypes, prejudice, and discrimination.

Key Terms

anticipatory set
between group differences
brand image
brand schema
categorization
color-in-context theory
consideration set
context variables
cue selection
demographic
   characteristics
discrimination

event schema
expectancy confirmation
extended inference
identity cues
impression formation
individual difference
   variables
individual stereotypes
interpretative inference
mili
mola
perceiver variables

person perception
person schema
prejudice
role schema
salience
schema
self-consciousness
self-help features
self-monitoring
self-schema
self-schematic
self-verification

social categorization
social cognition
social perception
social stereotype
statute
steampunk
stereotype
stimulus variables
store image
target
verbal report
within group similarity

Discussion Questions

1. Daycare providers may use parents' physical appearance and dress cues as they make their decisions concerning whether or not to accept a child into their daycare. Use Livesley and Bromley's four-stage person perception model to analyze the daycare provider's social perception process and provide examples. Describe the stages of cue selection, interpretative inference, extended inference, and anticipatory set respectively.

2. A Brazilian university expelled a twenty-year-old student who wore a mini-dress that sparked protests on campus ("Brazil college," 2009). She was escorted from campus by military police who protected her from the crowd of students standing by and chanting "whore." Use social perception theory to analyze the possible reason. List the possible stimulus variables, perceiver variables, and context variables involved in this event.

3. Make a list of stereotypes which you have experienced or heard about. Differentiate between the positive and negative ones. Explain their existence and maintenance using social categorization theory.

STUDIO™

Visit your book's STUDIO for additional quiz questions and vocabulary flashcards!

Suggested Readings

Elliot, A. J., & Maier, M. A. (2007). Color and psychological functioning. *Current Directions in Psychological Science, 16*(5), 250–254.

Glick, P., Larsen, S., Johnson, C., & Branstiter, H. (2005). Evaluations of sexy women in low-and high-status jobs. *Psychology of Women Quarterly, 29*, 389–395.

Stanforth, N. F., & Lennon, S. J. (1997). Customer expectations and store policies: Satisfaction, patronage and retail store service. *Clothing and Textiles Research Journal, 15*, 115–124.

Workman, J. E., & Johnson, K. K. P. (1989a). The role of clothing in extended inferences. *Home Economics Research Journal, 18*(2), 164–169.

References

Aaker, J. L. (1997). Dimensions of brand personality. *Journal of Marketing Research, 34*(3), 347–356.

Abbey, A., Cozzarelli, C., McLaughlin, K., & Harnish, R. (1987). The effects of clothing and dyad sex composition on perceptions of sexual intent: Do women and men evaluate these cues differently? *Journal of Applied Social Psychology, 17*(2), 108–126.

Adams, G. & LaVoie, J. (1975). Parental expectations of educational and personal–social performance and childrearing patterns as a function of attractiveness, sex, and conduct of the child. *Child Study Journal, 5*(3), 125–142.

Agnew, R. (1984). Appearance and delinquency. *Criminology, 22*(3), 421–440.

Allport, G. W. (1954). *The nature of prejudice.* Cambridge, MA: Addison-Wesley.

Anderson J.R. (1990). *Cognitive psychology and its implications* (3rd ed.). New York, NY: W.H. Freeman and Company.

Augustinos, M., & Walker, I. (1995). *Social cognition: An integrated introduction.* Thousand Oaks, CA: Sage.

Banner, L. W. (1983). *American beauty.* Chicago, IL: The University of Chicago Press.

Bardack, N., & McAndrew, F. (1985). The influence of physical attractiveness and manner of dress on success in a simulated personnel decision. *Journal of Social Psychology, 125*, 777–778.

Berlyne, D. E. (1960). *Conflict, arousal, and curiosity*. New York, NY: McGraw-Hill.

Brandt, B., Brown, D. M., Burns, L. D., Cameron, B. A., Chandler, J., Dallas, M. J., Kaiser, S. B., Lennon, S. J., Pan, N., Salusso, C., & Smitley, R. (1998). Development of a method to measure the individual and joint effects of visual and tactile perceptions of fabrics. *Journal of the Textile Institute, 89*(2), 65–77.

Brazil college back down on mini-dress expulsion (2009, November 10). *Sydney Morning Herald*. Retrieved from: http://www.smh.com.au/world/brazil-college-back-down-on-minidress-expulsion-20091110-i6e2

Brochu, P. M., & Morrison, M. A. (2007). Implicit and explicit prejudice toward overweight and average-weight men and women: Testing their correspondence and relation to behavioral intentions. *The Journal of Social Psychology, 147*(6), 681–706.

Bruner, J. (1957). On perceptual readiness. *Psychological Review, 64*, 123–152.

Bruni, F. (2014, June 30). A grope and a shrug: Dov Charney, American Apparel and sexual harassment. *New York Times*. Retrieved from: http://www.nytimes.com/2014/07/01/opinion/frank-bruni-dov-charney-american-apparel-and-sexual-harassment.html?_r=0

Buckley, H. M. (1983). Perceptions of physical attractiveness as manipulated by dress: Subjects versus independent judges. *Journal of Psychology, 114*, 243–248.

Buckley, H. M. (1984–85). Toward an operational definition of dress. *Clothing and Textiles Research Journal, 3*(2), 1–10.

Buckley, H. M. & Haeffner, J. E. (1984). The physical attractiveness stereotype using dress as a facilitator. *Journal of Consumer Studies and Home Economics, 8*, 351–358.

Burns, L. D., & Lennon, S. J. (1993). The effect of clothing on the use of person information categories in first impressions. *Clothing and Textiles Research Journal, 12*(1), 9–15.

Cavallier, A. (2016, January 22). Two teens arrested for allegedly attacking Bronx Muslim man while shouting 'ISIS, ISIS.' *PIX11 News*. Retrieved from: http://pix11.com/2016/01/22/two-teens-arrested-for-allegedly-attacking-bronx-muslim-man-while-shouting-isis-isis/

Clayton, R., Lennon, S. J., & Larkin, J. (1987). Perceived fashionability of a garment as inferred from the age and body type of the wearer. *Home Economics Research Journal, 15* 237–246.

Clifford, M. & Walster, E. (1973). Research note: The effect of physical attractiveness on teacher expectations. *Sociology of Education, 46*, 248–258.

Collett, J. L. (2005). What kind of mother am I? Impression management and the social construction of motherhood. *Symbolic Interaction, 28*, 327–247.

Cooper, J., Darley, J. M., & Henderson, J. E. (1974). On the effectiveness of deviant and conventional-appearing communicators: A field experiment. *Journal of Personality and Social Psychology, 29*, 752–757.

Dabbs, J. M. & Stokes, N. A. (1975). Beauty is power: The use of space on the sidewalk. *Sociometry, 38*(4), 551–557.

Damhorst, M. L. (1984–85). Meanings of clothing cues in social context. *Clothing and Textiles Research Journal, 3*(2), 39–48.

Damhorst, M. L., Eckman, M., & Stout, S. (1986). Cluster analysis of women's business suits. In R. H. Marshall (Ed.), *ACPTC Proceedings: National Meeting 1986*, Monument, CO: International Textiles and Apparel Association, 65.

Darley, J., & Cooper, J. (1972). The "Clean for Gene" phenomenon: The effects of students' appearance on political campaigning. *Journal of Applied Social Psychology, 2*, 24–33.

Davey, A. (1983). *Learning to be prejudiced: Growing up in multi-ethnic Britain*. London, England: Edward Arnold.

Davis, L. L. (1984). Judgment ambiguity, self-consciousness, and conformity in judgments of fashionability. *Psychological Reports, 54*, 671–675.

Davis, L. L. (1987). Effect of sex, inferred sex-role and occupational sex-linkage on perceptions of occupational success. *Perceptual and Motor Skills, 64*, 887–898.

DeLong, M. R., Minshall, B., & Larntz, K. (1986). Use of schema for evaluating consumer response to an apparel product. *Clothing and Textiles Research Journal, 5*, 17–26.

Dobni, D., & Zinkhan, G. M. (1990). In search of brand image: A foundation analysis. In M. E. Goldberg et al. (Eds.). *Advances in Consumer Research* (Vol. 17, pp. 110–119). Provo, UT: Association for Consumer Research.

Dress code, mandatory courtesy required for Montreal taxi drivers (2015, October 28). *CTV News Montreal*. Retrieved from: http://montreal.ctvnews.ca/dress-code-mandatory-courtesy-required-for-montreal-taxi-drivers-1.2631947

Dress for Success: About us (n.d.). Retrieved from: https://www.dressforsuccess.org/about-us/

EEOC v. Abercrombie & Fitch Stores, Inc. (2015). 731 F. 3d 1106, reversed and remanded.

Elliot, A. J., & Maier, M. A. (2007). Color and psychological functioning. *Current Directions in Psychological Science, 16*(5), 250–254.

Fenigstein, A., Scheier, M. F., & Buss, A. H. (1975). Public and private self-consciousness: Assessment and theory. *Journal of Consulting and Clinical Psychology, 43,* 522–527.

Ferro, S. (2015, October 9). American Apparel lawsuit is 'mother of all sexual harassment cases,' judge says. *Huffington Post.* Retrieved from: http://www.huffingtonpost.com/entry/american-apparel-lawsuit-dov-charney-sexual-harassment_us_5617c6dce4b0082030a2067d

Fiske, S. T., & Taylor, S. E. (1991). *Social cognition.* New York, NY: Random House.

Form, W., & Stone, G. (1957). Urbanism, anonymity, and status symbolism. *American Journal of Sociology, 62,* 504–514.

Forsythe, S. (1987). Effect of clothing on perception of masculine and feminine managerial traits. *Perceptual and Motor Skills, 65,* 531–534.

Forsythe, S., Drake, M. F., & Cox, C. (1984). Dress as an influence on the perceptions of management characteristics in women. *Home Economics Research Journal, 13,* 112–121.

Glick, P., Larsen, S., Johnson, C., & Branstiter, H. (2005). Evaluations of sexy women in low-and high-status jobs. *Psychology of Women Quarterly, 29,* 389–395.

Grabe, M. E., & Samson, L. (2010). Sexual cues emanating from the anchorette chair: Implications for perceived professionalism, fitness for beat, and memory for news. *Communication Research*, 38(4), 471–496. DOI: 0093650210384986.

Grossman, J. L. (2009, March 3). Sex-stereotyping and dress codes under Title VII: Why courts can't get it right. Retrieved from: http://writ.news.findlaw.com/grossman/20090303.html

Guéguen, N. (2012). Color and women attractiveness: When red clothed women are perceived to have more intense sexual intent. *The Journal of Social Psychology, 152*(3), 261–265.

Hamilton, D. L. (1979). A cognitive–attributional analysis of stereotyping. In L. Berkowitz (Ed.) *Advances in experimental social psychology* (Vol. 12, pp. 53–84), New York, NY: Academic Press.

Haq, H. (2015, August 12). Why is 'teflon' Trump still so popular? Retrieved from: http://www.csmonitor.com/USA/Politics/2015/0812/Why-is-Teflon-Trump-still-so-popular-video

Hartnett, J., Gottlieb, J., & Hayes, R. (1976). Social facilitation theory and experimenter attractiveness. *The Journal of Social Psychology, 99,* 293–294.

Hebl, M. R., & Mannix, L. M. (2003). The weight of obesity in evaluating others: A mere proximity effect. *Personality and Social Psychology Bulletin, 29,* 28–38.

Heider K.G. (1970). *The Dugum Dani: A Papuan culture in the highlands of West New Guinea.* Chicago: Aldine.

Higgins, E. T. (2000). Social cognition: Learning about what matters in the social world. *European Journal of Social Psychology, 30,* 3–39.

Higham, W. (2011, December 17). What the hell is steampunk? *Huffington Post.* Retrieved from: http://www.huffingtonpost.co.uk/william-higham/steampunk-what-the-hell-is-it_b_1015192.html

Jacoby, J., & Mazursky, D. (1984). Linking brand and retailer images: Do the potential risks outweigh the potential benefits? *Journal of Retailing, 60*(2), 105–122.

Jawahar, I. M., & Mattsson, J. (2005). Sexism and beauty-ism effects in selection as a function of self-monitoring level of decision maker. *Journal of Applied Psychology, 90,* 563–573.

Johansson, L., Ghaderi, A., & Andersson, G. (2005). Stroop interference for food- and body-related words: A meta-analysis. *Eating Behaviors, 6*(3), 271–281.

Johnson, B. H., Nagasawa, R. H., & Peters, K. (1977). Clothing style differences: Their effect on the impression of sociability. *Home Economics Research Journal, 6*(1), 58–63.

Johnson, K. K. P., & Roach-Higgins, M. E. (1987a). Dress and physical attractiveness of women in job interviews. *Clothing and Textiles Research Journal, 5*(3), 1–8.

Johnson, K. K. P., & Roach-Higgins, M. E. (1987b). The influence of physical attractiveness and dress on campus recruiters' impressions of female job applicants. *Home Economics Research Journal, 16,* 87–95.

Johnson, K. K. P., Schofield, N. A., & Yurchisin, J. (2002). Appearance and dress as a source of information: A qualitative approach to data collection. *Clothing and Textiles Research Journal, 20,* 125–137.

Jung, J., & Lennon, S. J. (2003). Body image, appearance self-schema, and media images. *Family and Consumer Sciences Research Journal, 32*(3), 27–51.

Kaiser, S. B. (1990). *The social psychology of clothing: Symbolic appearances in context* (2nd ed.). New York, NY: Macmillan.

Kaiser, S. B. (1997). *The social psychology of clothing: Symbolic appearances in context* (2nd ed., rev.). New York, NY: Fairchild.

Kamtsios, S., & Digelidis, N. (2008). Physical activity levels, exercise attitudes, self-perceptions and BMI type of 11 to 12-year-old children. *Journal of Child Health Care, 12*(3), 232–240.

Katz, P. A. (1982). Development of children's racial awareness and intergroup attitudes. In L. G. Katz (Ed.), *Current topics in early childhood education* (Vol. 4, pp. 16–54). New York, NY: Ablex.

Kiefer, A. K., & Sekaquaptewa, D. (2007). Implicit stereotypes, gender identification, and math-related outcomes: A prospective study of female college students. *Psychological Science, 18*(1), 13–18.

Kimle, P. A., & Damhorst, M. L. (1997). A grounded theory model of the ideal business image for women. *Symbolic Interaction, 20*(1), 45–68.

Laird, D. (1932). How the consumer estimates quality by subconscious sensory impressions. *Journal of Applied Psychology 16*, 241–246.

Lapitsky, M., & Smith, C. M. (1981). Impact of clothing on impressions of personal characteristics and writing ability. *Home Economics Research Journal, 9*, 327–335.

Lennon, S. J. (1990). Effects of clothing attractiveness on perceptions. *Home Economics Research Journal, 18*, 303–310.

Lennon, S. J. (1992). Categorization as a function of body type. *Clothing and Textiles Research Journal, 10*(2), 18–23.

Lennon, S. J., & Clayton, R. (1992). Age, body type, and style features as cues in nonverbal communication. *Semiotica, 91*(1/2), 43–55.

Lennon, S. J., & Davis, L. L. (1989). Clothing and human behavior from a social cognitive framework—Part I: Theoretical perspectives. *Clothing and Textiles Research Journal, 7* (4), 41–48.

Lennon, S. J., Davis, L. L., & Fairhurst, A. (1988). Evaluations of apparel advertising as a function of self-monitoring. *Perceptual and Motor Skills, 66*, 987–996.

Lennon, S. J., & Miller, F. G. (1984). Salience of physical appearance in impression formation. *Home Economics Research Journal, 13*, 95–104.

Lennon, S. J., & Miller, F. G. (1984–85). Attire, physical appearance, and first impressions: More is less. *Clothing and Textiles Research Journal, 3*(1), 1–8.

Littrell, M. A., & Berger, E. A. (1985–1986). Perceiver's occupation and client's grooming: Influence on person perception. *Clothing and Textiles Research Journal, 4*(2), 48–55.

Livesley, W. J., & Bromley, D. B. (1973). *Person perception in childhood and adolescence.* New York, NY: John Wiley & Sons.

Loken, B. (2006). Consumer psychology: Categorization, inferences, affect, and persuasion. *Annual Review of Psychology, 57*, 453–485.

Macapagal, K. R., Rupp, H. A., & Heiman, J. R. (2011). Influences of observer sex, facial masculinity, and gender role identification on first impressions of men's faces. *Journal of Social, Evolutionary, and Cultural Psychology, 5*(1), 92.

Man skirts are now a thing, but who will wear them? (2015, July). Retrieved from: https://www.yahoo.com/style/man-skirts-are-now-a-thing-but-who-will-wear-123373198968.html

Matera, C., Nerini, A., Giorgi, C., Baroni, D., & Stefanile, C. (2015). Beyond sociocultural influence: Self-monitoring and self-awareness as predictors of women's interest in breast cosmetic surgery. *Aesthetic Plastic Surgery, 39*(3), 331–338.

McGuire, W. J. (1976). Some internal psychological factors influencing consumer choice. *Journal of Consumer Research, 2*, 302–319.

McPeek, R., W., & Edwards, J. D. (1975). Expectancy disconfirmation and attitude change. *Journal of Social Psychology, 96*, 193–208.

Medin, D. L., Wattenmaker, W. D., & Hampson, S. E. (1987). Family resemblence, conceptual cohesiveness, and category construction. *Cognitive Psychology, 19*, 242–279.

Mehta, N., Rajiv, S., & Srinivasan, K. (2003). Price uncertainty and consumer search: A structural model of consideration set formation. *Marketing Science, 22*(1), 58–84.

Mervis, C. B., & Rosch, E. (1981). Categorization of natural objects. In M. R. Rosenzweig & L. W. Porter (Eds.), *Annual review of psychology* (Vol. 32, pp. 89–115). Palo Alto, CA: Annual Reviews.

Miller, C. (1991, February 4). Research reveals how marketers can win by a nose. *Marketing News*, pp. 1–2.

Miller, F. G. (1982). Clothing and physical impairment: Joint effects on person perception. *Home Economics Research Journal, 10*, 265–270.

Muslim man who was 'pummeled' by crowd shouting 'ISIS, ISIS' in the middle of the Bronx as his nine-year-old niece watched on in horror (2016, January 17). *Daily Mail.* Retrieved from: http://www.dailymail

.co.uk/news/article-3403818/Man-wearing-Asian-clothing-pummeled-crowd-shouting-ISIS-ISIS-New-York-nine-year-old-daughter-looked-on.html

Nelson, T. D. (2005). Ageism: Prejudice against our feared future self. *Journal of Social Issues, 61*(2), 207–221.

Neuberg, S. L. (1989). The goal of forming accurate impressions during social interactions: Attenuating the impact of negative expectancies. *Journal of Personality and Social Psychology, 56,* 374–386.

NYC votes to change taxi driver dress code (2011, January 21). Retrieved from: http://newyork.cbslocal.com/2011/01/21/nyc-votes-to-change-taxi-driver-dress-code/

O'Neal, G. S. (1998). African-American aesthetic of dress: Current manifestations. *Clothing and Textiles Research Journal, 16*(4), 167–175.

Pazda, A. D., Elliot, A. J., & Greitemeyer, T. (2014). Perceived sexual receptivity and fashionableness: Separate paths linking red and black to perceived attractiveness. *Color Research & Application, 39*(2), 208–212.

Posthuma, R. A., & Campion, M. A. (2009). Age stereotypes in the workplace: Common stereotypes, moderators, and future research directions. *Journal of Management, 35*(1), 158–188.

Price Waterhouse v. Hopkins, 490 U.S. 228 (1989).

Ramsey, P. (1987). Young children's thinking about ethnic differences. In J. Phinney & M. Rotheram (Eds.), *Children's ethnic socialization: Pluralism and development.* London, England: Sage Publications.

Rizzo, C. (2015, October 5). 9 women (and 1 man) share their worst slut-shaming stories at Amber Rose's slutwalk. Retrieved September 16, 2016 from: http://www.cosmopolitan.com/sex-love/a47241/slut-walk-slut-shaming-interviews/

Roberts, S. C., Owen, R. C., & Havlicek, J. (2010). Distinguishing between perceiver and wearer effects in clothing color-associated attributions. *Evolutionary Psychology: An International Journal of Evolutionary Approaches to Psychology and Behavior, 8*(3), 350–364.

Rosch, E. (1973). Natural categories. *Cognitive Psychology, 4,* 328–350.

Rosch, E., Mervis, C., Gray, W., Johnson, D., & Boyes-Braem, P. (1976). Basic objects in natural categories. *Cognitive Psychology, 8,* 382–439.

Rosenthal, R., & Jacobson, L. (1968). *Pygmalion in the classroom: Teacher expectations and pupils' intellectual development.* New York, NY: Holt, Rinehart & Winston.

Rowold, K. (1984). Sensitivity to the appearance of others and projection as factors in impression formation. *Home Economics Research Journal, 13,* 105–111.

Rupp, D. E., Vodanovich, S. J., & Crede, M. (2006). Age bias in the workplace: The impact of ageism and causal attributions. *Journal of Applied Social Psychology, 36*(6), 1337–1364.

Ryckman, R. M., Robbins, M. A., Thornton, B., Kaczor, L. M., Gayton, S. L., & Anderson, C. V. (1991). Public self-consciousness and physique stereotyping. *Personality and Social Psychology Bulletin, 7,* 400–405.

Scherbaum, C., & Shepherd, D. (1987). Dressing for success: Effects of color and layering on perceptions of women in business. *Sex Roles, 16,* 391–399.

Schneider, D. J., Hastorf, A. H., & Ellsworth, P. C. (1979). *Person perception.* Reading, MA: Addison-Wesley.

Schroeder, P. (2004, June 6). Nothing stuck to Teflon president. *USA Today.* Retrieved from: http://www.usatoday.com/news/opinion/editorials/2004-06-06-schroeder_x.htm

Shah, R., and Ogden, J. (2006) "What's in a face?" The role of doctors' ethnicity, age and gender on patient's judgements: An experimental study. *Patient Education and Counselling, 60,* 136–141.

Snyder, M., Berscheid, E., & Matwychuk, A. (1988). Orientations toward personnel selection: Differential reliance on appearance and personality. *Journal of Personality and Social Psychology, 54,* 972–979.

Snyder, M., Campbell, B. H., & Preston, E. (1982). Testing hypotheses about human nature: Assessing the accuracy of social stereotypes. *Social Cognition, 1,* 256–272.

Snyder, M., & Gangestad, S. (1981). Hypothesis testing processes. In J. H. Harvey, W. Ickes, & R. F. Kidd (Eds.), *New Directions in Attribution Research* (Vol. 3, pp. 171–196). Hillsdale, NJ: Erlbaum.

Snyder, M., & Swann, W. B. (1978). Hypothesis testing processes in social interaction. *Journal of Personality and Social Psychology, 36,* 1202–1212.

Snyder, M., Tanke, E. D., & Berscheid, E. (1977). Social perception and interpersonal behavior: On the self-fulfilling nature of social stereotypes. *Journal of Personality and Social Psychology, 35,* 656–666.

Stanforth, N. F., & Lennon, S. J. (1997). Customer expectations and store policies: Satisfaction, patronage and retail store service. *Clothing and Textiles Research Journal, 15,* 115–124.

Stangor, C., Lynch, L., Duan, C., & Glass, B. (1992). Categorization of individuals on the basis of multiple social features. *Journal of Personality and Social Psychology, 62*(2), 207–218.

Steampunk picnic at park. (2015, August 25). *Hucknall Dispatch.* Retrieved from: http://www.hucknall dispatch.co.uk/news/local/steampunk-picnic-at -park-1-7427883

Swann, W. B. (1984). Quest for accuracy in person perception: A matter of pragmatics. *Psychological Review, 91,* 457–477.

Swann, W. B. (1987). Identity negotiation: Where two roads meet. *Journal of Personality and Social Psychology, 53,* 1038–1051.

Swann, W. B., Griffin, J. J., Predmore, S. C., & Gaines, B. (1987). Cognitive-affective crossfire: When self-consistency meets self-enhancement. *Journal of Personality and Social Psychology, 52,* 881–889.

Takeda, M. B., Helms, M. M., & Romanova, N. (2006). Hair color stereotyping and CEO selection in the United Kingdom. *Journal of Human Behavior in the Social Environment, 13*(3), 85–99.

Taylor, S. E., Fiske, S. T., Etcoff, N. L., & Ruderman, A. J. (1978). Categorical and contextual bases of person memory and stereotyping. *Journal of Personality and Social Psychology, 36,* 778–793.

Thornton, G. R. (1944). The effect of wearing glasses upon judgments of personality traits of persons seen briefly. *Journal of Applied Psychology, 20,* 203–207.

Thurston, J. L., Lennon, S. J., & Clayton, R. V. (1990). Influence of age, body type, currency of fashion detail, and type of garment on the professional image of women. *Home Economics Research Journal, 19*(2), 139–150.

Title VII of the Civil Rights Act of 1964, 42 U.S.C. Sec. 2000e, et seq.

Traut-Mattausch, E., Schulz-Hardt, S., Greitemeyer, T., & Frey, D. (2004). Expectancy confirmation in spite of disconfirming evidence: The case of price increases due to the introduction of the Euro. *European Journal of Social Psychology, 34*(6), 739–760.

Walline, J. J., Sinnott, L., Johnson, E. D., Ticak, A., Jones, S. L., & Jones, L. A. (2008). What do kids think about kids in eyeglasses? *Ophthalmic and Physiological Optics, 28*(3), 218–224.

Ward, J. C., Bitner, M. J., & Barnes, J. (1992). Measuring the prototypicality and meaning of retail environments. *Journal of Retailing, 68*(2), 194–220.

Ward, P., Davies, B. J., & Kooijman, D. (2007). Olfaction and the retail environment: examining the influence of ambient scent. *Service Business, 1*(4), 295–316.

Wingate, S., Kaiser, S., & Freeman, C. (1985–86). Salience of disability cues in functional clothing: A multidimensional approach. *Clothing and Textiles Research Journal, 4*(2), 37–47.

Workman, J. E. (1984–85). Effects of appropriate and inappropriate attire on attributions of personal dispositions. *Clothing and Textiles Research Journal, 3*(1), 20–23.

Workman, J. E. (1987). Fashionable versus out-of-date clothing and interpersonal distance. *Clothing and Textiles Research Journal, 5*(3), 31–35.

Workman, J. E. (1991). Improving uniform design for foodservice workers: Criteria and prototypes. *Journal of Home Economics, 83*(3), 17–22.

Workman, J. E., & Johnson, K. K. P. (1989a). The role of clothing in extended inferences. *Home Economics Research Journal, 18*(2), 164–169.

Workman, J. E., & Johnson, K. K. P. (1989b). The role of clothing in perpetuating ageism. *Journal of Home Economics, 81,* 11–15.

Wyer, R. S. (1980). The acquisition and use of social knowledge: Basic postulates and representative research. *Personality and Social Psychology Bulletin, 6*(4), 558–573.

Yu, J., & Bairner, A. (2012). Confucianism, baseball and ethnic stereotyping in Taiwan. *International Review for the Sociology of Sport, 47*(6), 690–704.

Zimmer, M. R., & Golden, L, L. (1988). Impressions of retail stores: A content analysis of consumer images. *Journal of Retailing, 64*(3), 265–293.

5 DRESS AND IMPRESSION FORMATION

After reading and reflecting on the content of this chapter students should be able to:

- **Evaluate the role of dress in the attribution process.**
- **Analyze behavioral consequences of impression formation using the S-O-R Model, symbolic interaction, and Livesley and Bromley's model of person perception.**
- **Explain impression formation using Implicit Personality Theory.**

INTRODUCTION

In this chapter, we continue with the same general topic of social cognition. In Chapter 4, "Dress and Social Cognition" we introduced the concept of impression formation. In this chapter we expand our discussion on impression formation to include attribution, Implicit Personality Theory, impression management, and dramaturgy. We also include a discussion of role theory as it relates to social perception, look at the rise and fall in popularity of casual business dress, examine some of the behavioral consequences of social perception, and apply Livesley and Bromley's explanation of the process of person perception to clarify such behaviors. We also introduce the S-O-R Model and symbolic interaction as ways to explain behavioral consequences of dress in impression formation.

ATTRIBUTION

The process of **attribution** focuses on the perceived causes of behaviors and therefore is part of social perception. In general, people are curious about what causes other individuals to engage in certain behaviors because knowing

what causes behaviors in the present helps people to predict future behaviors. Choice is an important concept in attribution because freely chosen behavior (e.g., the clothes we wear, the modifications we make to our bodies) can suggest some information about those individuals engaged in the behavior. If something happens to an individual as a result of chance or luck the event is unpredictable. But if something happens as a result of an individual's effort, we think we can predict when it might happen again or perhaps work to prevent the event from happening at all. According to attribution theory, past behavior is informative about future behavior to the extent that the behavior is freely chosen.

Attribution Theories

Several different **attribution theories** provide models for how we try to find causes for our behavior and the behavior of others. The focus of these attribution theories is explaining why an outcome occurred, especially outcomes that are negative (Gordon & Graham, 2006). For example, suppose you fail an examination. According to attribution theory you would ask yourself "why did I fail this test?" You might attribute failing the test to being unlucky (e.g., I did not wear my lucky T-shirt when taking the test). You might attribute failing to the instructor not liking you (e.g., This teacher has not liked any of my answers.) You might think you did not study enough for this test or you might attribute your failing to not being intelligent enough to fully understand the course material. Any number of attributions to the causes of this behavior or any other individual's behavior can be made. The possibilities are endless.

Attribution theory, however, has focused primarily on three underlying causes or casual dimensions: locus of causality, stability, and controllability. **Locus of causality** is concerned with the location of the cause. It tried to answer the question of whether the cause was external or internal to the individual. **Stability** is concerned with whether the cause is temporary (unstable) or permanent (stable). **Controllability** refers to whether or not the cause is regulated by the individual. Continuing with the above example, if an individual thinks he or she was sexually harassed because of bad luck, the cause is external to the individual, unstable, and uncontrollable.

Attributions of Victim Responsibility as a Function of Dress

Researchers have used attribution theory to explain and predict how aspects of appearance (e.g., dress, cosmetics) affect attributions of victim responsibility for a crime (Johnson, 1995; Johnson & Workman, 1992; 1994; Lewis & Johnson, 1989; Workman & Orr, 1996). In these studies, the researchers were interested in determining to what extent people were willing to attribute responsibility for a sexual assault or for sexual harassment to women based on their dress or their use of cosmetics. While a sexual assault can certainly happen at random and be attributed

to bad luck, the researchers found support for the belief that women cause (i.e., are responsible for) their own sexual assaults and their sexual harassment because they wear revealing clothing and/or heavy makeup (Figure 5.1). These results are also consistent with a much more recent study of child sexual assault from the UK (Rogers, Lowe, & Reddington, 2016). In that experimental research like earlier studies, the victim of the assault was judged more to blame for the sexual assault when she wore revealing dress and makeup as compared to when she wore non-revealing dress and no makeup.

Why might people be willing to attribute responsibility for a sexual assault or sexual harassment to a woman in revealing clothing or one who is wearing lots of makeup? It might be because they view the incident as caused by something freely chosen by the woman (her body-revealing dress or the heavy makeup). They could infer that not wearing revealing dress or heavy makeup might protect them from similar incidents. This type of inference is an example of **blaming the victim** of the event for the incident. When you blame the victim of a crime for the crime, you create the illusion of control. By blaming the victim, you think you can control whether these types of events

Figure 5.1

As a function of short skirts, research participants have attributed responsibility for sexual assault and sexual harassment.

will happen to you because you can control whether or not you will engage in the activities that were similar to those of the victim. In this case you think you can control whether you will be sexually harassed because you control whether or not you wear body-revealing clothing. In other words, we blame victims because they threaten our view of the world as safe. We are threatened when good people suffer misfortune, because that means that we, too, might suffer misfortune.

However, there is evidence that such attitudes and attributions toward female rape victims may be changing. Recent research has found that college students did not attribute responsibility for a sexual assault to a woman as a function of her revealing dress (Maurer & Robinson, 2008). More recently, women's revealing dress and experiences of sexual violence have been studied (Moor, 2010). The author found no relationship between wearing revealing dress and actual experiences of violence such as sexual assault. In that study, the percentage of female victims and non-victims of violence who reported wearing revealing clothing was nearly identical. "Between 60–64% of the former reported wearing such attire from time to time in comparison to 63–65% of the women who were never victimized" (p. 122). Moor concluded that since victims and non-victims of violence did not differ in wearing revealing dress, women's responsibility for sexual violence is unrelated to wearing revealing dress. Another very recent study also found that undergraduates did not assign responsibility for a sexual assault to a woman as a function of her revealing dress (Johnson, Ju, & Wu, 2016).

Why might attitudes and attributions toward female sexual assault victims be changing? It is hard to know for sure, but changing attitudes may be due to publicity surrounding (a) Title IX violations on university campuses and (b) the Slutwalk movement. See Chapter 4, "Dress and Social Cognition" for more information about Slutwalk. Title IX bans sex discrimination, which includes sexual assault and sexual misconduct, in US educational institutions; universities and colleges face potential loss of federal funding for Title IX violations ("What is Title IX?," n.d.). As of July 2015 there were 124 universities and colleges under investigation for violations of Title IX and the handling of sexual assault complaints (Kingkade, 2015). Many of the named universities have established programs to educate students and employees about sexual assault and making sexual assault complaints. These programs clarify that complainants are not responsible

for their sexual assaults. For example, the Harvard Law School was found in violation of Title IX and as part of their settlement the school agreed to (among other things) notify complainants of their right to file a Title IX complaint, notify employees and students about the school's Title IX coordinators and provide their contact information, provide training for staff, educate students regarding policies and procedures relating to complaints, and conduct yearly assessments of the school's climate ("Harvard Law School found," 2014).

Changing attitudes and attributions toward female sexual assault victims may be also due to the publicity surrounding slut shaming and Slutwalk, which promotes an end to slut shaming and victim blaming (Rizzo, 2015). Slut shaming occurs when we judge people based on assumptions about their sexual activity or on their actual sexual activity; such assumptions may be due to what they wear, what they look like, or rumors (Kohli, 2016). Slutwalk began in Toronto, Canada, in 2011 ("Toronto 'slut walk' takes," 2011). The original Slutwalk was organized in response to provocative comments made by Toronto police officer Michael Sanguinetti, who told a class in personal security that, "women should avoid dressing like sluts in order not to be victimized." Later the Toronto police chief said that Sanguinetti's comments "place the blame upon victims, and that's not where the blame should ever be placed." As of 2015 Slutwalk had reached 250 cities across the world, which both promotes the movement and underscores how universal victim blaming and sexual violence is (Townes, 2015).

Attributions Concerning Hiring and Dress

A few other researchers have used attribution theory to examine the influence of dress in employment interviews (Goudge & Littrell, 1989; Workman, 1984–85). An assumption in these studies was that people freely choose what to wear to an interview. For example, how dress might influence causal attributions concerning why people were hired was the focus of one study (Goudge & Littrell, 1989). Research participants were businessmen who were asked to make attributions about why someone was hired. They rated job skills (internal causal dimension) as most important, dress as slightly above neutral in importance (internal, controllable causal dimension), and luck (uncontrollable, external dimension) as slightly unimportant. Although study participants rated dress as relatively neutral as a factor in hiring, it is common for websites offering job interview advice to urge applicants to take care in how they dress and groom themselves.

IMPRESSION FORMATION

Gilbert (1998) refers to the term *impression formation* as **ordinary personology** or the way people come to know about each other. Often impression formation refers to the process integrating various bits of information about another person to form an overall impression of the person. While we know that people use cues in forming impressions of others, which specific cues evoke which impressions has received little study (Gerrard & Dickinson, 2005). See Table 5.1 and Figure 5.2 for some examples. People are able to form very complex impressions when given limited information, and when they form those impressions people believe that certain traits occur together (Gilbert, 1998). For example, people might assume that a skillful person is also intelligent or that a person who is athletic is also coordinated.

Processes for Investigating Relationships Between Dress and Impression Formation

Using Multiple Dress Cues

Researchers interested in relationships between dress and impression formation have studied it by examining the simultaneous effect of multiple dress cues. For example, in one study researchers were interested in how dress influenced impressions formed of taxi drivers (Workman & Johnson, 1989a). Their manipulation consisted of items they labeled appropriate clothing (a white shirt with a collar, dark pants, and shoes) and those they labeled inappropriate clothing (a white T-shirt, dark shorts, and sandals). They showed pictures of the outfits to participants and found that dress affected impressions. However, what specific aspects of their dress manipulation actually influenced their participants' impressions was left undetermined. A more recent example of use of multiple cues is a study in which the stimulus person's appearance was described verbally (Johnson, Ju, & Wu, 2016). Because

BLACK FRIDAY VIOLENCE AND ATTRIBUTION

The day after Thanksgiving in the US is called Black Friday and serves as the kickoff to the US holiday shopping season. On Black Friday 2011, several incidents of consumer misbehavior occurred at Walmarts across the country (Black Friday violence, 2011). At an upstate NY Walmart, a fight broke out when Black Friday shopping began at midnight; a man was charged as shoppers were pushed to the ground and fights broke out resulting in minor injuries. At an LA Walmart, a woman pepper sprayed a group of Black Friday shoppers when they pushed and tried to cut in line to get Xbox 360s. At a Walmart in South Carolina, a woman was shot during an attempted robbery. In California, a Black Friday shopper was critically injured from a gunshot during a robbery near a Walmart. Apparently the shopper was walking to the car with Black Friday purchases when gunmen approached and demanded the packages. In Connecticut, when a Walmart shopper cut in line ahead of twenty people and resisted arrest, he was tasered (Martinez, 2011). In addition, it was only three years before, on Black Friday 2008, that a Walmart worker was trampled and killed as shoppers rushed to get into a Valley Stream, NY Walmart (Carr, 2008).

After reading about so many incidents of consumer misbehavior on Black Friday at Walmarts, you might attribute Black Friday misbehavior to something about Walmart. In other words, it seems that there might be something about Walmart (e.g., policies for crowd control, policies for how promotions are handled) that evokes consumer misbehavior on Black Friday.

Figure 5.2
One first impression situation where dress is likely to influence attributions is speed dating.

TABLE 5.1

EXAMPLES OF RESEARCH FINDINGS RELATING SPECIFIC DRESS CUES AND THEIR EFFECT ON FIRST IMPRESSIONS

Dress Cues	Affects Judgments of:	Author and Year of Publication
Age	Physical attractiveness	Mathes, Brennan, Haugen, & Rice, 1985
	Attractiveness, likelihood of encouraging questions, friendliness, likelihood of developing rapport, likelihood of expecting good work, likelihood of assigning too much work.	Wilson, Beyer, & Monteiro, 2014
	Memory loss	Workman & Johnson, 1989b
Attractiveness	Hostility, trustworthiness, competence, health	Zebrowitz & Franklin, 2014
	Perceived intelligence, perceived academic performance, perceived consciousness	Talamas, Mavor, & Perrett, 2016
	Course evaluations	Riniolo, Johnson, Sherman, & Misso, 2006
Baldness	Dominant, dynamic, and masculine	Butler, Pryor, & Greider, 1998
	Maturity, age, unattractiveness, less aggressive	Muscarella & Cunningham, 1996
Beards	Attractiveness, parenting, health, masculinity	Dixson & Brooks, 2013
	Masculinity, aggressive, socially mature, older	Neave & Shields, 2008
Body Type/Size	Attractiveness	Taniguchi & Lee, 2015
Clothing Attractiveness	Intelligence, morality, adjustment	Buckley & Haefner, 1984
	Competence, sociability	Lennon, 1990
Clothing Fashionability	Elite, competence	Workman, 1990
Clothing Formality	Status, role	Damhorst, 1984–85
Clothing Similarity	Structure, values	Sontag, & Schlater, 1995
Clothing Style	Self-control, reliability, attractiveness, individualism, social ease, dependency	Paek, 1986
Cosmetics	Attractiveness, femininity, morality	Workman & Johnson, 1991
	Perceived age, social skills, academic performance, dating success, occupational success, attractiveness, financial success, relationship success, athletic success	Dayan, Cho, Siracusa, &Gutierrez-Borst, 2015
Eyeglasses	Scholastic ability/intelligence	Behling, & Williams, 1991
	Smarter, more honest	Walline, Sinnott, Johnson, Ticak, Jones, & Jones, 2008
Facial Disfigurement	Confidence	Christman, & Branson, 1990 Stevenage & McKay, 1999
Facial Jewelry	Age, extroversion, interest in extreme sexual behavior	Ferguson, 1999

TABLE 5.1

EXAMPLES OF RESEARCH FINDINGS RELATING SPECIFIC DRESS CUES AND THEIR EFFECT ON FIRST IMPRESSIONS (continued)

Dress Cues	Affects Judgments of:	Author and Year of Publication
Fragrance/Perfume	Warmth, friendliness, intelligence, likeableness	Baron, 1983
Garment Type	Intelligence, attractiveness, popularity	Bell, 1991
Grooming	Impressions	Miller, 1970
Hair Color	Expressive nature, intelligence	Behling, & Williams,1991
Hair Color and Cosmetics	Competence, salary	Kyle & Mahler, 1996
Muscularity	Strength, masculinity	Wells & Siegle, 1961
Obesity/Overweight	Likability, intelligence	Lennon & Miller, 1984
	Appearance, carelessness, professionalism	Ruggs, Hebl, & Williams, 2015
Shoes	Age, gender, income, attachment anxiety	Gillath, Bahns, Ge, & Crandall, 2012
	Sexy, pretty, elegant	Guéguen, Stefan, & Renault, 2016
Smile	Credibility	Hareli, Harsuh, Suleiman, Cossette, Bergeron, Lavoie, Dugay, & Hess, 2009
Tallness	Leadership	Higham & Carment, 1992
	Persuasiveness	Young & French, 1996
	Leadership, success, income, performance	Judge & Cable, 2004
Tattoos on Women	Physical attractiveness, sexuality, alcohol consumption	Swami & Furnham, 2007

the stimulus person was described as dressed in a body-hugging short red dress that showed cleavage with killer heels and black stockings, it is impossible to determine which specific aspects of her appearance affected respondents' impressions.

Using a Single Dress Cue

A few researchers have focused on examining the influence of a specific aspect of dress. In one such study, researchers varied one piece of information about clothing, skirt length of the stimulus person, for its effect on impression formation (Workman & Orr, 1996). They found that skirt length alone did affect impressions. (See Table 5.1 for dress cues used in impression formation research and the impressions those cues conveyed at the time of the research).

Is it important to know what specific cues convey what specific types of information? In some instances, the answer is yes. For example, costume designers and novelists are interested in knowing which specific dress cues convey specific information (Lennon & Burns, 1993). When designing costumes for stage or screen actors, costume designers must be knowledgeable regarding the impressions conveyed by various dress cues. This is necessary because the designers need to construct appearances that are consistent with the characters for whom they are designing. In addition, they need to construct appearances that accurately and quickly convey the characters' core personalities to the audience. Similarly, authors need to know what dress cues convey specific information, so when they describe the characters in their novels, readers can easily relate to the type of individual being described.

Classic Process for Investigating Impression Formation

Often impression formation deals with the manner in which multiple pieces of information about a person are combined into a general impression. In classic impression formation studies, researchers presented people with a list of adjective traits and then asked them to form an impression of the person being described by those adjectives (e.g., Asch, 1946). See Table 5.2 for an example of a task that researchers might ask a participant to do when conducting this type of study.

Implicit Personality Theory

Researchers using the classic research approach exemplified in Table 5.2 assume that people expect certain traits to co-occur. This assumption is the basis for **implicit personality theory** (Schneider, 1973). According to implicit personality theory our impressions of people consist of specific traits and additional traits that we anticipate the person will have (i.e., trait inferences). For example, suppose you just met an attractive young woman named Emma who is very friendly to you. Her specific traits that you recognize are attractiveness and friendliness. Because you know from past experience that attractive people are popular and extroverted you also expect that she is probably popular and extroverted as well. Traits (i.e., attractive, friendly) and the additional trait inferences (i.e., popular, extroverted) are part of your own theory of what traits tend to appear together. In other words, you have implicit personality theories that you have developed over time based on your experiences that link traits together. Once you know a person has a specific trait, you can use your theories to infer additional traits he/she is likely to have.

As described in the previous example, we form mental constructs of expected behavioral traits based on our observations and past experience. These expected traits help us organize information and suggest other traits people might have (e.g., Emma is popular). We form these theories because we have frequently found in our experience that certain traits tend to occur with each other; thus, we begin to expect certain traits will occur together (Rosenberg, Nelson, & Vivekananthan, 1968). The theories help us organize information about people and help us better understand and predict the behavior of others (Bruner & Tagiuri, 1954). In documenting that people use some traits to infer other traits, most researchers have focused on relationships between various traits (friendly goes with popular) or between behaviors and inferred

---

TABLE 5.2

INSTRUCTIONS IN AN IMPRESSION FORMATION STUDY

John is intelligent, skillful, industrious, cold, determined, practical, and cautious. Please indicate the extent to which you think the items in the following list are also characteristic of John by circling the appropriate numbers on the scale provided.

	John							
Not generous	1	2	3	4	5	6	7	Generous
Not good-natured	1	2	3	4	5	6	7	Good natured
Not happy	1	2	3	4	5	6	7	Happy
Not humorous	1	2	3	4	5	6	7	Humorous
Not sociable	1	2	3	4	5	6	7	Sociable
Not important	1	2	3	4	5	6	7	Important
Not restrained	1	2	3	4	5	6	7	Restrained
Not popular	1	2	3	4	5	6	7	Popular

Take a look at the person in the photo in Figure 5.3. There are several dress and appearance cues that people can use when forming an impression. Is it the driver's shirt, beard, eyes, smile, or body type that shapes the judgments formed about him?

Using your implicit personality theories, identify several traits that you are confident this person has. Which traits did you use initially to infer additional traits?

Figure 5.3
Perceivers use dress cues to form impressions of this bus driver according to their implicit personality theories.

traits (helping goes with friendly). However, according to implicit personality theory, any attribute of a person (e.g., dress) could be used in forming your implicit personality theory (Schneider, 1973).

Using Photos, Drawings, or Videos

Instead of using lists of trait-descriptive adjectives to study the effects of dress on impression formation, researchers have used photos, drawings, or videos of people dressed differently as stimuli. For example, in an impression formation study discussed in Chapter 3, "Conducting Research on Dress," people were asked to view photos and make judgments of a person (i.e., the retail manager) depicted in the photos (Johnson, Crutsinger, & Workman, 1994). In that study the female stimulus person wore a white button-down collar shirt with a navy blue jacket. In one condition, the female stimulus person simply had the neck of the shirt unbuttoned, in the second condition a scarf was worn around the neck, and in the third condition a necktie was worn. The researchers developed rating scales for respondents to use to indicate their ratings of the stimulus person. Rating scales typically consist of a series of statements and a set of choices along which to rate the stimulus person. (See Table 5.3 for examples of rating scales and the traits along which a stimulus person was rated). By selecting a number, participants could indicate their ratings of each trait. In the examples, the rating scales have seven choices and respondents choose a number from 1 to 7 when using the scale. The traits to the left and right of the numbers are called the **endpoints**; in these rating scales the endpoints are *likely* and *not likely*. The **number of discriminations** (or choices) is 7.

Using Combinations of Dress Cues

Other researchers have varied dress cues to study impression formation, building on the work of Asch (1946). Researchers have varied dress cues in the same way that Asch varied personality traits (Lennon & Miller, 1984; 1984–85). Their reasoning was as follows: (a) people form impressions of others based on what the others wear (e.g., business suit = professional), (b) people also form impressions of others based on lists of traits, then (c) dress cues may operate like the trait descriptive adjectives in shaping impressions. Applying this reasoning, researchers have substituted dress cues for pieces of adjective trait information. Instead of providing lists of adjective traits, these researchers provided stimuli consisting of combinations of dress cues such as dress ensembles (Johnson, 1995; Lennon & Miller, 1984; 1984–85). Other research has used lists of clothing items one owns as stimuli (Workman, 1988). Although these different forms of stimuli (visual, verbal) do affect impressions, recently scholars in Germany as well as Hong Kong have warned researchers that the two types of stimuli may not be interchangeable since they are processed in fundamentally different ways which could influence research results (Kuzmanovic, Bente, Cramon, Schilbach, Tittgemeyer, & Vogeley, 2012; Wyer, Hung, Jiang, 2008).

In a series of studies, researchers used combinations of dress cues and implicit personality theory to determine if the theory could be extended from applying to traits and trait inferences to dress cues (Clayton, Lennon, & Larkin,

TABLE 5.3

EXAMPLE OF RATING SCALES FROM JOHNSON, CRUTSINGER, AND WORKMAN (1994)

Participants in the research were asked to: "indicate the likelihood that the manager pictured possesses each trait" (p. 28).

		Dependable						
Likely	7	6	5	4	3	2	1	Not Likely
		Conscientious						
Likely	7	6	5	4	3	2	1	Not Likely
		Ambitious						
Likely	7	6	5	4	3	2	1	Not Likely
		Helpful						
Likely	7	6	5	4	3	2	1	Not Likely
		Professional						
Likely	7	6	5	4	3	2	1	Not Likely
		Trustworthy						
Likely	7	6	5	4	3	2	1	Not Likely

1987; Thurston, Lennon, & Clayton, 1990). They reasoned that three attributes of dress people might use in making trait inferences were age, body type or size, and clothing. They found that all three attributes were used in forming impressions of garment fashionability and impressions of women's professional image.

Using Verbal Descriptions

In addition to using photos of people or lists of traits as stimuli in impression formation research, verbal descriptions of appearance have also been used. These verbal descriptions have also influenced impressions. For example, in one study the stimulus person Amy described herself as wearing an "off-the-shoulder, body hugging, short, red dress that showed a good deal of my cleavage . . ." and "killer heels and black silk stockings" (Johnson, Ju, & Wu, 2016, p. 133). In another study conducted in France, research participants were verbally provided with information about a stimulus person's physical characteristics such as sex and attractiveness (Przygodzki-Lionet, Olivier, & Desrumaux, 2010).

IMPRESSION MANAGEMENT

As we have seen in the previous section, researchers have used a variety of materials to study what people use to form impressions. These researchers have also documented that people form impressions of others based on very little information, and the impressions, once formed, can have some serious consequences. Since we know that others form impressions of us based on how we dress, we can select what we wear very carefully to try to control the kinds of impressions others form of us, a process called **impression management**. For example, when you carefully select a suit to wear to an interview to convey an overall impression of professionalism, you are attempting to manage the impressions others form about you. When you try to manage the information you convey about yourself, the activity is called **self-presentation**.

We can also try to shape the impressions formed of other people as well as impressions formed of products. You might have a job where it is your responsibility to use appearance to shape the impressions formed about a new product (e.g., brand manager). You might have a responsibility to use appearance to shape impressions of a political candidate. For example, when in the course of a political campaign a campaign staff attempts to **spin** or reinterpret in a positive way what the candidate said or did, they are engaging in impression management (of the candidate). Regardless of the object of the impression, through impression management we actively regulate information in order to influence the impressions formed by others (Schlenker & Weigold, 1992).

Dramaturgy

Impressions of self can be managed by manipulating clothing and other props according to sociologist Erving Goffman (1959). Basing his work in symbolic interactionism (see Chapter 9, "Dress and the Self" for a discussion of this perspective), he described how people want to know, in advance, what others expect of them and what to expect of others. A **role** is the behavior that we expect of others who occupy certain social positions. Knowing how the situation one has entered is defined, what roles are being enacted, and what type of behavior is expected, people quickly know how they need to act to get the desired response from others. For example, suppose you were invited to someone's home for a meal. Upon arriving for the meal, you are directed by your friend who is wearing a swimsuit and coverup to the backyard where a swimming pool is located along with a picnic table set up with paper plates and plastic silverware. You immediately assume that behaviors will be informal and you will be asked to serve yourself. Compare this to another invitation for a meal where when you arrive you are escorted to a dining room where the table is set with crystal and cloth napkins. You immediately have a different set of expectations for your behavior and the behavior of your hosts.

There are many sources of information possible about others (e.g., past experience, Facebook page, gossip, Instagram) but in a first encounter situation, information can be limited to appearance cues such as dress. Because people infer information about others on the basis of their dress and appearance, we can control how we are treated by others by making the "right" presentation of self to others (Goffman, 1959). Another way to describe making the right presentation is to say that people can enact a role and give a **performance** to attempt to manage how others treat them. A performance was described as "all the activity of a given participant on a given occasion which serves to

influence in any way any of the other participants" (Goffman, p. 15).

By talking about people's interactions with others as performances, he was able to explain everyday behaviors by drawing analogies between theater performances and everyday performances, hence his use of the term *dramaturgy* (Goffman, 1959). **Dramaturgy** is a term used to describe the representation of the main elements of drama on the stage. Sociological dramaturgy refers to the idea that who you are is dependent on time, place, and audience. In other words, just like an actor or actress takes on a role and makes a performance of a specific individual for a play, in everyday life people are taking on roles and performing for each other. Generally, the role is the particular position and associated image that a single individual wants to convey to others. "It is the essence, the contrived sense of self, that the individual wants to project to the world" (Kivisto & Pittman, 2007, p. 274).

Performances of self change depending on who the audience is, the context of the performance, and the time. For example, in your history your parents probably have asked you on at least one occasion to be on your best behavior when relatives were visiting. Or perhaps you change your behavior when you go on a date as compared to when you are attending class. In each instance you were managing your presentation of self. For example, you may have behaved a little better than you might have otherwise when the relatives were visiting or were a little shyer than you might otherwise be in a dating situation versus a classroom. Changing your behavior based on the situation does not suggest you are a completely different person from context to context, but it does suggest that people manage what aspects of the self to present to specific people. People can be sincere or authentic in their presentations because they want the audience members to believe that they are who they say they are (Goffman, 1959). An individual can also be cynical in the performance and not care what the audience members believe about him or her and the performance.

The term **front** has been used to talk about all of the materials needed to make a performance (Goffman, 1959). Again thinking about a theater performance, we can think about the front as the context for the performance and all the required props such as the furniture, the decorations, and other background items. The term **personal front** is used to describe all of the items that we specifically connect with the individual including dress, age, gender, facial expressions, and the like. Some of these items do not typically vary over time (e.g., gender) and some may change over the course of a performance (e.g., facial expression). You can think about a person's personal front as a mask that is worn for the performance. Because cues such as dress and other items (e.g., furniture) are assigned meanings, people can manage the impressions formed about them.

Passing

Assigning meaning to dress cues allows us the ability to announce to someone else a specific role we are playing (e.g., leader) or identity we have (e.g., athlete). Because people will rely on these cues and generally do not question them, this process of assigning roles and identities to others allows for the possibility of deception. You can, at least for a short time, have others believe you are someone (i.e., have an identity) that in reality, you are not. The term used to describe this is **passing** or **impersonation**. For example, suppose you want someone else to believe that you are high status and wealthy. You can get a credit card, buy a designer outfit, rent a Mercedes Benz, and meet the person you intend to deceive at an exclusive restaurant. You can control the contact you have with this individual and thus, present all the cues to this specific audience member to deceive him or her into thinking you are high status and wealthy. A recent controversial case of passing was reported in June 2015 (Pérez-Peña, 2015). Rachel Dolezal, a blond white woman, passed as being partly of black descent. As such she became president of the NAACP (National Association for the Advancement of Colored People) in Spokane, Washington. After her white ancestry became public, she was pressured to resign from that position. Although the NAACP has had white officials in the past, in this instance Ms. Dolezal's credibility was the issue.

Managing the impressions that others form of you requires that you control the contact and information

Figure 5.4

The sexual assaults on the Fort Apache Indian reservation in Whiteriver, Arizona were committed by someone wearing clothing that identified him as a police officer.

individuals have about you. Arenas where that type of control is possible, making deception possible as well, include online dating sites, classified advertisements, and Facebook. All three arenas provide a context where the individual controls the information that is available about his/her and who has access to that information. Individuals could develop different personalities under false names with the intention of deceiving others about their true identities and characteristics.

Evidence that individuals do attempt to pass and that this behavior can have serious consequences comes from a report of sexual assaults. A man was able to pose as a police officer by wearing a dark shirt and hat with the word *police* on them. He raped ten girls and a young woman after "arresting" them on the Fort Apache Indian reservation in Whiteriver, Arizona. The victims were vulnerable because they trusted that someone dressed as a police officer legitimately was a police officer. In effect, they expected someone dressed as a policeman to behave in a way that was consistent with the part for which he was dressed (Figure 5.4).

Restrictions to Passing

There are barriers you may have to overcome to be able to successfully pass. Not all individuals have access to the props that are needed to convince someone else you have an identity that in reality you do not. For example, there can be intrinsic restrictions to passing. It may simply not be possible for an individual to gain access to the items

---

IN-CLASS ACTIVITY
Passing

Identify one movie where a character in that movie engaged in passing. What are the outcomes frequently associated with passing as depicted by the movie?

needed. In our previous example, if you do not have access to credit, it would be extremely difficult for you to pass as wealthy.

There are also **moral restrictions** against passing. For some, it is simply immoral behavior to pretend to be someone that you are not. To do so may be harmful to others. For example, suppose you are a student studying to be a lawyer. You tell a stranger that you actually are a lawyer. You even give him some legal advice. It turns out that your advice was inaccurate and results in a lawsuit. Thus, even though you may have been well-intentioned, your advice resulted in harm.

There are other restrictions to passing. Organic restrictions are linked to the body. **Organic restrictions** are present when there are aspects of your body that are inconsistent with the identity you are trying to claim for yourself. Returning to our original example, which was a desire to pass as wealthy and as high status, having un-manicured, rough, and calloused hands from outdoor work would make it difficult to pass for high status and wealthy. High-status people do not generally engage in outdoor manual work. They hire other people to do this work for them.

Finally, there can be **knowledge restrictions** that prevent someone from passing. Continuing with a desire to pass as wealthy and high status, a knowledge restriction indicates that there may be information obtained through cultivation and socialization that someone with this identity has that you do not have. This information could come from having had life experiences as a result of their wealth (e.g., extensive travel, friendships) that are simply not as available to other individuals.

Role Distance

Our discussion of acting and using dress to take on roles with the possibility of deception raises the question of when are individuals being sincere in their presentations of self and when are they only acting? Perhaps we can best answer this question with the concept of role distance. **Role distance** is the perceived difference between your true self and the role you are playing. All of us have experienced at one time or another, a distance between the way we were feeling and the way we were acting. For example, suppose you are a flight attendant. One of the key aspects of your position is to be friendly and helpful to passengers. One day you wake up with a headache. By the time you get to work, you still are not feeling well. Regardless

of how you actually feel, you have to act helpful and be friendly. Therefore, you experience a distancing from your thoughts about yourself and your actual behavior. In this instance, the distancing may only be temporary. Eventually your headache will go away and you will act in a way that is consistent with your feelings. But what if the distance you experience is not temporary?

Since it is more demanding to play a role that is not consistent with your true self than it is to play a role that is consistent with your true self, one might expect that the greater distance you experience from your true self and a role you enact, the more strain you will experience and the greater difficulty you will have in maintaining that role and your thoughts about who you are. The solution may be to give up the role or avoid acting in those types of roles to begin with. You might also somehow learn to deal with the conflict you experience either by becoming cynical or changing your ideas about who you really are. Since it is probably not realistic to give up your ideas about who you really are, if the distancing is a result of a work role you play, you might decide to quit that job and find another. If you think that you will not be able to find another job, you might see cynicism as the best alternative, taking the view that you can do this work role because it means you will be able to keep paying your bills and also recognizing that it is a role that is not reflective of your true self.

Dress and Impression Management

Some researchers have explicitly studied the role of dress variables in impression management. In a study of "artificial" tanners (that is, people who tanned using tanning beds), researchers were interested why people tan in light of the medical information that tanning is linked to cancer (Vannini & McCright, 2004). They found that "artificial" tanners perceived tanned skin as connoting health, sociability, fitness, attractiveness, and affluence. Research participants noted that they tanned because they wanted to be seen as having those qualities (i.e., to manage the impressions they conveyed to others); they believed that tanned skin was a way to manage impressions of health, sociability, fitness, attractiveness, and affluence. However, a recent incident in the media has resulted in negative press for salon tanning. In April 2012, New Jersey resident Patricia Krentcil, also known as "Tanning Mom" (Martinez, 2012), captured media attention over tanning. New Jersey school officials had observed burns on Krentcil's five-year-old daughter's legs and notified authorities ("Grand jury says no indictment," 2013) (Figure 5.5). Krentcil was arrested for child endangerment for allegedly permitting her daughter to use a tanning bed. At the time New Jersey law banned children under fourteen from using tanning salons. Although the charges were eventually dropped, the case did inspire new legislation in New Jersey that now bars children under seventeen from using the salons.

Other researchers have studied how dress is used to manage impressions of workplace role performance (i.e., to purposely convey certain information to others) (Rafaeli, Dutton, Harquail, & Mackie-Lewis, 1997). They found that dressing appropriately for one's role was a way to convey an impression of willingness to serve client needs. They concluded that employees actively worked to manipulate dress symbols to communicate to others and themselves.

Managing one's presentation to others is not limited to the formal workplace. Researchers studied the extent to which MBA students used workplace attire to manage other's impressions (Peluchette, Karl, & Rust, 2006). Instead of studying how dress is perceived by others, as is done in impression formation research, these researchers examined the extent to which the students used dress to influence the impressions they conveyed or to achieve

certain goals. They found that not everyone used dress for impression management purposes. However, those who valued dress used it for impression management purposes and believed it had a positive impact on work-related outcomes. The researchers also measured self-monitoring and found that respondents high in self-monitoring (i.e., those who attempt to control how they present themselves to others) were more likely than those low in self-monitoring to believe that their dress positively affected both their power and influence at work.

Managing Another's Appearance to Impact Perceptions of Self

Most studies of impression management focus on the way people manage their own appearances to affect impressions of themselves. However, one researcher found that mothers used their children's appearances to affect others' impressions of them (the mothers) (Collett, 2005). In a study of mothers of young children, she found that mothers were concerned about how their children looked. As a result, they attempted to manage the impressions conveyed by their children because they believed that those impressions reflected on them. Mothers believed that their children's appearances were important for communicating the characteristic of being a "good" mother. Thus, these women used impression management both to convey desirable impressions and to reinforce this aspect of themselves. These studies of dress and impression management reveal that dress is used to convey desired impressions (willingness to help clients, health, sociability, fitness, attractiveness, and affluence) and to affect outcomes (power and influence in the workplace). Dress is also used to reinforce one's persona (mother). If these studies are representative, then impression management appears to be used in several aspects of daily life (i.e., in the workplace, in the home, and in leisure activities).

CASUAL BUSINESS DRESS

Since people make attempts to manage how they are perceived by others using dress, it follows that some businesses and organizations might attempt to manage the impressions formed by patrons of the business or organization. One way to control such impressions is for companies to develop **dress code** guidelines for their employees' dress and overall appearance. This practice is consistent with

Figure 5.5
Patricia Krentcil was suspected of taking her five-year-old daughter into a tanning booth. Vannini and McCright (2004) found that artificial tanners like Krentcil perceived tanned skin to be healthy and attractive.

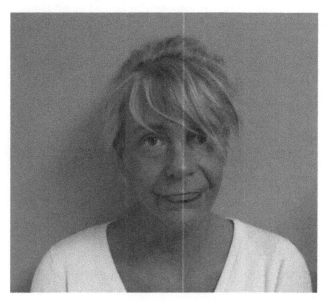

research that has shown that the inferences people convey to others extend to the companies for which they work (Workman & Johnson, 1989a). This process is described in detail in Chapter 4, "Dress and Social Cognition."

When we think of dress codes we often think of companies that require uniforms of some type. The classic men's suit (i.e., jacket, shirt, tie, pants) was for many years the required "uniform" of a businessman. As women entered the workforce in the 1970s and 1980s the skirted suit was frequently presented as appropriate dress for women in business (Figure 5.6).

Some organizations develop very specific guidelines for their employees. They develop **formal dress codes** that prohibit individuals from wearing some styles of dress at work and require other styles to be worn. The term *formal* was used to describe these dress codes because the overall appearance of an employee was formal rather than casual.

Figure 5.6

Contemporary professional dress for women.

Given the research demonstrating that we use dress to manage impressions, it is perhaps surprising that so many businesses in the US adopted casual business dress (CBD) codes in the late 1990s.

With all the attention paid to CBD in the popular press, some researchers focused on studying it. In one study, researchers surveyed Fortune 500 companies regarding their reasons for instituting CBD (Foust et al., 1999). The most important reason cited to establish the CBD codes was to improve employee morale. Other reasons for adopting a CBD code were that it was an added benefit at no cost to the company and that it would improve productivity. Most respondents agreed that CBD would save employees money and that it would function as a status leveler. In other research, companies that had CBD were found to have less absenteeism than companies without CBD (Yates & Jones, 1998).

On the other hand, some researchers have found that formality of workplace dress was positively related to desirable outcomes in the workplace (Norton & Franz, 2004). For example, employees who dressed formally reported high conscientiousness. As compared to employees who did not prefer formal dress policies, those who did had higher job satisfaction, reported more time commitment, had higher-level jobs, and supervised more employees.

Other researchers conducted a field experiment wherein they investigated the effects of interventions on employee performance (Raj, Nelson, & Rao, 2006). Forty employees were asked to suggest an incentive that would improve their performance; twenty-three picked CBD and seventeen picked flexible hours. All employee performance was observed for three weeks to establish a **baseline**, or beginning performance level. Then employees were allowed to wear CBD or to establish flexible hours, whichever they had selected for three weeks (treatment period). During this period their performance was monitored to determine the effect of the treatment (CBD or flexible hours). Finally, they were all monitored for six months, the post treatment period, to assess continuing performance. What the researchers found was that both incentives improved performance even six months later and both incentives were related to increased job satisfaction. The researchers pointed out that neither of these incentives cost the company money to implement. However, they also noted that the incentives themselves might have been effective, not due to the nature of the incentives per se, but rather due to the fact that they were self-selected by the employees.

Two researchers specifically studied the change from wearing a formal (suit) uniform to a casual one (khakis and t-shirt) for flight attendants (Adomaitis & Johnson, 2005). The thirty-seven flight attendants who were interviewed first wore formal uniforms, then casual ones, and then returned to wearing the formal ones. The flight attendants shared that the formal uniform enhanced their abilities to perform their role, communicated their flight attendant role, and conveyed authority. Attendants reported that the casual uniforms hindered their ability to perform their job, limited their effectiveness, and reduced their authority. The researchers concluded that the casual uniform actually created barriers for these workers. Since the researchers demonstrated that attendants' clothing affected their behavior and feelings, the research provides support for opting for formal dress in the workplace.

To summarize, the research on CBD is mixed. Some researchers have found that casual dress in the workplace improves employee productivity and job satisfaction. Other researchers have found that casual dress was a hindrance to employees' ability to perform their jobs. Whether or not CBD is truly associated with all the advantages or disadvantages noted in the popular press is questionable.

ROLE THEORY

One way to explain some of the research findings on workplace dress and impression formation is through the use of role theory. In fact, much of the research in dress and human behavior which has focused on the effects of dress on others' behaviors has used the theoretical framework of role theory (e.g., Bickman, 1974; Geffner & Gross, 1984). **Role theory** helps to explain why we think people should dress in a certain way (Sarbin, 1954). It is a theory from sociology and begins with the notion of a status, a socially recognized position in a social system. A role is defined as the behavior generally expected of one who occupies a particular status. The word *role* is another metaphor from theater. According to role theory, within a society a certain position or status has associated with it a set of norms and expectations. A norm is an expectation for how people are supposed to act, think, or feel in specific situations; this includes expectations for how people should dress. These norms and expectations specify the behavior of the person in that role toward others and specify the behavior of others towards the person in that role.

As we enact roles, how we act (behave) and how we appear (what we look like) is very important because what we wear, the makeup we put on, and our hairstyles help to reinforce the role being enacted. As we discussed in the previous section on dramaturgy, dress helps us play a part and helps us to be perceived by others as fitting that part. Clothing, makeup, accessories, and hairstyles are props that facilitate or hinder enactment of our roles (Goffman, 1959).

Wearing the correct dress for the role helps us manage our impressions. Looking the part conveys to others that you have the skills and knowledge to perform the expected behaviors. This concept is evident in the study of flight attendant dress, noted earlier in this chapter, because when dressed in the casual uniforms the attendants felt hindered in their ability to perform their flight attendant role and they felt limited in their effectiveness and authority (Adomaitis & Johnson, 2005).

Dressing-Out-of-Role

Role theory also explains why dressing out of role helps people "hide in plain sight." People can hide by dressing out-of-role, because that type of dress evokes expectations for role congruent behaviors. Consider the movies *Sister Act, U.S. Marshalls,* and *Mrs. Doubtfire*. In each of these movies a main character is able to assume a different role by wearing clothing that is out-of-role for their typical selves but consistent with the new role. Because we

---

Figure 5.7

In the movie *Mrs. Doubtfire*, Robin Williams dressed out-of-role as a woman to be able to work as a live-in nanny for his children.

expect people to dress consistently with their roles we do not consider that a lounge singer might be disguised as a nun or that a US marshall would opt to wear a big chicken suit, or that an estranged dad would adopt the appearance of a middle-aged female housekeeper (Figure 5.7). The fact that these movie characters do adopt these appearances is funny precisely because they are out-of-role and unexpected.

Thus far in this chapter we have discussed various social cognitive processes and how they are affected by dress and related variables. In the next section, we present research that outlines how dress affects actual behaviors and some models to illustrate the nature of that process.

BEHAVIORAL CONSEQUENCES OF SOCIAL PERCEPTION

Dress Affects the Behavior of Others

Although most research on social psychological aspects of dress focuses on social perception, there is a body of research that addresses how one's dress affects the actual behaviors of others and of oneself. Research strategies used to study the effects of dress on behaviors include laboratory experiments, field experiments, and fieldwork. For example, researchers have found that the dress of customers in retail stores affected the speed that they were served by salespeople (Kim & Lennon, 2005; Lennon & Davis, 1989b). These two studies revealed that what someone wears affects how others behave towards her/him.

Recently researchers have studied dress color to determine if it has behavioral consequences. They showed men a picture of a woman wearing a red T-shirt or the same woman wearing a blue T-shirt (Kayser, Elliot, & Feltman, 2010). When the men expected to interact with the woman wearing the red T-shirt they placed their chairs significantly closer to where she was expected to sit, as compared to the men who expected to interact with the woman wearing the blue T-shirt. In another study, male drivers were found to be more likely to pick up female hitchhikers when they wore red T-shirts as compared to T-shirts of other colors (Guéguen, 2012). In an online study, when a woman was depicted wearing a red T-shirt she received more requests for contact than when wearing

any other color T-shirt (Guéguen & Jacob, 2013). In all three of the studies, men behaved differently when women wore red clothing as compared to other colors.

Dress Affects One's Own Behaviors

A few researchers have found that one's own clothing can affect one's own behaviors. For example, researchers found that female research participants who donned a swimsuit and then took a math test performed worse on the math test than female participants who donned a sweater and then took the math test (Fredrickson, Roberts, Noll, Quinn, & Twenge, 1998). In a subsequent study from Australia, gay men who wore and evaluated a pair of Speedo briefs performed differently from other gay men who wore and evaluated a turtleneck sweater in an experimental task (Martins, Tiggemann, & Kirkbride, 2007). In these studies, the clothing participants wore affected their performance on experimental tasks. In another study, researchers wondered whether wearing black uniform jerseys might predispose the wearer to be more aggressive (Frank & Gilovich, 1988). They found that participants wearing black jerseys choose to play more aggressive games than participants wearing white jerseys. In each of these studies, the dress manipulations affected the behavior of the person wearing the clothing.

More recently, researchers determined that when clothing is worn that has symbolic meaning for the wearer, it has behavioral consequences (Adam & Galinsky, 2012). The researchers took an "enclothed cognition" perspective. They maintained that for one's own clothing to affect one's own behavior two conditions must be met: (a) the person must be wearing clothing with symbolic meaning and (b) the symbolic meaning must be understood by the person (and relevant to the experimental task). In their study, participants put on a white lab coat (Figure 5.8). Half of them were told that it was a doctor's coat and the other half was told that it was a painter's coat. Another group of participants saw the white lab coat spread out on a table and were told it was a doctor's coat, but did not wear the coat. The experimental task involved selective attention to details in a diagram (i.e., ability to focus on relevant details and ignore irrelevant details), which is important for physicians, but not for painters. Results showed that participants who wore the doctor's coat noted

Figure 5.8
Adam and Galinsky (2012) in their research used coats like these, which can be worn by doctors or painters.

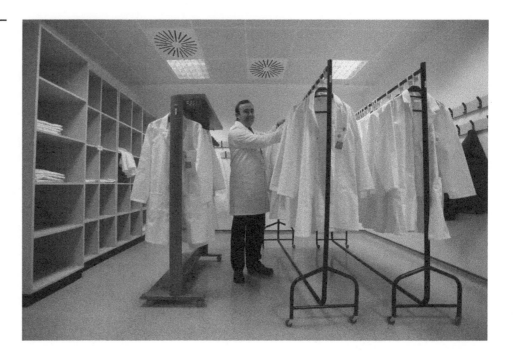

more details than participants who saw the doctor's coat, who in turn noted more details than participants who wore the painter's coat. In this study what the participant wore and understood about it, affected their performance on the experimental task.

Finally, researchers studied the effects of wearing designer sunglasses on one's own behaviors (Gino, Norton, & Ariely, 2010). Although all participants were given authentic Chloe sunglasses to wear, half the participants were told that the sunglasses were counterfeit Chloe sunglasses and the rest were told the sunglasses were authentic Chloe sunglasses. While counterfeits convey status to others, they also are a reminder to the wearers that they are conveying an inaccurate impression (i.e., they are pretending to have enough money to purchase authentic Chloe sunglasses). Those who thought their sunglasses were counterfeit cheated more on two experimental tasks than those who thought they were wearing authentic designer sunglasses. Thus, the dress variable (sunglasses) affected the behavior of those who wore them.

To summarize, researchers have demonstrated that there are behavioral consequences to social perception. What a person wears affects how others behave toward that person (Kim & Lennon, 2005; Lennon & Davis, 1989b). In addition, researchers have also found that what people wear affects their own behavior (Adam & Galinsky, 2012; Frank & Gilovich, 1988; Fredrickson et al., 1998; Gino et al., 2010; Martins et al., 2007).

In an attempt to summarize the research on how dress affects actual behavior, researchers content analyzed ninety-three studies published in journal articles over a fifty-year period from 1955 to 2004 (Johnson, Yoo, Kim, & Lennon, 2008). They focused only on research that investigated the effects of dress on behavior. Dress significantly affected the behavior of others in 85.3 percent of the research analyzed. The most common behavior studied in that research was helping behavior. Other frequently investigated behaviors as a function of dress were obedience, invasion of interaction territory, disclosure, and aggression.

Perspectives That Explain Why Dress Influences Behavior

Johnson and her colleagues offered symbolic interaction, Livesley and Bromley's model of impression formation, and the S-O-R Model as perspectives that could be used to frame research about behavior as a function of dress (2008). **Symbolic interaction** maintains that one's dress communicates information to others because people attribute meaning to dress cues (Stone, 1962). Stone suggested that dress might affect behaviors, but did not go so far as to articulate how that might happen. (Symbolic interaction as a perspective to understand how dress is used and can influence behavior is discussed in detail in Chapter 9, "Dress and the Self").

Figure 5.9
The S-O-R Model applied to dress stimuli.

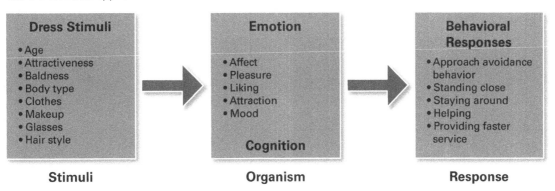

In one model of impression formation, discussed in the last chapter, the final stage of person perception is called anticipatory set or verbal report (Livesley & Bromley, 1973).

According to their model, the expectations evoked at that stage could take the form of the perceiver's behavior toward an individual. The model seems to suggest that for dress to affect behavior it would first have to be selected as a cue, then would have to evoke an inference (i.e., social perception), and then could evoke behavior. However, this sequence is not explicitly articulated or tested, so it is also possible that once dress is selected as a cue it could directly affect behavior without first evoking an inference.

The **S-O-R Model** was developed to explain how environments affect behavior (Mehrabian & Russell, 1974). The S-O-R Model posits that stimuli (S) in the environment evoke affective states in the organism (O) in the forms of pleasure, arousal, and dominance and the affective states in turn evoke responses (R) in the form of approach-avoidance behaviors. Recently researchers (Eroglu, Machleit, & Davis, 2001) have modified the model to include cognitive states in addition to affective states as part of the organism (O).

In their discussion of social perception and dress, researchers suggested that dress could affect impressions, which in turn could affect behaviors (Lennon & Davis, 1989a). Applying that suggestion to the S-O-R Model, dress is an example of stimuli (S), impressions are an example of cognition (O) and behaviors are an example of a response (R). (See Figure 5.9 for a diagram of this relationship). Since dress is the near environment for the body, the S-O-R Model can be used to explain how dress affects behavior according to Johnson and her colleagues (2008). According to this model, dress would first evoke affective (or cognitive) states in the organism (O) and then that evoked state would precipitate a behavioral response (R). Thus this model suggests that dress does not affect behavior directly, unlike the approach suggested by Livesley and Bromley (1973).

Chapter Summary

Social cognition is the study of how we process information about people and includes social perception. Discussed in this chapter as part of social cognition are attribution, dramaturgy, impression management, and impression formation. We considered two models of impression formation: Livesley and Bromley's model, and the S-O-R Model. The S-O-R Model, symbolic interaction, and Livesley and Bromley's model can also explain the behavioral consequences of impression formation. Implicit personality theory and role theory were also discussed. Finally, rating scales, number of discriminations, and scale endpoints were discussed in the context of social perception research.

Key Terms

attribution	formal dress codes	number of discriminations	role theory
attribution theories	front	ordinary personology	self-presentation
baseline	impersonation	organic restrictions	S-O-R Model
blaming the victim	implicit personality theory	passing	spin
controllability	impression management	performance	stability
dramaturgy	knowledge restrictions	personal front	symbolic interaction
dress codes	locus of causality	role	
endpoints	moral restrictions	role distance	

Discussion Questions

1. Identify your own impression management strategies. Discuss your strategies with a partner, and identify common strategies.

2. What is passing? Use the movie or theater production you identified in the In-Class Activity earlier in the chapter to explain and provide examples of the following terms as they relate to passing: role, role distance, personal front, front region, and back region.

3. Identify a context where you were required to follow a formal dress code. How was this code developed? In what ways might the presence of a formal dress code enhance your impression of a business when you apply for a job?

4. Role theory helps to explain why we think people should dress in a certain way. Consider yourself as a manager of a department store. Describe appropriate dress for yourself while at work.

5. A research study found that people who dressed in an attractive way might receive more friendly services from the salesperson than people who dressed in a less attractive way. Use the S-O-R Model to explain this result.

STUDiO™

Visit your book's STUDIO for additional quiz questions and vocabulary flashcards!

Suggested Readings

Adam, H., & Galinsky, A. D. (2012). Enclothed cognition. *Journal of Experimental Social Psychology, 48*, 918–925.

Fredrickson, B., & Roberts, T., Noll, S., Quinn, D., & Twenge, J. (1998). That swimsuit becomes you: Sex differences in self-objectification, restrained eating, and math performance. *Journal of Personality and Social Psychology, 75*, 269–284.

Guéguen, N., & Jacob, C. (2013). Color and cyber-attractiveness: Red enhances men's attraction to women's internet personal ads. *Color Research & Application, 38*(4), 309–312.

Johnson, K. K. P., Yoo, J.-J., Kim, M. J., & Lennon, S. J. (2008). Dress and human behavior: A review and critique. *Clothing and Textiles Research Journal, 26*, 3–22.

References

Adam, H., & Galinsky, A. D. (2012). Enclothed cognition. *Journal of Experimental Social Psychology, 48*, 918–925.

Adomaitis, A., & Johnson, K. K. P. (2005). Casual versus formal uniforms: Flight attendants' self-perceptions and perceived appraisals by others. *Clothing and Textiles Research Journal, 23*, 88–101.

The Arizona Republic (2006). *11th victim ID'd in Whiteriver serial rape case*. Retrieved from http://www.seattletimes.com/nation-world/arizona-reservation-terrorized-by-rapist-posing-as-policeman/

Asch, S. E. (1946). Forming impressions of personality. *Journal of Abnormal Social Psychology, 41*, 258–290.

Baron, R. (1983). "Sweet smell of success"? The impact of pleasant artificial scents on evaluations of job applicants. *Journal of Applied Psychology, 68*, 709–713.

Behling, D. U., & Williams, E. A. (1991). Influence of dress on perception of intelligence and expectations of scholastic achievement. *Clothing and Textiles Research Journal, 9*, 1–7.

Bell, E. L. (1991). Adult's perception of male garment styles. *Clothing and Textiles Research Journal, 10*, 8–12.

Bickman, L. (1974). The social power of a uniform. *Journal of Applied Social Psychology, 4*(1), 47–61.

Black Friday violence: 2 shot in armed robberies, 15 others pepper-sprayed (2011, November 25). Retrieved from http://usnews.nbcnews.com/_news/2011/11/25/9012057-black-friday-violence-2-shot-in-armed-robberies-15-others-pepper-sprayed

Bruner, J. S., & Tagiuri, R. (1954). The perception of people. In G. Lindzey (Ed.), *Handbook of social psychology* (Vol. 2, pp. 634–654). Reading, MA: Addison-Wesley.

Buckley, H. M. & Haeffner, J. E. (1984). The physical attractiveness stereotype using dress as a facilitator. *Journal of Consumer Studies and Home Economics, 8*, 351–358.

Butler, J., Pryor, B., & Grieder, M. (1998). Impression formation as a function of male baldness. *Perceptual and Motor Skills, 86*, 347–350.

Carr, D. (2008). Media and retailers both built Black Friday. *New York Times*. Retrieved from http://www.nytimes.com/2008/12/01/business/media/01carr.html?_r=1&ref=media

Christman, L. A., & Branson, D. H. (1990). Influence of physical disability and dress of female job applicants on interviewers. *Clothing and Textiles Research Journal, 8*, 51–57.

Clayton, R., Lennon, S. J., & Larkin, J. (1987). Perceived fashionability of a garment as inferred from the age and body type of the wearer. *Home Economics Research Journal, 15*, 237–246.

Collett, J. L. (2005). What kind of mother am I? Impression management and the social construction of motherhood. *Symbolic Interaction, 28*, 327–247.

Damhorst, M. L. (1984–85). Meanings of clothing cues in social context. *Clothing and Textiles Research Journal, 3*(2), 39–48.

Dayan, S. H., Cho, K., Siracusa, M., & Gutierrez-Borst, S. (2015). Quantifying the impact cosmetic make-up has on age perception and the first impression projected. *Journal of Drugs in Dermatology, 14*(4), 366–374.

Dixson, B. J., & Brooks, R. C. (2013). The role of facial hair in women's perceptions of men's attractiveness, health, masculinity and parenting abilities. *Evolution and Human Behavior, 34*(3), 236–241.

Eroglu, S. A., Machleit, K. A., & Davis, L. M. (2001). Atmospheric qualities of online retailing: A conceptual model and implications. *Journal of Business Research, 54*, 177–184.

Ferguson, H. (1999). Body piercing, *British Medical Journal, 319*(7225), 1627.

Foust, S., Cassill, N., Herr, D., & Williamson, N. (1999). Adoption of the casual workplace by United States Fortune 500 companies. *Journal of the Textile Institute, 90 Part 2*(2), 147–162.

Frank, M. & Gilovich, T. (1988). The dark side of self and social perception: Black uniforms and aggression in professional sports. *Journal of Personality and Social Psychology, 54*, 74–85.

Fredrickson, B., & Roberts, T., Noll, S., Quinn, D., & Twenge, J. (1998). That swimsuit becomes you: Sex differences in self–objectification, restrained eating, and math performance. *Journal of Personality and Social Psychology, 75*, 269–284.

Geffner, R., & Gross, M. (1984). Sex-role behavior and obedience to authority: A field study. *Sex Roles, 10*, 973–985.

Gerrard, S., & Dickinson, J. (2005). Women's working wardrobes: A study using card sorts. *Expert Systems, 22*, 108–114.

Gilbert, D. T. (1998). Ordinary personology. In D. T. Gilbert, S. T. Fiske, & G. Lindzey (Eds.), *The handbook of social psychology* (4th ed., Vol 2, pp. 89–150). New York, NY: McGraw-Hill.

Gillath, O., Bahns, A. J., Ge, F., & Crandall, C. S. (2012). Shoes as a source of first impressions. *Journal of Research in Personality, 46*(4), 423–430.

Gino, F., Norton, M. I., & Ariely, D. (2010). The counterfeit self: The deceptive costs of faking it. *Psychological Science, 21*(5), 712–720.

Goffman, E. (1959). *The presentation of self in everyday life.* Garden City, NJ: Doubleday.

Gordon, L.M., & Graham, S. (2006). Attribution theory. In N. Salkind (Ed.) *The Encyclopedia of Human Development* (Vol 1, pp. 142–144), Thousand Oaks, CA: Sage Publications.

Goudge, B., & Littrell, M. (1989). Attributions for job acquisition: Job skills, dress, and luck of female job applicants. *Clothing and Textiles Research Journal, 7*(4), 19–26.

Grand jury says no indictment for mom in tan salon visit by daughter, 5 (2013, February 27), CNN.com. Retrieved from http://www.cnn.com/2013/02/26/justice/new-jersey-tanning-case/

Guéguen, N. (2012). Color and women attractiveness: When red clothed women are perceived to have more intense sexual intent. *The Journal of Social Psychology, 152*(3), 261–265.

Guéguen, N., & Jacob, C. (2013). Color and cyber-attractiveness: Red enhances men's attraction to women's internet personal ads. *Color Research & Application, 38*(4), 309–312.

Guéguen, N., Stefan, J., & Renault, Q. (2016). Judgments toward women wearing high heels: A forced–choice evaluation. *Fashion and Textiles, 3*(1), 1–7.

Hareli, S., Harush, R., Suleiman, R., Cossette, M., Bergeron, S., Lavoie, V., Dugay, G., & Hess, U. (2009). When scowling may be a good thing: The influence of anger expressions on credibility. *European Journal of Social Psychology, 39*, 631–638.

Harvard Law School found in violation of Title IX, agrees to remedy sexual harassment, including sexual assault of students (2014, December 30). Retrieved from http://www.ed.gov/news/press-releases/harvard-law-school-found-violation-title-ix-agrees-remedy-sexual-harassment-including-sexual-assault-students

Higham, P. A., & Carment, W. D. (1992). The rise and fall of politicians: The judged heights of Broadbent Mulroney and Turner before and after the 1988 Canadian federal election. *Canadian Journal of Behavioral Science, 24*, 404–409.

Johnson, K. K. P. (1995). Attributions about date rape: Impact of clothing, sex, money spent, date type, and perceived similarity. *Family and Consumer Sciences Research Journal, 23*(3), 292–310.

Johnson, K. K. P., Crutsinger, C., & J. E. Workman (1994). Can professional women appear too masculine? The case of the necktie. *Clothing and Textiles Research Journal, 12*(2), 27–31.

Johnson, K. K. P., Ju, H. W., & Wu, J. (2016). Young adults' inferences surrounding an alleged sexual assault: Alcohol consumption, gender, dress, and appearance schematicity. *Clothing and Textiles Research Journal, 34*(2), 127–142. DOI: 10.1177/0887302X15624550.

Johnson, K. K. P. & Workman, J. E. (1992). Clothing and attributions concerning sexual harassment. *Home Economics Research Journal, 21* (2), 160–172.

Johnson, K. K. P. & Workman, J. E. (1994). Blaming the victim: Attributions concerning sexual harassment based on clothing, just-world belief, and sex of subject. *Home Economics Research Journal, 22* (4), 382–400.

Johnson, K. K. P., Yoo, J.-J., Kim, M. J., & Lennon, S. J. (2008). Dress and human behavior: A review and critique. *Clothing and Textiles Research Journal, 26,* 3–22.

Judge, T. A., & Cable, D. M. (2004). The effect of physical height on workplace success and income: Preliminary test of a theoretical model. *Journal of Applied Psychology, 89,* 428–441.

Kayser, D. N., Elliot, A. J., & Feltman, R. (2010). Red and romantic behavior in men viewing women. *European Journal of Social Psychology, 40*(6), 901–908.

Kim, M., & Lennon, S. J. (2005). The effects of customers' dress on salesperson's service in large-sized clothing specialty stores. *Clothing and Textiles Research Journal, 23*(2), 78–87.

Kingkade, T. (2015, July 24). The U.S. Department of Education's Office for Civil Rights is investigating 124 colleges and universities and 40 elementary and secondary schools over how they have handled sexual assault among students. *Huffington Post.* Retrieved from http://www.huffingtonpost.com/entry/schools-investigation-sexual-assault_us_55b19b43e4b0074ba5a40b77

Kivisto, P., & Pittman, D. (2007). Goffman's dramaturgical sociology: Personal sales and service in a commodified world. In P. Kivisto (Ed.) *Illuminating social life,* 5th ed. (pp. 271–290). Thousand Oaks, CA: Sage Publications.

Kohli, S. (2016, February 22). The problem with slut shaming in schools. *Los Angeles Times.* Retrieved from http://www.latimes.com/local/education/lausd/la-me-edu-slut-shaming-20160218-story.html

Kuzmanovic, B., Bente, G., von Cramon, D. Y., Schilbach, L., Tittgemeyer, M., & Vogeley, K. (2012). Imaging first impressions: distinct neural processing of verbal and nonverbal social information. *Neuroimage, 60*(1), 179–188.

Kyle, D., & Mahler, H. (1996). The effects of hair color and cosmetics use on perceptions of a female's ability. *Psychology of Women Quarterly, 20,* 447–455.

Lennon, S. J. (1990). Effects of clothing attractiveness on perceptions. *Home Economics Research Journal, 18,* 303–310.

Lennon, S. J., & Davis, L. L. (1989a). Clothing and human behavior from a social cognitive framework, Part I: Theoretical perspectives. *Clothing and Textiles Research Journal, 7*(4), 41–48.

Lennon, S. J., & Davis, L. (1989b). Customer service as a function of customer appearance and salesperson goals. *Home Economics Forum, 9,* 9–11, 18.

Lennon, S. J., & Miller, F. G. (1984). Salience of physical appearance in impression formation. *Home Economics Research Journal, 13,* 95–104.

Lennon, S. J., & Miller, F. G. (1984–85). Attire, physical appearance, and first impressions: More is less. *Clothing and Textiles Research Journal, 3*(1), 1–8.

Lewis, L., & Johnson, K. K. P. (1989). The effect of dress, cosmetics, sex of subject, and causal inference on attribution of victim responsibility. *Clothing and Textiles Research Journal, 8,* 22–29.

Livesley, W. J., & Bromley, D. B. (1973). *Person perception in childhood and adolescence.* New York, NY: John Wiley & Sons.

Martinez, A. (2011, November 26). Black Friday, blue bruises. Retrieved from http://www.newsy.com/videos/black-friday-blue-bruises/

Martinez, E. (2012, May 10). 'Tanning mom' Patricia Krentcil banned from over 60 tanning salons, report says, CBSNews.com. Retrieved from http://www.cbsnews.com/8301-504083_162-57431758-504083/tanning-mom-patricia-krentcil-banned-from-over-60-tanning-salons-report-says/

Martins, Y., Tiggemann, M., & Kirkbride, A. (2007). Those Speedos become them: The role of self-objectification in gay and heterosecual men's body image. *Personality and Social Psychology Bulletin, 33,* 634–647.

Mathes, E. W., Brennan, S. M., Haugen, P. M., & Rice, H. B. (1985). Ratings of physical attractiveness as a function of age. *Journal of Social Psychology, 125*(2), 157–168.

Maurer, T. W., & Robinson, D. W. (2008). Effects of attire, alcohol, and gender on perceptions of date rape. *Sex Roles, 58*(5-6), 423–434.

McCurry, J. W. (1996). Piazza: Casual dress trend threatens hosiery. *Textile World, 146*(11), 25.

Mehrabian, A., & Russell, J. A. (1974). *An approach to environmental psychology.* Cambridge, MA: MIT Press.

Miller, A.G. (1970). Role of physical attractiveness in impression formation. *Psychonomic Science, 19,* 241–243.

Moor, A. (2010). She dresses to attract, he perceives seduction: A gender gap in attribution of intent to women's revealing style of dress and its relation to blaming the victims of sexual violence. *Journal of International Women's Studies, 11*(4), 115–127.

Muscarella, F., & Cunningham, M. R. (1996). The evolutionary significance and social perception of male pattern baldness and facial hair. *Ethology and Sociobiology, 17*, 99–117.

Myers, A. L. (2006, October 10). Arizona reservation terrorized by rapist posing as policeman. *The Seattle Times*. Retrieved from http://www.seattletimes.com/nation-world/arizona-reservation-terrorized-by-rapist-posing-as-policeman/

Neave, N., & Shield, K. (2008). The effects of facial hair manipulation on female perceptions of attractiveness, masculinity, and dominance in male faces. *Personality and Individual Differences, 45*(5), 373–377.

Norton, S. D., & Franz, T. M. (2004). Methodological issues in research on business casual dress. *Journal of American Academy of Business, 5*(1/2), 130–137.

Paek, S. L. (1986). Effect of garment style on the perception of personal traits. *Clothing and Textiles Research Journal, 5*, 10–16.

Peluchette, J. V., Karl, K., & Rust, K. (2006). Dressing to impress: Beliefs and attitudes regarding workplace attire. *Journal of Business and Psychology, 21*, 45–63.

Pérez-Peña, R. (2015, June 15). Rachel Dolezal leaves N.A.A.C.P. post as past discrimination suit is revealed. *New York Times*. Retrieved from http://www.nytimes.com/2015/06/16/us/rachel-dolezal-quits-naacp-in-spokane.html?action=click&contentCollection=U.S.&module=RelatedCoverage&region=Marginalia&pgtype=article

Professionalism in the workplace (2013). Retrieved from http://www.ycp.edu/media/york-website/cpe/York-College-Professionalism-in-the-Workplace-Study-2013.pdf

Przygodzki-Lionet, N., Olivier, J., & Desrumaux, P. (2010). The effects of facial attractiveness, sex, internality of applicants on hiring decisions for managerial and non-managerial jobs. *Studia Psychologica, 52*(1), 53.

Rafaeli, A., Dutton, J., Harquail, C. V., & Machie-Lewis, S. (1997). Navigating by attire: The use of dress by female administrative employees. *The Academy of Management Journal, 40*(1), 9–45.

Raj, J. D., Nelson, J. A., & Rao, K. S, P (2006). A study of the effects of some reinforcers to improve performance of employees in a retail industry. *Behavior Modification, 30*, 848–866.

Riniolo, T. C., Johnson, K. C., Sherman, T. R., Misso, J. A. (2006). Hot or not: Do professors perceived as physically attractive receive higher student evaluations? *Journal of General Psychology, 133*(1), 19–35.

Rizzo, C. (2015, October 5). 9 women (and 1 man) share their worst slut-shaming stories at Amber Rose's SlutWalk. *Cosmopolitan*. Retrieved from http://www.cosmopolitan.com/sex-love/a47241/slut-walk-slut-shaming-interviews/

Rogers, P., Lowe, M., & Reddington, K. (2016). Investigating the victim pseudomaturity effect: How a victim's chronological age and dress style influences attributions in a depicted case of child sexual assault. *Journal of Child Sexual Abuse, 25*(1), 1–19.

Rosenberg, S., Nelson, C., & Vivekananthan, P. (1968). A multidimensional approach to the structure of personality impression. *Journal of Personality and Social Psychology, 9*, 283–294.

Ruggs E., Hebl M., & Williams A. (2015). Weight isn't selling: The insidious effects of weight stigmatization in retail settings. *Journal of Applied Psychology, 100*(5), 1483–1496.

Sarbin, T. R. (1954). Role theory. *The hand-book of social psychology, 1*, 223–258.

Schlenker, B. R, & Weigold, M. F. (1992). Interpersonal processes involving impression regulation and management. *Annual Review of Psychology, 43*, 133–168.

Schneider, D. J. (1973). Implicit personality theory: A review. *Psychological Bulletin, 79*, 294–309.

Sontag, M. S., & Schlater, J. D. (1995). Clothing and human values: A two-dimensional model for measurement. *Clothing and Textiles Research Journal, 13*, 1–10.

Stevenage, S. V., & McKay, Y. (1999). Model applicants: The effect of facial appearance on recruitment decisions. *British Journal of Psychology, 90*(2), 221–234.

Stone, G. P. (1962). Appearance and the self. In A. M. Rose (Ed.), *Human behavior and social processes: An interactionist approach* (pp. 86–118). New York, NY: Houghton Mifflin.

Swami, V., & Furnham, A. (2007). Unattractive, promiscuous and heavy drinkers: Perceptions of women with tattoos. *Body Image, 4*(4), 343–352.

Talamas, S. N., Mavor, K. I., & Perrett, D. I. (2016). Blinded by beauty: Attractiveness bias and accurate perceptions of academic performance. *PloS one, 11*(2), 1–18. e0148284.

Taniguchi, E., & Lee, H. E. (2015). Individuals' perception of others' self-esteem, psychological well-being and attractiveness: Role of body size and peers' comments among Japanese and Americans. *The Social Science Journal, 52*(2), 217–228.

Toronto 'slut walk' takes to city streets (2011, April 3). Retrieved from http://www.cbc.ca/news/canada/toronto/toronto-slut-walk-takes-to-city-streets-1.1087854

Townes, C. (2015, October 3). The feminist 'Slutwalk' movement just landed the perfect celebrity spokesperson. *Think Progress.* Retrieved from http://thinkprogress.org/culture/2015/10/03/3708674/amber-rose-slut-walk/

Thurston, J. L., Lennon, S. J., & Clayton, R. V. (1990). Influence of age, body type, currency of fashion detail, and type of garment on the professional image of women. *Home Economics Research Journal, 19*(2), 139–150.

Vannini, P., & McCright, A. M. (2004). To die for: The semiotic seductive power of the tanned body. *Symbolic Interaction, 27*(1), 309–332.

Walline, J. J., Sinnott, L., Johnson, E. D., Ticak, A., Jones, S. L., & Jones, L. A. (2008). What do kids think about kids in eyeglasses?. *Ophthalmic and Physiological Optics, 28*(3), 218–224.

Wells, W., & Siegel, B. (1961). Stereotyped somatotypes. *Psychological Reports, 8,* 77–78.

What is Title IX? (n.d.). Retrieved from http://www.sadker.org/TitleIX.html

Wilson, J. H., Beyer, D., & Monteiro, H. (2014). Professor age affects student ratings: Halo effect for younger teachers. *College Teaching, 62*(1), 20–24, DOI: 10.1080/87567555.2013.825574

Workman, J. E. (1984–85). Effects of appropriate and inappropriate attire on attributions of personal dispositions. *Clothing and Textiles Research Journal, 3*(1), 20–23.

Workman, J. E. (1988). Trait inferences based on perceived ownership of designer, brand name, or store brand jeans. *Clothing and Textiles Research Journal, 6*(2), 23–29.

Workman, J. E. (1990). Status characteristics theory: An application to clothing research. *Clothing and Textiles Research Journal, 8,* 49–54.

Workman, J. E., & Johnson, K. K. P. (1989a). The role of clothing in extended inferences. *Home Economics Research Journal, 18*(2), 164–169.

Workman, J. E., & Johnson, K. K. P. (1989b). The role of clothing in perpetuating ageism. *Journal of Home Economics, 81,* 11–15.

Workman, J. E., & Johnson, K. K. P. (1991). The role of cosmetics in impression formation. *Clothing and Textiles Research Journal, 10,* 63–67.

Workman, J. E., & Orr, R. L. (1996). Clothing, sex of subject, and rape myth acceptance as factors affecting attributions about an incident of acquaintance rape. *Clothing and Textiles Research Journal, 14,* 276–284.

Wyer, R. S., Hung, I. W., & Jiang, Y. (2008). Visual and verbal processing strategies in comprehension and judgment. *Journal of Consumer Psychology, 18,* 244–257.

Yates, D., & Jones, G. (1998). Casual dress days: Are there bottom-line impacts? *Organization Development Journal, 16*(1), 107–110.

Young, T. J., & French, L. A. (1996). Height and perceived competence of U. S. presidents. *Perceptual and Motor Skills, 87,* 321–322.

Zebrowitz, L. A., & Franklin Jr, R. G. (2014). The attractiveness halo effect and the babyface stereotype in older and younger adults: Similarities, own-age accentuation, and older adult positivity effects. *Experimental Aging Research, 40*(3), 375–393.

CHAPTER
6 DRESS AND PHYSICAL APPEARANCE

After reading and reflecting on the content of this chapter students should be able to:

- Analyze the presentation of self using the Rudd and Lennon (1994) model of body aesthetics.
- Explain how faces and bodies contribute to judgments of attractiveness and subsequent behavior.
- Evaluate how and why people purposefully manipulate their bodies.

INTRODUCTION

In this chapter we discuss aspects of our physical selves and dress. Two particular aspects of our physical selves affect our own and others' perceptions of us; these two aspects are our faces and our bodies (shape or size) and both contribute to attractiveness. We will see that our faces and bodies also affect others' behavior toward us, as well as our own behavior toward ourselves and toward others. Faces and bodies are stimuli in social cognition, or how we think, perceive, judge, and make inferences about people in the world around us. We also sometimes choose to purposefully manipulate our facial and bodily appearance; such manipulations are examples of dress as defined in Chapter 1, "Why Study Dress?" First we consider social comparison theory (Festinger, 1954). This social psychological theory has been used to explain appearance comparisons. Then we introduce a model of body aesthetics from Rudd and Lennon (1994). Other topics covered in this chapter include facial and body attractiveness, obesity stigma, and various purposeful manipulations of the body.

SOCIAL COMPARISON THEORY

Social comparison theory explains that as human beings we are motivated to self-evaluate, to know how well we are doing in various aspects of life. In social comparison we compare ourselves to objective standards (Festinger, 1954), but if objective standards are not available we will compare to other people, called **comparison targets**. For example, as a swim team member you know your school's records in the events you swim. After you finish swimming your events, you can compare your speed with your school's records. This represents an objective standard to which you can compare your performance. On the other hand you can also compare your speed to the speed of your teammates. In this instance, you are making a social comparison because you are comparing to other people. The theory was developed to explain opinion and ability comparison, but since has been used to explain appearance comparison (Richins, 1991). For example, if you want to determine if a new dress style is likely to become fashionable, you might seek out others to see if they have adopted that particular dress style.

Early researchers also found a link between social comparison and self-esteem (Morse & Gergen, 1970). In that research when an individual compared herself with someone more attractive (the comparison target), she experienced a decrease in self-esteem. If the comparison target was less attractive, the individual making the social comparison experienced an increase in self-esteem. Although we know that other factors affect the social comparison process (e.g., the domain of comparison), the theory is as valid today as it was in 1954 and recently has been used to explain how mothers use their adolescent daughters and how retail shoppers use other retail shoppers as comparison targets in terms of clothing consumption behaviors (Dahl, Argo, & Morales, 2012; Gentina, Decoopman, & Ruvio, 2013).

RUDD AND LENNON MODEL OF BODY AESTHETICS

The **Rudd and Lennon model** of body aesthetics holds that the body is an important contributor to personal appearance and judgments of overall attractiveness (Rudd & Lennon, 1994). This model (see Figure 6.1) explains the active construction of bodily appearance as a function of the US (or Western) **cultural aesthetic ideal,** or cultural ideal of beauty. In this case, since the model focuses on body aesthetics, it pertains to the cultural ideal of beauty with respect to the body. Rudd and Lennon acknowledge that clothing might also be important in their model, but do not address its importance.

The model suggests that people within a culture internalize the cultural aesthetic appearance standard and create and compare their appearances based on that standard through the process of social comparison (Festinger, 1954). In US culture such a standard might be represented by fashion models in the media. In fact, young women do report

comparing to fashion models in ads (Adomaitis & Johnson, 2008). Consider your own bodily appearance. According to the model, there is a US or Western ideal of beauty (perhaps exemplified by fashion models) that you presumably learn through socialization. You use that ideal as a frame of reference as you actively create your appearance; hence you compare to that ideal. When your evaluations of your appearance approximate the ideal, you feel good about yourself. This in turn is thought to lead to stronger personal and social identity and contributes to self-image.

IN-CLASS ACTIVITY
Cultural Ideal

Do you think that there is a cultural ideal of beauty for women and men in the US? What is it? In other words, what features or characteristics do you feel pressure to maintain to be attractive?

Figure 6.1
Graphic of the Rudd and Lennon model.

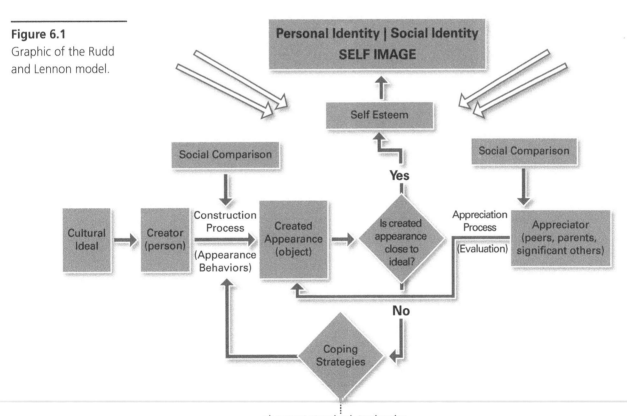

If you are not satisfied with your appearance (i.e., your appearance does not come close enough to the appearance ideal), you take steps, called **coping strategies** (e.g., dieting), to re-create your appearance so that it will more closely approximate the appearance ideal according to the Rudd and Lennon model (1994). As applied to bodily appearance, coping strategies can have positive or negative effects and include tanning, dieting, exercising, tattooing, purging, and cosmetic surgery (Figure 6.2). The model also recognizes that others' opinions about how you look affect the steps you take to change and remake your appearances. For example, researchers found that family feedback on appearance was positively related to frequency of using risky appearance-management behaviors

to change appearance (Lee & Johnson, 2009). Others' opinions of your appearance can be positive or negative and both can impel you to remake your appearance. For example, being told you are fat (negative comment) might make you start using diet pills to lose weight, while being told you look great in your bathing suit (positive comment) might make you continue taking diet pills to maintain that look. In fact, researchers have found that both negative and positive comments about appearance have detrimental effects (Calogero, Herbozo, & Thompson, 2009). Both kinds of comments are negatively associated with body image which will be discussed in more detail in Chapter 7, "Dress and Body Image."

Negative (and sometimes positive) perceived assessments lead to a feedback loop in the model. The feedback loop models the way people cope with not coming close enough to the cultural ideal. There are four possible coping strategies: you can try harder, perhaps utilizing more coping strategies (e.g., dieting and exercising); you can give up and feel bad about how you look; you can change your own personal standard of what is beautiful; or you can change the cultural standard. Continuing with the previous example, respondents were trying harder to approximate the cultural ideal by engaging in the risky appearance behaviors (Lee & Johnson, 2009). The strategies of (a) trying harder or (b) giving up can sometimes have detrimental consequences. An example of detrimental consequences of trying harder is the case of eighteen-year-old Stephanie Kuleba who had a reaction to anesthesia during breast augmentation surgery and died (Rivero & Brady, 2008). To summarize the model, you internalize the cultural ideal of beauty, compare yourselves to the cultural ideal (via social

Figure 6.2
Nicki Minaj has reportedly had breast and buttock implants. In the Rudd and Lennon model of body aesthetics, these surgeries would be considered coping strategies.

IN-CLASS ACTIVITY
Coping Strategies

What coping strategies do you use? Can you think of any feedback you have received from family or peers on your appearance? Has that motivated any subsequent coping strategies? Have the coping strategies been successful? Have you purchased any products to aid in the coping strategies? Have any of your strategies been "successful," but not healthy (e.g., disordered eating, steroid use, or tanning)?

comparison), create your appearance accordingly, present that appearance to others, internalize others' responses, and finally sometimes engage in coping strategies to re-create your appearance when you are not satisfied with the created appearance and/or others' assessments of it.

In the next section we consider the kinds of information conveyed by faces. Facial attractiveness research will be reviewed and specific features found to judge facial attractiveness will be discussed. Use of attractive models in advertising will be considered, and finally we discuss how people manipulate their faces through the use of cosmetics and non-invasive (or minimally invasive) cosmetic surgical procedures.

FACES

Human faces convey a great deal of information including sex, age, ethnicity, emotion/mood, abilities or personal characteristics, and direction of gaze (Macrae, Quinn, Mason, & Quadflieg, 2005). As such they are very important visual stimuli (Kanwisher & Yovel, 2006). In fact, people form impressions of others based on facial appearance in about one-tenth of a second (Willis & Todorov, 2006). In one study that illustrates how faces convey information, undergraduates viewed facial photos of fifty CEOs from the twenty-five highest- and the twenty-five lowest-ranked companies in the Fortune 1000 list (Rule & Ambady, 2008). In looks the CEOs were similar, all were men, about the same age, and appeared to be Caucasian. Each photo was rated on leadership ability. Results showed that CEO leadership ratings were strongly related to actual company profits. Thus, not only do people extract information from faces (i.e., leadership ability), sometimes that information is related to an objective measure (i.e., company profits). In other words, if a CEO is judged to be high in leadership ability, you might expect him to lead a profitable company.

In a follow-up study, female CEOs were investigated (Rule & Ambady, 2009). Objective measures of the women's compensation and their companies' profits were also obtained. Undergraduates viewed the faces of the 20 Fortune 1000 female CEOs and rated them for a variety of traits including leadership ability, competence, and dominance. Results showed that the female CEOs rated as more competent and higher in leadership ability also led companies that were more profitable. In addition, ratings of dominance were related to female CEOs' cash

compensation and total compensation. In both studies of Fortune 1000 CEOs, we do not know what specific physical features led to the ratings of leadership and dominance, we only know that the ratings (based only on facial information extracted from photos) were related to actual company profitability. It is not surprising that we extract these kinds of information from faces because every day we deal with others in social interactions and we focus on faces in those interactions (Fiske & Taylor, 2008).

Faces express emotions and we can reliably recognize some emotions from others' faces. Researchers have demonstrated that across cultures people are able to "read" emotion from faces (Ekman, 1993; Ekman, Sorenson, & Friesen, 1969; Izard, 1971). Research also shows that we extract trait information from faces. One study found that symmetric faces, as compared to less symmetric faces, are perceived to be healthier, more attractive, more sociable, more intelligent, more lively, more self-confident, and more balanced (Fink, Neave, Manning, & Grammer, 2006).

Another line of research has investigated specific features of the face and the kinds of impressions those features convey. In particular, adults with baby-faced features (i.e., large eyes, short noses and chins, big foreheads) are perceived to have more childlike qualities (more naïve, honest, submissive, warm, and less strong) than adults with more mature features (see Zebrowitz & Montepare, 2005). To the extent that cosmetics are used to enhance our features (e.g., make our eyes look larger or our noses shorter), such intentional manipulations of the body are examples of dress manipulations.

Facial Attractiveness

One very obvious aspect of our physical appearance that is revealed in our faces is our facial attractiveness.[1] Attractiveness of stimuli (in this case, faces used in research studies) refers to judgments concerning the beauty or aesthetic appeal of the stimuli. Researchers have investigated the effects of attractiveness compiling a large body of work that has been reviewed many times (e.g., Jackson, Hunter, & Hodge, 1995; Langlois, Kalakanis, Rebenstein, Larson, Hallam, & Smoot, 2000). In this work, many of the studies have examined facial attractiveness and typically used

---

[1]Sometimes when researchers have studied attractiveness, they have not distinguished between facial attractiveness, body attractiveness, and/or both. Hence it may be impossible to know which aspect of attractiveness was manipulated.

yearbook photos or **headshots**. For example, to investigate potential influences of attractiveness, researchers have conducted pretests using a panel of judges to determine what comprises *facially* attractive and less attractive stimulus persons (Johnson & Roach-Higgins, 1987a, 1987b). The attractive and less attractive photos are used to manipulate the variable "attractiveness." (Please refer to Chapter 4, "Dress and Social Cognition" for more information on stimuli, variables, and pretests.) However, some research does not distinguish between faces and bodies or examines topics more globally. For example, some attractiveness research treats faces and bodies together and does not separate the effects of each.

With attractiveness manipulations such as headshots or full-body photos which include the face and body, researchers have repeatedly documented that physically attractive individuals receive positive rewards (e.g., Jackson et al., 1995; Langlois et al., 2000). For example, in a seminal study (Dion, Berscheid, & Walster, 1972) research participants were given three photos (one attractive, one average in attractiveness, one unattractive). As compared to unattractive persons, the attractive stimulus persons were judged to be more socially desirable, to have a more prestigious occupation, to be a more competent spouse, to have a happier marriage, to have a better social life, to marry sooner, and to have more happiness in their lives. The authors explained these results as evidence for a "What is beautiful is good" stereotype. This attractiveness advantage appears to hold true whether attractiveness is

due to another's inborn beauty, as shown by these studies, or due to dress manipulations as reviewed in Chapter 4, "Dress and Social Cognition." However, researchers have now shown that it is not so much an attractiveness advantage that is responsible for such effects, but rather an unattractiveness disadvantage (Griffin & Langlois, 2006; Hammeresh & Parker, 2005). In other words, people who are considered to be unattractive may suffer detrimental social and personal consequences.

In general, the research on the effects of physical attractiveness, whether based on faces or faces and bodies, shows that people tend to rate attractive others better than unattractive others. As compared to unattractive adults, attractive adults are perceived to be more occupationally competent, to have more social appeal, to be more interpersonally competent, and to be better adjusted (Langlois et al., 2000). In one very early study (Dion, 1972), research participants read a description of a child committing a transgression. Half the participants were shown a small photo of an attractive child accompanying the description and the other half was shown a photo of an unattractive child. The research participants judged the unattractive child to be more antisocial and more likely to commit a similar transgression in the future than the attractive child. Furthermore, other researchers have shown that attractive children are judged to be more academically competent than unattractive children (Langlois et al., 2000) (Figure 6.4). These kinds of effects carry over to daily life. For example, attractive professors receive higher course ratings

Figure 6.3
Republican Presidential Debate in Detroit, MI on March 3, 2016. Candidate attractiveness is often influential in political elections.

Figure 6.4

Langlois et al. (2000) found that attractive children were judged to be more academically competent than unattractive children.

than unattractive professors (Riniolo, Johnson, Sherman, & Misso, 2006). In Riniolo et al., students judged their own professors' "hotness" and a positive relationship was found between hotness and course evaluations. The attractiveness effect also influences political elections. In one study, candidate attractiveness has been shown to affect the outcome of a mock election, but only among uninformed voters (Stockemer & Praino, 2015) (Figure 6.3).

The fact that attractive people are judged to possess more positive qualities than unattractive people is unfortunate and undemocratic. However, more unfortunate is the fact that attractiveness also affects social interactions (i.e., how you are treated by others). In other words, your level of attractiveness affects your daily life. In their review of 919 research studies focusing on attractiveness,[2]

[2]In these studies since study participants interacted with attractive others, attractiveness could be based on facial attractiveness, body attractiveness, or both and it is impossible to disentangle the effects.

researchers showed that as compared to unattractive people, attractive people are actually treated better by others (Langlois et al., 2000). Attractive adults received more attention, received more rewards, were provided more help, and had more positive interactions than unattractive adults. Attractive children received more attention, received higher evaluations of competence in school, and had more positive interactions and fewer negative interactions with others than unattractive children. Many of the studies reviewed by the researchers appear to have used experimental designs in controlled laboratory settings (please refer to Chapter 3, "Conducting Research on Dress" for more information). Next, we consider non-experimental attractiveness research that measures its real-life consequences on income, evaluations, and success at getting elected. See Table 6.1 for a summary of this research and examples of how attractive people are treated better than unattractive people.

TABLE 6.1

IMPRESSIONS AND BEHAVIORS AS A FUNCTION OF ATTRACTIVENESS

Inferences Made about	Results for Attractive People as Compared to Unattractive People	Authors
Attractive Adults	More socially desirable More prestigious occupation More competent spouse Have a happier marriage Have a better social life Expected to marry sooner Have a happier life	Dion, Berscheid, & Walster (1972)
Attractive Adults	More occupationally competent Have more social appeal More interpersonally competent Better adjusted	Langlois et al. (2000)
Attractive Children	More social Less likely to commit a transgression in the future	Dion (1972)
Attractive Children	More academically competent	Langlois et al. (2000)
Behaviors Aimed at	Results for Attractive People as Compared to Unattractive People	Authors
Attractive Adults	Received more attention Received more rewards Given more help Had more positive interactions	Langlois et al. (2000)
Attractive Adults	Earn more money	Hamermesh & Biddle (1994)
Attractive Male Attorneys	Made more money	Biddle & Hamermesh (1998)
Attractive Han Chinese Women	Earn more money	Hamermesh, Meng, & Zhang (2002)
Attractive Economists	More likely to be elected to an office in a professional organization	Hamermesh (2006)
Attractive Professors	Receive better teaching evaluations from their students	Hamermesh & Parker (2005)
Attractive Children	Receive more attention Receive higher evaluations of competence in school Have more positive interactions	Langlois et al. (2000)

Attractiveness and Real Life Outcomes

A series of articles about the importance of attractiveness[3] on actual income conducted by economists underscores the effects of attractiveness on real life outcomes. Scholars analyzed data collected in three very large consumer surveys of employed adults from the US and Canada (Hamermesh & Biddle, 1994). The survey information was collected by interviewers who gathered information on income, occupation, and attractiveness (among other things). Each interviewer rated each interviewee on a 5-point scale with endpoints of 1 = strikingly handsome or beautiful and 5 = homely. Results of the analysis clearly show that more attractive people actually earned more money than less attractive people.

The same researchers studied the effect of attractiveness on attorneys' incomes (Biddle & Hamermesh, 1998). They obtained photos of each entering law school student who graduated between 1971 and 1978 and between 1981 and 1988. Each photo was rated by four independent raters using the same scale as used by Hamermesh and Biddle (1994). The law school also provided access to survey information collected from about 2,000 students five years and again fifteen years after graduation. From the surveys, the researchers were able to determine starting salaries, income at five years after graduation, and income fifteen years after graduation. Results showed that attractive male attorneys made more money than less attractive male attorneys (there were not enough women in the sample to get a precise estimate of the relationship). These results demonstrate that attractiveness pays off in terms of higher income.

Subsequently, a multinational team of researchers from the US, Australia, and Hong Kong examined whether the use of attractiveness-enhancing products (clothing, cosmetics) would also be related to receiving higher incomes (Hamermesh, Meng, & Zhang, 2002). The researchers interviewed 853 married Han Chinese women who worked at least thirty hours per week in Shanghai, China. The researchers obtained information about income and about household expenditures including those for her clothing and cosmetics. The researchers also rated the women's attractiveness[4] on a five-point scale with endpoints of 1 = very pretty and 5 = ugly. As with the previous studies, the more attractive women earned significantly more (about 10 percent more) than those whose looks were average or below average. Results also showed a small effect for spending on clothing and cosmetics on income; for every yuan (the Chinese currency) spent on clothing and cosmetics, earnings increased 15 percent. Thus, the use of attractiveness-enhancing products does pay off in terms of higher income. These results demonstrate that even folks not born attractive can attain some of the benefits by using attractiveness-enhancing products.

More recently, research by Hamermesh and his colleagues has examined other outcomes of attractiveness including economists' success at being elected in a professional association and actual teaching evaluations of university professors (Hamermesh, 2006; Hamermesh & Parker, 2005). Among the economists in one professional organization, 312 candidates for office were evaluated from 1.25-inch by 1.5-inch photos[5] as either above or below average in attractiveness (Hamermesh, 2006). Of those rated above average, 55 percent were elected; of those rated below average only 45 percent were elected, demonstrating that candidate looks affected election outcomes. The extent to which professors' attractiveness was related to actual teaching evaluations of them was investigated by Hamermesh and Parker. They examined 16,957 teaching evaluations at one university from 463 classes. Photos of each professor were rated on attractiveness by six raters and the average of these ratings was entered into the analyses. It is unclear from the study whether or not the photo was a facial photo or a full body photo. Results showed more attractive professors received higher teaching evaluations and that relationship between attractiveness and evaluations was stronger for men than women. The authors note that since teaching evaluations are used in tenure and promotion decisions, one's attractiveness can have important life outcomes.

[3]In this study since the interviewer interacted with study participants, attractiveness could be based on facial attractiveness, body attractiveness, or both and it is impossible to disentangle the effects.

[4]In this study, since the researchers interviewed study participants, attractiveness could be based on facial attractiveness, body attractiveness, or both and it is impossible to disentangle the effects.

[5]Although not specified in the article, since the photos were so small, it seems likely that they were facial photos and not full body photos. However, in the actual elections it is likely that many of those casting votes would have interacted with candidates, so that attractiveness could be based on facial attractiveness, body attractiveness, or both.

APPEARANCE DISCRIMINATION

Retailers hire workers they think will convey the image of the company. That strategy has proven problematic for Abercrombie and Fitch. The retailer was accused of racial discrimination in hiring by former employees and job applicants (Leung, 2003). They charged that they were fired or not hired because their ethnic looks (blacks, Asians, Latinos) were inconsistent with Abercrombie's all-American look. According to one former employee, several Asian-American salespeople were fired and replaced with white males. When blacks, Asians, and Latinos were employed at Abercrombie, they mostly worked in the stockroom. A Stanford University student was purportedly told that he could not be hired because the store already employed too many Filipinos. In 2004 Abercrombie and Fitch was ordered by the court to pay $50 million to former employees and job applicants who brought the discrimination charges (Strasburg, 2004). The company was also required to begin a series of programs and adopt policies to promote diversity and prevent discrimination.

Those programs must not have been effective because two Muslim women more recently sued Abercrombie for discrimination; they wore headscarves for religious reasons. One was denied a job and the other was fired from her job at Abercrombie. The court ordered Abercrombie to pay $71,000 and attorney fees. The company also agreed to make changes to its looks policy to allow workers to wear headscarves for religious reasons (Associated Press, 2013). However, the problems continue for Abercrombie. The latest discrimination case against Abercrombie went all the way to the Supreme Court in *EEOC v. Abercrombie & Fitch*. In 2008 Abercrombie choose not to hire Samantha Elauf as a sales associate because her hijab did not conform to their looks policy. However, Elauf was not told about the looks policy. In June 2015 the Supreme Court decided, 8-1, that Abercrombie's failure to accommodate Elauf was a violation of her civil rights to have religious accommodation (LeVine, 2015).

Another real life outcome related to attractiveness is discrimination against women who do not conform to appearance norms. In Chapter 4, "Dress and Social Cognition," discrimination was discussed and defined as negative behaviors taken with respect to a social group, such as people with non-normative appearance. In her 2010 book *The Beauty Bias*, law school professor Deborah Rhode draws on an impressive amount of appearance-related research (including attractiveness research), legal scholarship, and case histories. She highlights the many forces that contribute to appearance-related bias, such as the media, the cosmetic industry, and the plastic surgery industry. Arguing that discrimination against unattractive women is as widespread as discrimination based on sex, race, ethnicity, religion, and age, her book offers a framework for challenging appearance discrimination. Rhode explains how appearance laws work in the one state and handful of municipalities that have them. She advocates extending the reach of appearance laws to remedy appearance discrimination.

Attractiveness and Advertising

Since attractiveness has many positive real life outcomes, attractiveness research has some important implications for advertising. A comprehensive review of attractiveness research found that as compared to unattractive people, attractive people are more successful at selling products, more successful at influencing people, and are more successful at getting people to like them (Patzer, 1985). For example, attractive spokespersons are judged to be more credible and more persuasive than less attractive spokespeople (Chaiken, 1979; Kamins, 1990). Other researchers found that ads, advertised products, and ads' messages are evaluated more favorably when attractive models are used in the ads (Baker & Churchill, 1977). More recent research has found some limitations of the attractiveness effect. For example, highly attractive models are not always superior to normally attractive models in terms of perceived trustworthiness or expertise (Bower & Landreth, 2001). Nevertheless, because of these results it is not surprising that unattractive spokespersons are seldom used to advertise products.

A closer reading of some of these studies illustrates a problem with interpreting some of the attractiveness research: it is sometimes impossible to tell if study participants are reacting to facial attractiveness, body attractiveness, or both (Baker & Churchill, 1977; Bower & Landreth, 2001; Chaiken, 1979; Kamins, 1990). In the Kamins study the spokespersons were well-known celebrities, so participants may have been using their own knowledge of the celebrities' facial and body attractiveness in their ratings, although photos of the celebrities in business suits were featured in the ads. In Chaiken's study the spokespersons interacted with study participants, so both facial and body attractiveness could have influenced the result. In the Baker and Churchill study, photos of models were used and it is unclear whether or not both faces and bodies were present in all photos. In Bower and Landreth's research, photos of models were used and it is unclear whether or not both faces and bodies were present in all photos.

What Aspects of Facial Appearance Contribute to Attractiveness?

The research literature presented thus far describes the effects of attractiveness, but it does not explain the particular features that are found attractive. Are there discrete facial features that predict judgments of attractiveness? In fact, there are. Three characteristics of attractive faces that are found in the literature are sexual dimorphism, averageness, and symmetry.

Sexual Dimorphism

Sexual dimorphism, characteristics of physical features that distinguish men from women, is evident in faces after puberty and includes full lips, small noses, small ears, high cheekbones, and small chin/jaw (feminine features) for women and square jaws, larger cheekbones and brow ridges (masculine features) for men (Rhodes, 2006) (Figure 6.5). Full lips, small noses, small ears, high cheekbones, and small chin/jaw are also called **neotonous** features (i.e., features associated with infants or neonates). The facial features of adult US women in photos were rated by male judges on attractiveness (Cunningham, 1986). Results

showed that higher attractiveness ratings were received by women with larger eyes, wider cheekbones, and smaller noses (i.e, more feminine characteristics). Those results have been extended to other cultural contexts (Jones et al., 1995). Jones and his colleagues collected data from five different cultures; within each culture men rated the attractiveness of photos of women from the same culture. Facial measurements were taken of each photo by the researcher. Across the five populations, women were seen as more attractive by men when they had large eyes, small noses, and full lips (i.e., more typically feminine characteristics reflecting sexual dimorphism). A meta-analysis of this line of research has been performed (Rhodes, 2006). In a **meta-analysis**, such as the one performed by Rhodes, a researcher amasses a large literature review and statistically is able to determine which results are consistent

Figure 6.5
George Eads from *CSI* has a square jaw, large cheekbones, and brow ridges; all are considered masculine sexually dimorphic features.

across the literature. In her meta-analysis Rhodes found that women judged to have feminine features are also judged as more attractive than women who lack those features; for men, the results are weaker, but men who are rated as more masculine are also rated as more attractive. Thus, women having feminine sexually dimorphic features are rated more attractive than women who do not have those features.

Average Faces

Researchers also discovered that faces with "average" features were judged to be more attractive than less average faces (Langlois & Roggman, 1990). In their research, they used computer generated faces that were created by averaging faces; they hypothesized that the average faces were more attractive than the faces used to create them. Adults rated the physical attractiveness of the individual faces and the composite averaged faces. For both men and women, the composite faces were rated more attractive than the individual faces. Others have found similar results. For example, in one study male and female Caucasian Australian adults rated faces and composite images that were averaged from those faces (Rhodes, Halberstadt, Jeffery, & Palermo, 2005). Half the faces were Caucasian and half were Japanese. Results showed that the faces averaged from two faces were rated as more attractive than the two original faces; furthermore, faces averaged from six faces were rated as more attractive than the faces averaged from two faces. Thus, as faces became more average, they were rated higher in attractiveness.

Facial Symmetry

Another line of research shows that symmetric faces are judged more attractive than less symmetric faces.

IN-CLASS ACTIVITY
Averaging Faces

Search online for *face research average demos*. That site allows you to practice averaging faces together. You can even upload your own face if you like. Then (1) average two faces together and (2) average six faces together. Which averaged face do you think is most attractive, 1 or 2?

Symmetry is established by drawing an imaginary line down the center of the face and determining how well each side of the face lines up. A research team from Australia and New Zealand manipulated faces to be vary in symmetry and assessed attractiveness (Rhodes, Proffitt, Grady, & Sumich, 1998). Judgments of attractiveness increased with increased manipulated symmetry. They also found that natural variations in facial symmetry were related to attractiveness. Other research on symmetry has used computer generated faces constructed to vary in symmetry (e.g., Fink et al., 2006); faces high in symmetry received significantly higher ratings of attractiveness than faces that were lower in symmetry. Researchers from Australia and Japan varied both the averageness and the symmetry of Japanese and Chinese faces and measured attractiveness (Rhodes et al., 2001). Chinese and Japanese participants rated average faces as more attractive than less average faces. In addition, symmetric faces were rated more attractive than less symmetric faces (Figure 6.6). Thus, the attractiveness of average faces and symmetric faces extend to non-Western cultures.

So given all of this evidence about facial features and attractiveness, you may wonder which features (sexually dimorphic features, average features, or symmetric features) are more important in influencing attractiveness

Figure 6.6
Rhodes et al. (2001) found that faces high in symmetry such as this one received significantly higher ratings of attractiveness.

ratings? To answer this question a meta-analysis of the research in support of the three characteristics that have been shown to influence facial attractiveness judgments was performed (Rhodes, 2006). Rhodes found that, across all studies analyzed, each of the three characteristics affected judgments of attractiveness of male and female faces, with femininity (i.e., feminine sexually dimorphic traits) being the strongest component of female attractiveness. Researchers from Scotland conducted an experiment to jointly study the contributions of symmetry and averageness to women's attractiveness (Jones, BeBruine, & Little, 2007). To do this, they used the computer to create faces that systematically varied the symmetry and averageness of women's photos. They found that, in judgments of women's attractiveness, the contribution of symmetry was slight in comparison to the contribution of averageness. Taken together, the two studies suggest that sexually dimorphic characteristics (i.e., feminine features), averageness, and symmetry (in that order) contribute to judgments of women's attractiveness.

Some scholars take an evolutionary approach to attractiveness and suggest that the characteristics we find attractive might offer some evolutionary advantage to the species (i.e., attractive characteristics might signal good health and fertility in a potential mate) (e.g., Jones et al., 1995; Rhodes, 2006; Thornhill & Gangestad, 1999). For example, symmetric faces are taken as signs of the absence of disease and sexual dimorphic features are a result of the production of sex-related hormones associated with fertility. An evolutionary view of attractiveness contrasts with the view that attractiveness is based on arbitrary standards that differ by culture.

MANIPULATIONS OF FACES

Aging Faces, Anti-Aging Products, and Non-Invasive Procedures

It is apparent from this previous review of facial attractiveness research that attractiveness is a valuable characteristic and offers advantages. As a result, when people do not think they are facially attractive enough for whatever reason, they may elect to alter or manipulate aspects of their faces. One reason people might elect to alter aspects of their faces is because of visible signs of aging such as sagging, wrinkling, and graying (Calasanti, 2005). Age (Yarmey, 1985) is a stimulus characteristic that has been shown to affect judgments in impression formation studies. In a study focused on physical attractiveness, age was found to be an important component of it (Wilson, Beyer, & Monteiro, 2014). For example, age has been shown to be related to teaching evaluations of university professors. The effects of age and gender of professors on student evaluations and judgments of attractiveness were investigated by Wilson, Beyer, and Monteiro (2014). In their experiment, undergraduates were presented a photo of a male or female professor. In addition, the photos had been digitally altered to look older, so that there were a total of four photos: a young male, a young female, an altered image of the male made to look older, and an altered image of the female made to look older. Each participant saw and evaluated only one of the photos. Students rated the female images to be more attractive than the male images. Not only were older professors rated less attractive than younger professors, they were also rated as less likely to encourage questions, less likely to exhibit friendliness, and less likely to develop more rapport with students. On the other hand, older professors were perceived to be more likely to expect good work and to assign too much work. In other words, younger professors received more positive evaluations than older professors. In summary, research shows that as a woman's age increases, her perceived attractiveness declines. Hence, youthful looks for women (and men) are culturally valued in the US and having visible signs of facial aging is undesirable.

DRESS IN THE NEWS
A Price to Pay for Looking Old?

Debra Moreno, a fifty-four-year-old office coordinator for Hawaii Healthcare Professionals, Inc. was terminated by company owner, Carolyn Frutoz-De Harne in 2008. Frutoz-De Harne ordered that Moreno be fired and told the manager that Moreno "sounds old on the telephone," "looks old," and is "a bag of bones." Although the manager indicated that Moreno was efficient and thorough, Frutoz-De Harne said that Moreno was not the type of person she wanted to represent Hawaii Healthcare Professionals. After an investigation the US Equal Employment Opportunity Commission (EEOC) filed suit charging age discrimination. The court found in favor of Moreno and she was awarded over $190,000 ("Court orders," 2012).

To manage the signs of aging, a large and profitable cosmetic surgery products industry has evolved in the US that is worth $2.6 billion (Cosmetic Surgery Products to 2014, 2010). The desire for a young-looking appearance by an aging population fuels the demand in the US for non-invasive cosmetic procedures. Facial injections, which are considered non-invasive, are expected to be the fastest growing type of procedure (to $1,066,000,000) by 2014 due to the lack of recovery time and of obvious signs of surgery. The second fastest growing type of procedure is predicted to be implants (to $494,000,000).

The five most frequently used types of minimally invasive (or non-invasive) procedures in 2014 were Botulinum Toxin Type A (Botox or other brand), soft tissue (dermal) fillers, chemical peels, laser hair removal, and microdermabrasion (American Society of Plastic Surgeons, 2014). See Table 6.2 for the frequencies with which people undergo these procedures.

Botulinum Toxin Type A (yes, it is a toxin) is injected into facial muscles associated with wrinkles. The toxin blocks nerve signals to the muscles and may weaken the muscle that causes the wrinkle. As long as the muscle does not contract, no wrinkle is formed. Estimated cost of a treatment based on a national average in 2014 was $324. Usage of Botulinum Toxin Type A increased approximately 5,407 percent from 1997 to 2014 according to the American Society of Aesthetic Plastic Surgery ("Cosmetic surgery national data bank," 2014). Botulinum Toxin Type A is also marketed to treat incontinence and chronic migraine.

Dermal fillers are used to fill wrinkles and can be temporary or semi-permanent as a function of the filler (American Society of Plastic Surgeons, 2010). Temporary fillers include fat (removed from your body with liposuction), collagen, hyaluronic acid, and others. A semi-permanent filler is polymethylmethacrylate or PMMA. The advantage of dermal fillers is that there is no recovery down time. The American Society of Plastic Surgeons estimated that the average cost of dermal fillers in 2014 was $592 ("Cosmetic surgery national data bank," 2014). Use of one's own fat as a filler may be more expensive because the price would also include the cost of liposuction.

A **chemical peel** is a chemical solution which is applied to the skin to remove the outer layers (American Society of Plastic Surgeons, 2010). A deep chemical peel requires a sedative and anesthetic. For this procedure recovery is two weeks and a risk is that the ability to tan may be lost. Estimated cost of a chemical peel is $574 based on a 2014 national average ("Cosmetic surgery national data bank," 2014).

Information from the Mayo Clinic website provided details about laser hair removal (Laser hair removal, n.d.). **Laser hair removal** uses intense pulsed light or IPL. Heat from the light is absorbed by pigment in the hair damaging the hair follicle, which slows hair growth. Treatments must be repeated and work best on people with light skin and dark hair. No information was provided on the Mayo Clinic website about treatment cost. The 2014 national average for laser or pulsed light hair removal was $311 ("Cosmetic surgery national data bank," 2014).

Microdermabrasion uses an instrument that "sands" the skin (American Society of Plastic Surgeons, 2010). A diamond tipped wand or other device may be used to remove the top layer of skin. The procedure is thought to stimulate new skin growth and collagen production. An advantage is the absence of recovery time. Estimated cost of microdermabrasion is $129 based on a 2014 national average ("Cosmetic surgery national data bank," 2014).

TABLE 6.2

FREQUENCIES OF THE TOP FIVE US MINIMALLY INVASIVE COSMETIC PROCEDURES IN 2014

Procedure	Frequency
Botulinum Toxin Type A	6.7 million
Soft tissue (dermal) filler	2.3 million
Chemical peel	1.2 million
Laser hair removal	1.1 million
Microdermabrasion	881,905

Source: American Society of Plastic Surgeons

Research on the Use of Anti-Aging Products and Non-Invasive Procedures

Age prejudice has been claimed to be "one of the most socially-condoned and institutionalized forms of prejudice" in the US (Nelson, 2005, p. 208). Hence, it is not surprising that aging women attempt to stave off the ravages of age through the use of many types of potions, creams, dyes, and even non-surgical procedures. A Canadian research team interviewed forty-four women (from ages fifty to seventy) about aging, body image, and non-surgical cosmetic procedures (Hurd Clarke & Griffin, 2008). Most of the women used some type of appearance management strategy (e.g., makeup, hair dye, wrinkle cream, non-surgical procedures). Those who endorsed altering themselves considered natural aging to be unattractive and undesirable. Other researchers investigated 304 Canadian women's (mean age = 40.5) perceptions and purchase of anti-aging skin care products (Muise & Desmarais, 2010). The women were also asked how acceptable it was to use makeup, hair dye, Botox, dermal fillers, and chemical peels. They found that anxiety about aging and importance of appearance each predicted purchase of anti-aging skin care products. When asked, the women reported that the most important reason for using anti-aging skin care products was to retain a young-looking appearance. The women distinguished between use of anti-aging skin care products and intent to have cosmetic surgery. They equated use of anti-aging skin care products with use of makeup and hair dye. Both cosmetic surgery and non-invasive procedures were viewed as more drastic. These results are consistent with those from another Canadian study in which interviewees viewed the use of anti-wrinkle creams, cosmetics, and hair dye as part of natural aging, but saw the use of cosmetic surgery and non-invasive procedures as part of unnatural aging (Hurd Clarke & Griffin, 2007). Thus, anti-aging skin care products, makeup, and hair dye are viewed as normative, but use of cosmetic surgery and non-invasive procedures are viewed as drastic measures for maintaining physical attractiveness.

Research on Use of Cosmetics

Although the use of non-invasive facial procedures is viewed as a drastic way to change one's appearance, an easy way to alter facial appearance is through the application of cosmetics. According to Kline and Company, the dollar value of US sales of cosmetics and toiletries in 2008 was over $35 billion and more than $7 billion of that was due to cosmetic sales (Cosmetics and toiletries USA 2008, 2009), Hence, the cosmetic industry in the US is alive and well. Kline and Company also predicts a growth of 2.2 percent through 2014. Women's use of cosmetics has been cited as an inexpensive, easily available, and quick means to increase their physical attractiveness (Franzoi, 2001).

Researchers have studied the effects of cosmetics on perceptions of self and found mixed results. In one study researchers found women's cosmetic product use positively related to dissatisfaction with appearance, suggesting that women wear cosmetics when dissatisfied with their appearance (Cash & Cash, 1982). Women unconcerned with physical appearance wore cosmetics in fewer situations than those women who were concerned. In a survey college women provided information about their cosmetic use and their facial image (Guthrie, Kim, & Jung, 2008). Facial image was assessed by asking participants to rate five areas of the face plus the entire face on degree of satisfaction and importance. Higher scores reflected more positive facial images. Results showed that quantity of cosmetic use was affected by perceived facial image, such that a more positive facial image was related to more cosmetics being used. In another study women were interviewed about their reasons for cosmetic use (Rudd, 1997). Creating a strong and positive self-image was the most important motivation; participants believed that cosmetics served as an extension of the self in their presentation to others, and they wore cosmetics to try to look their best for themselves, as well as for others. Another strong motivation was transforming or "normalizing" the appearance of the face by correcting perceived flaws such as short eyelashes or blemishes or a prominent nose with strategic use of foundation, mascara, blush, and other products.

In other research, women were more satisfied with their faces and overall appearance and thought they would be judged as more attractive by their peers when wearing cosmetics than when cosmetics free (Cash, Dawson, Davis, Bowen, & Galumbeck, 1989). Further analyses revealed that men, but not women, judged women to be more attractive when wearing cosmetics. However, that research found that women tend to overestimate the extent to which cosmetics actually improves their judged attractiveness.

Cosmetics have been found to affect more than simple attractiveness judgments. We have seen that physical attractiveness is positively related to judgments and evaluations; thus, it makes sense that if cosmetics increase attractiveness, then cosmetic use should also correlate positively with judgments that correlate with attractiveness. A research team from France and the UK recently studied this issue (Nash, Fieldman, Hussey, Lévêque, &

Pineau, 2006). Caucasian women were stimulus persons for the researchers and were photographed with and without cosmetics. With cosmetics the women were judged to be healthier, more confident, to have greater earnings potential, and to have a higher status profession than without the cosmetics. These are all characteristics that have been associated with attractive people.

However, use of cosmetics does not always lead to more positive perceptions. Early research found that when a woman wore lipstick she was perceived as more sociable and attractive, but less conscientious, more anxious, more frivolous, and more interested in men (McKeachie, 1952). Other researchers have also studied impression formation as a function of cosmetics use. When a woman wore no makeup compared to when she was wearing heavy makeup, she was perceived to be more moral, but less attractive and less feminine (Workman & Johnson, 1991). French researchers used twelve women as stimulus persons who were photographed both with and without ordinary cosmetics (Huguet, Croizet, & Richetin, 2004). Consistent with the previous studies' results, women were judged to be more attractive when wearing makeup than when not. However, when wearing makeup the women were also judged to be more vain, unfaithful, and shallow and less kind, honest, and confident than when not wearing makeup.

Because the face is so important to attractiveness and to identity, makeup may play an important role in Western culture (Negrin, 2000). However, cosmetics are also important in a recently Westernized culture. Makeup was investigated using qualitative research conducted in Bulgaria (Ghodsee, 2007). She found that the introduction of a capitalist economy into the previously communist country led to a preference for spending on cosmetics, perfume, and hair dye over almost any other type of goods. The author explained that under communism in Bulgaria, beauty and fashion products were scarce and the state attempted to convince women that beauty and fashion were irrelevant to their identities. In communist Bulgaria, most Bulgarians had producerist identities, determined by their relationship to work as producers. However, under the free market system with its media and advertising industries, and easy availability of products, people's identities came to be based less on producing things and more on consuming things. With this movement to consumption identities, women began to see material things as necessary for a "normal" life. Similar to what US women experience, Ghodsee found in her interviews with Bulgarian women, that the widespread availability of cosmetics under the free market system together with media promotion and advertising may have fueled comparison to media images and celebrities, and created beauty standards for women that were nearly impossible to achieve.

Another standard that is nearly impossible to achieve is white or light skin preferred by many dark skinned people around the globe (Ashikari, 2005; Glenn, 2008). A qualitative researcher located in the UK studied the success of Japanese companies' skin-whitening cosmetics (e.g., Shiseido) and their popularity (Ashikari, 2005). Ashikari observed, interviewed, and surveyed urban middle-class Japanese women and found that the popularity of skin whitening cosmetics among Japanese women is due to the globalization of a Caucasian ideal of beauty. She found a preference for white skin, which she demonstrated is related to consumer culture. While skin color was important, eye color and hair color were not. Furthermore, white skin was considered ideal for women, but dark skin was considered ideal for men. Ashikari explains that in the Japanese language the word for color (*iro*) means skin tone when used in reference to people. The Japanese word for the color white (*shiro*) is used to describe a Japanese person with light skin. Hence the sentence *Ashikari-san wa iro ga shiroi* means that "Mr. Ashikari has fair or pale skin." However, it does not mean that, "Mr. Ashikari is Caucasian."

Does the proliferation of skin-lightening cosmetic use around the world suggest a growing significance of colorism? Glenn (2008) believes that it does. **Colorism** is social stratification based on skin color between and within ethnic groups. A book about discrimination as a function of color particularly among African Americans, but also among other dark-skinned peoples, was written by Russell, Wilson, and Hall (1993). They researched people from Africa, India, Japan, and Arab countries, among others. In all cases they found that lighter skin was considered more beautiful and desirable than darker skin. Likewise, Glenn traced skin lightening around the world and found it used in India, Africa, the Philippines, Japan, China, Korea, and Latin America. Glenn indicts large multinational cosmetics and pharmaceutical companies for increasing the desire for lightening products through their advertising and marketing. Glenn contends that such companies create the need for the products by portraying dark skin as a burden and handicap. In counterpoint, in one recent instance as reported by Amnesty International (2016), light skin color was not desirable. The report highlighted the plight of **albinos** (i.e., individuals with no pigmentation in their skin, hair, and eyes), who are discriminated against and murdered in East Africa. Given this attention, perhaps some enterprising cosmetic company will market a skin-dyeing product that could permanently color albino skin.

Tanning

Ironically although dark-skinned individuals may wish to have lighter skin, many in Western cultures desire the look of darker skin achieved via tanning. There are three methods of tanning: sun tanning, indoor tanning using tanning beds, and sunless tanning using products that can be rubbed or sprayed on the skin. The Mayo Clinic website considers sunless tanning to be a practical alternative to sun tanning because sunless tanning products provide a tanned look without exposure to ultraviolet (UV) rays (Mayo Clinic Staff, n.d.). The active ingredient in most sunless tanning products is dihydroxyacetone or DHA. DHA has been approved by the FDA for external application and works by reacting with dead skin cells to darken the skin. These products are considered safe if used as directed.

However, sun tanning is not considered safe according to the FDA website ("The risks of tanning," n.d.). Both sun tanning and indoor tanning risk sunburn, which is a sign of skin damage and UV exposure. Research demonstrates a connection between severe sunburn and the most deadly form of skin cancer, melanoma. According to the FDA, no tan is safe. Once skin is exposed to UV radiation, melanin is produced in an attempt to protect the skin, which may cause the skin to darken. The increase in melanin and change in skin color is actually a sign of skin damage. Hence, tanning increases the risk of skin cancer. Likewise indoor tanning is not considered safe by the FDA because indoor tanning devices expose the user to UV radiation and also pose risks to eye injury, in addition to skin damage and skin cancer ("FDA proposes," n.d.). Evidence also suggests that indoor tanning by children and young adults is especially risky. Indoor tanners are 59 percent more likely to develop skin cancer than people who have never tanned indoors.

Research supports the risks of indoor and sun tanning. A researcher from the Netherlands found that UV exposure from sunlight is carcinogenic and, particularly among Caucasians, has contributed to observed increases in skin cancer (de Gruijl, 1999). The International Agency

for Research on Cancer declared in 2009 that tanning beds are carcinogenic for humans (Reinberg, 2009). Tanning bed exposure and melanoma have been reported among dermatology patients (Ting, Schulz, Cac, Peterson, & Walling, 2007). These researchers found a high incidence of melanoma in a survey of more than 500 dermatology clinic patients. Tanning bed exposure was reported by 88 percent of respondents; those with tanning bed exposure were significantly more likely to have developed melanoma. Adolescents are also at risk given their practice of indoor tanning (Cokkinides, Weinstock, Lazovich, Ward, & Thun, 2009). Attitudes toward indoor tanning, parental permission to tan indoors, and parental use of indoor tanning predicted adolescents' use of indoor tanning in that study. However, recently researchers have found that among undergraduates those who recognized the perceived negative health effects of tanning were less likely to tan by any method (Yoo & Kim, 2013).

Given the serious risk associated with tanning, why do people continue to tan? The short answer is that tanned skin confers social benefits: it is fashionable and attractive. In qualitative research conducted by a Canadian-US team, people with tans were perceived as healthy, sociable, fit, attractive, and affluent by indoor tanners (Vannini &

DRESS IN THE NEWS
Hot or Not

In an attempt to understand why people continue to tan given the harmfulness of the practice, Vinh Chung, a doctor with Vanguard Dermatology and Skin Cancer Specialists of Colorado, recently used the Hot or Not website to study the effects of tanning on attractiveness judgments (Naquin, 2011). The research team conducted an experiment and their manipulation was whether or not the depicted stimuli appeared to be tanned or not. Photos of five women were uploaded to the website. For each woman one photo was considered a baseline photo depicting her as she actually looked. The other photo was altered using Photoshop software to make her appear tanned. All ten photos were then rated by visitors to the site. The results were that when "tanned" the women were rated more attractive as compared to the baseline photos. The research this story was based on was published in *Dermatologic Surgery* (Chung, Gordon, Veledar, & Chen, 2010).

McCright, 2004). Attractiveness was identified as a rationale for a tan in other research (Cafri, Thompson, Jacobsen, & Hillhouse, 2006). In a study of late adolescent women, researchers found that those who believed tanned women were fashionable naturally also had positive attitudes about tanning (Cho, Lee, & Wilson, 2010). In that study tanned women were perceived to be fashionable and fit. Another benefit to tanning is increased body satisfaction (Yoo & Kim, 2013).

BODIES

Overall attractiveness is not only based on facial attractiveness, as seen in the section on attractiveness and advertising. A recent study by Australian researchers has determined that the current Western standard of ideal beauty is based on both facial and body attractiveness for both women and men (Peters, Rhodes, & Simmons, 2007). For men, face attractiveness contributed more strongly to overall attractiveness than body attractiveness did, while for women face attractiveness and body attractiveness contributed to overall attractiveness relatively equally. Other research challenges those findings and suggests that body shape is important when women judge men's attractiveness. German researchers studied the relationship among physical attractiveness of the face and body and actual physical fitness in men (Hönekopp, Rudolph, Beier, Leibert, & Müller, 2007). They assessed men's

physical fitness using a physical fitness test that included six different types of exercises. One group of women rated photos of the men on physical attractiveness (of faces and of bodies), while another group rated them on masculinity. Actual physical fitness correlated highly with ratings of body attractiveness, but facial attractiveness did not. Other analyses demonstrated that men who scored higher on actual physical fitness were rated as more masculine and that masculinity ratings predicted higher ratings of body attractiveness.

After puberty women gain body fat in the hips and thighs; this distribution of body fat is quantified by the **waist to hip ratio or WHR**. Before puberty boys and girls have similar WHRs (Henss, 2000). Healthy women have WHRs from .67 to .80 (before menopause), while for men it ranges from .85 to .95. Women with small waists in comparison to hips (more of an hourglass figure) will have lower WHR than women who are less curvy with smaller difference between waist and hips. See Table 6.3 for comparisons of WHRs for various combinations of measurements. As can be seen from the table, similar hip to waist differences result in similar WHRs.

Cathie Jung holds the record for the smallest waist on a living woman. She reports her measurements as: 39, 15, 39. She achieved that 15-inch waist through corset training, which included sleeping in a tightly laced corset. If these measurements are correct, then Cathie's WHR is a mere .38! Search online for *Cathie Jung official site* and read Cathie's story.

TABLE 6.3

WHR COMPARISONS

Bust Measurement	Waist Measurement	Hips Measurement	Difference (H-W)	WHR
38	26	38	12	.68
35	23	35	12	.66
34	26	34	8	.76
35	25	35	10	.71
40	30	40	10	.75
30	30	30	0	1.00
40	40	40	0	1.00

Researchers contend that women with smaller WHRs signal reproductive potential and hence are judged as more attractive than women with larger WHRs (Henss, 2000; Singh, 2002). Since men and women differ in WHR after puberty it can be considered a sexually dimorphic feature. Researchers from the UK examined two sexually dimorphic features in women, one evident in the face (feminine or neotonous features) and one evident in the body (WHR) (Furnham & Reeves, 2006). In this study feminine (or neotonous) features and WHR were systematically varied in an experiment. Participants were asked to judge women's attractiveness and were shown full-body photos. Manipulating the face (through the manipulation of feminine [neotonous] features) had a significant effect on attractiveness ratings, whereas manipulating the body (WHR) had no effect on attractiveness. However, the possibility remains that other body manipulations such as weight or **body mass index or BMI**: (weight in kilograms divided by height in meters squared, which is a measure of body fatness) could impact judgments of attractiveness.

Scholars have also investigated the impact of attractiveness by manipulating the grooming (including WHR) of one female television news anchor (Grabe & Sampson, 2011). The researchers were interested in whether the grooming of the anchor would affect (a) the amount of information recalled from a news broadcast and (b) the perceived professionalism of the anchor. The researchers reasoned that WHR is a compelling cue to a woman's physical attractiveness and that clothing, makeup, and accessories also contributed to judgments of attractiveness and professionalism. Based on this rationale, the manipulation of grooming consisted of two conditions combining various aspects of WHR, clothing, makeup, and accessories. A twenty-four-year old news anchor (anchorette) with brown hair and of normal weight served as a stimulus person. In what the researchers called the sexualized condition, she was depicted dressed "in a tight fitting dark blue jacket and skirt that accented her (low) hip-to-waist-ratio.

She also "wore bright red lipstick and a necklace" (p. 479). In the other grooming condition (unsexualized), she wore "a shapeless and loose-fitting dark blue jacket and skirt which deemphasized her waistline" (p. 479); in this condition she wore no lipstick or necklace. Participants watched the stimulus person in one of the two grooming conditions reading local news stories in a news studio. The presentation of the stimulus person showed her upper body (head, chest, upper thighs, waist, and hips), so that the manipulation was visible. As compared to women, men rated the sexualized anchorette as more professional. Men also recalled significantly more news information from the unsexualized anchorette than the sexualized anchorette. In this study because the authors manipulated WHR using a clothing manipulation it is not clear if the effects are due to WHR or the clothing differences. Also since jewelry and lipstick differed between conditions, one or both of those variables could have been the cause of the results.

Other research confirms the importance of faces and bodies in self-assessments of physical appearance. Instead of asking people to assess their own attractiveness, we might ask them how satisfied they are with their bodies and assume that satisfaction and self-perceived attractiveness might be related. For example, one researcher asked men and women to indicate how satisfied they were with various parts of their bodies (Tucker, 1981; 1985). Two of the dimensions of appearance that were isolated in the research reflected facial appearance and bodily appearance. Both men and women rated face and overall appearance as one significant component of their satisfaction. In addition, both men and women considered items related to their body structure as important to their satisfaction. For men, the items reflected strength, muscularity, and the shape of the upper body; and for women, the items reflected weight and lower body shape. In these studies, facial appearance was considered part of overall appearance.

Instead of asking people directly to report on aspects of appearance they are satisfied with or having them rate people on attractiveness, **implicit measures** can be used. Implicit or indirect measures are ways to assess the variable of interest (in our case the variable of interest is attractiveness) without directly asking about the variable. We can assess what attributes people consider to be desirable implicitly by studying responses to heterosexual personal advertisements. In such studies researchers have found evidence for the importance of faces and bodies to overall attractiveness (e.g., Goode, 1996; Pawlowski & Koziel, 2002). In these studies researchers prepare phony personal ads, vary the physical attributes used to describe the bogus advertiser, and then measure the number of responses or **hit rate**. This way they can assess which personal physical attributes influence the hit rate. For example, Polish researchers found that women's weight was negatively related to hit rate (i.e., as advertised weight increased, the hit rate decreased) suggesting that heavier women were not considered desirable as potential mates (Pawlowski & Koziel, 2002). Goode found that men responding to ads were more influenced than women by the attribute of attractiveness, while women were more influenced than men by descriptions of financial success. In Goode's study the desirable advertisers were described as handsome, athletic, broad-shouldered (for men) and beautiful, shapely, and slender (for women). Thus, attractiveness as defined for the research included aspects of faces and bodies.

Body Type

Body type refers to a person's overall shape or silhouette. Some researchers studying dress and social perception have focused their work on the body as a stimulus variable. This makes sense, considering that bodies form the scaffolding for the clothes you wear and, depending on fashion, your clothes more or less conform to your body's shape. Body type has been manipulated and defined in a number of ways by researchers. For example, body type has been presented to research participants using verbal descriptions, drawings, and photos of stimulus persons. In general, large-sized individuals are rated less positively than thinner individuals. For example, researchers from the UK (2013) conducted a study with men and women from the UK, Hong Kong, and China (Mo et al., 2013). Participants judged real women who differed in body size as measured by BMI. Results showed that higher BMIs were associated with lower ratings of attractiveness and healthiness. In an experiment out of Australia, participants were shown images of a woman before and after weight loss and formed impressions of her (Fardouly & Vartanian, 2012). After weight loss the stimulus person was rated both less sloppy and more competent. In a recent review of the literature related to weight bias, researchers demonstrate the prevalence of bias as well as stereotyping for obese individuals (Puhl & Huer, 2009).

DRESS IN THE NEWS
Wedding Reality Shows

Many reality TV shows now focus on weddings (McKay, 2011). Some of the titles include: *Bridezillas* (WE network), *Say Yes to the Dress* (TLC), *Bridalplasty* (E!), *Bulging Brides* (WE), *Buff Brides* (Fit TV), *Wedding Wars* (VH1), *Rich Bride, Poor Bride* (WE), *My Big Friggin' Wedding* (VH1), and *Shedding for the Wedding* (CW). According to McKay, any woman feeling the pressure of planning a wedding and looking good has enough to worry about without being inundated with images of women attempting unrealistic appearance changes. By hyping the superficial aspects of weddings some think that reality wedding TV could trigger women to take unhealthy drastic measures to change how they look. One expert believes that such shows encourage the belief that everything about a wedding must be perfect and ignore the true focus of weddings—the commitment to another person.

Overweight Stigma

Since the Western ideal of beauty for women and men includes the absence of body fat, it is not surprising that Americans (men and women) spend about $58 billion a year on weight-loss programs, diet foods, diet cookbooks, and weight-loss drugs to achieve that ideal (Rothblum, 2009). In such an environment, what happens to people who are overweight, fat, or obese? Research suggests that they are stereotyped and stigmatized. A **stigma** is a deeply discrediting attribute (Goffman, 1963). Stigmas result from violations of major norms (Cusack, Jack, & Kavanagh, 2003). An example of a major norm is the cultural ideal of beauty. Hence, someone who is overweight has violated the norm of ideal beauty (Figure 6.7).

In an attempt to determine if obese men are stigmatized in the same way as women, researchers devised an experiment (Hebl & Turchin, 2005). Stimuli consisted of photos of black or white men and women. The participants were black and white men. Both black and white men rated obese men more negatively than medium and thin men. Hence, the men did stigmatize obesity in others. In a qualitative study of weight stigma, participants were recruited from a weight loss organization (Puhl, Moss-Racusin, Schwartz, & Brownell, 2008). Results showed that stigma was experienced by obese individuals in many domains of life. The most common source of stigmatizing comments was people who should have known better: friends, parents, and spouses. The state of being overweight is visible and cannot be hidden as some other stigmas can and it does affect social interaction. People also blame themselves for being overweight; in other words, it is our own "fault" if we are overweight (Puhl et al., 2008). This fact plus its visibility makes the stigma of being overweight especially onerous.

Research in a variety of fields demonstrates bias against overweight or large-sized people, called **overweight bias**. Overweight bias occurs when overweight people are viewed less positively than others simply because they are overweight. Overweight individuals are rated less positively on social traits than thinner individuals (Hebl, Ruggs, Singletary, & Beal, 2008). That experimental research showed that large-sized people are viewed as less happy, less successful in relationships, and less popular/sociable than thinner individuals. Large-sized women are even perceived to be less fashionable than thinner women

---

Figure 6.7

Being overweight violates the cultural norm of ideal beauty; hence it is a stigma for men, women, and children within many cultures.

when wearing the very same clothing style (Lennon & Clayton, 1992)!

Large-sized people are also rated less positively on workplace characteristics. In a study of professional image, thinner women were judged as more professional than larger women (Thurston, Lennon, & Clayton, 1990). Larger people are judged to be less intelligent and to have less job aptitude than thinner people (Hebl et al., 2008). Compared to thinner people, larger individuals are judged to be less successful (Smith, 1985). In an attempt to determine if stereotypes of negative personality traits associated with obese employees have any real basis in working-age US adults, researchers assessed relationships between personality traits and BMIs in a large national sample of working-age US adults (Roehling, Roehling, & Odland, 2008). Results of the study failed to find any practically significant relationships between BMIs and the negative personality traits. These results were confirmed in a follow-up study with college students. What this research demonstrates is that personality stereotypes of obese employees are not based on fact. Yet, in the US prejudice, stereotypes, and discrimination are targeted toward obese and overweight individuals (Rhode, 2010). Taking a different approach Rhode used popular press accounts, research findings, and cited **case law** (legal decisions made by judges) to demonstrate that obese and overweight individuals face discrimination in the workplace, education, health care, provision of goods and services, and in interpersonal situations.

However, overweight bias does not hold for all ethnic groups in the US. When asked to rate same-race women of various body types, African American men were more likely than Caucasian men to rate women with larger bodies as powerful, attractive, and ambitious (Jackson & McGill, 1996). Caucasian men were more likely to rate them negatively as lazy, disgusting, uneducated, unhealthy, lacking in willpower, depressed, and sloppy. When assigning physical characteristics related to being attractive, African American men were more likely than Caucasian men to pick round buttocks and wide hips as attractive, and less likely to select slim figures. Other researchers were interested in the thinness obsession in the US and reasoned that there might exist differing levels across ethnic groups (Hebl & Heatherton, 1998). They devised an experiment using photos of nine African American female models and nine Caucasian American female models. Within each ethnic group, ⅓ of the models were thin, ⅓ were average, and ⅓ were large; however, all photos were taken from fashion magazines and catalogs so all models were within the normal size range. Participants were African American and Caucasian American women who judged the models on personal traits. Results revealed a strong size bias for the Caucasian models, but not for the African American models. These studies demonstrate that impression formation is affected by very small differences in body size (since all were fashion models), although not necessarily for all ethnicities.

Overweight bias can lead to discrimination. For example, obese children are at risk for peer victimization such as pushing, kicking, teasing, and ignoring (Gray, Kahhan, & Janicke, 2009). Over 50 percent of obese children report this kind of discrimination (Warschburger, 2005). Some researchers have studied discrimination in simulated hiring decisions and found that large-sized people were more likely to be discriminated against (Swami, Chan,

Wong, Furnham, & Tovee, 2008). Recently, researchers conducted a meta-analysis of twenty-five experimental studies on weight-based bias in employment (Rudolph, Wells, Weller, & Baltes, 2009). They found weight-based bias across workplace outcomes (i.e., hiring decisions, promotions, and performance evaluations). Weight was negatively related to all workplace outcomes, that is, overweight workers were systematically devalued in comparison to non-overweight workers. When real overweight people are asked about the extent to which they experience weight-based discrimination, researchers find that perceptions of weight-based bias has increased from 7 percent reporting it in 1996 to 12 percent in 2008 (Andreyeva, Puhl, & Brownell, 2008).

In the US, some types of discrimination are banned by law in certain situations. For example, Title VII of the Civil Rights Act of 1964 bans employment discrimination as a function of race, color, religion, sex, or national origin, but not appearance or weight. Michigan is the only state to have a law banning discrimination based on appearance in hiring situations. Nevertheless, discrimination occurs. Scholars have reviewed research on obesity, bias, and discrimination and found evidence of stigmatization and sometimes discrimination in employment, education, and health care (Puhl & Brownell, 2001).

Haskins and Ransford (1999) were interested to determine if people's actual size affected their life circumstances. They surveyed women working in the aerospace industry. The women reported income, current occupation, age, race, education, weight, height, and how they felt about their weight. The researchers hypothesized that income and occupational status would be affected by weight. They found that women's weight was negatively related to income, but only at the entry-level and only for professional and managerial positions. Thus, starting salaries for professional and managerial positions were higher for thinner women, demonstrating discrimination.

The Politics of Body Size

Kwan (2009) studied meanings associated with fat bodies. She noted that social problems are related not only to objective conditions but also to **collective definitions** (i.e., definitions by various groups). She did an analysis of organizational materials from the Centers for Disease Control and Prevention (CDC), the National Association to Advance Fat Acceptance (NAAFA), and the Center for

Consumer Freedom (CCF), a food industry group. She found that each group characterized fat people and fat bodies differently. For example, the CDC characterized obesity as an epidemic in the US with many health risks. NAAFA does not accept that obesity is linked to disease. The food industry (CCF) takes yet a different perspective; they argue that obesity is not related to disease and that the weight loss industry has a vested interest in linking obesity to disease. In other words, the food industry wants to keep people eating more food, while the weight loss industry wants people to eat less, buy diet pills and exercise equipment, and memberships in Weight Watchers or Jenny Craig. It is clear from this research that fatness is politicized. Kwan did not study fashion publications, but if she had she might have found that fatness is considered unaesthetic. In fact, recent research found that college women's anti-fat attitudes (e.g., "Fat people are physically unattractive") are positively correlated with time spent reading fashion magazines (Lin & Reid, 2008).

Inscribed Bodies

In Chapter 1, "Why Study Dress?" you learned about body modifications as a subcategory of dress. Changes to the surface of the body are examples of body modifications and one such type of modification is tattooing. Tattoos often feature in articles in the online media. In October 2015, the *BBC News Magazine* published a feature that wondered if Western world leaders were tattooed. They were only able to verify that Justin Trudeau, prime minister of Canada, has a tattoo and President Obama and Vladimir Putin do not, at least not on their chests (Barford, 2015). While it is common to see sports figures and media celebrities with tattoos featured in the media, we do not often see forehead tattoos used as advertising. Andrew Fisher sold his forehead as advertising space for over $37,000 on eBay (Associated Press, 2005). Another tattoo trend seen on social media is for women who have had breast cancer to have their breasts tattooed to cover scars and for psychological benefits (James, 2015; Kim, 2015).

People have been tattooing their bodies for thousands of years (Lake, 2015). Lake provided a number of statistics about tattoos. Once considered the purview of servicemen and motorcycle gang members, today 20 percent of Americans have at least one tattoo. Greater percentages of women (58 percent) have tattoos than men (41 percent) in the US. Roughly 25 percent of Americans regret getting their tattoos and close to 33,000 sought tattoo removal in 2013, with nearly 73 percent of those for women. The tattoo removal industry is expected to reach $83 million by 2018, which is small in relation to the entire tattoo industry in the US that made $3 billion in revenue in 2014.

Schildkrout (2004) reviewed the literature in anthropology and related disciplines about inscribed bodies or writing on skin. She includes tattooing, piercing, branding, and body paint as types of inscriptions. Schildkrout finds that inscribing human flesh is **pan-human** (characteristic of humans everywhere around the world) and represents personal and cultural differences. In particular, inscriptions signal identity and convey boundaries between groups, between oneself and society, and between man and god. In the past in anthropological literature, body inscriptions were a sign of not being civilized and were often characterized as deviant (Figure 6.8). Writers in both psychology and medicine viewed body inscriptions as a symbol of individual **pathology** or disease. However, by 2000 tattoos became a fashion statement and piercings in the earlobe were commonplace. For example, researchers surveyed 1,375 college students and found that 47 percent of the women had piercings in locations other than the earlobe and 46 percent of the men (in ears or elsewhere); in addition 25 percent of the women and 26 percent of the men had permanent tattoos (Tate & Shelton, 2008).

One researcher was interested in body modifications and how they were represented in the media (Adams, 2009). For example, are certain types of procedures promoted as normative in the attempt to approximate the cultural ideal of beauty and others presented as more deviant? Adams analyzed seventy-two newspaper articles that dealt with tattooing, piercing, and cosmetic surgery. Procedures such as cosmetic surgery and tattooing were presented as means of self-expression and as lifestyle choices, whereas body piercing was more often presented as self-destructive and unhealthy.

In fact, researchers have investigated body piercing and cultural deviance (Bui, Rodgers, Caihol, Birmes, Chabrol, & Schmitt, 2010; Mayers & Chiffriller, 2008; Nathanson, Paulhus, & Williams, 2006; Roberts, Auinger, & Ryan, 2004). French researchers completed a database search for research about body piercing and high-risk behaviors (Bui et al., 2010). They found that piercing was associated with drug use in men and women, with high-risk sexual behaviors (e.g., unprotected sex, sexual promiscuity), and with alcohol use and smoking (Figure 6.9). Roberts, Auinger, and Ryan (2004) surveyed over 4,000 adolescents from thirteen to eighteen about body piercing at a location other than the ear. The researchers found that adolescents who reported piercings at other locations than the ear also were more likely to report several high-risk behaviors (peer substance use, sexual intercourse, smoking, marijuana use, and suicide attempts). Others have also found relationships between piercing and medical

Figure 6.8
Maria Jose Cristerna from Mexico, known as "Vampire Woman," holds the Guinness World Record for being the woman with the most tattoos and body modifications.

Figure 6.9
A French research team found that piercing was associated with drug use, with high-risk sexual behavior, and with alcohol use and smoking.

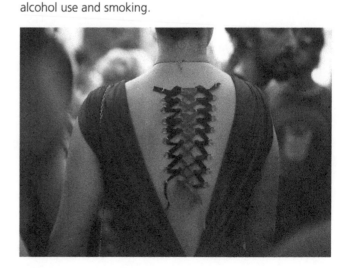

complications. Mayers and Chiffriller found that 19 percent of college students with body piercings had medical complications and 9 percent had infections.

Scholars have also conducted research by manipulating tattoos on experimental stimuli (Wohlrab, Fink, Kappeler, & Brewer, 2009). Female stimuli with tattoos were rated as less healthy than those without tattoos and male stimuli with tattoos were rated as more dominant than those without tattoos. College students' perceptions of women with tattoos were investigated in experimental research that varied the number of tattoos visible on a female stimulus person (Swami & Furnham, 2007). Overall they found negative perceptions as a function of tattoos. Also ratings of physical attractiveness decreased as number of tattoos increased. In addition, as number of tattoos increased, ratings of promiscuity and perceptions of alcohol consumption both increased.

Body Modifications in Applied Settings

Having a visible tattoo can impact both the service you receive as a customer as well as your employment opportunities in some professional fields. In research with health care providers and medical and nursing students, researchers found that both physicians and nurses rated tattooed individuals less positively than did students studying to be future health care providers (Stuppy, Armstrong, & Casals-Ariet, 1998). Women's attitudes were generally less positive than those of men, particularly toward tattooed professional women. Attitudes toward tattooed adolescents were even more negative than attitudes toward tattooed adults. That this bias exists is important since holding a negative attitude toward an individual with a visible tattoo may impact the care that is provided to tattooed individuals by these professionals.

Is this negative bias concerning tattooed individuals limited to health care professionals? In the mid-1990s researchers conducted a telephone survey of employers representing the hospitality, beauty, retailing, and office sectors (Bekhor, Bekhor, & Gandrabur, 1995). These researchers also reported a bias against the hiring of people with visible tattoos. Less than 30 percent of the 242 employers surveyed indicated they would employ a person with a tattoo.

As having a tattoo has gained in popularity has the bias toward people with tattoos found in research conducted in the 1990s disappeared? Or do these negative attitudes toward tattooed individuals continue to persist? The answer appears to be yes, the bias has continued at least in some professions. Researchers investigated restaurant managers, human resource managers, and college recruiters in the hospitality industry who reported that visible body modifications including both tattoos and body piercings would be viewed negatively and that individuals with visible tattoos would be unlikely to be hired (Brallier, Maguire, Smith, & Palm, 2011; Swanger, 2006). In other research, patients at a rural Maryland hospital rated health care workers with visible tattoos as less professional than workers without visible tattoos (Westerfield, Speroni, Stafford, & Daniel, 2012). Similarly, undergraduates indicated visible tattoos were not appropriate for tax service providers and workers in finance but were appropriate for those employed as mechanics and bartenders (Dean, 2011). Other researchers have also repeatedly reported that people with tattoos or body piercings are associated with negative attributes (Brallier et al., 2011; Degelman & Price, 2002; Seiter, & Hatch, 2005; Swami & Furnham, 2007).

Co-workers with facial body art (tattooing and piercing) are also undesirable in the workplace (Miller, Nicols, & Eure, 2009). Business students were asked to indicate the extent to which a stimulus person with two facial piercings and one facial tattoo would be an acceptable work partner. Results showed that persons with facial art were more acceptable work partners when the job did not require face-to-face customer contact and if one's rewards did not depend on the efforts of the person with facial art.

With the growing popularity of such body modifications, what are the implications for college students and gaining access to employment as a professional? Should having a visible tattoo or body piercing matter? The research on the perception of individuals who possess body modifications such as tattoos and body piercings suggests that public perception continues to lag behind the actual movement of these body modifications into the cultural mainstream. Although employers are unlikely to admit that they discriminate against individuals with tattoos or piercings, employers are determining how well prospective employees fit with the company image and some people continue to be uncomfortable around others exhibiting multiple tattoos and piercings. Are there employers who do not care? The answer is probably yes for employment in positions in which workers do not have high contact with the public. Working in a call center or behind a computer in an office cubicle are examples that come to mind.

It may take time for ideas about tattooed and body pierced individuals to change. Ultimately, the degree of fit between prospective employees and the company image may guide decisions about hiring employees with multiple tattoos and piercings. As was discussed in Chapter 4, "Dress and Social Cognition," employers are concerned about the link between the appearance of employees and the resulting extended inferences about their companies. Research is needed to confirm that extended inferences would actually be negative if employees had tattoos and visible body piercings. Regardless, undergraduates seem to be aware of this negative bias concerning tattooed individuals and indicate as one strategy to deal with it that they plan to cover their tattoos when interviewing for post-graduation positions and/or remove piercing jewelry when possible (Foltz, 2014).

In summary, although tattooing and piercing have become more common, they still have negative connotations in some contexts. As compared to non-tattooed women, tattooed women are perceived negatively: as less healthy, less attractive, more promiscuous, and likely to be heavier drinkers. In addition, people prefer not to work with others who have facial art, especially in face-to face contact positions or as team partners. Negative perceptions of people with facial art abound in health care, hospitality, beauty, retailing, and office sectors.

Aging Bodies

Just as visible signs of aging are visible in the face, the body is also a marker of age because of how we feel and how we look (Calasanti, 2005). Visible signs of aging in the body include age spots, loss in height, increase in weight, loss of lean muscle mass, and sagging breasts (for women). See Table 6.4 for a summary of visible signs associated with aging of the body. Researchers have also studied visible bodily changes associated with aging. Canadian researchers interviewed thirty-six women aged between seventy-one to ninety-three about body changes and clothing (Hurd Clarke, Griffin, & Maliha, 2009). The interviewees identified physical changes of weight gain, altered body shapes, sagging arms (bat wings), and sagging necks (turkey wattles) that they attempted to compensate for with their clothing. These aging women reported that their clothing choices were limited because of weight gain or because of inappropriate styles and colors available in the marketplace.

Classic styles in navy, beiges, and pastels were preferred by the women in the research by Hurd Clarke et al. (2009).

TABLE 6.4

VISIBLE BODILY CHANGES ASSOCIATED WITH AGING

Body Feature	Visible Changes
Hair	Thinning, balding, graying. Women experience growth of facial hair; men experience growth of nose hair and eyebrow hair.
Skin	Skin loses elasticity, becomes sun-damaged, and can develop "age spots."
Height	Height increases until age 40, and by 80 people may lose up to 2 inches of height. This loss is due to forward bending of the spine and compression of disks.
Weight	For men, weight increases until about age 50, then declines. For women, weight increases until the late 60s, then declines slowly.
Body Fat	The proportion of body fat to weight doubles between ages 25 to 75.
Fat Distribution	Fat is redistributed from just under the skin to deeper parts of the body.
Lean Muscle Mass	Without exercise, women (men) lose 22% (23%) of their lean muscle mass between 30 and 70.
Breasts	As women age, breasts become smaller, less firm, less full, and lose support.

Sources: Aging changes in the breast (2011) and Changes with aging (n.d.).

They also reported using their clothing to mask their bodies' changes. They wore long sleeves to hide sagging arms. They selected pants instead of skirts to hide varicose veins and swelling or to avoid having to wear pantyhose. They avoided sleeveless and strapless styles, sundresses, and dresses with spaghetti straps. They also avoided low-cut tops and tried to select things that were easy to get on and off. Some of the interviewees commented that they do not have as many choices when buying apparel because there is little available that fits an older body. Yet, even though they felt their choices were limited, the women thought it was important to pay attention to their appearances to avoid negative social judgments and ageist assumptions. They also noted that lack of attention to appearance might convey dependence—that they need assistance. They wanted to avoid the impression that they were frail, incompetent older women. Thus, for these women clothing was used strategically as a socially acceptable way to hide the visible signs of an aging body, just as they might use cosmetics to mask the changes of facial aging.

Cosmetic Surgery for Faces and Bodies

The Freedonia Group conducts market research on the use of cosmetic surgery products and predicts that the industry will grow 7.4 percent annually through 2014 (Cosmetic Surgery Products to 2014, 2010). See Table 6.5 for frequencies and increases in types of cosmetic surgery reported by the American Society of Aesthetic Plastic Surgery and Table 6.6 for the frequencies with which men and women elect various types of cosmetic surgery reported by the American Society of Plastic Surgeons. As can be seen from Table 6.5, four popular cosmetic surgery types have increased dramatically since 1997. Given these increases and increases in the use of minimally-invasive procedures (see Table 6.2), researchers have developed an instrument to assess attitudes about the acceptance of cosmetic surgery in the general population (Henderson-King & Henderson-King, 2005). They used the term *cosmetic surgery* and did not distinguish it from non-invasive procedures. Using this instrument the authors surveyed 169 college men and women and found that the more young people feared becoming unattractive in the future (presumably due to aging), the more they endorsed cosmetic surgery. In another study reported in the same article, the authors surveyed 261 college men and women; they found that the more people approved of using makeup, the more accepting they were of cosmetic surgery. Together this research suggests that cosmetic surgery and non-invasive (or minimally invasive) cosmetic surgical procedures are becoming socially acceptable among the young (Figure 6.10).

TABLE 6.5			
FREQUENCIES AND INCREASES OF SELECTED COSMETIC SURGERY PROCEDURES, 1997–2014			
Procedure	*Frequency in 1997*	*Frequency in 2014*[6]	*Percent Change*
Breast Augmentation	101,176	286,694	183.4%
Liposuction	176,863	342,494	93.6%
Eyelid Surgery	159,232	165,714	4.1%
Tummy Tuck	34,002	164,021	382.4%
Breast Reduction (in women only)	47,874	114,470	139.1%

Source: American Society for Aesthetic Plastic Surgery, 2014.

[6]Frequencies reported in Tables 6.5 and 6.6 do not always agree and are from different sources: the American Society of Plastic Surgeons (ASPS) and the American Society of Aesthetic Plastic Surgery (ASAPS), respectively. The ASPS only includes plastic surgeons, whereas the ASAPS includes plastic surgeons, as well as dermatologists and other providers who perform plastic surgery.

Figure 6.10

Justin Jedlica, the human Ken doll, has reportedly had over 190 cosmetic procedures.

Assuming that people elect specific cosmetic surgical procedures to more closely approximate the cultural ideal, we might infer from Table 6.6 that large breasts, thinness, and youthfulness are part of that ideal for women and are achieved respectively via breast augmentation, liposuction and tummy tucks, and eyelid surgery. For men, we might infer that youthfulness and absence of body fat are part of that ideal and are achieved respectively via eyelid surgery, liposuction, and breast reduction. Since one's nose has a prominent position on the face, it is not surprising that nose surgery is one of the top five cosmetic surgeries for men.

What Predicts Why Some People Endorse Cosmetic Surgery and Others Do Not?

In the next section we discuss factors that predict why some people are more likely than others to endorse cosmetic surgery as a viable means to change the appearance of their faces and bodies. Such factors include male female differences, personality differences, and media influence.

Male–Female Differences

From Table 6.6, it is clear that women outnumber men for four of the top five categories of cosmetic surgery. Men outnumber women for hair transplantation. Objectification

TABLE 6.6

TOP FIVE COSMETIC SURGERIES BY SEX IN 2014

Women		Men	
Procedure	Frequency	Procedure	Frequency
Liposuction	302,028	Liposuction	40,466
Breast Augmentation	286,694	Nose Surgery	32,641
Tummy Tuck	156,449	Eyelid Surgery	27,765
Eyelid Surgery	137,949	Breast Reduction	24,234
Breast Lift	132,908	Face-lift	15,019

Source: American Society of Plastic Surgeons. Report of the 2014 plastic surgery statistics (2015).

theory was used to guide research conducted in the UK to explain why women are more likely to have cosmetic surgery to change physical appearance than men (Calogero, Pina, Park, & Rahemtulla, 2010). Objectification theory will be discussed in more detail in Chapter 9, "Dress and the Self." Objectification theory holds that Western societies sexually objectify women and, more recently and to a lesser extent, men (Hebl, King, & Lin, 2004). According to the theory, people evaluate themselves from an external perspective from observations of others using unrealistic cultural standards (Fredrickson & Roberts, 1997). Sexual objectification occurs when people are defined by sexual body parts. Calogero et al. hold that positive attitudes toward cosmetic surgery among women result from sociocultural conditions that lead to objectification. Results showed that women's acceptance of cosmetic surgery to change physical appearance can be explained by sexual and self-objectification.

Personality Differences

Research suggests that personality traits predict the use (or intent to use) cosmetic surgery to enhance physical attractiveness (Davis & Vernon, 2002). The researchers were interested in attachment anxiety as a personality trait; people high in attachment anxiety are dependent on their (romantic) partner's approval, may be concerned about abandonment, and accordingly may be more likely to be concerned with their appearance. A large sample of men and women who ranged in age from fifteen to seventy-one completed questionnaires. Results showed that women were more likely than men to have (or intend to have) any facial or body cosmetic surgery, but men were more likely to have (or intend to have) any hair procedure. Across all procedures, those higher in attachment anxiety were more likely to have (or plan to have) a cosmetic surgery procedure.

Media Influence

One reason cosmetic surgery may be becoming more acceptable among young people is due to media influence. What we see in the media influences our perceptions of beauty and how we think we should look according to the Rudd and Lennon (1994) model of body aesthetics. The influence of the media is illustrated in research findings. In one study college women were surveyed about whether or not they would consider cosmetic surgery (Swami, 2009). Results showed that greater media influence was related to higher scores for consideration of cosmetic surgery. Australian researchers surveyed more than 100 women who ranged in age from thirty-five to fifty-five; results showed that television exposure was directly related to positive attitudes toward cosmetic surgery for social reasons (to earn rewards from others) and to consideration of having cosmetic surgery in the future (Slevec & Tiggemann, 2010). Hence, it is possible that media influence may be fueling increases in cosmetic surgery procedures among college students and middle-aged women.

DRESS IN THE NEWS
Men's Cosmetic Surgery

Today more men in Western countries are electing cosmetic surgeries to tighten their necks, remove body fat, and reshape their noses (Hodgkinson, n.d.; Landro, 2011). David Culpepper elected to have a face-lift and chin implant, and like many men who opt for such procedures, did so when he found himself back in the dating game and was encouraged by a partner, fiancée, or girlfriend (Hodgkinson, n.d.; Landro, 2011). Baby boomers like Culpepper, who are seeing the effects of aging, seek cosmetic surgery as a way to look youthful. This is especially important for men seeking to maintain an edge in the work environment. Mr. Culpepper was back to work in two weeks after his surgery and he wed his fiancée Cindy Galardi shortly thereafter.

Younger men also elect cosmetic procedures although the procedures are not usually covered by insurance. For young men such procedures are viewed as a way to fix embarrassing or unmanly characteristics, which not surprisingly, give them a more attractive appearance. For example, for male breast reduction (See Table 6.6), which was elected by 18,000 men in 2010 in the US, nearly 75 percent were teens from thirteen to nineteen. Due to advancements in techniques used, some cosmetic surgeries are done on an outpatient basis, and newer minimally invasive procedures (e.g., Botox or fillers) only require an office visit.

It has been suggested that the proliferation of cosmetic surgery reality television programs and other media depictions such as stories about celebrities having cosmetic surgeries may explain the increase in cosmetic surgery to change physical appearance (Slevec & Tiggemann, 2010). Recent research supports that suggestion. College students (101 women and 69 men) were surveyed about reality television shows featuring cosmetic surgeries and use of cosmetic surgery to alter features of their faces and bodies (Markey & Markey, 2010). Those who had positive views of reality television shows that featured cosmetic surgery also had more favorable attitudes toward using cosmetic surgery to alter both their (a) bodies and (b) faces. The researchers then designed an experiment to determine if one exposure to a reality television program depicting cosmetic surgery would make people more likely to want cosmetic surgery to alter their bodies and faces. Undergraduate men and women either viewed twenty minutes of *Extreme Makeover* or of *Sell this House*. People who watched *Extreme Makeover* were more likely than people who watched *Sell this House* to want to use cosmetic surgery to alter their faces and bodies.

In other research undergraduate men and women were surveyed about frequency of viewing reality television shows depicting cosmetic surgery and likelihood of engaging in a variety of behaviors including wearing makeup, breast augmentation, breast reduction (only asked of women), dermabrasion, hair coloring, laser hair removal, Botox, face-lift, exercising, and dieting (Nabi, 2009). Over half the sample had seen *I Want a Famous Face*, *Extreme Makeover*, or *The Swan*. Results found that frequency of viewing reality television depicting cosmetic surgery was significantly related to likelihood of both invasive (Botox, face-lift) procedures and minimally invasive (e.g., laser hair removal, hair coloring, demabrasion) procedures. More viewing predicted greater likelihood of having the procedures. In a second part of the research, the author surveyed 320 college students (85 percent women). Survey results found that frequency of viewing reality television depicting cosmetic surgery was related to

likelihood of engaging in invasive procedures, minimally invasive procedures, and non-invasive procedures (e.g., diet and exercise). Taken together these studies demonstrate that reality television programs depicting cosmetic surgery may be related to increases in invasive and minimally invasive cosmetic surgery.

Celebrity Worship

Another possible reason for increases in both types of procedures is celebrity worship. Celebrities are often featured in gossip magazines telling all about their cosmetic surgeries. People who emulate such celebrities might be influenced by them to also elect cosmetic surgery to alter their faces and bodies. In a study conducted in the UK, undergraduate British women were surveyed about celebrity worship and the likelihood that they would consider cosmetic surgery to change their appearance (Swami, Taylor, & Carvalho, 2009). Results showed that women who scored higher on celebrity worship had more positive attitudes toward cosmetic surgery and were more likely to consider having such surgery.

To summarize, in this section you have seen that (a) women are more likely than men to endorse cosmetic surgery and cosmetic surgical procedures, (b) personality differences are related to endorsement of cosmetic surgery and cosmetic surgical procedures, and that (c) various types of media exposure is related to endorsement of cosmetic surgery and cosmetic surgical procedures. In particular, reality television depicting cosmetic surgery and celebrity worship are related to endorsement of cosmetic surgery to alter physical appearance.

IN-CLASS ACTIVITY
Minimally Invasive Procedures

Would you ever consider having cosmetic surgery or one of the minimally invasive procedures? Why, or why not?

Chapter Summary

Two characteristics of our physical selves that affect our own and others' perceptions of us are our faces and our bodies (shape or size); both contribute to judgments of attractiveness. Faces and bodies are stimulus variables in social cognition; hence faces and bodies influence how we think, perceive, judge, and make inferences about people in our daily lives. We can purposefully manipulate facial and bodily appearance; these manipulations are examples of dress as defined in Chapter 1, "Why Study Dress?" Topics covered include the Rudd and Lennon Model of Body Aesthetics (1994), facial and body attractiveness, obesity stigma, and various purposeful body manipulations.

Key Terms

albinos
body mass index or BMI
body type
Botulinum Toxin Type A
case law
chemical peel
collective definitions

colorism
comparison target
coping strategies
cultural aesthetic ideal
dermal fillers
headshots
hit rate

implicit measures
laser hair removal
meta-analysis
microdermabrasion
neotonous
overweight bias
pan-human

pathology
Rudd and Lennon Model
sexual dimorphism
social comparison theory
stigma
waist to hip ratio or WHR

Discussion Questions

1. In discussing the Rudd and Lennon model of body aesthetics, we made the assumption that people create their appearances in order to more closely approximate the cultural ideal of beauty. But sometimes people create their appearances in ways that do not bring them closer to the cultural ideal (a Goth appearance, a Mohawk haircut). How could you modify the Rudd and Lennon model to accommodate such appearances?

2. Using the four coping strategies outlined in the Rudd and Lennon model, classify the following statements using those coping strategies: (a) Even though I would like to be ten pounds lighter, I am comfortable in my body; (b) I eat right, I take care of my kids, and exercise when I can. I do not have the body of a teenager; (c) My stomach is not as flat as I would like, so I go to the gym every day; (d) I made the decision to have my nose reshaped because I think it is too big.

3. Think of a man and a woman who you find physically attractive. List the physical characteristics they exhibit that you consider attractive. Can you categorize these characteristics as aspects of facial attractiveness or aspects of body attractiveness? Do they have other physical characteristics that are attractive, that do not fit these two categories?

4. Interview someone who has made purposeful modification of his/her body. Determine the motivations for the body modifications, whether or not dissatisfaction with natural looks plays a part, and the extent to which a significant other influences the decision.

STUD!O

Visit your book's STUDIO for additional quiz questions and vocabulary flashcards!

Suggested Readings

Andreyeva, T., Puhl, R. M., & Brownell, K. D. (2008). Changes in perceived weight discrimination among Americans, 1995–1996 through 2004–2006. *Obesity, 16*(5), 1129–1134.

Biddle, F. E., & Hamermesh, D. S. (1998). Beauty, productivity, and discrimination: Lawyers' looks and lucre. *Journal of Labor Economics, 16*(1), 172–201.

Calogero, R. M., Pina, A., Park, L. E., & Rahemtulla, Z. (2010). Objectification theory predicts college women's attitudes toward cosmetic surgery. *Sex Roles, 63*, 32–41.

Davis, D., & Vernon, M. L. (2002). Sculpting the body beautiful: Attachment style, neuroticism, and use of cosmetic surgeries. *Sex Roles, 47*, 129–138.

References

Adams, J. (2009). Bodies of change: A comparative analysis of media representations of body modification practices. *Sociological Perspectives, 52*(1), 103–129.

Adomaitis, A. D., & Johnson, K. K. P. (2008). Advertisements: Interpreting images used to sell to young adults. *Journal of Fashion Marketing and Management, 12*, 182–192.

Aging changes in the breast (2011, December 13). *Medline Plus*. Retrieved from http://www.nlm.nih.gov/medlineplus/ency/article/003999.htm

American Society of Aesthetic Plastic Surgery (2010). Surgical procedures: A 14-year comparison. Retrieved from http://www.surgery.org/sites/default/files/2010-14yrcomparison_0.pdf

American Society of Aesthetic Plastic Surgery (2015). Top 5 cosmetic surgeries by gender. Retrieved from http://www.surgery.org/sites/default/files/2014-Gender.pdf

American Society of Plastic Surgeons (2010). Report of the 2010 plastic surgery statistics. Retrieved from http://www.plasticsurgery.org/Documents/news-resources/statistics/2010-statisticss/Top-Level/2010-US-cosmetic-reconstructive-plastic-surgery-minimally-invasive-statistics2.pdf

American Society of Plastic Surgeons (2014). Top 5 cosmetic minimally-invasive and cosmetic surgical procedures. Retrieved from http://www.plasticsurgery.org/news/2015/plastic-surgery-statistics-show-new-consumer-trends.html

Amnesty International (2016). "We are not animals to be hunted or sold": Violence and discrimation against people with albinism in Malawi (2016). Retrieved from https://www.amnesty.org.uk/sites/default/files/we_are_not_animals_-_malawi_report_-_final_formated.pdf

Andreyeva, T., Puhl, R. M., & Brownell, K. D. (2008). Changes in perceived weight discrimination among Americans, 1995–1996 through 2004–2006. *Obesity, 16*(5), 1129–1134.

Ashikari, M. (2005). Cultivating Japanese whiteness: The "whitening" cosmetic boom and the Japanese identity. *Journal of Material Culture, 10*(1), 73–91.

Associated Press (2005, January 25). $37,375 payday: That's using your head! *NBC News*. Retrieved from: http://www.nbcnews.com/id/6867209/ns/us_news-weird_news/t/payday-thats-using-your-head/#.V9xnrHJLKDY

Associated Press (2013, September 23). Abercrombie & Fitch settles discrimination lawsuit over head scarves. *NY Daily News*. Retrieved from http://www.nydailynews.com/life-style/fashion/abercrombie-settles-discrimination-suit-article-1.1464996

Baker, M. M., & Churchill, G. A. (1977). The impact of physically attractive models on advertising evaluation. *Journal of Marketing Research, 14*, 538–555.

Barford, V. (2015, October 21). Is Canada's new PM the only world leader with a tattoo? Retrieved from: http://www.bbc.com/news/magazine-34585178

Bekhor, L., Bekhor, P. S., & Gandrabur, M. (1995). Employer attitudes toward persons with visible tattoos. *Australian Journal of Dermatology, 36*, 75–77.

Biddle, F. E., & Hamermesh, D. S. (1998). Beauty, productivity, and discrimination: Lawyers' looks and lucre. *Journal of Labor Economics, 16*(1), 172–201.

Bower, A. B., & Landreth, S. (2001). Is beauty best? Highly versus normally attractive models in advertising. *Journal of Advertising, 30*, 1–12.

Brallier, S., Maguire, K., Smith, D., & Palm, J. (2011). Visible tattoos and employment in the restaurant service industry. *International Journal of Business and Social Science, 2*(6), 72–76.

Bui, E., Rodgers, R., Caihol, L., Birmes, P., Chabrol, H., & Schmitt, L. (2010). Body piercing and psychopathology: A review of the literature. *Psychotherapy and Psychosomatics, 79*(2), 125–129.

Calasanti, T. (2005). Ageism, gravity, and gender: Experiences of aging bodies. *Generations, 29*(3), 8–12.

Calogero, R. M., Herbozo, S., & Thompson, J. K. (2009). Complimentary weightism: The potential costs of appearance-related commentary for women's self-objectification. *Psychology of Women Quarterly, 33*, 120–132.

Calogero, R. M., Pina, A., Park, L. E., & Rahemtulla, Z. (2010). Objectification theory predicts college women's attitudes toward cosmetic surgery. *Sex Roles, 63*, 32–41.

Cash, T. F., & Cash, D. W. (1982). Women's use of cosmetics: Psychosocial correlates and consequences. *International Journal of Cosmetic Science, 4*, 1–14.

Cash, T. F., Dawson, K., Davis, P., Bowen, M., & Galumbeck, C. (1989). Effects of cosmetics use on the physical attractiveness and body image of American college women. *The Journal of Social Psychology, 129*(3), 349–355.

Chaiken, S. (1979). Communicator physical attractiveness and persuasion. *Journal of Personality and Social Psychology, 37*(8), 1387–1397.

Changes with aging (n.d.). Retrieved from http://www.antiaging-wellness.com/Pages/Aging/Changes/physical.php

Cho, H., Lee, S., & Wilson, K. (2010). Magazine exposure, tanned women stereotypes, and tanning attitudes. *Body Image, 7*(4), 364–367.

Chung, V. Q., Gordon, J. S., Veledar, E., & Chen, S. C. (2010). Hot or not—Evaluating the effect of artificial tanning on the public's perception of attractiveness. *Dermatologic Surgery, 36*(11), 1651–1655.

Cokkinides, V., Weinstock, M., Lazovich, D., Ward, E., & Thun, M. (2009). Indoor tanning use among adolescents in the US, 1998 to 2004. *Cancer, 115*, 190–198.

Cosmetic surgery national data bank statistics (2014). The American Society for Aesthetic Plastic Surgery. Retrieved from http://www.surgery.org/sites/default/files/2014-Stats.pdf

Cosmetic surgery products to 2014 (2010, December). Retrieved from http://www.freedoniagroup.com/brochure/27xx/2712smwe.pdf

Cosmetics and toiletries USA 2008: Factsheet. (July 2009). Retrieved from http://www.klinegroup.com/reports/cia4g.asp

Court orders Hawaii HealthCare Professionals and its owner to pay over $190,000 for age discrimination (2012, July 19). Retrieved from http://www.eeoc.gov/eeoc/newsroom/release/7-19-12.cfm

Cunningham, M. R. (1986). Measuring the physical in physical attractiveness: Quasi–experiments on the sociobiology of female facial beauty. *Journal of Personality and Social Psychology, 50*, 925–935.

Cusack, M., Jack, G., & Kavanagh, D. (2003). Dancing with discrimination: Managing stigma and identity. *Culture and Organization, 9*, 295–310.

Dahl, D. W., Argo, J. J., & Morales, A. C. (2012). Social information in the retail environment: The importance of consumption alignment, referent identity, and self-esteem. *Journal of Consumer Research, 38*(5), 860–871.

Davis, D., & Vernon, M. L. (2002). Sculpting the body beautiful: Attachment style, neuroticism, and use of cosmetic surgeries. *Sex Roles, 47*, 129–138.

Dean, D. (2011). Young adult perception of visible tattoos on a white-collar service provider. *Young Consumers, 12*(3), 254–264.

Degelman, D., & Price, N. D. (2002). Tattoos and ratings of personal characteristics. *Psychological Reports, 90*, 507–514.

de Gruijl. F. R. (1999). Skin cancer and solar UV radiation. *European Journal of Cancer, 35*, 2003–2009.

Dion, K. (1972). Physical attractiveness and evaluation of children's trangressions. *Journal of Personality and Social Psychology, 24*, 207–213.

Dion, K., Berscheid, E., & Walster, E. (1972). What is beautiful is good. *Journal of Personality and Social Psychology, 24*, 285–290.

Ekman, P. (1993). Facial expression of emotion. *American Psychologist, 48*, 384–392.

Ekman, P., Sorenson, E. R., & Friesen, W. V. (1969). Pan-cultural elements in the facial displays of emotions. *Science, 164*, 86–88.

Fardouly, J., & Vartanian, L. R. (2012). Changes in weight bias following weight loss: The impact of weight-loss method. *International Journal of Obesity, 36*(2), 314–319.

FDA proposes new safety measures for indoor tanning devices: The facts (n.d.). Retrieved from http://www.fda.gov/forconsumers/consumerupdates/ucm350790.htm

Festinger, L. (1954). A theory of social comparison processes. *Human Relations, 7*, 117–140.

Fink, B., Neave, N., Manning, J. T., & Grammer, K. (2006). Facial symmetry and judgements of attractiveness, health and personality. *Personality and Individual Differences, 41*, 491–499.

Fiske, S. T., & Taylor, S. E. (2008). *Social cognition: From brains to culture.* New York, NY: McGraw-Hill.

Foltz, K. (2014). The Millenial's perception of tattoos: Self expression or business faux pas? *College Student Journal, 4,* 589–602.

Franzoi, S. L., (2001). Is female body esteem shaped by benevolent sexism? *Sex Roles, 44,* 177–188.

Fredrickson, B., & Roberts, T. (1997). Objectification theory. *Psychology of Women Quarterly, 21,* 173–206.

Furnham, S., & Reeves, E. (2006). The relative influence of facial neoteny and waist-to-hip ratio on judgements of female attractiveness and fecundity. *Psychology, Health, and Medicine, 11*(2), 129–141.

Gentina, É., Decoopman, I., & Ruvio, A. (2013). Social comparison motivation of mothers' with their adolescent daughters and its effects on the mother's consumption behaviour. *Journal of Retailing and Consumer Services, 20*(1), 94–101.

Ghodsee, K. (2007). Potions, lotions and lipstick: The gendered consumption of cosmetics and perfumery in socialist and post-socialist urban Bulgaria. *Women's Studies International Forum, 30,* 26–39.

Glenn, E. N. (2008). Yearning for lightness: Transnational circuits in the marketing and consumption of skin lighteners. *Gender & Society, 22*(3), 281–302.

Goffman, E. (1963). *Stigma: Notes on the management of spoiled identity.* New York, NY: Simon & Schuster.

Gold, G. (2011, February 25). Celebrity cosmetic surgery red carpet secrets revealed. Retrieved from http:// www.stylelist.com/2011/02/25/celebrity-cosmetic -surgery-red-carpet-secrets-revealed/

Goode, E. (1996). Gender and courtship entitlement: Responses to personal ads. *Sex Roles, 34,* 141–169.

Grabe, M. E., & Samson, L. (2011). Sexual cues emanating from the anchorette chair: Implications for perceived professionalism, fitness for beat, and memory for news. *Communication Research, 38,* 471–496.

Gray, W. N., Kahhan, N. A., & Janicke, D. M. (2009). Peer victimization and pediatric obesity: A review of the literature. *Psychology in the Schools, 46*(8), 720–727.

Griffin, A. M., & Langlois, J. H. (2006). Stereotype directionality and attractiveness stereotyping: Is beauty good or is ugly bad? *Social Cognition, 24,* 187–206.

Guthrie, M., Kim, H. S., & Jung, J. (2008). The effects of facial image and cosmetic usage on perceptions of brand personality. *Journal of Fashion Marketing and Management, 12*(2), 164–181.

Hamermesh, D. S. (2006). Changing looks and changing "discrimination": The beauty of economists. *Economic Letters, 93,* 405–412.

Hamermesh, D. S., & Biddle, J. (1994). Beauty and the labor market. *American Economic Review, 84,* 1174–1194.

Hamermesh, D. S., Meng, X., & Zhang, J. (2002). Dress for success: Does primping pay? *Labour Economics, 9,* 361–373.

Hamermesh, D. S., & Parker, A. (2005). Beauty in the classroom: Instructors' pulchritude and putative pedagogical productivity. *Economics of Education Review, 24,* 369–376.

Haskins, K. M., & Ransford, H. E. (1999). The relationship between weight and career payoffs among women. *Sociological Forum, 14*(2) 295–318.

Hatfield, E., & Sprecher, S. (1986). *Mirror mirror: The importance of looks in everyday life.* Albany, NY: State University of New York Press.

Hebl, M. R., & Heatherton, T. F. (1998). The stigma of obesity in women: The difference is black and white. *Personality and Social Psychology Bulletin, 24*(4), 417–426.

Hebl, M. R., King, E. B., & Lin, J. (2004). The swimsuit becomes us all: Ethnicity, gender, and vulnerability to self-objectification. *Personality and Social Psychology Bulletin, 30,* 1322–1331.

Hebl, M. R., Ruggs, E. N., Singletary, S. L., & Beal, D. J. (2008). Perceptions of obesity across the lifespan. *Obesity, 16*(S2), S46–S52.

Hebl, M. R., & Turchin, J. M. (2005). The stigma of obesity: what about men?. *Basic and Applied Social Psychology, 27*(3), 267–275.

Henderson-King, D., & Henderson-King, E. (2005). Acceptance of cosmetic surgery: Scale development and validation. *Body Image, 2,* 137–149.

Henss, R. (2000). Waist–to–hip ratio and female attractiveness: Evidence from photographic stimuli and methodological consideration. *Personality and Individual Differences, 28,* 501–513.

Hodgkinson, D. (n.d.). Male cosmetic surgery. Retrieved from http://www.cosmeticsurgeryoz.com/Male –Cosmetic–Surgery.htm

Hönekopp, J., Rudolph, U., Beier, L., Leibert, A., & Müller, C. (2007). Physical attractiveness of face and body as indicators of physical fitness in men. *Evolution and Human Behavior, 28,* 106–111.

Huguet, P., Croizet, J–C., & Richetin, J. (2004). Is "What has been cared for" necessarily good: Further evidence for the negative impact of cosmetics use on impression formation. *Journal of Applied Social Psychology, 34*(8), 1752–1771.

Hurd Clarke, L., & Griffin, M. (2007). The body natural and the body unnatural: Beauty work and aging. *Journal of Aging Studies, 21,* 187–201.

Hurd Clarke, L., & Griffin, M. (2008). Visible and invisible ageing: Beauty work as a response to ageism. *Aging & Society, 28,* 653–674.

Hurd Clarke, L., Griffin, M., & Maliha, K. (2009). Bat wings, bunions, and turkey wattles: Body transgressions and older women's strategic clothing choices. *Ageing & Society, 29,* 709–726.

Izard, C. E. (1971). *The face of emotion.* New York, NY: Appleton Century–Crofts.

Jackson, L. A., Hunter, J. E., & Hodge, C. N. (1995). Physical attractiveness and intellectual competence: A meta–analytic review. *Social Psychology Quarterly, 58,* 108–122.

Jackson, L. A., McGill, O. D. (1996). Body type preferences and body characteristics associated with attractive and unattractive bodies by African Americans and Anglo Americans. *Sex Roles, 35,* 295–307.

James, E. (2015, December 8). Breast cancer survivor covers mastectomy scars with intricate floral tattoos in order to reclaim control of her body after undergoing two surgeries and six rounds of chemo. *Daily Mail.* Retrieved from http://www.dailymail.co.uk/femail/article-3351204 /Breast-cancer-survivor-covers-mastectomy-scars -intricate-floral-tattoos-order-reclaim-control-body -undergoing-two-surgeries-six-rounds-chemo.html

Johnson, K. K. P., & Roach Higgins, M. E. (1987a). Dress and physical attractiveness of women in job interviews. *Clothing and Textiles Research Journal, 5*(3), 1–8.

Johnson, K. K. P., & Roach Higgins, M. E. (1987b). The influence of physical attractiveness and dress on campus recruiters' impressions of female job applicants. *Home Economics Research Journal, 16,* 87–95.

Jones, D., Brace, C. L., Jankowiak, W., Laland, K. N., Musselman, L. E., Langlois, J. H., . . . & Symons, D. (1995). Sexual selection, physical attractiveness, and facial neoteny: Cross-cultural evidence and implications [and comments and reply]. *Current Anthropology, 36*(5), 723–748.

Jones, B. C., DeBruine, L. M., & Little, A. C. (2007). The role of symmetry in attraction to average faces. *Perception & Psychophysics, 69,* 1273–1277.

Kamins, M. A. (1990). An investigation into the "match-up" hypothesis in celebrity advertising: When beauty is only skin deep. *Journal of Advertising, 19*(1), 4–13.

Kanwisher, N., & Yovel, G. (2006). The fusiform face area: A cortical region specialized for the perception of faces. *Philosophical Transactions of the Royal Society B, 361,* 2109–2128.

Kim, E. K. (2015, October 19). Meet the tattoo artist making breast cancer survivors feel 'whole again.' Retrieved from http://www.today.com/health/meet-tattoo -artist-making-breast-cancer-survivors-feel-whole -again-t48276

Kwan, S. (2009). Framing the fat body: Contested meanings between government, activists, and industry. *Sociological Inquiry, 79*(1), 25–50.

Lake, R. (2015, June 13). Tattoo statistics: 23 facts you won't regret reading. Retrieved from https://www.credit donkey.com/tattoo-statistics.html

Landro, L. (2011, May 24). Gym, Check. Diet, Check. Face, Lift. *Wall Street Journal.* Retrieved from http:// online.wsj.com/article/SB10001424052748704816604 576335162883878514.html#

Langlois, J. H., Kalakanis, L., Rebenstein, A. J., Larson, A., Hallam, M., & Smoot, M. (2000). Maxims or myths of beauty? A meta–analysis and theoretical review. *Psychological Bulletin, 126,* 390–423.

Langlois, J. H., & Roggman, L. A. (1990). Attractive faces are only average. *Psychological Science, 1,* 115–121.

Laser hair removal (n.d.). Retrieved from http://www .mayoclinic.com/health/laser–hair–removal/MY00134

Lee, J., & Johnson, K. K. P. (2009). Factors related to engagement in risky appearance management behaviors. *Clothing and Textiles Research Journal, 27,* 163–178.

Lennon, S. J., & Clayton, R. (1992). Age, body type, and style features as cues in nonverbal communication. *Semiotica, 91*(1/2), 43–55.

Leung, R. (2003, December 3). The look of Abercrombie and Fitch. Retrieved from http://www.cbsnews.com/ stories/2004/11/24/60minutes/main657604.shtml

LeVine, M. (2015, June 1). Supreme Court rules against Abercrombie in hijab case. *Politico.* Retrieved from http://www.politico.com/story/2015/06/ambercrombie –fitch–hijab–case–supreme–court–ruling–118492 .html

Lin, L., & Reid, K. (2009). The relationship between media exposure and antifat attitudes: The role of dysfunctional appearance beliefs. *Body Image, 6,* 52–55.

Macrae, C. N., Quinn, K. A., Mason, M. F., & Quadflieg, S. (2005). Understanding others: The face and person construal. *Journal of Personality and Social Psychology, 89,* 686–695.

Markey, C. N., & Markey, P. M. (2010). A correlational and experimental examination of reality television viewing and interest in cosmetic surgery. *Body Image, 7*(2), 165–171.

Mayers, L. B., & Chiffriller, S. H. (2008). Body art (body piercing and tattooing) among undergraduate university students: Then and now. *Journal of Adolescent Health, 42,* 201–203.

Mayo Clinic Staff (n.d.). Sunless tanning: What you need to know. Retrieved from http://www.mayo clinic.org/healthy-lifestyle/adult-health/in-depth /sunless-tanning/art-20046803

McKay, H. (2011, March 14). Do wedding-themed reality shows make a mockery of marriage? *Fox News.* Retrieved from http://www.foxnews.com /entertainment/2011/03/14/wedding-themed-reality -shows-making-mockery-sacred-tradition-marriage

McKeachie, W. J. (1952). Lipstick as a determiner of first impressions of personality: An experiment for the general psychology course. *Journal of Social Psychology, 36,* 241–244.

Miller, B. K., Nicols, K. M., & Eure, J. (2009). Body art in the workplace: Piercing the prejudice? *Personnel Review, 38,* 621–640.

Mo, J. J., Cheung, K. W., Gledhill, L. J., Pollet, T. V., Boothroyd, L. G., & Tovée, M. J. (2013). Perceptions of female body size and shape in China, Hong Kong, and the United Kingdom. *Cross-Cultural Research, 48*(1), 78–103. DOI: 10.1177/1069397113510272.

Morse, S., & Gergen, K. J. (1970). Social comparison, self-consistency, and the concept of self. *Journal of Personality and Social Psychology, 16*(1), 148–156.

Muise, A., & Desmarais, S. (2010). Women's perceptions and use of "anti-aging" products. *Sex Roles, 63,* 126–137.

Nabi, R. L. (2009). Cosmetic surgery makeover programs and intentions to undergo cosmetic enhancements: A consideration of three models of media effects. *Human Communication Research, 35*(1), 1–27.

Naquin, S. (2011, November 2). Hot or not: Does a tan make you more attractive? Retrieved from http://www .kktv.com/home/headlines/Hot_Or_Not_-_Does_A _Tan_Make_You_More_Attractive_133088623.html

Nash, R., Fieldman, G., Hussey, T., Lévêque, J-L., & Pineau, P. (2006). Cosmetics: They influence more than Caucasian female facial attractiveness. *Journal of Applied Social Psychology, 36*(2), 493–504.

Nathanson, C., Paulhus, D. L., & Williams, K. M. (2006). Personality and misconduct correlates of body modification and other cultural deviance markers. *Journal of Research in Personality, 40,* 779–802.

Negrin, L. (2000). Cosmetics and the female body: A critical appraisal of poststructuralist theories of masquerade. *European Journal of Cultural Studies, 3,* 83–101.

Nelson, T. D. (2005). Ageism: Prejudice against our feared future self. *Journal of Social Issues, 61,* 207–221.

Patzer, G. L. (1985). *The physical attractiveness phenomena.* New York, NY: Plenum Press.

Pawlowski, B., & Koziel, S. (2002). The impact of traits offered in personal advertisements on response rates. *Evolution and Human Behavior, 23,* 139–149.

Peters, M., Rhodes, G., & Simmons, L. W. (2007). Contributions of the face and body to overall attractiveness. *Animal Behavior, 73,* 937–942.

Puhl, R., & Brownell, K. D. (2001). Bias, discrimination, and obesity. *Obesity Research, 12,* 788–805.

Puhl, R. M., & Heuer, C. A. (2009). The stigma of obesity: A review and update. *Obesity, 17*(5), 941–964.

Puhl, R. M., Moss-Racusin, C. A., Schwartz, M. B., & Brownell, K. D. (2008). Weight stigmatization and bias reduction: perspectives of overweight and obese adults. *Health Education Research, 23*(2), 347–358.

Reinberg, S. (2009, July 28). Tanning beds get highest carcinogen rating. Retrieved from http://health usnews.com/health-news/family-health/cancer /articles/2009/07/28/tanning-beds-get-highest -carcinogen-ratingRhode, D. L. (2010). *The beauty bias: The injustice of appearance in life and law.* New York, NY: Oxford University Press.

Rhodes, G. (2006). The evolutionary psychology of facial beauty. *Annual Reviews of Psychology, 57,* 199–226.

Rhodes, G., Haberstadt, J., Jeffery, L., & Palermo, R. (2005). The attractiveness of average faces is not a generalized mere exposure effect. *Social Cognition, 23,* 205–217.

Rhodes, G., Proffitt, F., Grady, J. M., & Sumich, A. (1998). Facial symmetry and the perception of beauty. *Psychonomic Bulletin and Review, 5,* 659–669.

Rhodes, G., Yoshikawa, S., Clark, A., Lee, K., McKay, R., Akamatsu, S. (2001). Attractiveness of facial averageness and symmetry in non-Western cultures: In search of biologically based standards of beauty. *Perception, 30*(5), 611–625.

Richins, M. L. (1991). Social comparison and the idealized images of advertising. *Journal of Consumer Research, 18*(1), 71–83.

Riniolo, T. C., Johnson, K. C., Sherman, T. R., & Misso, J. A. (2006). Hot or not: Do professors perceived as physically attractive receive higher student evaluations? *The Journal of General Psychology, 133,* 19–35.

Rivero, T., & Brady, J. (2008, March 25). Florida teen dies after complications during breast surgery: Doctors believe a reaction to anesthesia may have caused death. *ABC News.* Retrieved from http://abcnews.go.com/GMA/story?id–4520099

Roberts, T. A., Auinger, P., & Ryan, S. A. (2004). Body piercing and high-risk behavior in adolescents. *Journal of Adolescent Health, 34,* 224–229.

Roehling, M. V., Roehling, P. V., & Odland, L. M. (2008). Investigating the validity of stereotypes about overweight employees: The relationship between body weight and normal personality traits. *Group & Organization Management, 33*(4), 392–424.

Rothblum, E. (2009, November 22). Weight-loss industry masks its economic interests with bogus health concerns. *The San Diego Union Tribune.* Retrieved from http://www.signonsandiego.com/news/2009/nov/22/weight-loss-industry-masks-its-economic-interests-/

Rudd, N.A. (1997). Cosmetics consumption and use among women: Ritualized activities that construct and transform the self. *Journal of Ritual Studies, 11*(2), 59–77.

Rudd, N. A., & Lennon, S. J. (1994). Aesthetics of the body and social identity. In M. DeLong and A. M. Fiore (Eds.), *Aesthetics of textiles and clothing: Advancing multi-disciplinary perspectives* (pp. 163–175). Monument, CO: ITAA.

Rudolph, C. W., Wells, C. L., Weller, M. D., & Baltes, B. B. (2009). A meta-analysis of empirical studies of weight-based bias in the workplace. *Journal of Vocational Behavior, 74,* 1–10.

Rule, N. O., & Ambady, N. (2008). The face of success: Inferences from chief executive officers' appearance predict company profits. *Psychological Science, 19,* 109–111.

Rule, N. O., & Ambady, N. (2009). She's got the look: Inferences from female chief executive officers' faces predict their success. *Sex Roles, 61,* 644–652.Russell, K., Wilson, M., & Hall, R. (1993). *The color complex: The politics of skin color among African Americans.* New York, NY: Harcourt Brace Jovanovich.

Schildkrout, E. (2004). Inscribing the body. *Annual Review of Anthropology, 33,* 319–344.

Seiter, J., & Hatch, S. (2005). Effects of tattoos on perceptions of credibility and attractiveness. *Psychological Reports, 96,* 1113–1120.

Singh, D. (2002). Female mate value at a glance: Relationship of waist-to-hip ratio to health and attractiveness. *Neuroendocrinology Letters, 23*(4), 81–91.

Slevec, J., & Tiggemann, M. (2010). Attitudes toward cosmetic surgery in middle-aged women: body image, aging anxiety, and the media. *Psychology of Women Quarterly, 34,* 65–74.

Smith, L. (1985). *Media images and ideal body shapes: A perspective on women with emphasis on anorexics.* Paper presented at the Annual Conference of the Association of Education in Journalism and Mass Communications, Memphis, TN.

Stockemer, D., & Praino, R. (2015). Blinded by beauty? Physical attractiveness and candidate selection in the US House of Representatives. *Social Science Quarterly, 96*(2), 430–443.

Strasburg, J. (2004, November 10). Abercrombie to pay $50 million in bias suits. *SF Gate.* Retrieved from http://articles.sfgate.com/2004-11-10/business/17451475_1_abercrombie-fitch-job-candidates-tom-lennox

Stuppy, D., Armstrong, M., & Casals-Ariet, C. (1998). Attitudes of health care providers and students toward tattooed people. *Journal of Advanced Nursing, 27*(6), 1165–1170.

Sutin, A. R., Stephan, Y., & Terracciano, A. (2015). Weight discrimination and risk of mortality. *Psychological Science, 26*(11), 1803–1811.

Swami, V. (2009). Body appreciation, media influence, and weight status predict consideration of cosmetic surgery among female undergraduates. *Body Image, 6,* 315–317.

Swami, V., Chan, F., Wong, V., Furnham, A., & Tovee, M. J. (2008). Weight-based discrimination in occupational hiring and helping behavior. *Journal of Applied Social Psychology, 38*(4), 968–981.

Swami, V., & Furnham, A. (2007). Unattractive, promiscuous and heavy drinkers: Perceptions of women with tattoos. *Body Image, 4*, 343–352.

Swami, V., Taylor, R., & Carvalho, C. (2009). Acceptance of cosmetic surgery and celebrity worship: Evidence of associations among female undergraduates. *Personality and Individual Differences, 47*(8), 869–872.

Swanger, N. (2006). Visible body modification (VBM): Evidence from human resource managers and recruiters and the effects on employment. *International Journal of Hospitality Management, 25*, 154–158.

Tate, J. C., & Shelton, B. L. (2008). Personality correlates of tattooing and body piercing in a college sample: The kids are alright. *Personality and Individual Differences, 45*, 281–285.

The risks of tanning (n.d.). Retrieved from http://www.fda.gov/Radiation-EmittingProducts/Radiation EmittingProductsandProcedures/Tanning/ucm 116432.htm

Thornhill, R., & Gangestad, S. (1999). Facial attractiveness. *Trends in Cognitive Sciences, 3*, 452–460.

Thurston, J. L., Lennon, S. J., & Clayton, R. V. (1990). Influence of age, body type, currency of fashion detail, and type of garment on the professional image of women. *Home Economics Research Journal, 19*, 139–150.

Ting, W., Schulz, K., Cac, N. N., Peterson, M., & Walling, H. W. (2007). Tanning bed exposure increases the risk of malignant melanoma. *International Journal of Dermatology, 46*, 1253–1257.

Tucker, L. A. (1981). Internal structure, factor satisfaction, and reliability of the Body Cathexis Scale. *Perceptual and Motor Skills, 53*, 891–896.

Tucker, L. A. (1985). Dimensionality and factor satisfaction of the body image construct: A gender comparison. *Sex Roles, 12*(9/10), 931–937.

Vannini, P., & McCright, A. M. (2004). To die for: the semiotic seductive power of the tanned body. *Symbolic Interaction, 27*(3), 309–332.

Warschburger, P. (2005). The unhappy obese child. *International Journal of Obesity, 29*, S127–S129.

Westerfield, H., Stafford, A., Speroni, K., & Daniel, M. (2012). Patients' perceptions of patient care providers with tattoos and/or body piercings. *Journal of Nursing Administration, 42*(3), 160–164.

Willis, J., & Todorov, A. (2006). First impressions: Making up your mind after a 100-ms exposure to a face. *Psychological Science, 17*, 592–598.

Wilson, J. H., Beyer, D., & Monteiro, H. (2014). Professor age affects student ratings: Halo effect for younger teachers. *College Teaching, 62*(1), 20–24, DOI: 10.1080/87567555.2013.825574

Wohlrab, S., Fink, B., Kappeler, P. M., & Brewer, G. (2009). Perception of human body modification. *Personality and Individual Differences, 46*, 202–206.

Workman, J. E., & Johnson, K. K. P. (1991). The role of cosmetics in impression formation. *Clothing and Textiles Research Journal, 10*, 63–68.

Yarmey, A. D. (1985). Older and younger adults' attributions of responsibility toward rape victims and rapists. *Canadian Journal of Behavioral Science, 17*, 327–337.

Yoo, J. J., & Kim, H. Y. (2013). Perceived negative health effect of tanning: The interface between tanning attitudes and behaviors. *Clothing and Textiles Research Journal, 32*(1), 6–19. DOI: 10.1177/0887302X13510601

Zebrowitz, L.A., & Montepare, J.M. (2005). Appearance DOES matter. *Science, 308*, 1565–1566.

Zimmerman, R. (2015, November 6). Fatal fat shaming? How weight discrimination may lead to premature death. Retrieved from http://www.wbur.org/commonhealth/2015/11/06/weight-discrimination-premature-death

CHAPTER 7

DRESS AND BODY IMAGE

After reading and reflecting on the content of this chapter students should be able to:

- Explain the concept of body image and its influence on thoughts about the self as well as appearance management behaviors.
- Apply theories that explain relationships between body image and self-perceptions.
- Apply tools for assessing body image (e.g., perceptual, attitudinal, behavioral).
- Analyze differences in body image among various populations of people (e.g., adult men and women, children and adolescents, homosexual men and women, athletes).
- Identify how body image impacts consumption decisions about dress.
- Identify and critique social activism campaigns that promote positive media images of the body.

INTRODUCTION

As you learned in Chapter 6, "Dress and Physical Appearance," the body is a very important vehicle in the public presentation of oneself to others. We make assessments of others on the basis of body characteristics and configurations, we categorize others (often unknowingly) based on their body size, color, attractiveness, or other physical features, and we often make evaluations and judgments about their worth (real or imagined) once we have assessed and categorized them. The previous chapter went into depth about two particular aspects of appearance, faces and bodies, and how they contribute to perceptions of attractiveness, stigma, and manipulations of the body. There are certainly several industries devoted to consumer interest in the body (e.g., beauty pageant industry, diet product industry, physical fitness industry, cosmetics industry).

Equally important to this public presentation of self to others is the personal perception of one's physical appearance, including both our face and body. In this chapter, we discuss the phenomenon of body image and how it influences our individual self-feelings, self-worth, and the amount of effort we put into grooming, making body improvements, and other appearance management behaviors as well as our shopping, eating, and other habits related to managing our appearance.

DEFINITION AND COMPONENTS OF BODY IMAGE

Several authors have written about body image and developed slightly different definitions. The field of body image research has greatly expanded from the 1980s to the present, with researchers working in disciplines including psychology, neuroscience, consumer sciences, gender studies, and media studies. Definitions used in these studies have incorporated psychological elements such as attitudes toward the body, satisfaction or dissatisfaction with the body, mood as affected by the body, rational or irrational beliefs about the body, and behaviors related to the body. For example, the earliest scholar to identify **body image** described it as "the picture of our own body which we form in our mind, that is to say, the way in which the body appears to ourselves" (Schilder, 1950, p. 11). A more contemporary definition of body image is, "one's perceptions, thoughts, and feelings about the body" (Grogan, 2008, p. 3).

So, how does body image operate? Because it is the mental construct you hold of your body, your body image has both a cause component and an affect component. How you perceive your physical body causes feelings of satisfaction or dissatisfaction, which then affects behaviors you engage in (e.g., the clothing and cosmetics you use, food you eat, and exercise you follow to maintain or change your body).

Perceptual Component

Let's examine each of these three components of body image: perceptual, attitudinal, and behavioral. The **perceptual component** of body image is "cognitive," referring to what we know or think we know about the body. This is a low level of cognition because it is based on input from our senses and is not based on higher order thinking about the body. Examples of this level of cognition include looking at ourselves in the mirror or at our reflection in a store window, information we get when we step on a bathroom scale, observing people's responses to our appearance and listening to their comments (sometimes complimentary, sometimes not) about our appearance, and recognizing our own experiences and feelings about living in our skins. All of these perceptions lead us to certain "knowledge" about our bodies which we can believe to be true regardless of how others see us.

Consider for a moment what you know about your own body using the characteristics listed in Table 7.1. How would you describe yourself on each characteristic? This information probably comes from your five senses—sight, sound, taste, touch, and smell. Then, given your answers, what do you believe about your own appearance? Do your beliefs fit with how others perceive you?

After completing this self-appraisal, one person might answer that she was of average height (5'4"), thick in the middle with a rounded shape in the bust and hips without very defined muscles, overweight but proportioned, has

curly hair, brown eyes, a nice smile, moves quickly when walking, has good posture, strong legs, and is generally healthy. This sounds like a positive perception. But if she believes what the fashion industry tells her through their garment sizing or their advertising images, she feels more negative about herself because she is not a standard size and does not see many images of body shapes like hers in advertisements.

Let's consider another person completing this simple activity. This second person may describe himself as tall (6'3") of average build, flat in the behind but with a broad chest and well-developed arm muscles, overweight but with very low body fat, curly hair, a red beard, a nice smile, walks confidently, has good posture, and is very strong. This person would seem to have a positive perception of his body, which is reaffirmed by the fitness magazines he reads, even though his body shape makes it difficult to find apparel that fits because his upper body is so much larger than his lower body. From these two people, we see how individual perceptions can vary dramatically and how they may be influenced by culture, society, peers, advertising images, and even inanimate objects such as scales.

Attitudinal Component

The **attitudinal component** of body image is "affective", referring to the emotional responses or feelings connected to thoughts about the body, or opinions held about the body. Feelings could be those of pride or shame; attitudes could be that one should diet or undergo cosmetic surgery to try to improve one's appearance to approximate cultural ideals of beauty. One typical feeling that individuals have is either satisfaction or dissatisfaction with the body. **Body satisfaction** results from positive thoughts and feelings about one's body, while **body dissatisfaction** results from negative thoughts and feelings about one's body (Grogan, 2008). Body satisfaction or dissatisfaction may also involve perceptions of similarity or dissimilarity between one's real body and one's ideal body (Cash & Szymanski, 1995).

Behavioral Component

The **behavioral component** of body image refers to responses we make to our perceptions and feelings about our bodies, including eating, exercise, substance use, grooming, and cosmetic procedures. These **appearance**

TABLE 7.1
CHARACTERISTICS OF THE BODY

Characteristic	Features
Size	Big, small, short, tall, thick, thin
Shape	Round, flat, defined muscles or not
Weight	Underweight, average weight, overweight, obese
Features	Hair, skin, smile, eyes, nails, etc.
Movement	Quick, slow, gestures, carriage
Performance	Strength, agility, endurance, speed, health

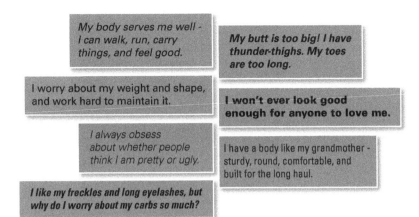

My body serves me well - I can walk, run, carry things, and feel good.

My butt is too big! I have thunder-thighs. My toes are too long.

I worry about my weight and shape, and work hard to maintain it.

I won't ever look good enough for anyone to love me.

I always obsess about whether people think I am pretty or ugly.

I have a body like my grandmother - sturdy, round, comfortable, and built for the long haul.

I like my freckles and long eyelashes, but why do I worry about my carbs so much?

Figure 7.1
Attitudes and feelings we may have about our body.

management behaviors can be categorized as routine and non-routine. Routine behaviors are practiced frequently, often daily, and may or may not carry a risk to one's health, such as bathing, using deodorant or body lotion, cosmetic use, washing and styling the hair, shaving, wearing high heel or platform shoes, and clothing the body. Non-routine behaviors are practiced less frequently, and also may or may not carry some health risk (i.e., tattooing, piercing, hair dyes, tooth whitening). Some non-routine behaviors can carry considerable health risk, as in the case of cosmetic surgery, disordered eating or exercise, and use of substances to change appearance such as steroids, human growth hormones, diuretics, or diet products with ephedra (Lee & Johnson, 2009; Rudd & Lennon, 1994).

Body image is intimately connected to self-esteem and self-presentation to others. As we will read in Chapter 8, "Dress and the Self," self-concept is a very complex and multi-faceted concept. As will be discussed in more detail in Chapter 8, William James (1890) was an early psychologist who studied the self and formulated the idea of a unified self. He acknowledged that this unified self brings together three distinct components of the self: the **material self** (including the body, its appearance and functioning), the **social self** or your connections with others, and the **spiritual self** or "existential" self in contemporary terms (how you see yourself in relation to the world around you.) Any of these components may dominate your feelings of "self" at any point in time (i.e., your bodily self

---

IN-CLASS ACTIVITY
Reflect On and Evaluate Your Emotional Responses to Perceptions of Yourself

Take a moment to reflect on and evaluate your emotional responses to the following perceptions of yourself in these situations. How might your responses affect your body image? Do you tend to be critical of your own body, or ashamed? If so, does that feeling make you feel depressed or dissatisfied with your body?

Observe others on the treadmill in my gym: _____

Have a bad hair day: _____

Wake up with a pimple: _____

View attractive models in magazine ads: _____

Run faster than others on my team: _____

Am shorter/larger than my peers: _____

Compare my attractiveness with my peers: _____

Take a moment to list aspects of your daily routine that reflect the motivating influence of external/internal stimuli on your appearance management behaviors. Also think about what risky behaviors you would consider and why.

Behavior	How Often Practiced	Motivating Influence/Reason
(ex., shower)	(ex., daily)	(ex., cultural norm)
(ex., ear piercing)	(ex., one time)	(ex., sister gave me earrings)
(ex., breast augmentation)	(ex., never, but considered)	(ex., smaller than the norm)

may be more important than your social self). Consider for a moment what percentage each of these components contributes to your general sense of "self." The total should equal 100 percent. For example, the diagram in Figure 7.2 might represent your current feelings about yourself.

Ideas and concerns about the body are very present and real issues that may impact the self. Attending to the body, or spending much time worrying about its care and presentation to others, may be top priority for many of us, and thus leave less time for us to attend to other aspects of the self, such as school, work, or family. Many of us suffer from some level of body image disturbance.

Figure 7.2

Components of general sense of self.

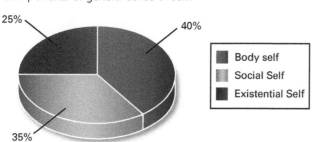

- Body self
- Social Self
- Existential Self

BODY IMAGE DISTURBANCE

Most of us are pleased with some aspects of our body and less pleased with others. Because of this, body image is best conceptualized on a continuum, with levels of dissatisfaction or disturbance ranging from none or minimal worry about the body, to severe concern and worry about the body. An extreme level of concern about the body may indicate a body image disturbance that is often accompanied by disordered behaviors and impaired social or physical functioning. **Body image disturbance** (or disorder) is defined as "a persistent report of dissatisfaction, concern and distress that is related to an aspect of physical appearance; some degree of impairment in social relations, social activities, or occupational functioning must be present" (Thompson, 1992, as cited in Thompson, Heinberg, Altabe, and Tantleff-Dunn, 1999, p. 11). Most of us fall in the middle of this continuum, meaning that we experience a moderate degree of concern or dissatisfaction. The researchers caution that it is not easy to tell where normal concern about appearance becomes a disturbance leading to distress or clinical diagnosis. The continuum, from low body distress to severe distress, may be depicted as follows:

Figure 7.3

Continuum of body distress described by Thompson, 1992.

LOW 1   2   3   4   5 **SEVERE**

1. Healthy body image with occasional worries
2. Body image dissatisfaction
3. Weight/size/shape preoccupation
4. Yo-yo Dieting or other risky behaviors
5. Disordered behaviors (anorexia, bulimia, muscle dysmorphia, self cutting, body dysmorphic disorder, etc.)

The pervasiveness of body image disturbance is undocumented, but we do know that many individuals experience some level of body image disturbance at various stages in their life. For example, a qualitative study of 95 undergraduate women investigated their thoughts about appearance, behaviors practiced, and self-esteem. Students wrote about these "lived experiences" in essays that were a couple of pages long. Themes emerged from the essays, including that many of these women routinely engaged in social comparisons concerning their appearance and were influenced by the opinions of others. This may have contributed to their dissatisfaction about their bodies, and perhaps motivated their disordered behaviors. Read through the themes that the researchers identified from the essays in Table 7.2 (Rudd and Lennon, 2000).

While unsolicited by the researchers, the women volunteered that they engaged in behaviors that would make them feel better about their bodies. They practiced eating behaviors that they thought would qualify as eating disorders (including anorexia and bulimia); they also practiced other appearance management behaviors that they assumed were risky, such as engaging in prolonged exercise or smoking/drinking/using laxatives or diuretics to lose weight. Some of the comments also revealed how invested these women were in their body image: one student said she was more or less content with her appearance except when she was around prettier girls, another wanted to look more the size of models she sees, and another had a problem with her skin being olive when the skin of those around her was pale white.

Severe body image disturbances include clinically diagnosed eating disorders, as well as other manifestations of body hatred such as self-cutting, muscle dysmorphia, and body dysmorphic disorder (APA, 2013). **Eating disorders** involve serious disturbances in eating behavior marked by extreme and unhealthy decreases in food intake, or extreme overeating often accompanied by purging behaviors, and feelings of distress or extreme concern about weight or body shape. The main types of eating disorders are *anorexia nervosa* (extreme food restriction) (Figure 7.4) and **bulimia nervosa** (bingeing followed by purging). A third type, **EDNOS** (Eating Disorders Not

---

TABLE 7.2

THEMES IDENTIFIED IN BODY IMAGE AMONG UNDERGRADUATE WOMEN (RUDD & LENNON, 2000)

Theme	# Responses	Percent
Social Comparison	35	19.44
World View	25	13.90
Influence of Others	17	9.44
Eating Disorders	18	1000
Coping Mechanisms	14	7.78
Frequent Behaviors	26	14.44
Hazardous Behaviors	33	18.33
Appearance & Social Interaction	6	3.33
Health Concerns	6	3.33
Total	**180**	**99.99%**

Figure 7.4
This young woman suffers from one type of eating disorder, Anorexia Nervosa, and is restricting her eating to water and bread.

Otherwise Specified) includes all other types not fitting the exact characteristics of anorexia or bulimia. Another type is **binge eating disorder (BED)**, or eating very large amounts of food on a regular basis without any purging behavior. Other extreme behaviors include **self-cutting** (using a knife to make many cuts in the limbs or trunk of the body), **muscle dysmorphia** (an obsession with weight lifting and sometimes supplement use) to gain muscle mass, and **body dysmorphic disorder** (intense hatred with a body part, often resulting in extreme measures to change that part or refusal to go out in public). Another behavior that has gained attention is **orthorexia** (a compulsion with eating healthy foods, sometimes focusing only on a few food groups). These behaviors currently

DRESS IN THE NEWS
Dangerous Runways

There has been much controversy over designer runway shows that feature very thin models. In September 2006, organizers of Fashion Week in Madrid, Spain instituted a ban on the use of runway models that fell below a body mass index (BMI) of 18. This ban was put into place after a runway model in South America, Uruguayan model Luisel Ramos who was twenty-two years old, died of heart failure immediately after stepping off a runway. Her sister Eliana, age eighteen and also a model, died a few months later of a heart attack as well, sparking great outrage. To put this into perspective, a BMI of 18 is the lowest BMI in the category of average weight. Below 18 is considered underweight, and average weight is considered to fall between a BMI of 18 and 24. By comparison, many runway models have a BMI of 16, which would be the equivalent of being 5'9" tall and weighing 110 pounds (Klonick, 2006).

In response to the Spanish ban on very thin models, other countries have considered their own bans. England considered a ban, but stopped short of an out-and-out ban. They advised individual designers to make healthy choices regarding their own models, and did not want to get involved in legislating standards of aesthetics. Australia enacted guidelines in 2010 that included banning anyone younger than sixteen from modeling; banning models below a BMI of 19 and male models that are considered too muscular; carrying a wide variety of sizes in stores; and using more body shapes, sizes and ethnicities in advertising campaigns. Bans or voluntary guidelines have also been discussed and implemented in Milan (Italy), Montreal (Canada), and Paris (France). Response from the Council of Fashion Designers of America (CFDA) was in the form of guidelines released in 2011 that recommended greater awareness of eating disorder symptoms on the part of designers and model agencies, and a ban on models younger than age 16. However, these guidelines are completely voluntary at this point. (Pearson, 2011; Taber, 2006).

incur much discussion in study groups among professionals, including the Academy for Eating Disorders and the American Psychological Association, and there is much ongoing research to study their causes, effects, and effective treatments.

HOW IS BODY IMAGE MEASURED?

There are many assessment tools that are used to study the components of body image. For convenience, we have grouped them into the same categories of body image identified previously: perceptual measures, attitudinal measures, and behavioral measures.

Perceptual Measures

Perceptual measures typically assess the accuracy of the individual's perception of their size or shape. These measures often provide individuals with a series of drawings on a single dimension of small to large body size (Thompson & Gray, 1995) or using a matrix of figures that vary on two dimensions such as body weight and muscle (Frederick & Peplau, 2007; Gruber, Pope, Borowiecki, & Cohane, 1999). On scales that assess one dimension such as body size, participants select one image that represents their current size, and another image that represents their ideal body size, so that a measure of satisfaction or dissatisfaction is calculated between what the participant indicates is "real" and what he/she indicates as "ideal." On scales that use two dimensions, participants also choose their current body size and muscularity and their desired body size and muscularity. These scales allow researchers to see which dimension (weight or muscle) participants want to change, and how much difference exists between current and desired body characteristics (Figure 7.5). In both instances, greater difference usually indicates that the individual has a negative or poor body image (Thompson, Penne, & Altabe, 1990 in Cash & Pruzinsky, 1990).

Other perceptual scales include: (1) light beams or drawings that participants adjust to their body size and that are compared to physical tools used to measure actual body width (Thompson, Penne, & Altabe, 1990) and (2) technology such as three-dimensional body scanning to provide images of body shape and size. Body scanners have been utilized by researchers to study body image and satisfaction among different audiences (Connell, Ulrich, Brannon, Alexander, & Presley, 2006), and to study garment fit for different body types. Please use this link to see three different women who all wear a size 10 pant, and have different body shapes (http://bodyscan.human.cornell.edu/scene7354.html).

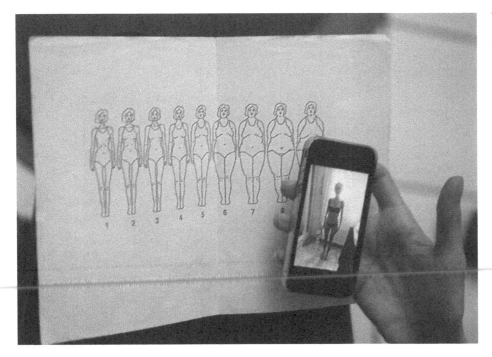

Figure 7.5
As part of her ongoing treatment, a patient uses an image of her body to position herself on a perceptual rating scale.

Attitudinal Measures

Attitudinal measures typically assess how happy or unhappy we are with body shape, attractiveness, or weight; in other words, aspects of body satisfaction or dissatisfaction. These measures typically consist of statements that the respondent evaluates using a Likert-type rating scale. A total score is calculated that reflects an individual's degree of satisfaction or dissatisfaction. The Multidimensional Body-Self Relations Questionnaire (MBSRQ) is a well-respected example of this type of measure. The questionnaire includes ten subscales that evaluate aspects of appearance such as personal investment in appearance, overall evaluation of appearance, evaluation of specific body parts, weight satisfaction, weight attitudes, and evaluations of fitness. Sample questions concerning investment in appearance include "Before going out in public, I always notice how I look" (Cash, 2000). Another example is the Body Esteem Scale (Frost, 2013) which includes questions dealing with body part satisfaction as well as general aspects of the body such as upper body strength and physical conditioning.

There are many other attitudinal scales. Some of these measure attitudes toward muscularity and personal satisfaction with muscularity (i.e., Drive for Muscularity Scale by McCreary, Sasse, Saucier, & Dorsch, 2004), men's body attitudes (i.e., The Male Body Attitudes Scale by Tylka, Bergeron, & Schwartz, 2005), degree of comparison to media images or peers (i.e., Sociocultural Attitudes Toward Appearance Questionnaire by Thompson, van den Berg, Roehrig, Guarda, & Heinberg, 2004), and types of feedback received from others (i.e., Perception of Teasing Scale by Thompson, Cattarin, Fowler, & Fishe, 1995).

Quantitative scales (such as discussed in Chapter 3, "Conducting Research on Dress") are not the only way to assess attitudes and feelings about the body; in fact, sometimes quantitative measures do not assess the true depth of feeling or experience that people have with their bodies. Qualitative assessments (please refer to Chapter 3 for examples) such as interviews or essays are able to deeply probe these attitudes and feelings. For example, as discussed earlier in this chapter, college women's feelings and behaviors related to their bodies were explored through essays (Rudd & Lennon, 2000). In another study, these same researchers interviewed forty-two women of varying ages and ethnicities in order to explore their "lived experiences" in their bodies, how those positive and negative experiences impacted their self-esteem, and their perceptions of social power or control. These interviews revealed a depth of emotion that would not have been captured using quantitative measures. The women who participated shared how they felt about their bodies, as well as their interpretation of their appearances as either successes or failures. They indicated they frequently went to great lengths to pursue a thin or attractive appearance, sometimes taking health risks (Rudd & Lennon, 1999).

Another qualitative study interviewed twenty mothers and their teenage daughters about diet-related behaviors and attitudes, and found a distinction between dieting behaviors and "watching" what one eats (Ogle & Damhorst, 2000). They concluded that mothers' influence on their daughters' behaviors was not a simple relationship but was related to such things as how strongly the daughter identified with her mother and the nature of verbal comments made by her mother. The advantage of such interviews is that the researchers could explore new

---

DRESS IN THE NEWS
Confidently Beautiful

Miss USA, Deshauna Barber from Washington DC who was crowned on June 5, 2016 on live television, was asked the following question as a finalist:

What does *confidently beautiful* [the pageant's motto] mean to you?

This was her response:

To me, confidently beautiful means understanding it's not always about your appearance. It's not always about who you are around and how they feel you look, where they feel you come from or your economic background. Serving in the military has taught me that being confidently beautiful is about being able to earn respect from people regardless of what you look like. As a woman in the military, people associate beauty with weakness and they learn very quickly that I'm extremely strong, and though I'm small, I'm powerful. Confidently beautiful is being myself and being very happy with who I've become. (Yahoo news, 2016)

relationships among variables and hear these narratives in the subjects' own powerful words.

Behavioral Measures

Behavioral measures assess behaviors undertaken to manage the appearance of the body and include eating, exercise and weight training, substance use, cosmetics use, grooming, clothing selection, tanning, and surgical cosmetic procedures. There are many of these measures discussed in the research literature on body image.[1]

Eating is the one behavior that has been studied the most and over the longest period of time, perhaps because everyone eats and everyone is believed to be able to control their eating habits by choosing what foods to eat, how and when to eat, and it is general knowledge that food intake affects body size and ultimately impacts body image. Some well-known measures of eating behavior evaluate behaviors such as food restriction, bingeing and purging tendencies, and other related behaviors that respondents self-rate on a scale of always to never (Clausen, Rosenvinge, Friborg, & Rokkedal, 2011).

Measures of appearance management behaviors have also been developed. For example, a landmark study used a scale with two subscales to measure **routine behaviors** that carry little or no risk (e.g., cosmetics use, lotion use, cutting and styling hair, etc.) and **risky behaviors** that are non-routine and carry some risk (e.g., binge eating and purging, tattooing, breast or chest implants, etc.). In this study of 194 college women, routine grooming behaviors (shaving, cosmetics use, lotion use, hair styling, and nail polish), engaging in strenuous exercise, and utilizing false hair (extensions, eyelashes) were common practices of college women (Lennon & Rudd, 1994). Less common but also practiced were cosmetic procedures (liposuction, breast implants, lip injections, teeth straightening) and body sculpting through diet or exercise or fasting. A subsequent study found that the most commonly practiced behaviors among 287 women in an internet survey were use of body lotion, shaping eyebrows, cutting and styling hair, and shaving; most commonly practiced risky behaviors were ear piercing and teeth straightening (Reilly & Rudd, 2009).

WHAT WE KNOW ABOUT BODY IMAGE AMONG VARIOUS POPULATIONS

Body image has been studied in many different populations over the past few decades. In this section, we will provide an overview of body image in some of the most-studied populations—adult women, adult men, children and adolescents, African American and other ethnic populations, gay men and women, and athletes. We will highlight a few important research studies for each population, including both domestic and international research, with the understanding that this area of research is rapidly growing in scope and an entire book could be dedicated to the topic of body image. We draw your attention to a research journal entitled *Body Image* that is dedicated to the topic of body image that you could refer to for research on this important topic.

Body Image in Adult Women

Among adult female populations in American and Westernized cultures, the following summary drawn from a range of studies paints a consistent picture of body image concerns. Research findings indicate[2]:

- Women are valued for youthful and thin appearances.
- Thinness is a primary component of female beauty.
- A majority of women report feelings of body dissatisfaction.
- Women routinely want to lose weight, regardless of their actual body.
- A majority of college women practice some type of eating-behavior problem such as chronic dieting, bingeing, and/or purging.
- Women are often dissatisfied with their muscle tone; the greatest body dissatisfaction was with the lower body (stomach, hips, thighs) and weight; the most satisfaction was with breasts and facial attractiveness.

---

[1] For an overview, readers are directed to the writings of Grogan (2008), Striegel-Moore & Smolak (2001), or Thompson et al. (1999).

[2] Cash, 1997; Harper & Tiggemann, 2008; Heatherton, Mahamedi, Striepe, Field & Keel, 1997; Mintz & Betz, 1988; Oehlhof, Musher-Eizenman, Neufeld, & Hauser, 2009; Olivardia, Pope, Borowiecki, & Cohane, 2004; Schaefer et al., 2015; University of Alberta Health Centre, 2001.

Threats to body image include puberty, pregnancy, and menopause. These facts show that body concerns and body dissatisfaction are experienced by a majority of women in American and Westernized cultures. Dissatisfaction with the body puts health at risk and may also contribute to disordered eating, depression, low self-esteem, and other negative psychological concerns. For example, we know that certain groups are at higher risk than others for developing eating disorders because of the emphasis placed on having the "right" body (e.g., dancers, models, elite athletes in certain sports), or feeling external pressures to achieve, and those with certain psychiatric disorders such as depression, addiction, and a history of abuse. Of those with eating disorders, about 90 percent are women and about 10 percent are men (Eating Disorders Awareness and Prevention, 1993; Fairburn, Welch, Doll, Davies, & O'Connor, 1997; Grabe & Hyde, 2006; Grabe, Hyde, & Lindberg, 2007; Grogan, 2008; Johnson & Wardle, 2005; Tiggemann, 2005).

Dissatisfaction may be with weight, body shape (e.g., small breasts and large hips), body features (e.g., hair, toes), muscularity, and the way the body functions (e.g., the way one runs or walks) among other things. Depending on the sample of women studies, estimates of body dissatisfaction are as low as 50 percent of women (Thompson et al., 1999) and as high as 95 percent of women (Cash, Winstead, & Janda, 1975; Fallon & Rozin, 1985: Heatherton, Mahamedi, Striepe, Field, & Keel, 1997). From these data, we can infer that dissatisfaction rather than satisfaction with their bodies or appearance is typical for women. Body dissatisfaction is so prevalent in women that some scholars refer to it as "**normative discontent**" (Rodin, Silberstein, & Striegel-Moore, 1985), meaning that so many women are discontented with their bodies that it is considered to be the norm or normal behavior.

Women become so concerned about their size, that they frequently over-estimate (i.e., think they are bigger than they really are) both their weight and certain body parts. For example, women think their lower body parts such as abdomen, butt, and thighs are bigger than they are and often think their waists and breasts are smaller than they are (Emery, Benson, Choen-Tovee, &Tovee, 1995) (Figure 7.6). Women commonly think they are heavier than they are (McCabe, Ricciardelli, Sitaram, & Mikhail, 2006). This fact is interesting because researchers believe that one's perception of their own body size is a better predictor of their satisfaction than other indicators such as

Figure 7.6
Girl's perception about size of tummy.

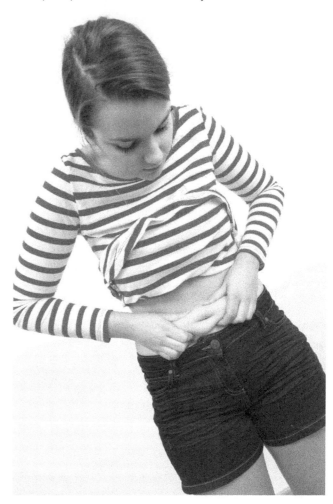

body mass index (BMI), the relationship between weight and height used to classify people as underweight, average weight, overweight, or obese (Tiggemann, 2005).

Women in international studies share very similar perceptions and feelings overall, yet socio-economic status is thought to have an important influence in some non-Western cultures. These are some key findings reported in literature on body image[3]:

- In twenty-six countries across ten geographic regions of the world, there were differences due to exposure to Western ideals of beauty; higher socio-economic status and greater exposure to Western

[3]Becker, 2004; Ember, Ember, Korotayev, & de Munck, 2006; Forbes et al., 2012; Frederick, Forbes, & Berezovskaya, 2008; Frederick et al., 2016; Grogan, 2008; Lennon, Rudd, Kim, & Sloan, 1999; Swami et al., 2010; Tiggemann, 2004.

media were related to more body dissatisfaction and desire to be thin.

- Larger body size is accepted in some non-Western, lower socio-economic cultures and may be associated with positive psychological variables and with access to food security.
- Among college women in international samples, body dissatisfaction was a significant problem in Argentina, Brazil, Singapore, Korea, England, and Australia, as well as several samples in the US.
- Asian women in the US report greater body and face dissatisfaction than non-Asian women, particularly with respect to eyes, overall facial attractiveness, and overall body weight and shape.
- Comparison to similar others in one's culture tends to predict higher satisfaction than comparison to dissimilar others (i.e., idealized Western models).

A number of behaviors related to appearance management also shed light on how women feel about their bodies, include dieting, eating disorders, exercise, and cosmetic surgery.[4] Please refer to Chapter 6, "Dress and Physical Appearance" for more information on procedures to alter the body and face. Dieting is a common method used to change body weight, and it is typically advocated by fashion and health magazines. In fact, the most frequently appearing messages on the covers of health magazines involve a thin appearance, exercising for appearance reasons, dieting, and weight loss. Estimates of dieting as a way to change one's body are high; 95 percent of women in England and America had dieted in their lives. Being on a diet or watching what you eat should not be simply viewed as bad behavior. There is a big difference between being on a diet wherein you are practicing healthy portion control with a balance of food groups and "dieting" for the purpose of losing weight that involves extreme calorie restriction or that direct one to restrict certain food groups or eat only one type of food (i.e., all-fruit diets, cabbage soup diet, no carbohydrates diet). Dieting behavior may be dangerous because it can begin at a young age when individuals may not understand all the implications and outcomes of their decision to restrict food. For example, people who are treated with eating disorders such as anorexia, bulimia, binge eating, and other disorders often have a long history of dieting.

[4]Bazzini, Pepper, Swofford, & Cochran, 2015; Ogden, 1992; Patton, Johnson-Sabine, Wood, Mann, & Wakeling, 1990.

Body Image in Adult Men

Among men, body image concerns are somewhat different than among women, as illustrated by this sampling of research findings[5]:

- Boys are fairly satisfied with their bodies until puberty; after puberty, there is an increase in dissatisfaction with some men.
- Men often want to be taller and have defined biceps, abdominals, and pectoral muscles; in one study, men wanted about twenty-five more pounds of muscle and about eight pounds less body fat than they had. Dimensions of male body satisfaction include face, upper body strength, and overall conditioning.
- Male pattern hair loss and weight gain become concerns in adulthood.
- An estimated 50,000 teen boys/male athletes engage in one risky appearance management behavior, that is, use of steroids.

Men tend to be more satisfied overall with their bodies than adult women, perhaps in part due to the Western cultural value accorded to "doing versus being" previously discussed. If men value their bodies more because of what their bodies will do, and how they will perform physically, rather than how they look, then they are likely to be less invested in attractiveness and presenting their appearance in a certain, prescribed way. However, the researchers also acknowledge that perhaps the pressure to appear attractive, thin, and muscular is growing and causing men to have greater concern about presenting their appearance in a certain way. Body dissatisfaction is reported particularly related to muscularity. For example, among men in Western Europe and the United States, many men preferred a body that had about twenty-eight pounds of muscle greater than what they currently had.

Poor body image in men has been linked to several psychological variables such as negative feelings, perfectionism, and low self-esteem. Men who internalized social messages about appearance, and who felt greater social pressure to look a certain way, were dissatisfied with their body fat and with their muscularity (Grammas & Schwartz, 2009). Men who struggle with body image

[5]Cash, 1997; Frederick, Forbes, Grigorian, & Jarcho, 2007; Furnham & Greaves, 1994; Grogan, 2008; Olivardia, Pope, Borowiecki, & Cohane, 2004; Pope et al., 2000; Schrof, 1992; Thompson & Cafri, 2007.

concerns may feel shame or anxiety because body dissatisfaction is typically considered to be a women's issue in Western culture; thus, men may question their masculinity in terms of cultural standards. Such feelings of gender-role conflict may lead to unhealthy eating or exercise behaviors (Berger, Levant, McMillan, Kelleher, & Sellers, 2005). Perfectionism and teasing about weight are related to low body satisfaction in men (Bardone-Cone, Cass & Ford, 2008).

Of course, variation in body image exists among men just as it exists among women. Specific subsets of men have strong variations in appearance orientation, appearance evaluation, and body satisfaction. When athletically active men were compared to bodybuilders and weight trainers, it was found that bodybuilders and weight trainers had higher investment in their appearance, higher evaluations of their appearance, and were more satisfied with their upper torsos and muscle tone than were average men who were athletically active (Pickett, Lewis, & Cash, 2005). There was also a greater prevalence of eating disorders among the body builders and weight trainers than among the athletically active men; however, competitive body builders held stronger body images and higher self-esteem than did their counterparts. Earlier researchers (Mangweth et al., 2001; Olivardia, Pope & Hudson, 2000) found that competitive body builders were similar to other individuals with eating disorders due to their obsessive eating and exercising habits, albeit focused on gaining weight and muscle mass; the men in those studies had low body image. In general, among men with eating disorders, there is often great body dissatisfaction (Anderson, 1990). Yet, body dissatisfaction has also been found among men without diagnosed eating disorders (but with some questionable eating behaviors) and men who suffer from muscle dysmorphia or who are extremely dissatisfied with their muscle mass (Pope, Olivardia, Gruber, & Borowiecki, 1999).

Compensatory behaviors to prevent weight gain and to maintain current body size and shape differ by gender. When men and women were compared on weight and shape salience, on compensatory behaviors practiced to prevent weight gain, and on drive for thinness (Anderson & Bulik, 2004), women had a greater drive for thinness, placed greater importance on weight and shape, and engaged in more compensatory behaviors such as aerobic exercise, calorie counting, dancing, gastroplasty surgery, use of diet programs (e.g., Herbal life, Jenny Craig, Nutrisystem, Optifast), smoking, and being on a vegetarian diet. Men also engaged in compensatory behaviors including use of amino acids, creatine, and protein supplements, dehydration, weight lifting, and martial arts. Behaviors such as eating less, cutting down fats and sugars, eating fewer meals, fasting, skipping meals or fasting, were practiced by both genders.

Body Image in Children and Adolescents

Your life stage, or age, may influence how important your body image is to you. Because the body undergoes a tremendous amount of physical change during adolescence, it is not too surprising that during adolescence many individuals are very concerned with their appearance and may suffer from body dissatisfaction as some of these statistics indicate[6]:

- About twice as many young girls as young boys are unhappy with their weight (66 percent of girls and 33–42 percent of boys) (Figure 7.7).
- A majority of adolescent girls ages 10–14 reported learning that an ideal body is attractive and slender from fashion magazines, peers, and family members.
- Adolescent boys are more interested in gaining muscularity than adolescent girls, while girls are more concerned with weight loss (Figure 7.8).
- Estimates are that .3 percent of teens are anorexic, .9 percent are bulimic, and 1.6 percent have binge eating disorder; in addition, another 3.3 percent have some form of sub-threshold eating disorder. Among adults, about 0.5 to 3.7 percent of women suffer from anorexia nervosa, about 1.1 to 4.2 percent of women have bulimia nervosa, and about 2–5 percent of Americans experience binge-eating disorder in a six-month period.
- Another study revealed 80 percent of 4th grade girls reported dieting, and girls as young as nine want to lose weight.
- Among girls as young as five to eight, about 40 percent wanted to have a thinner body and expect to diet if they were to gain weight.

[6]Dohnt & Tiggemann, 2006; Levine, Smolak, & Hayden,1994; McCabe, Ricciardelli, & Finemore, 2002; Mellin, Irwin & Scully, 1992; Moore, 1990, 1993; Schur, Sanders, & Steiner, 2000; Swanson, Crow, LeGrange, Swendsen, & Merikangas, 2011; The National Institute of Mental Health, 2002.

Figure 7.7
Teen girls want to lose weight.

Figure 7.8
Teen boys want to gain muscle.

that 35 percent of boys wanted to be thinner, but 19 percent wanted to be heavier (Schur et al., 2000); muscularity is valued by boys just as it is by adult men (Grogan & Richards, 2002).

Girls tend to engage in "fat talk," or talk that focuses on how fat they feel and strategies to lose weight or hide perceived flaws (Nichter, 2000). This type of talk can be reaffirming in some sense, in that it can be a means of bonding with others over a commonly held concern. Yet, it can also deter young women from focusing on other elements of themselves that are more meaningful, and it may perpetuate the stereotype that one's worth is derived primarily from one's appearance.

Racial and Ethnic Differences in Body Image Among Women and Men

Race and ethnicity seem to account for some of the differences found within male and female populations. While investigation of differences is in its infancy, some

We know that body image concerns are experienced by teens and by younger children. In one study of eight-year-old girls and thirteen-year-old girls (Grogan & Wainwright, 1996), girls at both ages wanted to be thin as children and also when they grew up. They worried about gaining weight and too much muscle, which would draw attention from boys. Other researchers report that even five-year old girls prefer bodies that are thinner than they are, and know they can count calories to lose weight (Wheatley, 2006; Williamson & Delin, 2001). The same was found to be true of boys ages 9-12 in a large study, in which 20–40 percent of the boys wanted to lose weight and 14–44 percent had already tried to do so (Maloney, McGuire, Daniels, & Specker, 1989).

The nature of body dissatisfaction in young boys and girls may be different. While girls in general want to lose weight to be thinner, some boys want to lose weight and others want to be larger and muscular. Researchers found

researchers have documented that African American women tend to have a higher body image than Caucasian American women, perhaps because a wider range of body sizes is valued (Ackard, Croll, & Kearney-Cooke, 2002; Grabe & Hyde, 2006; Lennon et al., 1999) or because their ethnic identity somehow protects them from absorbing media messages portraying a Euro-American ideal of beauty (Mastria, 2002). Some researchers have suggested that behaviors resulting from poor body image, such as eating disorders, occur less often among African-American women than among other ethnic groups (Wildes, Emery, & Simons, 2001), yet other researchers have found that there is little difference in eating disorders among Euro, African, Hispanic, and Asian American women (Grabe & Hyde, 2006; Shaw, Ramirez, Trost, Randall, & Stice, 2004).

Some African American girls define beauty differently than Euro-American girls; for instance, in one study African American girls described their "ideal" girl in terms of traits such as style, attitude, confidence, and pride, while Euro-American girls described their "ideal" in terms of physical characteristics such as tall, thin, blond, and having high cheekbones (Parker et al., 1995).

Asian American women have not been widely studied in terms of body image investment, evaluation, or behaviors; Hispanic women have also received little attention in the body image literature (Grabe & Hyde, 2006). The research that exists shows mixed results, with some researchers finding body dissatisfaction levels equivalent to that among Euro-American women and other researchers finding less dissatisfaction. Asian American women tend to accept standards of beauty similarly to Euro-American women (Evans & McConnell, 2003), and to devalue certain ethnic characteristics of their eyes and face (Mintz & Kashubeck, 1999.) Other research demonstrates that Asian American women have a greater fear of becoming fat than Euro-American women (Sanders & Heiss, 1998). Some researchers have found no differences in body satisfaction among different Asian ethnic groups including Koreans, Chinese, Japanese, and Hawaiians (Yates, Edman & Arguete, 2004), but other researchers have found differences among Koreans and Singaporeans (Lennon et al., 1999).

Studies investigating body image among Hispanic women in the United States are few and findings are inconsistent. Some researchers found that Hispanic women are more satisfied with their bodies than Euro-American women (Barry & Grilo, 2002), but other researchers found

that Hispanic college women have a stronger drive to be thin than their Euro-American counterparts (McComb & Clopton, 2002). However, another study reported that Latina-American women spend three times more on personal care and beauty products, engage in more cosmetic surgery, and have higher rates of eating disorders than other ethnic groups in the US (Gil, 2011). It may be that Hispanic women also are somewhat protected by cultural values, but that their individual ethnic heritage may determine how important ideals of beauty are to them.

A large study analyzed results from 98 articles representing 42,667 women and reporting research about body satisfaction with these four ethnic groups (Grabe and Hyde, 2006). Even though there were significant differences between Euro-American and African American women, other differences in body dissatisfaction among the four groups were quite small. Body dissatisfaction among Hispanic women and Asian American women was similar to Euro-American women. So more research is needed to understand reasons for these differences, as well as to understand factors that may lead to greater risk of poor body image among all women. As a more recent study found, perhaps exposure to Western media and socio-economic status account for more variation than just ethnicity alone (Swami et al., 2010).

Research on racial differences in men is also in its infant stage, with most researchers focusing their attention on college men. Ethnic groups studied include Asian or Asian American populations; African American populations; Hispanic or Latin populations; Pacific Islander/Hawaiian populations, but none have been reported with Native American or Native Alaskan men. Variables commonly measured are weight, physical appearance, appearance evaluation, appearance orientation, and appearance surveillance.

African American men seem to have a greater investment in appearance than Euro-American men, as well as a greater satisfaction with their appearance (Smith, Thompson, Raczynski, & Hilner, 1999). Euro-American men appear to be more satisfied with their bodies than Asian and Hispanic men; but when controlling for body mass index, differences existed between Euro-American and Hispanic men only (Frederick, Forbes, Grigorian & Jarcho, 2007). Asian, African American, Euro-American, and Hispanic men want to be toned and muscular (Altabe, 1998). Pacific Islander young adult men and adolescent boys (Fiji, Tonga, Samoa) report very similar concerns with muscularity as their Western counterparts (Lipinski

& Pope, 2002; Ricciardelli et al., 2007); other researchers report that a large and robust body size is preferred by many Pacific Islander men (Craig, Swinburn, Matenga-Smith, Matangi, & Vaughan, 1996). College men in Hong Kong had lower body satisfaction than those in the US, and both were dissatisfied with their muscularity (Jung, Forbes & Chan, 2010). Therefore, scholars suggest that there is much additional research yet to be conducted with all ethnic populations to identify meaningful differences, if any exist.

Body Image in Gay Men and Women

It has been reported that gay men sometimes feel more dissatisfied with their bodies than heterosexual men (Beren, Hayden, Wilfey & Grilo, 1996), although that difference may not be great. Researchers who examined the findings of twenty-seven other studies conducted with 5,220 men found a relatively small, but statistically significant, difference between the two populations (Morrison, Morrison, & Sager, 2004). Possible reasons for this discrepancy may be that the "body aesthetic," or the ideal of attractiveness to which gay men aspire, may be more important to their potential male partners, whereas attractiveness for heterosexual men may not be as important to their potential female partners as other personal characteristics (Rudd, 1996; Sergios & Cody, 1986). Another reason is that men may internalize society's prejudice against them (**internalized homonegativity**) and be more critical of their bodies and appearance. Indeed, Reilly and Rudd (2006) found that such internalization of societal prejudice contributed to somewhat lower body satisfaction, lower self-esteem, and slightly higher incidence of eating disturbance in their sample of 213 gay men. It has also been found that gay men have a more pronounced desire to be muscular than straight men (Yelland & Tiggemann, 2003); this drive for muscularity is an important component of masculine identity in general (McCreary & Saucier, 2009).

Tanning may be another appearance management behavior that is more important to gay men than to heterosexual men. In one study of gay men, over half engaged in sun, salon, or cosmetic tanning (Reilly & Rudd, 2008). A difference existed, however, in the type of tanning practiced by those who were strongly invested in their appearance versus the tanning practiced by those who were satisfied with their appearance. Men strongly invested in their appearance practiced risky tanning (sun or salon

tanning), while men who were satisfied with their appearance practiced safer methods (cosmetic tanning).

Regarding removal of body hair from parts other than the face (e.g., back, chest, legs, abdomen, and groin), a majority of both gay men and heterosexual men engaged in this behavior (Martins, Tiggemann, & Churchett, 2008). Salient reasons were cleanliness, sex appeal, and looking more muscular (Boroughs, Cafri & Thompson, 2005).

Research findings concerning lesbian women are also inconsistent. Some researchers have reported that lesbian women seem to suffer less from negative body image because they are not as focused on a thin ideal body type as are heterosexual women (Moore & Keel, 2003) and in fact hold positive body images (Owens, Hughes, & Owens-Nicholson, 2002). In another study, researchers found very similar levels of body dissatisfaction among lesbians and heterosexual women, but lesbian women had a higher level of body "surveillance," or body checking, than did heterosexual women (Kozee & Tylka, 2006). Yet other researchers found no real differences between lesbians and heterosexual women in their preferences for attractiveness or thinness in a partner (Legenbauer, Vocks, Schäfer, Schütt-Strömel, Hiller, Wagner, & Vogele, 2009). With these inconsistent findings, there is need for further research to tease apart differences in perceptions, attitudes, and behaviors related to body image.

FACTORS THAT INFLUENCE BODY IMAGE

What are some factors that are known to influence body image? We discuss a few of the known reasons: (1) media exposure to unrealistic ideals of beauty, (2) social comparisons, (3) self-esteem, and (4) gender ideology.

Media Exposure

Media exposure is considered to be a common influence on people's thoughts about how bodies should appear. Because celebrities and others featured in the media are glamorized, idealized, and portrayed as extremely popular and desired by others, people often aspire to have the same attributes, including their bodies (Figure 7.9). Celebrities do not reflect diversity in appearances. They often have similar body types. Most are thin. If they are not thin, then there is much celebration about any weight loss; the celebrity may become a spokesperson to endorse the plan they

Figure 7.9
Celebrities and others featured in the media are often portrayed with idealized attractiveness.

have utilized to lose weight, as in the case of Jennifer Hudson, award-winning recording artist and Broadway actor, and now a publicized spokesperson for Weight-Watchers®.

These media images are sometimes not true representations. Even though celebrities and professional apparel models have been photographed which typically results in accurate images, computer technology has allowed editors to remove any attributes that are less than desirable. Images are perfected and set forth as genuine. Repeated exposure to these similar and often corrected media images representing a narrow range of possibilities and this, a singular ideal (e.g., thin, large breasts, small hips, no blemishes) may cause viewers to accept this singular ideal as an accurate representation of reality, a phenomenon called **cultivation theory** (Gerbner, Gross, & Morgan, Signorielli, & Shanahan, 2002) The more we see certain representations of reality (e.g., thin, flawless skin, shapely legs and arms, perfect teeth, luxurious hair), whether or not they are actually authentic, the more we "cultivate" the idea that bodies should look a certain way and the more intensely we may desire these characteristics for ourselves. Adopting these representations as the ideal for women's bodies may contribute to body dissatisfaction (Levine & Harrison, 2004), as viewers compare their imperfect bodies to the "perfect" bodies seen in the media. Thus, as the pattern of presenting the same ideal repeats over time, it becomes a cultural guide.

How many of us see images similar to ourselves in fashion magazines, or health and fitness magazines, or in spokespersons for products on television? When we do, how do we feel? When we do not, do we feel any differently? What messages do these images send us?

We constantly receive messages about our bodies and respond internally to them, even if our responses are not realistic or rational. Nevertheless, we do respond, and often on a subconscious level we begin to feel dissatisfaction, which may lead us to take some form of action to alter our bodies to come closer to some ideal appearance.

Let's complete an assessment of the following list of body characteristics. What body parts are you satisfied with, and what body parts are you not satisfied with? For those parts you are dissatisfied with, how would you consider changing them? Then consider how realistic or safe the specific options are. Feel free to add your own body parts or characteristics; for example, in a study conducted by Rudd and Lennon (2000), one respondent said how dissatisfied she was with her toes. This list has been inspired by items in the Body Areas Satisfaction Subscale of the Multidimensional Body-Self-Relations Questionnaire (Cash,1997) and the Physical Appearance State & Trait Anxiety Scale (Thompson & Thompson, 1999). Use the bolded example responses to guide your own assessment.

Now, complete this list of routine and non-routine appearance-management behaviors (Lennon & Rudd, 1994; modified by Reilly & Rudd, 2009) that you currently practice or would consider undertaking. Please add any other behaviors you engage in related to your appearance.

Do you notice any connection between the behaviors you practice, or would consider, and your feelings of body satisfaction/dissatisfaction? How do you explain this connection?

Social Comparison

Social comparison occurs when people compare themselves to others on characteristics they consider to be important to them, such as appearance. You also saw how this process works in the model in Chapter 6, "Dress and Physical Appearance." So people compare themselves with relevant other people, and tend not to compare themselves with irrelevant other people. But what constitutes relevance, particularly on the aspect of appearance? Some people may tend not to compare their attractiveness or bodies with professional models because they realize that these people are not typical of the average person

However, other people may see such models as relevant targets of comparison). If we view magazine models as relevant targets of comparison, greater exposure to media images may lead to greater body dissatisfaction and more negative feelings like depression, anxiety and objectification (Bazzini, Pepper, Swofford, & Cochran, 2015; Cash, Cash, & Butters, 1983; Heinberg & Thompson, 1995; Tiggemann & McGill, 2004).

People can engage in upward social comparisons or downward social comparisons. An **upward social comparison** occurs when the target of comparison is better on the comparison attribute than you are. An example of upward social comparison is when the average person compares their physical abilities to those of professional athletes, which might push the individual to work harder on the comparison attribute (running faster, lifting more weight, etc.) to bring them closer to the target. Comparison can increase your motivation to achieve. If you are

---

IN-CLASS ACTIVITY
Keep a Record for One Week

Keep a record for one week of the images you pay attention to in any magazines or television ads. Note how similar or dissimilar they are to you, your feelings, and the messages you interpret about bodies in general or your own body in particular.

How Similar/Dissimilar to Me	My Feelings	Messages about Body
(ex., tall, thin, long blond hair, flawless skin)	(ex., concern because I am short, not thin, have freckles, and have dark hair)	(ex., you aren't beautiful unless you look how the model looks, regardless of other qualities)

Body Part or Characteristic	Aspect	Satisfied or Dissatisfied	How I Would Consider Changing	Realistic or Safe
Hair	Color Length Texture Style			
Ex., Hair	Color Length Texture Style	D S D D	Too dark, get highlights ——— Too curly, straighten Cut short	Pretty safe ——— Unrealistic Unrealistic
Facial Features	Nose Eyes Lips Attractiveness			
Shoulders	Width Slope			
Breasts/chest	Size Shape			
Stomach/waist	Size Shape			
Ex Stomach/waist	Size Shape	Too Big Tummy Pooch	Diet, Exercises Body shaper, many sit-ups	Unrealistic Maybe a Shaper
Hips/buttocks	Size Shape			
Legs	Length Shape			
Feet	Size Shape			
Weight	Overall How proportioned			
Muscle tone	Overall Specific areas			

Routine Behavior	1 = very infrequently, 5 = very frequently
Wearing slenderizing undergarments	
Wearing slenderizing apparel	
Makeup	
False nails	
Hairpieces or wigs	
False eyelashes	
Body lotions	
Nail polish	
Shaping or plucking eyebrows	
Cutting hair	
Styling hair	
Coloring hair	
Perming or straightening hair	
Shaving	
Aerobic or other exercise	
Weight lifting/training	
Non-Routine Behavior	**1 = very unlikely, 5 = very likely**
Dieting	
Binge eating and purging	
Fasting	
Facelift	
Liposuction	
Lip injection	
Ear/nose piercing	
Other body part piercing	
Breast/chest implants	
Breast/chest reduction	
Electrolysis	
Teeth straightening	
Mole/blemish removal	
Tattooing	

SOCIAL COMPARISON WHEN SHOPPING

We discussed in this chapter that social comparison may influence how we feel about our bodies. Does social comparison related to appearance influence you when you are shopping? Three researchers (Darren Dahl, Jennifer Argo, and Andrea Morales, 2011), were interested in how comparative information influences decision-making when shopping for apparel. In other words, the researchers were interested in how consumers react when another customer or a sales associate is wearing the same item that a shopper is interested in. Does social comparison result in the consumer wanting the item more or less than if the comparison did not occur? These researchers focused their attention on women with low self-esteem. They reasoned that since individuals low in body esteem generally have negative reactions to appearance comparisons, they would be most influenced by the behavior of an attractive person when purchasing clothing. The researchers speculated that these individuals will negatively evaluate a product they are interested in purchasing when an attractive customer is viewed wearing or trying on the product. The negative response is a result of an upward social comparison. The researchers found that their reasoning was supported after conducting a series of experiments. Specifically, the researchers found that if a low self-esteem consumer saw an attractive customer wearing the same apparel item, the consumer's reaction to the item was negative. Put another way, if you are interested in a dress, and you see a customer who is more attractive than you wearing that dress in the store, it is as if you say to yourself, "that dress is cute and attractive, but compared to her, I look terrible in this dress." The low esteem shopper makes an upward social comparison that reduces her own evaluation of the product.

---

not as good as a professional, you can seek advice from a coach or increase your practice hours to get closer to the abilities of the target. Another possible outcome, however, could be that you can think negative thoughts about yourself and experience a decrease in self-esteem.

People can also compare themselves to people whose abilities are lower than their own. This process is called **downward social comparison**. A downward social comparison typically results in individuals feeling better about themselves as a result of the comparison. As in our previous example, if an experienced volleyball player (someone in their senior year) compares their athletic ability with someone who is new to the team (a freshman) and new to the game, regardless of how good the experienced person actually is, they are going to feel better about their abilities. It is believed that women compare themselves with unrealistic images more-so than do men (Strahan, Wilson, Cressman, & Buote, 2006). This behavior is not surprising since there are more messages about physical appearance in women's than in men's magazines, including health magazines (Bazzini et al., 2015; Malkin, Wornian, & Chrisler, 1999). However, researchers have also shown that body dissatisfaction is prevalent in men, particularly related to muscularity (Frederick, Fessler, & Haselton, 2005; Karazia & Crowther, 2009). They found that men tend to compare to people similar to themselves (e.g., peers) as well as to those with desirable physical characteristics (e.g., athletes). Men and women differ in whom they consider "reasonable targets" of comparison. Women rated their family and friends as reasonable targets for appearance information, while men rated their classmates and celebrities as reasonable (Heinberg & Thompson, 1992).

Self-Esteem

What factors may encourage or discourage a healthy body image and the practice of certain appearance-management behaviors? We typically think of self-esteem as contributing to a healthy sense of oneself (please refer to Chapter 9, "Dress and the Self"). For example, we know that a stronger self-esteem may protect women from negative body image attitudes and behaviors (Lennon & Rudd, 1994); respondents with low self-esteem were more likely to consider risky appearance-management behaviors than those with higher self-esteem. Indeed, in a study across four ethnic groups, strong self-esteem was associated with stronger body image in general among Caucasian American, African American, Korean, and Singaporean women (Lennon, Rudd, Sloan, & Kim, 1999). Conversely, low self-esteem is generally related to poorer body image in women (Lennon, Lillethun, &Buckland, 1999), men (Reilly & Rudd, 2006), and adolescents (Koff, Rierdan, & Stubbs, 1990).

Gender Ideology

As will be discussed in Chapter 10, "Dress and Identity," gender is socially constructed, meaning that our culture and our social groups establish expectations for how men and women behave. Many authors have written about this distinction, and specifically how women are held to stricter standards of attractiveness and attention to appearance (Grogan, 2008; Thompson et al., 1999; Wolf, 1990). They argue that cultural aspects of gender are the key to understanding body image disturbances and the negative behaviors and self-feelings that often accompany them (Wooley, 1995). So if women internalize cultural norms of appearance that are restrictive, they develop negative self-thoughts about appearance and perhaps self-doubts about their attractiveness, (Bergner, Remer, & Whetsell, 1985).

We learn these gender role expectations (ideology) from those we interact with and observe, including family, peers, and the media. We astutely observe the near environment around us, and learn from an early age what it means to be male or female—what ways to walk, sit, gesture, speak, adorn and care for our bodies, and monitor our behavior.

Traditional gender expectations in Western culture differ for girls and boys; girls are often expected to "be" (pretty, quiet, respectful, happy, loving), while boys are expected to "do" (sports, crazy stunts, take risks, take control) (Freedman, 1986; Kaiser, 1990). Girls learn from an early age to pay attention to their appearance and to monitor it and control it; some writers refer to this as the "disciplined body" (Bordo, 2003; Domzal & Kernan, 1993). They suggest that common behaviors demonstrated by those with disciplined bodies include rigid control of dieting, exercising, cleanliness, and grooming. Boys learn to test body capabilities through physical activity, and do not worry about monitoring it or controlling it. So, if you hold traditional attitudes concerning gender ideology, you probably believe in these differences and your beliefs guide your actions related to your body. However, if you hold more egalitarian beliefs about gender roles and believe that any gender can do or be anything they desire, then women can do or be anything they want (e.g., athletes, corporate executives, coal miners, soccer players), just as men can do or be anything they want (e.g., caretakers, nurses, ballet dancers, preschool teachers). These egalitarian attitudes are likely to filter into your attitudes about your body and appearance as well.

Social and cultural pressures or expectations to look a certain way can strongly impact boys and men, just as they do girls and women. For example, sports participation can serve as a protective factor in how individuals view themselves and encourage healthy ways of training and eating (Smolak, Murnen, & Ruble, 2000). Yet, for some athletes, sports participation may be a risk factor because it does not build self-confidence but instead may contribute to perfectionist tendencies, internalization of an "ideal" body type for the sport, or social comparison to others on the team, thus leading to poor body image and unhealthy behaviors (Streigel-Moore & Smolek, 2001). Men and women who compete in sports that emphasize leanness, such as swimming, diving, track and field, tennis, and gymnastics, worry about maintaining a thin body shape that is associated with success in their sport (Rudd & Carter, 2006).

Having an attractive appearance is more important to women who hold traditional attitudes concerning gender ideology than to women holding non-traditional attitudes. Holding traditional attitudes also influences the connection between appearance and self-esteem. If women hold traditional attitudes and are attentive to their appearance, they feel good about themselves. The self-esteem of women with nontraditional attitudes is not as tied to appearance, meaning that they tend to place less importance on and give less attention to their clothing and grooming behaviors.

Other writers (Bartky, 1990; Grogan, 2008; Moradi, 2010) believe that both men and women are active agents in constructing their own ideals of beauty within the range of options present in their culture. If they have a strong social support network for that appearance, even if it is outside of the norm (e.g., female bodybuilders or intense grooming in men), they feel satisfied.

Chapter Summary

The construct of body image is composed of many complex and distinct components, including perceptions, attitudes, and behaviors. Perceptions can often be distorted, causing individuals to view themselves more critically and less objectively than others view them. In addition, attitudes toward the body are shaped by culture, peers, family, and media, and thus often make us feel inadequate in appearance. We may think that we need to be thinner, or taller, or more beautiful, or more muscular. We then engage in behaviors related to managing our appearance—controlling what we eat, how and how often we exercise or train with weights, what supplements we may use, what surgery we may consider or actually undergo, and what products we use to create our appearances. The outcome of these behaviors may or may not actually strengthen our body image, nor our self-esteem.

Key Terms

anorexia nervosa	body image	EDNOS (eating disorder not otherwise specified)	perceptual component
appearance management behaviors	body image disturbance	internalized homonegativity	risky behaviors
attitudinal component	body satisfaction	material self	routine behaviors
behavioral component	bulimia nervosa	muscle dysmorphia	self-cutting
binge eating disorder (BED)	cultivation theory	normative discontent	social comparison
body dissatisfaction	downward social comparison	orthorexia	social self
body dysmorphic disorder	eating disorder		spiritual self
			upward social comparison

Discussion Questions

1. Is the media to "blame" for poor body image among women and girls, or men and boys? Why, or why not?

2. To what extent do families encourage good or bad feelings about the body and resulting appearance management behaviors?

3. In what ways can we give value to people based on characteristics other than physical appearance? Do YOU evaluate others primarily based on appearance?

4. How can the fashion industry promote positive body image?

STUDiO™

Visit your book's STUDIO for additional quiz questions, vocabulary flashcards, and chapter worksheets!

Suggested Readings

Bazzini, D., Pepper, A., Swofford, R., & Cochran, K. (2015). How healthy are health magazines? A comparative content analysis of cover captions and images of *Women's and Men's Health* magazine. *Sex Roles, 72*, 198–210.

Reilly, A. & Rudd, N.A. (2009). Social anxiety as predictor of personal aesthetic among women. *Clothing and Textiles Research Journal, 27*(3), 227–239.

References

Ackard, D., Croll, J., & Kearney–Cooke, A. (2002). Dieting frequency among college females: Association with disordered eating, body image and related psychological problems. *Journal of Psychosomatic Research, 52,* 129–136.

Altabe, M. (1998). Ethnicity and body image: Quantitative and qualitative analysis. *International Journal of Eating Disorders, 23,* 153–159.

American Psychiatric Association (2013). *Diagnostic and statistical manual of Mental Disorders (DSM–5.)* Washington, DC: Author.

Anderson, A. (1990). *Males with eating disorders.* New York, NY: Bruner Mazel.

Anderson, C., & Bulik, C. (2004). Gender differences in compensatory behaviors, weight and shape salience, and drive for thinness. *Eating Behaviors, 5,* 1–11.

Bardone–Cone, A., Cass, K., & Ford, J. (2008). Examining body dissatisfaction in young men within a biopsychosocial framework. *Body Image, 5,* 183–194.

Barry, D. & Grilo, C. (2002), Eating and body image disturbances in adolescent psychiatric inpatients: Gender and ethnicity patterns. *International Journal of Eating Disorders, 32,* 335–343.

Bartky, S. (1990). *Femininity and domination: Studies in the phenomenology of oppression.* New York: Routledge.

Bazzini, D., Pepper, A., Swofford, R., & Cochran, K. (2015). How healthy are health magazines? A comparative content analysis of cover captions and images of *Women's and Men's Health* magazine. *Sex Roles, 72,* 198–210.

Becker, A. (2004). Television, disordered eating and young women in Fiji: Negotiating body image and identity during rapid social change. *Culture, Medicine and Psychiatry, 28,* 533–559.

Beren, S. E., Hayden, H. A., Wilfey, D. E., & Grilo, C. M. (1996). The influence of sexual orientation on body dissatisfaction in adult men and women. *International Journal of Eating Disorders, 20*(2), 135–141.

Berger, J. M., Levant, R., McMillan, K. K., Kelleher, W., & Sellers, A. (2005). Impact of gender role conflict, traditional masculinity ideology, alexithymia, and age on men's attitudes toward psychological help seeking. *Psychology of Men and Masculinity, 6,* 73–78.

Bergner, M., Remer, P., &Whetsell, C. (1985). Transforming women's body image: A feminist counseling approach. *Women and Therapy, 4,* 25–38.

Bordo, S. (2003). *Unbearable weight: Feminism, Western culture, and the body.* Berkeley, CA: University of California Press.

Boroughs, M., Carfi, G., & Thompson, J.K. (2005). Male body depilation: Prevalence and association features of body hair removal. *Sex Roles, 52*(9/10), 637–643.

Cash, T.F. (1997). *The body image workbook: An 8–step program for learning to like your looks.* Oakland, CA: New Harbinger Publications.

Cash, T. (2000). *Users manual for the multidimensional body–self relations questionnaire.* Available from the author on *http://www.body-images.com.*

Cash, T., Cash, D., & Butters, J. (1983). Mirror, mirror on the wall. . .? Contrast effects and self-evaluations of physical attractiveness. *Personality and Social Psychology, 9,* 359–364.

Cash, T. & Pruzinsky, T., eds. (1990). *Body Images: Development, deviance, and change.* NewYork, NY: Guilford Press.

Cash, T. F., & Szymanski, M. L. (1995). The development and validation of the Body–Image Ideals Questionnaire. *Journal of Personality Assessment, 64*(3), 466–478.

Cash, T., Winstead, B., & Janda, L. (1975). The great American shape–up: Body image survey report. *Psychology Today, 20*(4), 30–37.

Clausen, L., Rosenvinge, J., Friborg, O., & Rokkedal K. (2011). Validating the Eating Disorder Inventory–3 (EDI–3): A comparison between 561 female eating disorders patients and 878 females from the general population, *Journal of Psychopathology and Behavioral Assessment, 33*(1): 101–110.

Connell, L. J., Ulrich, P., Brannon, E., Alexander, M., & Presley, A. B. (2006). Body shape assessment scale: Instrument development for analyzing female figures. *Clothing and Textiles Research Journal, 24*(2), 80–95.

Craig, P. L., Swinburn, B. A., Matenga–Smith, T., Matangi, H., & Vaughan, G. (1996). Do Polynesians still believe that big is beautiful? Comparison of body size perceptions and preferences of Cook Islands, Maori and Australians. *New Zealand Medical Journal, 109,* 200–203.

Dahl, D., Argo, J, & Morales, A. (2011). Social information in the retail environment: The importance of consumption alignment, referent identity, and self-esteem. *Journal of Consumer Research,* Retrieved from http://www.jstor.org/stable/10.1086/660918

Dohnt, H. K. & Tiggemann, M. (2006). Body image concerns in young girls: The role of peers and objectification theory. *Body Image, 7,* 32–38.

Domzal, T. & Kernan, J. (1993). Variations on the pursuit of beauty: Toward a corporal theory of the body. *Psychology and Marketing, 10*(6), 495–511.

Eating Disorders Awareness and Prevention (1993). *Statistics: Eating disorders and their precursors.* Seattle, WA: Author.

Ember, C., Ember, M., Korotayev, A. & de Munck, V. (2006). Valuing thinness or fatness in women: Reevaluating the effect of resource scarcity. *Evolution and Human Behavior, 28,* 48–54.

Emery, J., Benson, P., Cohen-Tovee, E., & Tovee, M. (1995). A computerized measure of body image. *Brain Research Association Abstracts, 12,* 68.

Evans, P. & McConnell, A. (2003). Do racial minorities respond in the same way to mainstream beauty standards? Social comparison processes in Asian, Black, and White women. *Self & Identity, 2,* 153–167.

Fairburn, C., Welch, S., Doll, H., Davies, B., & O'Connor, M. (1997). Risk factors for bulimia nervosa: A community-based case-control study. *Archives General Psychiatry, 54,* 509–517.

Fallon, A. & Rozin, P. (1985). Sex differences in perceptions of desirable body shape. *Journal of Abnormal Psychology, 94*(1), 102–105.

Forbes, G., Jung, J., Vaamonde, J., Omar, A., Paris, P., & Formiga, N. (2012). Body dissatisfaction and disordered eating in three cultures: Argentina, Brazil, and the U.S. *Sex Roles, 66,* 677–694.

Frederick, D., Buchanan, G., Sadehgi-Azar, L., Peplau, L.A., Haselton, M, & Berezovskaya, A. (2007). Desiring the muscular ideal: Men's body satisfaction in the United States, Ukraine, and Ghana. *Psychology of Men and Masculinity, 8,* 103–117.

Frederick, D., Fessler, D., & Haselton, M. (2005). Do representations of male muscularity differ in men's and women's magazines? *Body Image, 2,* 81–86.

Frederick, D., Forbes, G., & Berezovskaya, A. (2008). Female body dissatisfaction and perceptions of the attractive female body in Ghana, the Ukraine, and the United States. *Psychological Topics, 17,* 203–219.

Frederick, D., Forbes, G., Grigorian, K., & Jarcho, J. (2007). The UCLA Body Project I: Gender and ethnic differences in self-objectification and body satisfaction among 2,206 undergraduates. *Sex Roles, 57,* 317–327.

Frederick, D., Mackenzie, C. K., Latner, J., Sandhu, G., & Tsong, Y. (2016). Body image and face image in Asian American and white women: Examining associations with surveillance, construal of self, perfectionism, and sociocultural pressures. *Body Image: 16,* 113–125

Frederick, D. A., & Peplau, L. A. (2007). The UCLA Body Matrices II: Computer-generated images of men and women varying in body fat and muscularity/breast size to assess body satisfaction and preferences. Presentation to the Society for Personality and Social Psychology, Memphis, TN.

Freedman, R. (1986). *Beauty bound.* Lexington, MA: Heath/Lexington Books.

Frost, Katherine (2013). Revising The Body Esteem Scale for the next quarter century. Dissertation, Marquette University. Paper 294. Retrieved from http://epublications.marquette.edu/dissertations_mu/294.

Furnham, A. & Greaves, N. (1994). Gender and locus of control correlates of body image dissatisfaction. *European Journal of Personality, 8*(3), 183–200.

Gerbner G., Gross L., Morgan M., Signorielli N., & Shanahan J. (2002). Growing up with television: Cultivation processes. In: Bryant, J., & Zillman, D., eds. *Media effects: Advances in theory and research.* Mahwah, NJ: Lawrence Erlbaum Associates, pp. 43–67.

Gil, L. (2011). Latina beauty obsession. *Huffington Post.* Retrieved from http://www.huffingtonpost.com/2011/12/01/latina-beauty-obsession_n_1123464.html.

Grabe, S. & Hyde, J. (2006). Ethnicity and body dissatisfaction among women in the United States: A meta-analysis. *Psychological Bulletin, 132,* 622–640.

Grabe, S., Hyde, J., & Lindberg, S. (2007). Body objectification and depression in adolescents: The role of gender, shame, and rumination, *Psychology of Women Quarterly, 31,* pp. 164–175.

Grammas, D. & Schwartz (2009). Internalization of messages from society and perfectionism as predictors of male body image. *Body Image, 6,* 31–36.

Grogan, S. (2008). *Body image: Understanding body dissatisfaction in men, women, and children* (2nd ed.). New York, NY: Routledge.

Grogan, S. & Richards, H. (2002). Body image: Focus groups with boys and men. *Men and Masculinities, 4,* 219–233.

Grogan, S. & Wainwright, N. (1996). Growing up in the culture of slenderness: Girl's experiences of body dissatisfaction. *Women's Studies International Forum, 19*, 665–673.

Gruber, A., Pope, H., Borowiecki, J., & Cohane, G. (1999). The development of the somatomorphic matrix: A biaxial instrument for measuring body image in men and women. In T.S. Olds, J. Dollman, & K. Norton (Eds.), *Kinanthropometry VI*. Sydney, Australia: International Society for Advancement of Kinanthropometry.

Harper, B. & Tiggemann, M. (2008). The effect of thin ideal media images on women's self-objectification, mood and body image. *Sex Roles, 58*, 649–657.

Heatherton, T., Mahamedi, F., Striepe, M., Field, A., & Keel, P. (1997). A 10-year longitudinal study of body weight, dieting, and eating disorder symptoms. *Journal of Abnormal Psychology, 106*, 117–125.

Heinberg, L. & Thompson, J.K. (1992). Social comparison: Gender, target importance ratings, and relations to body image disturbance. *Journal of Social Behavior and Personality, 7*, 335–344.

Heinberg, L.& Thompson, J.K. (1995). Body image and televised images of thinness and attractiveness: A controlled laboratory investigation. *Journal of Social & Clinical Psychology, 14*, 325,338.

James, W. (1890). *The principles of psychology* (2 vols.). New York, NY: Henry Holt (Reprinted Bristol, England: Thoemmes Press, 1999).

Johnson, F., & Wardle, J. (2005). Dietary restraint, body dissatisfaction, and psychological distress: A prospective analysis. *Journal of Abnormal Psychology, 114*, 119–125.

Jung, J., Forbes, G., & Chan, P. (2010). Global body and muscle satisfaction among college men in the United States and Hone Kong–China. *Sex Roles, 63*, 104–117.

Kaiser, S. (1990). *The social psychology of clothing: Symbolic appearances in context*. New York, NY: Macmillan Publishing Company.

Karazia, B. & Crowther, J. (2009). Social body comparison and internalization: Mediators of social influences on men's muscularity–oriented body dissatisfaction. *Body Image, 6*, 105–112.

Klonick, K. (2006, September 15). New message to models: Eat! *ABC News*. Retrieved from http://abcnews.go.com/Entertainment/story?id=2450069

Koff, E., Rierdan, J., & Stubbs, M.L. (1990). Gender, body image, and self-concept in early adolescence. *Journal of Early Adolescence, 10*, 56–68.

Kozee, H.B. &Tylka, T. L. (2006). A test of objectification theory with lesbian women. *Psychology of Women Quarterly, 30*, 348–357.

Lee, J. & Johnson, K.K.P. (2009). Factors related to engagement in risky appearance management behaviors. *Clothing and Textiles Research Journal, 27*(3), 163–178.

Legenbauer, T., Vocks, S., Schäfer, C., Schütt-Strömel, S., Hiller, W., Wagner, C., &Vogele, C. (2009). Preference for attractiveness and thinness in a partner: Influence of internalization of the thin ideal and shape–weight dissatisfaction in heterosexual women, heterosexual men, lesbians, and gay men. *Body Image, 6*, 228–234.

Lennon, S., Lillethun, A., & Buckland, S. (1999). Attitudes toward social comparison as a function of self–esteem, idealized appearance and body image. *Family and Consumer Sciences Research Journal, 23*(2), 94–117.

Lennon, S. & Rudd, N. A. (1994). Linkages between attitudes toward gender roles, body satisfaction, self–esteem, and appearance–management behaviors in women. *Family and Consumer Sciences Research Journal, 23*, 94–117.

Lennon, S., Rudd, N. A., Sloan, B., & Kim, J. S. (1999). Attitudes toward gender roles, self–esteem, and body image: Application of a model. *Clothing and Textiles Research Journal, 17*(3), 1–12.

Levine, M. P., & Harrison, K. (2004). Media's role in the perpetuation and prevention of negative body image and disordered eating. In J. K. Thompson (Ed.), *Handbook of Eating Disorders and Obesity* (pp. 695–717). New York, NY: John Wiley.

Levine, M. P., Smolak, L., & Hayden, H. (1994). The relation of sociocultural factors to eating attitudes and behaviors among middle school girls. *The Journal of Early Adolescence,14(4)*, 471–490.

Lipinski, J. P. & Pope, H. G. (2002). Body ideals in young Samoan men: A comparison with men in North America and Europe. *International Journal of Men's Health, 1*, 163–171.

Malkin, A.R., Wornian, K., & Chrisler, J. C. (1999). Advertising and social comparison: Consequences for female pre–adolescents and adolescents. *Psychology and Marketing, 10*, 513–530.

Maloney, M., McGuire, J., Daniels, S., & Specker, B. (1989). Dieting behavior and eating attitudes in children. *Pediatrics, 84*, 482–489.

Mangweth, B., Pope, H., Kemmler, G., Ebenbichler, C., Hausmann, A., DeCol, C., Kreutner, B., Kinzl, J., & Biebl, W. (2001). Body image and psychopathology in male body builders. *Psychotherapy and Psychosomatics, 70*, 38–43.

Martins, Y., Tiggemann, M. & Churchett, L. (2008). The shape of things to come: Gay men's satisfaction with specific body parts. *Psychology of Men & Masculinity, 9*(4), 248–256.

Mastria, M. (2002). Ethnicity and eating disorders. *Psychoanalysis and Psychotherapy, 19*, 59–77.

McCabe, M. P., Ricciardelli, L.A., & Finemore, J. (2002). The role of puberty, media and popularity with peers on strategies to increase weight, decrease weight and increase muscle tone among adolescent boys and girls. *Journal of Psychosomatic Research, 52*, 145–153.

McCabe, M., Ricciardelli, L., Sitaram, G., & Mikhail, K. (2006). Accuracy of body size estimation: Role of biopsychosocial variables. *Body Image: An International Journal of Research, 3*, 163–173.

McComb, J. & Clopton, J. (2002).Explanatory variance in bulimia nervosa. *Women & Health, 36, 115*–123.

McCreary, D., Sasse, D., Saucier, D. M., & Dorsch, K. D. (2004). Measuring the drive for muscularity: Factorial validity of the Drive for Muscularity Scale in men and women. *Psychology of Men and Masculinity, 6*, 83–94.

McCreary, D. & Saucier, D. (2009). Drive for muscularity, body comparison, and social physique anxiety in men and women. *Body Image, 6*, 24–30.

Mellin, L., Irwin, C., & Scully, S. (1992). Prevalence of disordered eating in girls: A survey of middle-class children. *Journal of the American Dietetic Association, 92*, 851–853.

Mintz, L. & Betz, N. (1988). Prevalence and correlates of eating disorders behaviors among undergraduate women. *Journal of Counseling Psychology, 35*(4), 463–471.

Mintz, N. & Kashubeck, S. (1999). Body image and disordered eating among Asian American and Caucasian college students: An examination of race and gender differences. *Psychology of Women, 23*, 781–796.

Moore, D. (1990). Body image and eating behavior in adolescent boys. *American Journal of Diseases in Children, 144*, 475–479.

Moore, F. & Keel, P. K. (2003). Influence of sexual orientation and age on disordered eating attitudes and behaviours in women. *International Journal of Eating Disorders, 34*, 370–374.

Moradi, B. (2010). Addressing gender and cultural diversity in body image: Objectification theory as a framework for integrating theories and grounding research. *Sex Roles, 63*, 138–148.

Morrison, M. A., Morrison, T.G., & Sager, C. (2004). Does body satisfaction differ between gay men and lesbian women and heterosexual men and women? A meta-analytic review. *Body Image, 1*, 127–138.

Nichter, M. (2000). *Fat talk: What girls and their parents say about dieting.* Cambridge, MA: Harvard University Press.

Oehlhof, M., Musher–Eizenman,D., Neufeld, J., & Hauser, J. (2009). Self-objectification and ideal body shape for men and women. *Body Image, 6*, 308–310.

Ogden, J. (1992). *Fat chance: The myth of dieting explained.* London, UK: Routledge.

Ogle, J. P. & Damhorst, M. L. (2000). Dieting among adolescent girls and their mothers: An interpretive study. *Family and Consumer Sciences Research Journal, 28*(4), 428–462.

Olivardia, R., Pope, H.G., Borowiecki, J. & Cohane, G. (2004). Biceps and body image: The relationship between muscularity and self-esteem, depression, and eating disorder symptoms. *Psychology of Men & Muscularity, 5*(2), 112–120.

Olivardia, R., Pope, H., & Hudson, J. (2000). Muscle dysmorphia in male weightlifters: A case–control study. *American Journal of Psychiatry, 157*, 1291–1296.

Owens, K. L., Hughes, T.L., & Owens-Nicholson, D. (2002). The effects of sexual orientation on body image and attitudes about eating and weight. *Journal of Lesbian Studies, 7*, 15–33.

Parker, S., Nuchter, M., Vickovic, N., Sims, C., & Ritenbaugh, C. (1995). Body image and weight concerns among African American and White adolescent females: Differences that make a difference. *Human Organization, 54*, 103–114.

Patton, G., Johnson-Sabine, E., Wood, K., Mann, A. & Wakeling, A. (1990). Abnormal eating attitudes in London school girls—a prospective epidemiological study: Outcome at twelve-month follow-up. *Psychological Medicine, 20*, 383–394.

Pearson, C. (2011, November 3). Fashion and eating disorders: How much responsibility does industry have? *Huffington Post.* Retrieved from http://www.huffington post.com/2011/09/13/fashion-eating-disorders-industry -responsibility_n_955497.html

Petrova, A. & Ashdown, S. (2008). Three-dimensional body scan data analysis. *Clothing and Textiles Research Journal, 26*(3), 227–252.

Pickett, T., Lewis, R, & Cash, T. (2005). Men, muscles, and body image: Comparisons of competitive bodybuilders, weight trainers, and athletically active controls. *British Journal of Sports Medicine, 39,* 217–222.

Pope, H., Gruber, A., Mangweth, B., Bureau, B., de Col, C., Jouvent, R., & Hudson, J. (2000). Body image perception among men in three countries. *American Journal of Psychiatry, 157,* 297–301.

Pope, H. H. , Olivardia, R., Gruber, A., & Borowiecki, J. (1999). Evolving ideals of male body images as seen through action toys. *International Journal of Eating Disorders, 26,* 65–72.

Reilly, A. & Rudd, N. A. (2006). Is internalized homonegativity related to body image? *Family and Consumer Sciences Research Journal, 35*(1), 58–73.

Reilly, A. & Rudd, N. A. (2008, July). Sun, salon and cosmetic tanning: Predictors and motives. *Proceedings of World Academy of Science, Engineering and Technology, 30,* ISSN 1307-1604, 391–397.Reilly, A. & Rudd, N. A. (2009). Social anxiety as predictor of personal aesthetic among women. *Clothing and Textiles Research Journal, 27*(3), 227–239.

Ricciardelli, L., McCabe, M., Mavoa, H., Fotu, K., Gounder, R., Schultz, J., Waqa, G., & Swinburn, B. (2007). The pursuit of muscularity among adolescent boys in Fiji and Tonga. *Body Image, 4,* 361–371.

Rodin, J., Silberstein, L., & Striegel-Moore, R. (1985). Women and weight: A normative discontent. In T. B. Sonderegger (Ed.), *Psychology and gender: Nebraska symposium on motivation* (Vol. 32) pp. 267–307. Lincoln, Nebraska: University of Nebraska Press.

Rosenberg M. (1965). *Society and the adolescent self-image.* Princeton, New York: Princeton University Press.

Rudd, N. A. (1996). Appearance and self-presentation research in gay consumer cultures: Issues and impact. *Journal of Homosexuality, 31*(1/2), 109–134.

Rudd, N. A. & Carter, J. (2006). Building positive body image among athletes: A socially responsible approach. *Clothing & Textiles Research Journal, 24*(4), 363–380.

Rudd, N. A., & Lennon, S. J. (1994). Aesthetics of the body and social identity. In M. R. DeLong & A. M. Fiore (Eds.), *Aesthetics of textiles and clothing: Advancing multi-disciplinary perspectives* (pp. 163–175). Monument, CO: International Textile and Apparel Association.

Rudd, N. A. & Lennon, S.J. (1999). Social power and appearance management among women. In K. K. P. Johnson & S.J. Lennon (Eds.), *Appearance and Power.* New York, NY: Berg, pp. 153–172.

Rudd, N. A. & Lennon, S. J. (2000). Body image and appearance-altering behaviors of college women. In S.

Michelman and S. Kaiser (Eds.), *Clothing and Textiles Research Journal, 18*(3), 152–162.

Sanders, N. & Heiss, C. (1998), Eating attitudes and body image of Asian and Caucasian college women. *Eating Disorders: The Journal of Treatment and Prevention, 6,* 15–27.

Schaefer, L., Burke, N.L., Thompson, J. K., Dedrick, R. F., Heinberg, L. J., Calogero, R. M., & Swami, V. (2015). Development and validation of the Sociocultural Attitudes Towards Appearance Questionnaire-4 (SATAQ-4). *Psychological Assessment, 27,* 54–67. Retrieved from http://dx.doi.org/10.1037/a0037917

Schilder, P. (1950). *The image and appearance of the human body.* New York, NY: International Universities Press. Schrof, J. (1992, June 1). Pumped up. *U.S. News & World Report,* pp. 54–63.

Schur, E. A., Sanders, M., & Steiner, H. (2000). Body dissatisfaction and dieting in young children. *International Journal of Eating Disorders, 27,* 74–82.

Sergios, P. & Cody, J. (1986). Importance of physical attractiveness and social assertiveness skills in male homosexual dating behavior and partner selection. *Journal of Homosexuality, 12*(2), 71–84.

Shaw, H., Ramirez, L., Trost, A., Randall, P., & Stice, E. (2004). Body image and eating disorders across ethnic groups: More similarities than differences. *Psychology of Addictive Behaviors, 18,* 12–18.

Smith, D., Thompson, J. K., Raczynski, J., & Hilner, J. (1999). Body image among men and women in a biracial cohort: The CARDIA study. *International Journal of Eating Disorders, 25,* 71–82.

Smolak, L., Murnen, S., & Ruble, A. (2000). Female athletes and eating problems: A meta-analysis. *International Journal of Eating Disorders, 27,* 371–380.

Strahan, E. J., Wilson, A.E., Cressman, K. E., & Buote, V. M. (2006). Comparing to perfection: How cultural norms for appearance affect social comparisons and self-image. *Body Image: An International Journal of Research, 3,* 211–228.

Striegel-Moore, R. & Smolak, L. (2001). *Eating disorders: Innovative directions in research and practice.* Washington, D.C.: American Psychological Association.

Swanson, S.A., Crow, S, J, LeGrange, D., Swendsen, J., & Merikangas, K. R. (2011). Prevalence and correlates of eating disorders in adolescents: Results from the National Comorbidity Survey Replication Adolescent Supplement. *Archives of General Psychiatry.*

Swami, V., Frederick, D., Aavik, T., Alcalay, L., Allik, J., Anderson, D. et al. (2010). The attractive female body weight and female body dissatisfaction in 26 countries across 10 world regions: Results of the International Body Project 1. *Personality and Social Psychology Bulletin, 36*(3), 309–325.

Taber, K. C. (2006, November 20). With model's death, eating disorders are again in spotlight—Americas. *New York Times*. Retrieved from http://www.nytimes .com/2006/11/20/world/americas/20iht-models .3604439.html

The National Institute of Mental Health: "Eating Disorders: Facts about Eating Disorders and the Search for Solutions." Pub No. 01-4901. Retrieved from http:// www.nimh.nih. gov/ publicat/nedspdisorder.cfm

Thompson, J. K. (1992). Body image: Extent of disturbance, associated features, theoretical models, assessment methodologies, intervention strategies, and a proposal for a new DSM-IV diagnostic category— Body image disorder. In M. Hersen, R. M. Eisler, & P.M. Miller (Eds.), *Progress in behavior modification, 28*, pp. 3–54. Sycamore, IL: Sycamore Press.

Thompson, J. K., Cattarin, J., Fowler, B., & Fishe, E. (1995). The perception of teasing scale (POTS): A revision and extension of the physical appearance related teasing scale (PARTS). *Journal of Personality Assessment, 65*(1), 146–157.

Thompson, J. K., Heinberg, L. J., Altabe, M., & Tantleff-Dunn, S. (1999). *Exacting beauty: Theory, assessment, and treatment of body image disturbance*. Washington, DC: American Psychological Association.

Thompson, J. K., Penne, L., & Altabe, M. (1990). Procedures, problems and progress in the assessment of body images, In T. F. Cash & T. Pruzinsky (Eds.), *Body Images: Development, deviance, and change* (pp. 21–48). New York, NY: Guilford Press.

Thompson, J. K. & Thompson, J. K. (1999). Physical appearance state and trait anxiety scale: Trait. In J.K. Thompson, L. Heinberg, M. Altabe, & S. Tantleff-Dunn, *Exacting Beauty: Theory, assessment and treatment of body image disturbance*. Washington, DC: American Psychological Association, p. 81.

Thompson, J. K., van den Berg, P., Roehrig, M., Guarda, A. & Heinberg, L. J. (2004). The Sociocultural Attitudes Towards Appearance Scale-3 (SATAQ-3): Development and Validation. *International Journal of Eating Disorders, 35*, 293–304.

Thompson, K. & Cafri, G. (2007). (Eds.) *The muscular ideal: Psychological, social and medical perspectives*. Washington, DC: American Psychological Association.

Thompson, M. & Gray, J. (1995). Development and validation of a new body-image assessment tool. *Journal of Personality Assessment, 64*, 258–269.

Tiggemann, M. (2004). Body image across the adult life span: Stability and change. *Body Image, 1*, 29–41.

Tiggemann, M. (2005). Body dissatisfaction and adolescent self-esteem: Prospective findings. *Body Image: An International Journal of Research, 2*, 129–36.

Tiggemann, M. & McGill, B. (2004).The role of social comparison in the effect of magazine advertisements on women's mood and body dissatisfaction. *Journal of Social & Clinical Psychology. Special Issue: Body Image and Eating Disorders, 23*, 23–44.

Tylka, T., Bergeron, D., & Schwartz, J. P. (2005). Development and psychometric evaluation of the Male Body Attitudes Scale (MBAS). *Body Image: An International Journal of Research, 2*, 161–175.

Wheatley, J. (2006). Like mother, like daughter: The young copycat dieters. *The Times, 11* August, 6–7.

Wildes, J., Emery, R., & Simons, A. (2001). The roles of ethnicity and culture in the development of eating disturbance and body dissatisfaction: A meta-analytic review. *Clinical Psychology Review, 21*, 521–551.

Williamson, S. & Delin, C. (2001). Young children's figural selections: Accuracy of reporting and body size dissatisfaction. *International Journal of Eating Disorders, 29*(1), 80–84.

Wolf, N. (1990). *The beauty myth*. London, UK: Vintage.

Wooley, S.C. (1995). Feminist influences on the treatment of eating disorders. In K.D. Brownell & C.G. Fairborn (Eds.), *Eating disorders and obesity: A comprehensive handbook* (pp. 294–298). New York, NY: Guilford.

Yahoo news (6 June, 2016). What Miss USA said last night that has everyone talking. Retrieved from http://www .yahoo.com/news/miss-usa-said-last-night -121400192.html

Yates, A., Edman, J., & Arguete, M. (2004). Ethnic difference in BMI and body/self dissatisfaction among White, Asian subgroups, Pacific Islanders, and African Americans. *Journal of Adolescent Health, 34*, 300–307.

Yelland, C. & Tiggemann, M. (2003). Muscularity and the gay ideal: Body dissatisfaction and disordered eating in homosexual men. *Eating Behaviours, 4*(1), 107–116.

8 DRESS AND PERSONALITY

After reading and reflecting on the content of this chapter students should be able to:

- **Explain how different theories of personality can be used to understand individual differences in dress.**

- **Differentiate between theories of personality reflecting the conflict perspective and those representing the fulfillment perspective.**

- **Describe defense mechanisms and how they may impact decision making concerning dress.**

- **Identify how human needs could be fulfilled using dress.**

- **Identify the dark triad of personality and how these traits are related to dress.**

INTRODUCTION

In Chapter 1, "Why Study Dress?" we noted that why you look the way you do and the choices that you make to dress your body and thereby modify your appearance is a result of three major influences: the culture and environment that you are living in, the social groups that you participate in, and the combination of individual characteristics that make you a unique individual. In this chapter, we focus our discussion on an individual characteristic, the psychological concept of personality, and how it can shape our behaviors and decision making concerning dress. You will quickly see that research on relationships between personality and dress spans several decades.

WHAT IS PERSONALITY?

The term *personality* comes from the Latin word *persona* meaning "mask." Masks were worn in the theater by actors

in ancient Greece and Rome to depict the characters of a play. The term **personality**, however, is used today to mean an enduring and somewhat stable characteristic of an individual. If you were sitting in a job interview and the interviewer asked you to describe yourself, you might think about words that described your physical characteristics (e.g., tall, brown hair, blue eyes, long fingers, small nose) as well as words to describe the activities that you like to do (e.g., skiing, spending time with friends, going to the movies) and words to describe your personality (e.g., outgoing, conscientious, creative). Although individuals can share similar personality traits with others, we often think about personality as an attribute that sets them apart from other individuals and makes them unique (Kalat, 2014). But it is not just that people differ from each other on the basis of their personality, one's personality is a lasting inner motivation that directs people to desire to achieve certain goals, thus it is another factor that underlies behavior including decisions and actions we take concerning dress.

To understand individuals' decision-making concerning dress and how those decisions might be related to personality, there are personality theories. These theories can be categorized as reflecting two basic perspectives: the conflict perspective and the fulfillment perspective.

THE CONFLICT PERSPECTIVE

The **conflict perspective** suggests that an individual's personality is the result of two opposing forces that are continuously in conflict with each other (Maddi, 1996). People can be both lazy and ambitious, giving and selfish, or caring and indifferent. Think about it, there are times when you have worked very hard to achieve a specific goal (maybe you ran for election as a class officer) and at the same time did not work hard at another specific goal (you did not study for an examination). If a person only saw you in the first situation, he might describe you as ambitious. If he only saw you in the second situation, he might describe you as lazy.

According to the conflict perspective, the best that can be accomplished in terms of the type of life you might lead is a compromise between continuous opposing characteristics of you. Leading an ideal life would suggest you have the ability to find a balance between these opposing forces with both being equally expressed. An example of an individual finding balance between opposing parts of a personality might be an apparel designer who makes a lot of money by being demanding with employees (bossy) and then donates a large portion of the profits of the company to a social cause (giving). If a person denied expression of one of these opposing forces, this denial could result in feeling inner tension that would need to be addressed.

One historically important individual that represents the conflict perspective in the study of personality is Sigmund Freud. Freud was an Austrian physician who lived in the early part of the twentieth century. His theory, labeled **psychodynamic theory**, related personality to the relationship of conscious as well as unconscious internal forces that were primarily in a state of conflict within each individual.

Psychodynamic Theory

Early in his career, Freud (1991; 1968) developed the idea that each individual's mind is divided into two parts: conscious and unconscious. Freud reasoned that people were well aware of the conscious aspects of our mind but the unconscious was a part of the mind that contained memories and emotions that were illogical but impacted people's behavior even though they could not easily talk about them or their influence. According to Freud, it was the unconscious part of the mind that was the basis for mental health problems. A good visual image of the conscious and the unconscious is to think about the human mind as if it were an iceberg. The part of the mind you are aware of is the part of the iceberg that is above water and what you are not aware of is below the surface of the water. Freud believed that traumatic experiences would force thoughts and emotions into the unconscious. The goal of psychoanalysis (Freud's therapy) was to bring those unconscious thoughts and emotions into the conscious. This process was proposed to produce a **cathexis** or release of emotional tension which would relieve the mental distress or illness. Once we understood the unconscious aspects

of our psychological illnesses, these illnesses could be treated. Throughout his career, Freud struggled to find empirical evidence for his theories. Regardless of his inability to locate evidence, he continued to speculate on the probable causes underlying an individual's "abnormal" behaviors.

The Components of Personality

Freud suggested that an individual's personality consisted of three parts: id, ego, and superego. The **id** is comprised of our biological drives and includes such things as need for food (hunger) or sex that demanded gratification. The **ego** is composed of the rational, decision-making part of our personality. One possible interpretation of the ego is that it is the part of personality that balances between our needs and the societal rules that exist for how to satisfy them. The **superego** consists of our memory of all the rules (i.e., the *shoulds*, the *oughts*) that we were taught growing up by our parents and other important members of society (e.g., teachers, doctors, peers) through the socialization process. With this structure, you can imagine it would be quite possible for these aspects of personality to be in conflict with each other. The id wanting to satisfy a need (e.g., I want to pierce my nose), the ego trying to decide how that need could be satisfied (e.g., having a small ring inserted), and the superego imposing restrictions (e.g., My mother thinks nose piercings are ugly). Freud was also not able to find evidence to support his view of personality. Nevertheless, people may experience inner conflict as they make decisions about how they want to appear and what items of dress they want to wear.

Applying ideas of the id, ego, and superego to decisions concerning dress and appearance, individuals may also feel in conflict with the dominant fashion of the day and may react to those fashions in a variety of ways (Kaiser, 1997). For example, following the current fashion of a time period necessitates conforming behaviors. Even though people may think they are being individualistic in their choices concerning dress, if they are participating in fashion, they are copying others and presenting the accepted fashion of a given time and place. The result is that everyone begins to look very similar. Suppose you want to stand out. You have a desire to use your dress to indicate to others that you are different. You are not like everyone else and you do not want to look the same. So you chose to wear dress items that are unique or practice a body modification that your peers or family members do not. Using Freud's terms, this desire to appear different from others reflects what the id wants. Your consideration of potential negative or positive reactions of your friends and family members to your "appearing different from others" reflects your superego. Concerns that these important people might react negatively and be less accepting of you if you wear these dress items or get the body modification can result in inner tension as what you want (id) to do may be in conflict with what you believe others want (superego) you to do. The ego part of personality is concerned with finding the balance between doing what you want (id) and what you think others would want you to do (superego). Luckily, dress can facilitate expression of a variety of ideas and allow individuals to craft appearances that make possible **ego differentiation** or the expression of a unique personality (Kaiser, 1997).

Another use of the term *ego* that does not reflect finding a balance is **ego-screaming**. Presenting extremely different appearances has been labeled as ego-screaming behavior or the attempt to create shock value and demand attention through one's appearance (Kaiser, 1997). Perhaps we can think of ego-screaming as an expression of the frustration experienced when one cannot find the balance between the appearance the id wants and the appearance their super-ego demands. They decide they cannot find a balance and ultimately, ignore their superego. The result is an appearance that is so out-of-the-ordinary it demands the visual attention of others. For example, evidence of ego-screaming can occur at many fairs and concerts where people have the opportunity to use hairsprays to change the color and shape of their hair creating messy and attention grabbing hairstyles. Reactions of some to the unique body modifications associated with punk or goth groups might have, at one point in time, be viewed as ego-screaming because of their high attention grabbing value (Brill, 2008; Sklar, 2013).

IN-CLASS ACTIVITY
Ego-Screaming

Any appearance that is designed for its shock value or with achieving a reaction of wonder or bewilderment from others may qualify as an example of ego-screaming. Identify an example of ego-screaming from your personal experience. In addition to ego-screaming, what other explanations exist for people presenting such appearances?

Defense Mechanisms

Aspects of Freud's work that continue to enter into everyday conversations are his ideas concerning defense mechanisms. Freud suggested that the ego defended itself against feeling tension or uncomfortable by transferring unpleasant thoughts to the unconscious part of personality. These unpleasant thoughts, according to Freud, often dealt with sexual or aggressive impulses. As a way of dealing with such tension and impulses, Freud posited the existence of defense mechanisms. **Defense mechanisms** are strategies people use to separate themselves from the unpleasant thoughts and feelings they may have as a result of their own behaviors. All psychologists have not accepted the view that personality is based on efforts to deal with sexual or aggressive impulses. They do however, recognize that people defend their self-concepts against threats to esteem and suggest that defense mechanisms may function as a means to protect one's self-esteem. (For a review of research findings relative to defense mechanisms see Baumeister, Dale, & Sommer, 2010).

Several defense mechanisms have been identified. What follows is brief descriptions of each supplied by Kalat (2014) and how each might relate to decision-making and behaviors concerning dress.

Denial

Denial refers to the refusal to accept reality or fact. When in a state of denial, a person simply asserts that the information concerning him or her is incorrect. For example, someone who is extremely thin and suffering with an eating disorder may insist that he or she is too fat. He or she is in denial about the true state of the body and may continue to behave as if that view is accurate.

Rationalization

Individuals are practicing **rationalization** when they attempt to prove that their behavior is justifiable and therefore, acceptable. They may try to explain their actions by getting an individual to view their behavior from a different perspective. Suppose you want to buy a pair of shoes for a date night. These shoes will add to your 100-plus shoe collection. Your significant other has made it known that she or he thinks you do not need any additional shoes. You buy the shoes. When confronted about your purchase, you tell your significant other that you did not buy the shoes to please yourself but rather you bought the shoes so that you would look good for her/him. Your purchasing may

Figure 8.1

Does this look familiar? Some consumers justify owning large and possibly excessive amounts of apparel and accessories using rationalization.

not be limited to shoes. Rather you may find your closet filled to overflowing because of your outstanding ability to rationalize your purchases (Figure 8.1).

Displacement

Displacement occurs when a behavior that should be directed at one person is directed towards another. Suppose you and a friend agree to go shopping because your favorite store is offering unbelievable discounts on their merchandise until noon. Your friend arrives late and you get to the store later than planned. All of the merchandise you were interested in has been sold. As a result, you are frustrated and disappointed because you told all your other friends you were going to get these great deals.

Instead of directing your frustration at the store manager for not having enough merchandise available or at other customers for buying up all of the available items, you displace your frustration by becoming angry at your friend for not arriving at the scheduled time. Another example of displacement may occur when people go shopping as a method of dealing with conflict. Suppose your boss is angry with you because you arrived late to work. You may feel frustrated or disappointed because your boss does not accept your reason for your tardiness. You deal with your disappointment by buying new clothing to make yourself feel better.

Regression

Regression involves a return to an earlier stage of development. By acting like a young child, an adult can sometimes escape the responsibilities of their adult roles. The television program *Bridezillas*[1] features several young women who pout, stomp their feet, and act like children when they do not get everything exactly the way they want it for their special day. During the 1990s some ravers[2] wore pacifiers around their necks or in their mouths borrowing forms of dress from their infant/toddler identities as they participated in the parties of the techno culture (Szostak-Pierce, 1999) and escaped from their everyday experiences as adults.

Projection

Attributing your own undesirable characteristics to other people who do not have these faults is known as **projection**. Perhaps individuals project their undesirable traits to others because they are uncomfortable with knowing that they have these traits. For example, perhaps you criticize your roommate for being too concerned about her appearance because she spends so much time getting ready in the morning when in fact you are complaining because you want more time than you are getting in the bathroom to get ready for your day.

---

[1] A bridezilla (a *neologistic portmanteau* of bride and Godzilla) is a difficult, unpleasant, perfectionist bride.

[2] A raver is a member of the 1990s techno culture. The techno culture experience is described as being a means of constructing one's reality through computers, appearance, electronic music, psychedelic drugs, and pagan-like rituals (Rushkoff, 1994) popular with some youth and young adults around the world but most closely linked to Europe and the United States.

Defense mechanisms were developed as psychological concepts many years ago. Are they still in evidence today? Are defense mechanisms used more during childhood than during adulthood? Can you think of an example when you recently practiced a defense mechanism? Do you use more of one type of defense mechanism over other types?

Reaction Formation

Reaction formation entails presenting yourself as the opposite of what you really are to hide or conceal the truth either from yourself or from others. Evidence of reaction formation might consist of a modest person who wears clothing that is extremely body revealing (Figure 8.2) or a shy person who wears bright colors and patterns to attract the visual attention of others.

Sublimation

The channeling of unacceptable impulses into acceptable ones is called **sublimation**. For example, if you had strong impulses to go shopping but in place of shopping you went to work out at the gym, you could be sublimating your shopping impulses.

THE FULFILLMENT PERSPECTIVE: NEEDS

In contrast to the conflict perspective of personality is the **fulfillment perspective**. The fulfillment perspective suggests that there is one force, one underlying tendency that is at the core of individual differences in behavior. For example, if the force was selfishness, your behavior over time would reflect this inborn tendency. This perspective suggests that anyone can achieve his or her inner potential or be what they want to be. You accept and value who you are and make every attempt to express this viewpoint in your daily life.

An example of a psychologist that represents the fulfillment perspective is the American psychologist Carl R.

Figure 8.2
Kim Kardashian-West. Celebrities may be engaging in reaction formation as they wear sheer clothing to attract the visual attention of others.

Rogers. Rogers thought that at the center of personality was the core tendency of humans to actualize their inherent potentialities. Rogers believed that people were basically good and that they had a drive (or internal force) to strive to be the best that they could be. This self-actualizing force was thought to be the drive behind the development of personality (McLeod, 2014a).

At about the same time that Rogers was developing his ideas about **self-actualization**, another American psychologist, Abraham Maslow (1970) was developing his ideas about personality and self-actualization. Maslow studied people that he regarded as mentally healthy. Maslow suggested that there exists a hierarchical order of human needs (i.e., psychological drives) that he believed individuals sought to satisfy (Figure 8.3).

Often depicted as a pyramid, at the bottom of his original hierarchy of needs were physiological needs and at the top was self-actualization. The hierarchy initially consisted

Figure 8.3
Maslow's hierarchy of needs indicating what desires had to be satisfied on one's journey to self-actualization and transcendence.

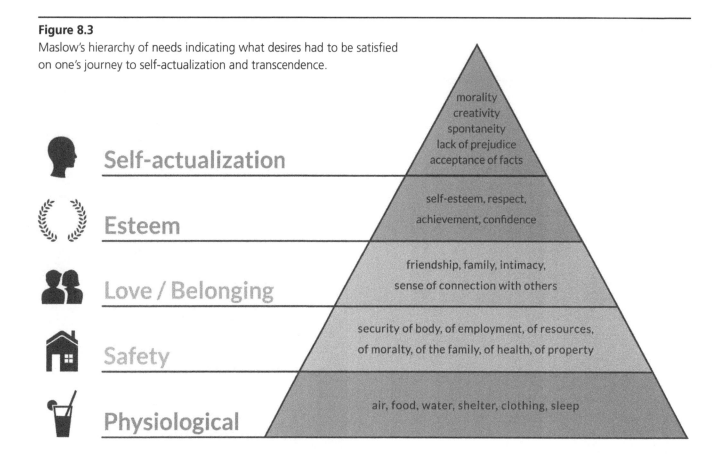

Self-actualization
morality
creativity
spontaneity
lack of prejudice
acceptance of facts

Esteem
self-esteem, respect,
achievement, confidence

Love / Belonging
friendship, family, intimacy,
sense of connection with others

Safety
security of body, of employment, of resources,
of morality, of the family, of health, of property

Physiological
air, food, water, shelter, clothing, sleep

of five layers. Maslow indicated that the four foundational layers contained deficiency needs. These levels were physiological, safety, love/belonging, and esteem. Maslow suggested that needs at these levels must be satisfied before an individual is motivated to satisfy the higher order need of self-actualization or being need (McLeod, 2014b).

Maslow was interested in human potential and how it was fulfilled. People were to be viewed as always on a journey to becoming self-actualized. Everyone has the potential to reach the highest level of self-actualization, and a self-actualized individual was doing all that she or he was capable of. As each person is unique, the journey of self-actualization led people in different directions. For some people, being self-actualized may lead them to create music, art, or design while for others the journey might take them to sport, business, or education. Whatever journey a person was on, life experiences such as divorce or job loss may result in people fluctuating between levels of the hierarchy or impede their progress towards self-actualization. By the 1970s, the initial hierarchy had been modified to include three addition levels. These levels

were labeled cognitive needs, aesthetic needs, and transcendence needs.

Maslow identified need deprivation and need gratification as the two motivating forces that linked needs to behavior (Wahba & Bridwell, 1976). The concept of deprivation was used to establish supremacy within his hierarchy. When lower order needs went unsatisfied, they were said to dominate the individual's personality. Gratification of a need resulted in activation of higher level needs allowing this level to dominate and organize the personality so that instead of being fixated with meeting lower order needs one could be occupied with meeting the needs of the next higher level. For example, an individual must first meet physiological needs such as hunger or thirst. If you fail to meet these needs, you are stuck at this level because all you can think about is eating and drinking. Once you have met these needs, they become subordinate and the next level of needs, in this case safety needs, can be addressed. This dynamic cycle of deprivation → domination → gratification → activation continues until all needs have been satisfied.

There is limited application of Maslow's ideas to understanding how and why we dress. However, what follows is a discussion of Maslow's hierarchy and how motivations for dress might be tied to satisfaction of needs at each level.

The first level of needs, physiological, are the requirements for human survival. If these needs are not met, the human body cannot function. **Physiological needs** include food, air, water, sex, and sleep. Motivations for dressing the body to meet physiological needs could include wearing dress items for protection from the elements and supernatural forces. We might apply insect repellent to protect our bodies from insect bites, wear mittens to protect our hands from the cold, or wear sun block to prevent our skin from sunburn. At this level we might also use dress to enhance our appearance for the purpose of attracting a sexual partner. Although technology has provided us with options that impact our ability to have children (e.g., artificial insemination), our ability to attract the sexual attention of another and procreate is fundamental to our survival.

Once physiological needs are met, an individual can begin to satisfy safety needs. **Safety needs** include achieving a sense of personal and financial security as well as needs for health and property. These needs might be met through health insurance policies, savings accounts, and job security. Motivations for dress that might meet safety needs could include wearing uniforms for work that keep you safe from injury while working (e.g., kevlar vests, steel-toed shoes). Another possibility is the wearing of business suits and other informal uniforms by service professionals including bankers and attorneys. These informal uniforms can assist in communicating that the wearer is trustworthy and respectable, enhancing the ability to fulfill one's work-related responsibilities and succeed (i.e., have job security).

Safety needs are followed by **love and belonging needs**. We all need to experience emotionally-based relationships including friendship and love. Acceptance and a sense of belonging can come directly from other individuals including parents and close friends as well as from participation in any of a variety of social groups including sports teams, fraternal organizations, gangs, professional organizations, and religious groups. Thus, the dress associated with any of these groups can be worn to both satisfy and signify needs for love and belongingness (Figure 8.4). Other dress items can be worn to attract others to you as when individuals conform to the clothing styles of a group

Figure 8.4

Dressing like other group members not only symbolizes group membership but can fulfill needs for belonging.

in order to participate in the group as well as attract potential partners. Once a relationship has been established, dress items can be worn to signify those love and belonging relationships including jewelry with BFF initials (i.e., best friend forever), engagement and wedding rings, and promise jewelry.

After meeting love and belonging needs, you can move onto meeting needs for **esteem**. Maslow (1970) believed that we all have a need to be respected by others and to respect ourselves. People need to believe that they are contributing to something, they are accepted by others, and they need to gain recognition for their efforts. But gaining recognition by others is not enough as people must accept themselves internally (i.e., self-esteem). Chopdar (2010, p. 2) suggested that esteem needs might be the motivation behind the images associated with what he termed *stealth-wealth*. *Stealth-wealth* was a term he used to describe "the clothing choices of an idealized million-aire playboy or aristocrat at rest as adapted to their own upper-middle class lives." Put another way, esteem needs might be reflected in dress choices that communicate the confidence and self-assurance of the wearer. Individuals that present confident appearances put forward images that are well-coordinated, neat and clean, and flattering to their body types.

After meeting esteem needs, an individual moves to **cognitive needs**. These are needs tied to desire for knowledge and self-awareness. Knowledge needs relative to dress might be demonstrated by those individuals who are opinion leaders and arbitrators of taste concerning how people ought to look. These individuals seek knowledge of fashion trends and share their opinions via fashion editorials, blogs, and work as image consultants.

From cognitive needs, individuals move to fulfilling **aesthetic needs**. These needs reflect one's ability to search for and appreciate beauty. Concerning dress, aesthetic needs might be met through viewing dress as a beautiful object. When one thinks of items of dress with high aesthetic value, one might think of a Japanese kimono that is worn on the body but also hung on the wall to adorn a room. Fulfilling aesthetic needs might be met by developing the ability to assemble items of dress that enhance one's appearance. Not every clothing style or accessory is equally flattering to all body types and sizes. Thus, aesthetic needs might be met by being able to select those apparel styles and accessories that are most flattering to one's body to present to self and others. Aesthetic needs might also be met by showing appreciation for others' well-crafted appearances.

Self-actualization needs follow aesthetic needs. This level of needs is concerned with recognizing what your full potential is and meeting that potential. Maslow described this need as the desire to become everything that you are capable of becoming. In order to achieve this level, you must meet and master the previous levels of needs. Dress that could be motivated by self-actualization needs might consist of items of dress that are truly expressive of the values and beliefs of the person wearing them. These individuals do not construct appearances to satisfy the desires of others or to follow fashion but use dress to express their unique inner nature. A possible example might be individuals who value the environment so they select clothing items that are environmentally friendly (i.e., recycled) but not necessarily fashionable.

Finally, the highest level of needs is transcendence needs. **Transcendence needs** are met by helping others achieve self-actualization. While it is difficult to image how dress might directly be used to help others achieve self-actualization, dress might be useful to assist others on their journey to meeting other needs and thus, indirectly, assist in achieving self-actualization. For example, others might meet their esteem needs or aesthetics needs by receiving donated items of dress. Rather than selling unwanted or slightly used dress items, donating them to women's shelters and other organizations that provide support to people in times of need would enable you to assist someone else on their self-actualization journey.

Need for Uniqueness

One specific need that may influence decision making concerning clothing that Maslow did not address in his hierarchy is need for uniqueness. **Need for uniqueness theory** (Snyder & Fromkin, 1980) suggests that people are constantly assessing their similarity and dissimilarity to others and that they act on these assessments. Individuals' desired state of being is to be not too similar to others and also not too dissimilar from others.

Dress is one means for individuals to express their uniqueness without provoking extreme reactions from others and violating social norms for appearance. One way to express need for uniqueness is through individuality in dress. Individuality could be achieved through the acquisition of distinctive clothing items (e.g., hand crafted) or repurposed items that are altered from their original state yet appear like the clothing that others are wearing. Vintage clothing stores, resale shops, craft and art fairs are several locations wherein individuals may locate distinctive clothing items (in the form of wearable art) that are also normative.

Another way that people meet their need to be unique is through consumption. Distinct individuals might be the first in their social group or community to purchase and wear a new style. However, being unique is tied to context. Each context exerts restraints concerning what to wear and how to appear. For example, you might be quite comfortable wearing your workout clothes to your class but not to a job (unless you work at a store that sells workout clothing). Another constraint on your ability to appear unique is how important it is to you to be approved of by others. If your desire for approval and acceptance by others is high, you might not adopt dress items that result in giving you a distinct appearance because you may suffer rejection from your peers and important others (Ruvio, 2008).

Two types of body modifications that have repeatedly been linked to need for uniqueness in research are tattooing and piercings. Tiggeman and Hopkins (2011) reasoned that as compared to individuals without tattoos or piercings, tattooed individuals as well as those with multiple piercings, would score higher on a need for uniqueness as well as scoring higher on appearance investment and on distinctive appearance investment. For their research, these researchers recruited customers from a music store located in Australia. Customers with tattoos scored higher on need for uniqueness than individuals without tattoos. Similarly, individuals with facial or body piercings scored higher on need for uniqueness than individuals with no piercings or conventional ear piercings. Additionally, participants who expressed an interest in getting a tattoo in the future also scored higher on need for uniqueness than participants not interested in a tattoo. This second finding points to need for uniqueness serving as a motivation for getting a tattoo rather than as a result of becoming tattooed.

Next, these researchers looked for differences between the body modified groups (both tattooed and piercings) on their appearance investment. **Appearance investment** refers to "the degree of an individual's beliefs about the importance, meaning, and influence of appearance in their life" (Cash, Melnyk, & Hrabosky, 2004, p. 306). There are two parts to the concept. One part reflects the extent to which one's appearance is integral to one's sense of self and self-worth. The second part reflects the effort invested in maintaining or improving one's appearance (Prichard & Tiggeman, 2011). For example, one particular point in life that tends to evoke considerable concern

about and investment in appearance for women are weddings. Many engaged women report a desire to lose up to twenty pounds prior to their weddings (Prichard & Tiggeman, 2008; 2009) suggesting their appearance is particularly important to them on that day and that they are willing to invest considerable effort to alter their appearance. **Distinctive appearance investment** refers to the desire of an individual to look different and stand out from others (Tiggeman & Golder, 2006). This concept refers to the level of investment an individual is willing to make to appear out of the ordinary and dissimilar to others (Figure 8.5). Again, weddings for some women are an event wherein they are willing to spend upwards of $10,000 for a dress they will wear once, and having multiple dresses for the event is not out-of-the-ordinary (White, 2016).

Returning to our research example, Tiggeman and Hopkins (2011) found that the people with tattoos as well as facial and body piercings seemed to have absorbed appearance ideals to the same degree as individuals without these body modifications. However, the relationship between need for uniqueness and likelihood of a future tattoo was mediated by distinctive appearance investment. This means that need for uniqueness did not necessarily translate into getting a tattoo. Rather, an individual had to have both a high need for uniqueness and a high need for a distinctive appearance for them to obtain a tattoo.

Figure 8.5

Although an individual can make a choice to engage in extreme body modifications for a variety of reasons, a high need for uniqueness may be related to tattooing and piercing as forms of dress, as these body modifications enable individuals to construct one-of-a-kind appearances.

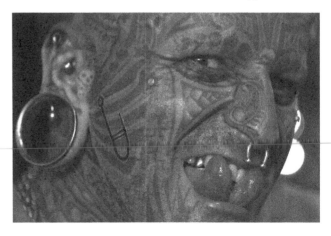

In related research, Swami (2011) obtained research findings suggesting that need for uniqueness may not only be a motivation for obtaining a tattoo but also an outcome of obtaining a tattoo. Swami had people complete assessments of their need for uniqueness along with their distinctive appearance investment, social physique anxiety, appearance anxiety, body appreciation, and their self-esteem. If you have social physique anxiety, you feel uncomfortable about evaluations of your physical self (your body) (Hart, Leary & Rajeski, 1989). Appearance anxiety refers to how anxious, tense, or nervous an individual feels at a particular point in time about sixteen different body sites (Reed, Thompson, Brannick, & Sacco, 1991). Body appreciation is degree of positive body image (Avalos, Tylka, & Wood-Barcalow, 2005). These assessments were completed before, immediately after, and three weeks after research participants got their first tattoo. Once an individual had obtained a tattoo there were significant positive changes to attitudes concerning their bodies. Contrary to Tiggeman and Hopkins' (2011) findings, both women and men reported significant increases in their distinctive appearance investment. They also reported increases to their self-ascribed uniqueness. Reductions in dissatisfaction with their appearance and anxiety about their appearance were also outcomes of obtaining a tattoo. Although men reported a decrease in social physique anxiety, women reported an increase. The researchers explained this difference as possibly being related to the fact that as compared to men, tattooed women experience negative attributions (Swami & Furnham, 2007) that in turn may increase their anxiety.

FULFILLMENT PERSPECTIVE: TRAITS

Psychologists distinguish between long lasting personality attributes of people and temporary characteristics. To describe consistent, long lasting tendencies, the term **trait** is used. To describe a temporary condition, the term **state** is used (Kalat, 2014). For example, being nervous immediately before you are to give a speech indicates you are in a nervous state; being nervous all the time is a trait. Both *trait* and *state* are terms used to describe behavior, not to explain it.

Trait psychologists have been interested in identifying and measuring those characteristics that people demonstrate consistently over their lifetimes. Over the years, to identify these characteristics that people demonstrate, many different terms have been used. As you know, many different terms can be used to describe the same thing. For example, suppose you want to use the word *kind* to describe a friend. You could also use the words *nice, gentle, thoughtful, compassionate, humane, caring, sympathetic,* and *benevolent.*

Psychologists have developed many different scales or instruments to measure numerous personality traits. However, measuring many different traits at the same time is unfeasible. Individuals are not interested in completing scale after scale to measure different aspects of their personalities. So some psychologists became interested in identifying a relatively short list of fundamental traits that could be used to assess personality. Key to this process were three psychologists, Gordon Allport, H.S. Odbert, and Raymond Cattell (John & Srivastava, 1999).

To begin this process of identifying fundamental traits, Allport and Odbert (1936) carefully examined words listed in a dictionary to identify 18,000 words that could be used to describe personality. They then deleted words from their list that were evaluative (e.g., mean) and terms referring to temporary states (e.g., puzzled). After this step, they looked for synonyms and groups of similar terms. They kept only one term from each group of terms they identified. When they identified antonyms, they also kept only one term, as antonyms are differences in extremes of a single trait and not different traits. After this process, Raymond Cattell (1965) further reduced their original list to thirty-five traits.

Getting the list reduced from 18,000 to 35 was a significant step, but thirty-five traits were still considered to be too many to be useful in assessing personality. To further reduce the number of traits and eliminate overlap, a data analysis technique called **factor analysis** was used resulting in five major groups of personality traits. These major clusters consisted of traits that were highly related or correlated to each other indicating they were measuring similar or the same trait.

The psychologists called their final results the five factor model of personality (Costa, McCrae & Dye, 1991; McCrae & Costa, 1987). The **Big-Five model** reflects these researchers thinking that most individual differences in human personality can be classified into five broad dimensions. These dimensions are labeled neuroticism, extraversion, agreeableness, conscientiousness, and openness to new experience (Kalat, 2014). Each dimension represents a collection of specific components that, in turn, subsume a large number of specific traits (Gosling, Rentfrow, & Swann, 2003). For example, extroversion represents a collection of component parts (e.g., sociability, enthusiasm) that represent other specific traits (e.g., talkative, outgoing). Researchers have not always agreed on what terms to use to label each dimension. However, the five categories are typically described as follows (Kalat, 2014). Accompanying each description are *possible* ways that each category might be tied to behaviors concerning dress. To know for certain whether or not such possible relationships actually exist, research is needed.

Extraversion is a tendency to seek stimulation and to enjoy the company of others. The opposite of extroversion is introversion. Other traits linked to this category include excitability, sociability, assertiveness, and talkativeness. Extraverts tend to be risk takers (Martsh & Miller, 1997). Applied to dress, people who are extroverts might be willing to freely share their opinions about new styles of dress and might also be one of the first people in their social group to wear new styles of clothing.

Agreeableness is a tendency to be concerned about others. This dimension is linked with terms such as *trust, helping, kindness*, and *affection*. People that are high in agreeableness generally trust other people and expect other people to trust them. Applied to dress, agreeable people might dress similar to others in their social group so that they easily fit in or they might quickly change their appearance when entering into a new group if they think that their appearance does not fit well with others' appearances.

Conscientiousness is a tendency to show self-discipline and to strive for achievement and competence. People high in this personality dimension typically apply themselves and follow through with the jobs that they say they will perform. Other terms linked to this personality dimension include *goal-directed, organized*, and *non-impulsive*. Applied to dress, people who are conscientious might make certain that their clothing is well cared for. For example, they might fold all of their sweaters to prevent them from losing their shape and hang up their clothing immediately after wearing.

Openness to experience is a tendency to enjoy new intellectual experiences and ideas. As you can imagine, this personality dimension is difficult to observe. Other traits linked with this personality dimension include

Figure 8.6
Lady Gaga has consistently demonstrated her willingness to be open to new experience with her dress as she wears innovative styles and materials to construct her appearance.

imagination, insight, and thought-provoking. Applied to dress, an individual who was open to experience might be willing to try innovative materials in their dress (e.g., meat) as well as innovative forms of dress (Figure 8.6).

Neuroticism is a tendency to experience unpleasant emotions frequently. If you put neuroticism on one end of a continuum, emotional stability would be located at the other end. In other words, an individual who is high in neuroticism would be low in emotional stability. Other traits linked to this category include anxiety, moodiness, and irritability. Applied to dress, high scores on neuroticism have been linked to binging behaviors, which has been linked to compulsive buying of clothing (Trautman & Johnson, 2007). Thus, an individual who is neurotic may have a larger-than-needed collection of clothing.

Researchers (Booth-Kewley & Vickers, 1994) have attempted to link the five broad dimensions of personality as indicated by the Big Five model with broad health behaviors including wellness behaviors linked to the body (e.g., exercise, good diet), accident control (e.g., knowing first aid), substance-related risk taking (e.g., alcohol consumption, smoking) and traffic risk taking (e.g., speeding). Not too surprising was their finding that conscientiousness was positively related to wellness behavior, accident control, and negatively related to traffic risk taking. Extraversion was positively related to wellness behaviors and accident control; Agreeableness was positively related to accident control and traffic risk taking; and openness to experience was positively related to substance risk taking. Openness to experience as a personality dimension may also be linked to individuals' willingness to engage in risky appearance management behaviors (e.g., excessive exercising, purging). Associations between personality and both risky and non-risky appearance management behaviors have not fully been investigated and are an area for future research.

Even though researchers in the 1970s and 1980s conducted numerous studies concerning the content of inferences people are willing to make about others based on their dress (See Damhorst, 1990 for a review of this research), how an individual's personality impacts his/her own clothing choices has received less attention. There have, however, been some researchers interested in whether one's personality relates to management of appearance. **Appearance management** encompasses "all attention, decisions, and acts related to one's personal appearance" (Kaiser, 1997, p. 5). Appearance management includes not only what we do to our bodies but also the planning needed to make what we do possible. All

DRESS IN THE NEWS
Dressing to Impress or Not

Dr. Baumgartner, a clinical psychologist who is based in the US, believes that your clothing is an indication of your thoughts and feelings (Bates, 2012). According to the doctor, women's showing too much cleavage means they are power hungry and have a need to control. Dr. Baumgartner, who is also a wardrobe consultant, shared typical errors that women make in her book *You Are What You Wear: What Your Clothes Reveal about You.* Typical mistakes include buying only designer labels, wearing office clothing all of the time, buying too much clothing, and not changing your style often enough.

Dr. Baumgartner suggested that the dress of Helena Bonham Carter (Figure 8.7) may be a sign of guilt or exhaustion. Dr. Baumgartner contends that all of our behaviors from the food we eat to the clothing that we wear are motivated by internal factors. So what internal factors are motivating your dress choices? Is your appearance always reflective of your personality? Why, or why not?

Figure 8.7
Helena Bonham Carter shopping in London, England.

individuals engage in some form of appearance management on a daily basis.

Appearance emphasis is an aspect of appearance management. **Appearance emphasis** includes the importance one places on one's looks and the extent of grooming behaviors in which one engages (Davis, Dionne, & Shuster, 2001). To examine how personality relates to appearance emphasis, Johnson, Francis, and Burns (2007) had undergraduate women complete a nine-item measure of appearance emphasis (See Table 8.1 for appearance emphasis items) and a measure of the five personality factors of the Big-Five model. Three of the five personality factors were moderate predictors of appearance emphasis: neuroticism, extraversion, and openness to experience. Specifically, individuals who placed a high emphasis on their appearance were also nervous and tense (high in neuroticism), down to earth, had a narrow range of interests, were conventional (low in openness to experience), and were extroverted. What does this mean? These findings suggest that your personality does impact at least one component of appearance management, that is, the emphasis or importance you place on your appearance. The connection between neuroticism and emphasis on appearance suggests that people who are anxious and are prone to worry in general are also likely to worry about their appearance. Similarly, extroverts placed an emphasis on their appearance along with those individuals who were low in openness to new experiences.

Perhaps these connections between personality and appearance emphasis have implications for shopping behaviors concerning dress. Participation in fashion can assist individuals in their quest to fit in with others and be accepted by them; thus these personality factors and their link to appearance emphasis may, to different degrees, reflect a strategy that is being used to fulfill a desire to be sociable, to fit in, and be accepted by others. It might be interesting to determine if relationships exist between personality and other aspects of appearance management

---

TABLE 8.1 — **STUDIO**

APPEARANCE EMPHASIS SCALE

The appearance emphasis measure was developed by Tricia Widner Johnson, Sally, K. Francis, and Leslie Davis Burns at Oregon State University, USA. The measure is designed to assess the importance an individual places on his or her looks and the extent of grooming behaviors in which an individual engages. People taking this measure indicate their degree of agreement with each statement using a scale anchored at one end with 1 = disagree strongly and the other end with 5 = agree strongly. A score is obtained by adding together your score on all of the items. The higher the score, the greater the emphasis placed on appearance. Take the measure and see how much you emphasize your appearance.

Statement	Score
1. I worry about judgments people make related to my appearance.	
2. I spend considerable time thinking about my personal appearance.	
3. Compared to other people I know, I pay more attention to my personal appearance.	
4. I give my personal appearance a lot of attention every day.	
5. I will not add an item to my wardrobe unless it is fashionable.	
6. I am afraid of what others will think of me if I don't dress fashionably.	
7. I feel more confident in myself when I give my personal appearance a lot of attention.	
8. I add an item to my wardrobe if it is something that I have seen my peers wearing.	
9. It is important that the items I add to my wardrobe be attractive.	

Source: Johnson, T., Francis, S., & Burns, L. (2007). Appearance management behavior and the five factor model of personality. *Clothing and Textiles Research Journal, 25*(3), 230-243. Reprinted by permission of the International Textile and Apparel Association.

including decision making concerning what specific forms of dress (i.e., tattoos, gauging, purging) will be used.

DOES DRESS ACCURATELY CONVEY PERSONALITY?

Earlier, we provided some examples of how personality traits might be communicated to others using behaviors related to dress (see discussion of Big Five personality traits). But all of that was supposition. Can we accurately infer another's personality using their dress? Are we correct when we make these inferences about others' personalities on the basis of their appearances some of the time or all of the time? How accurate are you when making inferences about strangers? Addressing the question of whether dress and/or other aspects of appearance can accurately convey specific personality traits of complete strangers was the focus of research by Naumann, Vazire, Rentfrow, and Gosling (2009). These researchers measured accuracy in making judgments of personality using appearance in two different conditions: one where participants were asked to assign personality traits from viewing a posed photograph and the other where people assigned traits from viewing a photograph where the person in the photo was allowed to pose in any manner he/she wanted. Personality of the people in the photographs was evaluated using a measure of the Big Five traits along with a range of single item measures including likeability, self-esteem, loneliness, liberalism, and religiosity. The researchers found that of the Big Five personality traits people could make accurate judgments of extraversion and openness to experience but not of agreeableness or conscientiousness. Judgments of self-esteem and religiosity were also very accurate. Interestingly, the accuracy of judgments increased when people viewed the "pose in any manner" photos as compared to the posed photographs. Useful indicators of the personality trait of extroversion included looking stylish, healthy, and smiling. People who were "agreeable" also smiled and stood in a relaxed manner. Conscientious people looked neat, healthy, smiled, and appeared energetic. People who were open to experience were likely to have a distinct style of dress and looked away from the camera. Individuals with high self-esteem had a neat, stylish, and healthy looking appearance. Lonely individuals appeared tense, sickly, messy, and unstylish. All in all, research participants' judgments of personality based in appearance were accurate.

So when it comes to making judgments of personality, perhaps using another's appearance is not a bad idea at all.

In the previous research, the research participants were allowed to use several appearance cues (dress, facial expression) to make their judgments of the personality of a stranger. Do we need several appearance cues or can we make accurate judgments of others personality based on a single cue? This was the question for a team of researchers (Gillath, Bahns, Ge, & Crandall, 2012) interested in whether people could infer the personality of a stranger using only their shoes. These researchers had people take photographs of the shoes they wore most often and then had them complete measures of their personality, political beliefs, attachment anxiety, and background characteristics. Another set of individuals then viewed the photographs of the shoes and rated the shoe owners on all of the same attributes. Unlike the earlier research (Naumann, Vazire, Rentfrow, & Gosling, 2009) where people

DRESS IN THE NEWS
What Does the Color of Your Clothes Say about Your Personality?

The colors we wear regularly may be sending messages that others use to infer our personality. Alex Myles (2015) assembled a guide to colors and what attributes that people might associate with them. Check to see if your favorite clothing color (the one you wear the most) is listed and whether the characteristics listed reflect your own.

Black: power, elegance, sophistication, control, authority, independence
Blue: trust, peace, loyalty, humor
Brown: authenticity, reliability, trust, intelligence, emotional stability
Gray: sophistication, too much means dull and depressed
Green: calm, charismatic, sensitive
Orange: social, popular
Pink: feminine, affectionate
Purple: wealth, royalty, creative, artistic
Red: aggressive, impulsive, sensual, extroverted
White: pure, clean, simple, open, confident, courageous
Yellow: intelligent, consistent, logical

could use several aspects of appearance simultaneously in making their inferences of personality, only the inferences concerning agreeableness as a personality trait were accurate. And inferences concerning agreeableness were not the most accurate overall. The most accurate inferences were those concerned with the wearer's background characteristics (e.g., gender, income, age).

When making their inferences, the viewers used specific attributes of the shoes as the basis for their judgments. For example, they used the height of the shoe and the masculinity of the shoe as cues to their judgments of agreeableness. Gender of the wearer was cued by the masculinity, fashionableness, and perceived price of the shoes. The attractiveness and fashionableness of the shoes cued inferences of the wearer's income. Thus, if you are interested in making inferences of personality, it appears you can use shoes to infer agreeableness but not other personality traits.

Earlier, we noted that need for uniqueness as a single trait might be a meaningful distinction between people with and without tattoos. However, the question remains as to whether or not tattooed people actually differ from non-tattooed individuals in terms of their personality. To answer this question, Tate and Shelton (2008) had over 1,000 undergraduates' complete measures of the five personality constructs along with a uniqueness measure and a measure of social desirability. The need for uniqueness measure assessed the degree to which a person had a healthy need to be different from others and the social desirability measure assesses the desire to be perceived favorably by other people.

The undergraduates were divided into groups based on whether or not they had a tattoo or a body piercing, and on the basis of their gender (Tate & Shelton, 2008). For men, any piercing qualified as a body piercing but for women the piercing had to be in a place other than the earlobes. Nearly a quarter of the participants had at least one tattoo and nearly half of them had at least one body piercing. Non-tattooed participants scored significantly higher on agreeableness and conscientiousness than did tattooed participants. Body pierced participants scored significantly higher on openness to experience and lower on conscientiousness than non-pierced participants. Tattooed individuals also scored higher on need for uniqueness but there were no differences on social desirability. The researchers noted that although differences did appear, the **effect sizes** were small. An effect size is

a quantitative measure of the strength of a phenomenon. A small effect size indicates that real world differences on these dimensions are likely to be minor. Thus, these researchers concluded that people with tattoos or body piercings did not actually differ in their personalities or in their need for uniqueness from those who do not have such body modifications.

However, in research conducted with individuals recruited from a tattoo parlor located in England, Swami (2012) reported significant differences in personality between individuals who actually obtained a tattoo and those who left the parlor without one. Those individuals who decided to get a tattoo were significantly less conscientious and more extroverted than those who left sans tattoo. But again the effect sizes were small to moderate suggesting the differences in personality may not be that meaningful. Those who got tattoos also scored higher than those without tattoos on willing to engage in casual sexual relations and in sensation seeking. As sensation seeking may be a primary trait inherent to extroversion, additional research is needed to determine whether any real difference is due to extroversion or to lower order facets such as sensation seeking, risk taking, and the like.

Canadian researchers have investigated relationships among personality characteristics, risky behaviors, body modifications, and other appearance characteristics (Nathanson, Paulhus, & Williams, 2006). They suggest that the body modifications do not cause high-risk behaviors, but rather that they are both effects of individual personality characteristics. College students completed questionnaires regarding what the researchers termed *cultural deviance markers*, which included number of piercings not

IN-CLASS ACTIVITY
Appearing Any Way You Want

As noted in your text, public perception of individuals with extreme body modifications lags behind the movement of these forms of dress into acceptance by the general public. Although retailers may not admit that they do not wish to hire such individuals in their stores, individuals may be denied employment because of these modifications. Should people be taking this idea into account when they make decisions to modify their bodies in such extreme ways? Why, or why not?

in ears, number of tattoos, and other appearance characteristics (profanity on clothing, shaved head, revealing clothing). First students completed personality inventories, demographic information, and reported information on their use of cultural deviance markers. Several months later the students estimated the extent of their high-risk behaviors (e.g., drug abuse, crime). Cultural deviance markers were related to drug abuse, even after personality characteristics were taken into account. However, cultural deviance markers were not related to other high-risk behaviors, whereas three personality characteristics (psychopathy, openness to experience, and self-esteem) were related to high risk behavior in the form of drug abuse.

AVERSIVE PERSONALITY TRAITS: THE DARK TRIAD

The topic of personality, as presented thus far in this chapter, has been mostly focused on discussion of socially positive personality traits. Personal traits that are socially negative have also been identified and may play a role in decision making concerning dress. These socially negative traits are labeled *Machiavellianism, narcissism*, and *psychopathy*. Referred to as the **dark triad**, Lee and Ashton (2005) define these traits as follows. **Machiavellianism** refers to individual differences in manipulativeness, insincerity, and callousness. **Psychopathy** refers to manipulation and exploitation of others. **Narcissism** is characterized by supremacy, exhibitionism, and manipulation as well as feelings of superiority and entitlement. It has been viewed as a normal trait. Even though the three dark traits appear to share some elements (manipulation, exploitation), they are distinct enough traits to be treated individually (Paulhus & Williams, 2002). Interestingly, researchers have documented that people who are particularly effective at enhancing their level of attractiveness using dress also tend to score high on these dark personality traits (Holtzman & Strube, 2012). We focus our discussion on the dark trait of narcissism as this trait has been featured in research concerning dress.

A team of researchers (Vazire, Naumann, Rentfrow, & Gosling, 2008) proposed several reasons why narcissism should be discernible using a person's appearance. First, because narcissists are defined as vain individuals, it is reasonable to assume that narcissists would pay special attention to their appearance. The special attention paid to appearance could include wearing fashionable clothing,

wearing items that match and are coordinated, and wearing items that fit well. In other words, narcissists are likely do all they can to make the best possible physical presentation of themselves.

Narcissists also like to be the center of attention. Thus, these researchers reasoned that narcissists might attempt to attract attention by wearing flashy or body-revealing clothing. They might also attempt to gain the attention of others by adopting forms of dress that are unique (e.g., tattoos, piercings, insertions). The researchers' final reason for why narcissists probably were identifiable from their appearance related to narcissists' concern with status. These researchers proposed that designer label clothing and other expensive dress items were likely to be worn by narcissists to communicate their actual or desired socio-economic status.

To test whether narcissism was actually identifiable through a person's appearance, Vazire et al. (2008) focused on three questions: How accurate are snap judgments of narcissism? Which components of narcissism (i.e., authority, exploitativeness/entitlement, self-absorption/self-admiration, arrogance/superiority) are manifested in physical appearance? And what are the valid cues to narcissism and what cues do observers use to judge narcissism? To answer these three questions, the researchers recruited undergraduates. All participants were photographed. In the first phase of a three-phase study the researchers collected self-ratings (the personality measures). In the second phase they had a group of individuals called informants, identified by the target persons as people who knew the targets well, look at the photographs and provide ratings of the personalities (including narcissism) of the target persons. In the last phase, a group of trained coders recorded the physical cues of the target persons.

How accurate were judgments of narcissism from appearance? The participants were very accurate in their judgments of narcissism. Which facets of narcissism were manifested in appearance? The observers identified three of the four facets of narcissism: authority, exploitativeness/entitlement, and self-absorption/self-admiration (Figure 8.8). Observer's judgments were most strongly correlated with the self-absorption/self-admiration component of narcissism, the part of narcissism linked with conceit and concern for one's appearance. And finally, what appearance cues did participants use as a basis for their ratings of narcissism? The narcissism ratings were associated with wearing expensive and stylish clothing, presenting an appearance that appeared to take a great

Figure 8.8

Narcissistic individuals are self-absorbed as well as self-admirers. As such, they are likely to capture their every move with the aid of a selfie stick and a cell phone camera (although not everyone that takes a selfie is narcisstic). In consideration of safety issues (being hit by a stick or walked over when someone else is taking a selfie) and due to the inconvenience caused to others, the selfie stick has been banned and/or restricted at several popular public venues.

deal of preparation, and attractiveness. Among the targets that were women, ratings of narcissism were also related to looking feminine, wearing cosmetics, having plucked eyebrows, and showing cleavage. Among the targets who were men, ratings of narcissism were linked to not wearing glasses. It was overall narcissism rather than components of narcissism (i.e., exploitativeness, self-absorption) that was most strongly related to the appearance cues. Thus narcissism, as one of the dark triad of personality traits, does seem to be evident in dress and appearance.

It may not be narcissism alone that accounts for effort put into maintaining an attractive appearance. Holtzman and Strube (2012) were interested in how the three dark personality traits linked to attempts to be physically attractive. They reasoned that people that were high in any or all of these traits may manage their dress in ways to be attractive to others. To test this hypothesis, the researchers photographed men and women who were undergraduates in two conditions: one adorned (as they appeared publicly everyday) and one unadorned (participants changed into gray sweatpants, a gray t-shirt, removed all jewelry, removed makeup, women pulled their hair away from

IN-CLASS ACTIVITY
Selfies and Narcissism

Why do young adults post so many selfies on the web? Some individuals have claimed the reason is that young adults today demonstrate increased levels of narcissism over previous generations of young adults (Figure 8.9). While that might be true, it is a difficult question to answer as for previous generations the technology was not available to share images and photographs in the way that is possible today. Digital cameras in smartphones have made the process of posting an image almost instantaneous. However, it still might be interesting to see what the relationship is between posting your selfies and your level of narcissism. Does the number of selfies posted increase with level of narcissism? Let's find out. You know how many selfies you post in a typical week. (Do not cheat on this number). Next, google "Narcissistic Personality Inventory" and take this measure of narcissism online to determine the relationship between your posting activity and your own level of narcissism.

Figure 8.9

Ben Stiller as the narcisstic supermodel Derek Zoolander. What aspects of dress are being used to communicate the message that he is a narcissist?

NARCISSISM AND CONSUMPTION

How might fashion retailers make use of the concept of personality? A team of researchers interested in how narcissism may relate to consumption reasoned that because narcissists were swayed by self-image motives, they were the consumer group most likely to strive to purchase high prestige products (Sedikides, Gregg, Cisek, & Hart, 2007). These researchers reasoned that narcissists were likely to interpret the consumption of products as an opportunity to sustain and even elevate their superiority. They proposed that narcissists are interested in the extent to which products purchased can make them feel and look good, thus they will be more interested in a product's symbolic value rather than its utilitarian value. What does this mean for fashion retailers who sell apparel items with high symbolic value?

---

their face, men shaved). These participants completed self-report measures of personality and also had a set of their peers rate them on the personality scales. Another set of participants rated the photographs for their attractiveness. All of the photographed individuals who scored high on the dark triad traits of personality were rated as more physically attractive when presenting their everyday appearance (adorned) than when in their unadorned state. Of the three dark traits, psychopathy was the most important. The researcher's explanation for this outcome was that individuals, scoring high in the dark traits, may derive more satisfaction and experience higher self-esteem from the additional attention they receive when they appear in an adorned state than when they appear in an unadorned state. This satisfaction and self-esteem may compel them to continue to present themselves to others in an adorned state because doing so facilitates their manipulative and exploitative tendencies.

Narcissists and Problem Consumption

Narcissists, as noted, are likely to be interested in purchasing items that will meet their needs for getting attention, exhibitionism, and uniqueness. Thus, they may be (a) interested in innovative products and activities as well as expensive products including designer label apparel, (b) be persuaded by advertisements featuring celebrities and other "great people" like themselves, and (c) be interested in brand loyalty programs that offer exclusive promotions to their "special" customers. They may also (d) be prone to be merchandise borrowers and a problem for fashion retailers. **Merchandise borrowing**, also referred to as deshopping (Johnson & Rhee, 2008; Piron & Young, 2001), is behavior similar to what you do when you "borrow" a library book from a university library. You borrow the book, use it by reading it, and then return it. You have no intention of keeping it at the time you borrow it. Applying this idea apparel and other items and you have people who purchase an apparel item or something for their home like an expensive flat screen television set. They have no intention of keeping the item. Rather they want to use the item and then return it to the store for a full refund or for store credit. In 2005, the cost of merchandise borrowing was estimated at around $16 billion a year (Merrick & Brat, 2005). It is higher now.

Estimates on how many people engage in merchandise borrowing are inconsistent. Typically researchers have found that about 20 percent of a sample they draw reports having borrowed merchandise in the past at least once (Johnson & Rhee, 2008; Piron & Young, 2001). Consumers frequently borrow fashion-related products such as clothing and accessories. Reasons for practicing apparel borrowing include wanting to wear something nice for a special event (e.g., weddings, graduations) and wanting to have expensive items, if only for a short period of time, and being unable to afford them.

Depending on their financial capabilities as their never ending need for the newest and the latest may test their financial resources, narcissists are good candidates for being merchandise borrowers as this practice may be a means to continuously display novel and expensive dress and other products linked to status and prestige. However, to know this for certain, research is needed.

Chapter Summary

Distinct qualities and characteristics of each person can influence their decision-making concerning their dress and appearance. One such characteristic is personality. There are several personality theories that are useful for understanding individual's decision making concerning their dress. An example from the conflict perspective of personality is psychodynamic theory developed by Sigmund Freud. The conflict perspective suggests that an individuals' personality is the result of opposing forces that are continuously in conflict with each other. Psychodynamic theory relates personality to the relationship of conscious as well as unconscious internal forces that are primarily in a state of conflict within each of us. The structure of personality consisted of the id, ego, and superego. Freud also suggested that the ego defended itself against feeling anxious or uncomfortable by transferring unpleasant thoughts to the unconscious part of personality. Defense mechanisms were a means to understand how people separate themselves from unpleasant thoughts and feelings they have as a result of their own behaviors. Several defense mechanisms have been identified including repression, denial, rationalization, displacement, regression, projection, reaction formation, and sublimation. Each defense mechanism can be linked to behaviors concerning dress.

Theories representing the fulfillment perspective are Abraham Maslow's hierarchy of needs and the Big Five model of personality. Maslow suggested that there existed a hierarchical order of human needs (i.e., psychological drives) that he believed individuals sought to satisfy. At the bottom of his hierarchy of needs were physiological needs and at the top was self-actualization. When lower order needs went unsatisfied, they were said to dominate the individual's personality. Gratification of a need resulted in activation of higher level needs allowing this level to dominate and organize the personality so that instead of being fixated with meeting lower order needs one could be occupied with meeting the needs of the next higher level. Each need level could be met with dress. One specific need that may influence decision making concerning clothing that Maslow did not address in his hierarchy is need for uniqueness. Need for uniqueness theory suggests that people are constantly assessing their similarity and dissimilarity to others and that they act on these assessments. Individuals' desired state of being is to be not too similar to others and also not too dissimilar from others. Dress is one means for individuals to express their uniqueness without provoking extreme reactions from others.

Another theory representing the fulfillment perspective is the five factor model of personality. The Big-Five model suggests that most individual differences in human personality can be classified into five broad dimensions. These dimensions are labeled neuroticism, extraversion, agreeableness, conscientiousness, and openness to new experience. Even though research linking decision making concerning dress and these personality dimensions is limited, there is some evidence that these dimensions are related to appearance emphasis as a component of appearance management.

Narcissism as one of the dark triad of personality traits has been investigated in relationship to appearance. Researchers have found that narcissism as a personality trait is accurately identified through appearance and that general cues to judgments of narcissism include wearing expensive and stylish clothing, presenting an appearance that appeared to take a great deal of preparation, and attractiveness.

Key Terms

aesthetic needs	conflict perspective	effect size	id
agreeableness	conscientiousness	ego	love and belonging needs
appearance emphasis	dark triad	ego differentiation	Machiavellianism
appearance investment	defense mechanisms	ego-screaming	merchandise borrowing
appearance management	denial	esteem	narcissism
Big Five model	displacement	extraversion	need for uniqueness theory
cathexis	distinctive appearance	factor analysis	neuroticism
cognitive needs	investment	fulfillment perspective	openness to experience

personality	psychopathy	safety needs	sublimation
physiological needs	rationalization	self-actualization	superego
projection	reaction formation	self-actualization needs	trait
psychodynamic theory	regression	state	transcendence needs

Discussion Questions

1. According to Freud's psychodynamic theory of personality, your personality is a result of conflict between the id, ego, and superego. Explain these three component parts of personality and then provide an example of how they may influence decisions concerning what you might wear to go on a date.

2. Defense mechanisms are a means to understand how people separate themselves from unpleasant thoughts and feelings they have as a result of their own behaviors. Explain each defense mechanism. Identify examples (different from those supplied in the text) of how appearance management may reflect one or more of these defense mechanisms.

3. Describe the hierarchy of needs model and how it relates to personality. Identify how dress could be used to meet needs at each level using examples other than those listed in the text.

4. Need for uniqueness was not included in Maslow's original model. Where would you place this need in Maslow's hierarchy, and why would you put it there? How can dress be used to satisfy a need for uniqueness?

5. Of the dark triad of personality traits, why is narcissism easily identified by dress? How might the other two dark personality traits be communicated using dress?

STUDIO™

Visit your book's STUDIO for additional quiz questions and vocabulary flashcards!

Suggested Readings

Johnson, T., Francis, S., & Burns, L. (2007). Appearance management behavior and the five factor model of personality. *Clothing and Textiles Research Journal, 25*(3), 230–243.

Moody, W., , P., & Sinha, P. (2010). An exploratory study: Relationships between trying on clothing, mood, emotion, personality, and clothing preference. *Journal of Fashion Marketing and Management, 14*(1), 161–179.

Sklar, M. (2013). *Punk style*. New York, NY: Bloomsbury.

References

Allport, G., & Odbert, H. S. (1936). Trait names: A psycholexical study. *Psychological Monographs, 47* (Whole No. 211).

Avaloa, L., Tylka, T. L., & Wood-Barcalow, N. (2005). The body appreciation scale: Development and psychometric evaluation. *Body Image, 2*(3), 285–297.

Bates, D. (2012). Dressing to impress: How what a woman wears can reveal more than she ever intended about her personality. Retrieved from http://www.dailymail.co.uk/femail/article-2120233/That-womans-clothes-say-personality.html#ixzz2ouAOxUXN

Baumeister, R., Dale, K., & Sommer, K. (2010). Freudian defense mechanisms and empirical findings in modern social psychology: Reaction formation, projection, displacement, undoing, isolation, sublimation, and denial. In D. Funder & D. Ozer (Eds.), *Pieces of the personality puzzle* (pp. 280–297). New York, NY: W.W. Norton & Co.

Booth-Kewley, S., & Vickers, R. (1994). Major domains of personality and health behavior. *Journal of Personality, 62*(3), 281–298.

Brill, D. (2008). *Goth culture.* New York, NY: Brill.

Cash, T. F., Melnyk, S. E., & Hrabosky, J. I. (2004). The assessment of body image investment: An extensive revision of the Appearance Schemas Inventory. *International Journal of Eating Disorders, 35*, 305–316.

Cattell, R. B. (1965). *The scientific analysis of personality.* London, UK: Penguin.

Chopdar, C. (2010). A hierarchy of sartorial needs. Retrieved from http://beyondanomie.wordpress.com

Costa, P., McCrae, R., & Dye, D. (1991). Facet scales for agreeableness and conscientiousness: A revision of the NEO Personality Inventory. *Personality and Individual Differences, 12*(9), 887–898.

Damhorst, M.L. (1990). In search of a common thread: Classification of information communicated through dress. *Clothing and Textiles Research Journal, 8*(2), 1–12.

Davis, C., Dionne, M., & Shuster, B. (2001). Physical and psychological correlates of appearance orientation. *Personality and Individual Differences, 30*, 21–30.

Freud, S. (1991; 1968). *On metapsychology, the theory of psychoanalysis: Beyond the pleasure principle, the ego, the id, and other works.* London, UK: Penguin Random House.

Gillath, O., Bahns, A., Ge, F., & Crandall, C. (2012). Shoes as a source of first impressions. *Journal of Research in Personality, 46*(4), 423–430.

Gosling, S., Rentfrow, P., & Swann, W. (2003). A very brief measure of the Big-Five personality domains. *Journal of Research in Personality, 37*, 504–528.

Hart, E. H., Leary, M. R., & Rajeski, W. J. (1989). The measurement of social physique anxiety. *Journal of Sport and Exercise Psychology, 11*, 94–104.

Holtzman, N., & Strube, M. (2012). People with dark personalities tend to create a physically attractive veneer. *Social Psychological and Personality Science, 4*(4), 461–467.

John, O. P., & Srivastava, S. (1999). The big five trait taxonomy: History, measurement, and theoretical perspectives. In L. A. Pervin & O. P. John (Eds.), *Handbook of personality: Theory and research* (2nd ed., pp. 102–139). New York, NY: Guilford Press.

Johnson, K. K. P., & Rhee, J. (2008). An investigation of consumer traits and their relationship to merchandise borrowing with undergraduates. *Journal of Family and Consumer Sciences Education, 26*(1), 1–13.

Johnson, T., Francis, S., & Burns, L. (2007). Appearance management behavior and the five factor model of personality. *Clothing and Textiles Research Journal, 25*(3), 230–243.

Kaiser, S. (1997). *The social psychology of clothing* (2nd ed.revised). New York, NY: Fairchild.

Kalat, J. (2014). *Introduction to psychology* (10th ed.). Boston, MA: Cengage Learning.

Lee, K., & Ashton, M. (2004). Psychopathy, machiavellianism, and narcissism in the five-factor model and the HEXACO model of personality structure. *Personality and Individual Differences, 38*, 1571–1582.

Maddi, S. (1996). *Personality theories* (6th ed.). Pacific Grove, CA: Brooks/Cole Publishing Company.

Martsh, C., & Miller, W. (1997). Extraversion predicts heavy drinking in college students. *Personality and Individual Differences, 23*, 153–155.

Maslow, A. H. (1970). *Motivation and personality* (2nd ed.). New York, NY: Harper & Row.

McCrae, R., & Costa, P. Jr. (1987). Validation of the five factor model of personality across instruments and observers. *Journal of Personality and Social Psychology, 52*, 81–90.

McLeod, S. A. (2014a). Carl Rogers. Retrieved from www.simplypsychology.org/carl-rogers.html

McLeod, S. A. (2014b). Maslow's hierarchy of needs. Retrieved from www.simplypsychology.org/maslow.html

Merrick, A., & Brat, I. (2005, December 15). Taking back that blender gets harder; Sears is the latest retailer to tighten returns policy; how to avoid being refused. *Wall Street Journal*, (Eastern edition), D.1

Myles, A. (2015). What the color of our clothes say about our personality. Retrieved from elephantjournal.com/2015/09

Nathanson, C., Paulhus, D. L., & Williams, K. M. (2006). Personality and misconduct correlates of body modification and other cultural deviance markers. *Journal of Research in Personality, 40,* 779–802.

Naumann, L., Vazire, S., Rentfrow, P., & Gosling, S. (2009). Personality judgments based on physical appearance. *Personality and Social Psychology Bulletin, 35*(12), 1661–1671.

Paulhus, D. L., & Williams, K. M. (2002). The Dark Triad of personality: Narcissism, machiavellianism, and psychopathy. *Journal of Research in Personality, 36,* 556–563.

Piron, F., & Young, M. (2001). Retail borrowing: Definition and retailing implications. *Journal of Retailing and Consumer Services, 8,* 121–125.

Prichard, I., & Tiggemann, M. (2008). An examination of pre-wedding body image concerns in brides and bridesmaids. *Body Image, 5,* 395–398.

Prichard, I., & Tiggemann, M. (2009). Unveiled: Pre-wedding weight concerns and health and beauty plans of Australian brides. *Journal of Health Psychology, 14,*1027–1035.

Prichard, I., & Tiggemann, M. (2011). Appearance investment in Australian brides-to-be. *Body Image, 8,* 282–286.

Reed, D. L., Thompson, J. K., Brannick, M. T., & Sacco, W. P. (1991). Development and validation of the Physical Appearance State and Trait Anxiety Scale (PASTAS). *Journal of Anxiety Disorders, 5,* 323–332.

Revio, A. (2008). Unique like everyone else? The dual role of consumers' need for uniqueness. *Psychology & Marketing, 25*(5), 444–464.

Rushkoff, D. (1994). *Cyberia: Life in the trenches of hyperspace.* San Francisco, CA: Harper Collins.

Sedikides, C., Gregg, Aiden, Cisek, S., & Hart, C. (2007). The I that buys: Narcissists as consumers. *Journal of Consumer Psychology, 17*(4), 254–257.

Sklar, M. (2013). *Punk style.* New York, NY: Bloomsbury.

Snyder, C. R., & Fromkin, H. L. (1980). *Uniqueness: The human pursuit of difference.* New York, NY: Plenum.

Swami, V. (2012). Written on the body? Individual differences between British adults who do and do not obtain a first tattoo. *Scandinavian Journal of Psychology 53,* 407–412.

Szostak-Pierce, S. (1999). Even further: The power of subcultural style in techno culture in K. K. P. Johnson & S. J. Lennon (eds). *Appearance and Power* retrieved from http://dx.doi.org.ezp2.lib.umn.edu/10.2752/9781847887221/AANDPOWER0011

Tate, J., & Shelton, B. (2008). Personality correlates of tattooing and body piercing in a college sample: The kids are alright. *Personality and Individual differences, 45,* 281–285.

Tiggemann, M., & Golder, F. (2006). Tattooing: An expression of uniqueness in the appearance domain. *Body Image, 3,* 309–315.

Tiggemann, M., & Hopkins, L. (2011). Tattoos and piercings: Bodily expressions of uniqueness? *Body Image, 8,* 245–250.

Trautmann, J., & Johnson, T.W. (2007). Binge eating behaviors, neuroticism, and compulsive clothing buying: Are they related? *Research Journal of Textiles and Apparel, 11*(2), 75–84.

Vazire, S., Naumann, L., Rentfrow, P., & Gosling, S. (2008). Portrait of a narcissist: Manifestations of narcissism in physical appearance. *Journal of Research in Personality, 42,* 1439–1447.

Wahba, A., & Bridgewell, L (1976). Maslow reconsidered: A review of research on the need hierarchy theory. *Organizational Behavior and Human Performance, 15,* 212–240.

White, H. (2016). How much does the average wedding dress cost? Popsugar. Retrieved from http://www.popsugar.com/smart-living/How-Much-Should-You-Spend-Wedding-Dress-8077374

CHAPTER
9
DRESS AND THE SELF

After reading and reflecting on the content of this chapter students should be able to:

- Define the concept of self.
- Explain how dress is tied to reflective consciousness as an experience of selfhood.
- Describe how dress is linked to interpersonal aspects of self as an experience of selfhood.
- Illustrate how dress is connected to the executive function of self as an experience of selfhood.
- Discuss how distinct approaches to the self are tied to behavior related to dress.

INTRODUCTION

How do you think about yourself on an individual basis? You may have ideas about yourself as a physical being. For example, you may like your weight but not your skin. You may love your hair but not your nails. You may also have ideas about yourself as a dressed being. How do you look in jeans? In a uniform? With your hair colored? You may also have ideas about your inner personality.[1] What type of person am I? What do you believe people think is true about the type of person you are? What type of person do you think you are? Combining all of your answers to these types of questions together results in both a self-concept and a self-image. **Self-concept** is a term that is used to describe an individual's general thoughts about him or herself. Self-concept is also sometimes referred to as **self-knowledge** or all the knowledge we have about the self. **Self-image** is a related term in that it refers to the mental picture that an individual has about him or herself. All of these terms imply both a description and an evaluation of oneself.

For example, Rachel (age seven) described herself by saying, "My name is Rachel, I live in Minnesota, my favorite color is purple, my hair is blond, and my favorite store is Target" (Figure 9.1). In this example, Rachel's self-knowledge concerning her appearance includes descriptive characteristics (e.g., my hair is blond). Older children might also think about themselves in terms of how their appearance and their abilities compare to their peers.

Figure 9.1
At age seven Rachel described herself by mentioning her name, her favorite color, that her hair was blonde, and where she lives, demonstrating that her self-knowledge at age seven included descriptive characteristics.

[1]Relationships between dress and personality as discussed in Chapter 8.

Three processes underlie the development of self-knowledge or a self-concept. These are social comparison (discussed in Chapter 6, "Dress and Physical Appearance" and Chapter 7, "Dress and Body Image") reflective appraisal or social feedback, and self-perception. In this chapter, we first define the concept of self. Next, the processes of reflective appraisal and self-perception are discussed. We follow with relationships between dress and the thoughts individuals have about their inner self. Finally, we discuss ideas about how and why individuals use dress to publicly and privately present their "self" to others.

SELF DEFINED

The self is a construct. The human **self** is a dynamic interactive system of beliefs, feelings, and motives that characterizes an individual. There is a physical self (i.e., the human body) and three important experiences of selfhood (Baumeister, 1998): reflexive consciousness, interpersonal aspects of self, and the executive function of self.[2] Relationships between dress and the human body are discussed in Chapter 6, "Dress and Physical Appearance." Relationships between dress and specific identities are discussed in Chapter 10, "Dress and Identity." In this chapter, we focus on the three patterns of experience that comprise selfhood and how they are implicated in dress.

Before we begin, it is our stance that the self is not directly known. Instead, an individual with the help of others develops an organized body of beliefs about the self (Higgins, 1996). We develop such beliefs over time through social interaction. Some of these beliefs may be related to appearance and dress. For example, I believe that I look good in this blue sweater because my mother and my sister tell me so. This process of developing beliefs over time results in a construction of the self. In Chapter 5, "Dress and Impression Formation" you learned that dress influences social interaction. In this chapter you will see that social interaction influences your "self."

Because the self is a process developing over time rather than a product, the self is a dynamic construct, having the potential to change over one's lifetime. For example, think back to the individual you were in junior high school. You

are most likely a different person in many ways now from the person you were then. Yet there are also likely elements of your self that have also remained the same since that time. The process of changes to the self can be reflected in different dress practices at different stages of development. For example, one of your authors had a three-year-old daughter who insisted on selecting her own clothes every morning, without her mother's help. This practice resulted in some extremely clashing and discordant outfits (e.g., rust and brown plaid pants worn with purple striped shirt) that she wore to preschool; yet ten years later when she was in junior high her fashion sense was highly developed and her outfits were tasteful. Clearly, what she wore was important to her and she wanted to be in control of what she wore, but through social interaction received feedback on her appearance that she incorporated into her self-presentation.

Our approach also reflects the idea of a **unified self**. W. James wrote "a man has as many social selves as there are individuals who recognize him and carry an image of him in their mind" (1892, p. 179). This quote suggests that people may act differently depending on who they are with so that one person may know you as fun-loving and playful while another person may know you as competent and professional. The fun-loving and playful aspects of the self may be perceived by others when you wear certain types or styles of clothing such as bright colors and patterns for casual activities. The competent and professional aspects may be reflected in formal business wear since many researchers have found that people wearing formal business clothing are perceived to be more professional, to be more competent, and to have more occupational success than people dressed casually (Johnson & Roach-Higgins, 1987a, 1987b; Kwon & Johnson-Hillery, 1998; Scherbaum & Shepherd, 1987; Thurston et al., 1990). We contend that what others may know about you can vary so that two different people, if asked to describe you, might come up with conflicting descriptions (think of what your relatives know about you as a person versus what your friends at school or work might know).

Although people may appear as if they have completely different selves, across situations and over time, there is a core unified self. If each person that knew someone, knew a totally different self, it is likely those people could not talk about the person as the same individual (Baumeister, 1998). It is plausible, however, that some friends might not know the individual to the same extent or may know

[2]Some researchers also use the term *identity* to refer to this construct (e.g., Baumeister, 1998); however, we, like many researchers interested in dress and appearance, distinguish between the terms *self* and *identity* (e.g., Roach-Higgins & Eicher, 1992; Stone, 1962).

Compare your "self" then and now on these characteristics.

Characteristics	Your "Self" in Junior High	Your "Self" in College
Body		
Friendships		
Future Plans		
Abilities		
Fears		
Favorite Clothing		

about different components of the individual than other friends. Individuals within this group of friends may even disagree about some attributes of the individual but overall those friends will be relatively consistent in their appraisal of attributes. Thus, we contend that an individual's self is a unified construct, that it may not be totally knowable by others, and that it is a broad concept reflecting different components including relationships to others (e.g., employer, mother, uncle, knitter, runner, pianist) and reflecting personal characteristics (e.g., thrifty, aggressive, bold, introverted). Researchers have found that various personal characteristics are conveyed by a person's dress (see Table 5.1) as well as one's relationships to others (Damhorst, 1985). Recall from Chapter 8, "Dress and Personality" that the personal trait of narcissism is one that can be very accurately judged from appearance. Hence some of the different components of the self are conveyed by dress.

There has also been discussion of possible selves (Markus & Nurius, 1986). When reflecting on their lives, people can have numerous ideas concerning what they might someday be, such as someday I will be famous, someday I will be fit, someday I will be a reporter, or someday I will be a parent. Upon reflection, you can see these can all be ideas concerning the same self in different situations and with different traits. For example, me-as-thin or me-as-heavy is still the same "me." However, many people believe they will be another "person" once they have made dramatic changes to themselves such as losing fifty pounds or having cosmetic surgery (Figure 9.2). They

believe that they will have more dates, be more attractive, be happier, or more successful than they are in the present. These types of beliefs may indicate that these individuals do not have a firmly grounded or developed conception of their "self."

For example, In 2004 Lorrie Arias wanted to be a contestant on *The Swan*, a reality television program that

Figure 9.2

These before and after weight loss pictures demonstrates a dramatic change to this man's physical self, but what about changes to his core self? To what extent is the inner self changed when the physical self is transformed?

BEFORE   AFTER

aired that year (Duca, 2014). She had previously lost 150 pounds, but was dissatisfied with the extra skin she was left with after weight loss, and was hoping to get a tummy tuck. After she was selected to be on the program she had ten procedures, more than anyone else had had on the program. During the filming of the procedures she was not allowed to see how she had changed. After she saw what she looked like on the filming stage she was surprised, but as soon as filming stopped she screamed for the executive producer, "I want my face back!"

Arias said she was happier before the show and that she has had self-esteem issues all her life (Duca, 2014). Whether or not Arias has a firmly grounded or developed conception of her "self" is unknown. However, she has said she would consider more surgery such as breast augmentation, brow lift, facelift, and liposuction. Recall from Chapter 7, "Dress and Body Image" that body dysmorphic disorder is characterized by an intense hatred with a body part, often resulting in extreme behaviors to either change that part or to stay inside and avoid being seen in public. The fact that Arias has expressed desire for more surgeries and confines herself to her home may suggest she has developed body dysmorphic disorder. She may be striving for a possible self that is impossible for her to attain.

EXPERIENCES OF SELF: REFLEXIVE CONSCIOUSNESS

Reflexive consciousness is comprised of experiences wherein an individual's attention is focused on constructing a concept of oneself. Reflexive consciousness requires us to be self-aware. When individuals try to answer questions about what their own opinions are, or think about what sort of person they are—that is, determine what traits or characteristics they use to describe themselves as unique individuals—these are experiences that involve reflexive consciousness. For example, adolescents often wonder where they will attend college, what occupation they will pursue, and whether they will get married; these thoughts are examples of reflection. Wondering "Why did I buy that jacket?" or Why did I wear that dress?" demonstrate reflective consciousness about dress. Without reflexive consciousness, the self "would have no meaning or value and would hardly exist at all" (Baumeister, 1998, p. 680). The self begins when our awareness is directed

inward and in humans, this happens around the age of twelve months.

As we reflect on the self, often some of our thoughts are actual, while others thoughts are possibilities. You may think about yourself in terms of what is (i.e., actual self). Statements like "I am tall" or "I have green eyes" are examples of possible actual self statements. These self-representations of an individual's actual attributes are called the **real self-concept** (Harter, 1999). The **ideal self-concept** consists of representations of attributes that are possible or ones that we want to have. Statements such as "I want to have red hair" or "I want to have flat abdominals" are examples of possible ideal self statements.

You may also evaluate yourself (e.g., I like my eyes, I like my outfit, I have good skin). Your thoughts about your physical and mental self can result in being more or less satisfied. This resulting satisfaction with either your total physical appearance, specific aspects of your physical appearance as well as your mental thoughts about self may, in turn, influence your sense of worth or **self-esteem**.

Domains of the self are aspects or facets of the self that contribute to self-esteem. Another view of self-esteem is that it is a function of aspects of the self that are important to us and our success at achieving those aspects (James, 1892). This perspective maintains that every aspect or domain of the self is not equally important; consequently, self-worth is a function of how well we match up with our ideal self on those important aspects or domains of the self. For example, peer acceptance is important for most adolescents and researchers have found that being able to dress in fashionable clothing is important for peer acceptance (Hendricks, Kelly, & Eicher, 1968; Kelly & Eicher, 1970; Littrell & Eicher, 1973; Smucker & Creekmore, 1972; Williams & Eicher, 1966). We might be tempted to predict that an adolescent unable to dress fashionably might have lower self-esteem than one who could dress fashionably. However, the adolescent's level of self-esteem is an important variable in this context. People with high self-esteem are able to discount or devalue those domains of the real self in which they are unsuccessful or inadequate. Thus, a high self-esteem adolescent unable to dress fashionably might reason that if my friends do not like me for who I am instead of what I wear, I do not want to be friends with them. By the same token, low self-esteem individuals are unable to discount those domains on which they are unsuccessful in achieving their ideals.

Figure 9.3
Children, adolescents, and their peers consider the domain of athletic competence to be important to the self.

Hence a low self-esteem adolescent is likely unable to discount the importance of peer acceptance via fashionable dress. Consistent with this reasoning, research has been reported that found low self-esteem for people who perceived themselves as inadequate on domains they rate as important (Harter, 1999).

What domains of the self do people agree are important? Some domains are more important than others at predicting overall self-esteem. Most children and adolescents identify athletic competence, social acceptance, scholastic competence, appropriate behavioral conduct,

and physical attractiveness as highly important. The domains of athletic competence, social acceptance, and physical attractiveness are important to peers (Figure 9.3) and the domains of scholastic competence and appropriate behavioral conduct are important to parents. However, it is perceived physical attractiveness that is the most important domain of the self in predicting overall self-esteem across many age groups from as young as four and into middle age (Harter, 1999).

Why might physical attractiveness be so important? It might be because your physical attractiveness is constantly on display and is not situation specific like the other domains. Regardless, our outer self or what we look like and our inner self (our feelings of self worth or self evaluations) are very closely linked (Harter, 1999).

When our perceptions of our ideal self differ from our perceptions of our real self (i.e., self-perceptions), we call the gap between the two perceptions a **self-discrepancy**. According to **self-discrepancy theory**, when we perceive such discrepancies between actual or real self and ideal self, we are motivated to reduce the discrepancy because it arouses negative feelings (e.g., low self-esteem, disappointment, dissatisfaction, sadness) (Harter, 1999; Higgins, 1996). One way to reduce the negative feelings is to

IN-CLASS ACTIVITY
Domains of the Self

Think back to high school and middle school. Do you agree with Harter that athletic competence, social acceptance, scholastic competence, appropriate behavioral conduct, and physical attractiveness contributed to your self-esteem and were important domains of the self? Which of these domains are still important to you?

try to change actual self-attributes. For example, women might exercise and diet to lose weight and more closely approximate the cultural ideal of thinness; men might lift weights and use steroids to more closely approximate the cultural muscular ideal. Both men and women might use clothing to mask aspects of their bodies that they are unsatisfied with.

Whether we are thinking about our actual self or our ideal self, two theories have been used by dress researchers to explain how we might use dress to reflect on and answer questions about who we are. These theories are **self-perception theory** (Bem, 1972) and **symbolic self-completion theory** (Wickland & Gollwitzer, 1982).

Self-Perception Theory

According to self-perception theory, people assess their own behaviors after they occur, to determine their own traits. For example, assume you help a stranger select an outfit while you are shopping in a store. As result of your helping behavior, you might infer that you are a kind and caring person. If you do this, you are inferring your own attributes using the same method that you use to infer the attributes of others. Thus, people's experiences of their own opinions or traits are actually interpretations of their own behavior (Bem, 1972).

What impact might the items of dress that we wear have on our self-perceptions? To answer this question, a team of researchers conducted an experiment. The researchers reasoned that since variations in appearance cause people to assign different attributes to others, variations in one's own appearance should cause people to assign different attributes to themselves. They also theorized that

people who would be most susceptible to making these self-inferences would be individuals who were responsive to self-produced cues as opposed to situational cues. **Self-produced cues** are cues that arise from an individual's own actions and personal properties. Self-produced cues include expressive behaviors such as smiling or frowning. **Situational cues** are tied to the context and can consist of conventional definitions of how most people will or should feel in a given situation. Differences in responsiveness to self-produced cues versus situational cues stem from how people originally learn to identify their own attributes. For example, consider eating. If you eat because you are hungry, you are responding to a self-produced cue. If you eat because the clock says it is time to eat (i.e., noon time) you are responding to a situational cue.

For the experiment, undergraduates put on a pair of glasses and rated their own abilities. Participants also rated their abilities when not wearing the glasses. Although wearing glasses did not affect actual performance on an easy task, people who were responsive to self-produced cues did rate themselves as more scholarly and competent when wearing glasses than when not. This was true for both males and females. Thus, wearing or not wearing eyeglasses resulted in participants assigning different traits to themselves (Kellerman & Laird, 1982).

In contrast, Kwon (1994) used self-perception theory to indirectly investigate relationships between dress and self-perceptions. Rather than having her research participants actually wear different clothing styles and indicate their self-perceptions, she had participants rate how they thought they would feel if they were wearing proper as opposed to improper clothing for work. Participants indicated they believed that if they were dressed properly, they would feel they were responsible and competent in a work setting as compared to being dressed improperly. It appears that simply thinking about wearing items of dress impacts self-perceptions.

Another team of researchers (Hannover & Kühnen, 2002) were also interested in determining whether what you wore influenced how you thought about yourself (Figure 9.4). They reasoned that clothing styles would influence self descriptions because certain clothing styles prepare individuals to think of specific trait categories. Psychologists sometimes refer to this process as **priming**. For example, if you were wearing a jogging suit this might cause you to think of athletic traits (e.g., healthy, fit) to describe yourself whereas if you were wearing a school

Figure 9.4
Wearing athletic apparel may enhance your physical performance but it can also impact self definitions as an athlete.

uniform you might think of academic traits when describing yourself (e.g., intelligent, studious). These researchers reasoned that perceptions about the self are, to some extent, created on the spot. Therefore, judgments about you made by you could be expected to be consistent with the ideas you are having about yourself at the time you are asked to make these self-judgments.

To test their idea, they devised an experiment in which they asked people to dress in either formal or casual clothing (Hannover & Kühnen, 2002). When people appeared for the experiment, they were asked to describe themselves as quickly as possible using a list of adjectives and indicating which adjectives were descriptive of themselves. Participants wearing formal clothing did accept formal traits

as descriptive of themselves and processed these traits faster than casual traits. This pattern was reversed for participants who were casually dressed. Thus, the clothing worn by these individuals influenced their thoughts about themselves.

Symbolic Self-Completion Theory

The second theory used to study how dress might be used to understand who we are is symbolic self-completion theory. Symbolic self-completion theory proposes that people strive for **self definitions**. A self-definition is "an ideal or goal that is set up or pursued through the accumulation of relevant symbols" (Wickland & Gollwitzer, 1982, p.32). Having a self-definition means acquiring a readiness to enact certain types of behaviors. For example, if you have the self-definition of "biker," the behaviors you may be ready to enact include riding your motorcycle, reading about motorcycles, wearing "biker" clothing, or associating with other bikers. According to the theory, no one reaches an absolute level of completeness in terms of a self-definition. Thus, even the best bikers would have to continue to work toward developing their self-definitions as a "biker."

Self-definitions have two critical components. The first is that a self-definition is perceived "as a condition for potential behavior that will ideally become a permanent part of one's self" (Wicklund & Gollwitzer, 1982, p. 32). Going back to our biker example, the first component suggests that a self-definition of being a biker will eventually become a permanent aspect of the self. You may still view yourself as a biker even if you are not able to ride your motorcycle anymore. The second component is that the pursuit of a self-definition has "a goal directed character" (p. 32). This means that there is active movement on the part of an individual toward completing the self-definition.

Also important to achieving a self-definition is interaction with others. The knowledge that you actually have a specific self-definition evolves from your interaction with others. Referring to the biker example, if you want the self-definition of "biker," you need to know that others recognize you as a biker in order for you to be able to claim that self-definition. Important in this process of getting others to acknowledge that you have this particular self-definition is the use of symbols. Symbols can communicate to others that one has a specific self-definition because of the meanings tied to them. These symbols include behaviors as well as physical objects. Because of its symbolic nature, dress plays a role in acquiring and maintaining self-definitions (Figure 9.5).

Once an individual is committed to a self-definition, he or she can be blocked from achieving it. For example, in the aforementioned biker example, the individual may not ride as often, as good, or as long as other bikers and as a result, may experience incompleteness in terms of this biker self-definition. In this case, the individual may engage in self-symbolizing. Self-symbolizing involves presenting a symbol of the desired self-definition with the intention of evoking in others a response that affirms that self-definition. In other words, a dress symbol can be chosen that signifies to others the desired self-definition.

Continuing with the biker example, suppose you desired the self-definition of "biker." At the end of a summer, you only have logged a 1,000 miles on your bike and you know that real bikers can ride upwards of 10,000 miles on their bikes during the summer months. You are questioning whether you can define yourself as a biker. You might symbolize your biker self-definition by wearing a T-shirt with a brand logo (e.g., Harley Davidson, Honda) to work. If others, upon seeing your T-shirt, acknowledge your self-definition as a biker by their comments (e.g., "Did you ride your bike this past weekend?" or "Here comes the biker!"), you may increase your sense of completeness in this self-definition. In other words, because you were acknowledged by others as having the self-definition you desired as a result of a symbol you presented, you feel a higher level of completeness in that self-definition. Thus, when people experience a sense of incompleteness with respect to a desired self-definition, they can display symbols of the self-definition to increase their sense of completeness.

Symbolic self-completion requires more than just acquiring symbols of completeness. It also requires exerting control over one's own perceptions of self to create a personally acceptable picture of reality. Once you acquire the symbol of completeness you must believe that having it (the symbol) makes you complete. If you do not, you can fall into a never-ending consumption cycle of acquiring symbols and rejecting them because acquiring them did not change how you thought about yourself. In fact, researchers have suggested that symbolic self-completion theory provides one explanation for compulsive buying behavior (Yurchisin & Johnson, 2004).

Figure 9.5
According to symbolic-self completion theory, items of dress worn can influence our self-definition. This biker has pins that indicate the number of rides he has participated in. In this image, is the biker using dress to experience a sense of completeness in a role or is the dress worn for other reasons (e.g., functionality)?

The role of dress in the process of taking on new self-definitions is important when people enter into social organizations. In qualitative research on sororities, young women noted their use of clothing to demonstrate acceptance of and commitment to the sorority. As pledges transitioned into the sorority they frequently wore Greek letters on their clothing. Some displays of Greek letters were very prominent such as wearing sweatshirts or hoodies with large Greek letters while others were subtle as in the instance of wearing necklaces or pins. As they transitioned from pledge to full members of the sorority, clothing was used to symbolize their active involvement as some members wore Greek clothing exclusively. One young woman noted that all of her clothing had Greek letters. Some members even adopted permanent symbols of their membership as they had their bodies tattooed with sorority symbols. However, as the self-definition of sorority member became less important and the women transitioned out of fraternal life, so did the need for wearing symbols of the organization (Arthur, 1997). One might expect similar experiences when younger children are joining scout groups or clubs.

Dress can be important in assisting individuals to achieve a sense of completeness in a self-definition and it can also be important in achieving a sense of completeness when people experience physical incompleteness. For example, women who have had surgery (mastectomy) to remove breast cancer tumors may experience a change in their physical selves that may make them feel physically incomplete. This feeling of incompleteness may contribute to their wearing a prosthesis (a "fake" breast of silicone or other material) or to have breast reconstruction surgery. Researchers documented that this was the case. Women used a prosthesis even when they were unhappy with it. They also found that woman who were dissatisfied with their prosthesis were more likely to seek breast reconstruction than women who were satisfied. The researchers interpreted this finding as evidence that if the prosthesis did not provide a sense of completeness, then a woman was more likely to continue to seek ways to experience completeness, in this case, seek breast reconstruction (Feather, Kaiser, & Rucker, 1989).

EXPERIENCES OF SELF: INTERPERSONAL ASPECTS

Interpersonal aspects of self involve experiences with others. In social interaction we receive feedback from others often on our self-presentation such as "I like your outfit" or "I wish my hair was as shiny as yours." Interpersonal aspects of the self involves learning to see ourselves the way that others see us (Yeung & Martin, 2003). When you try to live up to others' expectations, make good impressions on others, attend social functions, join groups and quit them—these and similar experiences reveal interpersonal experiences of self (Baumeister, 1998). In other words, concern is with the interpersonal self when individuals try to locate themselves within a specific social context by making claims to social identities. As noted in Chapter 10, "Dress and Identity," these identity categories include individual (e.g., personable, athletic), relational (e.g., parents, occupation), and group identities (e.g., ethnicity, gender).

Stone (1962) used the term *identity* to describe this component of self as he commented "when one has identity, he is situated—cast in the shape of social object by the acknowledgment of his participation or membership in social relations" (p.93). It is as if you walk into a room and people publicly comment, "there is the president of the club," "there is the discussion leader," "there is a beautiful fashionable women," "that man over there is her father." People gain a sense of who and what they are in interaction with other people (i.e., they make claim to identities that need verification by others) and they have specific identities as members of different social groups (e.g., member, officer). These identities contribute to their overall self.

Clothing researchers have focused considerable attention on understanding relationships between experiences of the interpersonal self and dress (e.g., Roach-Higgins & Eicher, 1992). Much of the work has utilized symbolic interaction as a framework (Mead, 1934; Stone, 1962).

Symbolic Interactionism

Remember we said earlier that the self is not directly known. We said that the self was a dynamic construct, and to know and understand the self (i.e., what type of person you are), you need the help of others and that knowledge of the self occurs over time. Symbolic interactionism posits that the self is a social construction established, maintained, and altered through interpersonal communication with others. In everyday language this means that you are able to answer questions about what type of person you are as a result of talking and listening to other people. For example, a television news anchor who learns from audience feedback that she is looking old and tired might elect cosmetic surgery to appear more youthful. Such feedback is likely to be deemed important and acting on the feedback could affect news program ratings.

In addition to the idea of the self being socially constructed, Cooley (1902) argued that the social practices influencing the self center around seeing ourselves as we imagine others see us. In other words, our ideas about who we are are internalizations of other's ideas about us (Yeung & Martin, 2003). Cooley (1902) labeled this idea as the looking-glass self. This notion is not to suggest that the self is simply taking on any person's ideas about us. The other impressions that we take on generally are those that come from people that we admire or hold in high esteem. In addition, we need to be somewhat impressionable to accept their beliefs about us (Cooley, 1902; Yeung & Martin, 2003). Thus, people may use others' opinions as looking glasses to tell them how they should appear and behave in some circumstances but not others. For example, let's assume that you do not know what to wear to a formal barbeque. In fact the entire idea of a formal barbeque sounds like an oxymoron to you. You ask your best friend for his advice and he suggests you wear jeans and a polo shirt but that both should not look worn because when he thinks of you, he thinks of a casual, informal person. Thus, your best friend has made dress recommendations based on how he views you. You are likely to follow this advice because it is coming from someone who knows you well.

With the numerous modes of communication and travel that individuals make use of, people are exposed to many different ways of being. At such a time, adopting the perspective of a single individual concerning how we should appear may not be useful. Rather, it could be useful to consider numerous significant others, even if their views are incompatible with each other, to inform your decisions concerning how to appear (Gergen, 2000).

It is also possible for people to shape how they are seen by others. The term *externalization* has been used to describe this process (Yeung & Martin, 2003). For example, someone else that you hold in high esteem may believe you have the right qualities to become a fashion model. That person might make a comment to you to the effect of "I was thinking about you the other day and I think you would make a good fashion model because you have the right height, the right body size, and an interesting face." You might accept this impression of you. Likewise, if you see yourself as the type of individual who could make a good fashion model, you might try to shape other's impressions of you to be consistent with this idea you have of yourself. For example, you could tell your friends that you have the needed body build, height, and face to be a fashion model. People can affect the perceptions others have of them (Yeung & Martin, 2003) by focusing other's attention on certain attributes and getting them to ignore others.

Stone (1962), in his initial work, focused on investigating verbal communication as key to the construction of the self, extended communication to include appearance.

He noted that appearance was a form of communication and, because of this property, is at least as important as verbal communication in establishing and maintaining the self. Appearance is important to knowing oneself because appearance facilitates identification of individuals. When you identify someone, you determine who and where a person is situated within a social context. Aspects of appearance, including clothing, assist in identification of others because they are used as symbols.[3] For example, you might wear a helmet, snowsuit, and insulated rubber boots and others may use these items as symbols to identify you as a snowmobiler. You may wear an apron at a backyard barbeque and be identified as the cook.

Program

Stone (1962) discussed the process of establishing identities as component parts of the self. He proposed that individuals manipulate their appearance and select clothing to communicate the aspects of the self (the specific identities) they want to convey to themselves as well as to others. For example, if you are a young woman and like to wear sexy clothing, to establish the serious mother aspect of self at a parent–teacher conference, you might wear less body-revealing clothing than you typically wear.

As a step in this process of establishing the self, individuals consider their own appearance (e.g., check their appearance in a mirror or mentally go over what they are wearing), perhaps to ensure accurate communication of the aspect of self they want to convey. In this process they may imagine how important others may think of them (i.e., looking glass self) or what characteristics others may assign to them based on the appearance they present. One's response to one's own appearance is called a **program**. You might experience a program as the process of examining your appearance in a mirror and consequently making some appraisal of that appearance (e.g., good enough) before moving to other activities of the day.

As part of that appraisal process you may also consider the common expectations that anyone else could have for your appearance. Mead (1934) used the term **generalized other** to refer to the process of taking into consideration other's expectations for your behavior or imagining what others expect of you. The generalized other can reflect a

---

[3]That symbols communicate identities is also consistent with symbolic self-completion theory.

collection of input from a variety of individuals within a society (e.g., what would your parents expect, your teachers, your neighbors, your employer, your peers). For example, suppose you were going to interview for a store management position in a highly fashionable boutique. You want the hiring agent to view you as a store manager. You could decide to wear a black conservative suit to symbolize that aspect of self because that is what you think your potential employers will expect you to wear (i.e., the impact of the generalized other). Once you put that suit on, your program is your answer to the question, do I look like I am a store manager of a highly fashionable boutique?

With the development of communication technologies that make it easy for individuals to connect with numerous "others" rather than adopting the perspective of a single generalized other, individuals may consider numerous generalized others. The perspectives of these numerous others may be in sync. They may also indicate diverse perspectives that are conflict with each other. The term *multiphrenia* or *many minds* has been used to capture this latter experience (Gergen, 2000). When you post photos of yourself in a new outfit on Instagram or Facebook, your resulting "likes" could reflect the expectations of those you have friended or followed and thereby represent numerous generalized others.

DRESS IN THE NEWS
A Case of Self-Expression

A sixteen-year old boy Jonathan Escobar who had recently changed schools often dressed in women's clothing and wore makeup. Jonathan frequently wore wigs, vintage clothing, skinny jeans, and flats. According to Gillooly (2009), the feminine appearance evoked both positive and negative comments (reviews) from other students. An administrator told him he should dress in a more manly way. Jonathan was pulled out of class to speak to the school's police officer who expressed concern about the student's safety. When interviewed, Escobar said, "I'm not going to dress like a man. I'm not going to wear depressing boring clothes. I'm going to express myself." From his comments it seems clear that Escobar was interested in expressing his self through his dress. For example, he also commented that his appearance was art, "It's who I am. I'm an artist. This is how I express my art."

Empirical evidence supporting the notion that people have multiple generalized others comes from qualitative research with Saudi Arabian women. The women were interviewed about their use of dress in presenting the self within the private spheres (e.g., inside the home) of their lives. The women shared that they did reference multiple generalized others as they used dress to present their "selves." Numerous others identified included expectations of individuals (e.g., husbands, in-laws) as well as communication from cultural sources including mass media (Tawfiq & Ogle, 2013).

Review

The next step of the process in establishing the self involves others' reactions to an individual's appearance. This is called a **review**. Going back to our interview example, when you meet the hiring agent for the store, the hiring agent responds to you and provides a review of your appearance. The review could take the form of a verbal comment (e.g., "you look nice today" or "you look like you just walked out of the store!") or the review could be an aspect of your treatment (e.g., graciously, abruptly).

Stone contends that when a review matches with a program, the self is validated. Applied to our example, this means you thought your appearance symbolized you were a store manager when you wore a black suit. If the hiring agent treated you like a store manager, the store manager confirmed this aspect of self for you. However, when programs and reviews do not coincide, the self is challenged. Continuing on with our example, if the hiring agent did not treat you as a store manager, you might try to convince the hiring agent that store manager is one of your identities by sharing other information with the agent (e.g., management experience in other environments) or you might agree that store manager is not currently a part of your self. You might also abandon the store manager identity or claim a different identity (e.g., sales associate).

Review Process

Hunt and Miller (1997) explored Stone's (1962) ideas about the establishment and communication of identities through qualitative research with sorority women. The researchers asked questions about how dress and appearance were used to communicate identities and how sorority membership affected the women's appearances.

Sorority women used several methods to react to (review) the appearance of others as well as to react to their own appearances (program). These methods included the application of moral rules and neutralization techniques used in response to unfavorable reviews. The application of moral rules was evidenced by statements from sorority members indicating as a member one should pay attention to one's appearance, one should show respect for diverse appearances, and one should engage in basic hygiene practices. Program neutralization techniques referred to methods participants used to counterbalance negative reviews of their own appearances. Neutralization techniques identified were categorized as denial of responsibility and denial of injury.

Denial of responsibility was used when participants wanted to imply that unmanageable forces were responsible for their appearance. If on a particular day a member was having trouble with her hair, she might claim she was just "having a bad hair day" or if a member was caught with a food stain on her jacket, the stain was due to an accident.

Within the sorority, it was expected that one would pay attention to one's appearance. To not pay attention to appearance violated that expectation and that violation could negatively impact the broader identity of the entire organization. Denial of injury was applied when participants suggested that their "deviant" appearance did not cause any enduring harm to either themselves nor to the reputation of the sorority. Thus, wearing sweat pants and a T-shirt to a class where a sorority member did not know anyone was not viewed as causing any harm to the reputation of the organization. In a similar manner, appearing in pajama bottoms and T-shirt in public was also not damaging because the member was not wearing any indicators that she was a member of the sorority.

Participants also reported that they reduced the effect of negative reviews by contesting the power of the reviewer and appealing to higher loyalties. Contesting the power of the reviewer involved questioning the credentials of the individual conducting the review. Sorority members in this instance shared that members who wanted to play the role of the "fashion police" were individuals who violated the organization's norm of respect for diverse appearances. Appealing to higher loyalties described situations in which participants believed that one's dress and appearance were beyond judgment. This could happen because a specific appearance reflected an individual's commitment to different criteria for appearance, such as physical and psychological comfort (e.g., It is more important to me to be physically comfortable than to wear high heels).

Public, Intimate, and Secret Self

In writing about the self as communicated through dress, Eicher (1981) proposed that there are three conscious parts of the self that relate to clothing. She labeled these parts as public, intimate,[4] and secret self. The **public self** was described as rooted in reality and consisted of aspects of the self such as one's age, sex, and occupation. These are components of you that you are willing to share with everyone. Think about how you dress when going to work or school or for other public activities. You may dress to communicate your fashionability, your biological sex, or your age. In our previous discussion of program and review, we often think about establishing identities that we want most others to apply to us. Indeed, when we think about dress as a form of communication, we often think about communicating information about the public self.

The **intimate self** was described as the aspects of self that one shares with close friends and relatives. Eicher (1981) noted that dressing to communicate the intimate self can result in dressing for relaxation and for non-public events as backyard barbeques and other activities that take place in and around the home. These are activities that are less public than going to work or school so that you have clothing items that you wear only when you are at home or only with certain close friends or relatives (e.g., paint spattered and ripped shorts). This element of self is more difficult to measure than the public self and perhaps as a result, is not as commonly discussed (Kaiser, 1997).

The **secret self** are aspects of the self that may not be shared with other persons (Eicher, 1981). Eicher initially assumed that there might be relationships between the secret self[5] and fantasy dress. Fantasy dress might include dressing as a member of the opposite sex (i.e., cross dressing) or dressing up for masquerades (Figure 9.6). Dress that might also fall into this category included items of dress that were owned but not worn or dress items never worn in public spaces (e.g., a man wearing stiletto heels).

[4]Eicher later relabeled *intimate self* as *private self* (Eicher, Baizerman, & Michelman, 1991; Michelman, Eicher, & Michelman, 1991).

[5]According to Stone (1962), the secret self if not reviewed by others could not be an established aspect of self.

Figure 9.6

Skirts are more frequently worn by women than men. Thus, one possible interpretation of a man seen wearing a skirt could be an attempt to communicate aspects of the secret self.

Eicher took the view that the self was comprised of multiple identities. While she used the term self in describing her ideas, in later work with Mary Ellen Roach-Higgins, Eicher (1992) stated that their interest was in "how dress—as a medium of communication—relates to identity" (p.5). Thus, better labels for these concepts might be public, private, and secret identities.

There is evidence that individuals do associate their clothing with public, private, or secret aspects of the self. In research with adolescent psychiatric patients, a majority acknowledged they owned dress intended to communicate aspects of their public self. A few agreed that some of their dress was intended to communicate aspects of

their **private self** and very few noted having dress specifically to communicate their secret self (Michelman, Eicher, & Michelman, 1991).

In additional work with nonpsychiatric adolescents, dress was clearly linked to public self. Within the context of a high school, adolescents linked most of their clothing with the public self. Participants shared that the high school was comprised of different groups including jocks, freaks, preppies, nerds, and punks. Members of each group were distinguishable by their appearance. For example, descriptions of jocks included that they wore athletic clothing such as letter jackets, jerseys, and had short hairstyles. In contrast, nerds wore out-of-style clothing and did not take care of their hair. Participants did not differentiate between clothing they would wear to communicate aspects of their public self from clothing they would wear to communicate aspects of their private self. However, there was no evidence that this group of adolescents used dress to communicate a secret self (Eicher, Baizerman, & Michelman, 1991). Perhaps it is adults rather than adolescents that use dress to express the secret self. Additional research is needed to answer this question as well as how the idea of dress to communicate public, private, and secret self might apply in non-Western cultures.

The question of whether it is adults that use every day items of dress to express the secret self has not yet been fully answered, but there is some evidence that adults may use costumes, a particular category of dress. A **costume** is dress characteristic of another period, place, or person (Figure 9.7) that might be worn on the stage for a performance, at a party (e.g., Halloween), or for other special events. Wearing a costume suggests dress that is out of the ordinary (Roach-Higgins & Eicher, 1992).

In a study of adults that routinely dressed in costumes, people did indicate they associated feelings of fun with clothing and felt they dressed out their fun side when among family and close friends. Women were more likely than men to indicate any use of clothing to express sexual fantasies. Miller (1997) noted that Eicher's (1981) original ideas concerning what was evidence of dress that was public, private, or secret were insufficient in explaining her participants' use of costumes. As a result, she proposed that when an individual was dressing for reality, he or she was likely communicating aspects of the public self. Likewise when dressing for fun, he or she was also likely communicating aspects of the private self. However, when dressing for fantasy, Miller proposed that public, private,

Figure 9.7
Adults and children have an opportunity to express their secret selves at Halloween each year as they appear like their favorite characters from movies, television, comics, or other sources.

and secret aspects of the self might all be reflected in the costume used to construct an appearance.

In subsequent research Miller (1998) was interested in investigating the role of fantasy with individuals who dressed up in costumes. The personal fantasy in this instance could involve the dream of being an important historical figure (e.g., Jefferson Davis, Betsy Ross) or a dream of experiencing life at a different point in time. Participants came from a broad group of organizations whose members dressed up in costumes including English Country Dancers, Buckskinners (Fur Traders), and Historical Reenactors. Her primary research question was whether reenactment costuming "serves to educate others about historic events or if costuming is a result of a reenactor's personal fantasy?" Participants were asked to check reasons why they were interested in dressing in costume from a list supplied by Miller; they were also instructed to share anything they wanted the researcher to know about their use of costumes.

It was a love of history and an ability to assume another persona that were the most often cited reasons for dressing in costume. There were gender differences with more men indicating a love of history than women and more women indicating ability to assume another persona than men. A male participant noted that dressing in costume allowed him not to play history but to actually live it. Participants

were hesitant to acknowledge that fantasy played a part in their willingness to wear costumes, with men even more hesitant than women. However, the researcher noted that it is impossible to live history and, therefore, historical reenactors have an element of fantasy in both their behavior as well as in their attempt to use a costume to temporarily assume another persona.

Related to Miller's (1997; 1998) work on individuals' use of costume to express private and secret self is Belk and Costa's (1998) work on buckskinning. Buckskinners reenact important life events of the early nineteenth-century American west. Buckskinners do transform their identities through their clothing. The reenactors' denial of their clothing as a costume indicated that as they put on their buck skins, they transformed into mountain men and women. In addition, these aspects of self are established and maintained with the help of outsiders (tourists) who at designated times react to (review) the appearance of these temporary mountain people and subsequently authenticate (validated) their temporarily transformed selves.

The Collective Self

The **collective self** (Triandis, H.C. (1989). The self and social behavior in differing cultural contexts. *Psychological Review, 96*(3), 506–520.) involves one's membership in various social groups including cultural groups. Although whether and how clothing is used to establish and communicate aspects of the private and public self has been the focus of some researchers, relationships between clothing and the collective self have not been investigated. The impact of membership in a culture and how that membership influences formation and development of self is needed. Cultures vary in the relative emphasis they place on private, public, or collective self. For example, US culture tends to emphasize private and public while Asian cultures tend to emphasize the collective self. Therefore, it is important to determine the applicability of these three concepts (public, private, collective) as well as the secret self to a variety of cultures.

As the Self Changes, So Does Dress

If dress can be used to create and communicate identities, it can also signify identity change and subsequent changes to the self. For many years Roman Catholic nuns were required to wear a habit[6] (Figure 9.8). During the 1960s nuns were given the option to stop wearing them and adopt non-spiritual dress. There were several issues linked to wearing habits including that they were a barrier to nun's independence and ability to function in the world. Wearing a habit communicated one collective self, that of nun, and disallowed communication of any individual aspects of self. Habits may have interfered with a nun's ability to connect with others, as their appearance was definitely distinct from the everyday clothing of others in the Western world. However, wearing a habit also excused nuns from manipulating their appearance to achieve cultural expectations for attractiveness (e.g., cosmetic use, thinness) for women in US society.

The transition to everyday dress was not necessarily smooth. As nuns transitioned, skills and knowledge had to be gained, or relearned in some cases, to be able to present a desired appearance. Experiences of conflict and possibly frustration evolved as nuns worked to reconcile their religious vows (e.g., vow of poverty) with the materialism and money associated with participation in fashion. However, for some nuns, adopting everyday dress enabled

them to communicate a new personal and religious self (Michelman,1997).

Over the lifespan there may not be as dramatic changes as that of a nun but people do continue to grow and change and that fact suggests that dress that reflects the self at one life stage may no longer be reflective of the self at another. Or that there may be emerging aspects of the self that are communicable using dress. Empirical support for this idea comes from qualitative research from the UK with adult British women (Guy & Banim, 2000). At times, the women suggested that their clothing was insufficient to represent specific aspects of self that they wanted to project. They also indicated that they had grown away from particular aspects of self and thus, some clothing styles were no longer a psychological fit. For example, one woman spoke about clothing items that were left at her parent's home when she went to college because they were no longer relevant to her self. Changes to their bodies also meant giving up certain clothing styles. One woman noted, "as

---

Figure 9.8
Nun wearing a habit.

---

[6]A habit is the dress of a religious order of women worn in a convent. The habit typically consisted of a long black robe, large rosaries (e.g., a long necklace consisting of beads) and a crucifix (i.e., cross), and an elaborate headdress.

I age, I increasingly seek clothes that are serviceable and comfortable, which serve my body rather than express my body. That does not mean that style does not matter . . . style must follow comfort and purpose now, whereas I can easily remember a time when style came first" (Guy & Banim, 2000, p. 321). The research with these women suggests that as views of the self continue to evolve over the course of life so will the dress used to express their self.

Sincerity of Self-Presentation

As we have presented dress as a method to establish, maintain, and communicate to others aspects of self, an assumption could exist that people's efforts would be sincere and that there would not be attempts to use dress to deceive others about your true identities or to assume identities that you should not claim. In research from the UK this question of deception versus sincerity of self-presentation was examined with British women (Tseelson, 1992). She developed three propositions: (1) that a sincere self-presentation is reflected in an appearance that lacks effort when with familiar others; (2) that duplicity in self-presentation is present when an improved image is presented with unfamiliar others. (In other words, she contended that any attempt to enhance your appearance is a mispresentation); and (3) that paying attention to one's appearance is a conscious intention to deceive. None of Tseelson's propositions were supported. Participants' responses indicated that they cared about their appearance when interacting with both familiar and unfamiliar others and that the self presented to others was not necessarily an improved self. In some situations, participants did try to present an ideal self but participants were unwilling to appear deceptive

in the process. For these participants, paying attention to appearance was a way to generate self-confidence, not to deceive others. However, this is not to say that dress is never used to make false claims to identities or to deceive.

Is All Clothing Related to Communicating Aspects of Self?

If individuals use clothing to establish and communicate aspects of the self, then observers should be able to read and interpret the information communicated in reliable ways. But what happens when clothing styles, through the process of **brand management**, become associated with distinct personality characteristics? Do individuals select clothing to communicate the image of the clothing brand or to communicate aspects of the self?

Brand management is the planning and analyzes of how a brand is perceived in the market by consumers. To shape how a brand is perceived, a brand manager makes decisions about the product—its packaging, pricing, and any other aspects of the brand that may impact on the inferences that consumers might make about the brand. For example, a brand might use athletes as models in their advertisements to convey the idea that people should view the brand as having specific characteristics such as strong, powerful, and active.

Interested in whether the intended image of branded apparel actually carried over onto the people who wore the brand, two studies were conducted (Feinberg, Mataro, & Burroughs, 1992). In the first study the researchers explored whether the personal characteristics assigned to individuals on the basis of their clothing are the same personal characteristics they used to describe themselves. Two groups of people participated. One group wore clothing that they believed communicated their personal characteristics. The second group observed the first group and assigned personal characteristics to them such as formal, energetic, mature, cultural, and individualistic. Observers were able to accurately identify some of the personal characteristics of the individuals. Thus, the clothing did successfully communicate some of the personal characteristics of the people wearing the clothing.

In the second study, the researchers examined the relationship between the image that was linked through advertising with different brands of clothing (i.e., jeans) and the personal characteristics of actual people who wore the brand. Using similar adjectives as in their first study, participants were supplied with drawings of different brands of jeans and asked to infer the personal traits of the people that would wear each brand. People who preferred to wear one brand of jeans did not vary in personal characteristics from participants who preferred to wear a different brand of jeans. Although the brands conveyed different images, the wearers of the brands did not describe themselves differently. Thus, the characteristics tied to a clothing brand appear to not be reflective of the traits of the people that wear those brands (Feinberg, Mataro, & Burroughs, 1992).

EXPERIENCES OF SELF: EXECUTIVE FUNCTION

Baumeister (1998) proposes the **executive function** as experiences that demonstrate the self as an active agent and decision maker. This function of the self is making choices (e.g., what brands of clothing or makeup to buy), initiating action, and taking responsibility for that action. Behaviors such as deciding what to buy or what to become, acting on impulse, or putting forth your best effort all involve the executive function of self. The executive function is not always "on" because many behaviors can happen without active intervention of the self.

The executive function may be in evidence when people make decisions about items of dress based on the items' perceived relationship to self. Sirgy (1982) developed self-image product-image **congruity theory** to explain how connections between products and selves might influence purchasing. The basic premise of the theory is that people will be motivated to purchase products with images that are congruent with how they see themselves (i.e., actual self-image) or with how they would like to be (i.e., ideal self-image). They will avoid those products that are inconsistent with either their actual or ideal images.

Ericken and Sirgy (1989) used congruity theory to understand the role of achievement motivation and clothing behavior in a work setting. An individual was described as self-congruent if he or she experienced a match between the image projected by an outfit of clothing and actual self-image (i.e., my clothing appears professional and I am a professional). An individual was ideal-congruent if they experienced a match between clothing, actual self-image, and ideal self-image (i.e., clothing appears professional, I am a professional, and I want to be a professional). The researchers argued that achievement motivated women were more likely to see themselves as professional women and to experience self-congruity wearing professional clothing than non-achievement motivated women. Studying faculty and staff women drawn from three universities, the researchers found both self-congruity and ideal-congruity were related to attitudes concerning clothing behavior. Achievement motivated women were likely to see themselves as desiring to be professional and, therefore, wanting to wear professional clothing. Women who were achievement motivated reported wearing business clothing more often than women who were less achievement motivated. In addition, achievement motivated women wanted to see themselves as business-like and felt business-like when wearing professional clothing (i.e., were ideal-congruent).

This relationship seems to hold for adolescents as well. When asked about their use of clothing brands, adolescents shared that their favorite apparel brand was most similar to their perceived self (i.e., this brand reflects who I am), followed by their social (i.e., this brand reflects who I want others to think I am), and their desired self (i.e., this brand reflects who I want to be). (Rhee & Johnson, 2007).

ADDITIONAL RELATIONSHIPS BETWEEN THE SELF AND APPEARANCE

Proximity of Clothing to Self

Sometimes when you are shopping for clothing you might look at an item of clothing and say to yourself, that style is definitely not me or the reverse, that the item is you. To describe this idea, that is, that clothing could be viewed as psychologically close to the self or far from the self, a concept was proposed—**proximity of clothing to self (PCS)**—by Sontag and Schlater (1982). The PCS concept was designed to determine what connection, if any, that clothing could contribute to the quality of one's life. These researchers worked to clarify the meaning of the concept and developed a scale to measure the concept with a random sample of adults. They found that proximity of clothing to self was a multifaceted concept. PCS was indicated by the extent to which clothing was "perceived as one with the self, recognized as an aspect of appearance by which the self is established and validated, recognized as a significant symbol of an individual's mood or attitude, perceived as an expression of self-regard or self-worth, and recognized as a method of an affective response to self-evaluation (i.e., clothing affects self-feelings with possible behavioral consequences), and related to body cathexis" (p.3). Thus, the proximity of clothing to self concept includes experiences of self that reflected two of the categories Baumeister (1998) identified—reflexive consciousness and interpersonal aspects of selfhood. Reflexive consciousness aspects include perceptions of clothing as one with the self, as expression of self-regard or self-worth, and as an element of self feelings. The interpersonal component of the self includes the use of clothing as an aspect of appearance by which the self is established and validated and clothing as a symbol of self.

In studying proximity of clothing to self initially, Sontag and Schlater (1982) had people respond to the open-ended question "what are some of the most important reasons why you feel as you do about your clothing?" Responses were evaluated to determine whether or not they possessed one or more elements of the PCS concept. All six components (see components in aforementioned Sontag & Schlater, 1982) were identified in people's responses but few individuals responded that clothing was symbolic of the self. More men than women responded that there was a relationship between their clothing and both their self-regard and self-esteem. More women than men indicated that there was a relationship between their clothing and how satisfied they were with their bodies (i.e., body cathexis).

In later research, Sontag and Lee (2004) worked to refine the PCS instrument to make it appropriate for use across the lifespan and to verify content, construct validity, and reliability. These researchers had adolescents, young adults, and mature adults answer open-ended questions reflecting the PCS concepts. Adolescents' responses reflected only four of the original six dimensions. The strongest relationship between clothing and self for adolescents was in relationship to self-esteem. Relationships between clothing and the other dimensions of PCS were only moderate, perhaps reflecting developmental differences in the self between adolescents and adults.

The PCS concept identifies several relationships between clothing and two expressions of self—reflexive consciousness and interpersonal aspects of self. Sontag and Lee (2004) have proposed testable relationships between the self and clothing in their definitions of each dimension that could be material for future research. Clothing researchers might also pose research questions that relate PCS to other variables in the clothing literature especially variables related to Baumeister's (1998) experiences of self that reflect the executive function (e.g., decision making).

CONCEPTS TIED TO THE SELF USED TO EXAMINE OTHER BEHAVIORS RELATED TO CLOTHING

Our discussion of the concept of the self and its relationship to dress thus far in this chapter has centered on understanding how beliefs about the self are influenced by clothing or tied to clothing use. There are many terms that make reference to the self. Consider for example terms such as *self-efficacy* or *self-esteem*. For the remainder of this chapter we present a discussion of some of the research that links dress to various concepts tied to the self. These concepts include self-consciousness, self-monitoring, self-objectification, self-actualization, and self-esteem. You will see that the researchers interested in these concepts were not focused on explaining or understanding experiences of self but rather were interested in understanding whether various aspects of the self were helpful in explaining behaviors related to clothing. Researchers focused on understanding interest in clothing, how clothing was used, and decision making concerning clothing (Kwon, 1992; Kwon & Shim, 1999; Lee & Burns, 1993; Miller, Davis, & Rowold, 1982; Solomon & Schopler, 1982). What follows is a discussion of these aspects of the self as they relate to decision making and behaviors concerning dress.

Self-Consciousness Theory

Self-consciousness theory is concerned with the extent to which an individual's attention is focused on the inner (reflexive consciousness) or outer (interpersonal) aspects of self. According to self-consciousness theory, when self-consciousness is directed outward, focus is on oneself as a social object. This focus is called public self-consciousness. When self-consciousness is directed inward, one is likely to focus on one's inner feelings, moods, or beliefs. This focus is called private self-consciousness (Buss, 1980). There has been research conducted by dress scholars investigating self-consciousness and dress Kwon, 1992; Miller, Davis, & Rowold, 1982; Solomon & Schopler, 1982).

In early work, clothing researchers examined relationships between public self-consciousness, social anxiety, and clothing variables using undergraduate women (Miller, Davis, & Rowold, 1982). Not too surprisingly, they found that young women who were high in public self-consciousness were interested in and involved with clothing. They were also sensitive to their self-presentations and reported experiencing anxiety following criticism of their appearance and their knowledge of fashion.

In similar work, undergraduate men and women completed questionnaires designed to examine whether self-consciousness was related to three clothing measures; fashion opinion leadership, attitudes toward conformity, and clothing interest (Solomon & Schopler, 1982). Some of their findings were inconsistent with the first research team. Public self-consciousness showed a consistent correlation with clothing interest for men but not for women. Public self-consciousness also showed a consistent correlation with attitudes toward conformity in clothing for women, but not for men. Clearly, public self-consciousness has some relationship to being interested in clothing. Perhaps for women, interest in clothing is a given but for men, one has to be self-conscious to admit to one's clothing interest. For women, if interest in clothing is a given, when one is publicly self-conscious being conforming to others in one's clothing choices may reduce any discomfort one might experience when appearing in public.

Kwon (1992) also used self-consciousness theory to investigate relationships between women's attitudes towards clothing practices, self-consciousness, and body consciousness. Self-consciousness in her research was defined as self-awareness directed toward the internal aspects of the self. Publicly self-conscious people tend to focus on themselves as social objects. When people are socially anxious they are in a high state of public self-consciousness. Privately self-conscious people tend to be aware of covert aspects of self, including personal moods and feelings. Body consciousness is awareness of one's physical self. As compared to individuals low in public self-consciousness, individuals high in public self-consciousness agreed with statements indicating that clothing was important to them in presenting themselves. As compared to individuals low in both public and private self-consciousness, individuals high in both agreed with statements indicating that they had a high level of clothing interest[7] and were sensitive to people's clothing

Self-consciousness theory has also been used to investigate causal relationships between self-consciousness, weight satisfaction, and women's use of clothing to enhance mood (Kwon & Shim, 1999). The research built on earlier work (Kwon, 1992). Both public and private self-consciousness had direct and positive effects on women's use of clothing to enhance their mood, such that women

[7]Clothing interest refers to the attitudes and beliefs about clothing, the knowledge of and attention paid to clothing, the concern and curiosity a person has about his/her own clothing and that of others (Gurel & Gurel, 1979, p.12). Researchers studying clothing interest have frequently used a measure developed by Creekmore (1963). Gurel and Gurel factor analyzed Creekmore's (1963) measure of interests in clothing and identified five dimensions. These dimensions are concern with personal appearance, experimentation with appearance, heightened awareness of clothing, enhancement of personal security, and enhancement of individuality. In some studies of clothing interest, not all dimensions of clothing interest have been measured (Kwon, 1992; Perry, Schutz, & Rucker, 1983) which can contribute to inconsistent research results.

used their choice of clothing to enhance their mood and self-image on a daily basis. The effect of public self-consciousness was greater than private self-consciousness, suggesting women high in public self-consciousness alleviate their feelings of public self-consciousness through their clothing selection. This interpretation is consistent with the findings of Solomon and Schopler (1982) again pointing to the strategy of reducing or managing your self-consciousness when you are in a public setting by wearing clothing that you think will make you fit in with others (conform) or with the social situation.

Self-Monitoring

Self-monitoring is a term used to describe the extent to which individuals observe their verbal and nonverbal presentations to fit particular situations (Snyder, 1974). High self-monitors are attentive to situational and interpersonal cues that they use to observe and shape their own self-presentations. We propose that the concept of public self-consciousness and self-monitoring are related concepts. If you are publicly self-conscious it is likely that you would shape your appearance to fit a social situation. Thus, we propose that individuals who are high in public self-consciousness are likely to be high self-monitors. We have not, however, located empirical data to support our proposition.

Davis and Lennon (1985) investigated relationships between self-monitoring, fashion opinion leadership, and attitudes concerning clothing related to one's self-presentation. The attitudes concerning clothing measured the importance of wearing clothing that is socially appropriate (conformity), that projects an image of an assurance

---

IN-CLASS ACTIVITY
Self-Monitoring and Customer Service in an Apparel Store

One wonders if it is possible to judge whether or not a stranger is a high self-monitor by their appearance. Would, for example, most strangers that looked as if they paid attention to their appearance be high self-monitors? And if they were, what are the implications for how they might be treated as clothing shoppers?

(security), and that shows uniqueness (attention seeking). As compared to low self-monitors, individuals who were high self-monitors displayed fashion opinion leadership characteristics, placed more importance on wearing clothing that was socially appropriate, felt using clothing to communicate individual differences was important, and placed more importance on use of clothing to project an image of assurance. Their findings are consistent with the research addressing relationships between public self-consciousness and clothing attitudes discussed previously (Kwon, 1992; Kwon & Shim, 1992; Miller, Davis & Rowald, 1982; Solomon & Schopler, 1982).

Self-Objectification

Self-monitoring activity may be connected to **self-objectification**. Self-objectification is explained by objectification theory. Objectification theory (Fredrickson & Roberts, 1997) is based on the idea that we live in a society that sexually objectifies women and men (Grieve & Helmick, 2008; Strelan & Hargreaves, 2005). Sexual objectification occurs when a person's body or parts of the body (i.e., breasts, legs, chest, buttocks) become solely representative of that person, regardless of other traits or personal attributes the person has.

There are ample depictions of women and men in advertisements that them as mere bodies or body parts posed to highlight products (Adomaitis & Johnson, 2008; Archer, Iritani, Kimes, & Barrios, 1983). So there are ample opportunities to view examples of objectified people. As a result of experiencing objectification, a woman or a man may think she/he has reduced value unless she/he has whatever is designated as the ideal body or body parts. Objectification theory proposes that societal objectification of people teaches them to internalize an outsider's objectified view of themselves. Adopting a self-objectified view can result in continual self-monitoring of appearance because an object's appearance is very important. Adopting this view can also result in negative feelings and behaviors motivated by concerns about the body.

Researchers interested in studying self-objectification in women have focused their attention on how self-objectification influences thoughts about, and behaviors toward, the body. For example, in studying undergraduate women, several researchers have documented that women who self-objectify tend to engage in restrictive eating or other forms of disordered eating (Fredrickson, Roberts,

Noll, Quinn, & Twenge, 1998; Noll & Fredrickson, 1998; Tiggeman & Slater, 2001). People who self-objectify also have depressive symptoms (Muehlenkamp & Saris-Baglama, 2002). Holding negative feelings about the body has been shown to be related to women's willingness to engage in behaviors that are harmful such as cutting themselves or burning themselves (Muehlenkamp, Swanson, & Brausch, 2005).

Self objectification has also been related to activities such as engaging in exercise. Strelan, Mehaffey and Tiggemann (2003) studied women attending fitness centers and found that those who were self-objectifiers were likely to experience reduced body satisfaction, body-esteem, and self-esteem. In addition, women who self-objectified reported exercising more for appearance-related reasons (e.g., attractiveness, body tone, weight control) than for health, enjoyment, or fitness reasons.

Researchers interested in self-objectification within men have suggested that men's degree of self-objectification may be lower in comparison to women (Calogero, Davis, & Thompson, 2005). However, like women, men also engage in appearance-related activities. Men who self-objectified were just as likely as women to exercise for appearance-related reasons (Strelan & Hargreaves, 2005) and this exercise seemed to strengthen the impact of self-objectification on their self-esteem. Men who self-objectified were also found to have a greater drive for building muscle and symptoms associated with muscle dysmorphia, such as muscle disparagement and extensive weight training (Grieve & Helmick, 2008).

Although being able to lose yourself when you are totally immersed in a task has been connected to feelings of maximum happiness and flow (Csikszentmihalyi, 1988), spending prolonged periods of time thinking about the self can also be detrimental and impede your ability to function. A state of self-objectification is thought to lead to an interruption in focused concentration because part of one's attention is continuously allocated to viewing the self (especially the body) as an object. As a first test of whether self-objectification truly impeded performance, Fredrickson and her colleagues (1998) used clothing to manipulate states of self-objectification. They assumed that people would assume an outsider's or third-person perspective and to view their bodies as objects when wearing a one-piece swimsuit as compared to wearing a v-neck sweater. They found that college women as compared to men, after wearing a swimsuit, described themselves more in terms of their bodies, experienced greater body shame, and performed worse on a math test. Others also found that college women in a state of self-objectification demonstrated decreased performance on a color-naming task (Quinn, Kallen, Twenge, & Fredrickson, 2006). In subsequent research, wearing a swimsuit as compared to a v-neck sweater evoked a sense of being defined by one's body for both women and men (Quinn, Kallen, & Cathey, 2006). However, only women reported feeling shame and for those that experienced shame, the feelings of shame lingered after the objectifying stimulus, in this instance having to wear a swimsuit, was removed.

Calogero (2004) reasoned that situations may not have to be specifically body focused (e.g., wearing a swimsuit) to produce negative feelings. Rather, she posited that the anticipation of being the object of an observer's gaze either male or female triggers the negative consequences linked with self-objectification. In a test of her hypothesis with undergraduate women she found that the mere anticipation of being looked at by a male, as compared to a female, was sufficient to evoke some of the negative consequences associated with self-objectification specifically, body shame and anxiety about the body.

Self-Objectification and Adolescents

Adolescence is a time during which young people are developing an increased awareness of self, concerned with their appearance, and concerned with social acceptance (Harter, 1999). With its greater focus on the self, adolescence may be a critical time for the development of self-objectification. Slater and Tiggemann (2002) were interested in investigating whether the predictions of self-objectification theory were applicable to adolescent girls who participated in dance. The researchers compared the responses of young girls aged twelve to sixteen who previously had studied dance to a group of similar young girls who had never studied dance. They anticipated that the young girls that had studied dance would exhibit higher levels of self-objectification than non-dancers as a result of the large amount of time dancers spend performing on stage (where their bodies are looked at by others) as well as the large amount of time spent practicing in front of mirrors and analyzing their bodies. Interestingly, dancers did not exhibit higher levels of self-objectification or self-monitoring than did non-dancers. However, other predictions of self-objectification theory were supported.

Self-objectification did lead to self-monitoring as well as body shame and appearance anxiety. Self-monitoring in turn was predictive of body shame, and body shame led to disordered eating. Thus, objectification theory appears to be applicable to adolescent girls. Left unanswered is at what age self-objectification first appears in girls and whether girls at even younger ages than twelve experience the effects and consequences of self-objectification

Also interested in the effects of self-objectification during adolescence, Grabe, Hyde, and Lindberg (2007) conducted a longitudinal study to address consequences of self-objectification (e.g., depression) with boys and girls (at age eleven and thirteen) and possible mediators (i.e., body shame, rumination) of the relationship between self-objectification and depression. They reasoned that the constant self-surveillance that arises from self-objectification may increase body shame among girls because it highlights their inability to achieve an idealized body. They also reasoned that self-surveillance elicits a disruptive state of consciousness that is reflected by passive worry (i.e., rumination) and self-hindering thought patterns. These self-hindering thought patterns may focus on the areas of concern (e.g., I am too fat) and the resulting meanings of that concern (e.g., I have no value). Self-surveillance at age eleven was hypothesized to predict body shame and rumination at age thirteen, which in turn was hypothesized to predict depression. The thirteen-year-old girls reported higher levels of body surveillance, body shame, rumination, and depression than the thirteen-year-old boys. Self-surveillance did significantly predict depression for girls but not for boys. Both body shame and rumination did mediate the relationship between self-surveillance and depression for girls. In other words, both experiences of body shame and rumination explain the link between body surveillance and depression. For boys, the outcome was similar except that body surveillance only predicted body shame and depression. When boys experienced body shame they were also at risk to experience depression. Future researchers interested in the effects of self-objectification might focus their attention on identifying other consequences of a young boy's self-objectification.

Self-Actualization

Self-actualization is a concept that stems from Maslow's (1968) work on personality (see Chapter 8, "Dress and Personality" for additional discussion of this concept). Self-actualization is a stage in development reflecting that an individual had achieved his or her full potential. Perry, Schutz, and Rucker (1983) were interested in using the concept of self-actualization to explore the relationship between personality and clothing interest with adults. They found that as individuals became self-actualized, they exhibited low levels of clothing interest; that is, were unconcerned with their personal appearance and did not experiment with it. This finding suggests that on our way to being all that we can be, our interest and concern about dress, and even perhaps other material things, diminishes.

Self-Esteem

Self-esteem involves a subjective evaluation of one's traits resulting in a positive or negative attitude toward the self (Rosenberg, 1965). Research findings addressing relationships between dress and self-esteem have been inconsistent. Chowdhary (1988) investigated relationships between clothing choice and self-esteem. She reasoned that elderly

---

INDUSTRY APPLICATION

WEARING BRANDS AS INDICATOR OF SELF?

We noted in this chapter that when people wear clothing (e.g., sweatshirts) that clearly announce an apparel brand or a retail store (e.g., Gap), individuals who view and try to interpret the meaning of that apparel item and its relationship to the individual can question what the wearer is trying to communicate. Is the message something about oneself or have retailers simply convinced consumers to be walking advertisements for their brands? At least one individual has taken the approach that if he is going to advertise for a company he is going to get paid for it. Andrew Fischer, known as the forehead guy, claims to have earned $50,000 for wearing advertisements on his forehead (Gonsalves, 2006). Fischer is not the only person to offer part of his body as human advertising space, but he was one of the first. Is Andrew Fischer on to something?

individuals with low self-esteem would choose classic styles of clothing, as compared to elderly, with high self-esteem. She also contended that elderly individuals with youthful self-perceptions would select trendier clothing styles than elderly individuals with "old" self-perceptions. Neither self-esteem nor age-related self-perceptions influenced elderly individuals' clothing style preferences. Holloman (1989) also investigated the relationship between self-esteem and clothing attitudes among black adults to determine if differences existed between the responses of men and women. Clothing attitudes measured included the use of clothing to attract attention, to enhance and compliment an individual, to express awareness of others, to gain approval of others, to provide comfort and protect the body, to show uniqueness, and to demonstrate creativity. For both men and women, self-esteem was connected to the use of clothing to enhance and complement an individual and to provide comfort and protect the body. For men only, self-esteem was negatively related to using clothing to attract the attention and to express awareness of others or to gain approval of others.

Chapter Summary

Researchers studying relationships between dress and experiences of self that are signs of reflexive consciousness utilized two theoretical approaches and a limited number of expressions of self. Self-perception theory indicates that people could use their own clothing to make inferences about themselves. Symbolic self-completion theory proposes that when individuals experience a sense of incompleteness concerning an attribute, they will strive to obtain a symbol of that attribute and hence achieve a sense of wholeness.

During the past twenty-five years, self-esteem was the only experience of reflexive consciousness that was investigated relative to clothing. Baumeister (1998) identified other experiences of self that may be related to clothing. For example, what relationships might exist between clothing and self-awareness? Another experience of reflexive consciousness that may be related to dress is self-deception. How do people use dress to maintain high self-esteem and other inflated views of themselves?

In the past twenty-five years, researchers have focused their attention on relationships between interpersonal aspects of the self and dress from the perspective provided by symbolic interaction. They have documented that dress is used in constructing aspects of the self in the realm of make believe or pretend and that dress is used both to reveal and conceal alternate personae in everyday life. Attention has been paid to the use of dress to communicate public, private, and secret aspects of the self. Others interested in pursuing this line of research may want to use open-ended questions to explore individuals' use of clothing to communicate private and secret aspects of self and to determine the contexts within which these components of self are communicated publicly or privately.

Findings might also differ according to age, ethnicity, or sexual orientation.

Symbolic self-completion theory was also used in research concerning relationships between interpersonal aspects of self and clothing. As individuals move in and out of different organizations they both acquire and leave behind aspects of the self.

Dress is an important tool to enhance self-presentation. People purposefully achieve desired selves through use of dress. Such behaviors can be risky. For example, people suntan to look healthy and fashionable. The practice of suntanning is linked to skin cancer, but people continue to suntan. Although it has been documented that people engage in risky appearance management behaviors, what relationship engagement in risky appearance management behaviors has to the self remains uninvestigated.

Not all clothing that is worn is related to self. Clothing choice can often be an automatic process engaged in with little thought. Guy and Banim (2000) found that some women expressed ambivalence when making decisions about what to wear. How often and to what extent this is the case, may be worthy of our attention least we make too much of the importance of clothing to self.

Of the three experiences of self, reflexive, interpersonal, and executive (Baumeister, 1998), the executive function is a relatively unexplored area. Clearly, this is a potential research area. In addition to research concerning the role of self in decision making about what to buy, researchers might consider the role of the self in deciding what to wear. It might also be informative to study relationships between aspects of self and brand. Do consumers purchase certain brands to convey an existing self-image or to buy a new one?

Key Terms

brand management
collective self
congruity theory
costume
domains of the self
executive function
generalized other
ideal self-concept
interpersonal aspects of self
intimate self

looking-glass self
priming
private self
program
proximity of clothing to self (PCS)
public self
real-self concept
reflexive consciousness
review

secret self
self
self-concept
self-consciousness theory
self definitions
self discrepancy
self discrepancy theory
self-esteem
self-image
self-knowledge

self-monitoring
self-objectification
self-perception theory
self-produced cues
situational cues
symbolic self-completion theory
unified self

Discussion Questions

1. Using symbolic self-completion theory, explain how dress can be used in the process of taking on new self-definitions.

2. Explain how a "make-over" can be successful utilizing self-perception theory.

3. Assume you have just been hired as a new manager. Explain how dress could be used to assist you in assuming this leadership position using Stone's (1962) concepts of program, review, validation, and challenge.

4. It may be possible to identify high self-monitors by looking at their appearance. What indicators might be useful in determining whether a shopper is a high or low self-monitor?

5. What is self-objectification? How do clothing choices made by women contribute to their objectification and subsequent self-objectification?

STUDIO™

Visit your book's STUDIO for additional quiz questions, vocabulary flashcards, and chapter worksheets!

Suggested Readings

Chang, H-J., Hodges, N., & Yurchisin, J. (2014). Consumers with disabilities: A qualitative exploration of clothing selection and use among female college students. *Clothing and Textiles Research Journal, 32*(1), 34–48.

Fredrickson, B., & Roberts, T. (1997). Objectification theory. *Psychology of Women Quarterly, 21*, 173–206.

Johnson, K. K. P., Lennon, S., & Rudd, N. (2014). Dress, body, and the self: Research in the social psychology of dress. *Fashion and Textiles, 1*, 1–24.

References

Adomaitis, A., & Johnson, K. K. P. (2008). Advertisements: Interpreting images used to sell young adults. *Journal of Fashion Marketing and Management, 12*(2), 182–192.

Archer, D., Iritani, B., Kimes, D., & Barrios, M. (1983). Facism: Five studies of sex differences in facial prominence. *Journal of Personality and Social Psychology, 45,* 725–735.

Arthur, L. (1997). Role salience, role embracement, and the symbolic self-completion of sorority pledges. *Sociological Inquiry, 67*(3), 364–379.

Baumeister, R. (1998). The self. In Gilbert, D., Fiske, S., & Lindzey, G. (Eds). *The Handbook of Social Psychology, Vol. 1,* (4th ed.). (pp. 680–740). New York, NY: McGraw-Hill.

Belk, R. W., & Costa, J. A. The mountain man myth: A contemporary consuming fantasy. *Journal of Consumer Research, 25,* 218–240.

Bem, D. (1972). Self-perception theory. In L. Berkowitz (Ed.) *Advances in experimental social psychology Vol. 6* (pp. 1–62). New York, NY: Academic Press.

Buss, A. H. (1980). *Self-consciousness and social anxiety.* San Francisco, CA: W.H. Freeman.

Calogero, R. (2004). A test of objectification theory: The effect of the male gaze on appearance concerns in college women. *Psychology of Women Quarterly, 28,* 16–21.

Calogero, R., Davis, W. & Thompson, J. K. (2005). The role of self-objectification in the experience of women with eating disorders. *Sex Roles, 52,* 43–50.

Chowdhary, U. (1988). Self-esteem, age identification, and media exposure of the elderly and their relationship to fashionability. *Clothing and Textiles Research Journal, 7*(1), 23–30.

Cooley, C. (1902). *Human nature and the social order.* New York, NY: Scribner.

Creekmore, A. M. (1963). Clothing behaviors and their relation to general values and to the striving for basic needs. Ph.D. dissertation, Pennsylvania State University, University Park, PA.

Csikszentmihalyi, M. (1988). The flow experience and its significance for human psychology. In M. Csikszentmihalyi & I. S. Csikszentmihalyi (Eds.). *Optimal experience: Psychological studies of flow in consciousness* (pp. 15–35). New York, NY: Cambridge University Press.

Davis, L. L., & Lennon, S. (1985). Self-monitoring, fashion opinion leadership, and attitudes toward clothing. In M. Solomon (Ed.), *The psychology of fashion* (pp. 177–182). Lexington; MA: Lexington Books.

Damhorst, M. L. (1985). Meanings of clothing cues in social context. *Clothing and Textiles Research Journal, 3*(2), 39-48.

Duca, L. (2014, October 27). What it's really like to get extreme plastic surgery, from a former 'Swan' contestant. *Huffington Post.* Retrieved from http://www.huffingtonpost.com/2014/10/27/extreme-plastic-surgery_n_6036110.html

Eicher, J. B. (1981). Influences of changing resources on clothing, textiles and the quality of life: Dressing for reality, fun, and fantasy. Combined proceedings, Eastern, Central, and Western Regional Meetings of Association of College Professors of Textiles and Clothing, 36–41.

Eicher, J. B., Baizerman, S., & Michelman, J. (1991). Adolescent dress, Part II: A qualitative study of suburban high school students. *Adolescence, 26,* 679–686.

Erickson, M. K., & Sirgy, M. J. (1989). Achievement motivation and clothing behavior: A self-image congruence analysis. *Journal of Social Behavior and Personality, 4*(4), 307–326.

Feather, B., Kaiser, S., & Rucker, M. (1989). Breast reconstruction and prosthesis use as forms of symbolic completion of the physical self. *Home Economics Research Journal, 17*(3), 216–227.

Feinberg, R., Mataro, L., & Burroughs, W. (1992). Clothing and social identity. *Clothing and Textiles Research Journal, 11*(1), 18–19.

Fredrickson, B., & Roberts, T. (1997). Objectification theory. *Psychology of Women Quarterly, 21,* 173–206.

Fredrickson, B., & Roberts, T., Noll, S., Quinn, D., & Twenge, J. (1998). That swimsuit becomes you: Sex differences in self-objectification, restrained eating, and math performance. *Journal of Personality and Social Psychology, 75,* 269–284.

Gergen, K. J. (2000). *The saturated self: Dilemmas of identity in contemporary life.* New York, NY: Basic Books.

Gillooly, J. (2009, October 8). Teen, N. Cobb High clash over dress code. *Marietta Daily Journal.* Retrieved from http://www.mdjonline.com/pages/full_story/push?article-Teen-+N-+Cobb+High+clash+over+dress+code%20&id=3886905-Teen-+N-+Cobb+High+clash+over+dress+code&instance=special%20_coverage_right_column

Gonsalves, A. (2006). Forehead guy is ready to wear ads again. *Informationweek.* Retrieved from http://www.informationweek.com/forehead-guy-is-ready-to-wear-ads-again/d/d-id/1039429?

Grabe, S., Hyde, J., & Lindberg, S. (2007). Body objectification and depression in adolescents: The role of gender, shame, and rumination. *Psychology of Women Quarterly, 31,* 164–175.

Grieve, R. & Helmick, A. (2008). The influence of men's self-objectification on the drive for muscularity: self-esteem, body satisfaction and muscle dysmorphia. *International Journal of Men's Health, 7*(3), 288–298.

Gurel, L.M., & Gurel, L. (1979). Clothing interest: Conceptualization and measurement. *Home Economics Research Journal, 7,* 274–281

Guy, A., & Banim, M. (2000). Personal collections: Women's clothing use and identity. *Journal of Gender Studies, 9*(3), 313–327.

Hannover, B., & Kühnen, U. (2002). "The clothing makes the self" via knowledge activation. *Journal of Applied Social Psychology, 32*(12), 2513–2525.

Harter, S. (1999). *The construction of the self: A developmental perspective.* New York, NY: Guilford.

Hendricks, S. H., Kelley, E. A., & Eicher, J. B. (1968). Senior girls' appearance and social participation. *Journal of Home Economics, 60,* 167–172.

Higgins, E. T. (1996). The "self digest": Self-knowledge serving self-regulatory functions. *Journal of Personality and Social Psychology, 71,* 1062–1083.

Holloman, L. (1989). Self-esteem and selected clothing attitudes of black adults: Implications for counselling. *Journal of Multicultural Counselling and Development, 17,* 50–61.

Hunt, S., & Miller, K. (1997). The discourse of dress and appearance: Identity talk and a rhetoric of review. *Symbolic Interaction, 20*(1), 69–82

James, W. (1948/1892). *Psychology.* Cleveland, OH: World Publishing.

Johnson, K.K.P., & Roach-Higgins, M. (1987a). The influence of physical attractiveness and dress on campus recruiter's impressions of female job applicants. Home Economics Research Journal, 16, 87–95.

Johnson, K.K.P., & Roach-Higgins, M. (1987b). Dress and physical attractiveness of women in job interviews. *Clothing and Textiles Research Journal, 5,* 1–8.

Kaiser, S. (1997). *The social psychology of clothing* (2nd ed.). New York, NY: Fairchild.

Kellerman, J., & Laird, J. (1982). The effect of appearance on self-perceptions. *Journal of Personality, 50*(3). 296–315.

Kelley, E. A., & Eicher, J. B. (1970). Popularity, group membership, and dress. *Journal of Home Economics, 62,* 246–250.

Knibbs, K. (2014, March 23). Now you can get custom fashion advice based on your Instagram selfies. *Daily Dot.* Retrieved May 27, 2014 from http://www.dailydot.com/lifestyle/zappos-instagram-fashion/

Kwon, Y. (1992). Body consciousness, self-consciousness, and women's attitudes toward clothing practices. *Social Behavior and Personality, 20*(4), 295–307.

Kwon, Y. (1994). The influence of appropriateness of dress and gender on the self-perception of occupational attributes. *Clothing and Textile Research Journal, 12*(3), 33–39.

Kwon, Y., & Johnson-Hillery, J. (1998). College students' perceptions of occupational attributes based on formality of business attire. *Perceptual & Motor Skills, 87*(3), 987–994.

Kwon, Y., & Shim, S. (1999). A structural model for weight satisfaction, self-consciousness, and women's use of clothing in mood enhancement. *Clothing and Textiles Research Journal, 17*(4), 203–212.

Lee, M., & Burns, L. (1993). Self-consciousness and clothing purchase criteria of Korean and United States college women. *Clothing and Textiles Research Journal, 11*(4), 32–40.

Littrell, M. B., & Eicher, J. B. (1973). Clothing opinions and the social acceptance process among adolescents. *Adolescence, 8,* 197–212.

Markus, H. & Nurius, P. (1986). Possible selves. *American Psychologist, 41,* 954–969.

Maslow, A. (1968). *Toward a psychology of being.* New York, NY: John Wiley and Sons.

Mead, G. H. (1934). *Mind, self and society.* Chicago, IL: University of Chicago Press.

Michelman, S. (1997). Changing old habits: Dress of women religious and its relationship to personal and social identity. *Sociological Inquiry, 67*(3), 350–363.

Michelman, J. D., Eicher, J.B., & Michelman, S.O. (1991). Adolescent dress, Part I: Dress and body markings of psychiatric outpatients and inpatients. *Adolescence, 26,* 375–385.

Miller, F., Davis, L., & Rowold, K. (1982). Public self-consciousness, social anxiety, and attitudes toward the use of clothing. *Home Economics Research Journal, 10*(4), 363–368.

Miller, K. A. (1997). Dress: Private and secret self-expression. *Clothing & Textiles Research Journal, 15*(4), 223–234.

Miller, K. A. (1998). Gender comparisons within reenactment costume: Theoretical interpretations. *Family and Consumer Sciences Research Journal, 27*(1), 35–61.

Muehlenkamp, J., Saris-Baglama, R. (2002). Self-objectification and its psychological outcomes for college women. *Psychology of Women Quarterly, 26,* 371–379.

Muehlenkamp, J., Swanson, J., & Brausch, A. (2005). Self-objectification, risk taking, and self-harm in college women. *Psychology of Women Quarterly, 29,* 24–32.

Noll, S. M., & Fredrickson, B. (1998). A mediational model linking self-objectification, body shame, and disordered eating. *Psychology of Women Quarterly, 22,* 623–636.

Perry, M. O., Schutz, H. G., & Rucker, M. H. (1983). Clothing interest, self-actualization, and demographic variables. *Home Economics Research Journal, 11*(3), 280–288.

Quinn, D., Kallen, R., & Cathey, C. (2006). Body on my mind: The lingering effect of state self-objectification. *Sex Roles, 55,* 869–874.

Quinn, D., Kallen, R., Twenge, J., & Fredrickson, B. (2006). The disruptive effect of self-objectification on performance. *Psychology of Women Quarterly, 30,* 59–64.

Rhee, J., & Johnson, K. K. P. (2007). Investigating relationships between branded apparel and identity with adolescents. Paper presented at the International Textiles and Apparel Association annual meeting, Los Angeles, CA

Roach-Higgins, M. E., & Eicher, J. B. (1992). Dress and identity. *Clothing and Textiles Research Journal, 10,* 1–8.

Rosenberg, M. (1965). *Society and the adolescent self-image.* Princeton, NJ: Princeton University Press.

Scherbaum, C., & Shaperd, D. (1987). Dressing for success: Effects of color and layering on perception of women in business. *Sex Roles, 16*(7), 391–399.

Sirgy, M. J. (1982). Self-concept in consumer behavior: A critical review. *Journal of Consumer Research, 9*(3), 287–300.

Slater, A., & Tiggemann, M. (2002). A test of objectification theory in adolescent girls. *Sex Roles, 46*(9/10), 343–349.

Smucker, B., & Creekmore, A. M. (1972). Adolescents' clothing conformity, awareness, and peer acceptance. *Home Economics Research Journal, 1,* 92–97.

Snyder, M. (1974). Self-monitoring of expressive behavior. *Journal of Personality and Social Psychology, 30,* 526–537.

Solomon, M. R., & Scholper, J. (1982). Self-consciousness and clothing. *Personality and Social Psychology Bulletin, 8*(3), 508–514.

Sontag, M. S., & Schlater J. D. (1982). Proximity of clothing to self: Evolution of a concept. *Clothing and Textiles Research Journal, 1,* 1–8.

Sontag, M. S., & Lee, J. (2004). Proximity of clothing to self scale. *Clothing and Textiles Research Journal, 22*(4), 161–177.

Strelan, P. & Hargreaves, D. (2005). Reasons for exercise and body esteem: Men's responses to self-objectification. *Sex Roles, 53*(7/8), 495–503.

Strelan, P., Mehaffey, S., & Tiggeman, M. (2003). Self-objectification and esteem in young women: The mediating role of reasons for exercise. *Sex Roles, 48*(1/2), 89–95.

Stone, G. P. (1962). Appearance and the self. In A. M. Rose (Ed.), *Human behavior and social processes: An interactionist approach* (pp. 86–118). New York, NY: Houghton Mifflin.

Tawfiq, W., & Ogle, J. P. (2013). Constructing and presenting the self through private sphere dress: An interpretative analysis of the experiences of Saudi Arabian women. *Clothing and Textiles Research Journal, 31*(4), 275–290.

Thurston, J.L., Lennon, S.J., & Clayton, R.V. (1990). Influence of age, body type, fashion and garment typed on women's professional image. *Home Economics Research Journal, 19*(12), 139–150.

Tiggemann, M., & Slater, A. (2001). A test of objectification theory in former dancers and non-dancers. *Psychology of Women Quarterly, 25*, 57–64.

Teelon, E. (1992). Self-presentation through appearance: A manipulative vs. a dramaturgical approach. *Symbolic Interaction, 15*(4), 501–513.

Triandis, H.C. (1989). The self and social behavior in differing cultural contexts. *Psychological Review, 96*(3), 506–520.

Wickland, R., & Gollwitzer, P. (1982). *Symbolic self-completion*. Hillsdale, NJ: Lawrence Erlbaum.

Williams, M. C., & Eicher, J. B. (1966). Teenagers' appearance and social acceptance. *Journal of Home Economics, 58*, 457–461.

Yeung, K., & Martin, J. (2003). The looking glass self: An empirical test and elaboration. *Social Forces, 81*(3), 843–879.

Yurchisin, J., & Johnson, K. K. P. (2004). Compulsive buying behavior and its relationship to perceived social status associated with buying, materialism, self-esteem, and apparel-product involvement. *Family and Consumer Sciences Research Journal, 32*(3), 291–314.

3 SOCIOLOGICAL PERSPECTIVES ON DRESS

CHAPTER

10 DRESS AND IDENTITY

After reading and reflecting on the content of this chapter, students will be able to:

- **Evaluate the role of dress in identity construction.**

- **Explain how dress is used as a prop in negotiation of identity.**

- **Analyze how dress can be used to resist a stigmatized identity.**

INTRODUCTION

In Chapter 9, "Dress and the Self" we said that the self is a dynamic interactive system of beliefs, feelings, and motives that characterize you as an individual. But because humans are complex, our selves are multi-dimensional. In the mornings you attend classes (i.e., you are a student), on weekends you play basketball with other members of your team (i.e., you are an athlete). To acknowledge this diversity, we say that the self is composed of several identities. It is important to understand that scholars do not agree in their definitions of *identity*. For example, identity has been described as a concept that has not been precisely defined (Brown, 1985, p. 551). For the purposes of this book, think of an identity as an organized set of characteristics that express the various aspects of who you are (i.e., your self). The concept of identity recognizes the complexity of the self.

Think of yourself as a student, a retail employee, or an athlete. Each of these descriptors represents an identity that characterizes you. Think about how you behave and dress when you are participating in an athletic competition and compare that to how you behave and dress when you are in a classroom attending class. In an athletic competition, you might be wearing a basketball uniform and socks in your team colors, with basketball shoes while running up and down the court. In your classroom, you are probably sitting down and taking notes, while wearing jeans, a T-shirt or sweater (depending on the weather). We use our dress to **announce** or communicate our identities (Figure 10.1). That is, the basketball uniform and socks with basketball shoes communicates the athlete identity, while the jeans and T-shirt or sweater communicates the student identity when worn in a classroom. Table 10.1 contains instances of identities and examples of dress that announce those identities.

We can think of an identity as a "self-in-context" or a **situated self** (Kaiser, 1997). This means that in some contexts or situations you will dress and act differently than in others as a function of which identity is salient (important) in the given situation. Identities are developed through social interaction. Ordinarily you cannot just

Figure 10.1
This Muslim woman's burkini expresses her religious identity and her identity as a lifesaver on an Australian beach.

TABLE 10.1

IDENTITY DRESS

Type of Dress	Identity	Type of Identity
Class sweater	Member of sophomore class in high school	Collective (class, school member or alum)
Class ring	Student of a specific university	Collective (class, school member or alum)
Prep school ties	School specific	Collective (prep school student)
Individualizations of graduation attire	Personality expression	Personal
Hat, apron, plastic gloves	Food service worker	Role (occupational)
Tutu, toe shoes	Ballerina	Role (occupational or leisure)
Mother-daughter dresses	Parent, child	Role (relational)
Burqini or burkini (bathing suit that covers hair, arms, legs)[1] (Figure 10.1)	Muslim	Collective (religious)
Senior cords[2] (Figures 10.2 and 10.3)	High school/college senior in Indiana; personality	Collective, personal

[1]A burqini is a swim suit designed for Muslim women that is considered modest and covers the head, hair, arms to wrists and legs to ankles (National Post, 2009). See Figure 10.1 for a burkini.

[2]Senior cords are cream-colored corduroy pants/skirts worn by Indiana seniors (high schools, and some universities) until the 1970s. Senior cords were decorated with embroidery "paints" and designs were selected to reflect the wearer's personal interests and membership groups (Schlick & Rowold, 1991). See Figures 10.2 and 10.3 for pictures of senior cords.

Figure 10.2

Senior cords were worn by high school seniors and reflected their interests and identities. Interests indicated on the skirt are ice-skating, bowling, and the owner possibly worked at Frisch's Big Boy restaurant. Senior cords worn in Richmond, Indiana high school in the 1960s.

Figure 10.3

The back of the senior cords in Figure 10.2. Additional interests on the back of the skirt include the team mascot (Red Devils), the owner took shorthand, and she may have been a basketball cheerleader. Senior cords worn in Richmond, Indiana high school in the 1960s.

assume any identity you desire, others must acknowledge that you have the identity in question for it to be more than a fantasy or daydream on your part. We acquire an identity when we are located or placed as social objects by others who acknowledge us as having the identity in question (Stone, 1962). You are acknowledged as having an identity when you are treated as if that identity is part of who you are. Another way to say this is that your identity is established when the social category you announce for yourself is the same as the one you are placed in by others. Recall that categorization was discussed in Chapter 4, "Dress and Social Cognition." A **placement** is a category to which others assign you. Thus, categorization by others and by oneself is one process that establishes identity. See Figure 10.4 for individuals that we can place as serious cyclists.

Figure 10.4

Perceivers use these men's dress to place them as serious cyclists.

NEGOTIATION OF IDENTITY

When your announcement of an identity coincides with others' placements of you, the identity in question becomes a meaning of your self. For example, suppose that you take a job as a manager of a department in a store following graduation and your subordinates are all older than you. How should you establish your identity as a professional? Your age definitely works against you, because youth is associated with novice status. You need to behave in a professional way: treat everyone fairly and complete tasks in a well-organized way. You may decide to establish your identity by creating a professional appearance (e.g., wear tailored clothing). However, you can engage in a variety of behaviors including ordering people around but unless your subordinates respond to you as a manager, you have not established a manager identity. Treating everyone fairly, completing tasks in a well-organized way, wearing tailored clothing are behaviors that are part of the **identity negotiation process**. We say that identities are negotiated through interactions with others. It may take several attempts on your part, as well as some time, to successfully negotiate any identity.

Another way identity negotiation is referred to is with the term *self-verification*. Recall from Chapter 4, "Dress and Social Cognition" that self-verification is the process of trying to confirm one's own view of oneself (Swann, 1984, 1987). The idea is that we want others to see us as we see ourselves and we do this by attempting to get feedback that confirms or verifies our self-view. According to Swann, one way we can get confirming feedback (reviews) is by displaying identity cues. Identity cues are visible cues that allow us to "look the part." Effective identity cues must (a) be under the control of the person and (b) reliably evoke the desired response. Returning to the example of department manager, the visible cue of tailored clothing

is under your control, satisfying one condition of an identity cue. However, does this cue reliably indicate department manager to most people? If not, that might suggest that it is hard to negotiate a department manager identity using this identity cue. On the other hand, the identity of law enforcement officer is associated with visible cues to identity: a uniform in somber colors, holstered weapon, and insignia or badge. In describing how we can lay claim to identities by looking the part, Swann mentions various types of dress as possible identity cues: clothing, cosmetics, and wigs; body modifications cited are dieting, weightlifting, and cosmetic surgery.

We do not always receive feedback that confirms identities we acknowledge for ourselves. After receiving discrepant feedback, we might re-interpret it in a way that conforms to a desired identity (Swann, 1987). We also resist negative or discredited identifications. Sometimes people disassociate themselves from undesired identities through the use of consumer products that act as identity cues (Banister & Hogg, 2004; Berger & Heath, 2007; Freitas, Kaiser, Hall, Kim, & Hammidi, 1997; McCormick, 2003). McCormick conducted qualitative research among high school students. She found that teens acknowledged and resisted identities, partly through the use of clothing. Freitas et al. describe how, in addition to using clothing to negotiate identity, their respondents also managed clothing to negotiate who they were not (Figure 10.5). These researchers explained that people strive for favored identities given discredited or stigmatized labels, such as aging, homosexuality, or ethnicity. UK researchers Banister and Hogg made a similar argument based on their interviews with British consumers. Their view was that discarded consumer goods (i.e., clothing items) are rejected because the goods reflect a negative identity, such as membership in an undesirable group (e.g., "Essex boys,[3]" tart). So as a way to disavow the group identity, consumers negotiated identities by rejecting products associated with negative imagery (e.g., by avoiding wearing the "wrong" item). Berger and Heath began with the premise that not all products signal identity. For example, favorite music or hairstyle are mentioned as products that signal identity, whereas backpacks and toothpaste do not. They found that consumers often differentiate themselves from others to signal their identities and to avoid signaling undesired identities. They

[3]*Essex Boys* is a British crime film about drug dealers who were murdered in 1995.

Figure 10.5
Individuals can work to establish as well as disestablish identities (e.g., geek, nerd, loser) that others attribute to them.

suggest that product features which are non-functional or **afunctional** are more likely to serve as signals of identity than functional features. For example, shoes have a function but shoe brand and shoe style are less functional and, therefore, more likely to signal identity.

IDENTITY THEORY

Identity theory evolved from an extension of structural symbolic interaction (Stryker, 1968, 2007; Stryker & Serpe, 1982; Serpe, 1987). Identity theory is an **interactionist theory**. It focuses on interactions between two or more people. For this reason it is called a **microsociological theory** or a theory which studies small parts of society. Within any social system, there are socially recognized positions. Some examples are parent, child, lawyer, president, and teacher. Each social position has behavior associated with it called a role, which can include behaviors related to dress. The role of a parent includes acting in ways that are kind, gentle, loving, nurturing, helpful, and encouraging, but also providing and laundering clothing. Within different societies or groups, people place more or less value on different social positions. The term **stratification** is used to describe this process. As a result, each social position is linked to a status or specific place within a set of social positions.

The notion or view of how identities are linked with specific individuals has changed over time. Identity was once considered to be determined at birth according to an historic analysis (Zukin & Maguire, 2004). People were born into a family with siblings (or not). That family was also linked with a social class. Consequently, upon birth a female child assumed identities of daughter, sister, and possibly middle class family member. This view of identity is consistent with one stream of sociological thought which uses the term *identity* to describe social relationships between individuals such as mother/daughter and brother/sister (Stryker, 2007). These **relational identities** appeared to be lifelong identities and permanent because people cannot change their parents or their siblings; these identities can also be symbolized by wearing matching or coordinated outfits (Figure 10.6). Similarly, in some societies it is difficult if not impossible to move from one social class to another.

Sociologists considered the self to consist of a set of identities and each identity was thought to be related to a particular role (Stryker & Serpe, 1982; Stryker & Burke, 2000). Such identities, called relational identities, influence behavior because each one of these identities has a

IN-CLASS ACTIVITY
Role of a Teaching Assistant

You have all attended classes for which there were teaching assistants. If you were asked to serve as a teaching assistant, what behaviors do you think would be expected of you? Would you dress any differently in the role of a TA? Brainstorm with a partner and list at least four behaviors expected of a teaching assistant.

Figure 10.6

Prince William and his son Prince George; identities such as father–son can be symbolized by wearing matching or coordinating outfits.

related role with a set of behavioral expectations attached to it, which may include expectations for dress. In this tradition, identities are meanings that we (and others) attribute to ourselves in a role (Stryker & Serpe, 1982).

However, other scholars concede that we have identities that are not associated with social positions. These identities have been called **personal identities** or **individual identities** and are associated with traits (Rosenberg & Gara, 1985, p. 88; Stryker, 2007). Personality characteristics form the basis for specific personal identities. For example, some people are naturally sociable, funny, introverted, or helpful. Recall from Chapter 8, "Dress and Personality" that there are some personality characteristics that can be reliably judged from one's dress. A third type of identity is called collective, group, or social identity and its basis or source is group membership (Ashmore, Deaux, & McLaughlin-Volpe, 2004; Vignoles, Regalia, Manzi, Golledge, & Scabini, 2006). Examples of **collective identities** include ethnic, gender, and religious identities. These bases of identity are also mentioned in Chapter 9, "Dress and the Self."

Another example of a collective identity is a heavy rock music festival identity, an identity that people "shift into" or construct partly through dress when attending heavy rock music festivals (Chaney & Goulding, 2016). Qualitative researchers from the UK and France conducted participant observation and interviews at two heavy rock music festivals in Europe over a five-year period that included seven visits to the festivals. When participants attended the festivals they left their usual (normal, work day) identities behind and adopted mostly black clothing, T-shirts decorated with grisly images, and gothic makeup to signal their temporary collective identity. Some wore studded accessories such as belts and bracelets. The heavy rock music festival identity created by participants and expressed partly through dress was an escape from daily life. In like manner, college students who celebrate Halloween in the US and wear costumes do so because the costumes allow them to adopt a different identity and afford freedom from social norms for a day (Miller, Jasper, & Hill, 1991; Mueller, Dirks, & Picca, 2007).

Identity theory builds on the assumptions, definitions, and propositions of symbolic interaction. The two assumptions of the theory concern the relationships between the self and society (Serpe, 1987). The first is that the structure of the self is relatively stable over time when social relationships are stable. The second is that changes in the structure of the self are directly related to movement within the social structure. So according to the theory, change in the self is tied to change in the structure of social relationships. This change in the self may be symbolized by dress. For example, US college seniors wear academic gowns to their graduation ceremonies. The gown symbolizes a change in the self (i.e., student to [hopefully] employed worker).

Movement in the social structure (social relationships) can be freely chosen (e.g., when you decide to get married) or can be brought about by normal life circumstances (e.g., when a child becomes an adolescent). Identity theory would suggest that both of these movements are accompanied by changes in the structure of the self. Thus, you might acquire a new identity and put aside an old one. When you marry you acquire the spouse identity, which is a relational or role-related identity, and you no longer claim the single identity. When you transition into puberty, you put aside the child identity and associated activities and become an adolescent (see Figure 10.7).

We establish identities through the processes of apposition and opposition (Stone (1962). **Apposition** is the process of bringing a person together with others who are similar (i.e., who claim the same identity). Through apposition individuals develop a sense of belonging or similarity to other group members. This sense of belonging offers stability to members (Tajfel, 1972, p. 293). Continuing with the previous examples, after marriage you become a spouse. You then may have things in common with all other spouses (e.g., establishing a home) that may set you apart from those who are singles. After childhood when you become an adolescent you have things in common with other adolescents (e.g., listening to popular music, experimenting with appearance styles) that set you apart from children. These are examples of apposition.

The other process in establishing identity is opposition. **Opposition** describes how the new identity sets you apart from others. Distinctiveness in identity serves the need to be different from others (Brewer, 1991). So as explained earlier, as an adolescent you no longer had the identity of child. Perhaps on becoming an adolescent you recall feeling so much more mature than your siblings or cousins who were still children. In this way, through your level of maturity, your interest in music, and your experimentation with appearance styles, you were set apart from your previous child identity. Continuing with the marriage example, with your spouse identity you may no longer have time after work each day to go out with your co-workers. Thus, through apposition and opposition identities are formed as we identify and *identify with* others.

Figure 10.7
As children transition from childhood to adolescence, dressing in costume for trick-or-treating is typically no longer consistent with the adolescent identity.

HOW IDENTITY THEORY IS RELEVANT TO COSTUME DESIGN

Identity theory can be applied in the context of costume design. Characters' identities are conveyed to audiences through what the characters say, what they do, and what they wear. In literature, authors create characters. This is called **characterization** and is accomplished in various ways such as describing characters' dress, physical features, and nonverbal behaviors (Corbett, 1977, p. 192). Costume designers for theater, movies, and television must select symbols of dress, whose meanings are understood by audience members, to convey those desired characteristics of characters. Designers of theater costume say that the enhancement of characterization is the primary function of stage costume (e.g., Anderson & Anderson, 1985). Through characterization a designer can manage or control the impressions of a character's personality (i.e., aspects of personal identities) conveyed to an audience (Schlenker, 1986). Thus, a designer can effectively convey one or more personal identities of a character through costume design. In addition, since various roles have specific dress symbols associated with them, a designer can convey aspects of a character's relational identities through dress. A designer can even convey many collective identities via dress (including makeup and hairstyle manipulations) such as gender identity (e.g., by creating a very masculine ensemble for a female character), ethnic identity, or religious identity. The key to this process is selecting dress symbols that are well understood by the audience, because if they are not understood then the characterization will not be successful.

For example, if asked to design a costume for police in science fiction, it is not hard to visualize some possible characteristics. The costume first and foremost would feature a uniform to identify them and set them apart from civilians. A sober color such as blue (US) or brown or black would be a good choice. Then we would probably include some type of hat/helmet, a weapon of some sort, and a badge or insignia of some sort. These components of dress would likely be understood by many in Western culture to comprise the look of police of the future. In fact, this is exactly how Robert Blackman, costume designer for *Star Trek: The Next Generation* designed police uniforms (Warren, 1991). However, some characters might be much harder to design for precisely because no well-understood depiction exists. In such cases characterization is much more difficult. Another example from the work of Blackman for *Star Trek: The Next Generation* will be illustrative. One episode required designing for a group of terrorists. How do you visually depict terrorists for an audience when no well-understood image exists? Blackman created costumes that consisted of ankle-length jumpsuits in khaki or in green. Around their ankles the terrorists wore cartridges in cartridge belts, around their heads they wore head bands, and they carried clubs that looked like nightsticks. Although Blackman designed for the television series *Star Trek: The Next Generation* in the late 1980s and early to mid 1990s, the terrorist costumes were eerily similar to the photo circulated on the Internet in 2002 of a Palestinian toddler dressed as a suicide bomber wearing several miniature cartridge belts and a red Hamas headband (BBC News, 2002; CNN.com, 2002; Reeves, 2002).

In Chapter 9, "Dress and the Self," the concepts of program and review were discussed in the context of establishing an identity. Recall that when programs and reviews coincide, identity is said to be validated. When programs and reviews do not coincide, identity is challenged. In response to a challenged identity you may try some other strategies to validate the identity. Challenging often occurs during periods of transition in our lives, as we move through the social structure (Serpe, 1987). At such times, we are often transitioning from one identity to another or simply acquiring new identities. Transitioning through identities or acquiring new identities is often accompanied by changes to dress and appearance. In a qualitative study, the researcher found that about ⅔ of his participants had elected aesthetic cosmetic surgery as a function of transitioning from one relational identity (role) to another (Schouten, 1991). Examples of such transitions include going back to school, a career change, going through puberty, winning the lottery, getting married, graduating, divorcing, relocating, surviving rape, getting a new job, becoming a parent, and having cosmetic surgery.

Identities are also shaped by the social feedback we receive. Although not couched in identity terms, research in the general area of body image has focused on the effects of negative verbal commentary (i.e., social feedback) and personal identities such as being "attractive." Results attest to the power of social feedback in shaping personal identities.

IDENTITY AND DRESS

One way we form and express our identities is through consumption (Zukin & Maguire, 2004). Zukin and Maguire reviewed the literature on identity construction published after 1980. Taking a broad historic view of the growth of consumer culture, the authors link consumption of consumer goods to identity construction. They suggest that one way we create our "selves" is by creating or constructing identities via acquisition of consumer products such as clothing or body modifications such as building muscle. Thus, we not only recognize more bases for identity (i.e., relational, individual, and collective) as outlined in the previous section, the concept of identity has shifted over time from fixed to flexible.

Especially in Western cultures, we are free and even encouraged to self-actualize; for example, to become whatever and whoever we desire. Recall Maslow's hierarchical order of human needs, which originally positioned self-actualization at the apex of human needs, from Chapter 8, "Dress and Personality" (search online for "Maslow's hierarchy of needs changing minds" for a visual of the hierarchy of needs). Thus from that perspective, identity can be viewed as an individual project, fashioned by appearance and achievement. Slogans such as "be all you can be" from the US Army and "just do it" from Nike exemplify the notion that individuals can achieve identities of all-round soldier and elite athlete.

As the idea that you can achieve identities by simply consuming products took hold, it is not surprising that people would apply the idea to their bodies. In her book *The Body Project*, the author described how in contemporary society, girls view the body as malleable and something that can be created and controlled (Brumberg, 1997). Thus, according to the author, the body has become girls' primary **DIY (do it yourself) project** in their quest for an "attractive" and/or "popular" personal identity. In seeking the ideal or perfect body, women and girls engage in a variety of appearance

management behaviors such as exercising, wearing apparel that enhances appearance, dieting, and using cosmetics (Rudd & Lennon, 1994). The term **body work** is used to describe such complicated beauty regimens and body modifications (Zlatunich, 2009).

Evidence that girls and women are encouraged to create and control their appearance to communicate specific identities comes from Zukin and Maguire (2004). These researchers contend that the results of several empirical research studies, that is, studies based on collecting and analyzing data, show that the popular press frequently offers suggestions for how women can produce or construct identities. Recall from Chapter 3, "Conducting Research on Dress" that the popular press includes online and offline newspapers, magazines, television, and blogs. For example, in an qualitative study, prom magazines (i.e., popular press articles) were analyzed and many articles were found that offered advice for achieving "perfection" in the context of high school proms (Zlatunich, 2009).

Recall that according to identity theory we either freely choose identities or acquire them due to normal life circumstances. However, sometimes circumstances oblige us to acquire or change an identity (e.g., experience of being raped leads to a rape survivor identity, a traffic accident leads to a disabled identity). In these instances, people have used dress to conceal the acquired identity or acquire a new identity. In qualitative research, the experiences of forty-one rape survivors were studied by Johnson, Hegland, and Schofield (1999). The women, whose experiences varied from date rape to stranger rape at gunpoint, often made changes to their appearance after the rapes. Rationale underlying these changes to appearance emphasized self-protection. Rape survivors talked about changing their appearance as a strategy to protect themselves

> ### IN-CLASS ACTIVITY
> **Body Work**
>
> What body work do you engage in daily? Work with a partner and develop a list of such daily behaviors. What body work have you considered but elected not to do? Make a list of these behaviors. To what extent do you think of your body as a project? What aspects of your body and its abilities are you especially pleased or satisfied with?

from future rapes as well as from the comments of others. They spoke about not wanting to be noticed, trying not to call attention to themselves, and putting on a mask. Another researcher has also found that female survivors of sexual violence use clothing as a disguise to conceal an identity (Hipple, 2000).

Sexual violence can also be a triggering event for identity construction. In order to study identity and dispossession, qualitative researchers advertised that they were interested in studying people who had just made changes in consumption (Cherrier & Murray, 2007). In research, as noted in Chapter 3, "Conducting Research on Dress," we use the term *informant* to mean a person who understands or has insight into a particular issue. Informants can provide information to the researcher about issues of interest. One of the informants in the Cherrier and Murray study shared that for her, rape was the event that triggered the construction of a new identity. Eventually, she disposed of all her conventional clothing, became a vegetarian, and began making her own clothing. This example demonstrates that dress can be used to reveal (announce) a new identity.

A tragic news story described in Chapter 5, "Dress and Impression Formation" in the context of role theory also illustrates how dress can both reveal and conceal an identity (Myers, 2006). That story was about an alleged serial rapist on a Whiteriver, Arizona Apache reservation, who dressed as a police officer to pose as one. The rapist wore a shirt and cap with the word *police* on them, approached his victims at night, acted like he was conducting a records check on his victim, told the victims they had an outstanding warrant for arrest, handcuffed them, and took them to a remote area where the sexual assaults took place. The alleged victims believed the attacker was an officer because his dress announced (i.e., revealed) that identity and concealed his "true" identity.

IDENTITY CONSTRUCTION

We construct our identities daily through the decisions and choices we make. This is called **identity construction**. Researchers have studied the process of identity (re)construction by focusing on individual identities (e.g., Cherrier & Murray, 2007; Rubin, Shmilovitz, & Weiss, 1993; Schouten, 1991). One of the core aspects of anyone's identity is his or her appearance. Thus, it is not surprising to

think that identity construction or reconstruction might be related to appearance. In qualitative research men's and women's motivations for aesthetic cosmetic surgery were studied (Schouten, 1991). All but two participants were motivated by dissatisfaction with a body feature. For some in the study, the cosmetic surgery allowed them to feel comfortable with relational identities they had constructed (i.e., roles recently adopted). For others, the surgeries were part of a reconstruction of identity (identity project). One woman's surgery enhanced her self-esteem and self-confidence and, within a year, she had left her husband and begun her own career.[4] Overall, participants saw their surgeries as a way to exercise control over both their appearance and destiny. Schouten explained that people sometimes create personal **rites of passage**, ceremonies or events that mark a change in status or stage in life, as a way to shape new identities. See Chapter 14, "Dress and Ritual" for more information on rites. Thus, for some the surgery itself was a rite of passage aiding in the transition from one identity to another. These results support the idea that identities in contemporary society are flexible and that identities are formed and expressed via consumption (Zukin & Maguire, 2004).

Another example of rites of passage that occurs in the context of identity change comes from a study of people who elected to undergo gastric reduction surgery (Rubin, Shmilovitz, & Weiss, 1993). Israeli qualitative researchers interviewed thirty-six people after their surgeries and subsequent weight loss to understand how the changes in

---

[4]According to Swann (1987) people may resist changes to their identities because such changes may have unpleasant effects on relationships; that is, relationship partners are expected to honor the negotiated identities. So it is not surprising that identity reconstruction might covary with dissolution of relationships.

their appearance affected the social responses of others. All interviewees were defined as clinically obese; their surgeries were not considered cosmetic and were only performed with medical justification. Participants shared that they separated from their previous identities and constructed new ones. Rites of passage engaged in included writing "farewell letters" and wills, eating the "last meal," discarding "fat" clothes as a way to destroy the previous fat identity, keeping some old clothes as reminders of the previous identity, and burning old photos of their fat selves.

We recognized in Chapter 6, "Dress and Physical Appearance" that fatness is disparaged in Western culture. Thus, as participants lost weight, their appearance began to approximate the thin cultural ideal and there came a point when they could fit into traditional ready-to-wear sizes (Rubin et al., 1993). Being able to wear traditional sizes provided tangible evidence of changes in their identities. Changes in body size were so dramatic that it was common for participants to relate stories of non-recognition by acquaintances. The non-recognition was particularly fun and pleasurable for participants. The newly thin were enthusiastically received by friends and family. The purchase of new, smaller-sized clothing necessarily covaried with the construction of new identities.

Sociological research on identity construction has changed in focus from examining individual and/or relational identities, to a focus on collective identities (Cerulo, 1997). In the next section, we consider research that has addressed identity construction in the context of collective identities.

In contrast to the positive manner in which the newly thin are received, some identity construction related to appearance is not received with widespread social approval (Figure 10.8). Qualitative researchers studied identity in the context of radical drag appearance (Jacob & Cerny, 2004). The researchers studied four gay men who cross-dressed publically; their appearances were neither male nor female. All participants related that a key experience was the sense of difference from dominant heterosexual society. Through their social relationships and interactions with others they came to perceive themselves as not "real" men, but rather as feminine men. In interviews they expressed linkages between male femininity and "doing drag." The authors explained how the radical

---

Figure 10.8

Some identity construction related to dress is not received with widespread social approval. Here Model/Drag Queen Willam Belli walks the runway at Betsey Johnson during Mercedes-Benz Fashion Week on September 10, 2014 in New York City.

CORPORATE IDENTITY AND IDENTITY PROGRAMS

An **identity program** is a planned strategy to package a business or other organization. The overall goal of an identity program is to develop an image and extend it to tie all aspects of the business together and ensure that a company or organization always conveys the same identity. The underlying idea of an identity program is to focus all services on brand continuity and extension. An example of a firm that creates identity programs is: www.adiginfo.com. ADIG describes itself as "a vertically integrated, apparel design, product development, and marketing support company" that specializes in retail consultancy (ADIG Profile, 2009). By browsing their site, it is apparent that ADIG will design apparel products, collateral (e.g., hangtags, advertising, mailers, ad copy), an image, a logo or trademark, store layout, store fixtures, training manuals, training content, and websites. They have even developed a Twitter Starter Program that advises clients on strategies for the use of social media (Twitter and Facebook) to their advantage. Many universities also have recently instituted identity programs to better market their identities. Using a search engine to locate "identity program," seven universities were featured in the first ten hits.

drag queen appearances "reveal a gender category crisis where the gender order" (i.e., male and female) "does not accommodate or affirm their existences" (p. 131). Gay men are considered feminine and thus are disqualified from an authentic male identity, yet they are not women. This identity is reflected in radical drag queen appearances that are interpreted as neither male nor female. Like the research participants in other studies reviewed, these participants also used dress to create and announce their (feminized male) identities.

In most of the studies we reviewed thus far, identity construction has been related to consumption and appearance such that newly constructed identities were achieved or enhanced via the acquisition and use of products such as clothing. A different focus was taken by an Australian–US research team, who studied circumstances under which people were motivated to change their consumption lifestyles so that they consumed less or **downshifted** (Cherrier & Murray, 2007). The researchers interviewed twelve people who freely gave up some or most of their possessions. These authors linked dispossession to transitions in life and identity projects. They explained that identity construction is a process; it is not simply constructed and finished, but rather is a continuous process of negotiation. In the course of dispossession, five of the interviewees specifically reported disposing of clothing, not buying any more fashionable clothing, and disposing of all branded clothing. It is interesting that even in this research in which people divested themselves of consumer goods including clothing, identity construction was still defined in relation to consumption of consumer products.

Summarizing from studies of identity construction, we can point out some commonalities. There is often a triggering event or life transition that evokes a realization or recognition of a need for change. Examples of such events appear in Table 10.2 and in the studies reviewed here included relocation, rape, recognition of difference, recognition of unethical practices in the workplace, and severe obesity. After such events, individuals separated from old identities: they left their husbands, left jobs, decided to have drastic surgeries. As people separated from old identities, they began the transition to new identities, some considered possible identities, while others experienced pleasure in buying new clothes and with looking in the mirror. Finally, people worked to integrate the new identity into the self. This process is not always easy. Research informants often found it difficult to do without material possessions in Cherrier and Murray's study (2007).

ONLINE IDENTITIES

With the diffusion of virtual communication, the internet offers tremendous potential to researchers interested in dress and identity and various types of research are possible. Why? The Internet allows anonymous communication that facilitates identity construction and identity experiments. Researchers have explored the manner in which

TABLE 10.2

POSSIBLE STAGES OF IDENTITY CONSTRUCTION

	Schouten (1991)	*Cherrier & Murray (2007)*	*Rubin, Shmilovitz, & Weiss (1993)*
Triggering event/transition	Career change, childbirth, widowhood, relocation, return to school	Rape, husband retired, unethical practices at work	Severe obesity; body weight double the norm for height/build
Separation from old identity	Reject former identity; take control	Disposed of clothing, detached from husband, left job	Decision to separate from old fat identity; to have surgery
Transition to new identity	Formulate possible new identities	Affirming new identity	Destruction of old fat clothes & photos, buying new clothes, looking in mirror
Integration of new identity	Attempting to adopt to new identity	Striving to maintain new identity	Easily accepted as "non-deviant" thin person; feel reborn

people use the internet to claim and negotiate identities. For example Dutch researchers were interested in the extent to which youth participated in identity experiments online (Valkenburg, Schouten, & Peter, 2005). Questionnaires were completed by a large sample of young people from the Netherlands, who ranged in age from nine to eighteen. First participants were asked if they ever used instant messaging or chat. Those who answered yes were then "asked if they pretended to be someone else" (p. 388) while they were instant messaging or chatting. Many (41 percent) acknowledged that they did experiment with their identities online. Younger students were more likely than older ones to present themselves as beautiful online and girls presented themselves as older than boys did.

Qualitative researchers found that male-to-female cross-dressers also used the Internet to express their gendered identities (Hegland & Nelson, 2002). Presenting yourself as female when you are male (or passing) is much easier in the virtual world than it is in the real world. The websites they analyzed offered advice and reflections on how to dress as a woman and how to achieve a female sounding voice. Photos and sometimes photo albums of the female persona were posted on the websites. In their desire to express their feminine identities and pass as women, the men created hyper-feminine appearances. Many of the cross-dressers did not dress like typical women, but rather overdid their female "looks" by adopting all the female "trappings." Many dressed in

an extremely stereotypical feminine, overtly sexual way, taking perhaps what they viewed as the straight male perspective on what the female body should look like (objectifying) as they constructed their identities.

The internet has also been used in identity construction in pro-anorexia (pro-ana) **virtual communities** (online interest and/or support groups), using covert participant observation (Brotsky & Giles, 2007). Recall from Chapter 3, "Conducting Research on Dress" that participant observers are researchers who take part in activities of the group being observed. In this case, one of the authors of this UK–US research team participated in online pro-ana groups, posing as a twenty-year old woman with anorexia. Pro-ana sites have been characterized in the media as being anti-recovery and dangerous. Thus, a key focus of the research was to assess if the sites were as dangerous as they were portrayed in the media. The researchers analyzed discussions and identified three themes: support for members, group identity, and negative attributions. When the participant observer (researcher) finally exited the communities, she announced that she was leaving to seek treatment for anorexia at an in-patient facility. Community members were "overwhelmingly encouraging, supportive, and helpful" (p. 101). This outcome is at odds with media depictions of pro-ana sites. The authors concluded that support of members' decisions, no matter what the decisions are, may be the main function of the communities. However, what the authors did not mention, and what should be obvious, is community members are participating in the community because they want to be thinner than they are (i.e., want to look different).

To summarize, researchers have begun to study how issues of identity transpire on the internet. Research strategies used in these studies include survey methodology, non-reactive research (interpretive content analysis), and fieldwork (participant observation). The anonymity of the internet makes it an appealing site for identity experimentation for subcultures (e.g., anorexics, adolescents, and cross-dressers). Issues related to appearance surfaced in all these studies. This is not surprising since appearance is an important part of individual identity. In the next section we focus on discrediting or negative identities. It turns out that people can be fairly successful at managing negative or ambivalent identities. In this way they are able to resist, circumvent, and contest such identities.

IDENTITY AND STIGMA

In Chapter 6, "Dress and Physical Appearance," stigma was defined as a deeply discrediting attribute (Goffman, 1963). Stigmas represent major norm infractions (Cusack, Jack, & Kavanagh, 2003). According to Goffman there are three major types of stigma: abominations of the body, blemishes of individual character, and tribal stigma (e.g., race, nation). Several researchers have investigated stigma and identity, the meanings associated with stigmas, and how people contest or resist negative or ambiguous identities. In this section we discuss negative or ambiguous identities that are easily discerned because either the defining attribute is visible or the identity is a form of symbolic consumption and fairly visible.

A qualitative research team from the UK and Ireland has studied *Star Trek* fans and how the identity of being a *Star Trek* fan and its associated stigma were managed (Cusack et al., 2003). Perhaps because *Star Trek* is science fiction, fans are assumed to be social misfits, immature, and mindless nerds with lowbrow or common tastes. The associated stigma is a blemish of individual character. Fans, called Trekkies, are discredited due to what is seen as their deviant and rampant consumption of anything associated with *Star Trek*. Although being a fan is not visible, various *Star Trek* symbols (books, videos) and costuming reveals the fan identity. These researchers found that fans managed their stigmatized identity in several ways. They developed a new label—Trekker—to replace the negative connotations of the diminutive Trekkie label, they rationalized the benefits of the program, they learned to strategically manage symbolic *Star Trek* cues, and they escaped public gaze by only costuming on special occasions such as conventions. See Figure 10.9 for *Star Trek* fans dressed in costumes. *Star Trek* fans are also treated in Chapter 12, "Dress and Social Organizations."

Several researchers have studied fatness as a stigma in relation to identity (Chan & Gillick, 2009; Granberg, 2006; Rice, 2007). Fatness is an abomination of the body. The

Figure 10.9
Trekkies are stigmatized due to what is seen as their deviant and rampant consumption of anything associated with *Star Trek*.

major norm infraction in this instance is deviation from the cultural ideal of beauty. According to Chan and Gillick, fat people feel that they are coerced to find a solution for being fat and the coercion has affective consequences. In this qualitative research, seven individuals considered obese were interviewed. Interviewees vacillated between accepting and rejecting their fat identity. One identity management strategy utilized was to characterize the fatness as involuntary. They resisted the identity of being a disabled individual by arguing that only people who were fatter than they should be categorized as disabled.

A qualitative Canadian researcher conducted in-depth interviews with eighteen Canadian women who acknowledged their identity as fat (Rice, 2007). The women's personal body histories told via the interview process revealed how size stereotypes devalued them as unfit. In addition, the size stereotypes also contributed to disordered eating and avoidance of physical activity. To manage and resist the discredited fat identity, the women had improvised identities. Many focused on intellectual or artistic development, others took on a comedian role, and one made sure that she was selected as team captain to avoid being picked last for the team. All tried to resist the devaluation associated with the fat-unfit identity.

The most extreme way to resist stigma associated with an identity is to exit the identity. In qualitative research fourty-six men and women were interviewed (Granberg, 2006). Participants had decided to lose weight as a way to resist their fat identity, in effect exiting the identity. For them body weight was a highly salient identity. All participants lost enough weight so that were no longer considered obese, yet paradoxically they were not all pleased with themselves. In some cases they had unrealistic expectations of improved social relationships or aspired to perfect bodies that did not materialize. Granberg notes that when an identity transformation begins, people attempt to manage the new identity through the process of verification. When the feedback received through social comparison, self-attribution, and reflected appraisals did not verify the new identity, some people tried harder to lose weight through increased dieting and exercising. Others changed their expectations or relied on cognitive strategies (instead of labeling her hips as large, one participant labeled her waist as small). Others managed by changing their comparison standards ("the people who look wonderful in their clothes have the same little saggy things that you have" [p. 120]).

To summarize from these studies, people can resist or circumvent some stigmatized identities. In some cases it is easier to do this than in others because some stigmatized identities are not themselves visible and identity cues associated with these identities can be managed to resist the identity (e.g., being a fan). In the case of the fat identity this is not possible, so individuals can develop other means of resistance: characterizing fatness as involuntary, adopting new roles or interests, and exiting the identity. Across all of these studies participants were able to successfully use cognitive strategies to resist negative identities.

CONSUMPTION EVENTS

In their review of sociological and historical work on consumption, Zukin and Maguire (2004) maintain that people "experience consumption as a project of forming, and expressing, identity" (p. 173). In this section, we highlight instances of consumption of dress and related products that express identity and that are celebrated in contemporary US culture. We define a **consumption event** as a commercial opportunity (a) to buy products and experiences, (b) that impact identity, (c) that involve wearing special clothing and accessories which are used as props in identity assumption, and (d) in which product consumption and experience consumption reinforce the identity. Three such consumption events are *Star Trek* conventions, La Quinceañera celebrations, and American Girl Place (parties/dolls).

Star Trek conventions are organized gatherings of *Star Trek* fans, creators, writers, and sometimes cast members. Events include screenings of favorite episodes or movies, buying and selling of *Star Trek* paraphernalia (e.g., costumes, action figures, alien prostheses, games, videos, DVDs, books, comics, trading cards, plaques), participating in best costume contests, and presentations by stars and writers. For a significant amount of money you can have lunch with one of the stars or have your picture taken with one. Awards are given for the best costume and dressing in costume is an important aspect of experiencing the conventions because it allows individuals to assume their favorite fictional *Star Trek* identity. Because costumes and their accoutrements are easily available, assumption of the desired identity is facilitated.

La Quinceañera celebrations are coming of age rites of passage for Latina girls (Conger, n.d.; Palfrey, 1997). They

Figure 10.10

La Quinceañera celebrations and other rites of passage often involve special clothing and accessories.

mark the transition from child to woman and are celebrated on the girl's fifteenth birthday. The event marks a change for the girl from being ineligible for marriage to being marriageable. The most important part of the celebration is a mass, for which the girl may wear a formal, full length ball dress, typically in a pastel color. See Figure 10.10 for an example of the ball gown. She may be served by attendants (up to seven women and seven men). Godparents are important in the celebration and sometimes bear some of the expense. Favors are purchased for and distributed to guests. A party follows, often with live band music. The total expense of the event is related to the wealth of the parents and godparents. In many aspects the event is like a wedding. Important dress symbols are the ball gown, a crown, flat shoes, and high-heeled shoes. The birthday girl also receives gifts which may include a tiara, bracelet or rings, earrings, a cross or medal, and a bible or prayer book. An entire industry has grown up around this

Latina cultural milestone and one source documents costs for the celebration at around $30,000 (Quart, 2000). The celebration reflects important aspects of religious identity, ethnic identity, and gender identity.

Another consumption event involves American Girl dolls and their accoutrements. American Girl dolls and accessories are beautifully crafted and expensive. A package consisting of a doll, her book, one outfit, and one accessory is priced around $115 to $120. In 2014 revenue from American Girl products was $620.7 million (Newman, 2015). Along with being able to purchase via the website and catalog, there are now twenty stores where doll clothes, matching clothes for the girl (See Figure 10.11 for a girl and her doll dressed alike), accessories, and furniture can be purchased. In addition to selling products, the stores are theme parks for girls and sell experiences such as a live theater, doll hairstyling salons, a bookstore, and a café where girls can eat with their dolls. For a fee a girl can host a party for seven of her friends. Parents like that the books that accompany the historic dolls teach about history, that the dolls have wholesome values, encourage reading, and give girls an alternative to Bratz dolls ("How I stopped," 2012). Qualitative research was conducted with girls and their mothers (Acosta-Alzuru & Kreshel, 2002). Interviews with the mothers and girls established that girls create identities through their consumption of American Girl products. In fact, issues related to ethnic identity and class identity are evident in the stories of several of the historic dolls: Kaya, Kristen, Josefina, Rebecca, Addy, and

Figure 10.11
According to Acosta-Alzuru and Kreshel (2002) girls create identities through their consumption of American Girl products. Sarah Lisak wears a nightgown that matches her American Girl Doll's nightgown.

DRESS IN THE NEWS
American Girl Dolls

American Girl dolls and accessories are costly, but do give girls an appreciation for history, values, and girls' personal life circumstances (Beck, 2011). In addition, in reading Beck's column, it is clear that she began to consider and reflect on aspects of identity as a young girl through an AG doll's fictitious history.

Samantha. With the "Truly Me" line of dolls, girls can select dolls with skin color, eye color, and hair color and texture to match themselves. These dolls also come with books like the historic dolls, but these books are blank, in effect allowing girls to create the dolls' identities.

As a five-year old, Beck saw one of the dolls, Samantha Parkington, in a catalog. She realized that she and Samantha looked alike, and both had mothers who were artists. Beck's parents got her the book about Samantha as she was just beginning to read. She remembers reading with her parents and learning about Victorian times. Through Samantha's life experiences, Beck learned what it meant to be an orphan and what it might mean to grow up without parents. In addition, she learned about class differences

and child labor through Samantha's story. Beck credits the doll and her life story as the seed from which her interests in women's narrative within history grew.

According to Beck the value of the AG dolls goes beyond the physical objects (doll and accessories), and encompasses the message, the enduring quality, and the personal stories of the dolls. Hence, AG dolls and their experiences provide very positive and enriching alternatives to other dolls on the market. Through Samantha's story, Beck actually reflected on aspects of Samantha's identity (orphan, class) in opposition to her own identity.

IDENTITY DEVELOPMENT

Identity development begins with children's awareness of self (i.e., that they are unique individuals). Infants cannot express their recognition of themselves verbally but researchers have devised ways to assess self-awareness through self-recognition (Lewis & Brooks-Gunn, 1979). The assumption underlying such research is that a concept of self is necessary before one can recognize oneself. Evidence comes from studies of infants' responses to mirrors, videos of themselves and others, and self-representations (photos, slides of themselves). In one type of study, an infant's face is marked with rouge or a piece of tape and the infant's response to the mark is observed when the infant is placed before a mirror. Any behavior toward the mark instead of the mirror is taken as evidence of self-recognition or self-awareness. Some infants display self-recognition by fifteen to eighteen months of age. Most infants display self-recognition by twenty-one to twenty-four months of age. Researchers presenting stimuli using videos or pictures demonstrated the same level of self-awareness (Lewis & Brooks, 1975).

In addition, by two years of age it is common for children to use self-referents such as "me" and "mine."

Identity development continues during childhood and becomes especially important in adolescence (Erikson, 1968). Erikson has described the achievement of a coherent identity as an important goal of adolescence. Puberty heralds various physical changes that evoke adolescents' exploration of and concern about their bodies and sexuality. For girls, an important part of identity and worth comes from physical appearance. As girls traverse puberty, they gain body fat in preparation for childbirth; thus, their bodies are likely to deviate from the cultural ideal of beauty. However, as boys move through puberty, they gain muscle mass; thus, their bodies more closely approximate the cultural appearance ideal. Early development for boys may provide advantages in athletics and positive body image (Crockett & Petersen, 1987). However, for girls early maturation predicts a negative body image (Tobin-Richards, Boxer, & Petersen, 1983).

Identity development continues across the lifespan and is a personal process according to Erikson (1968). Because identities evolve over a lifetime and because each of us experience different social interactions, no two people will have the same identities. Thus, the identities you develop are ultimately unique, although the process by which identity develops is thought to be similar across individuals. Although identity development is most often associated with adolescence, re-evaluation and modification of identities is possible across the lifespan. In previous sections of this chapter, we discussed how dress is used to reveal and conceal identities. In the early twenty-first century some identities are especially central in Western culture, such as gender identity, ethnic identity, and religious identity. Both sex and ethnicity are usually considered to be immutable and both implicate identity in a fundamental sense (Rhode, 2010). In this section, gender identity is discussed and examples of how dress is used to reflect gender identity are provided.

GENDER IDENTITY

To understand gender identity, we first need to establish the difference between sex and gender. Sex refers to the biological categories of men and women. **Sex differences** then refer to biological differences between men and women. Men are typically taller than women and have greater upper body strength and muscle mass. Women typically have larger breasts, smaller hands and feet, and higher voices than men. Of course, men and women differ in terms of genitalia. Gender, on the other hand, is socially constructed, hence **gender differences** are socially constructed differences. For example, in Western culture wearing cosmetics is considered more appropriate for women than men. Gender is defined in terms of what activities and behaviors are considered appropriate for men and women within their cultural context. Across some cultures what it means to be male and female differs from Western culture. So gender identity describes how people define themselves, in terms of maleness or femaleness, within their culture.

How do people define themselves as masculine or feminine? In other words, what characteristics do we view as masculine and feminine? To assess people's self-descriptions in terms of masculine or feminine traits the Bem Sex Role Inventory was developed (Bem, 1974). Bem's view was that everyone has both masculine and feminine traits. People (usually men) with a masculine identity rate themselves highly on traits such as ambitious, dominant, and self-reliant (traits considered masculine) and low on traits such as affectionate, gentle, and understanding (traits considered feminine). Someone (usually a woman) with a feminine identity does the reverse. Someone with an **androgynous identity** would self-rate highly on both masculine and feminine traits. Perhaps because feminine traits are not highly valued in US culture, people who self-identify as masculine or androgynous have been found to be psychologically better adjusted (Alpert-Gillis & Connell, 1989). This reality can be problematic for women because qualities that lead to success in the workplace are often seen to be masculine (e.g., ambitious, self-reliant). Table 10.3 lists some traits that the respondents in Bem's (1974) study endorsed as masculine, feminine, and androgynous.

GENDER ROLES, GENDERED DRESS, AND GENDER STEREOTYPING

What society determines as appropriate behavior for men and women is known as their respective **gender roles**. Gender roles are the attitudes and behaviors that a culture

TABLE 10.3

SEX-TYPED AND ANDROGYNOUS TRAITS

Sex-Typed and Androgynous Traits from Bem (1974)		
Masculine traits	Feminine traits	Androgynous traits
Aggressive	Affectionate	Adaptable
Ambitious	Cheerful	Conceited
Assertive	Childlike	Conscientious
Athletic	Compassionate	Friendly
Competitive	Does not use harsh language	Happy
Dominant	Gentle	Helpful
Forceful	Loyal	Likable
Self-reliant	Tender	Reliable

IN-CLASS ACTIVITY
Designing for Television

Suppose you are designing costumes for a television show. The cast calls for a male actor to be macho (stereotypically masculine), and another to be effeminate (stereotypically feminine). With a partner, make a list of suggestions for what each actor should look like including items of dress and accessories and any other physical characteristics. If you think any particular brands of items should be featured in their appearance, identify them also. What occupations would you attribute to each actor?

expects of men and women. Thus, gender roles govern how people publically present themselves and serve as an active expression of gender identity. In Western culture gender roles govern how we dress as men and women, the length of our hair, whether we shave our legs or faces, the types of occupations we enter, the way we move our bodies, and whether we wear makeup or not (Fabricant & Gould, 1993). For adults most behaviors express masculinity or femininity. Usually, gender identity is consistent with anatomic sex and gender role (e.g., when a woman feels feminine and acts feminine by wearing makeup, fragrance, and feminine clothing).

Gender roles and gendered clothing is evident in the popular media, which serve to socialize viewers regarding how to dress. Television, movies, and other media are cultural products or cultural forms and represent abstract ideas within a culture/society such as gender roles (Johnson, 1986–1987). In one study of roles in a television series, relationships between dress, power, and gender roles on *Star Trek: The Next Generation* were studied (Lennon, 1999). She found that gender role stereotypes were evident. As compared to men's roles, the most important recurring roles for women were traditional helping (i.e., feminine) roles. Men performed more important tasks than women and held more positions of power. Also the

uniforms worn were gendered. For example, women's uniforms were more tight-fitting than men's. Because dressing according to gender role is expected, an effective way to make a plot unexpected is by featuring characters who dress as members of the opposite sex (e.g., *Tootsie, Bosom Buddies, The Birdcage, Mulan* [cartoon], *Some like it Hot, Mrs. Doubtfire*).

In many societies dressing in a manner considered appropriate for the opposite sex is a violation of social norms, rules about how one should behave. When people violate social norms, they may face a sanction. **Sanctions** are ways that society members enforce conformity to social norms and can be positive or negative. A **positive sanction** is a reward for behaving as one should or conforming to social expectations while a **negative sanction** is a punishment for nonconformity. We talked about the concept of the cultural ideal of beauty for women and that it includes thinness and being toned. Recent winners of the Miss America pageant are both thin and toned. The way winners are sanctioned for their conformity to these social norms is by receiving prize money and fame.

In the same way, our culture sanctions conformity and nonconformity to gendered appearances. Recall in Chapter 6, "Dress and Physical Appearance" we discussed how women with the most feminine features were considered the most attractive across cultures. This is an example of another way that members of a society positively sanction conformity to a gendered appearance. On the other hand, nonconformity is negatively sanctioned. In 1998, a 15 year-old cross-dressing boy Matthew McLendon was forced to quit his high school or face expulsion (Sewell, 1998). McLendon had been disciplined for wearing "female dress, makeup and hairstyle" to school. At a school board meeting, one parent expressed concern about the boy's potential effect on younger students. Because the school was private, administrators had more leeway in coming to their decision than would have been the case at a public school. In this case nonconformity was sanctioned with threatened expulsion from school.

Another example of negative sanctions concerned the inclusion of a student's photograph in a high school yearbook. The photograph of Florida high school senior Kelli Davis was banned from her school's yearbook ("Lesbian student shut out," 2005). The high school principal said he made the decision because Kelli was wearing boy's clothes in the picture. When they arrived at the photography studio, students were given the choice of wearing a "drape" or a tuxedo top in their senior pictures. Kelli selected the tuxedo top because she felt uncomfortable wearing the drape because it exposed her chest. Although Kelli's class was the first to graduate from the high school, there was apparently an unwritten social norm that boys should wear the tuxedo top and girls should wear the drape in their senior pictures. Kelli's mother did petition the school board to allow Kelli's picture to appear in the yearbook but the board upheld the principal's decision. In this example,

nonconformity to the norm was sanctioned by refusal to publish a photo in the yearbook. In this instance, as in the previous example, a social norm to dress in a way consistent with biological sex was enforced.

The norm to dress in a way consistent with biological sex also applies to fashionable clothing. There are many examples in the history of fashion when a new style is ridiculed or opposed if it involves a feature typically associated with the opposite sex. In fact, in the popular press—newspapers, magazines, advice columns, cartoons—people are often very vocal in their expression of opposition to such styles. For example, in the mid-1960s long hair for men became fashionable. In 1964, when the Beatles appeared on US television on *The Ed Sullivan Show*, their "long" hair shocked many Americans.

Gender differences are not apparent in infancy, but over time through socialization children develop a gender identity. Socialization is the process through which children learn the norms and values of the culture they live in and is the focus of Chapter 11, "Dress and Socialization." This includes the norms and values of their families, their peer groups, their schools, their religions, or any other group to which they belong. Children notice differences between men and women between ages two and three and are able to categorize people into the categories of men and women. They quickly learn whether they are boys or girls. They typically learn to identify with their same-sex parent and this identification guides them as they develop their gender identity. Along with an awareness of their own sex, they learn what articles of clothing are appropriate for wear and which ones are not appropriate. For example, boys do not usually wear skirts but girls do. In fact, the concept that only women wear skirts is so universal or pan-human, that the universal symbol for a women's restroom features a picture of a stylized woman apparently wearing a dress. In Table 10.4 are listed a few formerly gendered items of dress.

SEXUAL ORIENTATION AS COMPONENT OF GENDER IDENTITY

As noted previously, gender is socially constructed; that is, the differences we assign on the basis of gender would not exist had members of a society not agreed upon them. **Queer**, sexual diversity, or LGBT (lesbian, gay, bi-sexual, transsexual) studies is concerned with the analysis of issues

TABLE 10.4

ONCE GENDERED ITEMS OF DRESS IN THE LAST HALF OF THE TWENTIETH CENTURY

Item of Gendered Dress	Inappropriate
Pants	For women in the workplace until 1970
Purse	For men until circa 2000
Tie	For women until around 1980
Earrings	For men until around 2000
Long hair	For men until mid 1970s

related to gender identity and sexual orientation. Within queer studies is **queer theory**, a viewpoint that challenges socially constructed categories of sexual identity (Jagose, 1996). Not a term to indicate a new social identity, rather to *queer* something "is to analyze a situation or a text to determine the relationships between sexuality, power, gender, and conceptions of normal and deviant, insider and outsider" (Dilley, 1999, p. 458). Researchers utilizing queer theory might conduct an analysis of the lives and experiences of those considered non-heterosexual, they might juxtapose those lives with lives considered normal, or may examine why non-heterosexual lives and experiences are even considered outside the norm (Dilley, 1999).

Although these researchers did not position their research within queer theory per se, their research could be considered a project that looks at relationships between sexuality, power, and gender. Clarke and her colleagues utilized qualitative methods to analyze the experiences of gay men, lesbian women, and bi-sexual women with visually negotiating their sexual identities (Clarke & Turner, 2007; Clarke & Smith, 2015). In qualitative research from the U.K., researchers interviewed their participants to examine their use of appearance and dress in identifying others' sexuality as well as in emphasizing or de-emphasizing their own sexual identity (Clarke & Turner, 2007). Participants shared that they felt free to appear like a stereotypic lesbian or a gay man but that expectations for appearance were policed such that there was low tolerance for deviation. Participants noted that there were negative connotations associated with appearing "too gay" as

people should not lose their individuality in appearance. However, some participants reported experiencing negative feedback in the form of comments, receiving criticizing looks, or being ignored when their appearance tested traditional gender boundaries. While variation existed in what appearances and specific items of dress were interpreted as gay/lesbian, some participants identified specific brands and body modifications (e.g., piercings) as indicative of gay/lesbian sexuality rather than an overall appearance. They described gay/lesbian fashion as more relaxed than heterosexual fashion. Participants shared that overt visual displays of sexuality became less necessary over time as participants became secure with this aspect of their identity.

Subsequently, in other UK research a qualitative survey of gay men was conducted to address the question of how these men made sense of their clothing and appearance practices and to uncover any external pressures (pressure to conform) they experienced when constructing their appearances (Clarke & Smith, 2015). Their participants revealed that appearance norms for gay men existed and centered on specific "looks" as well as on making an investment in one's appearance. Two common looks were identified: the camp gay man and the fashion conscious gay man. The camp gay man was described as wearing tightly fitted clothing, often in feminine colors, and engaging in a range of grooming practices commonly linked with women. The fashion conscious gay man presented an image that reflected concern for appearance and fashionability. With the emergence of the metrosexual man, some participants questioned whether interest in appearance and clothing remained solely a gay concern. Participants also shared pleasures and risks experienced when conforming to gay appearance expectations. Pleasures included achieving correspondence between inner and outer selves and fitting in with members of the community. Risks included loss of personal identity when dressing to conform to gay appearances and the potential for appearing too gay. Both concerns had been identified earlier by Clarke and Turner (2007).

In other qualitative research the consumption experiences of queer women were investigated (Reddy-Best & Pedersen, 2015). Noting that appearance and dress were important to signaling sexual identities, these researchers were interested in the shopping experiences of queer women. They wanted to document where queer women looked for style inspiration and any experiences of discrimination or distress while shopping. Because they often

TABLE 10.5

MASCULINE AND FEMININE ELEMENTS AND PRINCIPLES OF DESIGN FROM WORKMAN AND JOHNSON (1993)

Element/Principle	Feminine	Masculine
Line: unidimensional element of design which connects two points (p. 94)	Curved lines, modified straight lines, thin, fuzzy, short or interrupted lines, upward movement of lines	Straight, angular, zigzag, thick, solid, sharp, long, continuous, unbroken, flattened curves, vertical, diagonal, downward movement of line, having large sharp distinct breaks, large full round curves
Shape and form: Shape is a two-dimensional space enclosed by a line; form is a three-dimensional area enclosed by a surface (p. 95)	Shapes enclosed by curved lines, bouffant full skirt, small waist, curved bodice, graceful flowing skirt, boleros, short capes, peplums, ruffles, small bustles, puffed sleeves, off-the-shoulder necklines, soft fluffy collars	Shapes enclosed by straight lines, long unbroken lines that combined the bifurcated silhouette with a wedge t-shaped silhouette
Texture and fabrics: Texture is the visual appearance and feel of the surface of a fabric (p. 95)	Smooth, soft, pliable, supple, thin, fine, wispy, fluffy, dull, crisp, sheer, napped, porous, delicate, slippery, transparent, lightweight. Fabrics considered feminine: lace, organdy, net, taffeta, soft sheer woolens, crisp cottons, silk	Bulky, thick, closed, coarse, rough, heavy, stiff, rich, shiny, luxurious Fabrics considered masculine included wool, heavy tweeds, firm suiting
Space: Space is the area within or between shapes (p. 95)	Small broken spaces, large areas of gathering, shirring, tucks, pleats, fluting, seaming, pockets	Large open spaces, plain unrelieved unbroken areas
Color: hue—the name of a family of colors (p. 95)	Shell pink, dusty rose, scarlet, apricot, orange, rust, gold, yellow, mint green, fuchsia, wine, white	Hunter green, turquoise, teal, baby blue, royal blue, navy, royal purple, beige, brown, black
Color: value—lightness or darkness of a hue (p. 95)	Subtle contrasts, in close value intervals, light pastel values	Dark value hues, strong value hues
Color: intensity—brightness or dullness of a hue (p. 95)	Soft grayed intensities	Bright intensities
Pattern: an arrangement o lines, spaces, or shapes on or in a fabric (p. 96)	Flower and plant motifs, shadowy abstracts, geometric patterns which blend with the background, small allover conventionalized floral designs, small scale dainty motifs	Stripes, plaids, animal and geometric motifs, bold motifs with sharp edges, large to medium size designs, sharply distinct figure and ground, and man-made objects

TABLE 10.5

MASCULINE AND FEMININE ELEMENTS AND PRINCIPLES
OF DESIGN FROM WORKMAN AND JOHNSON (1993) *(continued)*

Element/Principle	*Feminine*	*Masculine*
Balance: A feeling of evenly distributed weight (p. 96)	Formal symmetrical balance, except in small details	One breast pocket
Emphasis: the center of interest (p. 96)	Neck treatment (except shirt collar), a yokeline, hemline, waistline, or back of dress	Designs that focus on shoulder width, waistline, hipline
Rhythm: a feeling of organized motion (p. 96)	Smooth, gentle or interrpted, staccato rhythm as found in buttons that are paired creating different intervals of spacing	Long continuous rhythm, dynamic rhythm, regular marching rhythm as found in evenly spaced buttons with a continuous front opening
Proportion: the comparative relationships of distances, sizes, amounts, degrees, or parts (p. 96)	High heels	Natural body proportions may be exaggerated, shoulder pads, epaulets
Scale: the relation of sizes to each other and to the whole (p. 97)	Small scale items	Large scale items
Harmony: agreement in feeling (p. 97)	Combinations of pastel hues, curved lines, rounded shapes, small spaces, soft smooth textures. Embellishments such as lace, embroidery, ruffles, beading	Straight thick lines, large unbroken spaces, large solid shapes with sharp edges, dark values, rough stiff textures
Other aesthetic considerations		
Design features	Closures can be located anywhere; for center front closures—right goes over left	Trousers always open in front, shirts and jackets always button at center front except for double breasted ones. Closures go left over right
Articles of clothing	Bras, hosiery, petticoats, blouses, slips	Necktie, pockets
Accessories	Ballerina slippers, slings, t-strap shoes, high heels, cosmetics, jewelry, purses, hair ornaments (barrettes, headbands, elastic hair ties, ribbons, bows	
Fit	Ease is design ease	Ease is comfort ease

shopped in the men's department, participants shared that they were frustrated with not being able to locate apparel that fit. Participants shared that they looked to family members and peers for style inspiration along with other queer individuals and queer publications. Most participants reported never seeing fashion advertisements targeting queer women and expressed frustration because of the lack of such images. Many women reported experiencing distress while shopping. Although some of this distress (i.e., embarrassment, unease) was caused by difficulties experienced by women in general when shopping (e.g., negative body image, unavailability of styles), other causes included distress linked to shopping for clothing for themselves in the men's section, asking for different sizes in men's clothing, or being told that they were shopping in the wrong section of the store. Shopping in thrift stores where there were fewer distinctions between men's and women's areas of a store eliminated some of this distress for some participants. Experiences that were identified as positive included those wherein sales associates did not judge them or appeared to be openly supporting the gay community.

RESEARCH ON GENDERED ASPECTS OF DRESS

Researchers proposed a link between cultural aesthetics and the social construction that is evident in dress (Workman & Johnson, 1993). They explained that gender stereotypes are based on three types of attributes, one type of which is an identifying attribute and includes physical characteristics such as clothing, hairstyle, and body movement. The purpose of their research was to illustrate how the elements and principles of design could be used to create dress variations that serve as identifying attributes of gender in twentieth-century US. They point out that while what is considered masculine or feminine is subject to change (as Table 10.4 illustrates), people are socialized to view items of dress as masculine or feminine. The authors contend that there exist cultural associations of various elements and principles of design with masculinity and femininity and that knowledgeable designers can mix and match among the elements and principles to create masculine or feminine appearances. The authors analyzed information from three prominent aesthetics textbooks of the late twentieth century. Table 10.5 (see pp. 256–257) summarizes their findings from the textbook analysis.

Next the researchers analyzed the research literature to determine the extent to which information from the textbook authors was supported by findings from the research literature (Workman & Johnson, 1993). They actually found considerable research support that (a) aesthetic information conveyed by dress signals gender, (b) aesthetic information conveyed by dress affects traits assigned to the wearer, (c) aesthetic information conveyed by dress influences behavior toward the wearer, (d) aesthetic information conveyed by dress affects the behavior of the wearer. Table 10.6 summarizes a few of the studies cited by Workman and Johnson and delineates the aspects of dress found to be masculine or feminine. This information could be used by a costume designer interested in creating a masculine or feminine appearance for a character.

TABLE 10.6

FEMININE AND MASCULINE MANIPULATIONS OF APPEARANCE USED BY RESEARCHERS

Researchers	Feminine	Masculine
Davis (1984–1985)	Skirt with ruffle, blouse with lace, pantyhose, fingernail polish, eye makeup, 2-piece swimsuit, purse or sachel, shoulder length or longer hair, high heeled shoes, watch face less than 1-inch diameter	Athletic supporter, going shirtless, necktie, football jersey, basketball shoes, hiking boots, watch face larger than 1-inch diameter
Davis (1987)	Pleats, pastel colors, puffed sleeves, pink, sandals	Traditional suit, briefcase, dark color, necktie
Lennon (1990)	Flowing lines, draped details, light colors, patterned fabrics, soft fabrics, dress or skirt, lace, ruffles, bows, jewelry, bowtie, long hair	Angular lines, heavy/rough fabrics, blazer jackets, shirts (as opposed to blouses), shoulder pads, necktie, loose baggy pants, short hair
Shakin, Shakin, & Sternglanz (1985)	Pink, ruffles, puffed sleeves, lace, a dress, yellow	Blue

Chapter Summary

An identity is an organized set of characteristics that expresses various aspects of the self. The concept of identity recognizes the complexity of the self and can be thought of as a situated self. Through dress, identities are announced or communicated to others, so in some situations people will dress and act differently than in others as a function of which identity is salient (important) to the given situation. Identities are developed through social interaction. Identity development, identity negotiation, self-verification, identity construction, and identity reconstruction are all discussed in relation to dress.

Key Terms

afunctional	DIY (do it yourself) project	interactionist theory	queer theory
androgynous identity	downshifted	microsociological theory	relational identities
announce	gender differences	negative sanction	rites of passage
apposition	gender roles	opposition	sanctions
body work	identity construction	personal identity	sex differences
characterization	identity negotiation process	placement	situated self
collective identity	identity program	positive sanction	stratification
consumption event	individual identity	queer	virtual communities

Discussion Questions

1. What are some identities that have associated identity cues?

2. Give an example of an instance in which you have had to negotiate an identity. Were you successful?

3. Why is identity theory called an interactional theory?

4. Using the definition of consumption event, give an example of one that is not mentioned in this chapter. Tell what kinds of products and experiences you can purchase for this consumption event, how the event impacts identity, what special clothing and accessories are used as props for the identity, and how the product and experience reinforce the identity.

STUDiO™

Visit your book's STUDIO for additional quiz questions and vocabulary flashcards!

Suggested Readings

Brumberg, J. J. (1997). *The body project: An intimate history of American girls*. New York, NY: Random House, Inc.

Freitas, A., Kaiser, S., Hall, C., Kim, J W., & Hammidi, T. (1997). Appearance management as border construction: Least favorite clothing, group distancing, and identity . . . not! *Sociological Inquiry, 67*, 323–335.

Quart, A. (2003). *Branded: The buying and selling of teenagers*. New York, NY: Basic Books.

Rhode, D. L. (2010). *The beauty bias: The injustice of appearance in life and law*. New York, NY: Oxford University Press.

References

Acosta-Alzuru, C., & Kreshel, P. J. (2002). "I'm an American girl . . . Whatever that means": Girls' consuming Pleasant Company's American girl identity. *Journal of Communication, 52*(1), 139–161.

ADIG Profile (2009, March 12). Retrieved from http://www.adiginfo.com/pdf_files/ADIG%20profile.pdf

Alpert-Gillis, L. J., & Connell, J. P. (1989). Gender and sex-role influences on children's self-esteem. *Journal of Personality, 57*(1), 97–114.

Anderson, B., & Anderson, C. (1985). *Costume design.* New York, NY: Holt, Rinehart and Winston.

Ashmore, R. D., Deaux, K., & McLaughlin-Volpe, T. (2004). An organizing framework for collective identity: Articulation and significance of multidimensionality. *Psychological Bulletin, 130,* 80–114.

Banister, E. N., & Hogg, M. K. (2004). Negative symbolic consumption and consumers' drive for self-esteem. *European Journal of Marketing, 38,* 850–868.

BBC News (2002, June 28). 'Baby bomber photo' shocks Israel. BBC News. Retrieved from http://news.bbc.co.uk/2/hi/middle_east/2071561.stm

Beck, K. (2011, July 6). In defense of the American Girl doll cult. Retrieved from http://mommyish.com/childrearing/in-defense-of-the-american-girl-doll-cult/

Bem, S. L. (1974). The measurement of psychological androgyny. *Journal of Consulting and Clinical Psychology, 42,* 155–162.

Berger, J., & Heath, C. (2007). Where consumers diverge from others: Identity signaling and product domains. *Journal of Consumer Research, 34,* 121–134.

Brewer, M. B. (1991). The social self: Of being the same and different at the same time. *Journal of Personality and Social Psychology, 71,* 83–93.

Brotsky, S. R., & Giles, D. (2007). Inside the "pro-ana" community: A covert online participant observation. *Eating Disorders, 15,* 93–107.

Brown, R. (1985). *Social psychology* (2nd Ed.). New York, NY: The Free Press.

Brumberg, J. J. (1997). *The body project: An intimate history of American girls.* New York, NY: Random House, Inc.

Cerulo, K. A. (1997). Identity construction: New issues, new directions. *Annual Review of Sociology, 23,* 385–409.

Chan, N. K., & Gillick, A. C. (2009). Fatness as a disability: Questions of personal and group identity. *Disability & Society, 24,* 231–243.

Chaney, D., & Goulding, C. (2016). Dress, transformation, and conformity in the heavy rock subculture. *Journal of Business Research, 69*(1), 155–165.

Cherrier, H., & Murray, J. B. (2007). Reflexive dispossession and the self: Constructing a processual theory of identity. *Consumption, Markets and Culture, 10,* 1–29.

Clarke, V., & Smith, M. (2015). Not hiding, not shouting, just me: Gay men negotiate their visual identities. *Journal of Homosexuality, 62*(1), 4–32.

Clarke, V., & Turner, K. (2007). Clothes maketh the queer? Dress, appearance and the construction of lesbian, gay and bisexual identities. *Feminism and Psychology, 17*(2), 267–276.

CNN.com (2002, June 29). Photo of baby suicide bomber called a 'joke.' Retrieved from http://www.cnn.com/2002/WORLD/meast/06/28/baby.photo/

Conger, C. (n.d.). How Quinceañeras work. Retrieved from http://people.howstuffworks.com/culture-traditions/cultural-traditions/quinceanera.htm

Corbett, E. P. (1977). *The little rhetoric and handbook.* New York, NY: John Wiley & Sons, Inc.

Crockett, L. & Petersen, A. (1987). Pubertal status and psychosocial development: Findings from the Early Adolescence Study. In R. Lerner & T. Foch (Eds.), *Biological-psycho-social interactions in early adolescence: A life-span perspective* (pp. 173–188). Hillsdale, N.J.: Erlbaum.

Cusack, M., Jack, G., & Kavanagh, D. (2003). Dancing with discrimination: Managing stigma and identity. *Culture and Organization, 9,* 295–310.

Davis, L. L. (1987). Effect of sex, inferred sex-role and occupational sex-linkage on perceptions of occupational success. *Perceptual and Motor Skills, 64,* 887–898.

Davis, L. L. (1984–85). Sex, gender identity, and behavior concerning sex-related clothing. *Clothing and Textiles Research Journal, 3*(2), 20–24.

Dilley, P. (1999). Queer theory: Under construction. *International Journal of Qualitative Studies in Education, 12*(5), 457–472.

Erikson, E. H., (1968). *Identity, youth, and crisis.* New York, NY: Norton.

Fabricant, S. M., & Gould, S. J. (1993). Women's makeup careers: An interpretative study of color cosmetic use and "face value." *Psychology & Marketing, 10,* 531–548.

Freitas, A., Kaiser, S., Hall, C., Kim, J-W., & Hammidi, T. (1997). Appearance management as border construction: Least favorite clothing, group distancing, and identity . . . not! *Sociological Inquiry, 67,* 323–335.

Goffman, E. (1963). Stigma: Notes on the management of spoiled identity. Englewood Cliffs: NJ, Prentice-Hall.

Granberg, E. (2006). "Is that all there is?": Possible selves, self-change, and weight loss. *Social Psychology Quarterly, 69*109–126.

Hegland, J. E., & Nelson, N. J. (2002). Cross-dressers in cyber-space: Exploring the Internet as a tool for expressing gendered identity. *International Journal of Sexuality and Gender Studies, 7*(2/3), 139–161.

Hipple, P. C. (2000). Clothing their resistance in hegemonic dress: The Clothesline Project's response to violence against women. *Clothing and Textiles Research Journal, 18*(3), 163–177.

How I stopped worrying and learned to love the American Girl doll. (2012, December 30). Retrieved from http://mom-101.com/2012/12/learned-to-love-the-american-girl-doll.html

Jacob, J., & Cerny, C. (2004). Radical drag appearances and identity: The embodiment of male femininity and social critique. *Clothing and Textiles Research Journal, 22*, 122–134.

Jagose, A. (1996). *Queer theory: An introduction.* New York, NY: New York University Press.

James, S. D. (2011, April 13). J. Crew ad with boy's pink toenails creates stir. *ABC News.* Retrieved from http://abcnews.go.com/Health/crew-ad-boy-painting-toenails-pink-stirs-transgender/story?id=13358903

Johnson, K. K. P., Hegland, J. E., & Schofield, N. A. (1999). Survivors of rape: Functions and implications of dress in a context of coercive power. In K. K. P. Johnson and S. J. Lennon (Eds.), *Appearance and power* (pp. 11–32). New York, NY: Berg.

Johnson, R. (1986–1987). What is cultural studies anyway? *Social Text, 16*, 38–80.

Kaiser, S. B. (1997, 2nd edition revised). *The social psychology of clothing.* New York, NY: Fairchild Publications.

Kuhn, M. H., & McPartland, T. (1954). An empirical investigation of self attitudes. *American Sociological Review, 19*, 68–76.

Lennon, S. J. (1990). Clothing and changing sex roles: Comparison of qualitative and quantitative analyses. *Home Economics Research Journal, 18*, 245–254.

Lennon, S. J. (1999). Sex, dress, and power in the workplace: *Star Trek, The Next Generation.* In K. K. P. Johnson and S. J. Lennon (Eds.), *Appearance and power* (pp. 103–126). New York, NY: Berg.

"Lesbian student shut out of tradition" (2005, January 25). Retrieved from http://www.altweeklies.com/gyrobase/AltWeeklies/Story?oid=oid%3A143583

Lewis, M., & Brooks, J. (1975). Infants' social perception: A constructionist view. *Infant perception: From sensation to cognition, 2* (pp. 101–148). New York, NY: Academic Press.

Lewis, M., & Brooks-Gunn, J. (1979). Toward a theory of social cognition: The development of self. *New Directions for Child Development, 4*, 1–20.

McCormick, J. (2003). "Drag me to the asylum": Disguising and asserting identities in an urban school. *The Urban Review, 35*(2), 111–128.

Miller, K. A., Jasper, C. R., & Hill, D. R. (1991). Costume and the perception of identity and role. *Perceptual and Motor Skills, 72*(3), 807–813.

Mueller, J. C., Dirks, D., & Picca, L. H. (2007). Unmasking racism: Halloween costuming and engagement of the racial other. *Qualitative Sociology, 30*(3), 315–335.

Myers, A. L. (2006, October 10). Arizona reservation terrorized by rapist posing as policeman. *The Seattle Times.* Retrieved from http://www.seattletimes.com/nation-world/arizona-reservation-terrorized-by-rapist-posing-as-policeman/

National Post (2009, August 12). Paris pool bans woman from wearing "burqini" swimsuit. Retrieved from http://network.nationalpost.com/np/blogs/holy-post/archive/2009/08/12/paris-pool-bans-woman-from-wearing-burqini-swimsuit.aspx

Netburn, D. (2011). J. Crew and Jenna Lyons' pink toenail controversy. *Los Angeles Times.* Retrieved from http://latimesblogs.latimes.com/alltherage/2011/04/j-crew-and-jenna-lyons-pink-toenail-controversy.html

Newman, J. (2015, March 13). American Girl trims staff. *Wisconsin State Journal.* Retrieved from http://host.madison.com/wsj/business/american-girl-trims-staff/article_da7b0898-25c8-566a-b3ff-dada5fdaaef0.html

Palfrey, D. H. (1997, July 1). La Quinceañera: A celebration of budding womanhood. Retrieved from http://www.mexconnect.com/articles/3192-la-quincea%C3%B1era-a-celebration-of-budding-womanhood

Quart, A. (2003). *Branded: The buying and selling of teenagers.* New York, NY: Basic Books.

Reddy-Best, K., & Pedersen, E. (2015). Queer women's experiences purchasing clothing and looking for clothing styles. *Clothing and Textiles Research Journal, 33*(4), 265–279.

Reeves, P. (2002, June 28). 'Baby Bomber' in family album leads to propaganda war. Retrieved from http://www.independent.co.uk/news/world/middle-east/baby-bomber-in-family-album-leads-to-propaganda-war-130927.html

Rhode, D. L. (2010). *The beauty bias: The injustice of appearance in life and law*. New York, NY: Oxford University Press.

Rice, C. (2007). Becoming "the fat girl": Acquisition of an unfit identity. *Women's Studies International Forum, 30,* 158–174.

Rosenberg, S., & Gara, M. A. (1985). The multiplicity of personal identity. *Review of Personality and Social Psychology, 6,* 87–113.

Rubin, N., Shmilovitz, C., & Weiss, M. (1993). From fat to thin: Informal rites affirming identity change. *Symbolic Interaction, 16,* 1–17.

Rudd, N. A., & Lennon, S. J. (1994). Aesthetics of the body and social identity. In M. DeLong and A. M. Fiore (Eds.), *Aesthetics of textiles and clothing: Advancing multi-disciplinary perspectives* (pp. 163–175). Monument, CO: ITAA.

Schlenker, B. R. (1986). *Impression management* (2nd Ed.). Monterey, CA: Brooks/Cole.

Schlick, P. J., & Rowold, K. L. (1991). Senior cords: A rite of passage. In P. A. Cunningham & S. V. Lab (Eds.), *Dress and popular culture* (pp. 106–124). Bowling Green, OH: Bowling Green State University Popular Press.

Schouten, J. W. (1991). Selves in transition: Symbolic consumption in personal rites of passage and identity reconstruction. *Journal of Consumer Research, 17,* 412–424.

Serpe, R. T. (1987). Stability and change in self. A structural symbolic interactionist explanation. Social Psychology Quarterly, 50(1), 44–55.

Sewell, D. (1998, Oct. 30). *The Columbus Dispatch.* Crossdresser forced to quit school, p. 3A.

Shakin, M., Shakin, D., & Sternglanz, S. (1985). Infant clothing: Sex labeling for strangers. *Sex Roles, 12,* 955–963.

Stone, G. P. (1962). Appearance and the self. In A. M. Rose (Ed.), *Human behavior and social processes: An interactionist approach* (pp. 86–118). New York, NY: Houghton Mifflin.

Stryker, S. (1968). Identity salience and role performance. *Journal of Marriage and the Family, 30,* 558–564.

Stryker, S. (2007). Identity theory and personality theory: Mutual relevance. *Journal of Personality, 75,* 1083–1102.

Stryker, S., & Burke, P. J. (2000). The past, present, and future of an identity theory. *Social Psychology Quarterly, 63,* 284–297.

Stryker, S., & Serpe, R. T. (1982). Commitment, identity salience, and role behavior: Theory and research example. In W. Ickes and E. Knowles (Eds.), *Personality, roles, and social behavior* (pp. 199–218). New York, NY: Springer-Verlag.

Swann, W. B. (1984). Quest for accuracy in person perception: A matter of pragmatics. *Psychological Review, 91,* 457–477.

Swann, W. B. (1987). Identity negotiation: Where two roads meet. *Journal of Personality and Social Psychology, 53,* 1038–1051.

Tajfel, H. (1972). Social categorization. In S. Moscovici (Ed.), *Introduction a la Pasychologie Sociale: Vol. 1* (pp. 272–302). Paris, France: Larousse.

Thanawala, S. (2015, June 3). Native American student will get to wear eagle feather to graduation. Retrieved from http://ww2.kqed.org/news/2015/06/02/native -american-student-sues-for-right-to-wear-eagle -feather-to-graduation

Tobin-Richards, M., Boxer, A., & Petersen, A. (1983). The psychological significance of pubertal change: Sex differences in perceptions of self during early adolescence. In J. Brooks-Gunn & A.C. Petersen (Eds.), *Girls at puberty: Biological and psychosocial perspectives* (pp. 127–151). New York, NY: Plenum.

Valkenburg, P. M., Schouten, A. P., & Peter, J. (2005). Adolescents' identity experiments on the Internet. *New Media & Society, 7*(3), 383–402.

Vignoles, V. L., Regalia, C., Manzi, C., Golledge, J., & Scabini, E. (2006). Beyond self-esteem: Influence of multiple motives on identity construction. *Journal of Personality and Social Psychology, 90,* 308–333.

Warren, B. (1991, September). Robert Blackman: Costume designer. *Star Trek: The Next Generation,* pp. 30–36.

Workman, J. E., & Johnson, K. K. P. (1993). Cultural aesthetics and the social construction of gender. In S. J. Lennon & L. D. Burns (Eds.), *Social science aspects of dress: New directions* (pp. 93–109). Monument, CO: ITAA.

Zlatunich, N. (2009). Prom dreams and prom reality: Girls negotiating "perfection" at the high school prom. *Sociological Inquiry, 79,* 351–375.

Zukin, S., & Maguire, J. S. (2004). Consumers and consumption. *Annual Review of Sociology, 30,* 173–197.

11 DRESS AND SOCIALIZATION

After reading and reflecting on the content of this chapter, students will be able to:

- Identify the social positions that exist within groups and how dress is used to signify those positions.
- Explain how we are socialized to dress in a certain way.
- Analyze how you were socialized and how what you learned from socialization agents has affected the way you dress today.

INTRODUCTION

Key to the understanding of a society is the concept of **social position**. You will recall from Chapter 10, "Dress and Identity," that every society, regardless of its size, is comprised of a set of social positions. For example, typically there are individuals who formally or informally lead the members of the society (e.g., Presidents, chiefs, executives) and those who follow (e.g., citizens, members, employees). This example has two simple social positions: Leader and follower.

As we noted in Chapter 10, a status is a specific place within a set of social positions (Giddens, Duneier, Appelbaum, & Carr, 2009). In this example, the individuals who lead the society are attributed higher status (e.g., more importance) than are the individuals who follow. An individual, because of the number of societies he or she is a member of and due to the number of social positions that could exist within any one society, may hold a number of statuses at the same time as well as over his or her lifetime. One's social position is often signified by special dress items. For example, in Western Europe kings and queens wore crowns and crown jewels.

Ascribed and Achieved Statuses

Some statuses are obtained at birth. These statuses include your age, sex, or the order of your birth (e.g., oldest child, youngest child). We use the term **ascribed status** to describe statuses which you are unable to control or exert an influence over. Dress can contribute to the successful execution of an ascribed status. Consider the presentation of children by their parents. When George was born to Prince William of England and Duchess Kate, he acquired the status of prince. When President Barack Obama and first lady Michelle Obama visited Prince William and Duchess Kate at Kensington Palace in April, 2016, Prince George was there to greet them. He was described as "smartly attired for bedtime in a light-colored robe and pajama pants" (Durand, 2016). Put another way, his appearance reinforced his ascribed prince status as he appeared consistent with his status as prince and with meeting the president and first lady of the USA.

Other statuses you obtain as a result of your decisions and your effort. Examples representing this second category of statuses include being a college graduate, a parent, or the president of an organization. The term **achieved status** is used to designate this category of statuses. Dress can also play a part in an individual's ability to be successful within an achieved status. For example, Joanne Lublin (2011) in the *Wall Street Journal* shared the story of a woman holding a middle management position within an organization. The woman preferred to wear a ponytail, khakis, sweaters, little makeup, and loafers to work. She had trouble getting people who held positions within her company at high status levels to listen to her ideas. She underwent an appearance makeover making several changes to her dress; she upgraded her work clothing to dressy slacks and jackets, had her hair cut into a sophisticated hairstyle, and added additional makeup as well as coordinating accessories. She credited her new appearance to boosting her confidence that in turn, resulted in faster acceptance of her ideas by upper management. In other words, individuals holding higher status positions positively responded to her when she dressed in a manner that was consistent with her status within the organization.

Status Set

Every person occupies some combination of statuses. The term used to describe the combination of statuses is **status set** (Giddens et al., 2009). You, for example, are a student if you are enrolled in school, a son or a daughter, a friend to your peers, an employee if you have a job, and a citizen of some country. Your status set is important because it guides what you do and enables others to predict a significant amount of your behavior. Status sets guide behavior because, as we just learned, each status that you hold has a set of expectations for behavior as well as expectations for your dress and appearance. In general, students act and appear different from professors; adults act and appear different from children. Each group develops its own set of behavioral expectations.

Some of the time, a specific status is more important to how you see yourself and how you want others to view you than other statuses. This specific status, a **master status**, takes priority over other statuses. Your sex could be considered a master status because it impacts how others treat you. You recognize that a status has master standing for you when other statuses you have in your status set are ignored or are of less importance to you. In addition, the status that is most important to you can change based on the situation you are in. For example, suppose you are the captain of your university's basketball team. Being captain is a high status position on campus and perhaps you are afforded certain privileges (e.g., free tutors) as part of holding this status. However, when you leave campus and return to your family for the holidays, your captain status is diminished relative to your family status as the "baby" of the family. Thus, what status is a master status is closely tied to context or situation.

NORMS AND ROLES

As previously noted, any social position in a given society or group has a set of expectations for behaviors linked to it. These expectations for behaviors typical of any individual

within a social position are called norms.[1] Norms are general guidelines for behavior and include expectations for dress and appearance. Norms are tied to context as well as to status. For example, if you are going to the beach, the norm would be to wear a swim suit, sandals, a baseball cap or visor, use sunscreen, and so forth. If you were going to work at an upscale boutique, the norm could be to wear all black (e.g., pants, shirt, shoes).

A closely related term to norm is *role*. Recall that in Chapter 5, "Dress and Impression Formation" that role was defined as the behavior that we expect of others who occupy certain social positions. Or put another way, a role is the way a person in a particular position, that is, holding a specific status within a social organization, is expected to act (Zusman, Knox, & Gardner, 2009). Returning to our beach example, perhaps there are three people going to the beach: a grandmother, a mother, and her teenage daughter. A man viewing these three people may hold different expectations for the dress of the grandmother as compared to the teenager even though both are women because each represents a different age status.

---

[1]See Freeburg and Workman (2010) for a method to identify and validate social norms related to dress.

CONCEPTS RELATED TO STATUS AND ROLE

Prescribed Role

Sometimes confusion exists about a certain role. There may be differences in what is expected (i.e., role prescription), what is perceived, and what behaviors are actually performed. **Prescribed role** is a term to describe the set of behaviors that a group of individuals expect should be done when any individual assumes a status (Giddens et al., 2009). For example, in a university setting, any one professor is expected to come prepared to class, deliver course material, prepare and evaluate course assignments, provide feedback to students, conduct research, dress appropriately, and so forth. What it means to "dress appropriately" can vary a great deal between professors, but there are common expectations held by students concerning what a professor looks like.

James Lang (2005), an assistant professor of English at Assumption College, shared his ideas about looking like a professor and his students' expectations for a professor's appearance. He was teaching during summer session wearing Birkenstock sandals, short pants, and a short-sleeved golf shirt. When an adult student indicated that Lang "did not look like a professor," he began thinking about what it meant to look like a professor and about what a professor's clothing could mean to students. Clearly his outfit did not send the message that he was the person in charge of the classroom to the student who remarked on his appearance.

Role Perception

While a professor may recognize and understand role expectations for the status of a professor, he or she may think that not all of these behaviors are absolutely necessary. Put another way, he or she may differ in their **role perception** from the expectations of others. Continuing on with our example of Assistant Professor Lang (2005), clearly the professor's sandals, shorts, and golf shirt met the professor's own role perception for how to appear as a college professor. However, in his article Lang described a broad spectrum of appearances that professors presented to students on his campus noting that a range existed from sharp dressers at one end to slobs at the other. The sharp dressers were described as wearing ties to class every day that matched their shirts. They wore brown or black shoes and some even wore suits! On the other hand, the slobs wore T-shirts and shorts to class. Clearly there were not only differences between students and professors in role perceptions for dress but also differences between professors (Figure 11.1).

Figure 11.1
If one were to cast an individual in the role of a college professor, this individual may reflect the expected appearance (i.e., a man, as men continue to outnumber women as professors, wearing glasses to convey intelligence, wearing suit and tie, and mature in years).

Role Performance

Differences in role perception may generate differences in **role performance**. Role performance refers to the actual behavior of an individual in a role (Giddens, et al., 2009). Continuing on with our example of Assistant Professor Lang (2005), Lang shared that he believed his appearance matched with his activities as a professor and that dress was a key feature in his own role performance. Lang intended that by wearing shorts, sandals, and golf shirt, he signified to his students that in his role as professor he was not uptight and that contributions made by students in his classes would be welcomed. He also thought that wearing his button-down shirt was an indicator that he was the one who was assigning the grades. The overall intended message of his appearance could be summarized as welcoming student input but at the same time reminding students that status differences existed between Lang and his students. Put another way, looking similar to a student is not the same as being equal to a student. Lang noted that while he was attempting to use dress as a signal to his role performance (assisting learning, assigning grades), he was uncertain that the messages he intended to send through his dress choices were the same messages his students received.

Role performance may differ between individuals for a number of other reasons including level of commitment to the role. Perhaps for some individuals in the role of professor, being a professor is not as important as other statuses that they hold so they are less committed to the role than they could be. Perhaps they would rather run a business as an apparel designer than be a professor. Perhaps other roles are competing for the professor's time such as being a father or mother to children or a caregiver to elderly parents.

In addition to level of commitment, role performance may vary between individuals because there is sufficient flexibility with the status so that only some of the expected behaviors linked to the role need to be fulfilled in order for the role to be successfully performed. Consider the status of student and the associated role. Expected behaviors for a student may include reading assigned course material prior to class, attending all scheduled classes, wearing appropriate clothing to class, and studying an hour each night for a class. Because successful completion of a class is designated by a passing grade, not all students engage in all expected behaviors all of the time (e.g., they may skip class, study only immediately before a test, wear pajamas and slippers to class) and yet many are still able to be successful (i.e., receive a passing grade).

Role Ambiguity

Role ambiguity refers to a situation in which the expectations for a particular social status are unclear (Giddens et al., 2009). Consider when you started your first job. Perhaps the scope of your responsibilities, even though they were probably explained to you, was not as clear as you might have desired. You may be asked to manage individuals who are ten or twenty years older than you with significant experience. Do you tell them what to do or do you ask them what to do? Your age might suggest you should follow their direction but your status as a manager suggests you should be setting the direction. Or perhaps you are moving to a new job at a new company. Since the company is new the corporate culture of the company is under a state of development and role expectations have not been firmly established. Would a traditional suit or a casual appearance be the best choice to wear to work? This question might be best answered through a process of trial and error.

Role Strain

Role strain occurs when contradictory expectations exist about a given status or when there is a higher number of expectations associated with a status than anyone could

---

IN-CLASS ACTIVITY
Conflicting Role Expectations

Expected behaviors for a course instructor include expectations for appearance. With the acceptance of casual dress in many organizations, people often appear in casual dress for work. What do you expect your professors to wear when at work? Do your expectations vary based on the discipline of the professor? For example, would you expect a business professor to appear differently from a design professor? Why, or why not? Do your expectations for a professor's appearance impact your evaluation of the professor's knowledge and ability as a teacher? Why, or why not? Do your expectations for a professor's appearance impact how you treat your professor? Why, or why not?

reasonably expect to meet (Giddens et al., 2009). The strain can result from not having sufficient time to fulfill all of the expectations or the expectations may simply exceed your capabilities. For example, as a student you may have one set of expectations that stem from your parents (e.g., get good grades), one set that comes from your friends (e.g., partying), one set from your employer (e.g., work long hours), and expectations from your teachers (e.g., attend classes). Working long hours may be incompatible with attending classes and you experience role stain trying to do both.

You can experience role strain relative to your appearance as different individuals may have different expectations for what appearance you should present based on the social position you occupy. For example, when you were an adolescent you might have wanted to wear clothing styles or make modifications to your body (e.g., tattoos, piercings) that were not in agreement with the appearance expectations of your parents or the administrators of your school. Your parents may have suggested that the body modifications you wanted were not suitable for an adolescent or the school administrators may have indicated that a clothing style was not acceptable for the role of student. As a result of these conflicting expectations for your appearance, you may experience role strain.

For example, former child beauty pageant contestant, Brooke Breedwell, has related her experience with expectations attached to the status of child pageant contestant (Bindley, 2012). Some of those expectations included attending pageants each day, everyday practice that included makeup and hairspray, 20 minute tanning bed sessions three times per week, and having to use fake teeth called flippers. As a result Breedwell became anxious, stressed, and perfectionist.

These appearance management behaviors reported by Breedwell are consistent with results of research that studied child pageant contestants (Cartwright, 2012). According to Cartwright's observations, child pageant contestants may be made to train beyond their abilities and to maintain an unrealistic appearance. Some parents set on winning disciplined their youngsters "for poor performance, lack of enthusiasm, or a flawed appearance" (p. 1106). Extrapolating from these two sources, it is possible that Breedwell and other child pageant contestants experienced role strain as a result of unrealistic expectations (Figure 11.2).

Gabi Finlayson may also have experienced role strain related to expectations for her appearance at her Utah high

Figure 11.2
When young children participate in adult activities such as beauty pageants they may experience role strain including incompatible expectations for appearance, as young participants are often presented in clothing items and makeup more commonly worn by adult women than by children.

school dance. Gabi believed that she had selected a dress that was appropriate (Goorwich, 2015; Lindsay, 2015). She had been anticipating wearing the dress that she and her mother purchased in Paris while on a family trip. However, upon arrival at the dance, Gabi was told by a school official that she needed to cover her shoulders; so she had to wear her winter jacket all evening. In this instance Gabi thought she was in compliance with the school dress code expectations, but the school official had different expectations and deemed that Gabi was in noncompliance, causing the role strain. (To see the dress go online and search for "American school girl made to cover her shoulders").

A person can hold the same status in two different groups but be expected to behave and/or dress differently based on group membership. This happens because each group develops its own set of roles; thus, roles can vary between groups. For example, you could be the president of a fraternal organization and you could be expected to wear tailored clothing to weekly meetings. At the same time, you could be president of an environmental organization where members expect you to wear environmentally friendly clothing. Perhaps it is difficult for you to locate tailored clothing that both fits you and is made from environmentally friendly materials. Suppose both groups meet on Monday evenings. You wear your tailored suit to your fraternal organization and also to the meeting for your environmental group. For the first meeting, your appearance fits right in with other members and meets expected norms for looking presidential, but for the second meeting your appearance deviates from the norms for your role as president. From this example you can see that each group determines what are the appearance norms for that group and what is the norm for one group can be viewed as not the norm (i.e., deviant) for another group.

Role conflict occurs when the expectations tied to two or more statuses are incompatible (Giddens et al., 2009). For example, assume you are a dance student worker employed as a department receptionist in a dance department. As a student, you may want to wear your body-revealing dance attire so you can easily go from class to work. Your work supervisor may want you to wear more formal attire than your dance clothing since you will be greeting the public. Your friends may expect you to wear trendy apparel styles. Thus, recognizing the incompatible expectations that exist for your dress may be a source of role conflict.

The resulting conflict between expectations for your appearance stemming from your membership groups (e.g., work, family, school administration, friendship groups) and your own expectations for appearance can result in appearance labor. **Appearance labor** is defined as any "dissonance between what individuals are expected to wear and what they would prefer to wear" (Peluchette, Karl, & Rust, 2006). Experiencing this dissonance can result in immense time spent in trying to resolve the conflict. Continuing with the previous example of Gabi Finlayson, the fact that she had to wear her jacket over her dress at the dance may have reflected appearance labor. She relates that she was embarrassed and insulted when she was singled out and made to wear her jacket over her dress (Goorwich, 2015). In these kinds of situations, does

one forego participation in some forms of dress because of the appearance expectations of the workplace (or school dance) or does one try to change expectations for workplace (or school dance) appearance? We learned in Chapter 8, "Dress and Personality," that one strategy to deal with appearance labor is to hide body modifications (e.g., tattoos, body piercings) that evoke negative responses from others. But is this a viable long-term strategy to resolving appearance labor? As forms of dress continue to evolve, experiences of appearance labor may be continuous throughout the life span. Research is needed documenting how issues of appearance labor are effectively resolved in the long term.

SOCIALIZATION

Now that we understand how a society or any large or small group of individuals is structured and how complicated it can be to successfully execute a role within a society, how do we learn how about roles and social positions and the accompanying norms for behavior within the ongoing society that we are born into? Rules and norms about how to behave, including how to appear and what to wear are learned through the process of socialization (Kammeyer, Ritzer, & Yetman, 1992). Recall that in Chapter 10, "Dress and Identity," socialization was defined as the process through which children learn the norms and values of the culture in which they live. Through socialization members of groups (e.g., adults) impart to new members (e.g., children, youth) the habits and values of their culture through instruction and modeling (Baumrind, 1980). **Socialization agents** are the teachers of how to function in society; that is, they teach the norms.

Socialization theory is a theory about how socialization occurs. Through socialization we learn not only how we are expected to dress but also the consequences if we do not dress as expected. In addition, through socialization we learn the functions of dress within societies and social groups. Learning how to function in society includes learning appropriate traits, skills, and appearances needed for everyday life. For example, as a child you may have learned what colors looked good together, what you need to wear to stay warm on a January day, and how to tie your shoes (Figure 11.3).

We usually think of socialization in terms of children being socialized by adults. However, socialization occurs

Figure 11.3

Learning to function in society includes mastering important skills for daily life such as how to tie shoes.

throughout the lifespan as adults learn how to function in new contexts. Across the lifespan we assume new statuses and need to learn the roles associated with them. For example, a new job or the same job at a different employer requires that the employee learn "how things are done" at the new employer (e.g., who to go to for advice, how to get expenses reimbursed, how people are expected to dress for work).

Formal and Informal Socialization

Socialization can be formal or informal. Organized education is a formal type of socialization with a planned curriculum and learning goals, so it is deliberate. In **formal socialization** there is usually a knowledgeable person who instructs others in a classroom type of setting. Organized education includes grade, middle, and high school, as well as nursery school and college. Religious education is often formal.

There is also formal socialization within employment. Retailers may offer formal socialization in the form of training programs for new retail management trainees. Modeling schools formally socialize future fashion models for their occupation (Vaughn & Riemer, 1985). For example, for one model walking lessons were provided by a "runway coach" as part of her socialization as a new fashion model (Mears, 2011).

Sometimes we can be formally socialized about how to dress. In 1980 the book *Color Me Beautiful* was published and shortly thereafter department and specialty stores began offering color analysis promotions (Hilliker & Rogers, 1988; Radeloff, 1991). These promotions often featured fashion color consultants who analyzed consumers' skin tones, eye colors, and hair colors and recommended colors of clothing to harmonize with personal coloring. Such color analyses constitute formal socialization about what to wear.

Informal socialization can occur anywhere; it involves learning without a formal lesson and an institution is not involved. There is no planned effort to achieve a certain outcome and the people doing the socializing may be unaware of their actions. For example, pre-school teachers may be unaware that they give more praise (e.g., "you are so pretty today") to girls coming to school wearing frilly dresses than they do to girls wearing jeans and matching T-shirts.

It is common for small children to experiment with what they wear perhaps because they see what adults wear. If they receive feedback about their dress, they may use it to shape their future behavior. For example, in one study the researcher describes an incident he observed at a preschool where children were playing dress up (Cahill, 1989). Some children provided feedback to a boy wearing a dress and high heels ("You're a boy . . . Those are girl things" [p. 288]). The result of this feedback was that the boy took off the "inappropriate clothing." Cahill also observed a teacher's aide describing girls wearing gender-appropriate clothing (dresses, lace) as "pretty" and "sweet." In these ways, the children were informally socialized regarding how to dress.

The previous examples of verbal commentary illustrate positive and negative sanctions respectively. In Chapter 10, "Dress and Identity," a sanction was defined as a reward (positive sanction) or punishment (negative sanction) intended to encourage or enforce conformity to norms. Positive sanctions regarding appearance can vary from praise as in the previous example to monetary prizes and scholarships received by beauty pageant winners. Negative sanctions can vary from a raised eyebrow to arrest for appearing nude in public ("Former mayor slapped," 2009). Through socialization we learn not only how we are expected to dress, but also the consequences that can follow if we do not dress as expected.

Parents, siblings, and peers also use verbal commentary in the form of teasing as a means to socialize expectations for appearance. Teasing can be divided into two forms: playful and hurtful. Playful teasing is friendly and can actually be perceived as fun and an instance of joking. Playful teasing can be labeled as flirting in circumstances where it is reciprocal. More often, however, teasing is viewed as hurtful because it is intended to injure or upset the recipient. Appearance-based teasing occurs often during adolescence with a range of aspects of appearance (e.g., clothing, weight, height, hair, facial features, body) identified as the focus of the tease (Yoo & Johnson, 2007, 2008).

The outcomes linked to teasing are more often negative than positive. Teasing about body weight during adolescence has been linked to body dissatisfaction, low self-esteem and even thinking about and attempting suicide (Eisenberg, Neumark-Sztainder, & Story, 2003; Lawler & Nixon, 2011; Yoo & Johnson, 2007).

Similarly, researchers studying young girl adolescents found that the more the girls were teased or received criticism about their bodies, the lower their reported level of body satisfaction (Seock & Merritt, 2013). Unlike the aforementioned researchers, in their research with both Euro-American and African-American adolescents Yoo and Johnson (2007) found that experiences of teasing could be positive. Positive teasing by friends included instances where the teasing was interpreted as a joke or as appropriate behavior because it signaled friendship. Responses to being teased about appearance often resulted in attempts to modify or change the aspect of appearance that was the focus of the tease. Strategies include to stop wearing dress items that are the focus of a tease, initiate new appearance management behaviors (e.g., weight loss programs, working out) to eliminate/reduce the problem, and buying new products or items of dress (e.g., treatments, new clothing) (Yoo & Johnson, 2007).

Effects of teasing have also been found to be long-term and sometimes even permanent. In two separate studies of teasing and body image, individuals who reported being teased during adolescence about their appearance (e.g., weight) were likely to be dissatisfied with those aspects of their appearance as adults (Cash, 1995). In later research with adults who had anxiety disorders, researchers found that as reported teasing increased so did social anxiety, depression, and stress (McCabe, Miller, Laugeson, Antony, & Young, 2010). Thus, there is clear evidence that the effects of teasing as a form of informal socialization experienced during childhood can last into adulthood.

Informal socialization can also take place in the groups or collectives to which we belong. Two sororities at a western state university were studied by Arthur (1998). In that qualitative study she found that as new members, young women quickly learned and adopted the sorority girl image. Even before pledging most girls were thin and fit and wore classic conservative or preppy clothing from moderate to expensive stores. Learning how to look like a sorority member was achieved by observation of and advice from other members.

In another qualitative study, sorority members were interviewed. The researchers found that in particular contexts (e.g., formal dances, house dinners, rush) there were fairly specific rules for how members were to appear in public (Hunt & Miller, 1997). Such rules are often learned through informal socialization.

Identification

During socialization children learn about dress through a process called **identification**. Identification is a cognitive process in which a child views him or herself as similar to another person (Figure 11.4). As a result of a desire to possess similar characteristics, the child is motivated to copy some of the behaviors of the individual that he or she identifies with. The person identified with could be any of a number of individuals (e.g., a parent, a celebrity, a teacher, a story book character, a sibling, an athlete). You can easily imagine a young boy identifying with an athlete or an older sibling and deciding to wear matching items of clothing or perhaps wanting to engage in the same body modifications (e.g., tattoo). Or consider a young girl identifying with a celebrity and wanting to have a similar hair style or clothing.

Learning via identification does not end during childhood. There is a trend for young British men to have beard transplants in an attempt to have beards like David Beckham and Ben Affleck (Halkon, 2016).

Social Learning Theory

Key to the process of identification is **observational learning or modeling**. Albert Bandura, a sociologist who studied modeling with children, developed **social learning theory** to explain how individuals learn from observing the behaviors of others and the outcomes of those behaviors. He suggested that people serve as models for each other. In quantitative research with children, Bandura (1977) found that after watching the behavior of an adult, children could later imitate the same or similar behaviors. Some examples of dress related behaviors that children learn from modeling adults include applying makeup and shaving.

Key to the process of observational learning is the individual's attention to the behavior, retention of the behavior, ability to reproduce the behavior, and motivation to produce the behavior. Individuals need to pay attention to the details of the initial behavior in order to reproduce it. Consider trying to pay close attention to the behavior of someone else. There are many factors that can impact your ability including distracting noises present in the environment and personal factors such as whether or not you have a headache or a cold. Individuals must also remember details of the behavior in order to reproduce it. An individual must also have the physical ability and resources to reproduce the behavior. A young child can watch a parent getting dressed but may not have the balance or motor control to dress herself. Your ability to reproduce

a behavior can, of course, increase with practice. Finally, even if individuals know what the behavior is and have the resources and ability to reproduce the behavior, they still may not produce the behavior unless they are motivated to do so.

Behaviors that are copied are often those behaviors that are positively reinforced by others. For example, you would be more motivated to imitate the behavior of a friend who received a compliment on her dress than one who received criticism. A young girl may be interested in wearing feminine clothing styles to pre-school because she observes that girls who look "pretty" receive more attention from teachers than girls wearing T-shirts and pants (Cahill, 1989).

That young children are motivated to imitate the dress of others is evidenced in the following experience of one of your authors and her daughter. The then three year-old daughter expressed the desire to wear a "sign" on her pants one morning as she was getting ready for preschool. Her mother had no idea what type of sign the preschooler meant, so she drew a cute picture and pinned it to her daughter's pants pocket. Her daughter promptly dissolved into tears and getting her to attend the preschool that day was difficult. Upon arriving at the school, a teacher was asked whether she knew about a "sign" that the little girls were wearing. She did not, but then the daughter came up to her mother with her friend in tow and showed her mother the sign that her friend had on her jeans—it was a brand logo! The daughter had keenly observed what her friends were wearing and was highly motivated to wear the same thing; it was the mother who did not have the resources to purchase the jeans or the ability to reproduce the logo and thus, enable her daughter's desired behavior.

Real People as Models

The process of modeling discussed thus far occurs with real people or live models; consider for example a young child wearing the same outfits or participating in similar forms of body modification (e.g., getting their nails done, dieting, getting a piercing) as an older sibling or a parent. In this instance the model may be demonstrating the actual behavior or providing direct instruction about how to engage in the behavior. For example, we know that mothers can exert a significant influence on daughters. As discussed in Chapter 7, "Dress and Body Image," daughters who imitated their mother's dieting behaviors were children of mothers who took a very deliberate and proactive approach to instructing their child about dieting (Ogle & Damhorst, 2000).

Symbolic Models

Modeling can also occur with a symbolic model. **Symbolic models** include individuals who are outside the family such as real or fictional persons in movies, television programs, or online media as well as dolls. Evidence that symbolic models do exert a significant influence comes from news articles depicting young adults and adolescents adopting items of dress worn by their favorite celebrities. This process is enabled by fashion magazines such as *In Style* and *People* that not only feature celebrities as models and as the subject of articles, but also inform readers on where to purchase the items or how to achieve the desired look.

Dolls as Models

Barbie is a popular fashion doll and has been identified as one of the most successful dolls of the twentieth century as well as a beauty icon. The doll has long legs, tiny feet, large breasts, and a tiny waist. There is considerable disagreement over the impact of Barbie on the lives of young girls. Some researchers claim that Barbie is a negative symbolic model for young girls because the doll is presented as primarily being overly concerned with her looks and her clothing and has a figure that is unattainable by any real

person.[2] The concern is that young girls internalize this view of what women are supposed to be and express similar views (e.g., desire to be thin and overly concerned with appearance) as adults.

Several groups of researchers have tried to document the impact of Barbie on girls. One research team investigated the use of these dolls among nine young children as well as their mother's ideas about the impact of playing with Barbie in their lives. These researchers found that important aspects included the clothing or the accessories the doll wore or the doll's hair. There was no mention made of the doll's body. When playing with Barbie, play centered on dressing and grooming the doll to increase her attractiveness. The girls role-played activities including attending a special event, shopping, or participating in a wedding. The reported influence of Barbie in the lives of the mothers was mixed with about half of the mothers suggesting Barbie impacted their lives and the others reporting no impact. The type of influence of Barbie on the mothers' lives was also split with about half suggesting a positive influence and the others a negative one (Markee, Pedersen, Murray, & Stacey, 1994).

Nearly ten years later, another team of researchers held exploratory focus groups with sixth grade girls and asked them to share their experiences with Barbie dolls. All of the participants had at least two Barbie dolls, one had fifty. All of the girls shared that they imagined many glamorous activities with their dolls including having weddings, attending proms, and other glamorous events (e.g., fashion shows). Overall feelings toward Barbie included that her body was unrealistic (Kuther & McDonald, 2004).

In addition to the pretend positive life events, the researchers were surprised to learn that many of the participants engaged in torture play and/or anger play with their Barbies. Activities commonly reported included damaging their dolls by cutting off their hair, removing limbs, and painting them. Most of this type of play occurred with older children and in the presence of boys. When asked why they tortured their Barbie doll in particular, one participant shared she tortured her Barbie because "she is the only one that looks perfect" (Kuther & McDonald, 2004, p. 43). The researchers suggested that the torturing of Barbie by young girls may signal a loss of voice or their silencing. Further research is needed to fully understand the torture play with Barbie.

[2]If Barbie were an actual woman, she would be 5'9" tall, have a 39" bust, an 18" waist, 33" hips and a size 3 shoe (Katz, 2011).

MATTEL CREATES DIVERSE BARBIES

In February 2016, Mattel unveiled a big change in the iconic Barbie doll that has been around since 1959 (Dockterman, 2016). In addition to the "original" version with a disproportionately large bust for her tiny waist, and standing on tippy-toes that would never hold her up in real life, she now comes in a "curvy" version that is realistic in proportions (with slightly larger tummy and hips, thighs, and calves), as well as a "tall" version, and a "petite" version. She also comes in a variety of skin colors, hair colors and hair textures, and some of the new Barbies will have larger feet. Mattel never acknowledged that the doll's proportions could have a negative effect on girls. By the mid-2000s, parents abandoned Barbie in favor of other dolls with different proportions (Bratz, Elsa, Monster High), and by 2015 Mattel's sales were at an all-time low. Perhaps to answer the question of why, Mattel conducted extensive research with moms across the country and found that moms wanted diversity of color and body in their children's dolls, as well as dolls that could empower girls to be more than "pretty."

One of the major concerns about Barbie is whether the doll fuels the desire to be thin in young girls. To answer this question, an experiment with young girls between the ages of five and eight was conducted. The young girls read a story book that told a story about Mira and depicted her as having either one of two figure types developed using paper dolls (Barbie, representing a size 2; Emme, representing a size 16) or no information about body type (control). Body esteem was lowered and body size dissatisfaction was greater when the girls were shown Mira using the Barbie images than when Mira was depicted as Emme or given no information about body type. Girls exposed to the Barbie wanted a thinner body now and in the future as adult women. The Barbie doll effect was also age-related with girls between the ages of 5½ and 7½ years reporting a greater desire to be thin than older girls (ages 7½ to 8½) (Dittmar, Halliwell, & Ive, 2006). Therefore, the answer to the question of whether Barbie dolls fuel a desire to be thin appears to be "yes" with young girls.

Looking forward, clothing researchers may want to investigate the influence of the twenty-first century Bratz doll. The Bratz dolls are adolescent dolls that wear sexy clothing and makeup. Researchers have expressed concern over the self-sexualization of young girls within the US (Lynch, 2012; Starr & Ferguson, 2012). **Self-sexualization** includes valuing oneself based solely on sex appeal or treating oneself as a sexual object. An interesting and valuable area of future research is documenting whether playing with Bratz dolls contributes to the self-sexualization of young girls (Figure 11.5).

Figure 11.5

A four-year old girl playing with Bratz dolls. Could playing with these dolls contribute to self-sexualizing behaviors in children?

Primary Socialization

In addition to categorizing socialization processes as formal and informal, we also group socialization into primary processes and secondary processes. During **primary socialization**, children learn how to dress through direct instruction with caregivers. For example, in the US it is common for children to put on different clothes for sleeping (i.e., sleepwear: pajamas or nightgowns) than they wear during the day. They learn to change their clothing for night time or day time from their caregivers.

Stages of Primary Socialization: Pre-play.

Stone (1962) identified three stages of primary socialization: pre-play, play, and game stages. During the **pre-play stage** of primary socialization the infant becomes social and responds to the caregivers in a pre-verbal way. Stone noted that the appearance of an infant is imposed by caregivers, who tend to dress the infant in ways consistent with biological sex. We say that this stage is characterized by **investiture**, in which the child has no control over his or her dress. Someone else, usually the mother, selects the infant's clothing and hairstyle (assuming that the infant has hair).

Stone explained that the dress of a child conveys meaning. He commented that children dressed in pink are described as *darling* or *graceful*, while children dressed in blue are identified as *handsome* and *strong*. Similarly, the biological sex of infants is often inferred from the color of their clothing. In fieldwork girls were identified by clothing that was pink or yellow, or that contained ruffles, puffed sleeves, or lace (Shakin, Shakin, & Sternglanz, 1985).

Even though color is often a key dress differentiator between the sexes, other indicators are used as well in both children's and adult apparel to distinguish the sexes. These indicators include use and type of appliqués (e.g., trucks, flowers, puppies, kittens), fabric type, and closures. These secondary indicators are so ubiquitous that children, as young as two or three years of age, are able to categorize clothing items as for boys or for girls. Young children are also able to link specific clothing items with feminine (e.g., playing with dolls) or masculine (e.g., aggressive play) activities (Kaiser, 1989). But there is no evidence that the clothing worn by a child actually impacts the play activities in which a child engages. Young girls wearing skirts are just as likely to engage in masculine play activities as girls wearing pants (Kaiser, Rudy, & Byfield, 1985).

DRESS IN THE NEWS
When Did Pink Signify Girl and Blue Signify Boy?

Jo B. Paoletti, a historian at the University of Maryland who has studied the meaning of children's clothing for three decades, noted that for practical reasons children until about the age of six wore white dresses because they were relatively easy to keep clean; white cotton could be bleached (Maglaty, 2011). It was not until just before World War I that pastel colors arrived as colors for babies and even then the pink-blue gender dichotomy did not immediately take hold. Initially pink was deemed as suitable for boys as it was a stronger color and blue for girls because it was a dainty color. According to Paoletti, the color distinction we know today was not popular until the 1940s and was as a result of consumer preferences as interpreted by retailers and manufacturers. Thus, the baby boomers were the first generation to be raised in gender distinct apparel. Boys dressed like their fathers and girls like their mothers. The 1960s brought the women's liberation movement and gender neutral or unisex apparel for children. Gender neutral clothing remained popular until the mid-1980s when pre-natal testing became popular. As a result of parents being able to determine the sex of their child early, they were able to make sex appropriate purchases of apparel and other items in advance of the birth of their child. According to Paoletti, the more you can individualize clothing, the more you can sell, as pink items appropriate for one sex are not appropriate for the other.

Another important factor in the continuation of gender differentiation is consumerism. Advertising is directed toward young children that tend to reinforce social conventions. Young children learn through these portrayals what it means to be a girl or to be a boy and part of that knowledge includes expectations for appearance.

Has the practice of dressing infants using colors or other indicators to signal their biological sex continued? In the 1990s researchers examined the near environment of infants (five months to twenty-four months) to assess the emergence of gender differences in their appearance. They found girls wore more pink clothing and jewelry while boy's clothing was red, white, or blue. Girls had pink pacifiers, dolls, and yellow bedding while boys had blue pacifiers, sports equipment, and blue bedding (Pomerleau, Bolduc, Malcuit, & Cossette, 1990).

Although at the beginning of the twentieth century, boys and girls were dressed the same Figure 11.6), since the mid-1980s the market for children's clothing has been clearly divided into specific items for boys and for girls. Even if the style of apparel itself is not clearly linked to one sex or the other (i.e., bib overall, jeans, T-shirts), the item is modified using an array of techniques (e.g., color) to suggest it is more appropriate for one sex than the other. So even if parents wanted to dress their child in gender neutral clothing, it might be difficult to do so (Paoletti, 2012).

Because certain colors are so closely linked with one gender or the other, presenting one's infant in colors that are not typically associated with the sex of the child may be problematic. A team of researchers conducted an experiment testing the effect of color (pink versus blue) of male infant clothing on health decisions concerning the child (Ben-Zeev & Dennehy, 2014). Participants were asked to select between implementing two options to prevent the flu: one of the decision choices was riskier than the other. As compared to when the male infants were wearing blue, when the infants were wearing pink, the participants selected the riskier option. The researchers concluded that a male infant dressed in pink violated a gender norm and consequently incurred riskier decisions. Additional research is needed to clarify these findings but it does raise interesting questions about differences in care that children might receive as a result of meeting or not meeting gender expectations for dress and appearance.

Moving forward, it might be interesting to see if twenty-first-century mothers continue to differentiate either the near environment or the appearance (or both) of their infants and young children using dress, what items of dress are used, or if this practice of using dress to emphasize the biological sex of a child has diminished or increased overall. As noted earlier, if what clothing styles and colors are made available to parents and other caregivers by retailers is any indicator, the answer to this question may be yes because there are few alternatives unless one can make their children's clothing.

If as indicated, an infant or child is invested with clothing during the preplay stage of socialization, what is the child learning about dress during this stage? Overall, children are learning how to differentiate gender on the basis of dress and appearance cues. During the first year

of life children label people as male and female based on physical attributes such as voice and hair length (Leinbach & Fagot, 1993; Poulin-Dubois, Serbin, Kenyon, & Derbyshire, 1994). During the second year of life, children learn what labels, activities, and objects are commonly related to each sex. For example, at eighteen months of age, girls are aware of the stereotyping of various toys, associating dolls with girls and vehicles with boys (Serbin, Poulin-Dubois, Colburne, Sen, & Eichstedt, 2001). At two years of age children associate a suit and tie, shaving, and fixing cars with men. Dresses, putting on make-up, cooking, and vacuuming are linked to women (Poulin-Dubois, Serbin, Eichstedt, Sen, & Beissel, 2002; Serbin, Poulin-Dubois, & Eichstedt, 2002).

Figure 11.6

What is the sex of this child? Historically, it was not always clear what the biological sex of a child was, as children, regardless of their sex, wore the same style of clothing. This is a photo of a child approximately two years old circa 1900.

Given that children appear to be learning gender distinctions linked to dress and that part of that distinction is tied to color, do young children have a distinct preference for wearing pink versus blue apparel items? Researchers tried to answer this research question by conducting a series of experiments with young children ranging in age from infancy to five years of age (LoBue & Deloach, 2011). They found that by age two, girls selected pink items significantly more often than did boys. By age three, girls demonstrated a distinct preference for pink items and young boys showed a distinct avoidance of them. They explained these differences by pointing out that these color preferences develop at about the same time that children begin to seek out gender-related information (Zosuls et al., 2009). Exploring gender helps children form their own gender identities (Martin & Ruble, 2004). Thus, if the color pink is part of what children have learned signifies the concept of "girliness," then it is not surprising that girls at this age are attracted to this color and that the reverse would be true for boys.

Supporting the idea that children may be learning gender rules for dress at an early age is the phenomena of appearance rigidity. Sometimes children themselves insist on wearing dress items that are linked to one sex or avoiding dress items linked to the opposite sex. The term used to describe this behavior is **appearance rigidity**. Appearance rigidity appears earlier in girls than in boys but by age four, both are insisting on wearing specific items of dress and avoiding others regardless of their ethnic background (Halim et al., 2014).

How important are children's appearance to their parents? Results from a survey of parents who had children between the ages of two to sixteen years revealed that the child's appearance was important (Striegel-Moore & Kearney-Cooke, 1994). As compared to fathers, mothers were more likely to report being pressured by others to improve the appearance of their children. A variety of reasons were reported for this pressure but common reasons included a need to improve the child's clothing, hairstyle, or teeth. Correspondingly, mothers more often than fathers shared that they had made attempts to improve the appearance of their children. These efforts included treating acne, providing orthodontic treatment, and making changes to the child's hairstyle.

Stages of Primary Socialization: Play Stage

The next stage of primary socialization is the play stage. During the **play stage** the child takes on roles, experiments

with roles, and notes how others react to their role performance (Stone, 1962). Part of that experimentation can include clothing. If the roles are those the child can reasonably expect to assume (e.g., mother, nurse, teacher), this process is termed **anticipatory socialization**. During anticipatory socialization people rehearse for expected future experiences, roles, and occupations. In nursery school, children often have "dress-up" clothes that facilitate experimentation with common roles such as mother (high heels, hose, makeup), father (briefcase, tie), or police person (hat, gun, badge). Children also accompany their parents on shopping trips wherein they engage in anticipatory consumer socialization, and training for future consumer roles by trying on clothing and learning to make purchases.

Sometimes children experiment with roles that they cannot reasonably expect to assume, a process called **fantastic socialization**. Fantastic socialization requires wearing extraordinary dress or costume to allow children to "dress out" of their usual roles and experiment with imaginary or other roles they can never assume according to Stone (1962) (Figure 11.7). Children might dress

Figure 11.7

On Halloween children may experiment with roles they can never assume (e.g., ladybug, cat, and lion), a process called fantastic socialization.

as cowboys and cowgirls, Indians, or superheroes and superheroines. In both aspects of the play stage, children dress out of their actual roles and so are misrepresenting their selves.

Adults also engage in both anticipatory and fantastic socialization (Stone, 1962). Consider what you might plan to wear for a trip out of town or out of the country. Deciding which tops and bottoms to wear together, with what shoes and accessories is an example of anticipatory socialization. Trying on myriad outfits in preparation to go out on a date is another such example. In terms of fantastic socialization, consider the opportunity for adults to participate in groups that "dress out" in costume. For example, Civil War re-enactments, Buckskinning re-enactments, *Star Trek* conventions, and cosplay conventions described in more detail in Chapter 9, "Dress and the Self" and in Chapter 12, "Dress and Social Groups," provide opportunities for adults to engage in fantastic socialization using dress (Belk & Costa, 1998; Kozinets, 2001; Miller, 1998; Strauss, 2003).

Primary Socialization: Game Stage

During the **game stage** of primary socialization, children have learned some social norms and values. This stage may begin with the pre-teenage years when children are overly concerned with conforming to their peers. Since dress is visible, it can be a sign of conformity or deviance. It is not uncommon for preteen girls to phone their friends in the morning to determine what they are wearing to school that day. This stage is characterized by "dressing in," meaning that children dress in role or consistent with their identity (Stone, 1962). Thus, appearances in this stage may be true representations of their selves.

Presumably most of adult life is characterized by the game stage as we progress through various careers and life stages, wherein we dress in-role. It is also possible to consider the end of life as the adult version of the pre-play stage where investiture characterizes the aged. As people's lives are extended and they require long-term care, they may have no control over their appearances which may be left up to a caregiver.

HOW DO WE LEARN HOW WE SHOULD LOOK?

As previously mentioned we learn about how we are expected to appear from our socialization agents, who teach us how to function in society; that is, they teach the norms and values of our society through modeling and direct instruction. Parents are the primary socialization agents of their children, but children can also socialize their parents regarding trends in music, fashionable clothing, and technology (e.g., how to text, how to sync an iPhone to a Fitbit, or how to use the Wii).

Socialization Agents: Parents

As the primary socialization agents of their children, parents provide important socialization concerning dress which begins during infancy. We want to emphasize that it is mothers, perhaps more than other caregivers, that are particularly important to this process and that their instruction continues throughout the lifespan. In qualitative research with Russian mothers and daughters, researchers found mothers socialized their daughters into womanhood (Roudakova & Ballard-Reisch, 1999). One of the first things that the daughters learned was the **imperative** (i.e., important norm) to be attractive and feminine. They learned the importance of expending effort to do so. One respondent recalled being taught by her mother how to fix her hair, apply makeup, and combine colors in clothing ensembles. Daughters recalled being instructed to maintain a well-groomed, tidy appearance. Mothers recalled telling their daughters about the importance of looking good and of modeling that behavior for them. Mothers often sacrificed having expensive things (i.e., new clothes, beauty products) so that their daughters could have them.

Researchers have studied how young women are socialized by parents with respect to appearance norms (Johnson, Kang, & Kim, 2014). Participants related that one way their mothers socialized them was by modeling expected behaviors. For example, one young woman commented, "My mom worked out every day and was always thin and fit. I think that this had an impact on me which still is present in my life today" (p. 87).

Parents also socialize their children regarding the appearance of their bodies. Mothers and fathers teach their children about how aspects of their bodies should look by making verbal comments (Schwartz, Phares, Tantleff-Dunn, & Thompson, 1999). In reflecting on appearance socialization by her mother one young woman said, "While she never called me fat or made direct comments about my physical appearance, every day I got some sort of reminder that I couldn't afford to eat that, or I shouldn't wear that . . ." (Johnson et al., 2014). While parents' comments affect all children, they can be especially critical and harmful to appearance-impaired children (e.g., children who are near-sighted and wear thick glasses, who are obese, or who have severe acne) (Beuf, 1990). Ann Beuf was a medical sociologist who worked with appearance-impaired children and she found that mothers who espouse a traditional gender ideology often give greater value to appearance than non-traditional mothers (p. 96). Beuf also found that fathers' appearance-related comments affect their children.

In addition to the direct instruction approach, as we noted earlier in this chapter, socialization concerning dress and appearance may take other forms. Ogle and Damhorst (2003) documented that mothers and daughters interacted about one body modification, dieting, using direct instruction and additional three methods: the avoidance approach, the modeling approach, and the laissez-faire approach. The avoidance approach entailed avoiding a discussion of dieting and/or being extremely cautious about what was said. Two reasons were provided for taking this approach: to avoid hurting feelings and a desire to avoid over-emphasizing appearance related issues. The laissez-faire approach was described as leaving daughters alone with respect to issues of dieting primarily because of the belief that input about dieting was not needed. The modeling approach was an attempt by mothers to actively and consciously demonstrate the diet-related behaviors mothers desired their daughters to adopt.

Socialization Agents: Peers

Peers also socialize us about how to dress and how we should look. Early dress research established the importance of dressing fashionably to obtain peer acceptance among adolescents (Hendricks, Kelly, & Eicher, 1968; Kelly & Eicher, 1970; Littrell & Eicher, 1973; Smucker & Creekmore, 1972; Williams & Eicher, 1966). The researchers found that teens may conform to their peers as a way of being accepted by peers. More recently, researchers show that young women continue to conform in their choices of clothing for peer acceptance (Johnson et al., 2014). One participant in that study said, "I wanted to fit in with all other girls and in an effort to do so, I conformed to the way they dressed" (p. 87).

Korean researchers have documented that the young Korean women are influenced by what their peers buy (Baek & Choo, 2015). In other research, peer influence was related to the kinds of clothing that female high school students were likely to select (Seock & Merritt, 2013). These studies show that peers influence our clothing practices; however, our clothing practices (i.e., how we dress) also influence others. For example, researchers have found that clothing influences social interaction in the form of helpfulness (Kim & Lennon, 2005; Lennon & Davis, 1989). In those studies when people were dressed in a fashionable way, they received more helpful treatment. Hence, shoppers in that research learned that dressing in a fashionable way is likely to improve social interactions.

Researchers have examined young women's clothing practices and sources of influence and advice on clothing consumption (Abbott & Sapsford, 2001). The researchers conducted qualitative research using participant observation and in-depth interviews. They concluded that the young women studied were socialized by both their peers and mothers. They found that in selecting clothes, girlfriends and sometimes mothers were more influential than boyfriends. Participants revealed that girlfriends provided good advice about what clothes looked good. Boyfriends' preferences were also important in that the young women would not buy anything their boyfriends did not like.

As our peers, siblings also influence how we dress. Researchers have found that college women were socialized by siblings who modeled appearance-related behaviors (Johnson, Kang, & Kim, 2014). One participant illustrated her sister's influence by saying, "She was wearing deodorant, shaving her legs, wearing makeup, and coloring her hair . . . . it took Lucy's personality to convince me to start doing these things myself" (p. 87).

Another time that peers can be expected to influence us with respect to how we should dress and look is when entering the workforce or when changing jobs.

Researchers surveyed working women in the early 1980s when women's participation in the labor force had risen to more than 50 percent. They were interested in the sources of information these women used in making decisions about what to wear to work. At the time, little was known about career women's dress. Those women who believed career dress was important were socialized by peers and managers at work (i.e., women sought information from their peers and managers at work), as well as by the media (i.e., magazines, books) (Rabolt & Drake, 1985).

Socialization Agents: Personal Shoppers

Another agent of socialization with respect to what to wear is the personal shopper or wardrobe consultant. **Personal shoppers or wardrobe consultants** are trained to help shoppers select clothing. Results from a qualitative study of personal shoppers revealed that the personal shoppers were used when women were transitioning from one lifestyle to another, such as entering the workforce, and that women wanted to learn how to select clothing to enhance their overall attractiveness (Gillen, 2001), findings consistent with the results of Rabolt and Drake (1985). In offering advice about clothing, the personal shoppers are socializing their clients about what to wear to look good.

Socialization Agents: Retailers and Manufacturers

Retailers and manufacturers show us what to wear with respect to the types of clothing ultimately promoted and offered for sale to consumers. As such they serve as socialization agents regarding what we wear. A recent report by market research firm NPD Group suggests that the US is degenderizing (Blurred lines, 2015). One example of this as related to the apparel industry might be more gender neutral clothing for children such as the new GapKidsXED line, which was introduced in August 2015 by Ellen DeGeneres and Gap (Zarya, 2015). The collection consists of basic classic looks in gender neutral colors such as beige, grey, brown, and green (Browning, 2015). The line focuses on comfort and has been described as "normcore." The items in the line feature bold graphic prints and uplifting slogans. Whether or not this type of gender neutral clothing influences consumers remains to be seen.

INDUSTRY APPLICATION

IMAGE CONSULTANTS

According to the website of the Association of Image Consultants International (www.aici.org), image consultants or personal shoppers "counsel both individual and corporate clients on appearance, behavior, communication skills, etiquette and international protocol." As such, image consultants/personal shoppers serve as socialization agents. Image consulting is a growing field and retailers can offer it to differentiate from competing retailers (MacKaben, 2013). Online retailers such as Zappos and J. Crew.com are offering personal shopping services, and personal shopping is now offered by several online personal shopping firms such as Keaton Row, Shop it to Me, Stylit, and Stitch Fix.

Although retail gatekeepers promote merchandise to consumers, at times consumers reject the merchandise and the retailers' influence. The NPD report (Blurred lines, 2015) suggests that providing a shopping experience that is independent of gender offers business opportunities for retailers. One suggestion is to provide men's and women's dressing rooms and bathrooms on each floor, to make shopping easier for those women who shop in men's departments (or vice versa). Such suggestions are echoed researchers who studied large size women and their athletic clothing (Christel, O'Donnell, & Bradley, 2016). These women often shopped for athletic clothing in men's departments not because they did not like what retailers offered in women's departments, but because it did not fit them.

Socialization Agents: Media

Historical accounts also indicate that media (i.e., illustrations) socialize us about how to dress. Historical documents from the Ellis Island archives were analyzed to write about Jewish immigrant women, their clothing, and how they were socialized to be "American" women (Schreier, 1994). She studied the time period from 1880 to 1920. As were other immigrants to the US, these women were labeled "greenhorns." A **greenhorn** is a newly arrived immigrant or newcomer, who is unfamiliar with culture and customs. The Jewish immigrant women resisted the "greenhorn" identity by exiting it as quickly as possible, called "greening themselves out" (p. 92). Because they wanted to fit in, they were willing to make changes in their behaviors, which included wearing a different style of clothing than they were accustomed to wearing. Schreier says "that clothing was the first step" (p. 93) in greening themselves out. Schreier documents how social workers worked to transform immigrants by explicitly showing them how to dress. In an article written by one of the social workers entitled "Before and After" (p. 95), an illustration was provided which depicted how American women should look.

More recently researchers have investigated the influence of media (e.g., pressure to lose weight, pressure to change appearance as a result of media exposure) in young girls (Seock & Merritt, 2013). The greater the reported media influence, the more likely the girls were to select their clothing based on its ability to boost self-confidence and hide figure flaws. Thus, not only do media provide a powerful source of socialization about clothing, media also socialize us about how our bodies should look.

Researchers studied media effects on children's internalization of the media body ideal and body surveillance (Knauss, Paxton, & Alsaker, 2008). Participants were Swiss adolescent girls and boys who completed questionnaires in their classrooms. Perceived media pressure (e.g., "I have felt pressure from TV or magazines to have a perfect body" [p. 637]) was found to be strongly related to

internalization of the media body ideal (e.g., "I wish I looked like a model" [p. 637]). Media pressure was also related to body surveillance (e.g., "during the day, I think about how I look many times" [p. 636]). These results demonstrate that media socialize children regarding how they should look.

Socialization Agents: Professionals

Health care professionals, coaches, and physical education (PE) teachers also socialize children regarding appearance. In the course of her work with appearance impaired children, medical sociologist Beuf (1990) dealt with many children who reported being belittled by physicians and other health care professionals who considered their appearance concerns to be trivial. Coaches also play an influential role and may serve as teachers, disciplinarians, parents, psychologists, and mentors (Rosen, 1992; Smith & Ogle, 2006). Coaches can socialize players with thoughtless comments regarding weight and bodies which can have unintended results (Figure 11.8). For example, Smith and Ogle report an incident in which a coach made a remark about the size/fit of the team uniform that resulted in a female player feeling insulted. More recently Ignacio Quereda, Spain's women's national soccer team manager, stepped down in July 2015 after all twenty-three players wrote a public letter calling for his removal. He

Figure 11.8
Spain's women's national soccer team manager, Ignacio Quereda, allegedly routinely yelled at players, called them "little girls," and called them fat. He stepped down in July 2015 after all twenty-three players wrote a public letter calling for his removal.

allegedly often yelled at players, called them "little girls," and called them fat (Hailey, 2015; "Quereda's reign," 2015). These kinds of comments that draw attention to athletes' weight or body size can actually facilitate disordered eating when made publically (Thompson & Sherman, 1999).

PE teachers also socialize students and their feedback is known to affect student performance (Nicaise, Bois, Fairclough, Amorose, & Cogérino, 2007). Other practices of PE teachers can also negatively influence children as illustrated in a qualitative study by Reddy-Best and Harmon (2015). These researchers interviewed overweight children about athletic clothing and participation in physical activity. The children had all been issued a uniform for sport participation or for PE class. The coaches and PE teachers often required the children to state their uniform size aloud for all to hear. Revealing their uniform size in front of their peers caused discomfort and concern. If the child's size was unavailable it sometimes had to be special ordered. Possibly the worst case scenario was when special ordering was not an option resulting in a child having to wear a uniform of the wrong size. In these last two instances, participants were often uncomfortable and embarrassed.

Socialization Agents: Cultural Beliefs

In many cultures, including the US culture, there are written and unwritten norms regarding appearance (as discussed in Chapter 6, "Dress and Physical Appearance"). An example of an unwritten appearance expectation is that women should be attractive and have a thin body; when they deviate from this norm (i.e., are unattractive and/or overweight), they receive negative sanctions in the form of negative verbal commentary, such as name-calling and teasing. This may also occur when a man is thin and not muscular.

In Chapter 4, "Dress and Social Cognition" we noted another cultural belief that is, that people in the US should keep their clothing tidy and clean. So strong is this norm that psychologists and psychiatrists often use a person's appearance as an indication of mental health. *The Diagnostic and Statistical Manual of Mental Disorders* (1987) or *DSM III-R* was written by teams of psychiatrists describing mental disorders including their symptoms. An untidy appearance is listed as a symptom of three mental disorders in the *DSM III-R* (p. 520-521):

bipolar disorder, dementia, and schizophrenia. A sexually seductive appearance is listed as a symptom of several mental disorders including bipolar disorder, histrionic personality disorder, organic mood syndrome, and others (p. 548-549). These examples from the *DSM III-R* are only important insofar as they illustrate written norms about how "normal" people should NOT look and the negative sanctions that accompany those looks (i.e., diagnoses of mental disorders).

Socialization and Acquisition of Dress

Thus far in this chapter we have treated how we are socialized about how to dress. In this next section we extend our treatment of socialization and dress to include socialization regarding the acquisition of dress items. In other words, how do we learn what to look for in the apparel we wear and who does the socializing? Some of the things children learn to look for include brands, licensed characters, and various clothing evaluative criteria. Agents of socialization include peers, parents, and media.

How do children learn to acquire items of dress? Research suggests that this is accomplished through modeling and instruction, both formal from parents and teachers and informal from peers, siblings, and parents. Parents not only are gatekeepers of what their children wear, but they also teach children how to select and acquire items of dress. In terms of what to wear, parents may place value on achieving distinction through their children since children's appearance reflects on the parents (Collett, 2005). That is, what the child wears or plays with symbolically represents the parents' attitudes and tastes (Martens, Southerton, & Scott, 2004). In addition, many items of dress are acquired on behalf of unborn children, babies, and toddlers by others, even before they are socialized.

Researchers have studied the socialization of very young children (preschoolers and kindergartners) regarding clothing acquisition (Haynes, Burts, Dukes, & Cloud, 1993). They examined mothers' role and children's involvement in the children's clothing selection and the importance of brand name clothing. With children this young researchers often resort to questioning the mothers about the children. Nearly 75 percent of the children were reported to be interested in the acquisition of their clothing. Mothers of kindergartners reported more interest than mothers of preschoolers did.

The mothers reported that children were allowed to select 85.4 percent of their costumes, 79.4 percent of shoes, and 74.4 percent of their sportswear items (Haynes et al., 1993). However, kindergartners selected significantly more than preschoolers in two categories: dress clothing and dresses. Kindergartners were also more likely than preschoolers to select apparel that matched the mothers' preferences, in colors and styles the mothers' thought looked good on them. While 70 percent of the children never showed a brand preference, 78 percent preferred licensed characters (e.g., Barbie, Ninja Turtles) at least some of the time. Results support the idea that mothers serve as socialization agents regarding clothing acquisition.

Researchers have found that children are socialized by observing their parents using various criteria to evaluate clothing. See Table 11.1 for some examples of **clothing evaluative criteria**, criteria people use to evaluate clothing. Using a consumer socialization perspective, researchers administered a questionnaire to parents (Shim, Snyder, & Gehrt, 1995). Results showed that the more often parents took the children on shopping trips, the more conscious the children were of clothing brand, color, price, peers, and style. These results demonstrate that parents are strong socializers of their children for clothing acquisition.

Also the extent to which parents emphasized particular criteria was positively related to the child's use of the same criteria, assuming that the parents' perceptions of the criteria their children used were accurate.

More recently researchers used a consumer socialization approach to study mothers and their tween daughters by comparing them on variables that shaped their apparel preferences and consumption (Paff Ogle, Hyllegard, & Yan, 2014). The mothers and daughters were similar in the importance assigned to several clothing evaluative criteria: comfort, fit, aesthetics/design, use of socially responsible construction/production methods, and use of high performance technology. The similarity between mothers and daughters is evidence of consumer socialization by the mothers.

Research shows that in addition to parents, peers also socialize children about clothing acquisition. In qualitative research from the UK focus group interviews with tween girls were conducted (Grant & Stephen, 2006). They found that fashion purchases were influenced by parental and peer group approval. Purchasing was also influenced by brand associations. Mothers were reported to be an important influence as were older sisters. Other researchers surveyed mothers and their twelve-year old daughters about influences on clothing acquisition (Saunders, Samli, & Tozier, 1973). Sixty-five percent agreed that some clothing would not be purchased unless the girls' friends approved. Friends were known to influence brands purchased for coats, blouses, dresses, and scarves. Peer influence was important and affected brand choice.

A UK–US research team investigated evaluation of fashion branded goods among British children aged seven to ten and the role of social influences in affecting that evaluation (Hogg, Bruce, & Hill, 1998). In small groups the children were shown six branded actual T-shirts and sweatshirts and the term *brand* was explained. In groups the students were given one product from a brand that they recognized and were asked to make a collage of images that represented the brand. They then discussed why they selected the images and the influence they felt from parents, siblings, and peers when they acquired clothing. Then the students rated each brand on a series of items. Parents of the children also completed questionnaires about their own and their child's influence on clothing purchases. Branded sportswear was more highly regarded by the children than store brands. Peers were found to influence children's clothing purchases.

TABLE 11.1

CLOTHING EVALUATIVE CRITERIA

Intrinsic Criteria (cannot be changed without changing the garment)	Extrinsic Criteria
Aesthetics	Brand
Attractiveness	Designer label
Color	Price
Comfort	Store image
Construction quality	Use of high performance technology
Design	Use of socially responsible construction/production methods
Durability	
Ease of care	
Fabric content fabric weave	
Fabric quality	
Fit	
Licensed characters	
Style	

Media also affect consumer socialization. Three sources of socialization (television, parents, and peers) and preferences for branded apparel among Malaysian tweens were studied by a Malaysian team of researchers (Teo, Sidin, & Nor, 2013). The researchers collected data using interviews with the younger children and surveys for the older tweens. The three socialization agents significantly influenced preferences for branded apparel in the following order: peers, parents, and television exposure. Other researchers also found that children were socialized by television because the more frequently the children requested products seen on television, the more conscious they were of clothing brand, color, peers, and style criteria (Shim, Snyder, & Gehrt, 1995).

FASHION THERAPY

Fashion therapy is a form of socialization that teaches people how to dress and groom themselves, often to help them find jobs. The rationale behind the programs is that self-esteem of the participants will increase as a function of the new appearance and that as a result, participants' social relations will also improve. The mechanism by which fashion therapy works is as follows. Self-esteem is positively related to an attractive appearance (Harter, 1999). Clothing has been found to affect judgments of physical attractiveness (Buckley, 1983; Buckley & Haefner, 1984). Therefore, we expect increases in self-esteem if people can manipulate their appearances (including clothing) to be more attractive. A more attractive appearance is likely to improve social interactions since we have already established that appearance affects social interaction (Kim & Lennon, 2005; Lennon & Davis, 1989). Several researchers have devised fashion therapy research programs that rely on direct instruction (Callis, 1982; Fiore & DeLong, 1990; Graham & Kligman, 1984; Mulready & Lamb, 1985).

Researchers developed a fashion therapy program and worked with displaced homemakers to enable them to become gainfully employed (Fiore & DeLong, 1990). **Displaced homemakers** are women who need to return to the workforce due to divorce, a spouse's death, or a spouse's disability. The women in the program attended classes that focused on professional appearance. In other research a fashion therapy program was aimed at female chronic psychiatric patients (Callis, 1982). The program lasted several weeks and topics covered included: hair style, hair care, makeup application, clothing selection, accessory selection, grooming, and other related topics. Fashion therapy was also used with female chemotherapy patients (Mulready & Lamb, 1985). Chemotherapy patients received a makeover in an attempt to improve their feelings about interpersonal relationships, body satisfaction, and self-concept. These fashion therapy programs have proven effective with adults experiencing difficult transitions in life. In particular, the programs have resulted in higher interpersonal relationship scores, higher self-concept scores, and greater appearance satisfaction scores. These results demonstrate the effectiveness of the fashion therapy program.

Some popular outreach recovery programs use the same techniques to build confidence, self-esteem, and body image. The Reach to Recovery and Look Good, Feel Better programs of the American Cancer Society provide these same services for women who have had cancer surgery, and Locks of Love creates wigs for disadvantaged children who have hair loss due to any medical condition. Another organization that does similar work for women seeking employment is Dress for Success. That organization provides access to resources people need for success in the workplace; this includes their Suiting Program, which provides interview suits to disadvantaged women entering the workforce. Dress for Success is discussed in more detail in Chapter 3, "Conducting Research on Dress." The idea that fashion therapy can improve social interactions, self-concept, and appearance satisfaction is the basis for makeover programs on television. In the next section makeover programs are discussed.

MAKEOVER SHOWS

Since the turn of the twenty-first century, a type of television show called **reality television** has become popular. Reality television is a type of programming that features unscripted events using ordinary people instead of actors. Some examples of reality TV shows include *Ellen's Design Challenge, American Idol, Hoarders*, and *Fit to Fat to Fit*. Some reality programs socialize viewers and participants on the programs by focusing on makeover or self-improvement and feature people trying to improve their lives with advice from experts. Viewers of these programs are socialized by observing the experts' advice and the resulting appearance transformations.

Based on the programs, makeovers are needed for homes, makeup and hair, body parts, and clothing. Programs that dealt specifically with appearance include *Fit to Fat to Fit, How Do I Look?, Tim Gunn's Guide to Style, Style by Jury,* and *Love, Lust, or Run.* The premise behind the appearance-related shows is that the average American is out of shape, badly dressed, and has poor taste in clothing. Thus, whatever you look like or whatever you have is not good enough. One or more experts or gurus can help you solve your "problem." Participants are critiqued about their flaws, and then undergo some type of appearance manipulation (e.g., shopping for clothing and accessories, a new haircut, a weight loss regimen, and sometimes cosmetic surgery). The programs end with the participant's transformation unveiled to everyone.

These programs are popular because they are consistent with the American dream of equal opportunity, regardless of the looks we were born with. In fact, there is a striking parallel between the makeover as contemporary television and the makeover as national historical myth (see also the previous discussion about Jewish immigrants' "greening out" process) (Heller, 2006). The networks like reality shows because they are very inexpensive to produce, unlike programs that feature a cast of well-known actors. The shows are advertiser-friendly because makeovers require buying products (e.g., clothing, accessories, makeup, salon treatments). Finally, the shows allow the audience to indulge in the fantasy of the makeover.

Makeover shows have been criticized on the basis of encouraging voyeurism in prime time TV (Gibbons, 2004). Another criticism is that the makeover shows promote the fairy tale of living happily ever after (i.e., Cinderella) once the appearance manipulation is complete. In addition, due to judicious editing the programs make some very painful procedures seem like an easy instant fix (Ashikali, Dittmar, & Ayers, 2014). Sometimes the participants do not maintain the transformation that they underwent (e.g., weight loss), and they experience a sense of failure and shame; other outcomes are that the participants may experience negative social interactions with others in their new bodies and appearances. In fact, researchers studied fourteen previous *Biggest Loser* participants who had previously been monitored and tested (Fothergill et al., 2016). These participants had regained a significant amount of the weight they originally lost. Furthermore, their metabolisms slowed and remained slow even with the weight regain, which the authors say make weight maintenance difficult. Based on this new research, a former *Biggest Loser* contestant now asserts that the show damaged her life and health and has threatened to sue the show (Cullins, 2016).

Chapter Summary

In this chapter you learn that groups are made up of different social positions and each of these social positions reflect a specific status and corresponding role. Included in roles are expectations for dress, thus, dress is useful in the identification of different social positions.

This chapter also focuses on the role of dress in socialization. Formal socialization about dress includes direct instruction regarding how to dress (e.g., a management training program that includes information about dress codes or a session with a retail color analyst who offers advice on flattering wardrobe colors). Informal socialization involves modeling others' dress behaviors, as well as learning from the feedback of friends and others. How people are socialized about how they should dress and how their bodies should look are covered, as well as consumer socialization and fashion therapy.

Key Terms

achieved status
anticipatory socialization
appearance labor
appearance rigidity
ascribed status
clothing evaluative criteria
displaced homemakers
fantastic socialization
fashion therapy
formal socialization

game stage
greenhorn
identification
imperative
informal socialization
investiture
master status
observational learning or
  modeling

personal shopper or
  wardrobe consultant
play stage
pre-play stage
prescribed role
primary socialization
reality television
role ambiguity
role conflict

role perception
role performance
role strain
self-sexualization
social learning theory
social position
socialization agents
socialization theory
status set
symbolic models

Discussion Questions

1. Identify one of your master statuses. How does that status impact your decision-making concerning dress on a regular basis?

2. Who are you in terms of your status set? List several expectations for your dress based on your status set. From this, indicate whether you have experienced role conflict concerning your dress as a result of competing expectations.

3. List three non-family members who socialized you regarding how to dress. Were the experiences positive or negative and why do you think so? Have these experiences affected the way you dress today?

4. What negative and positive feedback did you receive growing up for how you dressed? What aspects of your dress were you motivated to change as a result of the feedback?

STUDiO™

Visit your book's STUDIO for additional quiz questions and vocabulary flashcards!

Suggested Readings

Hogg, M. K., Bruce, M., & Hill, A. J. (1998). Fashion brand preferences among young consumers. *International Journal of Retail & Distribution Management, 26*(2), 293–300.

Knauss, C., Paxton, S. J., & Alsaker, F. D. (2008). Body dissatisfaction in adolescent boys and girls: Objectified body consciousness, internalization of the media body ideal and perceived pressure from media. *Sex Roles, 59,* 633–643.

Poulin-Dubois, D., Serbin, L. A., Eichstedt, J. A., Sen, M. G., & Beissel, C. F. (2002). Men don't put on make-up: Toddlers' knowledge of the gender stereotyping of household activities. *Social Development, 11,* 166–181.

Schor, J. B. (2004). *Born to buy.* New York, NY: Scribner.

References

Abbott, P., & Sapsford, F. (2001). Young women and their wardrobes. *Through the wardrobe: Women's relationships with their clothes* (pp. 21–37). New York, NY: Berg.

Arthur, L. B. (1998). Dress and the social construction of gender in two sororities. *Textiles and Clothing Research Journal, 17,* 84–93.

Ashikali, E. M., Dittmar, H., & Ayers, S. (2014). The effect of cosmetic surgery reality tv shows on adolescent girls' body image. *Psychology of Popular Media Culture, 3*(3), 141–153.

Baek, E., & Choo, H. J. (2015). Effects of peer consumption on hedonic purchase decisions. *Social Behavior and Personality: An International Journal, 43*(7), 1085–1099.

Bandura, A. (1977). *Social learning theory.* Englewood Cliffs, N.J.: Prentice-Hall.

Baumrind, D. (1980). New directions in socialization research. *American Psychologist, 35*(7), 639–652.

Belk, R. W., & Costa, J. A. (1998). The mountain man myth: A contemporary consuming fantasy. *Journal of Consumer Research, 25*(3), 218–240.

Ben-Zeev, A., & Dennehy, T. (2014). When boys wear pink: A gendered color cue violation evokes risk taking. *Psychology of Men & Masculinity, 15*(4), 486–489.

Beuf, A. (1990). *Beauty is the beast.* Philadelphia, PA: University of Pennsylvania Press.

Bindley, K. (2012, September 14). Brooke Breedwell, former child pageant star, warns parents against pageant life. *Huffington Post.* Retrieved from http://www.huffingtonpost.com/2012/09/14/brooke-breedwell-former-child-pageant-star_n_1885132.html

Blurred lines: How retail is becoming less gendered, and why you should care (2015). The NPD Group, Inc. Retrieved from https://www.npd.com/lps/pdf/Content-Marketing-Blurred-Lines.pdf

Browning, B. (2015, August 31). Ellen DeGeneres and Gap launch new clothing line for girls that challenges stereotypes. *Advocate.* Retrieved from http://www.advocate.com/ellen-degeneres/2015/08/31/ellen-degeneres-launches-new-gapkids-clothes-challenge-gender-stereotypes

Buckley, H. M. (1983). Perceptions of physical attractiveness as manipulated by dress: Subjects versus independent judges. *Journal of Psychology, 114,* 243–248.

Buckley, H. M. & Haeffner, J. E. (1984). The physical attractiveness stereotype using dress as a facilitator. *Journal of Consumer Studies and Home Economics, 8,* 351–358.

Cahill, S. (1989). Fashioning males and females: Appearance management and the social reproduction of gender. *Symbolic Interaction, 12,* 281–298.

Callis, C. (1982). Appearance programs with female chronic psychiatric hospital patients: A comparison of sex-week and nine-week treatment interventions. *Journal of Rehabilitation, 48*(4), 34–39.

Cartwright, M. (2012). Princess by proxy: What child beauty pageants teach girls about self-worth and what we can do about it. *Journal of the American Academy of Child and Adolescent Psychiatry, 51*(11), 1105–1107.

Cash, T. F. (1995). Developmental teasing about physical appearance: Retrospective descriptions and relationships with body image. *Social Behavior and Personality: An International Journal, 23*(2), 123–130.

Christel, D. A., O'Donnell, N. H., & Bradley, L. A. (2016). Coping by crossdressing: an exploration of exercise clothing for obese heterosexual women. *Fashion and Textiles, 3*(1), 1–19.

Collett, J. L. (2005). What kind of mother am I? Impression management and the social construction of motherhood. *Symbolic Interaction, 28*, 327–247.

Cullins, S. (2016, May 28). Lawyers say weight loss class action against NBC would be a big loser. *Hollywood Reporter*. Retrieved from http://www.hollywood reporter.com/thr-esq/biggest-loser-contestant-class-action-897951

Diagnostic and Statistical Manual of Mental Disorders Revised (1987). Washington, DC: American Psychiatric Association.

Dittmar, H., Halliwell, E., & Ive, S. (2006). Does Barbie make girls want to be thin? The effect of experimental exposure to images of dolls on the body image of 5- to 8-year-old girls. *Developmental Psychology, 42*(2), 283–292.

Dockterman, E. (February 8, 2016.) A Barbie for every body. *Time, 187*(4), 44–51.

Durand, C. (2016, April 22). Prince George stays up to meet the Obamas at Kensington Palace dinner. Retrieved from: http://abcnews.go.com/Entertainment/prince-william-kate-harry-host-obamas-dinner-kensington/story?id=38603288

Eisenberg, M. E., Neumark-Sztainer, D., & Story, M. (2003). Associations of weight-based teasing and emotional well-being among adolescents. *Archives of Pediatrics & Adolescent Medicine, 157*(8), 733–738.

Fiore, A. M,, & DeLong, M. R. (1990). A personal appearance program for displaced homemakers. *Journal of Career Development, 16*(3), 219–226.

Former mayor slapped with nudity charge (2009, July 2). Retrieved from http://www.cbsnews.com/sections/crimesider/main504083.shtml?keyword=Mark+Musselwhite

Fothergill, E., Guo, J., Howard, L., Kerns, J. C., Knuth, N. D., Brychta, R. et al. (2016). Persistent metabolic adaptation 6 years after "The Biggest Loser" competition. *Obesity*. doi:10.1002/oby.21538

Gibbons, S. (2004, December 22). TV makeover shows are prime-time madness. *Women's Sense*. Retrieved from http://www.womensenews.org/story/commentary/041222/tv-makeover-shows-are-prime-time-madness

Giddens, A., Duneier, M., Appelbaum, R., & Carr, D. (2009). Introduction to sociology (7th ed.). New York, NY: W. W. Norton & Company.

Gillen, K. (2001). Choosing an image: The personal shopper. *Through the wardrobe: Women's relationships with their clothes* (pp. 71–93). New York, NY: Berg.

Goorwich, S. (2015, January 30). American school girl made to cover her shoulders at high school dance. Retrieved from http://metro.co.uk/2015/01/30/american-school-girl-made-to-cover-her-shoulders-at-high-school-dance-5043143/

Graham, J. & Kligman, A. (1984). Cosmetic therapy for the elderly. *Journal of the Society of Cosmetic Chemists, 35*, 133–145.

Grant, I. J., & Stephen, G. R. (2006). Communicating culture: An examination of the buying behaviour of 'tweenage' girls and the key societal communicating factors influencing the buying process of fashion clothing. *Journal of Targeting, Measurement and Analysis for Marketing, 14*(2), 101–114.

Hailey, B. (2015, June 26). Spain's women's team is a catastrophe, and it doesn't need to be. Retrieved from http://screamer.deadspin.com/spains-womens-team-is-a-catastrophe-and-it-doesnt-need-1714119233

Halim, M. L., Ruble, D. N., Tamis-LeMonda, C. S., Zosuls, K. M., Lurye, L. E., & Greulich, F. K. (2014). Pink frilly dresses and the avoidance of all things "girly": Children's appearance rigidity and cognitive theories of gender development. *Developmental Psychology, 50*(4), 1091–1101.

Halkon, R. (2016, May 13). Beard it like Beckham: New trend as British men fork out thousands to have facial hair transplants to look like star. Retrieved from http://www.mirror.co.uk/news/uk-news/beard-like-beckham-new-trend-7961883

Harter, S. (1999). *The construction of the self: A developmental perspective*. New York, NY: Guilford.

Haynes, J. L., Burts, D. C., Dukes, A., & Cloud, R. (1993). Consumer socialization of preschoolers and kindergartners as related to clothing consumption. *Psychology and Marketing, 10*(2), 151–166.

Heller, D. (2006). *The great American makeover*. New York, NY: Palgrave Macmillan.

Hendricks, S. H., Kelley, E. A., & Eicher, J. B. (1968). Senior girls' appearance and social participation. *Journal of Home Economics, 60*, 167–172.

Hilliker, J. A. S., & Rogers, J. C. (1988). Color analysis in the marketplace. *Clothing and Textiles Research Journal,* 6(3), 26–31.

Hogg, M. K., Bruce, M., & Hill, A. J. (1998). Fashion brand preferences among young consumers. *International Journal of Retail & Distribution Management,* 26(2), 293–300.

Hunt, S. A., & Miller, K. A. (1997). The discourse of dress and appearance: Identity talk and a rhetoric of review. *Symbolic Interaction,* 20(1), 69–82.

Johnson, K. K., Kang, M., & Kim, J. E. (2014). Reflections on appearance socialization during childhood and adolescence. *Clothing and Textiles Research Journal,* 32(2), 79–92. DOI: 10.1177/0887302X13518430

Kaiser, S. (1989). Clothing and social organization of gender perception: A developmental approach. *Clothing and Textiles Research Journal,* 7(2), 46–56.

Kaiser, S., Rudy, M., & Byfield, P. (1985). The role of clothing in sex role socialization: Person

perceptions versus overt behavior. *Child Study Journal,* 15, 83–97.

Kammeyer, K. C. W., Ritzer, G., & Yetman, N. R. (1992). *Sociology: Experiencing changing societies.* Needham Heights, MA: Allyn and Bacon.

Katz, N. (2011, April 21). Life-size Barbie's shocking dimensions (PHOTO): Would she be anorexic? *CBS News.* Retrieved from http://www.cbsnews.com/news/life-size-barbies-shocking-dimensions-photo-would-she-be-anorexic/

Kelley, E. A., & Eicher, J. B. (1970). Popularity, group membership, and dress. *Journal of Home Economics,* 62, 246–250.

Kim, M., & Lennon, S. J. (2005). The effects of customers' dress on salesperson's service in large-sized clothing specialty stores. *Clothing and Textiles Research Journal,* 23(2), 78–87.

Knauss, C., Paxton, S. J., & Alsaker, F. D. (2008). Body dissatisfaction in adolescent boys and girls: Objectified body consciousness, internalization of the media body ideal and perceived pressure from media. *Sex Roles,* 59, 633–643.

Kozinets, R. V. (2001). Utopian enterprise: Articulating the meanings of Star Trek's culture of consumption. *Journal of Consumer Research,* 28(1), 67–88.

Kuther, T. L., & McDonald, E. (2004). Early adolescents' experiences with, and views of, Barbie. *Adolescence,* 39(153), 39–51.

Lang, J. (2005, July 27). Looking like a professor. *The Chronicle of Higher Education.* Retrieved from http://chronicle.com/article/Looking-Like-a-Professor/45035

Lawler, M., & Nixon, E. (2011). Body dissatisfaction among adolescent boys and girls: the effects of body mass, peer appearance culture and internalization of appearance ideals. *Journal of Youth and Adolescence,* 40(1), 59–71.

Leinbach, M. D., & Fagot, B. I. (1993). Categorical habituation to male and female faces: Gender schematic processing in infancy. *Infant Behavior and Development,* 16, 317–332.

Lennon, S.J., & Davis, L. L. (1989). Customer service, customer appearance, and sales person goals: Qualitative and quantitative techniques. *Home Economics Forum,* 4, 9–11, 18.

Lindsay, R. (2015, January 29). Why school dress codes may be harmful to girls. *Christian Science Monitor.* Retrieved from http://www.csmonitor.com/The-Culture/Family/2015/0129/Why-school-dress-codes-may-be-harmful-to-girls

Littrell, M. B., & Eicher, J. B. (1973). Clothing opinions and the social acceptance process among adolescents. *Adolescence,* 8, 197–212.

LoBue, V., & DeLoache, J. (2011). Pretty in pink: The early development of gender-stereotyped colour preferences. *British Journal of Developmental Psychology,* 29, 656–667.

Lublin, J. (2011, April, 12). How to look and act like a leader. *Wall Street Journal.* Retrieved from http://www.wsj.com/articles/SB10001424053111904140604576498380000356032

Lynch, A. (2012). *Porn chic: Exploring the contours of raunch eroticism.* New York, NY: Berg.

MacKaben, K. (2013, October 21). More people turning to online 'personal' shopping services. *Baltimore Sun.* Retrieved from http://www.baltimoresun.com/features/bs-ae-online-personal-shopper-20131021,0,2840010.story#ixzz32y8yb9gn

Maglaty, J. (2011, April 7). When did girls start wearing pink? *Smithsonian.* Retrieved from http://www.smithsonianmag.com/arts-culture/when-did-girls-start-wearing-pink-1370097/

Markee, N. L., Pedersen, E. L., Murray, C. I., & Stacey, P. B. (1994). What role do fashion dolls play in socialization of children? *Perceptual and Motor Skills,* 79(1), 187–190.

Marks, D. (2016, February 2). Students defy gender norms to protest Clovis dress code. Retrieved from http://ww2.kqed.org/news/2016/02/02/students-defy-gender-norms-to-protest-clovis-dress-code

Martens, L., Southerton, D., & Scott, S. (2004). Bringing children (and parents) into the sociology of consumption: Towards a theoretical and empirical agenda. *Journal of Consumer Culture, 4*(2), 155–182.

Martin, C. L., & Ruble, D. (2004). Children's search for gender cues cognitive perspectives on gender development. *Current Directions in Psychological Science, 13*(2), 67–70.

McCabe, R. E., Miller, J. L., Laugesen, N., Antony, M. M., & Young, L. (2010). The relationship between anxiety disorders in adults and recalled childhood teasing. *Journal of Anxiety Disorders, 24*(2), 238–243.

Mears, A. (2011). *Pricing beauty: The making of a fashion model.* Berkeley, CA: University of California Press.

Miller, K. A. (1998). Gender comparisons within reenactment costume: Theoretical interpretations. *Family and Consumer Sciences Research Journal, 27*(1), 35–61.

Mulready, P. M., & Lamb, J. M. (1985). Cosmetics therapy for chemotherapy patients. In Solomon, M. R. (Ed.), *The psychology of fashion: From conception to consumption* (pp. 255–263). Lexington, MA: Lexington Books.

Nicaise, V., Bois, J. E., Fairclough, S. J., Amorose, A. J., & Cogérino, G. (2007). Girls' and boys' perceptions of physical education teachers' feedback: Effects on performance and psychological responses. *Journal of Sports Sciences, 25*(8), 915–926.

Ogle, J. P. & Damhorst, M. L. (2000). Dieting among adolescent girls and their mothers: An interpretive study. *Family and Consumer Sciences Research Journal, 28*(4), 428–462.

Ogle, J. P., & Damhorst, M. L. (2003). Mothers and daughters interpersonal approaches to body and dieting. *Journal of Family Issues, 24*(4), 448–487.

Paff Ogle, J., Hyllegard, K., & Yan, R. N. (2014). An investigation of mothers' and tween daughters' clothing preferences and purchase intentions toward a prosocial clothing company. *Journal of Fashion Marketing and Management, 18*(1), 70–84.

Paoletti, J. (2012). *Pink and blue: Telling the boys from the girls in America.* Bloomington, IN: Indiana University Press.

Peluchette, J. V., Karl, K. & Rust, K. (2006). Dressing to impress: Beliefs and attitudes regarding workplace attire. *Journal of Business and Psychology, 21*(1), 45–63.

Pomerleau, A., Bolduc, D., Malcuit, G., Cossette, L. (1990). Pink or blue: Environmental gender stereotypes in the first two years of life. *Sex Roles, 22*(5/6), 359–367.

Poulin-Dubois, D., Serbin, L. A., Eichstedt, J. A., Sen, M. G., & Beissel, C. F. (2002). Men don't put on make-up: Toddlers' knowledge of the gender stereotyping of household activities. *Social Development, 11*, 166–181.

Poulin-Dubois, D., Serbin, L. A., Kenyon, B., & Derbyshire, A. (1994). Infants' intermodal knowledge about gender. *Developmental Psychology, 30*, 436–442.

Quereda's reign as Spain coach ends after 27 years (2015, July). Retrieved from http://equalizersoccer.com/2015/07/31/ignacio-quereda-fired-spain-wnt-coach-jorge-vilda-hired/

Rabolt, N. J., & Drake, M. F. (1985). Information sources used by women for career dressing decisions. In Solomon, M. R. (Ed.), *The psychology of fashion: From conception to consumption* (pp. 371–385). Lexington, MA: Lexington Books.

Radeloff, D. J. (1991). Psychological types, color attributes, and color preferences of clothing, textiles, and design students. *Clothing and Textiles Research Journal, 9*(3), 59–67.

Reddy-Best, K. L., & Harmon, J. (2015). Overweight boy's and girl's experiences with and perception of athletic clothing and its relationship to physical activity participation. *Fashion and Textiles, 2*(1), 1–16.

Rosen, L. (1992, October/December). Treatment of athletes with eating disorders working with coaches. In L. Hill (Ed.,), *National Anorexic Aid Society Newsletter, 15*(4), 1–2, 6.

Roudakova, N., & Ballare-Reisch, D. S. (1999). Femininity and the double burden: Dialogues on the socialization of Russian daughters into womanhood. *Anthropology of East Europe Review: Central Europe, Eastern Europe and Eurasia, 17*(1), 21–34.

Saunders, J. R., Samli, A. C., & Tozier, E. F. (1973). Congruence and conflict in buying decisions of mothers and daughters. *Journal of Retailing, 49*(3), 3–18.

Schreier, B. A. (1994). *Becoming American women: Clothing and the Jewish immigrant experience, 1880–1920.* Chicago, IL: Chicago Historical Society.

Schwartz, D. J., Phares, V., Tantleff-Dunn, S., & Thompson, J. K. (1999). Body image, psychological functioning, and parental feedback regarding physical appearance. *International Journal of Eating Disorders, 25*(3), 339–343.

Seock, Y. K., & Merritt, L. R. (2013). Influence of body mass index, perceived media pressure, and peer criticism/teasing on adolescent girls' body satisfaction/dissatisfaction and clothing-related behaviors. *Clothing and Textiles Research Journal, 31*(4) 244–258. DOI: 10.1177/0887302X13498508

Serbin, L. A., Poulin-Dubois, D., Colburne, K. A., Sen, M. G., & Eichstedt, J. A. (2001). Gender stereotyping in infancy: Visual preferences for and knowledge of gender-stereotyped toys in the second year. *International Journal of Behavioral Development, 25*, 7–15.

Serbin, L. A., Poulin-Dubois, D., & Eichstedt, J. A. (2002). Infants' responses to gender-inconsistent events. *Infancy, 3*(4), 531–542.

Shakin, M., Shakin, D., & Sternglanz, S. (1985). Infant clothing: Sex labeling for strangers. *Sex Roles, 12*, 955–964.

Shim, S., Snyder, L., & Gehrt, K. C. (1995), Parents' perception regarding children's use of clothing evaluative criteria: An exploratory study from the consumer socialization process perspective. In F. R. Kardes and M. Sujan (Eds.), *Advances in Consumer Research:* 22 (pp. 628–632), Provo, UT: Association for Consumer Research.

Smith, P. M., & Ogle, J. P. (2006). Interactions among high school cross-country runners and coaches: Creating a cultural context for athletes' embodied experiences. *Family and Consumer Sciences Research Journal, 34*, 276–307.

Smucker, B., & Creekmore, A. M. (1972). Adolescents' clothing conformity, awareness, and peer acceptance. *Home Economics Research Journal, 1*, 92–97.

Starr, C. R., & Ferguson, G. M. (2012). Sexy dolls, sexy grade-schoolers? Media & maternal influences on young girls' self-sexualization. *Sex Roles, 67*(7–8), 463–476.

Stone, G. P. (1962). Appearance and the self. In A. M. Rose (Ed.), *Human behavior and social processes: An interactionist approach* (pp. 86–118). New York, NY: Houghton Mifflin.

Strauss, M. D. (2003). Identity construction among Confederate Civil War reenactors: A study of dress, stage props, and discourse. *Clothing and Textiles Research Journal, 21*(4), 149–161.

Striegel-Moore, R. H., & Kearney-Cooke, A. (1994). Exploring parents' attitudes and behaviors about their children's physical appearance. *International Journal of Eating Disorders, 15*, 377–385.

Teo, C. B. C., Sidin, S. M., & Nor, M. I. M. (2013). Exploring influences of consumer socialization agents on branded apparel purchase among urban Malaysian tweens. *Pertanika Journal of Social Sciences & Humanities, 21*(1), 1–16.

Thompson, R. A., & Sherman, R. T. (1999). Athletes, athletic performance, and eating disorders: Healthier alternatives. *Journal of Social Issues, 55*(2), 317–337.

Vaughn, J. L., & Riemer, J. W. (1985). Fabricating the self: The socialization of fashion models. *Sociological Spectrum, 5*, 213–229.

Williams, M. C., & Eicher, J. B. (1966). Teenagers' appearance and social acceptance. *Journal of Home Economics, 58*, 457–461.

Yoo, J. J., & Johnson, K. K. (2007). Effects of appearance-related testing on ethnically diverse adolescent girls. *Adolescence, 42*(166), 353–380.

Yoo, J. J., & Johnson, K. K. (2008). Self-objectification and appearance-based teasing during adolescence. *Journal of Family and Consumer Sciences Education, 26*(1), 14–28.

Zarya, V. (2015, August 18). Ellen DeGeneres' new GapKids line blows away gender stereotypes. *Fortune*. Retrieved from http://fortune.com/2015/08/18/ellen-degeneres-new-gapkids-line-blows-away-gender-stereotypes/

Zosuls, K. M., Ruble, D. N., Tamis-LeMonda, C. S., Shrout, P. E., Bornstein, M. H., & Greulich, F. K. (2009). The acquisition of gender labels in infancy: Implications for sex-typed play. *Developmental Psychology, 45*, 688–701. doi:10.1037/a0014053

Zusman, M., Knox, D., & Gardner, T. (2009). *The social context view of sociology*. Durham, NC: Carolina Academic Press.

12 DRESS AND SOCIAL ORGANIZATIONS

After reading and reflecting on the content of this chapter, students should be able to:

- Use social learning theory to explain group members' influence on decision making concerning dress.
- Describe the part that dress plays in the functioning of social groups.
- Analyze an individual's dress as related to participation in social groups.
- Explain how dress functions within total institutions.

INTRODUCTION

Individuals who live and interact with each other and share a set of beliefs—that is, share a culture—make up the basic features of a society. A society reflects an association of individuals that makes human behavior and relationships between individuals somewhat predictable and that enables members to solve problems. By *predictable*, we mean that human behavior within a society is patterned and can be discussed in terms of several interrelated parts. The size of the association of individuals can be small in number (e.g., book clubs, riding clubs) or large (e.g., Fashion Group International).

Some of the terms that we use to describe societies and other social organizations you have been previously introduced to in Chapter 11, "Dress and Socialization" and include the concepts of social status, norms, social positions, and role. Building on these concepts, in this chapter we discuss the concepts of group, organization, and institution as distinct components of societies and the part that dress can play in the formation and functioning of these societal components.

SOCIAL GROUPS

A **social group** is a number of people who share interests and have things in common as well as physically or socially interact with each other. Think for a minute about examples of social groups to which you belong. You might have recognized you are a member of a family, a student organization, a fraternal organization, a class, a club, or a sports team. Each of these groups shares common characteristics regardless of their size. These common characteristics include some type of interaction, shared interests, a sense of belonging, expectations for your behavior and your dress, and some type of structure. For example, college women hoping to be recruited into a sorority are advised to avoid plunging necklines, risqué miniskirts, gaudy makeup, glitter, and false eyelashes (Houta, 2015). Here the social group is a sorority and the dress expectations include avoidance of plunging necklines, risqué miniskirts, gaudy makeup, glitter, and false eyelashes.

The **social structure** of a group can be defined as the way the social positions that exist are organized relative to each other (Zusman, Knox, & Gardner, 2009). For example, a sport team can have the following positions: player, captain, coach, and team manager. Each of these positions has a different status and norms for behavior. Understanding the social structure of a group is important because different social structures can result in different outcomes. For example, if you were raised in a single-parent home the rules you learned about dress might be more permissive than if you were raised in a household with both of your parents and your grandmother.

Membership in some groups can last a lifetime (e.g., family, religious, professional) and memberships in other groups can last a short period of time (e.g., concert attendees). Because people can move in and out of groups, groups are dynamic and always in a state of change. The term *process* is used to describe how social organizations change

(Zusman, Knox, & Gardner, 2009). Thus, individuals may adopt and reject dress items as they participate in and then leave different social groups through their lifetime.

With every movement in and out of a social group, there is generally a change in one's behavior. For example, when an individual gets married, this represents an exit from one group (single man or woman) and the corresponding norms for behavior (e.g., dating different people) and an entrance into another group (married people) and the corresponding norms for behavior (e.g., discontinue dating). The new group and accompanying statuses shape the changes in behavior that a person demonstrates (Zusman, Knox, & Gardner, 2009). Such changes in behavior may be related to dress. For example, senior cords worn by Indiana seniors (see Chapter 10, "Dress and Identity") were no longer worn after graduation when students exited the "senior" group.

Subculture

We learned in Chapter 1, "Why study dress?" that *subculture* is another term for a *social group*, that is, a group of individuals who interact with each other and share a lifestyle, interests, and beliefs among other commonalities. Students attending a particular middle school can be considered a subculture of the larger group of all middle school students. Subcultures may have expectations for how to dress such as a middle school's dress code. While a social group in theory could entail all members of a society, a subculture is a group that is smaller in size than the dominant culture in which they exist. For example, we learned previously in Chapter 9, "Dress and the Self" that a high school can be divided into different smaller groups of students who share interests (e.g., jocks, nerds) so it serves as an example of a social group that has both a dominant culture and smaller subcultures.

The relationship between the dominant culture and a subculture is complex. Typically when we think of the dominant culture, we think of people, places, and the meanings of things defined by dominant consensus. Continuing with our high school example, there were rules that all students were asked to follow established often in conversations with administrators, teachers, students, and parents. These rules include expected behaviors (e.g., how to act, what to wear). Schools often develop a mission statement that reflects the direction they want students to take (e.g., "The mission of our high school is to educate,

empower, and enable all students to become caring, contributing citizens who can succeed in an ever-changing world").

Subcultures arise because, for whatever reason, the dominant culture has failed to meet the needs of some of the members of the society. In a high school setting, small student interest groups (e.g., theater, sports, leadership) develop out of a desire of students to learn more about a topic than they might ordinarily in their regular classes. Returning to the example of senior cords from Chapter 10, "Dress and Identity," seniors often decorated their cords to reflect their interest groups such as dance club.

When we think of a country as representing a culture, we can easily imagine numerous subcultures developing (e.g., anti-abortion groups, gun control groups, knitters, environmentalists). One example of a popular subcultural group is the hippie subculture that developed during the 1960s (Figure 12.1). While members of the dominant culture initially supported the Vietnam War, many youth were not interested in being drafted to fight in this war. The youth were also not interested in supporting the dominant values of the time. Out of this discontent, evolved the hippie subculture, a group that promoted the basic belief that life was about being happy. Interested in an alternative lifestyle and rebelling against a society grown increasingly repressive, hippies focused on freedom and getting back to nature. They developed a distinctive appearance. Hair for both sexes was worn long. Clothing was often loose and made of cotton and hemp. Anything handmade, whether sewn, knit or woven was prized. Gradually, hand-made extended to dyeing one's own clothes and tie-dye became popular (Bhaddock, 2011).

When subcultures begin to define the world according to their own terms, conflict can evolve between members

Figure 12.1
Members of the hippie
subculture often wore their
hair long, peace symbols,
flowers in the their, and hand-
made garments to distingusih
themselves from the dominant
culture of the period. These two
people are dressed as hippies
for the Jarama Circuit in Madrid,
Spain. The Jarama Vintage
Festival seeks to revive the
1960s, 1970s and 1980s.

of the subculture and the dominant culture. The conflict is made visible via style. Developing a distinct style (e.g., rebellious, radical) enables the subculture to make visible their resistance to mainstream culture and call attention to their unmet needs. The response of the dominant culture may initially be fear as the subculture may be calling into question basic beliefs and ways of behaving of the dominant culture. Several things can happen next nearly simultaneously. First the dominant culture can move to meet these unmet needs. Second, the dominant culture begins to assimilate the subculture's style. Entrepreneurs find a way to commodify the style of the subculture and soon the subculture's way appearing is available to the dominant culture. In this way the once unique or deviant way of appearing of the subculture is contained and the subculture begins to lose its power as the dominant culture assimilates and thus, nullifies the subculture's style. All subcultures experience this same process of differentiation and eventual assimilation (Hebdige, 1979). While the subculture may remain in some form, it no longer has the same power of resistance it had initially.

Continuing with the hippie example, as the subculture gained momentum; the dominant culture slowly began to assimilate the beliefs of the subculture and its appearance. The political leaders decided to withdraw from participation in the war in Vietnam and, of importance to dress, prominent fashion designers co-opted the hippie look in their expensive ready-to-wear lines. The result was to make the once unique hippie style, a style of the dominant culture.

Knowing what social groups individuals participate in is important because this information helps us make predictions about the individuals' behavior including their decision making concerning dress. Since groups are important to understanding decision making concerning dress, we next discuss different types of groups and how decision making concerning dress can be impacted by these groups.

TYPES OF SOCIAL GROUPS

Primary Groups

One important distinction concerning the type of groups people are members of is the distinction between primary and secondary groups. The term **primary group** is used to refer to small, informal collections of individuals who interact with each other in personal, direct, and intimate ways (Cooley, 1909). You have emotional ties with individuals in your primary groups. Good examples of members of your primary groups include parents, siblings, extended family members (e.g., aunts, uncles, grandparents) as well as close friends, some work associates, and some of your neighbors. Interactions that occur in primary groups tend to be personal and focus on feelings and experiences. The goal of a primary group is often the relationship between individuals rather than for achieving some other purpose. As you learned in Chapter 11, "Dress and Socialization," the individuals most involved in your socialization concerning dress are your parents, siblings, and peers. Hence, you are socialized by members of your primary groups.

In-Group Membership

A sense of belonging is a key characteristic of a group because those who belong to a group think of members as forming a distinct social unit. This distinct social unit can be small in size as in the instance where a young man shares a ring or a pin with a young woman (e.g., a group of two) or adolescents share jewelry (e.g., best friend forever [BFF] bracelets) or it can be large in size (e.g., fans of a team). This social unit has boundaries that separate those who are "in" the group from those who are "out" of the group. An **in-group** is a group wherein members feel that they share a common bond, share ideologies, come from a common background, or otherwise resemble other members of the group. Key to an in-group is a sense of togetherness with other members of the group. Family members can easily comprise an in-group of individuals as they share life experiences that are unique to them. Wearing the same or coordinated items of dress makes visible to others that in-group members are connected to each other in some way (e.g., family members, cancer survivors, surfers, war veterans) even if it is not obvious to observers what the connection is.

Friendship Groups

Friendship groups are another example of an in-group and they often exert an influence on dress and appearance. Friendship groups probably exert their greatest impact during adolescence, as it is very commonly reported that adolescents spend a significant amount of time hanging out with their friends and that within friendship groups there is a great deal of similarity in attitudes and behaviors (Tolson & Urberg, 1993). Friendship groups provide a means for adolescents to test out new ideas, interests, and behaviors and receive feedback in a context that is independent of the family. These groups also provide opportunities for sharing and a sense of belonging. A research team from Turkey and the UK studied the relationship of friendship groups and fashion consumption among British adolescent school girls (Yalkin & Rosenbaum-Elliott, 2014). Results showed that the adolescents gained skills and knowledge related to fashion by talking to peers in their friendship groups.

Large friendship groups in high schools often have names (e.g., cowboys, greasers, band geeks) and are identified by distinctive attributes of their dress. For example, in qualitative research with students of one high school the students identified distinct friendship groups based on their appearance: jocks, nerds, freaks, preppies, and punks. Jocks were described as wearing athletic clothing in general and letter jackets. One student referred to male jocks as mesh men, a reference to the fabric of some athletic apparel. Nerds were described as unconcerned about their appearance, wearing out-of-style clothing, or things that their parents had selected for them. Freaks were described as wearing black everything and leather clothing while punks wore similar clothing but it was torn and their hair was often dyed bright colors, shaved off in patterns, or spiked up. Preppies were described as wearing expensive, branded clothing. One student described preppies as "well ironed" (Eicher & Baizermann, 1991).

Even though adolescents may form large friendship groups and may develop similar outward appearances as a result of participation in these groups, the influence of friends and peers on appearance management decisions and behaviors has not received a great deal of research attention. Perhaps this is because clothing researchers think that it is obvious that adolescents influence each other's dress and appearance. However, one set of researchers did investigate the impact of high school friendship groups on one appearance management behavior, dieting. These researchers found that participation in friendship groups contributed to a high level of concern about body image. Participants not only engaged in weight loss behaviors but also talked about weight loss/dieting, reported comparing their bodies often, were the recipients of teases about weight from friends within the group, reported that their friends were important to their decision to diet, and perceived their friends to be preoccupied with dieting and weight loss (Paxton, Schutz, Wertheim, & Muir, 1999).

Using a different term, *peer crowds*, another team of researchers also documented that peer groups exert a significant influence on health-related behaviors including exercise and weight control behaviors. **Peer crowds** were described as large groups of peers that are similar in interests, appearance, or attitudes. What makes this team of researchers' work interesting is they divided their participants into groups based on the peer crowds with which they affiliated. They used groups that they claimed were observed most frequently in high schools: populars (socially oriented and outgoing), brains (enjoy academics), burnouts (often get into trouble), jocks (active in sports), and alternatives (rebel against mainstream culture). Health-related behaviors differed based on the group with which a participant affiliated. Participants who associated with burnouts and populars engaged in unhealthy eating and bulimic eating. Those associated with jocks and populars reported engaging in exercise while brains reported healthful eating (Mackey & Greca, 2007). Do these results surprise you or do they seem consistent with your school experience?

Cosplay Groups

Fan groups are another example of in-groups. **Cosplay**, a combination of the terms *costume* and *play*, is an activity that involves fans of popular culture (e.g., television, movies, games) getting together with other like-minded individuals to assume the appearance of their favorite characters (i.e., wear costumes) and engage in a performance.

Early examples of these types of group activities include individuals who dressed in period costumes to attend Renaissance fairs or fans of science fiction who dressed up as their favorite *Star Wars* or *Star Trek* character for conventions. Sometimes the cosplay performance is formal such as instances where there is a fashion show or where the individual role-plays the assumed persona in virtual environments or sometimes the performance is informal and includes socializing with others when in costume.

Often cosplay takes place in a discrete location such as a convention or get-together. Individuals often either make their own costumes or commission their costumes from other fans or from professional seamstresses and tailors. Costuming skills are critical because cosplayers are judged on their ability to authentically portray and enact their character. Fans can earn praise for their sewing skills as they participate in fashion shows and show off their costumes. In addition to fashion shows, costume is also central to photography sessions often held after shows. Cosplayers view requests for photographs as compliments to their ability to effectively execute a look or appearance. (Figure 12.2).

Most participants in cosplay conventions dress in costume, but not all. Not wearing a costume does not mean that these spectators do not signify their participation

DRESS IN THE NEWS
Comic Book Guys and Cosplay Women

Costume play (cosplay) seems to generate unease and anxiety among men. Why? Perhaps men feel threatened by women of all sizes and shapes appearing in superhero costumes, as the superhero comic world has long been dominated by men. Cosplay, dominated by women, opens up new and interesting ways to combine a love of fabric, sewing, and dressing up with a love of comic book characters. So, why so upsetting? Perhaps it is the sexuality of cosplay or perhaps it is because women players are perceived as not "real" fans of the characters whose appearances they emulate. Whether or not cosplay is yet another arena for male hegemony, if comics and superheroes are supposed to be for everyone, then cosplay should be an inclusive arena for people to wear whatever they wish.

Figure 12.2
Cosplayers dressed as Gandalf the Grey and Elves of Lord Of The Rings attend Film & Comic Con Manchester at Event City in Manchester, England. The festival attracts comics, manga, cosplay, films, and games fans.

using dress. Rather, through T-shirts, buttons, headbands or hats, and jewelry, these fans also use dress as a way to signify their character affiliations.

Cosplaying is also an embodied experience as it allows spectators to encounter fictional characters. As a fan practice, cosplay is concerned with embodying a character accurately. Thus, cosplayers often develop an increased awareness of their own bodies and choose a character that matches their own posture or body build. However, cosplayers also want to bring something of their self to the enactment of their characters. In this way, cosplay is also a form of self-expression (Lamerichs, 2011).

Cause-Related Dress

One type of distinctive apparel that can reflect in-group membership is cause- related dress. **Cause-related dress** is a term used to describe items of dress that have text, symbols or images that express an opinion or an affiliation with a cause. These items can be constructed by an individual or sold by a manufacturer (McElvain, 2008). The term has also been used to describe products that "raise money for a specific charity as well as awareness of the cause" (Yurchisin, Kwon, & Marcketti, 2009, p. 449). The dress items can reflect in-group status because it is assumed that all individuals who wear the items share in their support of the cause it represents.

The contemporary popularity of cause-related dress could be credited to the development of a rubber wristband by the Lance Armstrong Foundation to raise money for cancer research and promote awareness of cancer. The

wristband was introduced in the summer of 2004, was about ½ inch wide, yellow, had the word LIVESTRONG imprinted on it, and sold for one dollar.

The promotion was successful as the next three years produced 63 million dollars (Ruibal, 2007) from wristband sales. Many other organizations followed with their own rubber wristbands and their own messages. Soon individuals, including highly visible celebrities, were seen wearing multiple bracelets in a variety of colors. This practice raised questions about the sincerity of the individuals who wore the cause-related items and their actual support of the causes. In other words, did the people who wore the items actually support the causes or were the items adopted as a fashion statement?

To answer this question, undergraduates completed questionnaires about their purchasing habits related to the rubber cause-related bracelets as well as their participation in fashion and interest in celebrity culture. Participants were divided into two groups: those that owned at least one charity bracelet and those that did not. Participants who purchased charity bracelets were more involved in fashion and in celebrity culture than participants who did not own a bracelet. Interestingly, participants who owned charity bracelets were less involved in the causes the bracelets represented than were participants who did not own bracelets. The researchers concluded that the popularity of the charity bracelets was perhaps more an indication of following fashion and interest in celebrity culture than of support of the causes represented by the bracelets (Yurchisin, Kwon, & Marcketti, 2009).

This is not to say that individuals who wear cause-related dress do not generally support the cause. The instance of the rubber wristbands is one where the cause-related item was easily affordable and as a result, easily adopted. Others may invest greater financial resources than one dollar to obtain a cause-related dress item and therefore, may be committed to the cause or those individuals who are committed to the cause may be making direct financial donations to the cause rather than wearing cause-related dress items. Thus, one cannot simply assume an individual's level of commitment to a cause based on their decision to wear cause-related clothing.

Out-Groups

The converse of in-groups is out-groups. An **out-group** is a group to which people feel they do not belong. Individuals do not identify with out-groups or affiliate with their members. It is not unusual for in-group members to view out-group members as having undesirable characteristics (Zusman, Konx, & Gardner, 2009). However, out-group members may still impact dress and appearance because people may make conscious attempts to avoid looking like them. If your high school was composed of different groups of students, you probably experienced a desire to appear similar to members of in-groups and distance yourself from out-groups even though all individuals you encountered shared membership in the same school.

Some in-groups and out-groups form on the basis of demographic characteristics. For example, if the number of retailers dedicated to selling apparel to young women is any indication, the fashion industry treats young women as an in-group and women over fifty (or large-size women) as an out-group. Social movements or causes can also serve as the basis for in-group and out-groups. The popularity of social responsibility and environmental concern about how and where apparel is produced could produce an in-group (e.g., people that buy apparel that is not manufactured in a sweat shop with poor labor practices) and an out-group (e.g., people that do not care who makes their apparel). Both groups can develop group characteristics to help individuals identify each other and communicate their shared beliefs. One of these shared characteristics is adopting distinctive items of dress.

Gangs

One primary group that could be considered an out-group (at least distinct from the mainstream) and that can exert a considerable influence on the behavior of adolescents is a youth gang. According to the National Institute of Justice (2011), a gang is a self-formed association of peers with members that engage in criminal activities and identify themselves by adopting a group identity by employing one or more of the following: a name, a symbol, tattoo or other physical marking, style or color of clothing, hairstyle, hand sign or graffiti. Documented visual expressions of gang membership have included colors, baggy pants, baseball caps, tattoos, and Starter jackets (Hethorn & Kaiser, 1999). A gang may have distinct characteristics such as an identifiable leadership, control over a particular territory, may have rules for joining, and may protect its members from others. Although individuals may feel that they were born into a gang, typically individuals join gangs by choice and can exit them, thus gangs are an example of a voluntary group.

Interest in gangs and violence related to dress developed during the 1980s. One association between gangs and dress came from news reports in locations across the US that reported stories of elementary and middle school students as well as adults being attacked and sometimes killed as a result of the items of dress that they wore. A stereotype of perpetrators and victims of the attacks emerged with both groups frequently described as gang members, male, and African American but in reality, victims and perpetrators varied in gender, age, and ethnicity (O'Neal, 1997).

Sometimes the goal of the attacks was to steal the item. In this context, violence was attributed to a general desire by some to quickly obtain symbols of status that could not otherwise be afforded as well as to characteristics of perpetrators that included a lack of self-esteem and a desire to fit in with others (O'Neal, 1997; 1998). In other instances, the goal of the attack may have been to protect the area from infiltration by rival gang members. In 2015 police authorities believed California man, was the victim in a gang-related shooting because he was wearing red shoes, the color of a rival gang, in the wrong neighborhood (Lloyd & Klemack, 2015). Remedies to solve the problem of violence motivated by dress included advising individuals to halt wearing any dress items that might put them at risk along with schools to develop dress codes.

Violence related to gangs and dress is not a thing of the past. A nineteen year old man was fatally shot at a car wash in South L.A.in 2015 because he was wearing red shoes (Palmer & Wolfe, 2015). Three men were arrested and all three were gang members. Red clothing was also the reason that a man was killed in Baltimore ("Gang member," 2013). The victim was killed for wearing a red shirt in an area where blue was the dominant gang's color. A similar situation recently took place in the capital of Honduras, where a woman was knifed allegedly because her hair was blond (Dubove, 2015). Apparently the gangs there use hair color to identify women associated with them. Only gang members or their associates are allowed to wear black or animal print leggings, carry satchel handbags, or wear Nike shoes.

Clothing Deprivation

Some adolescents may refrain from trying to join social groups or participate in social activities because they believe that they do not have the "right" clothing to participate. **Clothing deprivation** is defined as "discontent with clothing in relation to peers, the feeling of not having enough clothing to be satisfied" (Francis, 1992, p. 29), as well as inability to purchase clothing. Adolescents who think they are clothing deprived relative to their peers believe there is a connection between their lack of clothing and both their social competence (popularity, attractiveness) and participation in groups (e.g., participation in sports) (Francis, 1992). However, this research was conducted over twenty years ago. With the ever decreasing cost of clothing over this same time period, the question is whether adolescents living in developed countries continue to experience clothing deprivation or if clothing deprivation is a thing of the past?

Secondary Groups

A **secondary group** is a group to which an individual has limited emotional ties, whose members interact with each other in formal ways, and whose members often come together for practical purposes. Secondary groups can be large or small in terms of membership. Examples of secondary groups include classrooms of students, committees, professional groups, and neighborhood groups. An example of dress associated with a secondary group is senior cords (see Figures 10.2 and 10.3 in chapter 10, "Dress and Identity"), which were cream colored corduroy pants/skirts worn by high school and university seniors in Indiana until the 1970s.

Differences between primary and secondary groups are differences in degree. Many formal secondary groups can have components of closeness and intimacy characteristic of primary groups and the reverse can also be true. Individuals working in close physical contact with each other may never share a personal conversation. They may also become close personal friends. Many primary groups

> **IN-CLASS ACTIVITY**
> **Clothing Deprivation**
>
> Take a moment to reflect on whether you have experienced clothing deprivation. What was the circumstance? Did not having the clothing you desired hinder your participation in a social group?

can develop from participation in secondary groups. Whether an individual is a member of a primary or secondary group shifts frequently because the closeness of relationships shifts over time. Consider the individuals you knew during high school. Some of these individuals have remained close friends while others have drifted away. Thus, it is ultimately up to the individual to identify those individuals that are members of their primary or secondary groups. Dress can be used to identify secondary groups. For example, food service may be identified by their aprons, hats, and plastic gloves. Also Disneyland tour guides wear a distinctive plaid costume, which for women includes a plaid skirt, a vest which might be plaid or a solid, and a white blouse (Doyle, n.d.; Myers, 2011).

Secondary groups are important because they help societies function effectively and allow people who do not know each other well to work effectively with each other. Secondary groups are also important because we spend a considerable amount of time living and working in secondary groups. Consider the amount of time you spend in school, working for a corporation, or living in a community. Secondary groups are also important because participation in them exerts an influence on our decision making concerning our dress. Continuing with the example of the Disneyland tour guides, all who work at a Disney Park are required to comply with the Disney Look, which is described as clean, natural, polished, and professional. It prohibits visible tattoos, tongue piercing or splitting, and earlobe expansion (The Disney look, n.d.).

School Dress Codes and Uniforms.

As we noted previously in Chapter 5, "Dress and Impression Formation," dress codes are used in the workplace as well as in schools to regulate dress and appearance. In this chapter we focus on the use of dress codes as well as uniforms in the school. As noted in the afore discussion on gangs and violence related to dress, for some schools and their administrators, interest in dress codes and in requiring students to wear uniforms during the 1980s and 1990s was in response to concerns about violence directed toward children and adolescents as a result of the clothing they were wearing, the increase in gang presence in the schools, and a desire to provide students with a safe learning environment.

A dress code is a set of rules that specify the required manner of dress in a school. Dress codes can be prescriptive or prohibitive. **Prescriptive dress codes** are regulations that detail exactly what must be worn. They are the most restrictive and are often associated with having to wear a school uniform (Figure 12.3). An example of a prescriptive dress code is a regulation indicating that all students must wear a plain white polo shirt. **Prohibitive dress codes** are regulations that indicate what items of dress are not to be worn by students. They are less restrictive because they in effect, allow students to wear any dress items except the prohibited ones. An example of a prohibitive dress code is a regulation indicating that students cannot wear jeans to school.

As uniforms, in general, are a method for groups to exert control over its members, when school officials decide to implement a dress code requiring students to wear a uniform, they are attempting to exert control over students. There are several key properties of uniforms (Joseph, 1986). First, a uniform is a group emblem. When a school adopts a uniform, the uniform becomes a symbol of that school and represents the attributes of that school. If the school is a prestigious school, the uniform can enhance the status of the student who wears it.

A uniform reveals and conceals statuses of the individual wearing it. Wearing a uniform conceals other statuses because only one status is represented by the uniform (e.g., student). The student status becomes a master status because symbols of other statuses (e.g., pins, patches) are often not allowed when wearing his or her school uniform.

By putting on the uniform, students declare their intention to follow the regulations of the school. The uniform certifies the individual as a representative of the school thus, the individual represents to others the attributes of the school when in uniform rather than a collection of individual attributes. Because all students in the school must wear the uniform, uniforms are a source of imposed conformity in appearance. Thus, uniforms suppress individuality and encourage conformity to expected behaviors.

In addition to the aforementioned properties and effects of uniforms, controlling students' appearance while they are in school is credited by many individuals (e.g., administrators, parents) with several positive outcomes

Figure 12.3
Uniforms can hide the individual social statuses of the children wearing them.

such as reducing theft and violence over designer and other expensive clothing (DeCosta, 2006). Dress regulations are credited with increasing the self-esteem of the students (Murray, 1997), promoting a collective identity (Tamura, 2007), being a social and economic equalizer as they reduce student competition over clothing (Gursky, 1996), increasing the academic performance of students (DeCosta, 2006), and perhaps teaching children that there is more to a person than the clothing that they wear. Uniforms have been endorsed because school officials believe they will increase student attendance, promote decorum, decrease dropout rates, and promote respect for authority (Vopat, 2010). They are also credited with enabling school officials to easily differentiate between students that belong on a campus from those who do not. Outside of the campus, dress regulations that require students to wear uniforms are said to help community members identify students as belonging to the school and in the neighborhood; therefore, they enable members to watch after these children (Paliokas, Fatrell, & Rist, 1996).

Opposition to dress regulations and the establishment of uniform requirements is derived from several beliefs including that such regulations limit student's freedom of expression due to their conforming nature, place an undue financial burden on families, and prohibit identity exploration (DeCosta, 2006). Vopat (2010) argued that dress codes intended for young children (five to eleven years of age) did not limit students' freedom of expression. He proposed that there were two types of expression: mere and substantive. Mere expression occurs when children select clothing items for their style or color, and/ or when they select clothing arbitrarily. These clothing choices are **mere expressions** because the student is not consciously attempting to use clothing to communicate anything to anyone else. Vopat proposed that young children were only capable of mere expression because they did not intend for their clothing choices to communicate anything to others. He also argued that because a child's clothing was typically decided upon by parents, what the clothing indicated was more about how parents wanted their children to be viewed rather than communicating a specific viewpoint of a child. Further, even in instances where a child was allowed to decide what clothing items to purchase, Vopat contended that children simply did not think about clothing as representative of any message other than mere expression. It was only when a child was capable of using their clothing for **substantive expression**, that is, the use of clothing to intentionally communicate

something to others, that a child's freedom of expression could be limited by a dress code regulation. Thus, according to Vopat, the issue of violating a student's freedom of expression could only be applied to children over eleven years of age.

Another major criticism of adopting policies that require students to wear uniforms is that there is no clear research evidence that school uniforms or dress code policies actually result in the positive outcomes that individuals claim for them. In fact, the research addressing the effect of dress codes on students has resulted in inconsistent findings. On the one hand there is research that links school uniforms with positive outcomes. For example, some researchers have reported that as compared to students not required to wear a uniform, uniformed students rated their school's climate as more positive and their attendance and student performance was better (Gregory, 1996; Murray, 1997). More recently, researchers used longitudinal data to study the effects of school uniforms (Gentile & Imberman, 2012). Results showed that when uniforms were adopted attendance increased (grades 6–12), but uniform adoption was not related to measures of discipline or scholastic achievement.

On the other hand, there is research that suggests there is no relationship between wearing school uniforms and positive self perceptions or improved school climate made by either students or their teachers. Wade and Stafford (2003) studied the effect of school uniforms with middle school students and their teachers comparing schools that had a uniform requirement to schools that did not. Students who were required to wear a school uniform did not rate themselves higher on measures of scholastic competence, social acceptance, physical appearance, behavior, or athletic competence than did students attending schools that did not require uniforms. In addition, neither students nor teachers in schools requiring uniforms rated their school's climate as better than students and teachers at schools without uniforms.

Furthermore, students are not completely in favor of school regulations requiring them to wear uniforms. DeCosta (2006) interviewed middle school students as they transitioned to a high school environment that required they wear a uniform. The interviews covered a range of topics but focused on the student's opinions concerning the uniform requirement and its effects on their school life. Students did not link their academic performance to wearing a uniform. The majority of the students opposed the policy for a variety of reasons including that it restricted their freedom, was expensive, and that the uniform requirement was pointless. In other words, the students did not believe that the outcomes attributed to wearing school uniforms were realized. Student reactions to having to wear a uniform included attempts to subvert the uniform policy by failing to comply and consequently having to wear an alternative uniform as punishment. The alternative uniform consequently became a popular symbol of student dissent. Other reactions included attempts to personalize the uniform.

Similar sentiments were expressed by high school students. The students were critical of the dress codes centering their critique at specific details of the regulations (e.g., not being allowed to wear tops with spaghetti straps) rather than being opposed to having regulations overall. Girls opposed aspects of the regulations that they viewed as not practical. For example, some items of dress were more comfortable to wear on hot days than others, thus prohibiting students from wearing these comfortable items was viewed as impractical. Complaints about the dress codes also stemmed from experiences wherein the rules were inconsistently applied (e.g., under-policed, over-policed) and subject to individual interpretation. Few girls viewed dress codes as constraining their freedom of expression. Dress codes were actually valued by some girls because they regulated body exposure and thus were viewed as a strategy to prevent peer or sexual harassment while attending school (Raby, 2010).

Clearly, researcher efforts have not produced consistent findings concerning how dress codes, particularly those requiring a uniform, impact students. Thus, we cannot with any certainty say what exactly is facilitated as a result of their adoption. However, Raby's (2010) research does suggest that dress regulations concerning body exposure may contribute to the maintenance of a non-hostile learning environment.

Regardless of any clearly documented advantage or disadvantage to requiring uniforms and applying other dress regulations in schools, if administrators and parents are interested in establishing them, the US courts have ruled that students do not give up their rights as they enter the campus. Thus, for any dress regulations to be valid they need to promote student safety and/or prevent disruption of other students in the classroom. School dress codes can be challenged in the courts if they are difficult to understand, too general in nature, and/or do not have a legitimate basis (Lennon, Schulz, & Johnson, 1999). For example, a rule that forbids students from wearing clothing styles that are too body revealing is general in nature and open to interpretation, thus it would likely be deemed invalid if challenged in the courts. On the other hand, a girl wearing a T-shirt with the following text on the front, "objects may be larger than they appear" may be sent home from school under a dress code that does not allow T-shirts with statements that generate a commotion that consequently disrupts the classroom. Thus, students have a right to dress as they choose and their dress for school can be limited only by regulations that are legitimate, promote student safety, and contribute to a positive learning environment.

Other Secondary Groups

Reference Groups

In Chapter 11, "Dress and Socialization" we discussed social learning theory and the role that models can have in decision making concerning dress. As we discussed this theory, we noted that individual people can serve as models for others' behavior. When a single individual serves as a model for you, the term **significant other** is used. When a group of people serves as a model for your behavior, the term **reference group** is used. You may or may not be a member of a group to use it as a reference group (Bandura, 1977) . For example, when you scan the pages of fashion magazines and attempt to imitate the dress of the models or the celebrities featured, these individuals are a reference group for you. On the other hand, if you are a member of the girls' volleyball team or the men's football team, the way in which the other members of the team appear may also guide your decisions about dress.

IN-CLASS ACTIVITY
Dress Codes in Schools

Research on how dress codes/uniforms impact the performance and overall school life of students is inconsistent. However, there exists an untested idea about relationships between having restrictions on dress and appearance and maintenance of a non-hostile learning environment (i.e., reducing sexually harassing comments about appearance). Does your own school experience support or rebut this idea?

SCHOOL UNIFORM POLICY DRIVES FASHION APPAREL SALES

While some fashion retailers may be wringing their hands when school districts require students to wear uniforms to school other retailers have found doing business in a school district actually contribute positively to profits. In the fall of 2013 more than 17,000 students attending school in the Allentown School District were required to wear uniforms to school. Retailers found that when parents come into the store to purchase uniforms for their children, they also purchase other items including fashionable items. "Suddenly people who would not have shopped here are coming in because they had a need . . . and they were buying other things as well," shared Edward McKeaney, Boscov's senior executive vice president of merchandising and advertising (Wescoe, 2013) (Boscovs' is a full-service department store located primarily in the states of Pennsylvania and New Jersey). Worried that the store might be perceived as a "uniform store" and not as a fashion forward retailer, Megan Watson, the buyer for two of Boscov's stores, said there are other economies in offering uniforms versus fashion clothing. "You can forecast the quantity you need much easier," she said. In contrast, when buying trendy apparel, if you do not buy correctly, you can quickly have overstocks and have to sell merchandise at a larger discount than anticipated—and lose money in the process. And, children grow and need new uniforms every year so offering customers uniforms is a consistent source of store traffic and income.

One's peers often serve as a reference group for ideas about dress. Students, as they transition from elementary school to middle school, use their knowledge about what is worn in middle school (i.e., new reference group, new peers) as a means to ease the transition from their old peer group into a new group in the middle school. Levi jeans were noted as a good transitional item of dress because "everyone wears them," so wearing Levi's in the new environment would be the safest way to fit in and not draw too much attention. Students also distanced themselves from previous reference groups whose members appeared in clothing that now appeared childish and unexciting (Waerdahl, 2005).

Reference groups can explain why some people do not appear the way we might expect them to. For example, we might expect that the teenage children of an upper class family might wear designer clothing similar to their parents but instead they wear items from a fashion discounter or perhaps a clothing resale shop. Their dress choices may indicate it is their peers that serve as their reference group rather than their parents.

Reference groups can help explain why some people are unhappy with their situation in life. Feelings of deprivation, including clothing deprivation described earlier in this chapter, can result from making comparisons to reference groups. This type of deprivation is called **relative deprivation**. You might experience relative deprivation when you see the size of other students' wardrobes and make comparisons to your own and determine that they have more clothing, nicer clothing, or more designer label clothing than you own. Experiences of relative deprivation can contribute to feeling inadequate and motivate coping behaviors.

Individuals are likely to have more than one reference group and reference groups often change over time. As a student, some of the reference groups that might have an impact on your dress probably include peers that share your major, your family members, your professors, and your roommates. Perhaps these groups encourage you to experiment with your appearance. Once you graduate and enter the workplace, you may find that a new reference group (e.g., other workplace members) assumes importance and shapes your decision making concerning dress accordingly.

Membership Groups

Membership groups are groups that require some type of credentials before membership is granted (Zusman, Knox, & Gardner, 2009). For example, membership in the Fashion Group International requires that you hold a position within the fashion industry, that you are a fashion educator, or that you are a student majoring in a fashion-related discipline. Entry into some membership groups is granted by simply having an interest and paying dues. For example, membership in the Red Hat Society requires that you be a woman fifty years of age or older.

Figure 12.4
Red Hat Society members.

DRESS IN THE NEWS
Red Hat Society and Changing Attitudes about Aging

Considered the largest social group in the world, the Red Hat Society was formed in 1989 when Sue Ellen Cooper and a group of friends met for tea wearing purple clothing and red hats. Membership has grown to include groups in all fifty of the United States and thirty other countries around the world. The goal of the organization is to have fun and change perceptions of aging women. Official membership begins at age fifty when women can wear the red and purple, but women can join at any age. Young women wear pink hats and lavender clothing.

Dress is important to this group as the signature purple clothing and red hats are a visible reminder that they are not invisible and not done living. The purple clothing indicates that members are in a group and connotes for outsiders their belongingness and their choice to spend time together and have fun. In a world of youth and beauty the group is a celebration of aging (Nass, 2012). Feeling good about aging includes feeling comfortable in your own skin, having fun, being fit, fulfilled, and free. Members participate in a range of activities including playing cards, discussing books, and having lunch.

Once you have joined a membership group, the group may require that you wear certain items of dress to meetings or you may simply want to wear items of dress similar to other members. Such is the case with the Red Hat Society that encourages its members to wear purple clothing items and red hats to meetings and other member events (Figure 12.4).

STRATIFICATION SYSTEMS

Thus far in this chapter, you have learned that one way you can study and understand individuals' decision making concerning their dress is to examine the groups that they participate in and those that they use as a point of reference. Members of some groups within a society have more power, prestige, and wealth than members of other groups. Some social positions within society are more valued and rewarded than others and may be associated with dress items. For example in Chapter 11, "Dress and Socialization," you learned that Western European royalty may have special dress items associated with their rank, such as a crown or crown jewels. *Social stratification* is the term used to describe a ranking of people from high to low status based on the social positions they occupy and to the continuation of this ranking over time (Zusman, Knox, & Gardner, 2009).

There are several criteria used for ranking individuals above or below each other including socioeconomic status, possessions, social knowledge, and ethnicity among others. **Socioeconomic status**, also known as **social class**, refers to ranking of people on the basis of income, education, and occupation. Because the education a person obtains strongly impacts one's occupation and subsequently income, these three factors are combined. The amount of money an individual is paid for performing a service (i.e., income) is a reflection of the value placed on that service by others as well as the value placed on the person who provides the service (Zusman, Knox, & Gardner, 2009). Thus, when we think of the high status of designer clothing, the cost of original designer apparel reflects the value we place on someone who contributes original and creative apparel to the marketplace. Income is also related to the types of possessions that one can afford. People want to possess certain items because they are indicators of high status within a society. Owning the right clothing and eating the right food are both related to social class.

The prestige of an occupation also contributes to social class. Prestige is the reputation that a person gets from holding an occupation that consequently translates into ability to influence others (Zusman, Knox, & Gardner, 2009). Wearing dress items that signify occupation or income—in other words, your social class—will impact how others behave towards you. Researchers have documented that people will defer to others than they infer are of a higher social class than their own (Fortenberry, MacLean, Morris, & O'Connell, 1978).

Because there are social classes, there is the possibility of social movement between classes. The term used to describe this is **social mobility**. A person born into a family at a particular social class may desire to move to a higher social class. Individual movement between social classes may or may not be permitted within a society. **Closed stratification systems** are systems where there is no or very little movement permitted between social classes. An example of a closed stratification system is a **caste system** found in historic and modern-day India. Membership in one's caste is signified by a caste mark, a mark often located on the forehead. Membership in a caste system occurs at birth and is determined by the position of the parents. Movement out of one's caste is forbidden. You may refer to Chapter 4, "Dress and Social Cognition" for more information on the caste system of India.

A caste-like system existed in the US when enslaved Africans were denied many of their rights including the right to vote. Important to keeping social distance between those of European descent and those of African descent was their dress. Even though the style of clothing might have been similar, clothing of enslaved Africans was frequently made from low-quality coarse materials, was drab, limited in number, and ill-fitting in contrast to the clothing of the upper caste slave owners that was made from silk and fine linens, closely fitted to the body, and clean. At least one state (e.g., South Carolina) went so far as to prescribe the materials that slave clothing could be made from. This is not to say that regulations concerning slave dress were enforceable, only that they existed, as slaves were often able to incorporate items of the upper caste into their dress (White & White, 1995).

Open stratification systems or class systems are systems that allow movement up and down social classes. Assignment to a position within a class system is achieved (i.e., achieved status) and is often based on the socioeconomic position of the family. Dress has been assumed to be an indicator of one's social class position primarily as it reflects ability to pay. Individuals wearing designer label clothing and diamond jewelry are assumed to have the income to be able to afford such items of dress, and therefore, are often assumed to be in a high social class. However, with the development and easy availability of credit in Westernized cultures, many individuals are able to obtain expensive items that otherwise would not be available to them without credit, thereby making differentiation of social classes based on dress items difficult.

ORGANIZATIONS

An **organization** is a large group of individuals that are trying to achieve specific goals. The organization has a range of social positions and accompanying statuses as well as rules (Kammeyer, Ritzer, & Yetman, 1997). Examples of organizations include a university, a police force, a hospital, or a business. Some organizations are public and some are private. Some organizations are local, others are national or international. Some are focused on social causes, others are focused on making money. Thus, many different types of organizations exist. For example, many US and Western European apparel retailers have expanded to international locations.

A **total institution** is an organization that is removed from the rest of society and forms a complete environment designed to meet all of the needs of its members. In a total institution all aspects of life are carried out under a single authority and in the presence of a large number of others. Examples of total institutions include prisons and mental institutions. Within a total institution there is a great deal of control exerted over the people that live within them so much so that upon entering a total institution people often have to be resocialized to the rules and roles that exist within them (Kammeyer, Ritzer, & Yetman, 1997). Dress is just one aspect of life that is controlled in total institutions.

In fact, one of the features of total institutions that make them unique is that upon entry individuals often lose their ability to control their appearance. Goffman (1962) in writing about total institutions noted that ordinarily individuals had access to their **identity kits** (i.e., clothing, cosmetics, and other grooming aids) that enabled them to manage their self presentation to others. Upon entering a total institution such as a prison, people often suffer a type of personal defacement, they are stripped of their identity as they are stripped of the ability to present their usual appearance as well as the items and equipment (i.e., their identity kits) needed to maintain that appearance. In other words, their social position as inmate or ward upon entry becomes a master status and this status is made clear by a requirement that they wear the uniform or the dress items required of an inmate. Within the US, this uniform appears to be a pair of unisex drawstring pants and v-neck, short-sleeved top in a solid color.

Not all prisoners are required to wear a uniform and thus, may continue to use their clothing as an indicator of social positions and accompanying statuses that were held outside the prison. In Europe for example, there are a number of ways prisoners obtain clothing. In some countries prisoners are allowed to wear their own clothing. This practice is dependent on the prisoner's financial situation outside prison and creates a hierarchy of inmates based on wealth. In Germany, prisoners not able to supply their own clothing, are provided with items that are specifically labeled as "not a uniform." The clothing is made in the prison and supplemented by items purchased outside of the institution. However, if they wear prison clothing, when the items are laundered prisoners frequently do not receive the same items back that they handed in for cleaning. This fact certainly makes it difficult to personalize clothing items. Similar procedures are followed in France (Ash, 2010).

Prison clothing in the US varies between institutions and states. The US has the highest number of incarcerated individuals in the world per population along with problems of overcrowding. Prison uniforms managed by the individual state are frequently ill-fitting, so prisoners need to develop inside knowledge on how to obtain clothing that is comfortable as well as sanitary. Clothing items are customized by the prisoners as a means to express individual identities, and regulations concerning uniforms are often tied to attempts to prevent gang identification. In two states, California and Texas, the punishment of male inmates is facilitated through the uniform requirement. In these states the inmates are issued pink clothing thus punished by their imprisonment as well as having to wear a uniform in a feminine color (Ash, 2010) (Figure 12.5).

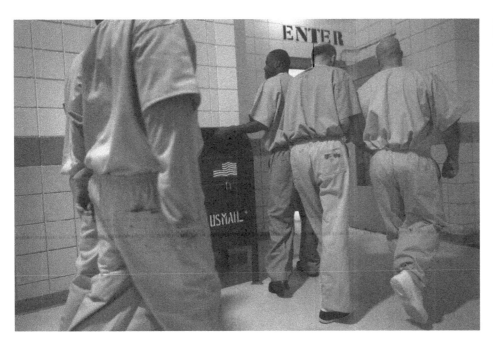

Figure 12.5
Total institutions often restrict the inmates' ability to manage their dress and appearance.

While male inmates may participate in gangs during incarceration, female inmates may join families. At California Valley State prison for women, the clothing is labeled "state blues" and consists of T-shirts, jeans, and flip-flop sandals. Different families are distinguished through the use of small items of dress (Ash, 2010).

In federal prisons within the US, regulations require that inmates leave their civilian clothing at the door. Inmates can either purchase appropriate clothing from approved retailers via websites or wear prison issued clothing that is made by inmates. Inmates also produce clothing for sale outside of the institution (Ash, 2010). For example, in 1989 the state of Oregon developed a facility for the production of jeans by inmates of the Eastern Oregon Correctional Institute. The Prison Blue® jeans along with select other items of apparel and accessories are made available to the public through approved regional retailers as well as designated websites (oce.oregon.gov).

There is also the orange jumpsuit that is frequently worn in maximum security prisons or when a prisoner, either male or female, is on death row. The design of the jumpsuit prohibits women from going to the bathroom and thus, is another layer of punishment for women (Ash, 2010).

Regardless of the provision of prison issue clothing, many prisoners within the US find themselves without appropriate clothing during their incarceration, a situation similar to prisoners in other parts of the world. It appears that prison clothing is both about control as well as an on-going means to humiliate the wearer.

Chapter Summary

Societies are made up of a variety of different types of social groups. Membership in social groups can exert an influence on decision making concerning dress. Groups are made up of different social positions and each of these social positions reflect a specific status and corresponding role. Included in roles are expectations for dress, thus, dress is useful in the identification of different social positions.

Knowing what social groups individuals participate in is important because this information helps us make predictions about that individual's behavior including decision making concerning dress. Social groups can be categorized as primary groups or as secondary groups. An important primary group is the family and family members are often responsible for teaching members about dress. Older family members often serve as models that are imitated by younger family members. Individuals can also imitate symbolic models. Another way to categorize social groups is as in-group versus out-group. An in-group is a group wherein members feel that they share a common bond, share ideologies, come from a common background, or otherwise resemble other members of the group. Key to an in-group is a sense of togetherness with other members of the group. Family members can easily comprise an in-group of individuals as they share life experiences that are unique to them. Wearing the same or coordinated items of dress makes visible to others that in-group members are connected to each other in some

way even if it is not obvious to observers what the connection is. An out-group is a group to which people feel they do not belong. Out-group members may still impact dress and appearance because people may make conscious attempts to avoid looking like them.

Secondary groups are important because they help societies function effectively and allow people who do not know each other well to work effectively with each other. Schools are an example of a secondary group and can implement dress codes to promote safe and effective learning environments. These dress codes can be proscriptive or prohibitive. Other groups that can exert an influence on decision making concerning dress include reference groups and membership groups.

Social stratification is the term used to describe a ranking of people from high to low status based on the social positions they occupy and to the continuation of this ranking over time. Socioeconomic status, also known as social class, refers to ranking of people on the basis of income, education, and occupation. Dress is often used as an indicator of social class but due to the availability of credit, may not be an accurate cue.

A total institution is an organization that is removed from the rest of society and forms a complete environment designed to meet all of the needs of its members. The clothing of individuals within a total institution is often determined by those in control and prevents individual expression.

Key Terms

caste system
cause-related dress
closed stratification system
clothing deprivation
cosplay
identity kit
in-groups

mere expression
open stratification or class
   system
organization
out-groups
peer crowds
prescriptive dress code

primary groups
prohibitive dress code
reference groups
relative deprivation
secondary groups
significant other
social class

social groups
social mobility
social structure
socioeconomic status
substantive expression
total institution

Discussion Questions

1. Provide examples of the two group types that have had the most consistent impact on your decision making concerning dress. Explain why these groups were the most important.

2. Several advantages and disadvantages have been posited for the use of uniforms in schools. Based on your experience, what are the advantages and disadvantages to requiring students to wear uniforms in school? As a future parent, would you want your child to have to wear a uniform to school? Why, or why not? Should teachers also be required to wear a uniform? Why, or why not?

3. Participation in a total institution restricts freedom of expression relative to dress. Not having to provide prison-issued clothing would be a significant savings to the government. What problems, if any, do you envision with allowing prisoners to wear their own (civilian) clothing during their incarceration?

4. How might the popularity of cosplay be explained? What does participation in these activities enable for individuals in addition to dressing in costume?

STUDiO™

Visit your book's STUDIO for additional quiz questions and vocabulary flashcards!

Suggested Readings

Ash, J. (2010). *Dress behind bars*. London, UK: I. B. Tauris.

Bennett, A., & Hodkinson, P. (2012) *Ageing and youth cultures*. New York, NY: Bloomsbury.

Craik, J. (2015). *Uniforms exposed*. New York, NY: Bloomsbury.

Lynch, A. (2012). *Porn chic*. London, UK: Berg.

References

Ash, J. (2010). *Dress behind bars*. London, UK: I. B. Tauris.

Bhaddock (2011, March 9). The Hippie counter culture movement. Retrieved from http://www.mortaljourney.com/2011/03/1960-trends/hippie-counter-culture-movement

Berlatsky, N. (2014). The comic-book guys quivering in fear of cosplay. *The Atlantic*. Retrieved from http://www.theatlantic.com/entertainment/archive/2014/12/why-comic-book-guys-are-quivering-at-cosplay-gender-insecurity/383617/

Cooley, C. H. (1909). *Social organization: A study of the larger mind*. New York, NY: Charles Scribner's Sons

DeCosta, K. (2006). Dress code blues: An exploration of urban students' reactions to a public high school uniform policy. *Journal of Negro Education, 75*(1), 49–59.

The Disney look (n.d.). Retrieved from http://cp.disneycareers.com/en/about-disney-college-program/disney-look/

Doyle, G. (n.d.). Disneyland VIP tour service reviewed . . . It is so fantastic! Disney Dose. Retrieved from http://disneydose.com/disneyland-vip-tour/#axzz4AMpORQcj

Dubove, A. (2015, May 21). Gangs prohibit Honduran women from going blond. *Panam Post*. Retrieved from https://panampost.com/adam-dubove/2015/05/21/gangs-prohibit-honduran-women-from-going-blond/

Eicher, J. B., & Baizerman, S. (1991). Adolescent dress, part II: A qualitative study of suburban high school students. *Adolescence, 26*(103), 679–686.

Fortenberry, J., MacLean, J., Morris, P., & O'Connell, M. (1978). Mode of dress as a perceptual cue to deference. *Journal of Social Psychology, 104*(1), 139–140.

Francis, S. (1992). Effect of perceived clothing deprivation on high school students' social participation. *Clothing and Textiles Research Journal, 10*(2), 29–33.

Gang member who killed man for wearing the wrong color gets life in prison (2013, September 26). Retrieved from http://www.abc2news.com/news/crime-checker /baltimore-city-crime/gang-member-who-killed-man -for-wearing-the-wrong-color-gets-life-in-prison

Gentile, E., & Imberman, S. A. (2012). Dressed for success? The effect of school uniforms on student achievement and behavior. *Journal of Urban Economics, 71*(1), 1–17.

Goffman, E. (1962). *Asylums: Essays on the social situation of mental patients and other inmates.* Chicago, Il: Aldine Publishing Co.

Gregory, N. B. (1996). Effects of school uniforms on self-esteem, academic achievement, and attendance (Doctoral dissertation, South Carolina State University). *Dissertation Abstracts International, 58*(8), 3035.

Gursky, D. (1996, March). "Uniform" improvement? *The Education Digest, 61*(7), 46–48.

Hebdige, D. (1979). *Subculture: The meaning of style.* New York, NY: Routledge.

Hethorn, J., & Kaiser, S. (1999). Youth style: Articulating cultural anxiety. *Visual Sociology, 14*(1), 109–125.

Houta, J. (2015). What to wear during recruitment. *Society 19.* Retrieved from https://www.society19.com/wear -recruitment

Joseph, N. (1986). *Uniforms and nonuniforms.* New York, NY: Greenwood Press.

Kammeyer, K., Ritzer, G., & Yetman, N. (1997). *Sociology: Experiencing changing societies* (7th Ed.). Boston, MA: Allyn and Bacon.

Lamerichs, N. (2011). Stranger than fiction: Fan identity in cosplay. *Transformative Works and Cultures, 7.* doi:10.3983/twc.2011.0246.

Lennon, S. J., Schulz, T. L., & Johnson, K. K. P. (1999). Forging linkages between dress and the law in the U.S., Part 2: Dress codes. *Clothing and Textiles Research Journal, 17*(3), 157–167.

Lloyd, J., & Klemack, J. (2015). Four arrested in shooting of man "killed over some red shoes." Retrieved from http://www.nbclosangeles.com/news/local/Tavin-Price -Simms-Car-Wash-Wrong-Red-Shoes-Shooting- Death-309351851.html

Mackey, E., & Greca, A. (2007). Adolescents eating, exercise, and weight control behavior: Does peer crowd affiliation play a role? *Journal of Pediatric Psychology, 32*(1), 13–23.

McElvain, J. (2008). *Wearing a cause.* Unpublished dissertation. University of Minnesota.

Murray, R. K. (1997). The impact of school uniforms on school climate. *NASSP Bulletin, 81*(593), 106–112.

Myers, B. (2011, July 28). Disneyland tour guides. Retrieved from http://www.disneydispatch.com /content/columns/its-all-in-a-nametag/2011/28 -disneyland-tour-guides/

Nass, S. (2012). Red Hat Society goal: Change attitudes on aging women. Retrieved from www.post-gazette.com.

National Institute of Justice. (2011). Gangs and gang crime. Retrieved from nij.gov/topics/crime/gangs-organized /gangs/definitions.htm

O'Neal, G. (1997). Clothes to kill for: An analysis of primary and secondary claims-making in print media. *Sociological Inquiry, 67*(3), 336–349.

O'Neal, G. (1998). Adolescent dress and risk taking. *Family Science Review, 11*(3), 190–202.

Paliokas, K. L., Fatrell, M., & Rist, R. (1996). Trying uniforms on for size. *The American School Board Journal, 183*(5) 32–35.

Palmer, M., & Wolfe, C. (2015, June 23). 3 men, 1 woman arrested in fatal South L.A. shooting of teen over his red shoes. Retrieved from http://ktla.com/2015/06/23 /multiple-people-arrested-in-fatal-south-l-a-shooting -of-teen-who-wore-red-shoes/

Paxton, S., Schutz, H., Wertheim, E., & Muir, S. (1999). Friendship clique and peer influences on body image concerns, dietary restraint, extreme weight-loss behaviors, and binge eating in adolescent girls. *Journal of Abnormal Psychology, 108*(2), 255–266.

Raby, R. (2010). "Tank tops are ok but I do not want to see her thong." *Youth and Society, 41*(3), 333–356.

Ruibal, S. (2007, July 17). Armstrong wristbands yield $63M. *USA Today,* p. 8C.

Tamura, Y. (2007). School dress codes in post scarcity Japan. *Youth & Society, 38*(4), 463–489.

Tolson, J. & Urberg. K. (1993). Similarity between adolescent best friends. *Journal of Adolescent Research, 8,* 274–288.

Vopat, M. (2010). Mandatory school uniforms and freedom of expression. *Ethics and Education, 5*(3), 203–215.

Wade, K. K., & Stafford, M.E. (2003). Public school uniforms: Effect on perceptions of gang presence, school climate, and student self-perceptions. *Education and Urban Society, 35*(4), 399–420.

Waerdahl, R. (2005). 'May be I'll need a pair of Levi's before junior high?': Child to youth trajectories and anticipatory socialization. *Childhood, 12*(2), 201–219.

Wescoe, S. (2013). School uniforms drive sales. Retrieved from http://www.lvb.com/article/20130812/LVB01/308089998/school-uniforms-drive-sales-and-traffic

White, S., & White, G. (1995). Slave clothing and African-American culture in the eighteenth and nineteenth centuries. *Past & Present, 148,* 149–186.

Yalkin, C., & Rosenbaum-Elliott, R. (2014). Talking fashion in female friendship groups: Negotiating the necessary marketplace skills and knowledge. *Journal of Consumer Policy, 37*(2), 301–331.

Yurchisin, J., Kwon, Y.J., Marcketti, S. B. (2009). Consumers of charity bracelets: Cause-supporters or fashion followers. *Journal of Fashion Marketing and Management, 13,* 448–457.

Zusman, M., Knox, D., & Gardner, T. (2009). *The social context view of sociology.* Durham, NC: Carolina Academic Press.

PART 4 ANTHROPOLOGICAL PERSPECTIVES ON DRESS

CHAPTER 13 DRESS AND CULTURAL AESTHETICS

After reading and reflecting on the content of this chapter, students should be able to:

- Explain the connection between cultural complexity and cultural patterns related to aesthetics, including technology and norms.

- Compare and contrast differences in levels of cultural complexity: folk, agrarian, urban-industrial, and mass.

- Analyze differences in aesthetics related to technology.

- Distinguish differences in aesthetics related to normative patterns: folkways, customs, mores, and laws.

- Explain how moral patterns regulate and constrain behavior related to dress.

- Identify cross-cultural aesthetic patterns in dress.

INTRODUCTION

As discussed in Chapter 1, "Why Study Dress?" culture is the predominant phenomenon that explains why humans behave in the ways they do, including the behavior of dressing. Cultural mentifacts (e.g., attitudes, beliefs, values, ideology) and sociofacts (e.g., social organizations including religious, education, government, family structure) help to explain cultural artifacts (e.g., clothing, appearance products, houses, household goods, vehicles, tools, equipment). In this chapter, we explore levels of cultural development and **patterns of culture**, or aspects of culture that shape our behavior, with respect to aesthetics concerning dress. We focus on specific types of patterns (i.e., technical and normative) in this chapter, and then discuss other cultural patterns (health and hygiene, ritual, religion, media) in the following chapter. All of these patterns, as well as our level of cultural complexity, influence the aesthetic choices we make as individuals and groups of people within a culture.

What is culture? As we noted in Chapter 1, culture is comprised of the traditions and customs that are transmitted from person to person through learning (Kottak, 2003). These traditions and customs play a large role in shaping the beliefs and behaviors of the people that are exposed to them. We learn these traditions and customs by growing up within a society. These traditions are developed over time, shared between individuals, are constantly undergoing change, and include beliefs about how people should look, how they determine right behaviors concerning dress from wrong behaviors, and what materials should be used for dress. Because all people are born into a culture, all people are "cultured."

On the basis of learning, we create, remember, and deal with ideas. Culture is a set of controls—plans, rules, instructions—for governing behavior. It is our culture that shapes how we deal with our basic needs (e.g., food, clothing, shelter). People everywhere dress their bodies, but it is the culture that shapes what materials will or will not be used in dress. For example, in China the furs of dogs and cats are used for trims and other items of dress while in Western cultures many consider using these animals as well as others (e.g., rabbits, mink, beaver) for items of dress to be unacceptable. (The reader is referred to the PETA.org website).

The term used to describe how people internalize these control mechanisms is called **enculturation**. Enculturation is important because, as individuals take on the beliefs of the culture(s) in which they participate, they use these beliefs to guide their behavior and their perceptions. Culture is not a simple collection of beliefs about how to act. One's culture reflects integrated collections or patterns of ideas, beliefs and values (Kottak, 2003). Changes in one set of patterns often result in changes in others. For example, thirty years ago many middle schools located in the US required sewing classes for girls (boys at that same time were required to take trade courses in woodworking, printing, mechanics, and so forth). This sewing requirement reflected a cultural belief about knowledge that was expected of women for their expected future work roles as homemakers. As ideas evolved about the role of women in society, especially changes in economic roles and expectations about careers outside of homemaking, sewing classes moved from being a required part of girls' curricula to an optional part elected by both boys and girls, to sewing classes being cut from many public school offerings altogether.

Often a set of core values integrates a culture and distinguishes it from others. For example, members of Western cultures, like the US, often reflect an individualistic value orientation. Holding an **individualistic orientation** means that Westerners tend to be self-centered, attribute their success to their individual efforts, promote themselves, and think in terms of "I." In contrast, members of Eastern cultures often reflect a collectivistic value orientation. Holding a **collectivistic orientation** means that Easterners tend to emphasize the importance of groups and think in terms of "we." Maintaining harmony and loyalty among individuals is important and confrontation is avoided. Collectivists recognize that the success of an individual is dependent on the success of the group. Even though members of a culture may know the behaviors expected of them, this is not to say that individuals always do what is expected of them or follow the rules. People use their culture actively; that is, they interpret the rules as individuals, challenge the rules, contest and reformulate

the rules or expectations for the dress of members of their culture. Many dress rules are violated, some regularly. For example, consider aesthetic "rules" learned in school or from family members about what color combinations are most attractive , how much skin should be exposed to be considered modest, or what types of dress can be worn for what ages or social situations. These so-called aesthetic rules are violated and reformulated regularly. The same is true for rules of dress that concern morality, hygiene, and ritual . For example, wearing a thong swimsuit thirty years ago on a public beach in the US might have resulted in getting arrested for indecent exposure. Today however, wearing the same swimsuit might only result in criticism based on one's body shape or size. Thus, some dress researchers find it useful to distinguish between the **ideal culture** beliefs of members of a culture concerning their dress (i.e., what they say people should do concerning their dress) versus **real culture** (i.e., actual observed behaviors concerning dress).

LEVELS OF CULTURE AND THE SPREAD OF CULTURE

As noted in Chapter 1, there are different levels of culture. The concept of subcultures, or small cultures within a larger complex culture, has already been presented. It is important for students to recognize that culture also exists on a large scale. The term **national culture** can be used to describe the beliefs and ways of behaving shared by citizens of the same nation. One example of a national cultural event within the US is celebrating the country's independence from Great Britain (i.e., 4th of July celebrations). Many cities across the nation celebrate independence with parades and individuals across the nation wear clothing often featuring the US flag, components of the flag (e.g., stars, stripes), or the colors of the flag (i.e., red, white, blue). This part of the US national culture is obvious, especially when US citizens are located outside of the US on July 4th and members of other nations are not engaged in such celebrations. Cultural beliefs can also be shared across cultures. The term *international culture* or **global culture** can be used to describe beliefs that are shared across national boundaries. Because of a common history or due to multinational organizations like the United Nations or the World Health organization, cultural beliefs can acquire a global scope. For example, female genital mutilation (also referred to as female circumcision) has been practiced for hundreds of years in parts of Africa as well as in cultures located in the Middle East, Southeast Asia, and South America (World Health Organization, 2012) and locations where immigrants from these regions reside. Often performed without anesthetic in unsanitary conditions by lay persons, the procedure involves the removal of a girl's external genitalia.

Cultural beliefs about beauty may also be shared across national boundaries. For example, contestants in the 2015 Miss Universe pageant represented eighty different countries, including those in the Americas, Europe, Asia, Africa, and island nations. One would thus expect to see great diversity in contestants from such diverse nations. However, little diversity was shown in body shapes and sizes, facial features, and hair styling. In fact, careful scrutiny of contestants in the annual pageant shows a majority of very thin and busty body types with long legs and European facial features. If one examines photos of pageant winners since the contest's beginning in 1952, there is also much similarity in appearance. While the choice of contestants to represent each country may not match what we consider to be the typical "look" or "body type" of the population of that country, perhaps it attests to a more ingrained idea of global beliefs about beauty—that beauty is primarily construed as being tall, thin, with large breasts, long legs, long and fairly straight hair, and European facial features (www.missuniverse.com).

Three additional terms are used to describe cultural behaviors and they indicate the extent to which a behavior is practiced across cultures. A **cultural universal** describes a practice that occurs in every culture. An example of a cultural universal is that all people engage in some form of dressing the body. A **cultural generality** is a practice that occurs in many but not all cultures. An example of a cultural generality is gender differentiation. In many cultures, some forms of dress are reserved exclusively for women and other forms are reserved for men. Finally, some behaviors are **particularities**; that is, they are practiced solely by particular cultural groups.

CULTURAL COMPLEXITY

Cultural complexity refers to the level of cultural development found in a culture, or how simple or complex the culture is in terms of its social organization, technology, labor and economic structure, and interaction among its members. Recognizing the level of cultural complexity is important because it impacts the tools that are available for converting physical materials into items of dress, the system of producing dress, and the level of interaction between members of differing cultures that impacts the adoption and rejection of items of dress. **Cultural scale theory** (scale of culture) allows us to distinguish among cultures that are domestic (tribes), cultures that are political states (ancient Egypt, Rome, much of feudal Europe), and cultures that are based on commercial economic trade (Bodley, 1994).

According to this conceptualization, domestic scale cultures are organized in small, ancestral groups often based on **kinship** (i.e., people related to each other based on descent or by marriage). They are homogenous in nature, since there is little interaction and co-mingling with outside group members. Power is widely shared by members in the group, with no class distinctions. Goods are distributed fairly evenly among members and all people share in decision making. In many cases, domestic scale cultures are nomadic and follow their animal food source from place to place. Examples of historic small-scale cultures are indigenous groups in the Americas (North and South American Indian groups), Europe (Saami or Lapps who live within the Arctic Circle and herd reindeer), and Asia (nomadic, horse-riding cultures). The role of dress in these historic cultures was protection as well as communication (group membership, role, and aesthetic preferences.)

Political state cultures are based on social classes, where those in a ruling class or land-owning class have greater power than those who work the land. These cultures are agrarian or farming cultures, and are thus larger and more heterogeneous than domestic cultures. Politics is what drives the production and distribution of goods, and therefore wealth. The ruling class uses the threat of force to direct the working class and to gain social power; opinions of the working class are basically not considered. Many political scale cultures do not last due to the imbalance of political power. Examples of such cultures are those of ancient Egypt and Rome, the Inca Empire of South America, and feudal economies of Asia and Europe.

Commercial scale cultures are based on wide-spread or global commerce, and those people who hold the greatest power are those who have the greatest shares of stock, or ownership in businesses or corporations. These cultures began to emerge during the Industrial Revolution in Europe and in the Far East as sources of power such as water and electricity began to be plentiful and were used to operate larger machinery to produce goods more rapidly and on a larger scale.

Anthropologists began to study the evolution of cultures based on their complexity in the mid-twentieth century. Based on the premise that cultures exist in varying levels of complexity, Redfield (1953, 1956) believed that cultures evolved from folk cultures to urban cultures. **Folk cultures** were considered to be small groups of hunter-gatherers who were basically not agrarian and followed their food source (somewhat nomadic). Folk cultures were small in size, isolated from other cultures, comprised of similar people, and typically not literate; social and cultural life was based on kinship patterns and sacred beliefs. The next level of culture, **agrarian cultures**, referred to a group of people who settled in one geographic area, raised their own food, and had a more complex economy, social organization, and political system. Finally, as cultures evolved in complexity and with the growth of the industrial revolution, they grew into **urban-industrial cultures** in towns or urban centers, based on the manufacture of goods; complex social, political, and economic systems evolved to distribute and trade these goods, and to govern people.

This continuum of cultural complexity was extended in the twenty-first century to include **mass cultures**, defined as commercial culture on a widespread level; that is to say, mainstream culture that is mass produced by mass media or mass manufacturing for mass consumption by the masses (Storey, 2006).

DRESS AS A CULTURAL SUB-SYSTEM

So, how do all components of culture work together to influence the dress of a cultural group? A pioneering article describes how technological, social, and ideological components of culture influence how individuals and groups express themselves through their dress and appearance. Let us first describe this model before moving into a discussion of technical, normative, and aesthetics patterns of dress (Hamilton, 1987).

There are three components of culture that meet various human needs: (1) technology helps to meet biological and material needs, (2) social systems meet social needs, and (3) ideology meets psychological needs. If we relate these to dress and appearance, technology includes knowledge to produce basic fabrics and garments, knowledge of agriculture to raise sheep for wool or grow cotton,

knowledge of distribution and marketing strategies to provide garments and other appearance products to consumers, knowledge of computer imaging capabilities to alter faces or bodies for advertising, and knowledge of techniques used in cosmetic surgery and other cosmetic procedures. Social systems related to dress include education (e.g., of professionals in design and business), religion (e.g., appropriate attire for religious ceremonies or officials), government (e.g., laws governing fair labor and working conditions), and economic markets (e.g., global trade agreements). Ideology related to dress might include ideas about dress that is immodest, the need to conform, what is fashionable , gender appropriateness of different body modifications, the importance of brands, and attitudes toward materialism.

We will discuss how cultural patterns influence the aesthetics of dress by examining each of these three basic components of culture: technology, social systems and norms, and aesthetic ideology.

TECHNICAL PATTERNS

Technical patterns concern the influence of technology on production of consumable goods within a culture. Technology influences the types of artifacts produced within a culture as well as the method of production. For example, if a culture has large animals in its environment and simple tools, then garments will be made of animal skins such as deer, whale, walrus, large fish, and seal. Producing these garments will include using a harpoon or gun to kill the animal and a large skinning tool to remove the skin from the animal, soaking the skin in urine to remove fat and remaining tissue, chewing the skin to make it soft and pliable, cutting the animal skin carefully (around four legs and a head) to piece together a garment to fit the human body, stitching it with tendon from the animal, and embellishing it with other animal parts such as hair, fur, bird beaks, or feathers. The forms of garments produced are influenced by both the raw materials used and the skill in producing them. Many garments such as parkas, coats, gloves, and boots from traditional Inuit or Eskimo cultures in the Arctic North were produced with these tools and methods (Fitzhugh & Crowell, 1988) (Figure 13.1).

By contrast, if a culture has an abundance of plants in its environment, as in the case of many island cultures, then garments will be made of leaves, grasses, bark, ferns,

Figure 13.1

Pieced and embellished skin garment, traditional tribal garment worn by Athabascan woman, Chena, Alaska, USA, 2009.

Figure 13.2

Tapa cloth from Fiji.

and flowers. Producing these garments will involve gathering the materials, cleaning and sorting them according to size, and assembling them to fit the style of the garment and the size of the wearer. For example, tapa cloth of Hawaii and other Polynesian islands, and bark cloth of the Ainu people in Northern Japan, is made of the soft, inner bark of the mulberry tree or other soft trees (Figure 13.2). Strips of bark are torn from the tree, softened by soaking in salty ocean water, scraped and pounded repeatedly to make it flat and felted, bleached, and dyed or stamped with color from clay or other plants (Kennett, 1995). The cloth is shaped into a garment that is wrapped around the body or that hangs loose from the shoulders over the body.

If we examine both body modifications and body supplements that are used in dress around the world, we find a wide variety of materials and processes that are used.

Tools, Processes, Skill, Inventions

Level of cultural complexity can influence the type of tools used in producing dress, as well as the processes employed, skills of the producers, and inventions that impact the production of dress. For example, dyeing fibers after they are spun into yarns and woven into a length of fabric requires less time and skill than dyeing individual yarns in a repeat pattern that eventually is woven into a fabric. Similarly, wrapping parts of fabric before dyeing it to create a tie-dyed pattern is easier than dyeing yarns and weaving them into a design.

Tools can also differ based on the level of skill in a culture. Participants in folk cultures may use simple tools made of stone, bone, or cactus needles, for example, to clean skins or plant fibers and sew them together. Complex tools would be needed to shape metal into jewelry, buttons, and other ornaments (Figure 13.7). Other complex tools would be required to carve wood into shoes, shields, or walking sticks, and to decorate them with ornate patterns (Figure 13.8).

The technology to create woven fabrics can vary from hand weaving on a simple hand loom (e.g., think of a simple square loom to make potholders), on a backstrap loom, or vertical loom, to electrically powered floor looms and computer-run industrial looms. Even if the technology is present within a culture, the quality of the end product can vary widely; for example, the time and skill required to hand-weave a fabric that is even on the edges and precise is much greater than the time and skill

TABLE 13.1

MATERIALS USED IN DRESS

Material	Example of Dress	Example Cultures
Animal gut	Gutskin kamlaykas (waterproof)	Inuit, Eskimo
Animal hide	Parkas, coats, shoes	Arctic, Europe, US, Asia, Africa
Animal parts (hair, fur, beaks, tails)	Fur trim, hair fringe, decoration	Arctic, Europe, American Indian nations
Beads	Collar, headdress, embellishment	American Indian, Africa
Beetles	Headdress, dress embellishment	Southeast Asia
Bone	Lip/nose inserts, jewelry, buttons	Africa, N & S America, Asia
Feathers	Capes, headdress, embellishment	American Indian, Hawaii
Fish skins	Protective parka or jumpsuit	Inuit, Eskimo
Flowers	Leis	Pacific cultures
Horn	Headpieces, attachments to garments	Africa, American Indian nations
Metal (bells, balls, thread, jewelry)	Embellishment	Most all cultures
Plant fibers (grass, bark, reeds, roots)	Whole garments or embellishments	East Asian & island cultures, American Indian nations
Quills	Bags, jewelry, leather ornamentation	Sioux nation (N America)
Shells	Embellishment	American Indian nations, Pacific islands
Stones (amber, turquoise, etc.)	Embellishment, jewelry	Southwest U.S., Africa
Teeth	Embellishment (ex., elk tooth dress)	Plains American Indians
Wood	Carved hats, purses, buttons	Tlingit (Canada)
Woven, knitted, or crocheted fabric (cotton, wool, silk, linen, synthetics)	Dresses, pants, capes, shawls, skirts, aprons, etc.	N. America, S. America, Asia, Europe, Africa, islands

Figure 13.3
West African tie-dye.

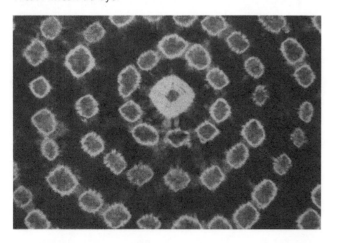

Figure 13.4
Malaysian ikat.

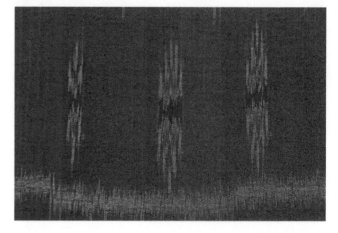

TABLE 13.2

DYES, PAINTS, AND METHODS OF CREATING PATTERNS USED IN CULTURAL DRESS WORLD-WIDE

Type	Description
Natural dyes	Indigo, lichen, madder-root, berries, cochineal (from crushed beetles) (Figure 13.6)
Chemical dyes	Synthetic dyes that yield bright, colorfast colors (Figure 13.5)
Tie dye	A method of resist dyeing where a thread or other substance is tied around fabric in a pattern, so the dye cannot color the area (e.g., a tie-dye tee shirt) (Figure 13.3)
Batik (or wax resist)	A method of resist dyeing where hot wax is stamped onto fabric or drawn by hand, so that dye cannot color the area
Ikat	Dyeing sections of yarn prior to weaving, creating a pattern when woven (Figure 13.4)
Surface embellishments	Appliqué, patchwork, embroidery, ribbon work (Figure 13.6)

Figure 13.5
US patchwork.

Figure 13.6
Peruvian crocheted mask.

Figure 13.7
Silver and turquoise bracelet requires complex tools.

Figure 13.8
Dutch carved wooden shoes require complex tools.

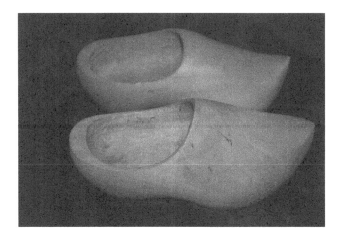

required to run an electrically powered or computer-run loom, in which the precision is built into the loom. Even though the technology itself may exist or be available to different cultures (e.g., power looms), some communities do not have the infra-structure (e.g., electricity, Internet) to use the technology available. Thus, in some cultures, hand-woven fabrics and hand produced items of dress are much more common than machine made items.

The technology needed to create patterns in fabric via weaving is quite different from the technology needed to create printed patterns. Weaving of different colored yarns was employed to create the plaid repeat pattern in a Scottish tartan in Chapter 1 (Figure 1.3), while the printed pattern in Figure 13.9 was created with a carved block dipped in dye (West African block print fabric).

It may take years of study with a family relative or a master artisan to gain the skill needed to produce quality items of dress that are used and treasured in the culture. For example, consider the skills required of the artisan who produces elaborate beaded collars of the Maasai people as seen in Figure 13.10, or embellished mirror work in the saris and accessories of the Gujurati region of India (Figure 13.11).

In mass or large-scale cultures, **virtual technology** can facilitate the sale of garments by allowing people to see how a garment will appear on the body without physically trying on the garment (Figure 13.12). "My virtual model™" introduced by the Land's End company in 2004 (Land's End first with new "My Virtual Model™" technology, 2004), or the "magic mirror" used by Macy's retailers in late 2010 (MacManus, 2010)), are computer programs that help an online shopper to virtually try on garments to see how they might look on his or her body. The Magic Mirror takes a photograph of your body, which is displayed on a screen in the store, and then you select the garments you want to virtually try on from a wide variety of apparel styles. You drag the items to the screen and place them on your image and then drag to expand the size to fit the photographed image. You can put several virtual garments on to create an outfit and determine how you might look. You can also send the image to your friends via Facebook text or email so that they can give you feedback.

In addition to "virtually trying on" apparel, there are 3-dimensional software programs that allow you to see how you might look with a certain cosmetic procedure, such as rhinoplasty (nose reshaping), liposuction (removal of body fat), or breast implants. Other 3-D modeling programs allow you to visualize how you might look after

Figure 13.10
Beaded collars of Maasai women, Kenya.

Figure 13.9
West African block print.

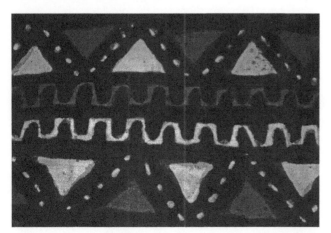

Figure 13.11
Mirror work purse, Gujurat, India.

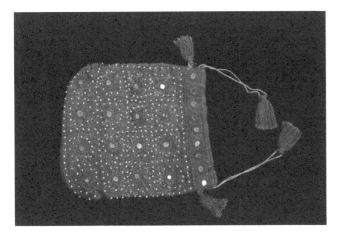

weight loss, or after using certain products to bulk up your muscles, or how you might appear with a new hairstyle. An Internet search will uncover many software applications, one of which is Photoshop, an imaging software program that allows anyone to change body size, shape, coloring, and texture of a scanned image. In fact, it is well known that most advertising images have been computer-enhanced, sometimes to the point of fantasy.

Technological developments have also made possible **fast fashion**. A fast fashion retailer quickly provides their customers with low-cost trendy items. Production lead times are short in duration because they use local sources rather than off-shore manufacturing facilities. This strategy enables the retailer to offer fashion items to their customers at the peak of demand. Customers learn that, if they want the item, they need to purchase it immediately rather than waiting for a price reduction or other type of promotion. Because customers purchase items at full price, clearance items are reduced and retailers' profits are increased (Cachon & Swenney, 2011). A fast fashion strategy provides consumers with new dress items on nearly a daily basis. However, fast fashion has also been described as throw-a-way fashion since investment in the items is low; many consumers purchase items that they intend to wear only once or for only a single season and then throw them away.

Smart Clothing

One of the emerging areas for the application of technology to apparel is the integration of electronics and clothing to create **smart clothing** or wearable technology (Dunne, 2011). Wearable technology systems consist of a combination of technologies including sensors, actuators, processors, and interfaces. Sensors can face towards the body or away from the body. When they face towards the body they can detect heart rate, temperature, and body

Figure 13.12
Model demonstrates virtual fitting room in Japanese apparel chain, *Urban Research*, June 2014.

position, among other signals. Outward facing sensors can detect factors in the environment such as sounds, temperature, and location. Using this information, a garment can record things about the wearer including his or her location, the weather, and how he or she may be feeling. Actuators can alter temperature, provide illumination, and produce sounds. Garments can be produced that light up or respond in other ways to the wearer (Figure 13.13). Processors are the link between sensors and actuators (i.e., understands the information gathered by the sensors and triggers the activators at the appropriate time).

Systems that only use sensors, activators, and processors run automatically. Sometimes the user wants to control the devices. In these circumstances, there are interfaces that allow the wearer to provide input and control the devices present in the clothing (Dunne, 2011). Combined, these systems allow the development of a range of smart clothing used in a range of areas (Berzowska, 2005) including medical monitoring (e.g., gives the wearer information about how well the body is doing, Figure 13.14), sports (e.g., record movements to improve technique), functional clothing (e.g., regulate body temperature), and fashion (e.g., clothing that responds to the wearer's emotions). Smart clothing requires an interdisciplinary approach to design as it requires both knowledge of apparel and knowledge of electrical engineering and computer science, and it offers innovation in dress in ways not previously envisioned.

We have noted that technology impacts the materials of dress, the design and functioning of dress, the manufacturing of dress, and how dress is marketed to consumers. Next, we turn to a discussion of gender roles in the production of dress.

Figure 13.13
These decorative flowers react to being touched. Touch their stamens and the flower startles, "touching" you back using a tiny vibrating motor.

Figure 13.14
A fiber-optic sensor placed down the center back of this shirt monitors spinal posture, reminding you to sit up when you've slouched for too long.

Gender Roles in Producing Dress

Worldwide, cloth is produced more commonly by women than men (Schneider & Weiner, 1989). Typically, in American culture, it is women who produce goods that are hand-knitted, crocheted, sewn, or feature another form of needle-work such as embroidery, cross-stitch, or appliqué. Often their work is taken for granted. However, when a man produces such goods, he is publicly acknowledged for his work (e.g., Roosevelt Greer, football player, noted for his needlepoint, crocheting, and knitting in the 1970s and 1980s).

Similarly, in other cultures, production tasks are differentiated between men and women. For example, in the many tribes that comprise the Kuba Kingdom in sub-Saharan Africa, weaving of raffia palm fiber into skirts is exclusively the responsibility of men (Darish, 1989). After the palms are harvested and the cloth is woven, then only men assemble and embellish wrapped skirts for men, and only women do the same for women. The embellishments that both sexes produce include embroidery, appliqué, patchwork, dyeing, dyeing of stitches, and tie-dyeing. Yet, only women practice specific embroidery techniques such as open-work and cut-pile (Darish, 1989).

By contrast, in Sumba (an eastern island in the Indonesian archipelago), young, unmarried women of the Kodi culture are responsible for producing the indigo dye used to color yarns woven into ikat fabric by chewing the indigo plants and other plants used in the dye (Hoskins, 1989). The actual dyeing is done by mature women who have borne children and have passed menopause, and the entire process is kept secret from men. Women weave the cloth on back-strap looms and decide on the geometric patterns that the colored yarns produce in the finished cloth.

In large-scale, industrialized cultures where textile production is a major part of the economy, gender roles in production may or may not be prevalent. In fabric manufacturing plants worldwide, men may commonly run the power looms to weave fabrics, or power saws and laser cutters used to cut fabric into garment pieces, whereas women may commonly operate the industrial sewing machines to stitch the pieces into finished garments. Men and women alike may finish, press, and package garments for shipping to markets, and work in distribution centers that ship the finished goods to individual stores. Creative and technical designers of garments, as well as merchandise buyers and planners for major design houses and corporations, are typically both men and women.

IN-CLASS ACTIVITY
Create and Describe a Culture

Your task is to create and describe a culture. The people live on an island with a climate like southern Alaska. It is close to glaciers, has lots of snow, and is cold throughout the autumn, winter, and spring. There is a short growing season in the summer. The island is forested and elk, deer, and bear, as well as many furred smaller animals live in the forest. Berries and many other edible plants grow on the island. The ocean is only two days walk from any point on land and is filled with fish, seals, and walruses.

Describe or make up a culture which is likely to develop on the island. Be sure to address universals of culture (e.g., technology/artifacts, ideologies [attitudes, values, beliefs], and social institutions).

SOCIAL SYSTEMS AND NORMATIVE PATTERNS

You learned in Chapter 12, "Dress and Social Organization" that norms are social habits that guide the functioning of a group of people. They are expectations of how people are supposed to act, think, or feel in specific situations. They guide the social interactions that people have, assist in regulating behavior or bringing order to behavior in a group of people, and serve as a sort of language by which we communicate with one another (Bicchieri, 2006). These **normative patterns** guide the functioning of a group of people by specifying behavioral expectations and defining correct and incorrect ways of responding to situations. Thus, cultural norms can guide many of our behaviors. Consider these cultural norms for behavior presented in Table 13.3, and see if you agree or disagree:

The most important cultural norms are those shared by a large segment of a culture. In fact, without cultural norms, chaos might result. Maintaining order requires the cooperation of members of a culture, so norms of loyalty, honesty, reciprocity, and promise-keeping are important for maintaining social order (Bicchieri & Muldoon, 2011). Norms vary with respect to duration, strength, and sanctions. Let's discuss each aspect.

TABLE 13.3

CULTURAL NORMS FOR BEHAVIOR

Content	Cultural norm (expected behavior)
How we talk to one another	One person speaks, then the other person
How we acknowledge a gift or kindness	Say thank you
How we eat	Use utensils for some foods and hands for others; chew with mouth shut
How we greet one another	Nod, smile, or say "hi," or "how are you," or "how you doing?"
How close we stand to one another	Close if a friend or partner, further away if a boss or unknown other person

Duration of norms refers to how stable or unchanging they are. There are some norms that are very stable over time, and others that change rapidly. Consider the difference between the norm of greeting one another and the norm of wearing mascara and eye liner among women in Western cultures. Greeting one another has been an accepted norm for a very long time in most cultures; thus, it is considered stable. In contrast, wearing mascara to darken the eyelashes has been practiced for a shorter period of time and is subject to change. At some times in history, the preferred color of mascara is black, at other times, brown, and yet at other times blue. The practice of wearing eye liner is also changing, with the thickness of the eye liner subject to change from season to season as well as the colors used, and the areas of the eye that are lined (Figure 13.15).

Strength of norms indicates whether the norm applies to a few people or to everyone in the group. Strength is also an indicator of whether the norm is enforced occasionally or always. Dress norms vary in strength; some norms apply to a few while others apply to everyone. Consider the use of cosmetics. If you never apply cosmetics, the norms for wearing them do not apply to you. If you are an avid cosmetics user, you would be expected to know and follow the norms for wearing cosmetics. For example, if you wear lipstick, it is expected that the lipstick be on your lips only and not your teeth or outside of your lips. Norms for dress can be enforced always or occasionally. Whether or not a norm is enforced is often tied to a specific situation. Consider the norm of covering a woman's breasts. When a woman appears in a public workplace, say a kindergarten classroom or a department store, it is expected by her employer and students or customers that she does not show breast cleavage. However, when a woman competes in a beauty pageant or goes to a club for dancing, this norm is usually not enforced. Complete baring of the breasts is typically allowed only on a public nude beach or attending a private nudist colony, but showing a lot of cleavage may be more acceptable in certain social situations, such as entertainment awards shows. Similarly, if someone is caught "streaking" across a public venue such as a football field during half-time performances of a band, or on a public street, for example, authorities would attempt to catch the individual and apply some form of reprimand. However, authorities working on nude beaches would permit the public display of nudity without repercussions.

Sanctions of norms refer to reactions by others that are designed to ensure compliance with a norm. Sanctions include both rewards (positive sanctions) or punishments (negative sanctions) intended to encourage or enforce conformity to norms and prohibit nonconformity.

Figure 13.15
The use of eye liner can change from season to season.

ANTI-AGING

Have you noticed the number of anti-aging products in television commercials and print ads, particularly in fashion magazines? These ads reflect a growing trend to market these cosmetic beauty products as pharmaceuticals that promise major changes in wrinkles, stretch marks, skin composition, and skin texture. Known as "cosmeceuticals," they often use claims that cannot be substantiated by research and ingredients that are made up or whose impact is exaggerated.

Anti-aging products may say "you will see results in eight weeks" and include footnotes from "clinical studies." (Who do you think owns the "clinic"?) There may be photo images of wrinkled skin before product use, and blurry wrinkles shown after product use, but no indication of the nature of the study, who participated, and how the "results" were found. Or there may be a doctor pictured next to the product, which lends credence to the claims of the product. Some creams may indeed contain ingredients that temporarily plump the skin and thus reduce the appearance of small lines, but this kind of statement is not very enticing.

At the core of such cosmeceutical advertising is the assumption that we can or should stop aging, as we could! We age from birth. The process of cellular aging is a natural part of life. Yes, major cosmetic companies (i.e., Lancôme, L'Oréal, Olay, Neutrogena, Elizabeth Arden, Mary Kay, Garnier) appeal to a huge market segment by encouraging all of us at any age to begin the fight against signs of aging by buying their products—the sooner, the better. This increases market sales tremendously if we buy into the promise that we can stave off the offensive signs of aging as early as possible.

There are also products that reduce age spots and freckles, implying that such "blemishes" are unattractive. These products carry high price tags! A "dark spot eraser" at $59 per fluid ounce may contain many long chemical compounds, none of which are proven to lighten spots, so it is basically a cosmetic concealer product!

Please analyze the appeals of cosmeceuticals that you have bought or considered buying. Why is it that we buy into these advertising claims, even though they may be unsubstantiated and lead us to spend huge sums on their purchase?

For some interesting reading on this industry trend, read:

Stewart, D. (April 20, 2009). *Sick & Twisted: "Anti-Aging" & "Cosmeceutical" Ads, Jezebel.com*. Retrieved from http://jezebel.com/5220066/sick—twisted-anti-aging—cosmeceutical-ads

Sanctions can be informal or formal. The nature of sanctions can vary from fairly weak and informal (e.g., negative comments, staring at someone's choice of dress) to severe and formal (e.g., imprisonment). Formal sanctions are applied by a specific group or agency (e.g., judicial system) to ensure that important cultural norms are followed. Informal sanctions are spontaneous and unorganized responses to nonconformity to a norm that may be applied by any member of the culture. Violating norms for dress that are extremely important to a culture *often* result in strong negative sanctions. For example, if you attend a school that requires a uniform, you may be suspended from the school for not wearing the uniform while in school. Wearing clothing in public is extremely important to US culture such that adults can be sentenced to jail time for failing to wear clothing when in public. When norms become so important that members of a culture codify them, we use the term *laws* to describe them. Nonconformity to laws will result in the application of formal sanctions.

Types of Norms

There are several different types of regulations or rules that vary in their duration, strength, and sanctions. We will explain each type briefly, and provide dress examples.

Folkways are weakly held expectations for behaviors concerning dress. They are not considered morally significant and not strictly enforced, but are predictable way of doing things. They are often long-standing and apply to large groups of people. Generally speaking, conformity to folkways is ensured by the use of gentle social pressure and learned through observation of others. Breaking or questioning a folkway does not result in severe sanctions but may cause the person to be laughed at, frowned upon, or scolded. In Western culture, folkways concerning dress include wearing undergarments, having clean fingernails, not having offensive body odor, and not having bad breath.

Folkways in Western culture are often tied to gender. For example, violation of a folkway may be a man wearing eye makeup. The sanctions applied to a young man who wears eye makeup include teasing, being laughed at, or being questioned. Wearing team colors or items with specific logos may be expected when attending sporting events on your campus or in your community and is another example of a folkway. If you do not wear these items, you may feel uncomfortable, feel that you stick out from everyone else, and you may receive criticism from your peers. This experience may motivate you to conform to the folkway and wear team colors at the next event or may cause you to avoid such events in the future.

Customs are social habits that are deeply rooted in tradition. They are handed down from generation to generation and are very slow to change. Customs may exist in language and communications, religion, health and grooming practices, and lifestyle behaviors that distinguish one social group from another. One anthropologist believed that the study of customs is very complex, noting that traditional customs around the world consist of a collection of specific behaviors more varied than that which would develop over time by any one person individually (Benedict, 2006). There are often more extreme sanctions for violating a custom than for violating a folkway. When individuals violate customs, it often makes others within the culture uncomfortable. Examples of customs in dress include brides wearing white for the color of their wedding dress (Figure 13.16). Wearing a white wedding gown in the US is so customary that it is quite difficult to find a wedding-style gown in another color such as red, blue, or black. The practice is tied to culture, however, as the customary color of traditional wedding dresses in China is red, the traditional color designating good luck. In northern parts of India, the traditional color of women's wedding garments is also red, a color symbolizing auspiciousness.

Although customs are slow to change, they do undergo change. A case in point is the academic garments worn by college professors. While at one time worn by learned professors at colleges and universities as part of their daily dress, **academic regalia** is commonly reserved for wear at graduation ceremonies. Academic dress generally consists

Figure 13.16
Custom of wearing a white wedding gown in the US.

of a gown with a hood and sometimes a cap (e.g., generally a mortarboard, tam, or a bonnet). The gown is typically black, although some schools allow use of the school's colors. The hood is made from velvet and the color of the velvet represents the discipline of your degree. Various universities have different shapes and patterns of hoods, in some cases corresponding to the styles or colors worn at the universities at the time they were founded, and in others representing a completely new design. The hood is often lined in a satin that is the color of the university where you obtained your degree. The sleeves of the gown signify the degree obtained by the wearer (e.g., bachelors, masters, doctorate). Please see example in Chapter 10, "Dress and Identity."

Male circumcision is a custom among many Western cultures, regardless of religious beliefs, and among Jewish cultures based on religious beliefs. Performed on a newborn male child in a hospital, or on an infant who is eight days old in a synagogue or a home in a special ceremony by a mohel (one who is trained in circumcision), many people are now questioning the traditional practice and refusing to have their male children undergo the process.

Mores are expected behaviors that are strongly held, considered essential, and strictly enforced. A subset of mores, called **taboos**, prevent a society's most outrageous behaviors (e.g., use of cat fur as mittens, flashing breasts). Such behaviors are usually formalized into laws that prohibit these behaviors.

Taboos have strong sanctions. Many sociologists believe that the informal social response of disgust and isolation of offenders on the part of family or citizens is more important than a formalized code. Mores related to dress include adults wearing clothing that reveals their genitals, wearing clothing with profanity, hate language, or disrespectful images, and children wearing styles that are too body-revealing for their age.

Laws are norms that have been enacted by a body of authority to regulate human conduct and as a result, guarantee social order. Laws can be **prohibitive** (prohibit certain behaviors) and designed to protect the interest of all members of a culture. Examples of prohibitive laws include rules concerning indecent exposure of the human body or what comprises pornography. Laws can be **regulative** (regulate certain behaviors.) This category includes legislation covering trade agreements and restrictions concerning textiles, apparel, and other materials used for making items of dress (e.g., furs, jewels). Laws can also be **promotive** (promote certain behaviors such as social policies.) Examples of laws that are promotive include social legislation regarding welfare programs that include money to be spent on clothing or regulations designed to keep people safe from potential risk (e.g., children's sleepwear

IN-CLASS ACTIVITY
Watch a Child Beauty Pageant

Watch a You Tube of four-year old Maddy Jackson competing on the show, *Toddlers and Tiaras*, dressed like a provocative Dolly Parton in her wig, size C cup fake breasts, and fake butt. Write a short one-page paper, answering the following points:

1. Is there a cultural more that has been violated?
2. Should there be sanctions, and if so, what should they be and for whom?
3. What impact does such behavior have on the child contestant and on society?

regulations, restaurant workers having to wash their hands before they return to work).

Sumptuary laws were specific laws governing who can wear what items of dress or otherwise regulating clothing and textiles. The laws dictated what color and type of clothing individuals were allowed to own and wear based on their social position within a culture. They were usually used for social discrimination. They also provided an easy way to identify rank and privilege.

The reign of Edward III of England in the 1330s provided the first national sumptuary legislation on record, which was continued by Edward IV in the 1400s. One act specified that nobility were allowed 24 in (61 cm) elongated pointed shoes (Figure 13.17); gentlemen could

Figure 13.17
English man's elongated shoes (1461–1483)

wear 12 in (31 cm) toe elongations and merchants 6.5 in (16 cm), while another stated that gold or purple silk could only be worn by women of royalty (Piponnier & Mane, 2000). Queen Elizabeth I enforced sumptuary laws called "Statutes of Apparel" which dictated what color and type of clothing individuals were allowed to own and wear, thus providing an easy and immediate way to identify rank and privilege. Bright and dark colors were generally expensive to produce and therefore, were limited to high status clothing. Only members of the Royalty were permitted to wear clothes trimmed with ermine and purple in color. Silks, velvets, and furs were the most expensive materials to produce and were also limited to high status clothing. Lesser nobles were allowed to wear clothing trimmed with fox and otter.

Other sumptuary laws in the US were enacted during World War II by the War Production Board in 1942 in an effort to conserve fabric in civilian clothing to avoid military shortages (Dear & Foot, 2001). The amount of fabric that manufacturers were allowed to use in women's dresses and other garments was restricted according to type of garment by the US Limitation Order L-85.

When regulations exist concerning clothing in contemporary times, they are often designed to protect the wearer's health. For example, regulations concerning children's clothing require that a child's pajamas and other sleepwear be flame retardant. Construction sites often have regulations concerning wearing hard hats for head protection and steel-toed footwear to protect the feet of workers. Historically, some cities have had regulations against cross dressing. **Cross dressing** is the practice of wearing clothing that is not associated with one's sex. From 1848 when Columbus, Ohio established an ordinance banning citizens from appearing in public in dress "not belonging to their sex," until 2011 when a man in New York City could be arrested for publicly wearing anything that impersonated a female, many cities had regulations against cross-dressing (News Desk, 2015). The primary reason for eliminating such regulations was that they served no purpose

Employers have wide discretion to establish conditions of employment—which include dress codes indicating expectations for their employees' clothing and grooming. Generally, a carefully drafted dress code will not discriminate and apply to all employees equally. However, this fact does not stop employees from questioning company dress code policies.

A school or a military institution may require specified uniforms; if it allows wearing regular clothes, it may place restrictions of when and where they may be worn. A school may also have a dress code even if it does not require the wearing of uniforms. Such a code is often prohibitive, specifying what cannot be worn to school. Examples will likely specify how long a skirt or pair of shorts must be on the leg, how much skin may be revealed (including how wide shoulder straps should be, or prohibiting tank tops), the wearing of head gear such as baseball caps, and the type of graphics or words that are prohibited on clothing worn by students. Dress codes such as these apply to all members of the organization, and violation usually results in sanctions of suspensions from school, or additional chores in the military. See Chapter 12, "Dress and Social Organizations," for examples.

AESTHETIC PATTERNS

Another type of cultural pattern that impacts dress relates to ideology, in this case aesthetic ideology, or what a group of people finds to be beautiful. Cultural complexity influences aesthetic patterns to the extent that simple cultures may have fewer materials or resources in processing dress, so there may be fewer options available on which to pass aesthetic judgment. Complex cultures may have a wide variety of materials available, as well as greater skill in processing them, resulting in more options available for people to use in creating their appearances than options available to simple cultures. With more options, there is a greater opportunity to establish specific cultural norms of beauty (i.e., what is and is not beautiful). In this section, we discuss the construct of aesthetics and what is "beautiful" and how ideals of beauty are manifested in dress. We provide a model for analyzing dress and the body and supply a few comparisons of aesthetic patterns.

What is aesthetics? **Aesthetics** is the study of beauty. It originated as a field of study in philosophy in the 1700s, although since ancient times in Greece (and probably many other cultures) people have considered the characteristics of beauty and have offered examples of what is thought to be beautiful. The ancient Greeks developed the Golden Mean (also called the Golden Ratio, Golden Section, Golden Rectangle), a mathematical construct usually attributed to the mathematician Pythagoras around 500 BCE (Riedweg, 2005). This construct suggested that

Favorite outfit (describe each feature below as you wear it)

Sight (i.e., colors, style features)_____

Smell (i.e., fragrance, odors)_____

Touch (i.e., textures, heat/cold) _____

Taste (i.e., flavored lip gloss)_____

Sound (i.e., swishy taffeta, dangly earrings) _____

Why wearing this outfit makes you feel happy or beautiful: _____

_____

_____

_____

unequal proportions were more attractive to the eye than equal proportions (specifically the proportion of 1 to 1.618). This relative proportion of unequal units was explained as existing in nature, in works of art and architecture, and in the human body. In ancient Greece, it is embodied in the beauty of the architectural wonders of the Parthenon and the Acropolis. However, there are many examples of this unequal proportion of units present in works of art considered to be beautiful in other cultures besides ancient Greece, and even before the time of Pythagoras, such as the Great Pyramid of Giza in Egypt built around 2500 BCE.

Aesthetics as a branch of philosophy was coined by a German philosopher named Baumgarten in 1735 (Kivy, 2004) to examine how people experienced their senses and drew conclusions about beauty. Other philosophers, such as Kant (1987) and Hume (1987) began to explore in the late 1700s how people decide what is beautiful. They concluded that study of what is beautiful relies on the five senses (i.e., sight, sound, touch, taste, smell), while judgments of beauty are a combination of sensory, emotional, and intellectual judgments. Take a moment to consider a favorite outfit in your wardrobe, and how it makes you feel happy or beautiful when you wear it.

Now examine how you arrived at your judgment of happiness or beauty. It was based in part on the information provided by your senses but may also have included an emotional response to the outfit (e.g., perhaps others complimented you when you wore it and you felt pleased) and an intellectual response to the outfit (e.g., the Lycra fiber in the skinny jeans accents the shape of your buttocks).

Now we will examine the concept of "beauty," compare a few different aesthetic ideals, discuss a framework for examining dress on the body, and analyze how we sometimes take a cultural element that is valued in a culture other than our own and incorporate it into our own aesthetic of beauty.

What is Beautiful

In Chapter 6, "Dress and Physical Appearance" and Chapter 7, "Body Image," we discussed the importance of attractiveness and body size/configuration in determining beauty. While these constructs may be defined in different ways among various populations, there is strong agreement that attractiveness is highly valued as a physical attribute and that certain body types or sizes are also highly valued. In many Western cultures or majority sub-cultures (i.e., Caucasian), that highly valued body type tends to be defined as thin and toned for women, and as thin and muscular for men. However, in non-Western cultures and in non-majority Western subcultures (i.e., people of color), those definitions may not hold up. For example, in late twentieth century studies among Caucasian 8th and 9th grade girls (a majority culture), ideal beauty was described as being tall, thin, blonde, with high cheekbones, while among African American girls of the same age, ideal beauty was described as being unique, creative, having style, attitude, pride, confidence, and a wide variety of body sizes (Collins, 1990; Parker, Nichter, Vuckovic, Sims, & Ritenbaugh, 1995). You can see that one set of characteristics focuses on specific physical attributes of the body, while the other set of characteristics focuses on ways in which the body is carried regardless of physical attributes.

Specific standards of beauty are somewhat different among various groups of women and men. Regarding specific body or facial features, the research literature has indicated that height, certain body features (breast size, arms), and certain facial features (eyes, face shape) are concerns among Asian American women (Mintz & Kashubeck, 1999) because they signal differences from the accepted standards of attractiveness in the majority culture (Hall, 1995). African American and Asian American women reported desiring lighter skin color as a beauty ideal, suggesting that body ideals may be "raced" (Orbe & Harris, 2015). Breast size has been found to be important to Caucasian women and Hispanic women, but not to African American women (See Grabe and Hyde, 2006 for a review of this research).

Among Western men, regardless of ethnicity, being thin and muscular is important. However, among male body builders, being large and very muscular ("shrink-wrapped") is the standard of beauty (Bridges, 2009). As one of the body builders observed, people are very invested in making themselves beautiful with clothing, jewelry, or other elements, whereas bodybuilders use time and effort in the gym to achieve the same goal.

Yet, there is another motivation, and that is power over others. Beauty contributes to **hegemony**, or a cultural process of domination of one group or person over others. The body builder study found that many body builders were well-respected in their gyms due to their extremely muscular physique and their strength. Distinctions may arise between bodybuilders who lift weights for

muscle definition and size, while power-lifters lift extreme amounts of weight to build strength. Thus, Bridges (2009) concluded that different types of "attractiveness" yield different types of power in the gym. So the question of beauty becomes complicated—is beauty seen in the actual body size and muscularity of the body, or is it seen in the confidence in the man's walk and body posture, or is it seen in the respect that the bodybuilder is accorded by others?

Thus, hegemonic masculinity as described in the bodybuilder study above may simply show how bodybuilders define their male gender publicly and use it to gain social power, just as other men may use athletic skill, intellectual accomplishments, or financial success to demonstrate their power. Women are equally skilled in using appearance to define their female gender publicly and use it to gain social power (hegemonic femininity), whether those appearance characteristics are thinness, large breasts, carefully applied cosmetics or nails, or high status brands of clothing and accessories.

Comparison of Different Aesthetic Ideals in Dress

We will compare a few specific aesthetic ideals of dress within different social and ethnic sub-cultures: African American aesthetics; Goth aesthetics; casual dress aesthetics in the workplace; and aesthetics at one well-known public celebration Then we raise the question of group aesthetics on social media.

African American Aesthetics

African American aesthetics of dress are not solely African, nor solely American, but a hybrid of both elements of style. The components of these aesthetic patterns were handed down in "cultural memory" from original peoples taken unwillingly from their African cultures to other cultures, including America, as slaves. These unique aesthetics included a multitude of different materials, colors, ways of decorating fabrics, accessories, etc. People captured and held in captivity were often stripped of their original clothing, and given drab and ill-fitting cast-off clothing once they reached their final destination. Besides this, they were thrown together with people from other groups who did not speak the same native language, so it is a wonder that any aesthetic traditions survived to be resurrected in their new environments.

Figure 13.18
Church hats for many African American women are statements of fashion as well as faith and group identity.

O'Neal (1998) wanted to determine what type of African American aesthetic of appearance survived in present-day American culture, and conducted interviews that focused on the characteristics that define this aesthetic. She concluded that there is clearly such an aesthetic, with defining characteristics such as (1) large scale designs and strong color, (2) stripes to construct and organize space, and (3) use of off-beat patterns and multiple rhythms. This aesthetic helps to unify the body, spirit, and the material, thereby creating a metaphysical connection; this aesthetic also creates a strong sense of ethnic identity, and validates triumph over extreme struggle. Another characteristic is the use of hats in church, sometimes called "crowns" (Marbury & Cunningham, 2000) (Figure 13.18).

Goth Aesthetics

A Goth aesthetic became noticeable as a social subculture in the 1980s. **Goth aesthetics** refers to an avoidance of materialistic or boring appearances, often through the use of dark clothing and use of black in body modifications. Referencing the Gothic period in medieval European history, the Goth subculture became known for their interest in mysterious or "dark" phenomenon such as dark romances, dark clothing, the supernatural, and the occult (Miklas & Arnold, 1999). It was, and still is, characterized as an aesthetic lifestyle that is counter to the perceived boring and materialistic lifestyle of the parents of Goth followers; Goths are typically young adults who want to distance themselves from the social norms of self-presentation exhibited by the majority culture. The culture is also associated with counter-culture behaviors such as acknowledging the pain and despair that many people feel, and particular Goth or Indie bands and music.

It is recognized that Goth followers wish to create an "extraordinary self," or a self that somehow transcends the boredom of everyday life. This extraordinary self is almost fantasy, in that it removes the individual from some of the worries and insecurities of life in the present, and also challenges some of the conventional categories of appearance as judged by others (gender, age, social status). One clear way to do this is through creating one's appearance, including dressing in black or dark jewel tones; dyeing the hair black; using black lipstick, eye color, or nail polish; wearing Doc Marten boots and unfitted clothing, among other things (Miklas & Arnold, 1999) (Figure 13.19).

Figure 13.19
Participant at Goth Weekend, Whitby, England.

Casual Dress Aesthetics

Where professional workplace dress once included the expectation of "business" attire for both men and women, many places of business have evolved into a more relaxed aesthetic of dress known as **casual dress aesthetics**. Instead of business suits or sports jackets for men, complete with long sleeved dress shirt and tie, and business or dress shoes, business dress for men may now include a wider range of acceptable clothing such as more casual pants worn with sweaters or casual shirts (no tie) and sneakers or casual shoes.

For women, "business" attire was once defined as wearing a nice dress or business suit with professional blouse and dress shoes (often with high heels) and hosiery. That aesthetic has evolved to include pants worn with sweaters or other tops, and casual shoes and socks. Even the amount of skin or body shape shown in women's clothing has changed dramatically over the past couple of decades. Where once it was unacceptable to reveal any bust cleavage, it has become more the "norm" to show cleavage. The same can be observed in the amount of leg revealed or the curvature of the butt or abdomen shown. Yes, such changes can be described as simply fashion change over time, but we argue that such changes may also be viewed as a change in aesthetics—from more formal and constrained, to more informal and relaxed. See Chapter 5, "Dress, Attributions, and Impression Formation," for more specific information about casual business dress.

IN-CLASS ACTIVITY
How Does Dress Impact the Work Environment?

How do you think dress in the workplace impacts the work environment? How does it affect interactions between employees and their bosses, between students and teachers, between sales associates and their customers? Does the way you are dressed at work impact the way you think of yourself and your responsibilities—for example, if you were dressed in shorts and a tank top with flip-flops, would you work as hard as if you were dressed more formally? Would your colleagues or your clients/customers take you seriously?

DRESS IN THE NEWS
Workplace Dress Codes

A server at a restaurant posted a photo of her bloody feet due to her company's requirement that she wear heels of 2.5 inches in height, causing blisters and the loss of a toenail. When she complained and tried to wear flat shoes, she was berated by her manager and told she would need to wear heels for her shift the next day. The company responded to this posting on social media by stating that their dress code for both men and women requires black shoes with a non-slip sole for safety reasons and with a heel of any height that is comfortable for them. Thus, it appears that both the employee and the employer are resorting to the "court of public opinion" in airing their cases, with the employee questioning the aesthetic code and the employer justifying the aesthetic code (Ricevuto 2016).

Burning Man Aesthetics

The Burning Man festival began in the mid-1980s on a beach near San Francisco as a festival that celebrated individuality, freedom, and artistic expression. It culminated with a giant effigy of a wooden man that was set on fire. Due to fire hazards, the celebration was subsequently moved to the Black Rock desert in Nevada, where it has continued to the present day. Some 55,000 people come together to create a city for the week-long series of events, and there has evolved an aesthetic for self-presentation among celebrants. This aesthetic encourages experimentation with "radical" or extreme self-expression (Kaiser & Green, 2008) and freeing oneself from typical social and workplace constraints of appearance, such as gendered garments or culturally understood aesthetics of color or body coverage.

The **Burning Man aesthetic** includes absurdity and nudity, meaning that any appearance is acceptable—appearing as aliens, as animals, as people from the future or the long-ago past, or in various states of undress or no dress (Figure 13.20). There are three main types of appearance creating activities: (1) creating things from scratch; (2) altering things via cutting, embellishing with found materials from the desert environment, or other means; and

Figure 13.20
Participants at Burning Man
festival, Black Rock City, Nevada.

(3) gifting appearance items or procedures to others. Various camps are established to facilitate each of these active ways of creating one's appearance. For example, the Fairyland camp offers workshops in creating fairy wings and tutus, an activity that draws more men than women, perhaps because these clothing items were readily available to young girls in their play, but were likely discouraged among young boys. Pandora's Lounge and Fix-It Shop encourages participants to alter garments by adding fake fur or buttons, string, feathers, and other items. Other camps provide gifts such as necklaces, goggles, body painting, or as in the case of Camp Furkini, a Speedo™ type bottom made of fake fur. Participants point out the transformative benefits in each of these cases (Kaiser & Green, 2008).

Social Media Aesthetics

We recognize that social media wield a strong influence on aesthetics and dress. Many people rely heavily on Facebook posts, Instagram photos, NSFW (Not Safe for Work) Tumblr blogs or other forms of social media to observe what people in their peer groups, or aspirational groups like celebrities, are doing and wearing. It is typical for individuals to post photos of themselves in various garments or in different social contexts just for the purpose of receiving feedback from others. Thus, a sense of group aesthetics of appearance and other behavior may be established. The

risk may be in using social feedback from others as a basis of comparison, which could result in a devalued sense of worth. For example, if you post photos of yourself in your new hot outfit for an upcoming social function, and other people comment on how "un-hot" you look, or how you shouldn't wear something like that because of your size, how might this judgment impact your feelings of self-worth? And if you compare your appearance to the thousands of images posted by Kim Kardashian, who doesn't look at all like you anyway, how likely are you to feel positive about yourself?

So, what we are beginning to see is that social media can create an "aesthetic" for us, such that we think certain appearance characteristics are valued as culturally relevant and should guide our decisions in presenting ourselves to others. Social media can then operate in much the same way as the cultural norms of these other reference groups do for their members and establish normative patterns of behavior. While those norms may not include bright and juxtaposed patterns as in the African American aesthetic, or dark clothing as in the Goth aesthetic, or radical self-expression as in the Burning Man aesthetic, they may include exaggerated provocative poses and "fish lips" faces, among other characteristics. In the same manner, then, social media may contribute to a certain expected aesthetic for our self-presentation. A current focus of research indicates that this aesthetic can be highly sexualized and toxic and leads to self-objectification (Manago et al., 2015), while other international research finds that some individuals see the posting of selfies as practicing freedom to be who they want to be, free of cultural restrictions ((Tildenberg and Cruz, 2015).

FRAMEWORK FOR EXAMINING DRESS ON THE BODY

Is there a framework or model that can guide our understanding of cultural patterns of aesthetic expression in dress? Hillestad (1980) developed such a model that examines appearance as a total concept of the body and dress. In this model, Hillestad differentiates the underlying structures of the body and dress via a linguistic approach. He examines the components and elements of each aspect of appearance just as a linguist examines components and elements of language. The body is composed of body forms, such as arms, legs, torsos, and heads; body surfaces such as skin and hair; and body motions such as walking, gesturing, and posture. Specific elements of these components include skin color and texture, hair color and texture, size and shape of various body parts, and sub-units of body movement. As one component changes, so too does overall expression of the body. For example, as one loses weight or grows taller, the body configuration changes and alters how the body moves or how it is perceived by others.

Dress can be analyzed by similar components and elements. Dress includes articles of clothing and other articles of adornment (such as shoes, jewelry, and other accessories). The elements of each include what materials are used, what processes are used to make them, and what techniques are used to embellish them. For example, **materials** could be natural or man-made (i.e., leather versus vinyl). The **processes** used to make them vary from simple to complex, and will determine how they appear and how they behave in the garment of accessory (i.e, knit T- shirt versus woven denim jeans). **Techniques of embellishment** result in unique artistic expressions (i.e., embroidery or tiny pleats).

Cultural Authentication

We can see that there are indeed cultural patterns related to aesthetic expression. Another example is what we call **cultural authentication**, which is the process of assimilating into a culture an item or idea or artifact that is not original to the culture (Eicher & Evenson, 2015). With respect to dress, this is the process of incorporating some element of dress from another culture into one's own culture so that it has aesthetic worth and meaning in one's own culture. This method of cultural diffusion of dress has occurred between Western and non-Western cultures, as well as among individuals in one culture who admire the aesthetic practices of another group and wish to incorporate aspects of those practices for themselves.

There are four stages of authentication, based on Eicher's extensive fieldwork (Erekosima & Eicher, 2015): (1) selection of an object or idea; (2) characterization of that object or idea, which refers to adopting the object or idea intact but attaching new meaning to the object and sometimes renaming it; (3) incorporating the object or idea into a specific context within the culture; and (4) transforming the object or idea physically or modifying its meaning or worth, thereby more fully integrating it into the new culture. These stages of authentication have been found to explain the assimilation of many items of dress from one culture to another, as demonstrated by research on assimilating European silk ribbons into the decorative handwork of Great Lakes American Indians (Pannabecker, 1988), the assimilation of jeans in Korea (Ingvoldstad, DeLong, & Koh, 1994), and assimilation of Western dress, called "holoku," that covered more of the female body in Hawai'i than traditional dress prior to the arrival of Christian missionaries (Arthur, 1997). Scholars are not certain that the four stages must be followed in exact order for an item to be considered authentic, yet this process does explain how fluid the process is in adopting new elements of dress and imbuing them with meaning unique to the culture.

I, one of the authors of this book, have a great fondness for cultural dress outside of my own culture, including American Indian jewelry, African textiles, and Japanese kimono. I don't feel completely comfortable wearing these items exactly as intended in their respective cultures because I feel like an imposter who is co-opting items that are not mine, but I do feel comfortable wearing them with my own twist. So I wear my Navaho, Zuni, and Lakota earrings with dressy garments, my African textiles made into a long duster and a short jacket worn with fitted pants, and my early twentieth-century Japanese kimono with silk pants and an obi sash that I designed and made. Thus, I have selected certain items that I admire in other cultures, transformed them by how I wear them (often creating new components to wear them with), incorporated them into my self-presentation, and characterized them by attaching new symbolic meaning and use to them.

Can you think of any items of dress that you have assimilated into your own self-presentation, or into your cultural group?

Chapter Summary

In this chapter, we have examined how the level of complexity in cultures can determine patterns of technology, norms, and aesthetic expression that are found. Technology establishes what materials and processes are available to dress the body, whereas normative patterns regulate, constrain, and order society. Aesthetic patterns of self-expression and group expression follow from technology and norms, and these aesthetic patterns continually change and transform what is produced. We can use models to examine the aesthetics of dress and ways in which we borrow aesthetic expressions from cultures other than our own into our own self presentation. In the next chapter, we will continue with an examination of cultural patterns and focus on patterns of health and hygiene, rituals, and media influence.

Key Terms

academic regalia
aesthetics
African American
   aesthetics
agrarian cultures
Burning Man aesthetics
casual dress aesthetics
collectivistic orientation
cross dressing
cultural authentication
cultural complexity
cultural generality
cultural scale theory

cultural universal
customs
duration of norms
enculturation
fast fashion
folk cultures
folkways
global culture
Goth aesthetics
hegemony
ideal culture
individualistic orientation
kinship

laws
mass cultures
materials
mores
national culture
normative patterns
particularities
patterns of culture
processes
prohibitive laws
promotive laws
real culture
regulative laws

sanctions of norms
smart clothing
strength of norms
sumptuary laws
taboos
technical patterns
techniques of
   embellishment
urban-industrial cultures
virtual technology

Discussion Questions

1. What is cultural complexity and why is it an important concept in the study of cultures?

2. What differences in technology related to production of dress would you expect to find in an isolated Inuit culture and a major metropolitan culture such as New York City?

3. What is one normative pattern that you might observe worldwide, and how would this norm vary in its duration, strength, and sanctions in different cultures?

4. How would you describe the aesthetics patterns of groups you belong to?

STUDiO™

Visit your book's STUDIO for additional quiz questions, vocabulary flashcards, and chapter worksheets!

Suggested Readings

Bridges, T. (2009). Gender capital and male bodybuilders. *Body & Society, 15*(1), 83–10.

Cachon, G., & Swinney, R. (2011). The value of fast fashion: Quick response, enhanced design, and strategic consumer behavior. *Management Science, 57*(4), 778–795.

Tildenberg, K. & Cruz, E. (2015). Selfies, image and the re-making of the body. *Body &Society, 21*(4), 77–102.

References

Arthur, L. B. (1987). Cultural authentication refined: The case of the Hawaiian holoku. *Clothing and Textiles Research Journal, 15*(3) 129–139.

Benedict, R. (2006 reprint). *Patterns of culture.* New York, NY: Houghton Mifflin Harcourt.

Berzowska, J. (2005). Electronic textiles: Wearable computers, reactive fashion, and soft computation. *Textile: The Journal of Cloth and Culture, 3,* 58–75.

Bicchieri, C. (2006). *The grammar of society: the nature and dynamics of social norms,* New York, NY: Cambridge University Press. Bicchieri, C. & Muldoon, R. (2011). Social norms. In Edward N. Zalta (Ed.), *The Stanford Encyclopedia of Philosophy (Spring 2011 Edition).* Retrieved from http://plato.stanford.edu/archives/spr2011/entries/social-norms/

Bodley, J. (1994). *Cultural anthropology: Tribes, states, and the global system.* London, UK: Mayfield.

Bridges, T. (2009). Gender capital and male bodybuilders. *Body & Society, 15*(1), 83–107.

Cachon, G., & Swinney, R. (2011). The value of fast fashion: Quick response, enhanced design, and strategic consumer behavior. *Management Science, 57*(4), 778–795.

Collins, P. H. (1990). *Black feminist thought: Knowledge, consciousness, and the politics of empowerment.* New York, NY: Routledge.

Darish, P. (1989). Dressing for the nest life: Raffia textile production and use among the Kuba of Zaire. In A. Weiner and J. Schneider (Eds.,), *Clothing and human experience,* Washington, D.C.: Smithsonian Institution Press, 117–140

Dear, I. C. B. & Foot, M. R. D. (2002). "War Production Board." *The Oxford Companion to World War II.* Oxford, England: The Oxford University Press.

Dunne, L. (2011). Wearable technology. In L. Welters & A. Lillethun (Eds). *The fashion reader.* New York, NY: Berg Publishers, pp. 613–616

Eicher, J. & Evenson, S. (2015). *The Visible Self* (4th ed.). New York, NY: Fairchild Books, an imprint of Bloomsbury Publishing, Inc.

Erekosema, T. & Eicher, J. (2015). The aesthetics of men's dress of the Kalabari of Nigeria. In Eicher, J. & Evenson, S. (2015), *The Visible Self*, (4th ed.). New York, NY: Fairchild Books, an imprint of Bloomsbury Publishing, Inc. pp. 349–361.

Fitzhugh, W. & Crowell, A. (1988). *Crossroads of the continents: Cultures of Siberia and Alaska*. Washington, D.C.: Smithsonian Institution Press.

Grabe, S. & Hyde, J. (2006). Ethnicity and body dissatisfaction among women in the United States: A meta-analysis. *Psychological Bulletin, 132*(4), 622–640.

Hall, C. (1995). Asian eyes: Body image and eating disorders of Asian and Asian-American women. *Eating Disorders, 3*, 8–19.

Hamilton, J. (1987). Dress as a cultural sub-system: A unifying metatheory for clothing and textiles. *Clothing and Textiles Research Journal, 6*(1), 1–7.

Hillestad, R. (1980). The underlying structure of appearance. *Dress, 5*, 117–125.

Hoskins, J. (1989). Why do ladies sing the blues? Indigo dyeing, cloth production, and gender symbolism in Kodi. In A. Weiner and J. Schneider (Eds.,), *Clothing and human experience*, pp. 141–173. Washington, D.C.: Smithsonian Institution Press.

Hume, D. (reprint 1987). "Of the Standard of Taste." In *David Hume, Essays: Moral, and Literary*. London, UK: George Routledge and Sons. Original publication year: 1870.

Ingvoldstad, A., DeLong, M., & Koh, A. (1994, October). Cultural authentication of jeans in the United States and Korea. Paper presented at the annual meeting of the International Textiles and Apparel Association, Minneapolis, MN.

Kaiser, S. & Green, D. (2008). Textiles, masculinities and spontaneous communities in the Burning Man Project. Textile Society of America Symposium Proceedings, 11th Biennial Symposium, September 4–7, 2008, Honolulu, HI, Paper 95. Lincoln, NE: Digital Commons at University of Nebraska. Retrieved from http://digitalcommons.unl.edu/tsaconf/95

Kant, I. (translated 1987). *The Critique of Judgment*. Translated by Werner S. Pluhar. Indianapolis, IN: Hackett Publishing Company.

Kennett, F. (1995). *Ethnic dress*. Great Britain: Reed International Books Limited.

Kivy, P. (Ed.) (2004). *The Blackwell Guide to Aesthetics*. Malden, MA: Blackwell Publishers.

Kottak, C. (2003). *Mirror for humanity* (3rd ed.). New York, NY: McGraw-Hill. Land's End first with new "My Virtual Model™" technology: Takes guesswork out of web shopping for clothes that fit. (Feb. 12, 2004). Retrieved from http://multivu.prnewswire.com/mnr/landsend/11847/

MacManus, C. (2010). Macy's mirror lets your reflection try on clothes. Retrieved from http:/www.cnet.com/news/macys-mirror-lets-your-reflection-try-on-clothes

Manago, A., Ward, L., Lemm, K., Reed, L., & Seabrook, R. (2015). Facebook involvement, objectified body consciousness, body shame, and sexual assertiveness in college women and men. *Sex Roles, 72*, 1–14.

Marbury, C. & Cunningham, M. (2000). *Crowns: Portraits of black women in church hats*. New York, NY: Bantam Dell Publishing Group.

Miklas, S. & Arnold, S. (1999). "The extraordinary self": Gothic culture and the construction of the self. *Journal of Marketing Management, 15*(6), 563–576.

Mintz, L.B. & Kashubeck, S. (1999). Body image and disordered eating among Asian American and Caucasian college students: An examination of race and gender differences. *Psychology of Women Quarterly, 23*, 781–796.

News Desk. (May 31, 2015). Arresting dress: A timeline of anti-cross-dressing laws in the United States. *PBS News Hour*. Retrieved from http://www.pbs.org/newshour/updates/arresting-dress-timeline-anti-cross-dressing-laws-u-s/

O'Neal, G. (1998). African American aesthetics of dress: Current manifestations. *Clothing and Textiles Research Journal, 16*(4), 167–175.

Orbe, M. & Harris, T. (2015). *Interracial communication: Theory into practice*. Los Angeles, CA: Sage Publication, Inc.

Pannabecker, R. (1988). The cultural authentication of ribbon: Use and test of a concept. *Clothing and Textiles Research Journal, 7*(1), 55–56.

Parker, S., Nichter, M., Vuckovic, N., Sims, C., & Ritenbaugh, C. (1995). Body image and weight concerns among African American and White adolescent females: Differences that make a difference. *Human Organization, 54*, 103–114.

Piponnier, F. & Mane, P. (2000). *Dress in the Middle Ages.* New Haven, CT: Yale University Press.

Redfield, R. (1953). *The primitive world and its transformation.* Ithaca, NY: Cornell University Press. Redfield, R. (1956). *Peasant society and culture.* Chicago, IL: University of Chicago Press.

Riedweg, C. (2005). *Pythagoras, His Life, Teaching and Influence.* Ithaca, NY: Cornell University Press.

Ricevuto, J. (2016, May 13). Waitress shares photo of her bloody feet highlighting sexist workplace codes. Retrieved from https://www.yahoo.com/beauty/waitresssharesphotoofherbloodyfeet123927941.html

Schneider, J. & Weiner, A. (1989). Introduction. In A. Weiner and J. Schneider (Eds.,), *Clothing and human experience, pp. 1–29.* Washington, D.C.: Smithsonian Institution Press.

Stewart, D. (2009, April 20). *Sick & Twisted: "Anti-Aging" & "Cosmeceutical" Ads,* Jezebel.com. Retrieved from http://jezebel.com/5220066/sick-twisted-anti-aging-cosmeceutical-ads

Storey, J. (2006). *Cultural theory and popular culture.* New York, NY: Pearson Education.

Tildenberg, K. & Cruz, E. (2015). Selfies, image and the re-making of the body. *Body & Society, 21*(4), 77–102.

World Health Organization. (2012). Female genital mutilation. Retrieved from www.who.int/mediacentre/factsheets/fs241.www.missuniverse.com

CHAPTER
14 DRESS AND CULTURAL RITUALS

After reading and reflecting on the content of this chapter, students should be able to:

- **Establish how dress is used as part of the functions of religion.**
- **Explain the stages of a ritual and how dress may be used to symbolize each stage.**
- **Describe how rituals related to dress reflect beliefs about health and hygiene.**

INTRODUCTION

As noted in Chapter 1, "Why Study Dress?" culture is the way that humans organize their world. It is the fundamental determinant of how we live as we do and how that life is shaped. When we contemplate how our lives are shaped, and how our lives are different from the lives of others, we see that they are shaped by our values and view of the world, our lifestyles, our traditions, and the products of human workmanship that we use and that surround us.

Every culture has some process among its members that assists them in ordering their world and provides them with meaning, identity, unity, peace of mind, and a sense of control over events. This cultural process is referred to as **religion**. Religion is a **human universal**, that is, all societies have a set of beliefs that can be identified as religion. Yet, religions between cultures and even within cultures show enormous variation (Nanda & Warms, 2004).

Even though not all beliefs are shared between religions, all religions have a set of shared characteristics. For example, all religions have a set of **sacred narratives** and symbols. Sacred narratives such as the Bible in the Christian religion are "stories that are believed to be true by members of a religious tradition. They document historical events, gods, spirits, and the origin of all things" (Nanda & Warms, 2004, p. 326).

Religious symbols can be expressed in material objects including dress (Figure 14.1). The cross and the Star of David are symbols of the Christian and Jewish faiths, respectively. When individuals wear these symbols, they may be identified as members of each of these respective religions whether they are indeed members or not. By having specific symbols such as these, individuals can identify believers from non-believers and can distinguish members of the group from non-members.

Figure 14.1
Wearing symbolism linked to a specific religion provides an opportunity to communicate one's faith to others. Both the item of dress (skull cap) and the pattern sewn into the item (Star of David) are symbols of Jewish faith.

Most religions also have a set of **rituals** during which members come together and celebrate the critical stories and symbols of their beliefs, communicate with the gods or other beings (e.g., spirits, ghosts), and/or try to exert influence on their physical and social world. Examples of rituals include weddings and baptisms. Most religions have methods to communicate with the supernatural world through prayer or magic. Finally, all religions have leaders or clerics that take leading roles in performing the rituals of the religion, and as noted previously, they may adopt specific and unique forms of dress to indicate their status as leader.

One of the important functions of religion is to provide meaning. Religion can explain aspects of the physical and social environment that are important to the lives of individuals. Even though religion does not answer all questions, religion often provides a **cosmology**, that is, a set of beliefs about a range of questions (e.g., What is the nature of life and death? Where did we come from? How are we to treat our world? How are we to treat each other?) that are sometimes not explained by science (Nanda & Warms, 2004). By providing people with a set of beliefs, which often evolve into moral codes, religion situates people's places within a society and provides perspective about the place of the group relative to the external world (Hamilton & Hawley, 1999); it unites people together, can provide people with a distinct identity (Druesedow, 2010), and exerts social control (Arthur, 1999) as well as provide a sense of belonging and meaning. Giving meaning to our lives and the world is fundamental to human existence (Frankl, 1946).

In this chapter we consider several different religions. We share how dress is used to provide people with a distinct religious identity, how it can visually unite people, and how dress exerts control over members. We begin by contrasting three distinct religions to illustrate how dress is used to enable to keep some religious groups quite separate (e.g., Anabaptist) from the dominant culture and another religious groups integrated (e.g., Mormonism) into the dominant culture. We continue to discuss links between functions of religion and how these functions are facilitated by dress. Next, we move into a discussion of rituals explaining the stages of a typical ritual and describing how dress may be used to symbolize each stage. We end the chapter with a discussion of how beliefs about health and hygiene underlie some of our everyday ritual behavior concerning dress and our appearances.

RELIGIOUS DRESS AND IDENTITY

Anabapists get their name from the belief of early practitioners that one should be rebaptised as an adult. There are four major groups of Anabaptists: Amish, Hutterites, Mennonites, and Brethren. Dress is important to these religious groups because it serves as a visible sign of their relationship to the external world; that is, to be viewed as separate from the practices of members of the dominant culture. In addition, dress is used to indicate humility over pride, to identity an affiliation with a specific church, and to indicate willingness to submit to the church (Druesdow, 2010; Hamilton & Hawley, 1999).

The primary means used to signify Anabaptists' separateness is through wearing **plain dress**.[1] Plain dress in this context means adherence to simplicity, modesty, orderliness, and equality; wearing items of clothing that do not conform to mainstream fashion and does not have embellishments or ornamentation (i.e., no showing off). Plain dress also includes wearing some type of head covering (Druesedow, 2010; Hume, 2013).

Old Order Amish

Amish people are located throughout the US and in Canada, with a distinct concentration in counties of the US state of Pennsylvania. The Amish resist modern life by maintaining barriers between their communities and others. Families are close-knit; they marry within their own kind and educate their children in community schools that focus on the Amish way of life and further insulate children from the influence of outsiders (Hume, 2013).

Change occurs within their communities but in ways that maintains their way of life. Variations occur between Amish communities such that they can be places on a continuum with "low" communities being the strictest (orthodox) to high communities (progressive) the least strict.

Just as there can be variation in terms of adherence to cultural norms, there can be variation in dress between Amish communities as it is individual communities that

---

[1]Because their dress enables them to be easily identified as Amish, and perhaps because of the influence of their religious beliefs on their dress, some authors have referred to the dress worn by the Amish as sacred dress (Hamilton & Hawley, 1999).

make decisions on the dress of its members. Among the Old Order Amish, a religious Anabaptist sect in the United States and Canada that immigrated from Europe, the prescribed aesthetic code is to wear "plain dress," or dress that is very basic and unadorned. This aesthetic pattern relates to living a simple rural lifestyle based on modesty, humility, and godliness, and one that is distinctly different from others in contemporary culture who they believe are living a profane and unworthy lifestyle. How the Amish dress is a small part of their larger belief system, but is indicative of a non-materialistic lifestyle that is focused on quiet contemplation, worship, and hard work (Scott, 2008).

In general, the plain dress of members of the Amish community includes the following for woman and men. A woman's clothing consists of an open-front bodice with a narrow band collar, elbow-length sleeves, and a skirt that comes to just below the knee for unmarried women and below the knee for married women depending on their age. Colors are muted. Pockets may be included but they are not easily visible. A prayer cap is worn in the home and outside a black bonnet is added over the cap. Black hose and black shoes are worn along with sweaters and capes that are dark in color. A matching apron worn over a dress indicates women are always ready to work. No makeup is worn. Hair is not cut but worn parted in the center and twisted along the sides of the head into a small bun in the back. Loose hair is interpreted as seductive; therefore a woman's hair is never worn loose in public. Typically, buttons are not used for garment closures only hooks and eyes or straight pins (Hamilton & Hawley, 1999; Hume, 2013).

Amish men wear denim pants and dress shirts with sleeve length dependent on the season. Suspenders are worn, along with a felt or straw hat (again depending on the season), and work boots. Married men wear full beards but no mustache. The man grows a beard when he joins the church, and his hair is cut in a bowl-shape. For the most part, items worn by any member of the community (i.e., men, women, children) are made by women rather than being purchased from a retailer. Their clothing reflects their humility with some members wearing old and worn clothing that is perceived as "more Amish" as wearing new might be perceived as vain. Children's clothing follow these same rules and mimics those of adults.

Even though great effort is made to not be influenced by developments in dominant (other) cultures, the impact of the external world is present. For example, the composition of the fabric that is used for garments has changed

DRESS IN THE NEWS
Hate Crimes

In 2011, a crime occurred in an Amish community in eastern Ohio, in which ten men and six women participated in hair- and beard-cutting attacks on members of their community as a way to shame them into adhering to the strict behavioral code of the community (Peralta, 2015). Because women are instructed to let their hair grow long, and men grow a beard as a symbol of following the Amish faith, the hair and beard have spiritual significance and it is forbidden to cut them. Therefore, cutting the hair and beard of their fellow members was considered to be a hate crime by the courts. The defendants were found guilty in March, 2013 and have been sentenced to prison.

This crime and sentencing has raised many questions, including:

- How will defendants cope with being deprived of wearing their prescribed dress when the men have to wear khaki or green prison uniforms and the women have to wear prison jumpers instead of their long dresses and prayer caps?
- Will they be offended or tempted to use technology that is forbidden, such as television, while in prison?
- Should local government get involved in a dispute in a community that has its own set of conduct and tries to remain separate from the larger community?

over time as man-made fabrics (e.g., polyester, nylon) were introduced in the external world. Again, adherence to dress rules do vary such that in communities styles present in the external world are worn under specific circumstances (e.g., only in the presence of women) or worn frequently but limited to specific categories of dress (e.g., underwear) (Hamilton & Hawley, 1999).

In sum, Amish dress highlights their efforts to publicly communicate a self that is distinct and separate from the dominant culture. Their dress as a method to make their religious beliefs visible (e.g., demonstrate lack of vanity, orderliness, equality) reflects their overall commitment to living a simple life and one that is clearly separate from the dominant culture.

Mormon Views

In stark contrast to the Amish, who desire to live apart from the dominant culture, are Mormons or members of the Church of Jesus Christ of Latter Day Saints. Mormonism as a religious view was highlighted during the 2012 US presidential race as Mitt Romney, the 70th governor of the state of Massachusetts, and practicing Mormon, became the first major party (Republican) presidential nominee.

Similar to the Amish, Mormons are a religious group characterized as having a strong commitment to family and a reliance on authority. However, variations exist in their individual adherence to policies that stem from the temple. The church encourages both thrift and modesty in dress and lifestyle. In fact, Mormons see a direct connection between modesty in dress and a woman's virtue. But the dress choices made by practitioners are not as closely monitored as they are with the Amish. Thus, there can be individual Mormons that strictly adhere to appearance policies and others who do not (Hamilton & Hawley, 1999; Salamone, 1999).

To understand their somewhat unique practice concerning dress (i.e., undergarments), it is important to understand some basic tenets of the religion. The church considers itself to be a restoration of the church of Jesus Christ. Members of the church are striving towards the goal of achieving eternal life and becoming a member of the Celestial Kingdom. Achieving eternal life means to become one with God, thus allowing members to become divine beings or "gods" themselves. Mormons believe that Jesus Christ leads the church by revealing his will to its president, whom members regard as a prophet and revelator. Central tenets within the community include a belief in the plurality of Gods, baptism for the dead, and marriage for eternity.

The sacred **garment or endowment** is given as a step toward being accepted into the Celestial Kingdom (Fischer, 1999). Although originally thought of as an undergarment used only for ceremonies, the garment is worn daily, next to the skin, and beneath street clothing. The garment functions as a constant reminder of the wearer's commitments. However, the garment is for the most part, invisible to outsiders and as a result, keeps the wearer protected from unwanted criticism.

The garment is available in one- or two-piece styles in a variety of fabrics. It is intended to cover the torso of the body down to the top of the knee. There is variety in necklines for both men and women but all garments have sleeves: a short sleeve for men and a cap sleeve for women. Other undergarments (e.g., brassieres) are worn over the garment. Because of its design, wearing the garment ensures that street clothing worn by either gender is modest. However, the garment may be removed for activities that require it such as swimming or hospitalization (Hamilton & Hawley, 1999).

Specific reasons Mormon women have provided for wearing the garment include a desire to be modest in appearance. The garment also represents previously made covenants to live life a certain way. Some women note that the garment "protects" them. This protection included protecting a woman from getting too intimate with a man and from being tempted to do things one is not supposed to do (Hamilton & Hawley, 1999).

Unlike the Amish who desire to live separate, Mormons seek to influence the external world. Thus, religious aspects of the self are not emphasized via items of dress worn every day and do not provide them with a distinct religious identity that functions to separate them from the external world. They are to be modest in their appearance, which can be achieved with a wide range of clothing styles, and their overall appearance is to be one that fits in with others. Rather than practicing a religion that requires dress that publicly separates and perhaps isolates them from outsiders, wearing the endowments of the Mormons, to some extent, enables them to separate and keep private their religious self from their everyday existence.

Islamic Views

In both of the previous examples of religious views, we noted that adherence to specific rules concerning dress varied by community (Amish) as well as by individual (Mormon). Some religions and their leaders tolerate little variance in the appearance of their members and prescribe dress for followers. Prescriptions for dress may apply equally to both genders or may be more or less restrictive for one gender. Negative sanctions may exist for not following these rules including being shunned or even expelled from the religious community (Tortora, 2010). Consider, for example, regulations concerning dress within the Islamic religion in the Republic of Iran.

Islam is one of the major religions of the world and its followers are referred to as Muslims. It was founded in the seventh century in an area of the world that today

Figure 14.2
Iranian women wearing orthodox hijab.

comprises western Saudi Arabia. Central to the beliefs within Islam is that the Qur'an, their holy book, is immutable, and the final revelation of God to humanity. To understand Islam within this region of the world, we need to understand a little of the history of the region.

Prior to the fall of 1979, Iran's political system was a monarchy ruled by a Shah. During this time period, a revolution occurred wherein the monarchy was replaced by the leaders of the Islamic Republic. Prior to and during the revolution the women were led to expect that they would gain new rights and opportunities as a result of their support. However, within a short time, new restrictions were placed on women that were said to be an attempt to protect a woman's honor and chastity (Shirazi, 2000).

The primary restriction on the appearance of women was the compulsory requirement that they wear **hijab**.[2] A hijab is a veil (sometimes referred to as a headscarf) that covers the head and chest. The Preamble of the Islamic Republic Constitution (1979) highlights the importance of a woman's role within society and mandates that exploitation of her body through public display is considered to be a sinful act (Shirazi, 2000).

Even though veiling has always been a part of Iranian culture, the enforcement of the hijab for women was part of the political reconstruction of Iranian social order into an Islamic society. According to Ayatollah Khomeini, the leader of the Islamic revolution, veiling was necessary because it distinguished revolutionary Islamic women from the women of the previous (corrupt) regime. The dress code set forth by the government and tied to religion indicated that all parts of a woman's body should be covered except her face and hands. Failure to wear the hijab could result in being denied service by shops as well as harsh treatment, humiliation, and possible arrest ("Iranian moral," 2011; Shirazi, 2000).

In the years since the revolution, two forms of hijab developed. Derived from the traditional form of Iranian chador, the traditional hijab is one piece, black, and when worn covers a woman's head and body but leaves her face exposed. Previously in use by religious Iranian women as proper attire to pray, enter, and visit holy sites, there are no fasteners within the garment, thus it requires use of one hand to hold it in place. If a women needs to use her hands to carry a child, groceries, or anything under her chador, the garment may be held in place with her teeth (Figure 14.2).

The second form of hijab consists of a head covering called the rusari and an outer gown known as the rupush. The **rusari** is a square head scarf that can be draped around the head and contains fashion elements such as sewn coins, design patterns, colors, and embellishments. The **rupush** can also be viewed as a fashion statement as it can also consist of a variety of colors and patterns as well as embellishments.

---

[2]There is no indication that there is a style of hijab that is shared or common among all women in Islamic cultures or that the meaning of the hijab is shared between these groups.

Even though in this example there appear to be strict rules concerning the dress of women, diverse styles of Islamic dress coexist in many places. Muslim women wear tunics and colorful headscarves that leave their faces uncovered and live near women wearing muted ankle-length dresses and face-covering veils. What might underlie this seemingly contradictory behavior for Muslim women? One explanation for the difference between these appearances can be attributed to attempts to communicate level of religious piety.

Piety in women is valued in many situations including the marriage market. Prior to the 1970s and 1980s simply wearing a headscarf was sufficient to communicate a woman's piety. However, during these two decades, women increasingly adopted the headscarf for a range of political and social reasons. It no longer clearly communicated religious piety. Thus, pious women adopted fundamentalist garments (headscarfs, wearing dark muted colors) to once again send a clear message of their religious devoutness (Patel, 2012).

Reflecting on all three religious views (Amish, Mormon, Muslim) we begin to see commonalities and differences. Policies concerning dress exist for all groups but adherence to those policies varies. Gender differences are present. The Amish have dress policies that denote differences based in gender as do Muslims while the Mormons differentiate much less in the style of their endowments based on gender. We see presenting a modest appearance is important to all three religious groups, but the manner

in which that goal is achieved is vastly different for each group and varies from wearing conservative clothing styles in public (e.g., Mormon) to being completed covered (e.g., Muslim). As we continue our discussion of functions of religion and the role that dress plays, we will continue to see the diverse ways religious groups meet common goals.

RELIGIOUS DRESS AND PERSONAL CONTROL

As we noted in our introduction to this chapter, an important function of religion is to increase individual's sense of personal control and reduce anxiety (Nanda & Warms, 2004). Within religious groups, people are taught to pray. **Prayer** is any conversation held with spirits or Gods. Prayers are often used to help oneself, others, or to bring aid to a community particularly in situations where outcomes are unpredictable. In prayer, people give thanks, praise, and blessings among other things (Levinson, 1996). For instance, if your community is in the path of an extreme weather event, such as a tornado or a hurricane, you may pray that the event misses your hometown or neighborhood. By doing so, you may feel a greater sense of control over an event that you, in reality, have no control over. You may feel this sense of control especially if what you requested in your prayers actually comes to pass.

Dress can be used as people pray. **Prayer beads** (also referred to as worry beads) are a form of dress that can be used to assist during prayer. They assist in keeping track of how many prayers have been said as well as the order of the prayers. They are typically fingered in an automatic manner and this enables the person praying to focus on the prayer rather than focusing on where he or she might be in the meditation. In addition to enabling prayer, these beads are also believed by some to aid their users by relieving stress and capturing negative energy.

Another item of dress that can be used to assist during prayer is a **prayer shawl**. Within the Jewish faith, men wear a shawl during morning prayers. The shawl is made from white wool or silk with black or blue strips at the ends. There are tassels located on all four corners and each tassel has four strings. Each corner has ten knots that are reminders to keep the Commandments. Women may also wear the shawl with some exceptions (Hume, 2010).

As a remedy to a distressful situation, even if prayer does not appear to work immediately, it may be effective in reducing the anxiety of an individual. Individuals may

---

IN-CLASS ACTIVITY
Islamic Women, Headscarves, and Migration

Often when people migrate into a new culture, they adopt the forms of dress worn by that culture. As Islamic women have migrated into Western cultures, many have continued to wear the headscarf. Continuing to wear a headscarf makes their appearance unique in some situations. Why might young women, in particular, continue to wear this form of dress when they are not forced to? Other than to signify religious affiliation, how might this clothing function for these women? How might it function for the people associated with these women?

simply feel better if they have made some attempt or have done all that they could to control those things in life that are intrinsically unpredictable (Nanda & Warms, 2004).

RELIGIOUS DRESS AND THE SOCIAL ORDER

Practicing a religion serves as a method of social control; put another way, religion works to preserve the social order (Nanda & Warms, 2004). Beliefs about what ideas and actions are good and what ones are bad are reinforced within the sacred stories and behaviors provided by religion. This process gives these beliefs a sacred authority that is difficult to question especially when one is raised from birth within a specific religious viewpoint. To maintain control, religious leaders may prescribe how individuals representing different statuses (i.e., leaders) within the religion should dress, as well as prescribe the dress of the followers of the religion so that roles and lines of authority are easily visible (Tortora, 2010).

Consider for example, **ecclesiastical dress**, clothing and other items of dress worn by leaders of the Christian church (as distinct from followers) from the early Christian era until the present. In addition to identifying individuals within the church hierarchy, the dress worn by church leaders functions to separate the ordinary from the sacred, to emphasize the glory of God through beautiful garments, and to express religious devotion and humility (Renne, 2005).

Dress Differentiates the Ordinary from the Sacred

The hierarchy of the different status positions within the clergy is symbolized through the use of different colors of garments so that only certain statuses are allowed to wear specific colors or dress with specific features. For example, only the Pope (i.e., the top leader of the Roman Catholic Church) is allowed to put his coat of arms on the sash that he wears in his ordinary dress (Figure 14.3). Status and social position within the church leadership are also communicated by restricting specific items of dress. For example, the color scarlet is reserved for the clothing of cardinals (cardinals are one status position below the Pope).

Since the articles of dress worn by Christian religious leaders typically are not contemporary styles but rather stem from the time of the ancient Romans, dress separates leaders from the **laity** (i.e., followers of the church) because of its distinct nature. That the dress of leaders closely resembles the dress of an early time period also suggests the enduring nature and continuity of the Catholic religion to contemporary followers.

Dress Glorifies

As the garments worn during ceremonies are often made from even more expensive fabrics than ordinary dress and are further embellished (threads of gold or silver), their beauty symbolizes glory to God. Many people who attend weekly church services and are not church leaders, reserve specific items of their "best" dress for these services, perhaps also to symbolize respect to God as well as for their fellow worshippers. This behavior is less obvious in contemporary times than it was fifty years ago.

Dress Expresses Devotion

In addition, items of dress worn by leaders within the Catholic religion are **sacramental**. In addition to setting leaders apart from followers, items may be blessed by church leaders for the purpose of exciting good thoughts and increasing devotion in those who see them as well as in those who wear them. Thus, the degree of religiousness of an individual may be inferred from their dress, with the most religious displaying all of the required dress items of a particular religion.

RELIGIOUS DRESS AND SOCIAL INTERACTION

The dress of the religious leaders and followers, especially when it serves to set them apart from the external world, may either facilitate social interaction with others or inhibit it. It can facilitate social interaction because it easily identifies members to other members. One can easily tell similar others even from strangers because of shared items of dress.

Dress can inhibit social interaction because one may feel obligated to be on one's best behavior when in the presence of religious individuals or even fellow church members. Thus, some informal conversations (e.g., gossip) and behaviors (e.g., consuming alcohol) may not take place in their presence.

RITUALS

A ritual is a social act that consists of a set of behaviors used for specific occasions. Rituals are formal, stylized, repetitive, and can make life changes significant. They are endowed with symbolic meanings. People perform them in special places and often at set times. Rituals include **liturgical orders**, sequences of words and actions invented prior to the current performance of the ritual in which they occur. In other words, rituals are not created in the moment but exist prior to being enacted, thus people often participate in rituals that they did not develop (Nanda & Warms, 2004).

Rituals convey information about the participants and their traditions. Repeated year after year and generation after generation, dress is a significant component of rituals as it is frequently used to mark the importance of the change as well as to convey enduring messages, values, and sentiments. By taking part in rituals, participants signal that they accept a common social and moral order that transcends their status as individuals.

Rituals are often part of religious organizations (i.e., sacred) and include weddings, baptisms, and Bat/Bar mitzvahs. They can also be secular. Examples of secular rituals include family reunions, graduation ceremonies, presidential inaugurations, political conventions, holiday shopping, Comicon, sweet sixteen birthdays, club events, carnivals, debutante balls, and sporting events (Birrell, 1981; Blanchard, 1988).

Common to many rituals are forms of dress that play an integral part in the ritual (Figure 14.4). The dress worn

Figure 14.3

Pope Francis in everyday dress (white cassock [ankle-length garment with long sleeves], pellegrina [short shoulder cape], white fringed fascia [white sash], pectoral cross [silver cross], and white zucchetto [skull cap]).

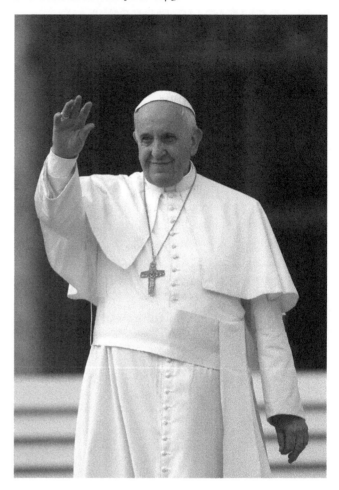

is often symbolic of the meaning of the ritual for the individuals involved in it and often marks a change in status for the individual(s) participating in the ritual. The status change may indicate that an individual is returning to an old status or acquiring a new one. For example, consider an induction into a leadership position such as becoming president of an organization. One person is assuming a new status (i.e., that of president) and another (the outgoing president) is returning to a previous status (i.e., member of the organization). The status change may be temporary, as in the previous case of taking on the role of president of an organization, or permanent. An example of a permanent status change is a high school or college graduation ceremony wherein an individual changes status from student to a graduate.

The specific content of religious rituals varies from culture to culture and organization to organization. There are two types of rituals that are extremely widespread: rites of passage and rites of intensification.

Rites of Passage

Rites of passage are public events that mark the transition of a person from one social status to another. Rites of passage are often linked to the life cycle of an individual as well as to life crises. People may participate in rites of passage as individuals or may participate as members of a group that are all experiencing the transition at the same time. (Kottak, 2003; Nanda & Warms, 2004).

Examples of transitions associated with the life cycle include birth, puberty, marriage, and death. Rites of passage are characterized by three stages: separation, transition (also referred to as liminality), and reincorporation. Often dress is used to emphasize one stage of the rite over other stages. In our discussion, we use an American marriage ceremony to illustrate the role of dress within each stage of a rite of transition but there are other examples that could be used from a range of cultures.

Stages in a Rite of Transition

Separation occurs when the individual(s) are disconnected from a former status. In marriage, separation can

be symbolized by an engagement ring (Figure 14.5). The engagement ring symbolizes a removal of a woman from an uncommitted status to the status of having made a promise to spend one's life with another individual. Other information can be communicated by the ring such as economic status (indicated by the type and size of stones present; type of metal used in the ring) or aesthetic preferences (indicated by the style of the ring) (Kottak, 2003).

Figure 14. 5
Engagement and wedding rings symbolize a separation from status as single individual to married individual. They often feature diamonds but can consist of other precious and semi-precious gems. Pictured here is a bride's engagement ring with coordinating wedding ring and groom's wedding band.

Transition is an in-between stage. The individual is not completely removed from the former status and has not achieved the new one either. To emphasize the ambiguity of this stage, symbols used often suggest nothingness or vagueness (Nanda & Warms, 2004). Returning to our marriage example, all of the activities surrounding the shopping for and purchase of a wedding gown and accompanying dress items can be symbolic of this stage wherein the individual is learning the bride status and accompanying role. This bride status in the marriage rite often lasts for only a few hours before a young woman undergoes the marriage ceremony and transitions to the new status of wife. In some instances, the new wife status is indicated as the bride changes from her wedding gown into a going-away outfit.

Reincorporation is the stage during which the movement from the previous status to the new status is completed (Kottak, 2003). Once reincorporation has occurred, the individual takes on the rights and responsibilities of the new status. Returning to the example of a marriage as a rite of passage, the wedding ring symbolizes a new status for both the bride and the groom. For the bride there may also be a bridal trousseau. The bride may have purchased or have been given new items of clothing to reflect her new status as wife. Consider for example, a gift of a negligee for her wedding night. The acquisition of the new status as wife may also involve changes to the ordinary or routine dress of both the husband and the wife as each exerts additional influence on the other's choices concerning their appearance (Yoo & Johnson, 2006).

As can be seen from our example, within a marriage ceremony between a man and a woman, often the emphasis is on the woman's dress rather than on the man's. The man's dress for the ceremony may be new but may also be rented. There is no expectation that the man needs to receive new clothing for his transition to his new status of husband. Perhaps this is because the transition is greater for women than it is for men. For example, in the United States a woman often changes her last name or adds a new last name to her original name but a man does not make similar changes.

An example of a secular rite of passage is the **debutante ball**. Debutante balls initially took place in Europe during the seventeenth century, a period of time characterized by class consciousness. Upper-class European families used the event to highlight the importance of heredity in establishing status. Women, who had reached a marriageable age and who were members of families of high social class and wealth, were presented to a select audience of men. This was an attempt to encourage marriage among members of similar social classes. Subsequently, debutante balls spread to the social elite of the US where they were again used to maintain class distinctions (Lynch, 1999).

Once only practiced by wealthy young women, making a debut has evolved into a coming-of-age experience for young men and women representing a range of incomes and ethnicities. Cultural versions of debutante events, such as the Hispanic Quinceañera, both introduce young people into society and celebrate cultural heritage. Making a debut no longer only signals a young woman's eligibility for marriage, but it is a rite of passage that denotes a transition to adult status (Haynes, 2005). Both debutantes and the fifteen-year-old Quinceañera honoree have similar dress expectations, including a long white formal gown, long gloves, elaborate hairstyle and makeup, and ornate accessories. In addition, Quinceañera honorees often have a court of assistants who are also elaborately dressed.

Sometimes participation in a rite of passage into a new status or group requires that the group identity transcend the individual member's personality. To achieve this, the organization may require that members wear a uniform to reduce physical distinctions such as those that exist based on age or gender. For example, The Heaven's Gate cult emerged in the 1970s as a new age religion that combined ideas from Christian doctrine and science fiction (particularly travel to other worlds) with ideas about evolutionary advancement. Several men in the group underwent castration to increase androgyny as a means to submerge individual members into a group identity ("One year later," 1998). The group became highly visible when members

---

IN-CLASS ACTIVITY
Rites of Passage

There are many rites of passage that people can participate in. Think about a rite of passage that you participated in that was very important to you. How was dress used in that rite? What stage of transition did the dress you wore highlight? Individuals often keep the dress items used for extended periods of time that are associated with rites of passage. Have you kept that item or those items of dress? Why, or why not?

TABLE 14.1

RITES OF PASSAGE, DRESS AND STAGE OF RITE EMPHASIZED

Rite of Passage	Item(s) of Dress	Stage of Rite Emphasized
Baptism	Baptismal gowns/new dress	Reincorporation into God's fold
Graduation	Cap and gown	Separation from student status
Initiation into sorority	White dress	Reincorporation into new group
Confirmation	New dress/white gown	Reincorporation into church as full member
Debutante	White gown and gloves	Separation from childhood
Quinceañera	Gown and high heels	Separation from childhood

committed mass suicide. Authorities found thirty-nine group members dressed in identical black shirts and sweat pants, black and white Nike Decades athletic shoes and armband patches that read "Heaven's Gate Away Team."

In what other rites of passage is there a special or new item of dress? And what aspects of the rite (e.g., separation, transition, reincorporation) are emphasized with the dress? Table 14.1 highlights some rites of passage wherein dress plays an important role.

Rites of Intensification

In addition to rites of passage, many groups have **rites of intensification**. These are rituals directed toward the well-being of the group or community rather than focusing on a status change of an individual. They often strengthen group identity. Through rites of intensification, groups maintain their connection to their past, enhance social unity, and renew the thoughts and feelings on which group cohesion is based (Nanda & Warms, 2004).

Rites of intensification can be either calendrical or critical. **Calendrical rites** take place at set intervals whether or not there is a need for immediate spiritual or supernatural help. These rites are scheduled well in advance and are performed for the benefit of all members of a religion, social organization, or community. Common examples within the US include New Year's Eve celebrations, Thanksgiving dinners, and Memorial Day events.

Critical rites are performed as needed, thus they are not held at stated intervals nor are they scheduled in advance. They often involve appeals to supernatural forces to overcome adversity. An example of a critical rite is a protest march. Protest marches enable participants to express their ideas and feelings about an issue to the larger society. Individuals may wear the same or similar items of dress to communicate their shared beliefs.

MAGIC

Even though individuals turn to religion as a means to gain a sense of control over events in life, we also find attempts to invoke magic in all types of societies. **Magic** refers to the use of supernatural techniques (e.g., spells, formulas, or incantations) to accomplish specific aims (Kottak, 2003). Magic is an attempt to use words and actions to compel spirits to behave in specific ways. Failure to achieve the desired outcome is typically thought to result from an incorrect performance of the ritual rather than because of a refusal of the spirits to act (Nanda & Warms, 2004). Magic is similar to religion in that it also can help people explain the inexplicable and it can serve emotion needs. For example, magic can reduce anxiety in times of crisis such as the death of a loved one.

There are two types of magic: imitative and contagious. In **imitative magic** the magician imitates the effect he or she is trying to achieve. Sticking pins into a voodoo doll that has the appearance of a specific individual for the purpose of harming that individual is an example of imitative magic (Nanda & Warms, 2004). **Contagious magic** rests on the idea that an object that has been in contact with an individual retains a magical connection with that person. Thus, if one can acquire that object, one can either receive the attributes of that individual or exert some type of influence on the individual. Sometimes practitioners of contagious magic use objects of dress from the potential victim of their efforts. They may use their hair or their nails for example. The spell performed on the dress item is believed to eventually reach the person.

Articles of dress are often attributed special power and importance once they have come into contact with famous or infamous individuals. Sports memorabilia (e.g., signed baseballs, jerseys), costumes worn by actors and actresses, or pens that have been used to sign important documents can be attributed to good fortune and, consequently, can be considered highly desirable.

Magic or good fortune can be summoned using items of dress. Good luck can be evoked by students particularly in situations where they feel unprepared. Consider for example that as a student you might invoke magic by wearing your "lucky" socks or by bringing a lucky charm (e.g., pencil, cap) to an examination in the hope that these dress items and/or behaviors will help your performance during the test.

Professional athletes may also use items of dress to invoke good luck when they compete. For example, good fortune may be summoned specifically by baseball players when participating in the two areas of baseball (e.g., hitting, pitching) that are the least predictable. Players might wear the same socks or cap, refuse to have their hair cut or shave their face, leave a button of their shirt undone, or refuse to have dress items cleaned to bring good luck and keep a hitting or pitching streak alive (Gmelch, 1995).

EVERYDAY RITUALS: HYGIENE/HEALTH

In addition to religion, another universal cultural pattern consists of behaviors that reflect ideas about hygiene or health. These ideas often develop into daily rituals as we use dress to manage our appearance and at times, contribute to our health (e.g., brushing and flossing teeth to reduce tooth decay and loss, wearing devices to monitor our physical activity or bodily functions).

When reflecting on beliefs that deal with dress and hygiene, there are two approaches. One approach is a **scientific approach**. This perspective is concerned with the maintenance of the physical health of the body and the prevention of disease itself or the spread of a disease. The

other approach is the **cultural approach**, which refers to how a culture defines being clean. Each approach is discussed further with a focus on how some of these beliefs contribute to everyday ritual behavior concerning dress.

Scientific Approach

There are several ways that dress contributes to human health. There are instances where dress provides a complete environment for humans that enables them to enter into what would be physically hostile and dangerous locations that would otherwise result in death. Space suits provide a complete environment that enables astronauts to enter into space while maintaining the functioning of their bodies. SCUBA (i.e., self-contained underwater breathing apparatus) suits allow divers to experience the ocean's depths without physical harm to their bodies (Figure 14.6). Firemen wear clothing that shields them from the extreme conditions of a fire and hazard suits protect workers from toxic chemical or biological environments. Indeed, health-protective apparel has been developed for most occupations that threaten physical well-being (Watkins, 2005) so that the donning and doffing of such items is a ritual part of worker behavior in these professions.

In addition to providing a complete environment for the body, dress can also supplement the body to enable people to remain in hostile environments for extended periods of time. Consider using items of dress to be able to tolerate the extreme cold of an Icelandic winter or the extreme heat of tropical summers.

Items of dress can also be used to maintain or enhance bodily functions, consequently contributing to maintenance of health. Compression stockings can be worn to enhance blood flow and reduce blood pressure. Individuals wear arch supports in their shoes to prevent or to treat ailments such as plantar fasciitis. An array of dress items can be worn to avoid sports injuries and become part of

Figure 14.6

Dress can maintain the health of an individual by providing an entire environment.

the ritual of preparing for participation. Take, for example, participation in cycling. A team of researchers interviewed cyclists who had crashed and were sent to hospital emergency rooms. Cause and prevention of injuries was tied to dress items worn rather than to the fabric or material that the item was made from. Injuries to arms and legs were linked to wearing short rather than long-sleeved tops and pants. Wearing open footwear contributed to foot and ankle injuries. Finally, cuts and abrasion injuries were prevented by wearing full cover gloves (deRome, Boufus, Georgeson, Senserrick, & Ivers, 2014).

One's health can be managed through wearing items of dress that monitor body processes or by simply wearing clothing that is comfortable because of fit or technological developments in fibers. The invention of devices such as fitbits® assist wearers with achieving fitness goals as it monitors number of steps taken daily, calories burned, heart rate, and sleep cycles.

Some items of clothing are worn because, at one point in time, they were believed to provide health benefits.

Even in the face of research that documented no such health benefits accrued from use, due to cultural beliefs, people continue to wear the clothing. Take for example, athlete supporters (jock straps) for men. The supporter was invented to offer the wearer relief from scrotal injuries, muscle strains, and fatigue. Developed in the 1800s to limit jostling felt by cyclists riding over cobblestone streets, the jock strap was never justified by physiology because it provided no discernable health advantage. Dolnick (1993) noted that most men believe the jock strap is overkill yet many men continue to wear them.

When reflecting on other forms of everyday dress that promote the health of individuals, what comes to mind is the use of items of dress to control the growth of bacteria, elimination of germs, or the treatment of dress items to do the same. In the marketplace we have several items of dress that are designed specifically to reduce the growth of bacteria or eliminate it. These items include hand sanitizers and bandages. Often when traveling in areas of the world where water is scarce or is not readily available, tourists can be seen ceremonially applying hand sanitizers prior to eating.

We also prevent the spread of disease or bacterial growth by cleaning our clothing with detergents and bleaches that are designed to remove dirt, germs, and bacteria. Specific items of dress may also be worn to prevent the spread of ailments. In several Asian countries (e.g., China, Korea, Japan), it is not uncommon to see people wearing masks to prevent the spread of colds to others or to prevent their catching someone else's cold.

Thus far, our focus has been on physical health. Dress items can also contribute to the mental health of individuals. Fashion rehabilitation programs exist in some areas for individuals recovering from mental illness. One example is the annual Fashion and Talent Showcase sponsored by the Mental Health Association in Tulsa, OK. The event is designed to celebrate participants' journey to wholeness. The event is designed to build self-esteem, as individuals recovering from mental illness are models in the fashion show and are able to socialize in a supportive environment. Models keep their outfits and many of the outfits are worn for subsequent job interviews and employment.

A state of undress or nudity can also be used for therapeutic benefits (Barcan, 2005). **Nudity** or nakedness[3]

---

[3]Some groups who practice nudity within social groups are referred to as nudists and others as naturists.

QUESTIONABLE CLAIMS AND HEALTH /BEAUTY PRODUCTS

Sometimes manufacturers make products claims concerned with improving health or enhancing physical beauty. Controversy has arisen over such "health" and "beauty" products that make these claims that cannot be substantiated by science. For example, do certain weight loss products really result in weight loss? If so, do they use safe ingredients? Several weight loss products have been taken off the market because the primary ingredient in them was ephedra (Chinese ma huang), known to be extremely risky to health because it causes heart attacks, stroke, and psychoses in high doses. Ephedra is an appetite suppressant because it acts as a powerful stimulant, especially in conjunction with caffeine (Hass, 2015). The US federal government banned ephedra in 2004, yet it is still available on the black market. Weight loss product manufacturers have also found many other powerful plant-based substitutes to manufacture similar products to replace those with ephedra.

While weight loss is touted as a healthy practice in the face of a rising obesity epidemic, does the end justify the means for many weight loss products on the market? In the larger, multi-billion dollar food supplement and weight training supplement industry, many products do not undergo ingredient testing by the FDA. Therefore, consumers may have no guarantee of the purity of ingredients in these supplements. What risks do consumers assume when they buy these products? What risks do advertisers and manufacturers assume?

The Federal Analog Act passed in 1986 is a part of the US Controlled Substances Act. It targets "designer drugs" that are chemically similar to any controlled substance listed in Schedule I or II of the act (for example, similar to heroin) if it is intended for human consumption (Sathappan, n.d.). Certain over-the-counter products have been found to have substances that are on the chemical watch list. As future retailers making decisions about what products you will offer to your customers, what obligations do you have to ensure product claims are valid?

is often believed to provide physical and mental health benefits. Early nudism was advocated as "a panacea for social ills and the detrimental effects of modern life on the human mind and body" (Woodall, 2002, p. 271). Although not a cure for all social ills, contemporary benefits include stress reduction, spiritual benefits (Story, 2000), development of healthy body image (Negy & Winton, 2008; Story, 1979), and the development of positive attitudes toward self (Sussman, 1977).

Cultural Approach

Another approach to thinking about health and hygiene is the cultural approach. Definitions of *clean* (i.e., hygienic) versus *dirty* vary by culture. These definitions can be influenced by scientific developments such as detergents and bleaches that make clothing "whiter than white" as well as by geographic constraints that can make cleaning the body and items of dress challenging. For example, if you lived in an area where water was not readily available, you might not bathe your body or wash your clothing as often as if you lived in a climate where water was plentiful. Thus,

cultural definitions are not completely removed from scientific ones.

Removal of Body Hair

One body modification presumably related to health and that varies between cultures is the removal of body hair (also referred to as **epilation** or **depilation**). Hair typically grows in many locations on the human body (e.g., head, face, arms, legs, armpits, pubic area, chest). Within the US, hair removal did not become an issue until the 1870s when the American Dermatological Association created a category for the treatment of excessive body hair (i.e., hypertrichosis) and labeled excessive body hair a problem for women that required treatment (Labre, 2002).

Toward the end of World War II, the removal of female body hair became normalized. Fashion magazines and beauty guides promoted the hairless ideal with the first focus on removal of armpit hair and the second on removal of leg hair (Labre, 2002). At this time, advertisements promoted the removal of hair as a means to increase attractiveness as well as to increase economic opportunities.

Hairlessness in women or in men has not been frequently addressed in research. What is known is that women in the US do routinely remove armpit and leg hair (Basow, 1991; Tiggemann & Kenyon, 1998) and that reasons provided for this hair removal include to avoid criticism, to follow social norms, to be feminine, and to be attractive. Indeed, in research with undergraduates, Basow and Braman (1998) found that hairless women were perceived as more attractive, positive, intelligent, and sociable and less aggressive, active, and strong than women with hair in their armpits and/or on their legs.

It is not too surprising that the battle against hair on women has spread to the pubic region (Tiggemann & Hodgsen, 2008). Pubic hair removal has been identified to have various benefits such as making women feel cleaner than when they are natural. One notable procedure to remove pubic hair featured and promoted within the media (e.g., fashion magazines, television shows, internet) is the Brazilian wax (Labre, 2002). One of the women credited with developing the technique claimed that waxing, and the Brazilian wax in particular, made women both clean and sexy (Labre, 2002). However, in promoting the removal of pubic hair, several important facts were left out including that the procedure was not popular with Brazilian women and that it did not contribute to cleanliness. Rather, it may actually contribute to health problems (Labre, 2002).

Pubic hair in women functions to protect the vulva from bacterial infections. Its removal can result in problems ranging from contact dermatitis to bacterial infections to the spread of viral infections (e.g., herpes) as the pores of the skin are left open for a period of time after the hair is removed. Open pores can be especially problematic if the women doing the procedure do not wash their hands before the procedure or wear sterile gloves (Tiggemann & Hodgsen, 2008; Tragar, 2006).

A somewhat hairless social norm also exists for US men. Even though men wear beards and mustaches, it is far more common for men to be clean-shaven. Hair is also removed from a man's groin, abdomen, and chest (Burroughs, Cafri, & Thompson, 2005). Reasons for hair removal include cleanliness, increasing sex appeal, making bodies appear muscular, and seeing other men practicing hair removal (Burroughs, Cafri, & Thompson, 2005). Thus, reasons for hair removal for both sexes appear to be tied more closely to aesthetic considerations than to maintaining health.

Body Cleanliness

Within the US, many people have cleanliness related rituals. In fact, some people may be viewed as having an obsession with body cleanliness. Many individuals shower more than once per day, wear deodorant or anti-perspirant (sometimes in combination with colognes, perfumes, aftershave), and brush their teeth more than after every meal. They use an array of products to scent the body, smooth their skin, and conceal skin blemishes. These products may also directly impact the health of the skin as they can have additional functions such as skin creams with SPF protection from the ultraviolent rays of the sun.

Although some cleanliness behaviors may be viewed as normal or even expected, others might be considered peculiar. Take, for example, blowing one's nose to remove mucous (Figure 14.7). Within the US, some individuals collect their mucous in swatches of fabric called handkerchiefs or hankies that must be subsequently laundered rather than use disposable facial tissues. In contrast, people in China simply remove the mucous from their noses by pressing against one of their nostrils and blowing hard through the other nostril. This practice is consistent with

Figure 14.7
Prince Phillip uses a handkerchief to collect his mucous.

How often do we clean our clothing?

Being clean is a relative term. For some individuals being clean means being in a state where there is no visible sign of dirt anywhere on the body and no body odor. This belief can result in daily showers or bathing. However, there are other people who believe this state of clean is not realistic. They may believe this for a variety of reasons. They may not have ready access to facilities so that they can keep their bodies in a state of clean or they may believe that washing the body removes good fortune. As a result, they may clean their bodies less frequently.

Just like there can be differences in what comprises a clean body, there are likely differences in what is considered clean clothing and how often clothing can be worn before it needs to be cleaned. For example, while people may decide to wear the same pair of jeans several times before washing them, they often change their underwear daily. Perhaps this is because underwear is worn close to the body and the impact of perspiring and other bodily functions that impact the cleanliness of underwear occurs sooner than it does to other items of clothing. Perhaps they were simply taught to change their underwear daily. While we might expect cultural differences in beliefs concerning clothing cleanliness, a survey conducted by Clorox revealed that within the US gender differences exist concerning how often clothing items can be worn before they need to be cleaned (Strickler, 2011).

The researchers reported that nearly 50 percent of men have no problem wearing clothing items, including underwear, several times before washing them. The research, done with 1,200 adults, found that when men do the laundry they rely on a "sniff test" to determine whether clothing actually needs cleaning. Blue jeans averaged five wearings between washing and underwear was worn twice (although 12 percent of the men indicated they often wear underwear three times before washing). If you think that single men clean their clothing more often (perhaps because they want to impress significant others), you would be wrong as it is men in relationships that tend to wear clothing that is cleaned more often than men not in relationships.

the belief that physical health is promoted by expelling bodily fluids. To members of both cultures, the corresponding practice could be viewed as unhygienic.

Chinese customs of expelling the bodily waste of children may also appear to be unhygienic to Western eyes. In China, babies and toddlers are often not diapered as they are in many Western cultures. Young children wear crotchless pants and are taught to squat where they stand when they have to urinate or defecate. This practice may appear to be unclean to some just as it could be considered unhygienic to collect urine and feces in diapers. Moreover, this latter practice can easily result in the formation of an unhealthy condition (e.g., skin rash) on children's bottoms.

DRESS AND THREATS TO HEALTH

There are also examples of items of dress that may be threats to physical health if worn over prolonged periods of time. For example, wearing certain types of shoes has been identified as a body modification that can result in negative effects. Perhaps the most extreme case of modified feet is the **lotus foot** of China. As noted in "Chapter 1: Why Study Dress?" Chinese footbinding had the effect of shortening feet and changing the location of support for body weight (Watkins, 2005). Some styles of lotus shoes enabled the weight to be carried on the heel of the foot removing any strain that could be placed on the toes. Although the practice did not break the bones of the foot, it made walking extremely difficult and running nearly impossible.

Not too dissimilar to the effects of the Chinese foot binding is the wearing of high-heeled shoes by women around the world. High-heeled shoes result in bending the toes up while slanting the foot down. Over time, wearing high-heeled shoes result in shortening part of the leg's calf muscle making wearing shoes with low heels difficult. Since weight is shifted toward the balls of the feet, these shoes can also result in blisters and compression on the toes depending on how long and how often the shoes are worn. Other ailments attributed to wearing high heels include bunions, hammertoes, and a range of knee problems. Regardless of the shoe worn, a glance at anyone's feet demonstrates that wearing shoes in general alters the shape of the foot and consequently, can impact its functioning.

Chapter Summary

Religion is the process humans use to assist in ordering the world and to provide meaning, unity, peace of mind, and a sense of degree of control over events. Dress plays an important role within religion as it provides a visible group identity, provides a means to exert social control over members of religious organizations, and enables the beliefs of members to be symbolized. An important component of religion is ritual wherein members can reinforce their beliefs. Dress is often a significant component of rituals as it is used to convey enduring messages, values, and sentiments of the participants. Even though individuals turn to religion as a means to gain a sense of control over events in life, we also find attempts to invoke magic in all types of societies. Magic refers to the use of supernatural techniques (e.g., spells, formulas, or incantations) to accomplish specific aims.

Religion is an important cultural pattern that shapes individuals' ideas and behaviors about dress. Health and hygiene is another important cultural pattern that affect ideas about dress. Cultural differences exist between beliefs about the relationship between dress and human health. Dress provides numerous health benefits to humans, including enabling them to experience environments not possible without specialized dress and enhancing body functions. Items of dress and dress practices can also harm the body.

Key Terms

calendrical rite	garment or endowment	plain dress	rusari
contagious magic	hijab	prayer	sacramental
cosmology	human universal	prayer beads	sacred narratives
critical rite	imitative magic	prayer shawl	scientific approach
cultural approach	laity	reincorporation	separation
debutante ball	liturgical orders	religion	transition
depilation	lotus foot	rites of intensification	
ecclesiastical dress	magic	ritual	
epilation	nudity	rupush	

Discussion Questions

1. Explain how dress can be used within the three stages of a rite of passage.

2. How does an item of dress become sacred?

3. Identify a secular ritual not discussed in the text in which dress is important. Explain how dress is used in this ritual.

4. In the text, examples were provided that detailed how dress can impact human health. Identify other examples of items of dress or practices related to dress that are not beneficial to human health and explain why.

STUD!O

Visit your book's STUDIO for additional quiz questions and vocabulary flashcards!

Suggested Readings

Dwyer-McNulty, S. (2014). *Common threads: A cultural history of clothing in American Catholicism.* Chapel Hill, NC; University of North Carolina Press.

Hume, L. (2013). *The religious life of dress: Global fashion and faith.* New York, NY: Bloomsbury Publishers.

Silverman, E. (2013). *A cultural history of Jewish dress.* New York, NY: Bloomsbury Publishers.

References

Arthur, L. (1999). *Religion, dress and the body.* Oxford, UK: Berg Publishers.

Barcan, R. (2005). Nudity. In V. Steele (Ed). *Encyclopedia of clothing and fashion* (pp. 458–460). Farmington Hills, MI: Thomson Gale.

Basow, S. (1991). The hairless ideal: Women and their body hair. *Psychology of Women Quarterly, 15,* 83–86.

Basow, S., & Braman, A. C. (1998). Women and body hair: Social perceptions and attitudes. *Psychology of Women Quarterly, 22,* 637–645.

Birrell, S. (1981). Sport as ritual: Interpretation from Durkheim to Goffman. *Social Forces, 60*(2), 354–376.

Blanchard, K. (1988). Sport and ritual—A conceptual dilemma. *Journal of Physical Education, Recreation, and Dance, 59*(9), 48–52.

Burroughs, M., Cafri, G., & Thompson, J. (2005). Male body depilation: Prevalence and associated features of body hair. *Sex Roles, 52,* 637–644.

de Rome, L., Boufous, S., Georgeson, T., Senserrick, T., & Ivers, R. (2014). Cyclists clothing and reduced risk of injury in crashes. *Accident Analysis and Prevention, 73,* 392–398.

Dolnick, E. (1993). Goodbye to an old supporter. *Health, 7*(2), 114–116.

Druesedow, J. (2010). Snapshot: Amish, Mennonites, Hutterites, and Brethen. In J.B. Eicher (Ed). *Berg encyclopedia of world dress and fashion, Vol 3- The United States and Canada.* Retrieved from http:/dx.doi.org.ezp2.lib.umn.edu/10.2752/BEWDF/ED.ch3066

Fischer, G. V. (1999). The obedient and disobedient daughters of the church: Strangite Mormon dress as a mode of control. In L. Arthur (Ed). *Religion, dress, and the body* (pp. 73–94). Oxford, UK: Berg.

Frankl, V. (1946). *Man's search for meaning.* Boston, MA: Beacon Press.

Gmelch, G. (1995). Baseball magic. In M. E. Roach-Higgins, J. B. Eicher, & K.K.P. Johnson (Eds). *Dress and identity* (pp. 251–259). New York, NY: Fairchild.

Haas, R. (2015). Appetite suppressant with ephedra. Retrieved from http://www.livestrong.com/article/496232-appetite-suppressant-with-ephedra/

Hamilton, J., & Hawley, J. (1999). Sacred dress, public worlds: Amish and Mormon experience and commitment. In L. Arthur (Ed). *Religion, dress, and the body* (pp. 31–51). Oxford, UK: Berg.

Haynes, M. (2005). Debutante dress. In V. Steele (Ed). *Encyclopedia of clothing and fashion* (pp. 348–350). Farmington Hills, MI: Thomson Gale.

Hume, L. (2010). Dress and religion. In J.B. Eicher (Ed). *Berg encyclopedia of world dress and fashion, Vol. 10: Global perspectives.* Retrieved from http://dx.doi.org.ezp1.lib.umn.edu/10.2752/BEWDF/EDch10010

Hume, L. (2013). *The religious life of dress.* New York, NY: Bloomsbury.

Iranian 'moral police' enforcing 'un-Islamic' dress code. (2011). *Fox News.* Retrieved from http://www.foxnews.com/world/2011/06/15/iranian-moral-police-enforcing-un-islamic-dress-code.html

Kottak, C. (2003). *Mirror for humanity: A concise introduction to cultural anthropology.* New York, NY: McGraw-Hill.

Labre, M. (2002). The Brazilian wax: New hairless norm for women. *Journal of Communication Inquiry, 26*(2), 113–132.

Levinson, D. (1996). *Religion: A cross cultural dictionary.* New York, NY: Oxford University Press.

Lynch, A. (1999). *Dress, gender and cultural change.* Oxford, UK: Berg.

Nanda, S., & Warms, R. (2004). *Cultural anthropology* 8th Ed. Belmont, CA: Thomson.

Negy, C., & Winton, S. (2008). A comparison of pro-and anti-nudity college students on acceptance of self and of culturally diverse others. *Journal of Sex Research, 45*(3), 287–294.

One year later, Heaven's Gate suicide leaves only faint trail. (1998, March 25). *CNN.* Retrieved from http://www.cnn.com/US/9803/25/heavens.gate/

Patel, D. (2012). Concealing to reveal: The informational role of Islamic dress. *Rationality and Society, 24*(3), 295–323.

Peralta, E. (2015). Judge reduces sentences for Amish involved in beard-cutting attack. Retrieved from http://www.npr.org/sections/thetwo-way/2015/03/02/390244303/judge-reduces-sentences-for-amish-involved-in-beard-cutting-attacks

Renne, E. (2005). Ecclesiastical dress. In V. Steele (Ed). *Encyclopedia of clothing and fashion* (pp. 395–400). Farmington Hills, MI: Thomson Gale.

Salamone, F. (1999). The Polynesian cultural center and the Mormon image of the body: Images of paradise on Laie, Hawai'i. In L. Arthur (Ed). *Religion, dress, and the body* (pp. 53–71). Oxford, UK: Berg.

Sathappan, H. (n.d.) The federal controlled substances analogue act: An antiquated solution meets an evolving problem. Retrieved from http://moritzlaw.osu.edu/students/groups/osjcl/amici-blog/the-federal-controlled-substances-analogue-act-an-antiquated-solution-meets-an-evolving-problem/

Scott, S. (2008). *Why do they dress that way?* New York, NY: Skyhorse Publishing.

Shirazi, F. (2000). Islamic religion and women's dress code: The Islamic Republic of Iran. In L. Arthur (Ed). *Undressing religion* (pp. 113–130). Oxford, UK: Berg

Story, M. (1979). Factors associated with more positive body self-concepts in preschool children. *Journal of Social Psychology, 108*, 49–56.

Story, M. (2000). The naturist society: A brief history. Retrieved from http://www.naturist.com/tns/about/History.html

Strickler, J. (2011, July 24). Real men wear dirty underwear. *Strib Express*, p. 1A.

Sussman, S. (1977). Body disclosure and self-disclosure—Relating two modes of interpersonal encounter. *Journal of Clinical Psychology, 33*(4), 1146–1148.

Tiggemann, M., & Hodgsen, S. (2008). The hairless norm extended. *Sex Roles, 59*, 889–897.

Tiggemann, M., & Kenyon, S. (1998). The hairless norm: The removal of body hair in women. *Sex Roles, 39*(11/12), 873–885.

Tortora, P. (2010). Religion and dress. In J.B. Eicher (Ed). *Berg encyclopedia of world dress and fashion, Vol 3- The United States and Canada.* Retrieved from http:/dx.org.ezp2.lib.edu./10.2752/BEWDF/ED.ch3064

Tragar, J. (2006). Pubic hair removal: Pearls and pitfalls. *Journal of Pediatric & Adolescent Gynecology, 19*, 117–123.

Watkins, S. (2005). Fashion, health and disease. In V. Steele (Ed). *Encyclopedia of clothing and fashion* (pp. 43–46). Farmington Hills, MI: Thomson Gale.

Woodall, E. (2002). The American nudist movement: From cooperative to capital, the song remains the same. *Journal of Popular Culture, 36*(2), 264–284.

Yoo, J., & Johnson, K. K. P. (2006). Clothing adoption: Application of a fashion adoption model to investigate spousal influences on clothing choices. *Clothing Research Journal, 4*(1), 5–9.

GLOSSARY

A

a priori reasoning or knowledge that comes from theoretical deduction rather than from observation or experience

a priori questions questions developed prior to conducting the research

academic regalia academic garments worn at academic ceremonies

acculturation cultural contact with another culture that in some way affects behavior

achieved status positions you obtain as a result of your decisions and effort

adornment making the body aesthetically pleasing

aesthetics the study of beauty

aesthetic needs needs that reflect one's ability to search for and appreciate beauty

African American aesthetics aesthetic patterns that are a hybrid of both African and American elements of style

afunctional not functional

agrarian cultures groups of people settled into one area who raise crops

agreeableness one of the Big Five personality dimensions and is a tendency to be concerned about others

albinos individuals with no pigmentation in their skin, hair, and eyes

analytic or explanatory surveys a type of survey research that is used to explain relationships among variables within a population

androgynous identity someone with an androgynous identity would self-rate highly on both masculine and feminine traits

announce the use of dress to communicate identity

anorexia nervosa a disorder associated with extreme food restriction

anticipatory set a stage of the person perception process in which expectations may be formed regarding how that person will behave based on inferences about a person and things associated with the person

anticipatory socialization usually during the play stage of socialization, when children rehearse for roles that they can reasonably expect to assume

appearance emphasis includes the importance one places on one's looks and the extent of grooming behaviors in which one engages

appearance investment refers to the degree of an individual's beliefs about the importance, meaning, and influence of appearance in their life

appearance labor dissonance experienced as a result of a discrepancy between what one is expected to wear and what one prefers to wear

appearance management encompasses all attention, decisions, and acts related to one's personal appearance

appearance management behaviors routine or non-routine behaviors related to management of our appearance

appearance perception observing and interpreting the appearance of oneself and others

appearance rigidity insistence on wearing dress items that are closely tied to one sex or avoiding dress items linked to the opposite sex

apposition a process in establishing identity; apposition is the process of bringing a person together with others who are similar and claim the same identity

archaeology the study of past civilizations and ancient people for evidence concerning early forms of dress

artifacts material items produced by a culture, such as tools, dress, housing, and furnishings

ascribed status a social position that is obtained at birth

assimilation when a smaller culture is gradually accepted into a larger culture

atheoretical not based on theory

attached dress items of dress that are either added to the body (such as earrings) or to an item of clothing (such as fringe)

attitudinal component our emotional responses or feelings about our body

attribution a process that focuses on perceived causes of behaviors

attribution theories theories about how we search for causes for our behavior and the behavior of others

B

baseline beginning performance level

behavioral component our behavioral response to our body image, including eating, exercise, and other appearance management behaviors

between group difference a characteristic by which one group is distinguished from another

Big Five model a view of personality that suggests that personality consists of five dimensions

binge eating disorder (BED) eating extreme amounts of food on a regular basis without purging behavior

blaming the victim in attribution theory, when one blames the victim of a crime for the crimebody dissatisfaction negative thoughts and feelings about one's own body

body dysmorphic disorder intense hatred of a body part and extreme coping mechanisms

body image the mental construct held of one's body

body image disturbance dissatisfaction and distress related to physical appearance that impairs social and occupational functioning

body mass index or BMI a ratio of height to weight used to categorize people as underweight, average weight, overweight, or obese

body modifications changes made directly to the body itself, either temporary or permanent

body satisfaction positive thoughts and feelings about our own body

body supplements additions of items to the body, such as jewelry, clothing, and accessories

body type a person's overall shape or silhouette

body work complicated beauty regimens and body modifications

Botulinum Toxin Type A a toxin that is injected into facial muscles to smooth wrinkles

brand image one's impression of a brand

brand management the planning and analysis of how a brand is perceived in the market by consumers

brand schema a partially integrated structure in memory consisting of consumers' knowledge about products and brands

bulimia nervosa an eating disorder associated with bingeing on food and then purging

Burning Man aesthetics absurdity and nudity in dress by people attending Burning Man festival

C

calendrical rite rites that take place at set intervals

case law laws that come into effect when judges make legal decisions

caste system a closed stratification system

casual dress aesthetics relaxed aesthetic concerning dress in the workplace

categorization the process we use to mentally classify things into groups so that non-identical things are treated as equivalent; a part of the perception process

cathexis used in psychoanalytic theory, the investment of emotional significance in an idea, object, or activity; release of emotional tension

cause-related dress a term used to describe items of dress that have text, symbols, or images that express an opinion or an affiliation with a cause

characterization the process by which characters' identities (in books, tv, movies) are conveyed to audiences through what the characters say, what they do, and what they wear

chemical peel a chemical solution which is applied to the skin to remove the outer layers of skin

class system an open stratification system

closed stratification systems systems where there is no or very little movement permitted between social classes

clothing deprivation discontent with clothing in relation to peers; the feeling of not having enough clothing to be satisfied

clothing evaluative criteria criteria people use in their decision-making regarding clothing

cognitive need needs tied to desire for knowledge and self-awareness

collective definition a definition shared by people in a group

collective (group/social) identity an identity whose basis is group membership (e.g., gender identity, ethnic identity, religious identity)

collective self involves one's membership in various social groups including cultural groups

collectivistic orientation when individuals in a culture tend to emphasize the importance of groups and think in terms of "we"

color-in-context theory a theory that proposes that color conveys meaning and its meaning varies based on its context

colorism social stratification based on skin color between and within ethnic groups

communication the exchange of information

comparison target in social comparison theory, the person we compare to

conceptual framework a perspective that provides us with a set of words to use to make sense out of our experiences

conflict perspective a viewpoint that suggests an individual's personality is the result of two opposing forces that are continuously in conflict with each other

congruity theory a theory developed to explain how connections between products and selves might influence purchasing

conscientiousness one of the Big Five personality dimensions, a tendency to be organized, dependable, and show self-discipline

consideration set a set of products or brands that an individual consumer considers interchangeable

consumption event a commercial opportunity (a) to buy, (b) that impacts identity, (c) that involves wearing special clothing, and (d) in which product consumption reinforces the identity

contagious magic the idea that an object that has been in contact with an individual retains a magical connection with that person

content analysis a method for summarizing any form of content by counting various aspects of the content and focuses on the content of media (either verbal or nonverbal)

context variables in social perception, context variables are variables contained in the setting within which the stimulus person is perceived

contextual perspective of dress one method to study social meanings of dress, combining perspectives of knowledge, symbolic interaction, and culture/history

control group in experimental research, a group that is not exposed to the manipulation of the independent variable

controllability in attribution theory, refers to whether or not a cause is regulated by the individual

coping strategy in the Rudd and Lennon Model, a step taken if one is not satisfied with her appearance, to re-create her appearance to more closely approximate the cultural ideal of beauty

cosmology a set of beliefs about a range of questions that are sometimes not explained by science

cosplay a combination of the terms *costume* and *play*

costume dress characteristic of another period, place, or person

costume historians scientists who focus on the social, political, and economic context of the time in which a particular type of dress was worn

critical rite rites that are performed as needed

cross dressing wearing dress that is typically associated with the opposite sex

cue selection a stage of the person perception process in which a perceiver selects, from information available about another person (i.e., stimulus), the particular information (i.e., cues) which will be used as a basis for forming perceptions

cultivation theory accepting distorted media images of people as real and desirable body characteristics for ourselves

cultural aesthetic ideal cultural ideal of beauty

cultural approach an approach that reflects cultural beliefs as opposed to scientific beliefs

cultural authentication the process of assimilating into a culture an item or artifact that is not original to the culture

cultural complexity the level of cultural development found in a culture

cultural generality a practice that occurs in many, but not all, cultures

cultural relativity finding worth in all cultural practices, even if different from one's own

cultural scale theory distinguishes among cultures on the basis of kinship, political states, and commerce

cultural universal a practice that occurs in every culture

culture a complex whole that includes such aspects as knowledge, beliefs, art, laws, capabilities, and habits that are acquired as members of society

customs ways of behaving that are deeply rooted in tradition

D

dark triad personal traits that are socially negative: Machiavellianism, narcissism, and psychopathy

database a digital collection of information stored in a computer system that is organized for easy access

database search uses a search engine and operates on material stored in a digital database

debutante ball an event wherein women were presented to a select audience of men; traditionally an attempt to encourage marriage among members of similar social classes

defense mechanisms strategies people use to separate themselves from the unpleasant thoughts and feelings they may have as a result of their own behaviors

demographic characteristics characteristics that can be used to describe a group or population; (e.g., sex, age, income)

denial a defense mechanism that consists of the refusal to accept reality or fact

dependent variable in experimental research this is the outcome variable that is observed to determine how it is affected by the independent variable

depilation removal of hair by mechanical or chemical means

dermal fillers temporary or semi-permanent wrinkle fillers that are injected into the skin

descriptive surveys a type of survey research that is designed to describe a population

diaspora a group of people who have moved to different locations from their original culture but still maintain strong connection to their cultural heritage

discrimination a process that occurs when negative actions are taken with respect to a social group or individuals; it is a behavior

displaced homemakers typically women who need to return to the workforce due to divorce, a spouse's death, or a spouse's disability

displacement a defense mechanism that occurs when a behavior that should be directed at one person is directed towards another

distinctive appearance investment refers to the desire of an individual to look different and stand out from others

DIY project do it yourself project

domains of the self aspects or facets of the self that contribute to self-esteem

downshifted a change in lifestyle in order to consume less

downward social comparison comparing oneself to others believed to be inferior on some attribute

dramaturgy the main elements of drama on the stage

dress the total arrangement of all outwardly detectable modifications of the body and all material objects added to it

dress codes expectations for dress as established by an entity such as an employer or school

duration of norms how long or short the time of the norm

E

eating disorder a serious disturbance marked by extreme and unhealthy decreases/increases in food intake and extreme concern about body weight or shape

ecclesiastical dress clothing and other items of dress worn by leaders of the Christian church

EDNOS (eating disorder not otherwise specified) various types of eating disorders that do not clearly fit other diagnostic categories

effect size a quantitative measure of the strength of a phenomenon

ego from psychoanalytic theory, part of personality that balances between our needs and societal rules for how to satisfy them

ego differentiation the expression of a unique personality

ego-screaming attempts to create shock value and demand attention through one's appearance

elements the group of things being studied in any study

empirical research research that involves collection of original data

enculturation the process by which people embrace cultural beliefs

endowment a name for Mormon undergarments

endpoints the words and corresponding numbers at the ends of a rating scale

epilation the removal of hair by the roots by any means

esteem part of Maslow's hierarchy of needs and motivation; a need to be respected by others and to respect ourselves

ethnocentrism judging another culture by one's own cultural standards

ethnographies written descriptions of ethnic groups, sometimes with drawings or photographs

event schema or scripts describe sequences of events for well-known situations

executive function experiences that demonstrate the self as an active agent and decision maker

expectancy confirmation if people expect others to possess certain characteristics or to act in a certain way, then they are likely to find those characteristics and interpret those behaviors in that way

experimentation a research strategy in which researchers vary one or more variables and determine their effect on some outcome

exploratory research research in which the researcher is just beginning to examine a phenomenon

extended inference a stage of the person perception process in which characteristics are thought to be assigned to people not on the basis of selected cues and immediate links to associated meanings, but on the basis of interpretative inferences

extraversion one of the Big Five personality dimensions, a tendency to be outgoing, talkative, and sociable

F

factor analysis a statistical procedure applied as a data reduction or structure detection method

fantastic socialization during the play stage when children experiment with roles they cannot reasonably expect to assume

fashion therapy a form of socialization that teaches people how to dress and groom themselves, often to help them find jobs

fast fashion producing new items of dress with very short production time

field experiment an experiment conducted in a naturalistic or real-life context; participants usually do not know they are participants in research

fieldwork a research strategy that involves the study of actions, behaviors, relationships, and situations of people in their everyday lives; also known as field studies or field research

fitted dress items of dress cut and shaped to fit the body through seams, darts, or other means

folk cultures small groups of hunter-gatherers

folkways norms that are weak expectations of behavior

formal dress codes specific guidelines developed by organizations that prohibit or prescribe desired workplace appearance

formal socialization a type of socialization for which a knowledgeable person instructs others in a classroom type of setting

front all the materials needed to make a performance

fulfillment perspective a viewpoint that suggests that there is one force, one underlying tendency that is at the core of individual differences in behavior

functions purposes that dress serves

G

game stage during primary socialization when children learn and follow established game rules, learn what their roles are, and learn what the roles of others are

gender differences socially constructed differences related to men's and women's expected behavior

gender roles attitudes and behaviors a culture expects of men and women

generalizable A characteristic of research results that allow the researcher to infer from particular results to a broader population than the sample studied

generalizations general statements which are obtained by inferring from specific research results

generalized other how you believe that others think you should behave

generation gap different opinions and understandings of people raised in different time periods

global culture beliefs or practices that are shared across national boundaries

Goth aesthetics avoidance of materialistic or boring appearances, often through the use of dark clothing and use of black in body modifications

greenhorn newly arrived immigrant or newcomer who is unfamiliar with culture and customs

H

handheld dress items of dress that are held in the hand, such as a cane or briefcase

headshot a photo similar to a yearbook photo which includes head, neck, and perhaps shoulders

hegemony a cultural process of domination of one group or person over others

hijab derived from the traditional form of Iranian chador, the traditional hijab is one piece, black, and when worn covers a woman's head and body but leaves her face exposed

hit rate number of responses to phony personal ads which are used in research

human universal all societies have this feature of culture; religion is an example

I

id from psychoanalytic theory, part of personality comprised of our biological drives

ideal culture how we say people should behave in a given culture

ideal self-concept representations of attributes that are possible or ones that we want to have

identification a cognitive process in which an individual views him or herself as similar to another person

identity an organized set of characteristics that express the various aspects of who you are; who one is as an individual and where one fits as a member of society

identity construction the way in which identity is created through the decisions and choices we make

identity cues cues used by a target to suggest to perceivers the target's desired identity and to increase the likelihood that perceivers will form impressions of the target that accurately predicts the target's behavior

identity kit an assemblage of objects that enable an individual to manage their presentation to others (e.g., brushes, cosmetics, shavers, combs, lotions)

identity negotiation process in social interaction the way in which we convey and others affirm the identity in question

identity program planned strategy to package a business or other organization to develop an image and extend it to tie all aspects of the business together

ideology the principle beliefs and values of a culture, a group, or a social movement

imitative magic when a magician imitates the effect he or she is trying to achieve

immodesty uncovering or revealing certain parts of the body usually to draw attention

imperative important norm

impersonation pretending to be someone other than yourself; *see* passing

implicit content indirect content

implicit measures ways to assess the variable of interest without directly asking about the variable

implicit personality theory the view that impressions of people consist of specific traits and additional traits that we anticipate the person will have

impression formation the process of integrating various pieces of information about another person to form an overall impression of her/him

impression management selecting what we wear very carefully to try to control the kinds of impressions others form of us

independent variable in experimental research this is the variable that is manipulated to determine its effect on some outcome

individual difference variables variables that differ between people, thus, individuals differ in the extent to which they exhibit these variables; otherwise known as perceiver variables

individual stereotype an exaggerated belief associated with a social group that justifies our conduct in relation to that social group

individual/personal identity an identity whose basis is personality characteristics or personal traits

individualistic orientation when individuals in a culture tend to be self-centered, attribute success to individual efforts, promote themselves, and think in terms of "I"

informal socialization learning without a formal lesson; there is no planned effort to achieve a certain outcome

informant a research participant who supplies information to the researcher

information literacy the set of abilities that includes finding, accessing, evaluating, and using information

in-group a group wherein members feel that they share a common bond, share ideologies, come from a common background, or otherwise resemble other members of the group

institutional review board a group of people or committee from a university that has been formed to approve, monitor, and review medical and behavioral research involving people

interactionist theory a theory that focuses on interactions between two or more people

internalized homonegativity internalized social prejudice against homosexual orientation

interpersonal aspects of self includes the use of clothing as an aspect of appearance by which the self is established and validated and clothing as a symbol of self

interpretative inference a stage of the person perception process in which a perceiver infers traits of the stimulus person presumably on the basis of the selectively perceived dress cue(s) and on the meaning(s) the individual has linked to the selected cue(s)

interviews a type of data collection in which the researcher asks questions in a one-on-one manner with a participant

intimate self the aspect of self that one presents via dress and demeanor to significant others, close friends, relatives, and one's intimates

investiture a situation where someone else is deciding on the dress of another

J

jargon special words used in a discipline that may be difficult to understand and may not be commonly used outside research publications in one's field

K

kinship people related to each other based on descent or by marriage

knowledge restriction (to passing) there may be information obtained through cultivation and socialization that someone who is trying to pass does not have

L

laboratory experiments an experiment for which research participants engage in tasks in a neutral environment such as a laboratory

laity the body of religious worshipers as distinguished from the clergy

laser hair removal method of hair removal that uses intense pulsed light which is absorbed by pigment in the hair damaging the hair follicle and slowing growth

latent content content that is not manifest; hidden content that is not obvious

laws ways of behaving defined as regulations to be followed by all members of a group and enforced with specific sanctions

liturgical orders sequences of words and actions invented prior to the current performance of the ritual in which they occur.

lived experience personal experience in living in one's body and clothing over a lifetime

locus of causality the location of the cause in attribution theories

looking-glass self imagining how important others may think of you, or what characteristics others may assign to you based on appearance

lotus foot the name given to the shape of a foot in China after having been bound

love and belonging needs part of Maslow's hierarchy of needs and motivation, achieving emotionally-based relationships including friendship and love

M

Machiavellianism refers to individual differences in manipulativeness, insincerity, and callousness

magic the use of supernatural techniques (e.g., spells, formulas, or incantations) to accomplish specific aims

mall intercept A study for which surveys are handed out to consumers at a mall

manifest content easily observable content that resides on the surface of communication

manipulation variation planned by an experimental researcher

mass cultures cultures that operate on a mass level (production, communication, media)

master status a status that takes priority over other statuses

material self the body; its appearance and its functioning

materials natural or man-made items used in dress

mentifacts guiding beliefs, mores, and values that shape a culture

merchandise borrowing the practice of buying an item, using the item, and then returning the item to a retailer for a merchandise credit or refund

mere expression when people select clothing arbitrarily, and do not consciously attempt to use it to communicate anything to anyone else

meta-analysis an analysis procedure for which a researchers amasses a large literature review and is able to determine which results are consistent across the research literature

method of enumeration how counting is done in content analysis

microdermabrasion a procedure which "sands" the skin to remove the top layer of skin to stimulate new skin growth and collagen production

microsociological theory a theory which focuses on explaining small parts of society

mili term for dark or cold colors in the language of the Dani of New Guinea

modeling copying the behaviors of someone else based on observing that behaviors and the outcomes of that behavior

modesty covering certain body parts out of a sense of shame or embarrassment

mola term for bright or warm colors in the language of the Dani of New Guinea

moral restrictions for some, it is simply immoral behavior to pretend to be someone that you are not

mores expected behaviors that are considered important and related to morals

mummies human remains that are usually intentionally preserved by the environment

muscle dysmorphia obsession with weight lifting and muscularity

N

narcissism a trait characterized by dominance, exhibitionism, and exploitation as well as feelings of superiority and entitlement

national culture beliefs and behaviors shared by citizens of the same nation

naturists a group that practices nudity

need for uniqueness theory a theory that suggests people are constantly assessing their similarity and dissimilarity to others and that they act on these assessments; individuals' desired state of being is to be not too similar to others and also not too dissimilar from others

negative sanction a punishment for nonconformity

neotonous features facial features associated with neonates or infants such as small ears and small noses

neuroticism the tendency to experience negative emotional states

non-probability sample a sample for which the researcher is unable to specify the probability for which each individual within a population will be included in the sample

non-reactive research an umbrella term for research that does not intrude on the people being studied

normative discontent a cultural norm that glorifies being dissatisfied with the body

normative patterns social habits that guide the functioning of a group of people

norms general guidelines for behavior

nudity nakedness

number of discriminations the number of choices that are possible on a rating scale

O

observation a data collection technique in which researchers watch and record the behavior of interest

observational learning or modeling another term for modeling

open stratification or class system system that allows movement up and down social classes

openness to experience a tendency to enjoy new intellectual experiences and ideas

opposition a process in establishing identity; opposition describes how the new identity sets you apart from others

ordinary personology the process by which people come to know about each other

organic restrictions (to passing) aspects of your body that are inconsistent with the person or identity you are trying to claim for yourself

organization a large group of individuals that are trying to achieve specific goals

origins of dress when and where people first began to wear clothing or adorn the body

orthorexia compulsion with eating healthy foods

out-group a group to which people feel they do not belong

outsider perspective a view of a phenomenon by someone not a member of the group being studied

overweight bias viewing overweight people less positively simply because they are overweight

P

pan-human characteristic that is universal among humans

paradigms perspectives or world views about what research is and how it should be conducted

participant observers researchers who participate in the activities of the group being observed

particularities behaviors practiced solely by specific cultural groups

passing impersonating someone

pathology disease

patterns of culture aspects of culture that shape behavior of members of the culture

peer crowds large groups of peers that are similar in interests, appearance, or attitudes

peer-reviewed or refereed an attribute of scholarly sources that have been evaluated by other experts in the discipline

perceiver variables aspects of the perceiver that affect what he/she perceives

perceptual component an aspect of body image focused on what we know about our own body based on input from our senses

performance a term used to describe an attempt to manage a presentation of self

person perception how and what we perceive about people; that part of social cognition that is concerned with perceptual processing of information including dress and appearance cues

person schema a mental knowledge that contains information on what traits seem to go together in people

personal front all of the items we specifically connect with an individual such as dress, age, gender, facial expressions, and so forth

personal identity an identity whose basis is personal characteristics such as personality traits; also called individual identity

personal shopper or wardrobe consultant a retail worker who is trained to help shoppers select products, usually clothing; also called wardrobe or image consultant

personality enduring and somewhat stable characteristics of an individual; the attributes that sets an individual apart from others and makes him/her unique

physiological needs part of Maslow's hierarchy of needs and motivation; need for food, air, water, sex, and sleep

pilot test or study a pretest used by experimental researchers for stimulus development

placement a category to which others assign you

plain dress wearing items of clothing that do not conform to mainstream fashion and do not have embellishments or ornamentation (no jewelry including wedding rings)

play stage in primary socialization when the child takes on roles, experiments with roles, and observes how others react to her/his role performance

popular press sources of information that are written for the general public as opposed to being written for a scholarly audience; some examples are blogs, newspapers, magazines

population in any study the groups of things being studied

positive sanction reward for conforming to social expectations

post-test only control group design an experimental design consisting of two groups in which only one of the groups is exposed to a manipulation of the independent variable

prayer any conversation held with spirits or gods

prayer beads an item of dress that can be used to assist during prayer; a string of beads

prayer shawl a shawl worn by men of the Jewish faith during morning prayers

prejudice a pre-judgment of others without learning about them through interpersonal contact

pre-play stage a stage of primary socialization during which infants become social and respond to the caregivers in a pre-verbal way

prescribed role a term to describe the set of behaviors that a group of individuals expect should be done when any individual assumes a status

prescriptive dress code regulations that detail exactly what must be worn

pretest trial run of an experiment or questionnaire

primary groups are small, informal collections of individuals who interact with each other in personal, direct, and intimate ways

primary socialization the learning and acceptance of norms and values that occurs during the process of socialization

priming exposure to stimuli that affects later responses

private self same as intimate self

probability sample a sample with human participants for which a researcher is able to specify the probability with which each individual in a population will be included in the sample

processes methods to manufacture dress by hand or machine

program one's response to one's own appearance

prohibitive dress code regulations that indicate what items of dress are not to be worn by students

prohibitive laws laws that prohibit certain behaviors in order to protect the interest of all members of a culture

projection a defense mechanism that involves attributing your own undesirable characteristics to other people who do not have these faults

promotive laws laws that promote certain behaviors such as social policies

protection dress that maintain physical comfort in hostile environments (e.g., extreme cold, heat, harmful) and dress that provides psychological comfort to ward off harm or bring good luck

proximity of clothing to self (PCS) an indicator of the psychological closeness to clothing to self

pseudomorph a false form or image that has formed over time on items such as tools and that represents an earlier fabric structure or ornamentation, such as twined feather fabric

psychodynamic theory developed by Sigmund Freud, a theory that related personality to the relationship of conscious as well as unconscious internal forces that were primarily in a state of conflict within individuals

psychology the study of individuals, who live in social groups within a larger culture, and focuses on the perceptions, motivations, and understandings of individuals that contribute to behavior

psychopathy refers to manipulation and exploitation of others

public self consists of aspects of the self such as one's age, sex, and occupation; components of your self that you are willing to share with everyone

Q

qualitative study an inquiry into a social problem that is aimed at developing a complex, holistic picture that uses words, reports detailed perspectives of informants, and is conducted in a natural setting

quantitative study an inquiry into a social problem, which is based on testing a theory of variables and their relationships

queer an umbrella term for individuals who identify as gay, lesbian, bisexual, or transgendered

queer theory a viewpoint that challenges socially constructed categories of sexual identity

questionnaire a written set of self-administered questions or items

R

random assignment or randomization the process of randomly allocating research participants to treatment conditions in experimental research

random selection occurs when every element of the population has an equal chance of being selected for the research

rating scale a format for collecting information that allows users to select a response from a set of choices; a method of assigning a value to a stimulus along a dimension

rationalization a defense mechanism that consists of attempts to prove that a behavior is justifiable and therefore, acceptable

reaction formation a defense mechanism that entails presenting yourself as the opposite of what you really are to hide or conceal the truth either from yourself or from others

real culture how people actually behave in a given culture

reality television a type of television programming that features unscripted events using ordinary people instead of actors

real-self concept self-representations of an individual's actual attributes

reference groups a group of people that serves as a model for individual's behavior

reflexive consciousness is comprised of experiences wherein an individual's attention is focused on constructing a concept of oneself

regression a defense mechanism that involves a return to an earlier stage of development

regulative laws laws that regulate certain behaviors

reincorporation a stage during a rite of passage; the stage during which the movement from the previous status to the new status is completed

relational (role-related) identities identity whose basis is social relationships between people

relative deprivation feelings of deprivation that result from making comparisons to reference groups

reliable content analysis is reliable when two people coding the same content achieve the same results

religion a set of beliefs that humans use to assist in ordering the world and to provide meaning, unity, peace of mind, and a sense of degree of control over events

research a systemic process in which scholars formulate questions, gather data, analyze and interpret that data, and formulate conclusions

review others' reactions to an individual's appearance

risky behaviors appearance management behaviors that carry some health risk

rite of passage public event that marks the transition of a person from one social status to another

rites of intensification rituals directed toward the well-being of the group or community rather than focusing on a status change of an individual

ritual an event wherein members can reinforce their beliefs

role the behavior that we expect of others who occupy certain social positions or statuses

role ambiguity a situation in which the expectations for a particular social status are unclear

role conflict occurs when the expectations tied to two or more statuses are incompatible

role distance the perceived difference between your true self and the role you are playing

role models individuals who we aspire to be like and who influence our behavior

role perception one's view of the expectations of a role

role performance refers to the actual behavior of an individual in a role

role schema sets of behaviors expected of a person in a particular social position

role strain occurs when contradictory expectations exist about a given status or when there is a higher number of expectations than anyone could reasonably expect to meet

role theory the idea that within a society a certain position or status has associated with it a set of norms and expectations including expectations for how to dress

routine behaviors appearance management behavior that carry little health risk

Rudd and Lennon Model a model of body aesthetics that explains the active construction of bodily appearance as a function the cultural ideal of beauty

rupush part of a hijab, the outer gown

rusari part of a hijab, a square head scarf that can be draped around the head and contains fashion elements such as sewn coins, design patterns, colors, and embellishments

S

sacramental items of dress worn by leaders within the a religion

sacred dress dress that is associated with a religion, worn due to religious beliefs

sacred narratives stories that are believed to be true by members of a religious tradition; documentation of historical events, gods, spirits, and the origin of all things

safety needs part of Maslow's hierarchy of needs and motivation, need to achieve a sense of personal and financial security as well as needs for health and property

salience relevant, noticeable, important

sample in research, a subset of the population being studied

sampling the procedure of selecting the subset of the population to study

sanction rewards or punishments given for following or not following a norm

sanctions of norms reactions by others that are designed to ensure compliance with a norm

schema a mental knowledge structure containing information about a concept or stimulus, including its attributes and how they are related to each other

scholarly source sources of material intended to disseminate research and academic discussion within a discipline, which are published in academic journals; they tend to be written and read by scholars and experts in the field

scientific approach a health perspective that is concerned with the maintenance of the physical health of the body and the prevention of the disease itself or the spread of a disease

secondary groups a group to which an individual has limited emotional ties, whose members interact with each other in formal ways, and whose members often come together for practical purposes

secret self aspects of self that may or may not be shared with other persons

self a dynamic interactive system of beliefs, feelings, and motives that characterizes an individual

self-actualization a stage in development reflecting that an individual had achieved his or her full potential

self-concept a term that is used to describe an individual's thoughts about him or herself

self-consciousness the degree to which a person's attention is focused on one's self

self-consciousness theory is concerned with the extent to which an individual's attention is focused on the inner or outer aspects of self

self-cutting harming the body via small cuts or burns

self-definition in symbolic self-completion theory, an ideal or goal that is set up or pursued through the accumulation of relevant symbols

self discrepancy discrepancies between actual or real self and ideal self

self-esteem sense of self worth

self-help feature features or aspects of clothing that make the clothing easy to put on and take off

self-image the mental picture that an individual has about him or herself

self knowledge another term for self-concept, or all the knowledge we have about the self

self-monitoring describes the extent to which individuals observe their verbal and nonverbal presentations to fit them to particular situations

self-objectification treating oneself as an object rather than a person

self-perception theory a viewpoint that suggests we infer our own attributes using the same method that we use to infer the attributes of others

self-presentation when you manage the information you convey about yourself

self-produced cues are cues that arise from an individual's own actions and personal properties

self-schema trait dimensions along which we have clear self-conceptions (i.e., we are self-schematic)

self-sexualization valuing oneself based solely on sex appeal or treating oneself as a sexual object

self-verification an interactive process in which we (as targets) attempt to confirm who we are with other people (i.e., perceivers) through negotiation

separation a stage within a rite of passage; the individual(s) are disconnected from a former status

sex differences biological differences between men and women

sexual dimorphism characteristics of physical features that distinguish men from women

significant other a single individual that serves as a model for you or point of reference

situated self self-in-context

situational cues cues tied to the context and can consist of conventional definitions of how most people will or should feel in a given situation

smart clothing wearable technology for monitoring body functions

S-O-R Model a model of the process by which stimuli in an environment affects a perceiver's internal states, which in turn affect subsequent behaviors

social categorization the process we use to mentally classify people into groups so that non-identical people are treated as equivalent

social class socio-economic status

social cognition the use of mental or cognitive processes to think, perceive, judge, and make inferences about people

social comparison comparing oneself to other people on any dimension

social comparison theory a theory that explains that people want to know how well they are doing in various aspects of life; objective standards are preferred, but in their absence we will compare to other people

social groups a collection of individuals; can be primary or secondary groups

social learning theory a viewpoint that explains how individuals learn from observing the behaviors of others and the outcomes of those behaviors

social mobility social movement between classes

social perception how and what we perceive about people; that part of social cognition that is concerned with perceptual processing of information including dress and appearance cues

social position the standing of an individual in a given society and culture

social psychology of dress the study of dress and adornment in the larger context of appearance in human behavior in general

social science various sciences that study human behavior

social self one's social connections with others

social structure the way the social positions that exist are organized relative to each other

social stereotype consists of social or cultural representations of a social group

socialization agents the teachers of how to function in society

socialization theory a theory about how socialization occurs

socioeconomic status social class

sociofacts social institutions and norms that direct human behavior

sociology the study of humans in groups that are smaller than entire cultures, focusing on social structures, organization, interaction, and deviance

spin the act of trying to reinterpret in a positive way the impression conveyed

spiritual self how you see yourself in relation to the world around you

stability in attribution theory, refers to a cause that is permanent rather than temporary

state a temporary condition

status a socially recognized position within a social system

status set a term used to describe a combination of statuses

statute laws passed by governing bodies

steampunk fashion deconstructed (the "punk" part) neo-Victorian looks that incorporate technological aspects from the nineteenth century (the "steam" part)

stereotypes mental representations of a group and its members; they derive from the cultural construction of social groups, are molded by and reflect the actual social position of groups, and operate in basic psychological ways

stigma a deeply discrediting attribute

stimulus person in impression formation laboratory experiments, the person about whom judgments are made

stimulus variables aspects of the stimulus person that affect social perception

store image one's impression of a store

strategy a research strategy is a plan for conducting research

stratification process by which societies or groups place more or less value on different social positions

strength of norms whether the norm applies to a few people or to many people

string skirts body supplements that were suspended from the waist and made of string; early body coverings similar to aprons made of linen fiber

structured interview an interview conducted using a list of questions developed before the interview

structured observation a type of observation for which researchers determine what specifically they are watching for before beginning to observe

subculture or society smaller groups of people who share geography, language, lifestyle and beliefs

sublimation a defense mechanism that entails the channeling of unacceptable impulses into acceptable ones

substantive expression the use of clothing to intentionally communicate something to others

sumptuary laws specific laws governing who can wear what items of dress

superego from psychoanalytic theory, part of personality that consists of our memory of all the rules that we were taught growing up by our parents and other important members of society through the socialization process

survey research a research strategy in which a group of people is asked to respond to questions or statements

suspended dress items of dress that hang from a body part, such as the neck, waist, or hips

symbolic interaction a viewpoint that posits that the self is a social construction established, maintained, and altered through interpersonal communication with others

symbolic models individuals who are outside the family such as real or fictional persons in movies, television programs or online media, as well as dolls that can impact an individual's behavior

symbolic self-completion theory a theory that explains use of symbols including clothing items to achieve a self-definition; it entails exerting control over one's own perceptions of self to create a personally acceptable picture of reality

T

taboos a subset of mores that is forbidden by a culture

target the person being perceived in social perception research

technical patterns the influence of technology on production of consumable goods

techniques of embellishment artistic ways to decorate dress

textile historian scientist who focuses on the materials and processes used in making textiles

theory a set of ideas that describe, explain, and predict outcomes and relationships and guide the development of hypotheses

total institution an organization that is removed from the rest of society and forms a complete environment designed to meet all of the needs of its members

trade publication these publications cover apparel and textile industry news, provide product information, and report trends in the field; authors tend to be authorities in the industry

traits consistent, long lasting tendencies

transcendence needs needs met by helping others achieve self-actualization

transition a stage within a rite of passage; an in-between stage when the individual is not completely removed from the former status and has not achieved the new one

treatment group in experimental research, the groups that is exposed to the manipulation of the independent variable

true insider when the researcher is a member of the group being studied, the researcher is a true insider

U

unified self a broad concept to describe the self, reflecting different components including relationships to others as well as reflecting personal characteristics

unit of analysis or recording unit this is what is being counted in content analysis

unobtrusive observation process of data collection in which the people being observed are unaware they are part of a research project

unstructured interview interview in which researchers do not use a set of predetermined list of questions, but rather have only an outline of suggested topics that they are interested in discussing

unstructured observation a process in which observations are recorded using descriptive words and avoiding evaluative ones; often used in conjunction with exploratory research

upward social comparison comparing oneself to others believed to be superior on some attribute

urban-industrial cultures cultures that manufacture goods

V

Venus figurines pottery remains of a female "earth mother" thought to be about 6,000 years old

verbal report see anticipatory set

virtual communities online interest or support groups

virtual technology technology that simulates what one looks like in clothing or with cosmetic surgery without actually trying it on or undergoing the procedure

visual representations images that depict dress, such as illustrations, photographs, tapestries, sculpture, films, websites, advertisements, magazines, etc.

W

waist to hip ratio or WHR waist to hip ratio; one measure of the distribution of body fat

within group similarities characteristics common to a group of non-identical objects

wrapped dress items of dress that wrap around the body and may be knotted or tied

written sources written records of dress, including historical records, diaries, travelers' accounts, novels, songs, poetry, and other written sources of information

INDEX

Impersonation, 106
Implicit content, 48
Implicit measures, 137–138
Implicit personality theory, 102–104
Impression formation
    attribution and, 95–98
    casual business dress and, 108–110
    classic studies of, 102
    combinations of dress cues in, 103–104
    implicit personality theory and,
        102–104
    multiple dress cues in, 98–101
    ordinary personology and, 98
    passing and, 106–107
    role distance and, 107
    role theory and, 110–111
    single dress cues in, 101–102
    social perception and, 68, 111–113
Impression management, 104–108
Independence, as mentifact, 11–12
Independent variable, 52
Individual difference variables, 77
Individual stereotypes, 86
Individualistic orientation, 312
Informants, 44, 244
Information literacy, 62–63
Information sources, about dress, 28–35
In-group, 294–297
Inscribed bodies, 141–143
Institutional review board (IRB), 42
Interaction, symbolic, 15–16, 112–113,
        215–218
Interactionist theory, 239
Interdependence, as mentifact, 11–12
Internalized homonegativity, 171
Internet. See Online identities
Interpersonal aspects of self
    brand management and, 222–223
    collective self and, 220–223
    costume and, 219–220
    defined, 215
    generalized other and, 216–217
    program in, 216–217
    review in, 217
    review process in, 217–218
    symbolic interactionism and, 215–218
Interpretative inference, 71–72
Interviews, 44, 45–46
Intimate self, 218
Investiture, 274
IRB. See Institutional review board (IRB)
Islamic views, 340–342

J

J. Crew, 254
James, William, 159

Jargon, 63
Jedlica, Justin, 146
Jespersen, Darlene, 87
Job interviews, 97–98
Jung, Cathie, 136

K

Kinship, 313
Knowledge restrictions, on passing, 107

L

Laboratory experiments, 52, 55, 61.
        See also Experimentation
Laity, 343
Laser hair removal, 132
Latent content, 47–48
Laws
    as norms, 325
    prohibitive, 325
    promotive, 325
    regulative, 325
    sumptuary, 325
Lean muscle mass, in aging, 144
Lesbians, body image in, 171
Line, as gendered design element, 256
Liposuction, 145
Literature, 32
Liturgical orders, 344
Lived experiences, 34–35
Locus of causality, 95–96
Looking-glass self, 215–216
Lotus foot, 352
Love needs, 190, 191

M

Machiavellianism, 200
Magazines, 34
Magic, 347–348
Makeover shows, 283–284
Makeup, 100, 133–134
Mall intercept, 58
Manifest content, 47
Manipulation, in experimentation, 52
Manufacturers, as socialization
        agents, 279
Masculine traits, 253
Maslow, Abraham, 189–190, 189–192
Mass cultures, 314
Master status, 264
Material self, 159
Materials, 332
Matoaka, 31
Media
    body image and, 171–173
    cosmetic surgery and, 147–148
    as socialization agent, 279–280

Membership groups, 302–303
Men
    body image in, 167–168
    circumcision of, 324–325
    cosmetic surgery in, 147
Mentifacts, 1, 11–12
Merchandise borrowing, 202
Merchandise catalogs, 32–33
Mere expressions, 300
Meta-analysis, 129
Method of enumeration, 50
Microdermabrasion, 132
Microsociological theory, 239
Mili, 81
Millennials, 7, 8
Modeling, observational, 271
Models, body types of, 162
Modesty, 26–27
Mola, 81
Moral restrictions, on passing, 107
Moreno, Debra, 131
Mores, 325
Mormon views, 340
Movies, 34
Mummies, 22–23
Muscle dysmorphia, 162
Muscle mass, in aging, 144
Music, 32
Myles, Alex, 198
Mystery shopping, 62

N

Narcissism, 200–202
National culture, 312
Need for uniqueness theory, 192–194
Negative sanction, 253
Negotiation of identity, 238–239
Neotonous, 129
Neuroticism, 195
Non-invasive procedures, 132–133, 140.
        See also Cosmetic surgery
Non-probability sample, 62
Non-reactive research, 46–52. See also
        Research
Normative discontent, 166
Normative patterns, 321–326
Norms, 1
    duration of, 322
    sanctions of, 322–323
    socialization and, 264
    strength of, 322
    types of, 323–326
Novel cues, 69
Novels, 32
Nudity, 349–350
Number of discriminations, 103

Proportion, as gendered design element, 257
Protection, as function of dress, 25–26
Proximity of clothing to self (PCS), 224
Pseudomorph, 30
Psychodynamic theory, 186–189
Psychology
    defined, 2
    social, of dress, defined, 2
Psychopathy, 200
Public self, 218
Purse, as gendered item of dress, 255
Pythagoras, 326

Q

Qualitative study, 41
Quantitative study, 41–42
Queer studies, 254–255
Queer theory, 255
Questionnaire, 57, 59
Questions, in fieldwork, 43
Quinceañera, 249–250

R

Race
    body image and, 169–171
    colorism and, 134–135
    overweight bias and, 139–140
Random assignment, 55
Random selection, 61
Randomization, 55
Rape, 96–97, 243–244
Rating scales, 51
Rationalization, as defense mechanism, 187–188
Reaction formation, as defense mechanism, 189
Reagan, Ronald, 74
Real culture, 312
Real self-concept, 210, 212
Reality television, 138, 283–284
Recording unit, 47
Red Hat Society, 303
Reference groups, 301–302
Reflexive consciousness, 210–215
Regression, as defense mechanism, 188
Regulative laws, 325
Reincorporation, in rites of passage, 346
Relational identities, 239
Relationship, as context, 13
Relative deprivation, 302
Relativity, cultural, 16–17
Reliability, in research, 47
Religion
    dress in, 338–342
    as human universal, 337

identity and, 338–342
magic and, 347–348
personal control and, 342–343
rites of intensification in, 347
rites of passage in, 345–347
rituals in, 338, 344–347
social interaction and, 343–344
social order and, 343
symbols in, 337
Research
    content analysis in, 46–47, 48–51, 61
    defined, 39
    descriptive surveys in, 60
    empirical, 39, 40
    experimentation in, 52–57
    explanatory surveys in, 60
    exploratory, 45
    fieldwork in, 42–46, 61
    generalization in, 61
    implicit content in, 48
    informants in, 44
    information literacy and, 62–63
    institutional review boards and, 42
    interviews in, 44, 45–46
    latent content in, 47–48
    mall intercept in, 58
    manifest content in, 47
    method of enumeration in, 50
    non-reactive, 46–52
    outsider's perspective in, 44
    paradigms and, 40–42
    participant observers in, 44
    population in, 60
    probability sample in, 61
    qualitative study and, 41
    quantitative study and, 41–42
    questions, 43, 49, 55
    random selection in, 61
    rating scales in, 51
    recording unit in, 47
    reliability in, 47
    sampling in, 60–62
    source material evaluation in, 63
    strategies, 42–60, 61
    structured observations in, 44
    survey, 57–60, 61
    theory and, 39–40
    unit of analysis in, 47
    unobtrusive observation, 44
    unstructured interviews in, 45–46
    unstructured observations in, 45
Retailers, as socialization agents, 279
Review, 217
Review process, 217–218
Rhythm, as gendered design element, 257
Risky behaviors, 165

Rites of intensification, 347
Rites of passage, 244–245, 345–347
Rituals
    everyday, 348–352
    religious, 338, 344–347
Rogers, Carl R., 189
Role(s)
    defined, 264
    dressing-out-of, 110–111
    gender, 252–254
    norms and, 264
    prescribed, 265
Role ambiguity, 266
Role conflict, 268
Role distance, 107
Role expectations, 266
Role models, 9, 272
Role perception, 265
Role performance, 266
Role schemas, 85
Role strain, 266–267
Role theory, 110–111
Routine behavior, 165
Rudd and Lennon model, of body aesthetics, 121–123
Rupush, 341
Rusari, 341

S

Sacrament, 343
Safety needs, 190, 191
Salience, 69–70
Sample, 60
Sampling, 60–62
Sanctions, 253
Sanctions of norms, 322–323
Sarkozy, Nicholas, 11
Satisfaction, body, 158
Scale, as gendered design element, 257
Schema
    brand, 84–85
    consideration sets and, 85
    defined, 83
    event, 85
    person, 85
    role, 85
    self, 85
    social cognition and, 83–85
Scholarly sources, 63
School dress codes, 298–301, 302
Scientific approach, 348–350
Secondary groups, 298, 301–303
Secret self, 218
Self. *See also* Identity
    appearance and, 224
    brand management and, 222–223

Socialization
    achieved status and, 263–264
    and acquisition of dress, 281–283
    agents, 268, 277–281
    anticipatory, 276
    appearance labor and, 268
    appearance rigidity and, 276
    ascribed status in, 263
    cultural beliefs and, 281
    defined, 9
    dolls in, 272–273
    fantastic, 276–277
    fashion therapy and, 283
    formal, 269
    game stage of, 277
    identification in, 270
    informal, 269–270
    makeover shows and, 283–284
    manufacturers in, 279
    master status and, 264
    media in, 279–280
    models in, 272–273
    norms and, 264
    parents in, 277–278
    peers in, 278–279
    personal shoppers in, 279
    play stage of, 276–277
    pre-play stage in, 274–276
    primary, 274–277
    professionals in, 280–281
    retailers in, 279
    role ambiguity and, 266
    role conflict and, 268
    role perception and, 265
    role performance and, 266
    role strain and, 266–267
    self-sexualization and, 273
    in social learning theory, 271–272
    social position and, 263
    status and, 263–264
    status set and, 264
    symbolic models in, 272
    theory, 268
Society, culture and, 8–9
Socioeconomic status, 304. *See also* Status
Sociofacts, 1, 11, 12, 13
Sociology, defined, 2
Songs, 32
S-O-R model, 113
Source material evaluation, 63
Space, as gendered design element, 256
Speed dating, 99
Spin, 105
Spirit Man Cave, 24

Spiritual self, 159
Stability, attribution and, 96
Statues, 33–34
Status
    achieved, 263–264
    ascribed, 263
    communication of, as function of dress, 28
    master, 264
    prescribed role and, 265
    socialization and, 263–264
    socioeconomic, 304
Status set, 264
Statutes, 87
Stealth-wealth, 191–192
Steampunk, 69
Stereotypes
    defined, 86
    gender, 253–254
Stereotyping
    discrimination in, 87
    individual, 86–87
    prejudice in, 86
    social, 87–88
    social cognition and, 86–88
Stigma, 138–140, 248–249
Stimulus person, 53
Stimulus variables, 70, 74–77
Store image, 69
Strain, role, 266–267
Strategy, in research, 42–60
Stratification, 239
Stratification systems, 303–304
Strength of norms, 322
String skirts, 22
Structured observations, 44
Style. *See* Clothing style
Subculture
    defined, 8
    social groups and, 292–293
Sublimation, as defense mechanism, 189
Substantive expression, 300
Sumptuary laws, 325
Suntanning, 135–136
Superego, 186
Superstition, 25–26
Survey research, 57–60, 61
Suspended dress, 5
Symbolic interaction, 15–16, 112–113, 215–218
Symbolic models, 272
Symbolic self-completion theory, 213–215
Symmetry, facial, 130–131

T
Taboos, 325
Tallness, as dress cue, 101
Tanning, 135–136
Target, in social perception, 70
Tattoos, on women, as dress cue, 101
Technical patterns, 314–321
Techniques of embellishment, 332
Television shows, 34, 51, 283–284
Terracotta Warriors, 33
Textile historians, 31–32
Textile science, 29–30
Textiles, categorization of, 82–83
Texture, as gendered design element, 256
Theory, 39–40
Tie, as gendered item of dress, 255
Title IX, 97
Titman, Christian, 240
Total institution, 304–305
Trade publications, 63
Traits, personality, 194–198, 200–202
Transition, in rites of passage, 346
Treatment group, 52
Trickle Down Theory, 40
True insider, 44
Trump, Donald, 74
Tummy tuck, 145
Tutankhamun, 23

U
Unified self, 208
Uniforms
    prison, 305–306
    school, 298–301, 302
Uniqueness, 192–194
Unit of analysis, 47
United Arab Emirates (UAE), 12
Unobtrusive observation, 44
Unstructured interviews, 45–46
Unstructured observations, 45
Upward social comparison, 173
Urban-industrial culture, 314

V
Vampire Woman, 142
Variables
    appearance, 76–77
    context, 70, 78
    in experimentation, 52
    perceiver, 70, 77–78
    stimulus, 70, 74–77
Venus figurines, 24
Verbal report, 73
Victim blaming, 96–97

Victim responsibility, 96–97
Videos, 34
Viewpoints, cultural, 16–17
Virtual communities, 247–248
Virtual technology, 318–319
Visual representations, as information
        sources, 33–34

W

Waist to hip ratio (WHR), 136, 137
Wardrobe consultants, 279

Wedding reality shows, 138
WHR. *See* Waist to hip ratio (WHR)
Within-group similarity, 81
Women. *See also* Gender
        attractiveness of, discrimination and,
                128
        blaming of, in sexual assault, 96–97
        bodies of, identity and, 243
        body image in, 165–167
        cosmetic surgery in, *vs.* men, 146–147
        cosplay and, 295

        hair in, 351
        Islamic, 342
        tattoos on, as dress cue, 101
Workplace professionalism, 98
Wrapped dress, 5
Written sources, 30–33

Z

Zappos, 223

CREDITS